17th Edition

FOUNDATIONS OF PHYSICAL EDUCATION, EXERCISE SCIENCE, AND SPORT

Deborah A. Wuest
Ithaca College

Jennifer L. Fisette
Kent State University

The McGraw·Hill Companies

Connect
Learn
Succeed™

FOUNDATIONS OF PHYSICAL EDUCATION, EXERCISE SCIENCE, AND SPORT,
SEVENTEENTH EDITION

Published by McGraw-Hill, a business unit of The McGraw-Hill Companies, Inc., 1221 Avenue of the
Americas, New York, NY 10020. Copyright © 2012 by The McGraw-Hill Companies, Inc. All rights reserved.
Previous edition © 2009. No part of this publication may be reproduced or distributed in any form or by any
means, or stored in a database or retrieval system, without the prior written consent of The McGraw-Hill
Companies, Inc., including, but not limited to, in any network or other electronic storage or transmission, or
broadcast for distance learning.

Some ancillaries, including electronic and print components, may not be available to customers outside the
United States.

This book is printed on acid-free paper.

2 3 4 5 6 7 8 9 0 DOC/DOC 1 0 9 8 7 6 5 4 3 2 1

ISBN 978-0-07-809578-8
MHID 0-07-809578-6

Vice President EDP/Central Publishing Services: *Kimberly Meriwether David*
Publisher: *Beth Mejia*
Sponsoring Editor: *Chris Johnson*
Marketing Manager: *Pamela Cooper*
Managing Editor: *Marley Magaziner*
Project Manager: *Melissa M. Leick*
Design Coordinator: *Margarite Reynolds*
Cover Designer: *Studio Montage, St. Louis, Missouri*
Cover Image: *Royalty-Free/CORBIS*
Buyer: *Kara Kudronowicz*
Media Project Manager: *Sridevi Palani*
Compositor: *Glyph International*
Typeface: 10/12 Times Roman
Printer: *R.R. Donnelley*

All credits appearing on page or at the end of the book are considered to be an extension of the copyright page.

Library of Congress Cataloging-in-Publication Data

Wuest, Deborah A.
    Foundations of physical education, exercise science, and sport / Deborah A. Wuest,
Jennifer L. Fisette.— 17th ed.
        p. cm.
    Includes bibliographical references and index.
    ISBN 978-0-07-809578-8 (alk. paper)
    1. Physical education and training. 2. Sports. 3. Physical education and
training—Vocational guidance. 4. Sports—Vocational guidance. I. Fisette, Jennifer L.
II. Title.
GV341.W85 2011
613.7'1—dc22

                                                                    2010048321

www.mhhe.com

BRIEF CONTENTS

CONTENTS

PART IV
Issues, Challenges, and the Future 509

CHAPTER 15

PREFACE

This is an exciting time to prepare for a career in physical education, exercise science or sport. Scientific evidence supports the significant contribution of physical activity to health, interest and participation in sport continues to grow, and physical education has the potential to help young people learn to be active for a lifetime. A multitude of opportunities await qualified professionals dedicated to providing quality experiences for participants in their programs.

We challenge students from the beginning of their careers to commit to ongoing development and growth as professionals in their fields. Students are encouraged to be advocates for physical activity and quality physical education, to value diversity and appreciate its many forms, and to work toward making opportunities to participate in physical activity available to all people throughout their lifespan. We hope that, as young leaders, they will work collaboratively with other dedicated professionals to address the issues facing us, the challenges ahead, and the realization of physical education, exercise science, and sport's potential to positively contribute to the lives of all people.

ORGANIZATION

The 15 chapters of this book are organized into 4 parts. Part I provides students with an orientation to the field. Chapter 1 focuses on the meaning and scope of contemporary physical education, exercise science, and sport. Emphasis is placed on understanding the scope of the discipline and committing to professional development. In Chapter 2, students are introduced to the philosophy, goals, and objectives of physical education, exercise science, and sport. The last chapter in this part, Chapter 3, discusses our role in society in relation to the changing demographics, wellness movement, and fitness and physical activity movement.

In Part II, the historical foundations of the field and an overview of some of the subdisciplines are presented. The historical foundations are covered in Chapter 4, including our heritage from other countries and the significant influences on the growth of the field in the United States. In Chapter 5, an overview of motor behavior is provided, including motor learning and motor development. This is followed by Chapter 6 on biomechanics and Chapter 7 on exercise physiology. In Chapter 8, an overview of sport sociology is presented, and Chapter 9 provides information on sport and exercise psychology. Chapter 10, Sport Pedagogy, is a new chapter providing information on curriculum, teaching, and assessment.

Part III, which consists of four chapters, addresses professional considerations and career opportunities, including enhancing professional marketability. Chapter 11 focuses on professional development, including professional responsibilities, ethics, leadership, and certification. Chapter 12, on teaching and coaching careers, shows how opportunities for these careers have broadened from the school setting and school-age population to nonschool settings and people of all ages. In Chapter 13, employment opportunities for professionals interested in fitness-and health-related careers are discussed. Careers in sport management, sport communication, performance, and other sport-related careers are described in Chapter 14.

Part IV explores issues and challenges confronting professionals today and looks ahead to the future. The final chapter, Chapter 15, addresses critical issues, specifically leadership in physical activity and youth sport, the growing field and our identity, and the gap between research and practice. Challenges facing professionals are identified. Providing high-quality daily physical education, advocacy, achievement of the national health goals, and lifespan involvement for all people are significant challenges that merit our attention and commitment. Societal trends and current developments are discussed. To prepare for the future, professionals must be willing to assume the responsibility for the leadership of our field and work to improve the way in which we provide services to people of all ages.

HIGHLIGHTS OF THIS EDITION

The 17th edition of *Foundations of Physical Education, Exercise Science, and Sport* continues its dual emphasis on providing students with an overview of disciplinary knowledge and encouraging them to explore the expanding career opportunities. This edition reflects the dynamic nature of the discipline today and is designed for use in introductory and foundations courses. This edition has been restructured to enhance the balance and emphasis placed on physical education, exercise science, and sport. The emphasis on education has been reduced and consolidated by adding a new chapter on sport pedagogy. Expanded

examples are used to increase relevancy to a wider audience of majors in exercise science and sport. While retaining its depth and breadth, the text has been streamlined, and boxes, tables, and charts used to highlight key concepts.

The text continues its focus on the role of physical education, exercise science, and sport professionals in promoting lifespan participation in physical activity for all people. This text emphasizes the need for culturally competent professionals to work with our increasingly diverse population. The responsibility of professionals to serve as advocates for historically underserved populations is stressed; this work is essential if our goal of lifespan involvement in physical activity is to be achieved.

Updated information and statistics are used to help students stay abreast of developments within physical education, exercise science, and sport. Key changes to this edition are highlighted below:

- The first three chapters have been restructured to provide students with a better introduction to physical education, exercise science, and sport. The first chapter covers the meaning and scope of the discipline, the second chapter outlines the philosophy of the subject to provide a framework for goals and objectives, and the third chapter focuses on the contributions to society made by experts and professionals in the field of exercise science.
- New examples broaden the book's scope and appeal. While previous editions highlighted the educational aspects of the field, this edition seeks to be more inclusive of exercise science and sport majors.
- A new Chapter 10, Sport Pedagogy, recognizes the importance of the subdiscipline and consolidates information pertaining to teaching physical education. This chapter covers curricular development, assessment, and teacher effectiveness, and will help students think critically about these topics regardless of whether they will be pursuing teaching careers.
- New end-of-chapter Discussion Questions are added to this edition and can be used by

instructors to engage students' critical thinking skills in the classroom. Other new features include information on critiquing web pages and on reading and understanding research.

- Key government reports and policies that have significant applications for professional practice, such as *The Surgeon General's Vision for a Healthy and Fit Nation* and *2008 Physical Activity Guidelines for Americans.*
- Since the future of physical education, exercise, and sport are closely related to the issues and challenges of today, this edition combines these topics in one final chapter.

Another major change in this edition is the addition of a new coauthor, Jennifer L. Fisette. As a young professional, Jen brings to this edition a contemporary understanding of physical education, exercise science, and sport.

We hope that readers will gain knowledge and inspiration through the topics and issues discussed in this text. We hope that they will aspire to be future leaders and agents of change as physical education, exercise science, and sport professionals.

SUCCESSFUL FEATURES

To facilitate use by instructors and students, the following pedagogical aids have been incorporated into this textbook:

Instructional Objectives. At the beginning of each chapter, the instructional objectives and competencies to be achieved by the student are listed. This identifies for the student the points that will be highlighted. Attainment of the objectives indicates the fulfillment of the chapter's intent.

Summaries. Each chapter ends with a brief review of the material covered, assisting the student in understanding and retaining the most salient points.

Discussion Questions. At the end of each chapter, discussion questions are provided to stimulate critical thinking. Students are encouraged to share their perspectives with their classmates and to explore different solutions to the problems and issues presented.

Self-Assessment Activities. Self-assessment activities are presented at the end of each chapter

to enable students to check their comprehension of the chapter material.

References. Each chapter provides up-to-date references to allow students to gain further information about the subjects discussed in the chapter.

Internet Resources. Each chapter begins with a *Get Connected* Box, which lists Internet sites that provide up-to-date information about relevant topics. The self-assessment exercises include activities that draw on these Internet resources.

Photographs. Carefully chosen photographs, many new, have been used throughout the text to enhance the presentation of material and to illustrate key points.

Writing Style. Foundations of Physical Education, Exercise Science, and Sport has been written in a style that students find readable and that provides them with important insights into the foundations and the roles of physical education and sport in the world today. Students will find substantial information about the career and professional opportunities that exist for knowledgeable, dedicated, and well-prepared professionals committed to the promotion of lifespan involvement in physical activity for all people.

COURSESMART eTEXTBOOKS

This text is available as an eTextbook from CourseSmart, a new way for faculty to find and review eTextbooks. It's also a great option for students who are interested in accessing their course materials digitally and saving money. CourseSmart offers thousands of the most commonly adopted textbooks across hundreds of courses from a wide variety of higher education publishers. It is the only place for faculty to review and compare the full text of a textbook online, providing immediate access without the environmental impact of requesting a print exam copy. At CourseSmart, students can save up to 50% off the cost of a print book, reduce their impact on the environment, and gain access to powerful web tools for learning, including full text search, notes and highlighting, and e-mail tools for sharing notes between classmates. For further details, contact your sales representative or go to www.coursesmart.com.

McGraw-Hill Create
www.mcgrawhillcreate.com

Craft your teaching resources to match the way you teach! With McGraw-Hill Create you can easily rearrange chapters, combine material from other content sources, and quickly upload content you have written, like your course syllabus or teaching notes. Find the content you need in Create by searching through thousands of leading McGraw-Hill textbooks. Arrange your book to fit your teaching style. Create even allows you to personalize your book's appearance by selecting the cover and adding your name, school, and course information. Order a Create book and you'll receive a complimentary print review copy in three to five business days or a complimentary electronic review copy (eComp) via e-mail in about one hour. Go to www.mcgrawhillcreate.com today and register. Experience how McGraw-Hill Create empowers you to teach *your* students *your* way.

Supplements

The 17th edition of *Foundations of Physical Education, Exercise Science, and Sport* features an instructor's website (www.mhhe.com/wuest17e) that offers a variety of resources, including an Instructor's Manual, PowerPoint presentations, and web links to professional resources. Please contact your McGraw-Hill sales representative for additional information and to gain access to the site.

Acknowledgements and Dedications

The authors extend their appreciation to the reviewers for their insightful comments and helpful suggestions. Each comment and suggestion was carefully considered during this revision. The reviewers of this edition include:

Philana-Lee Gouws, University of Nevada, Las Vegas
Elizabeth Kelly, Monroe Community College
Erica Morley, Mesa Community College
Tom Pellinger, Fitchburg State College
Pam Richards, Central College
Wendell C. Sadler, Tarleton State University
Mary Jo Sariscsany, California State University, Northridge
Frank Zaffino, Pennsylvania State University—Altoona

This textbook would not have been possible without the outstanding professionals at McGraw-Hill who contributed in many ways to the completion of this project. Special thanks are extended to Chris Narozny for his patience in answering our many e-mail queries and his editorial work that helped shape this edition. Thank you, Chris! We would like to thank the professionals at McGraw-Hill, specifically Melissa Leick and Marley Magaziner and our editor at Glyph International, Vipra Fauzdar.

This edition is dedicated to the memory of Charles A. Bucher, the author of many of the earlier editions of this *Foundations* text. Bucher died in 1988 after a long and illustrious career committed to educating future physical education, fitness, and sport professionals. Bucher was a professor at New York University for 35 years and, after retiring in 1979, a professor at the University of Nevada until his death. At the time of his death, he was president and executive director of the National Fitness Leaders Association. His work on the earlier editions of this book helped set the tone for the many editions that followed, and we are indebted for his pioneering efforts.

In closing, the authors would like to acknowledge the people who helped support them throughout this endeavor.

Deborah Wuest. I'd like to dedicate this edition to my daughter, Meriber, who has been supportive throughout this revision and the many that came before. At 18, she is pursuing her passion for soccer as a student-athlete. This book is also dedicated to my early-morning writing companions—my cats Jake, Rosie, Mia, and Mira, and my dog, Ally Goose. They were great company and, in their honor, a portion of the proceeds of this edition will be donated to the SPCA. Lastly, a special thank-you to my coauthor, Jen, for her enthusiasm for learning, her dedication to the myriad of details so important in a project like this, and her commitment to the profession. However, we would not have been able to complete this without her sense of humor and willingness to discuss "options." Working on this project with Jen was truly enjoyable. When I was a young professional, Charles Bucher extended me the opportunity to work as his coauthor. I am happy to "pay this forward" and look ahead to working with Jen on many more editions.

Jennifer L. Fisette. This edition is lovingly dedicated to my partner, Theresa Ann Walton, and my stepson, Quinn, who have shown me the true essence of life: family, love, laughter, balance, and the simple things. I am truly grateful for their continued support and belief in me, especially during the long days and nights while I worked on this edition. This book is also dedicated to my coauthor, mentor, and friend, Deb, who gave me this amazing opportunity to collaborate with her on this edition. Deb has greatly influenced my professional journey to academia and inspires me to be a grounded and successful person and professional as she is. I greatly enjoyed our weekly phone chats and discussions, and look forward to future collaborations with Deb.

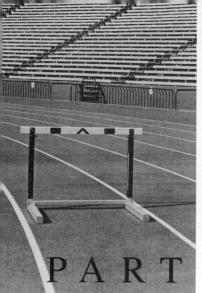

PART

I

Nature and Scope of Physical Education, Exercise Science, and Sport

Part I introduces the reader to physical education, exercise science, and sport. The first chapter sets the stage for the reader by providing definitions and an introduction to the specialized areas of study within physical education, exercise science, and sport. How to grow as a professional in physical education, exercise science, and sport concludes Chapter 1. The second chapter includes the influences of various philosophies on programs and provides the reader with information about the objectives of physical education, exercise science, and sport.

The contribution of physical education, exercise science, and sport to society and health, and the critical role of professionals delivering services to people of all ages are described in Chapter 3.

Physical education, exercise science, and sport represent a growing and expanding field. The growth of this field is reflected in the expanding knowledge base and the development of specialized areas of study. The expansion of physical education, exercise science, and sport has created a diversity of career options for professionals.

CHAPTER 1

MEANING AND SCOPE

OBJECTIVES

After reading this chapter the student should be able to—

- Discuss the nature of contemporary physical education, exercise science, and sport and show how it has evolved during the past five decades.
- Define the following specialized areas of study: sport philosophy, sport history, sport sociology, sport and exercise psychology, motor development, motor learning, biomechanics, exercise physiology, sports medicine, sport pedagogy, adapted physical activity, and sport management.
- Clarify the relationship between the discipline and the profession relative to the field of physical education, exercise science, and sport.
- Explain the relationship of physical education, exercise science, and sport to allied fields of study.
- Describe the different types of research reports and their application to physical education, exercise science, and sport.
- Identify social media resources that can inform the practice within the field of physical education, exercise science, and sport.

This is one of the most exciting, dynamic times in the history of physical education, exercise science, and sport. Unfolding before us is the vision of lifetime involvement in physical activity for all people. This is a powerful vision, one that is compelling for physical educators, exercise scientists, and sport leaders who choose to embrace it and extraordinary in its potential to affect the well-being and quality of life of people of all ages.

Contemporary physical education, exercise science, and sport have evolved from a common heritage—the traditional program of physical education designed to prepare teachers to serve children and youth in the school setting. Since the 1960s the foundation, scope, and focus of our programs have grown and changed tremendously. As physical education expanded, new disciplines of study—exercise science and sport—emerged. As the knowledge base comprising this multidimensional field grew, specialized areas of study evolved and exciting new career opportunities began to appear for qualified professionals. Today physical education, exercise science, and sport

GET CONNECTED

Newsletters, RSS feeds, and podcasts are just some of the ways to stay abreast of current news, research, and developments related to physical education, exercise science, and sport.

US Department of Health and Human Services—this site offers access to RSS feeds, podcasts, videos, and newsletters related to health. There are instructions on the site explaining how to subscribe to and access each of these media.

http://www.hhs.gov > Watch, Listen, Subscribe to access a wide variety of information on health and physical activity.

American College of Sports Medicine—ACSM Fit Society electronic newsletter for the general public, focusing on popular health, sport, nutrition, and fitness topics.

http://www.acsm.org > Fit Society Page > sign up to subscribe.

PELinks4U Newsletter—sponsored by PELinks4U, this website offers a monthly newsletter and articles on a variety of topics, primarily related to the teaching of physical education and the promotion of active lifestyles.

http://www.pelinks4u.org > Listservs/Newsgroups > PE-News. Also a directory of e-mailing lists and newsgroups for sport sciences, athletic training, wellness, and health.

professionals serve people of all ages in a diversity of settings. Our influence on participants' lives is greater today than it was before. This greater involvement and changing focus are evident from the descriptions of participants in some of our programs.

The crowd cheers as the player dribbles down the court toward the basket. With the score tied and only seconds to go on the clock, the player fakes left, drives around the opponent, and lays the ball up on the rim. Score! The buzzer sounds, ending the game. The crowd cheers, acknowledging the great performance of both teams, as the women walk off the court. Sports are not just for boys and men anymore!

Giving one final push, he raises his arms in triumph as he leans toward the finish line of the Boston Marathon—the first wheelchair racer to finish. Working closely with the athletic trainer after his shoulder surgery had brought him back to his pre-injury competitive level. The hard training was really worth it. Few things are more satisfying than winning a hard-fought race.

She practices her somersaults and then works on the balance beam. When the music begins, she joins her group at the mat. As the instructor presents different movement challenges, she responds eagerly, enjoying the chance to be creative and try new things. After the lesson is completed, the toddler runs across the gym to her mother. Although it is expensive, her mother thinks the Kidnastics preschool program is a wonderful contribution to her daughter's development.

He hustles out of the locker room, looking forward to his workout. Following warm-ups, he completes his weight-training program. After cooling down, he changes clothes and goes back to his office to finish the project that is due tomorrow. He makes a note on his desk calendar to attend the nutrition seminar tomorrow offered by the fitness center staff. The comprehensive employee fitness program is a great company benefit.

She mounts the medal stand—she has won the silver medal for the 100-meter freestyle swimming event at the state games. Not bad for a 76-year-old grandmother, she thinks

Career opportunities in physical education, exercise science, and sport range from teaching in the school setting to instructing in nonschool settings, such as leading aerobics classes in a community or corporate fitness setting.

to herself as her grandchildren and team-mates cheer! This is the healthiest she has felt in years, and she enjoys the new friends she has made in the program.

They work carefully, using the skinfold calipers to take each other's measurements at selected sites on their bodies. After they enter the measurements into the computer, the data analysis program produces a profile of their body composition. In another area of the gym, their peers engage in step aerobics, using heart-rate monitors to keep track of their work intensity. In the weight area, students work on their individualized training programs. High school physical education is changing!

The patient stands quietly as the electrodes are attached. The cardiac rehabilitation specialist checks his heart rate on the ECG monitor. He is nervous about starting to exercise so soon after his heart attack. After the specialist reassures him that everything looks fine, he begins his warm-up exercises. The other members of the group, all post–heart attack patients themselves, make him feel welcome with their positive comments and enthusiasm as they exercise beside him. He begins to feel better already.

Getting the family to eat dinner together is difficult. Someone is always rushing off to practice. Tonight it is Mom's turn to hurry off to volleyball practice at the school gymnasium. An active participant in the community sports program, Mom plays soccer in the fall and volleyball in the winter. She looks forward to learning to play golf in the spring; the instructors appreciate the enthusiasm of the adults who want to learn new sports to enjoy in their leisure time.

As you can see from reading the descriptions, participants of all ages, genders, and abilities are involved in today's physical education, exercise science, and sport programs.

Welcome to the field of contemporary physical education, exercise science, and sport. Providing an overview of the field is, quite admittedly, a challenge, for physical education, exercise science, and sport are expanding rapidly and the growth of knowledge within this dynamic field is

People of all ages enjoy athletic competition.

unprecedented. This virtual explosion of knowledge has led to the development of new areas of study that are highly specialized and discrete and yet, at the same time, highly interrelated and vitally connected. The expansion of the field has led to considerable debate among the field's members, focusing on such issues as the appropriate name for the discipline and how best to define the relationship between scientific research and professional practice. Despite the ongoing debate, the growing consensus is that the central focus of this complex, multifaceted field is human movement or, more generally, physical activity.

We now know that leading a physically active lifestyle can help prevent disease and positively contribute to health and well-being throughout the lifespan. If the health of our nation is to improve, physical education, exercise science, and sport professionals must make certain that all people have access to programs, regardless of their age, race, ethnicity, gender, sexual orientation, disability status, income, educational level, or geographic location. This is a challenge that awaits you as future professionals.

Physical educators, exercise scientists, and sport leaders need to know how to read scientific and practitioner-based research. As the field continues to grow and change, this knowledge base will inform your professional practice and provide a clearer picture of all individuals across the lifespan within today's society. Dramatic changes have

occurred over the last five decades in the field of physical education, exercise science, and sport. As we enter the next decade in the twenty-first century, new and more exciting opportunities and challenges await us.

CONTEMPORARY PHYSICAL EDUCATION, EXERCISE SCIENCE, AND SPORT PROGRAMS

The proliferation of physical education, exercise science, and sport programs during the last five decades has been remarkable. Programs have expanded from the traditional school setting to community, home, worksite, commercial, and medical settings. School-community partnerships bring sport instruction and fitness programs to adults in the community and offer increased opportunities for youth involvement. Community recreation programs offer a great variety of instruction and sport activities for people of all ages and abilities, such as tennis, golf, gymnastics, and karate clubs.

Health club membership is booming. Today, over 45.5 million people belong to a health club, compared with only 20.7 million in 1990.[1] Membership by people 55 years and older increased by over 300% during the past 15 years. Members take advantage of a myriad of fitness classes and participate in resistance and cardiovascular training and in one-on-one nutritional counseling. Personal trainers work with clients in health clubs and in their homes. Adults seeking the convenience of working out at home boosted the sales of home exercise equipment to $4.2 billion a year, up from $990 million in 1990.[2] Walkers move briskly through neighborhoods, intent on meeting the daily requirement of including 30 minutes of moderate-intensity physical activity into their lives. Joggers, bikers, and swimmers join the millions who have made daily physical activity an integral part of their lives.

Corporations offer employees comprehensive onsite health promotion programs, encompassing a wide range of fitness activities as well as cardiac rehabilitation and nutritional counseling. Many worksites offer smoking cessation, stress management, and occupational safety courses to their employees, who find it convenient to fit these health-enhancing opportunities into their busy schedules. Hospitals sponsor cardiac rehabilitation programs and increasingly offer fitness programs to community members. Sports medicine clinics treat injured sport and fitness participants of all ages, no longer limiting their practice to the elite adult athlete.

People of all ages are seeking out sport opportunities in many different settings. Youth sports involve more than 25 million children a year. Over 7.5 million athletes participate in interscholastic sports and over 6.5 million participate in intercollegiate sports.[3–5] Sport events such as the Empire State Games, AAU basketball, Senior Games, the Boston Marathon, and master's swimming competitions involve millions of adults in sport competitions. Community recreational leagues for basketball, softball, soccer, and volleyball provide increased opportunities for participation. Sport events such as the Super Bowl, the Olympics, the World Cup, and the National Collegiate Athletic Association basketball tournament capture the enthusiasm of millions of spectators. Girls and women are participating in sports and physical activities in record numbers.

School physical education programs focus on promotion of lifespan involvement in physical activity. Students learn the skills, knowledge, and attitudes that will enable them to participate in various physical activities throughout their lives. Elementary school physical education programs focus on helping children attain competency in the fundamental motor skills (e.g., throwing and catching) and movement concepts (e.g., balance) that form the foundation for later development of specialized games, sport, fitness, and dance activities. (See Chapter 5.) As children progress through school, skill and fitness development is accompanied by an increased knowledge and understanding of physical activity. High schools offer students the opportunity to choose from several different activities for their physical education program. Some instruction may take place in the community, increasing the range of activities that can be offered to students and encouraging students to use the community facilities during their leisure time. Courses in anatomy, exercise physiology, and athletic training may be included in the curriculum, further developing students' understanding and appreciation of physical activity. Intramural programs afford students of all skill levels the opportunity to compete against their classmates. Interscholastic athletics offer highly skilled boys and girls the chance to compete against students from other schools.

At the collegiate level, young adults enroll in courses in martial arts or tennis, work out at fitness centers, join aerobic dance classes, and take part in recreational sports programs. Intercollegiate athletic programs for men and women continue to expand, involving more participants and attracting greater interest from the public.

People are engaging in physical activity in record numbers. There is increased public recognition that being active is good for your health. Several national reports, such as *Healthy People 2010*[6] and *The Surgeon General's Vision for a Healthy and Fit Nation,*[7] present overwhelming evidence that people of all ages can improve their health and quality of life by including moderate amounts of physical activity in their daily lives. Although most people know that physical activity is good for them and participation in physical education, exercise science, and sport programs is at an all-time high, a closer look at the participation by children, adolescents, and adults reveals much cause for concern.

Despite the documented health benefits of physical activity, 40% of adults engage in no leisure-time physical activity.[6] Young children and adolescents are more active than adults are, but their activity levels decrease with age. Only 60% of high schoolers met current physical activity recommendations. In 2000, the US government issued the report *Promoting Better Health for Young People through Physical Activity and Sports.*[8] According to the report, "Physical inactivity has contributed to an unprecedented epidemic of childhood obesity that is currently plaguing the United States." Too many children and youth are inactive,

unfit, and overweight, placing them at increased risk to develop many chronic diseases.

In the United States, the prevalence of overweight and obesity among children, adolescents, and adults has risen at an alarming rate during the past 30 years. Concerned that health problems associated with overweight and obesity could reverse many of the nation's recent health gains, the US Surgeon General in 2010 issued a *Vision for a Healthy and Fit Nation.*[7] The Surgeon General called for individuals and groups across the United States to assist Americans in balancing healthful eating with regular physical activity. Ensuring daily, quality physical education in the schools, incorporating more physical activity into daily life, and increasing opportunities for physical activity at worksites were among the action priorities.

In 2004, with poor diet and physical inactivity identified as the second leading cause of preventable death in the United States, the Department of Health and Human Services again called for America to get active and eat healthier. This initiative, Healthy Lifestyles and Disease Prevention, encourages Americans to increase the amount of physical activity in their lives and to make healthier dietary choices.[9] This public health initiative reflects the important role of physical activity in health, not only in terms of quality of life but in leading a longer, healthier life.

Further examination of health status and physical activity patterns in the United States reveals health disparities and fitness inequities among different population groups. Age, socioeconomic status, race, ethnicity, gender, educational attainment, and geographic location were found to influence physical activity levels. Inactivity is greatest among women, minorities, the economically and educationally disadvantaged, people with disabilities, and the aged.[6] These populations have less access to services and face other barriers to the adoption and maintenance of physically active lifestyles.

Their limited opportunities for physical activity adversely affect their health, their quality of life, and, ultimately, their lifespan.

Involvement in physical activity should begin at an early age and continue throughout one's life. School physical education programs are the primary avenue for helping children and youth learn the skills, knowledge, and attitudes to lead a healthy, physically active lifestyle. Health policy reports recognize the important contribution physical education can make to health and call for daily, high-quality physical education for all students K–12.[6,10] Unfortunately, the number of children and youth participating in daily physical education programs is declining. Daily participation in physical education by high school students decreased from 42% in 1991 to 25% in 1995, and rose slightly to 30% in 2005.[11,12] Many lifelong habits (e.g., drug and alcohol abuse, smoking, lack of physical activity) and many diseases (e.g., type 2 diabetes, heart disease) have their roots in childhood. That's why it is important to develop positive health habits early in life. Over 55 million students are enrolled in public and private elementary and secondary schools in the United States.[13] Imagine the health benefits if each of these students had access to daily quality physical education pre-K–12. Increasing the number of children and youth that have the opportunity to participate in quality physical education programs on a daily basis is an important priority.

The phenomenal growth of physical education, exercise science, and sport programs—the expansion to new settings and the greater inclusion of people of all ages and abilities—has created a wide array of career opportunities for students interested in this exciting field. Employment opportunities range from the traditional career of teaching physical education and coaching in the schools to sport instruction and fitness-related careers in community and commercial facilities. Increasingly common are career opportunities in cardiac rehabilitation, athletic training, and worksite health promotion. Careers in sport marketing, sport management, and sport communication are growing in popularity.

The main challenges facing professionals are increasing the level of physical activity by people across the nation and addressing inequities in physical activity opportunities. As physical education, exercise science, and sport professionals, we must make a greater commitment to reach out to these populations and involve them in our programs. We must address the specific barriers that inhibit the adoption and maintenance of physical activity by different population groups, utilize new approaches that are sensitive to the needs of increasingly diverse populations, and improve access by developing quality public programs in schools, recreation centers, worksites, and health care settings. All people have the right to good health and the opportunity to be physically active throughout their lifespan.

As you begin your professional career, make a commitment to service. Commit yourself to creating opportunities for all people—regardless of age, income, education, race, ethnicity, gender, sexual orientation, geographic location, or ability—to enjoy and to benefit from lifespan participation in physical activity.

Physical Education, Exercise Science, and Sport Defined

Physical education, exercise science, and sport share a common focus—human movement or, more generally, physical activity. Physical activity is the cornerstone of this dynamic field.

Historically, physical education programs focused on teaching children and youths in the school setting. The traditional definition of physical education reflects this educational focus. Since the 1960s, a tremendous amount of change has occurred in physical education. The expansion of physical education beyond its traditional realm to nonschool settings and the development of programs to instruct people of all ages in physical activities require a more inclusive, contemporary definition.

Today, physical education is defined as an educational process that uses physical activity as a means to help individuals acquire skills, fitness,

PHYSICAL ACTIVITY CHALLENGE

Our challenge is to improve participation of populations with low rates of physical activity.

Current participation patterns:

- Women are generally less active than men at all ages.
- African Americans and Hispanics are generally less active than whites.
- People with low incomes are typically not as active as those with high incomes.
- People with less education are generally not as active as those with higher levels of education.
- Adults in the Northeast and South tend to be less active than adults in the North Central and Western states.
- People with disabilities are less physically active than people without disabilities.
- Participation in physical activity declines with age. By age 75, one in three men and one in two women engage in no physical activity.

Source: US Department of Health and Human Services. *Healthy People 2010: Understanding and Improving Health.* Washington, D.C.: US Government Printing Office, 2000.

knowledge, and attitudes that contribute to their optimal development and well-being. In this definition, the term *education* refers to the ongoing process of learning that occurs throughout our lifespan. Education, just like physical education, takes place in a variety of settings and is not limited to a specific age group. Homeschooling, continuing education through distance learning, worksite health promotion programs, and preschools are just some of the expanded settings for education and physical education programs. Teachers today may be called instructors, leaders, or facilitators. Today's students span the age range, from the very young exploring movement skills in a preschool program to the older adults learning how to play golf through a community recreation program.

Most physical education programs today are based on a developmental model. This model purports that physical education, through the use of carefully structured physical activity, contributes to the development of the whole person. Physical education includes the acquisition and refinement of motor skills, the development and maintenance of fitness for optimal health and well-being, the attainment of knowledge about physical activities, and the fostering

of positive attitudes conducive to lifelong learning and lifespan participation. As Ziegler states, "We have a 'womb to tomb' responsibility for the developmental physical activity for all citizens throughout their lives."[14]

Within the last five decades, there has been an increase in the scholarly study of physical education. Research continues to expand our knowledge with respect to the preparation of physical education teachers, teacher effectiveness, teaching methods, improvement of student learning, and it also provides us with new insights on coaches' and athletes' behaviors.

Exercise science is the scientific analysis of exercise or, more inclusively, physical activity. To study physical activity, exercise scientists draw upon scientific methods and theories from many different disciplines, such as biology, biochemistry, physics, and psychology. The application of science to the study of physical activity led to rapid expansion of the knowledge base of exercise science. As the knowledge base of exercise science grew, so did our understanding of the effects of physical activity on various systems of the body. The significant role that physical activity plays in preventing disease and promoting health became

Exercise physiologists study the body's short- and long-term adaptations to exercise.

clearer. Exercise's value as a therapeutic modality in the treatment of disease and the rehabilitation of injuries became better known. (See box for definitions of exercise, physical activity, physical education, physical fitness, and sport.)

Exercise science is a very broad area of study, encompassing many different aspects of physical activity. Through research, scholars gain new insights into how people's movements develop and change across their lifespan and further expand their understanding of how people learn motor skills. Analysis of the performance of motor skills using biomechanics leads to improvement in skill efficiency and effectiveness. Researchers' exploration of the limits and capacities of performers has enabled athletes of all abilities to perform at higher levels of achievement. The psychological effects of physical activity on well-being and strategies to enhance adherence to exercise and rehabilitation programs are some other areas of study within exercise science.

Sports are highly organized, competitive physical activities governed by rules. Rules standardize the competition and conditions so that individuals can compete fairly and achieve specified goals. Sports provide meaningful opportunities to demonstrate one's competence and to challenge one's limits. Competition can occur against an opponent or oneself.

People of all ages and abilities engage in sports for enjoyment, personal satisfaction, and the opportunity to attain victory and/or obtain rewards. The level of competition ranges from recreational sport to elite sport. When sport is highly developed, governing bodies regulate sport and oversee its management. *Athletics* refers to highly organized, competitive sports engaged in by skillful participants. At this level, coaches play a significant role, athletes are highly skilled, specially trained officials ensure the fairness of the competition, records are kept, events are promoted through the media, and spectators assume an important role. Sports occupy a prominent position in our society.

Since the early 1970s, there has been an enormous interest in the scholarly study of sport. These sport studies have focused on the significant role of sport in our society, its tremendous impact on our culture, and its effects on the millions of people who play sports and the millions more who watch and read about them. Scholars study the philosophical, historical, sociological, and psychological dimensions of the sport experience. Examples of areas of investigation include sport ethics, the influence of significant historical events on the sport experience, the inequities in sport opportunities for minorities, and the control of anxiety by athletes during performance. Other researchers have directed their attention to investigating the management of sport and its promotion. The growing popularity of sport and its prominent role in our society makes sport a vital area of study.

The realm of physical education, exercise science, and sport today embraces many different programs, diverse settings, and people of all ages. This recent growth of physical education, exercise science, and sport has been accompanied by an increased interest in its scholarly study. This research has led to the development of specialized areas of knowledge. The subsequent increase in the breadth and depth of knowledge provides a foundation for professional practice.

DEFINITION OF TERMS

- Exercise—physical activity done for the purpose of getting fit that increases energy expenditure above baseline levels. Exercise is planned, structured, and repetitive. The duration, frequency, and intensity of exercise can be measured.
- Physical Activity—bodily movement produced by the contraction of the skeletal muscles that substantially increase energy expenditure above baseline level. A broad term, it encompasses exercise, sport, dance, active games, activities of daily living, and active occupational tasks.
- Physical Education—subject matter taught in schools that provides K–12 students with opportunities to learn, have meaningful content and appropriate instruction. Quality physical-education programs focus on increasing physical competence, health-related fitness, self-responsibility, and enjoyment of physical activity for all students so that they can be physically active for a lifetime.
- Physical Fitness—capacity of people to perform physical activities; set of attributes that allow individuals to carry out daily tasks without undue fatigue and have the energy to participate in a variety of physical activities; state of well-being associated with low risk of premature health problems.
- Sport—well-established, officially governed competitive physical activities in which participants are motivated by internal and external rewards.

Sources: Adapted from the President's Council on Physical Fitness and Sport. Definitions: Health, fitness, and physical activity. 2000 (www.fitness.gov); US Department of Health and Human Services. *Healthy People 2010* (www.healthypeople.gov); National Association for Sport and Physical Education. *Moving into the Future: National Standards for Physical Education* (2nd ed.). Reston, Va.: Author, 2004; and Coakley, J. *Sport in Society: Issues and Controversies* (10th ed.). New York, 2009, McGraw-Hill.

The expansion of physical education, exercise science, and sport has led to a tremendous growth of career opportunities for enthusiastic and committed professionals.

Physical Education, Exercise Science, and Sport: The Field

Corbin[15] defines a *field* as a "combination of a well-established discipline and one or more professions that deliver a social service" and are "focused on common goals." Disciplinarians engage in research and scholarly endeavors to advance a knowledge base. This knowledge serves as a foundation for the professionals who deliver services to people.[15] Professionals use this knowledge and their skills to design and deliver programs to meet the unique and changing needs of the people they serve. As we continue to grow and become increasingly specialized, we must keep sight of our common focus on physical activity. Both the professional and disciplinary dimensions of the field enrich our understanding and ability to promote lifespan involvement in regular physical activity for all people.

The Profession

Physical education, exercise science, and sport can be described with reference to their status as a profession. A *profession* is an occupation requiring specialized training in an intellectual field of study that is dedicated to the betterment of society through service to others. Professionals provide services to others through the application of knowledge and skills to improve people's well-being.

Several characteristics help distinguish a profession from occupations that are not a profession, such as a trade or a craft. These characteristics include:

- An organized and continually expanding body of knowledge that forms the theoretical foundation for practice.
- Educational preparation that includes an extensive course of study focusing on the acquisition

Children with disabilities must have access to sport opportunities.

People of all ages are frequenting fitness centers and health clubs. Many work out on a regular basis. Regular physical activity contributes to good health and overall quality of life.

of knowledge, development of specialized skills, and attainment of needed competencies.

- Criteria for entry into the profession, which can include participation in an accredited program, a certification process, or licensing procedures.
- Formal associations and opportunities for communication among the membership.
- Established opportunities for continued development and enhancement of professional knowledge and skills.
- A professional code of ethics to govern the membership and provide guidelines for service.
- Recognition by society for the valuable contribution to the welfare of citizens.
- Dedication to helping others and serving people.

Physical educators, exercise scientists, and sport leaders possess a bachelor's degree and frequently pursue advanced study via graduate programs in the field. Their professional preparation programs include extensive study in the theoretical aspects of the field, skill development, and often practical experiences that allow them to apply their knowledge and use their skills under the guidance of qualified professionals. Additional requirements and certifications may be necessary to engage in professional practice.

Today there is increased recognition by society of the valuable contribution professionals in our field make to the lives of others. Our commitment to promoting lifespan physical activity for all

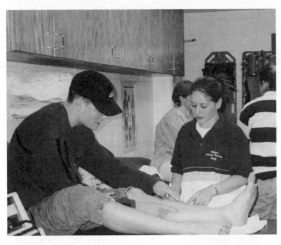

One of an athletic trainer's responsibilities is evaluating injuries.

members of society benefits the health of the nation. The expansion of physical education, exercise science, and sport programs to different settings and the involvement of people of all ages in our programs offer professionals increased opportunities to serve others and enhance their well-being.

Traditionally, physical education has been considered part of the teaching profession. Today, our professional emphasis continues to grow as our programs expand to teaching or activity-related careers in nonschool settings, health- and fitness-related careers, and sport-related careers. This is particularly true in regard to medical and health promotion programs as we collectively attempt to combat obesity and hypokinetic diseases that are negatively affecting our country. Never before has it been more important for physical education, exercise science, and sport professionals to promote the health and well-being of all individuals across the lifespan. In doing so, we need to go beyond our program settings and collaborate with the medical and health professions. The emergence of new professional opportunities has created a need for highly qualified professionals who possess a high level of skill, an appreciation and understanding of the needs of an increasingly diverse population, and a sound grasp of the knowledge of physical education, exercise science, and sport.

Throughout the remainder of this text, the term *professionals* will be used in place of "physical educators, exercise scientists, and sport leaders."

The Academic Discipline

Since the mid-1960s there has been a phenomenal surge in the scientific study of physical education, which advanced its status as an academic discipline. Henry[16] defines an *academic discipline* as

> an organized body of knowledge collectively embraced in a formal course of learning. The acquisition of such knowledge is assumed to be an adequate and worthy objective as such, without any demonstration or requirement of practical application. The content is theoretical and scholarly as distinguished from technical and professional.

An academic discipline has a focus, a conceptual framework that provides structure for the field, a unique scope in comparison to other fields, and distinct scholarly methods and modes of inquiry leading to the advancement of knowledge and deeper understanding. This body of knowledge is worthy of study for its own sake and does not need to have any immediate application to professional practice. Traditional academic disciplines include biology, psychology, philosophy, history, and mathematics.

The seminal point in the development of the discipline movement occurred in 1964 when Franklin Henry called for the "organization and study of the academic discipline herein called physical education."[16] His clarion call came at a time when forces in society were exerting pressure for educational reform, improved educational standards, and greater academic rigor in the preparation of teachers. Then, physical education teacher preparation programs focused on the application of knowledge and endured criticism for their lack of academic rigor, their emphasis on the learning of job-related skills, and their focus on performance courses, such as Basketball Fundamentals.[17]

Henry's call for an academic discipline stimulated greater scholarly activity by academicians at colleges and universities. Developing technologies, theoretical knowledge, and methods of scientific inquiry from other disciplines were directed to the study of physical education and increasingly to exercise and sport. The discipline of psychology, for example, provided the foundation for the development of motor learning and sport psychology. Sociology laid the groundwork for the growth of sport sociology. The proliferation of research and generation of scholarship led to the development of specialized areas of study, commonly called *subdisciplines*.

Subdisciplines of Physical Education, Exercise Science, and Sport

The discipline of physical education, exercise science, and sport consists of 12 subdisciplines. The cross-disciplinary nature of physical education, exercise science, and sport is evident from the names of the subdisciplines. Theories, principles, scientific methods, and modes of inquiry from many other academic disciplines were used by researchers and scholars in the development of these specialized areas of study. Knowledge and research methods from the hard sciences of biology, chemistry, physics, anatomy, physiology, and mathematics strongly influenced the development of the subdisciplines of exercise physiology and sport biomechanics. Psychology, sociology, history, and philosophy, often called the social sciences, formed the foundation for the development of sport and exercise psychology, motor development, motor learning, sport sociology, sport history, and sport philosophy. The rehabilitation sciences, particularly physical therapy, exerted an important influence on the development of sports medicine and adapted physical activity. Educational research significantly affected the development of sport pedagogy. In the subdiscipline of sport management, the influence of management, law, communication, and marketing is evident.

The growth of the subdisciplines broadens the scope of the field. Equally important, the interdependence between these growing areas offers us valuable knowledge and greater insight as we move toward the accomplishment of our goals. The 12 subdisciplines of physical education, exercise science, and sport are briefly described below.

Exercise physiology is the study of the effects of various physical demands, particularly exercise, on the structure and function of the body. The exercise physiologist is concerned with both short-term (acute) and long-term (chronic) adaptations of the

Biomechanists analyze the mechanical aspects of athletes' skill performance in order to help them improve.

various systems of the body to exercise. The effects of different exercise programs on the muscular and cardiovascular systems, the immune system, and the health status of different population groups such as children and the aged are just some areas of study within the field. Clinical exercise testing, design of rehabilitation programs for postcardiac patients, and planning of exercise programs to prevent cardiovascular disease are among the responsibilities of exercise physiologists. (See Chapter 7.)

Sports medicine is concerned with the prevention, treatment, and rehabilitation of sports-related injuries. Athletic trainers' responsibilities are broader than just administering treatment to the injured athlete on the playing field. From the standpoint of prevention, the athletic trainer works with the coach to design conditioning programs for various phases of the season, to correctly fit protective equipment, and to promote the welfare of the athlete, such as counseling the athlete about proper nutrition. With respect to treatment and rehabilitation, the athletic trainer assesses injuries when they occur, administers first aid, works collaboratively with the physician to design a rehabilitation program, provides treatment, and oversees the athlete's rehabilitation. (See Chapter 13.)

Sport biomechanics applies the methods of physics and mechanics to the study of human motion and the motion of sport objects (e.g., a baseball or javelin). Biomechanists study the effect of various forces and laws (e.g., Newton's laws of motion) on the body and sport objects. The musculoskeletal system and the production of force, leverage, and stability are examined with respect to human movement and sport object motion (e.g., spinning across the circle to throw a discus). Analysis of movements with respect to efficiency and effectiveness is used to help individuals improve their performance. (See Chapter 6.)

Sport philosophy examines sport from many different perspectives. Sport philosophy encompasses the study of the nature of reality, the structure of knowledge in sport, ethical and moral questions, and the aesthetics of movement. Sport philosophers critically examine the meaning of sport for all participants involved and enjoin us to question our beliefs and assumptions about sport. Sport philosophers engage in systematic reflection, use logic as a tool to advance knowledge and arrive at decisions, and seek to understand the relationship between the mind and the body. Sport philosophers debate questions of ethics, morals, and values. (See Chapter 2.)

Sport history is the critical examination of the past, with a focus on events, people, and trends that influenced the development and direction of the field. History is concerned with the who, what, when, where, how, and why of sport.[18] These facts, when placed in the social context of the time, help us better understand the present and gain insight regarding the future. (See Chapter 4.)

Sport and exercise psychology uses principles and scientific methods from psychology to study human behavior in sport. Sport psychologists help athletes improve their "mental game," that is, develop and effectively apply skills and strategies that will enhance their performance. Achievement motivation, regulation of anxiety, self-confidence, rehabilitation adherence, cohesion, and leadership are among the topics studied by sport psychologists. Recently, exercise psychology has attracted greater attention from researchers. Exercise psychology is concerned with exercise addiction, adherence, and other psychological issues affecting the well-being of people who are physically active. (See Chapter 9.)

Motor development studies the factors that influence the development of abilities essential to movement. The motor development specialist uses longitudinal studies (i.e., studies that take place over a span of many years) to analyze the interaction of genetic and environmental factors that affect an individual's ability to perform motor skills throughout their lifespan. The role of early movement experiences, heredity, and maturation on children's development of motor skills is an important focus of study. Professionals use theories of development to design appropriate movement experiences for people of all ages and abilities. (See Chapter 5.)

Motor learning is the study of changes in motor behavior that are primarily the result of practice and

Sport psychologists help athletes achieve optimal levels of performance.

experience. The effect of the content, frequency, and timing of feedback on skill learning is a critical area of study. Motor learning is concerned with the stages an individual progresses through in moving from a beginner to a highly skilled performer. The most effective conditions for practicing skills, the use of reinforcement to enhance learning, and how to use information from the environment to modify performance are investigated by motor learning specialists. Motor control, intimately related to motor learning, is concerned with the neurophysiological and behavioral processes affecting the control of skilled movements. (See Chapter 5.)

Sport sociology is the study of the role of sport in society, its impact on participants in sport, and the relationship between sport and other societal institutions. Sport sociologists examine the influence of gender, race, and socioeconomic status on participation in sports and, more recently, physical activity. Drug abuse by athletes, aggression and violence, the effect of the media on sport, and player–coach relationships interest sport sociologists. The experiences of the millions of children involved in youth sport has also drawn the attention of sport sociologists. (See Chapter 8.)

Sport pedagogy can be defined broadly to include the study of teaching and learning in school and nonschool settings. Sport pedagogy studies how physical educators and sport leaders provide an effective learning environment, achieve desired learning goals, and assess program outcomes. Sport pedagogy seeks to determine the characteristics and skills possessed by effective teachers and coaches and how these influence student/athlete activity and student/athlete learning. Curricular development, its implementation, and the preparation of teachers are major foci in sport pedagogy. (See Chapter 10.)

Adapted physical activity is concerned with the preparation of teachers and sport leaders to provide programs and services for individuals with disabilities. Specialists modify activities and sport to enable people with different abilities to participate. By federal law, adapted physical educators have a role in designing an individualized educational plan (i.e., IEP) for students with disabilities so that they can participate to the fullest extent they are able in school physical education. Advocacy to secure services and leadership to create more opportunities in physical education and sport are important aspects of this field. (See Chapters 10 and 12.)

Sport management encompasses the many managerial aspects of sport. These include personnel management, budgeting, facility management, and programming. Other aspects of sport management are law, policy development, fundraising, and media relations. Knowledge from this area can be used by professionals in many different aspects of the sport enterprise, including interscholastic and intercollegiate sports, professional sports, fitness and health clubs, community sport and recreation programs, and sporting goods sales. (See Chapter 14.)

Specialization and Integration

The emergence of subdisciplines led to specialization by both the academicians and practitioners in the field. The creation of new professional societies and scholarly journals provided a forum for professional dialogue, the dissemination of scientific findings, and the sharing of scholarly work.

At colleges and universities, curricular changes were implemented as new courses were developed and, eventually, new undergraduate majors were added, such as those in sport studies, athletic training, and fitness and cardiac rehabilitation. These new career options attracted an increasing number of students, and the number of graduates of these programs soon exceeded the number of graduates from the traditional teaching program. The graduates of these nonteaching programs often prefer to describe their occupation with reference to their specialized areas of study. Thus, these professionals refer to themselves as athletic trainers, exercise scientists, and sport managers rather than physical educators. The new graduate programs offered at the master's and doctoral levels, such as those in exercise physiology, sport pedagogy, sport management, and sport psychology, reflect the increasingly sophisticated, complex nature of the discipline.

The disciplinary movement will continue to expand our body of knowledge. As specialization

Sport sociologists study the behavior of people in sport situations—athletes, coaches, and fans—as well as the impact of sport on the community.

TABLE 1-1	Subdisciplines of Physical Education, Exercise Science, and Sport—Application to Fitness Instruction and Program Leadership
Subdiscipline	**Types of Questions**
Exercise Physiology	What frequency, duration, and intensity of exercise will yield health benefits? How long will it be before participants achieve a significant difference in their health status?
Sports Medicine	What exercises will prevent injury? How should exercise be modified for hot, humid weather?
Sport Biomechanics	What are the correct techniques for weight training? How can I evaluate a participant's gait?
Sport Philosophy	What is my role as a fitness leader in involving participants in the program? What is the responsibility of the participants in this program?
Sport History	What societal factors contributed to the fitness movement in the 1970s? How have cultural beliefs limited the participation of girls and women in fitness activities?
Sport and Exercise Psychology	What are the best strategies to help program participants adhere to or continue their involvement in the program?
Motor Development	What are the developmental needs of the participants? How can the program be designed to meet these needs?
Motor Learning	What are the best practice conditions for learning a skill? How does the frequency of feedback and praise influence participation?
Sport Sociology	What are societal factors that influence the activity choices of the program participants? What are the societal forces that influence their participation?
Sport Pedagogy	What are characteristics of effective teachers? What are guidelines for most effectively presenting instruction?
Adapted Physical Activity	How can the program be modified to meet individual needs or accommodate individuals with disabilities?
Sport Management	What is the best way to promote the program? How can I bring about a change in policy?

increases, it is important not to lose sight of the whole breadth of the field. Even though specialized areas have developed significant knowledge bases, they are not mutually exclusive. There is an overlap in content, ideas, and areas of inquiry, as we are based on a common focus, which has been increasingly defined as physical activity.

Table 1-1 shows how professionals can use knowledge from each of the subdisciplines to enhance the effectiveness of their programs. In this era of continued growth of the whole field

and increased specialization within the field, we should strive to make connections among the subdisciplines. Charles advises that when we eschew boundaries that define the subdisciplines, we can give isolated factors greater meaning by placing them in the perspective of the larger field.[19] Lumpkin suggests that as a field "we should commit to common goals, different roles, and a cross-disciplinary body of knowledge."[20] We must understand the significant contribution of each of these scholarly endeavors and the

Sport pedagogy studies behaviors of teachers and coaches, identifying those that contribute to an effective learning environment. Coach Mike Krzyzewski, Duke University, is recognized for his leadership and coaching excellence. Photo courtesy Duke University Sports Information Office.

important role each of us plays in achieving the goal of lifespan participation in physical activity for people of all ages. It is equally important to remember that as professionals working with people, we are dealing with the whole person— his or her mind and body in the context of society. We must be sensitive to society's changing needs and capitalize on them as an opportunity for growth. Charles states, "We must recognize and capitalize on indicators of cultural change that point toward a future society that places a premium on health and well-being and that values personal fulfillment through physical activity."[19] If we can do this, we can achieve our fullest potential as a significant force in society.

ALLIED FIELDS

Health, recreation and leisure, and dance are frequently referred to as allied fields of physical education, exercise science, and sport. These fields share many purposes with physical education, exercise science, and sport, namely the development of the total individual and concern for quality of life. However, the content of the subject matter of the allied fields and the methods used to accomplish their goals may vary from the subject matter and methods of physical education, exercise science, and sport.

Health

Health education concerns itself with the total well-being of the individual, encompassing physical, mental, social, emotional, and spiritual health. Three areas within health education are health instruction, provision of health services, and environmental health.

Health instruction focuses on teaching the basics of healthy living in many areas, including disease prevention, mental health, nutrition, physical fitness, stress management, and dealing with abuse of drugs and alcohol. Health services is concerned with developing and maintaining a satisfactory level of health for all people through services such as routine eye examinations, cholesterol and blood pressure monitoring, and cancer screening. Environmental health focuses on the development of healthful and safe environments where individuals are not needlessly exposed to hazards such as toxic chemicals and infectious materials.

Americans are becoming increasingly conscious of the instrumental role physical activity plays in one's health-related quality of life. Data supporting the health benefits of participation in appropriate physical activity on a regular basis continue to mount. Accrued benefits of regular physical activity include the prevention of coronary heart disease, hypertension, noninsulin-dependent diabetes mellitus, osteoporosis, obesity, and mental health problems.[6,11] Other benefits may include the reduction of the incidence of stroke and the maintenance of the functional independence of the elderly.[6,11] Additionally, it has been found that, on average, individuals who are physically active outlive individuals who are physically inactive.[6,11] The strong role regular and appropriate physical activity plays in the health and well-being of individuals further confirms the allied nature of health and physical education, exercise science, and sport.

Recreation and Leisure

Another area allied with physical education, exercise science, and sport is recreation and leisure. Recreation and leisure are generally thought of as self-chosen activities that provide a means of revitalizing and refreshing one's body and spirit. The spectrum of activities ranges from active to passive and from group to individual in nature. Recreation is important for individuals of all ages.

It is within recreation and leisure opportunities that individuals of all ages can simply play. The notion of play, whether formal or informal, is often lost after early childhood and youth. Denzin suggests that "the persistent effort to segregate work from play and leisure in modern western societies may rest on the felt conception that moments of play deny the self of the seriousness it somehow deserves. Only children appear to think otherwise."[21] Ask yourself, when was the last time that you played? How do you feel when you simply play? Most often, individuals have fun and feel a sense of enjoyment when they are free to play, create their own games and activities, and have the opportunity to express themselves through physical movement (or other forms of play).

Recreational opportunities abound. Schools, communities, and businesses offer a wide range of activities to meet the fitness and leisure needs of individuals. Worksite fitness programs, industrial sport leagues, commercial fitness programs, competitive recreational leagues, instructional clinics, and open facilities for drop-in recreation are increasing in number. During nonschool hours, school facilities are the site for various recreational offerings for people of all ages. Many individuals

Physical activity contributes to health and fitness throughout life. Bicycling is an excellent activity for people of all ages.

and families pursue recreational activities independently as well.

Therapeutic recreation focuses on providing a broad range of services for individuals of all ages who have disabilities. Through a diversity of interventions, the individual's quality of life is enhanced, the development of leisure skills is encouraged, and the integration of the individual into community recreational opportunities and life is emphasized.

Recreation and leisure, like physical education, exercise science, and sport, can contribute to the quality of an individual's life. They provide opportunities for individuals to engage in freely chosen activities, including physical activities that will yield beneficial health outcomes, during their leisure time.

Dance

The third allied area is dance. Dance is a popular activity for people of all ages and is both a physical activity and a performing art that gives participants an opportunity for aesthetic expression through movement.

People dance for a variety of reasons. Dance is used to communicate ideas and feelings and is considered a creative art form. As with all of the arts, dance should be an integral part of the educational experience. As a form of recreation, dance provides opportunities for enjoyment, self-expression, and relaxation. Dance also can be used as a form of therapy, providing opportunities for individuals to express their thoughts and feelings. It provides a means to cope with the various stresses placed on individuals. Dance is increasingly used as a means to develop fitness.

There are many forms of dance that are enjoyed by individuals—including ballet, ballroom, folk, clog, modern (e.g., salsa and hip-hop), square, and tap. Cultural heritage is reflected in and passed on through dance activities.

Health, recreation and leisure, and dance are allied fields to physical education, exercise science, and sport. The overall focus of these fields of endeavor is the development of the total

Adults can use a variety of physical activities to accumulate the recommended 30 minutes a day of moderate-intensity physical activity necessary for health benefits.

individual and the enhancement of each person's quality of life. Attainment of these aims involves health promotion, pursuit of worthy leisure-time activities, and creative expression through dance. These experiences, coupled with the movement activities that compose the realm of physical education, exercise science, and sport, offer the potential to enhance the lives of people of all ages. Fulfillment of this potential will depend on the quality of leadership provided by professionals in health, recreation and leisure, dance, physical education, exercise science, and sport.

GROWING AS A PROFESSIONAL IN PHYSICAL EDUCATION, EXERCISE SCIENCE, AND SPORT

As a future professional, it is important that you make a commitment to your field that goes well beyond your academic course work and practical experience. You might ask why it is important for professionals with bachelor's and graduate degrees to continue professional development throughout their careers. The primary reason is that our field is constantly changing, placing us in a position to continue our knowledge development based on the latest research, both scientific and practitioner-based. Research findings create opportunities for professionals to inform, change, modify, and enhance their practice. If you do not want to be that professional that is deemed "old school," then it is your ethical duty to stay current in the latest research, practice, and technologies to provide your students, clients, and players with the most accurate and effective instruction and practice.

Do you believe everything that you hear and read or do you draw your own conclusions? How do you know what to believe or not to believe (i.e., what is fact and what is falsified interpretation)? Throughout this text, we are going to educate you on how to read and critique research by guiding you through the "12 Steps to Understanding Research Reports" (see box). In the Self-Assessment Activities found at the end of each chapter, a specific activity will be provided that centers on one or more of the 12 steps as you learn how to read research reports found in professional journals. We will also emphasize how research can inform professional practice, and provide you with opportunities to apply research findings to your future profession.

Reading Research

Before you begin to read research reports, it is important for you to understand research terminology that will provide different perspectives from which you will analyze and critique reports in professional journals. First, it is important to distinguish between scientific and practitioner-based research. *Scientific research* is based on a systematic approach to gathering information that potentially answers an investigated question, whereas *practitioner-based research* focuses on how to apply the information learned within your instruction or area of practice.

Second, research reports are usually based on two paradigms (i.e., types) of research: quantitative and qualitative. *Quantitative research* is based on numbers, primarily the statistical analysis of numeric data that were gathered. Quantitative reports typically describe, correlate, predict, or explain a hypothesis that was posed at the beginning of a study. In contrast to quantitative research, *qualitative research* answers questions through words, images, and sounds. The purpose of this research is to learn more about the social context in which the participants live, which is conducted through the lens and interpretation of the researcher(s).[22] As you read quantitative and qualitative reports, Locke, Silverman, and Spirduso[23] suggest that you attempt to answer five basic questions:

1. What is the report about?
2. How does the study fit into what is already known?
3. How was the study done?
4. What was found?
5. What do the results mean?

12 STEPS TO UNDERSTANDING RESEARCH REPORTS

Steps	Questions
Step 1—Citation	What is the name of the study, who is the author(s), and where and when was it published? Report the complete reference citation using APA format.
Step 2—Purpose & General Rationale	What was the purpose of the study and how did the author(s) make a case for its importance? Is the study quantitative or qualitative in nature?
Step 3—Fit & Specific Rationale	How does the topic of the study fit into the existing research literature and how is that information used to make a specific case for the investigation?
Step 4—Participants	Who was studied (give number and characteristics) and how were they selected to participate in the study?
Step 5—Context	Where did the study take place? Describe important characteristics of the environment and setting (e.g., group demographics).
Step 6—Steps in Sequence	In the order performed, what were the major procedural steps in the study? Describe or diagram in a flowchart. Show a sequential order and any important relationships among the steps.
Step 7—Data	What data sources were used (e.g., test scores, questionnaire responses, or frequency counts for a quantitative study or field notes, interview transcripts, photographs, or diaries for a qualitative study), how were the data collected, and what was the role of the author(s) throughout the process?
Step 8—Analysis	What form(s) of data analysis was used and what specific questions was it designed to answer? What statistical operations and computer programs, if any, were employed?
Step 9—Results	What did the author(s) identify as the primary results (products or findings produced by the analysis of data)? In general, "what was going on there"?
Step 10—Conclusions	What did the author(s) assert about how the results in step 9 responded to the purpose(s) established in step 2, and how did the events and experiences of the entire study contribute to that conclusion?
Step 11—Cautions	What cautions does the author(s) raise about the study itself or about interpreting the results? Add here any of your own reservations, particularly those related to methods used to enhance validity and credibility (quantitative) or trustworthiness and believability (qualitative).
Step 12—Discussion and Application	What interesting facts or ideas did you learn from reading the report? Include here anything that was of value in regard to results, research designs and methods, references, data-collection instruments, history, useful arguments, or personal inspiration. How can the information learned be applied to improve professional practice? Or, what were the implications of this study for a practitioner?

Source: Adapted from Locke, L, Silverman, S, and Spirduso, WW. *Reading and Understanding Research*. Thousand Oaks, Calif.: Sage, 2004.

Quality research that is scientific and practitioner-based within the quantitative and qualitative paradigms has the potential to provide the reader with new knowledge that can inform the practice of all professionals.

Staying Up-to-Date with Technology

In today's society, technology influences many aspects of our lives and will play an important role in your professional endeavors. Technology helps professionals stay abreast of new developments in the field, facilitates communication among professionals, and plays a role in professional activities such as teaching, assessment, and research.

Electronic databases such as ProQuest, Academic Search Premier, and SportDiscus provide ready access to professional journals. RSS, Really Simple Syndication, lets you subscribe and receive up-to-date information from online newspapers, some electronic journals, and government initiatives. Additionally, professionals can subscribe to updates from the US Department of Health and Human Services (www.hhs.gov, click on the icon to subscribe to updates) to get the most current information and decisions on issues such as obesity, morbidity, nutrition, physical activity, and hypokinetic diseases. Smartphone applications can deliver this information directly to your fingertips.

Through the World Wide Web and the Internet, communication with other professionals can occur rapidly. E-mail is one of the most common ways to communicate. Real-time communication between professionals can occur using instant messaging programs, and other applications, such as Skype, let professionals engage in phone and video chat. Live web conferencing programs, such as Adobe Connect, allow professionals to share presentations and multimedia from their desktops and receive feedback from other professionals. Although having

CRITIQUING THE WEB

These are tips for evaluating the quality of content on the web. In recent years, the web has become a rich environment of pages, blogs, wikis, social networking sites, free research services, media, and more. It can be a challenge to figure out which content to trust. This information will help you identify the type of site you are visiting and evaluate its content.

Here are a few general tips for evaluating content on the web. Check that the . . .

- author has expertise on the topic.
- source of the content is stated, whether original or borrowed, quoted, or imported from elsewhere, and that the content can be independently verified from other sources. This is especially important if you cannot check on the expertise of the author or if the author is not identified.
- level and depth of the information meets your needs.
- site is currently being maintained. Check for posting or editing dates.
- information is up-to-date.
- links are relevant and appropriate, and in working order.
- site includes contact information.
- top-level domain in the site address is relevant to the focus of the material, e.g., .edu for educational or research materials, .org for profit or nonprofit organizations, .gov for government sources. Note that the top-level domain is not necessarily a primary indicator of site content. For example, some authors post their content on blog or wiki platforms hosted by companies with .com addresses.

Source: Adapted from: http://library.albany.edu/usered/eval/evalweb

such readily available information is convenient, you need to be critical consumers about the information that you get from the World Wide Web and the Internet. To help guide your critical analysis of web pages, see the Critiquing of the Web box.

Social media, such as Facebook, MySpace, Ning, and Tapped In (www.tappedin.org), lets professionals communicate with each other, form groups around common interests and readily exchange ideas. Blogging, the posting of commentary, video, and photos, gives professionals the opportunity to stay cognizant of current trends and issues as well as contribute to the discussion. Wikis, collaboratively built web pages, allow professionals to work together to develop new websites of professional interest. Social bookmarking sites, such as Delicious, invite people to bookmark websites of interest, tag them with descriptors, and choose to share them with other people.

Sharing of ideas, best practices, and research is easy and convenient. Websites such as PE Central and PELinks4U invite professionals to voice their opinions, share lesson plans, and post best practices, while providing a multitude of resources. YouTube provides individuals all over the world with video clips that range from children engaged in daily activity to the latest fitness techniques. Consumers (i.e., you) need to analyze and critique the information to determine what is and is not accurate or appropriate practice.

Continuing your professional development is an important responsibility of professionals. Webinars and podcasts offer the opportunity to stay on top of professional development opportunities. Online courses and degrees allow you to continue your education without having to be physically present in a classroom or educational institution.

There are also many computer applications that help professionals work more efficiently and effectively. Word processing, spreadsheet, and statistical applications facilitate writing and data collection and analysis. Smartphone applications conveniently provide professionals with access to a myriad of programs that help them perform their work. Sample applications include exercise prescription, tracking of client or student performance, and physical activity information.

Current technology, as well as new and emerging technologies, means that it is easier for professionals to remain abreast of developments in the field. Communicating and collaborating with colleagues, sharing ideas and resources, and taking advantage of professional development opportunities are just some of the ways in which technology helps professionals fulfill their responsibilities.

SUMMARY

Contemporary physical education, exercise science, and sport are rapidly changing, dynamic fields. Physical education is defined as an educational process that uses physical activity as a means to help individuals acquire skills, fitness, knowledge, and attitudes that contribute to their optimal development and well-being. Education is the ongoing process of learning that occurs throughout our lifespan. Education, just like contemporary physical education, takes place in a multiplicity of settings and reaches out to involve individuals of all ages. Exercise science is the scientific analysis of exercise or, more inclusively, physical activity. Sport is a highly organized, competitive physical activity governed by rules where the outcome is largely determined by skill and strategy. Rules standardize the competition and conditions so that individuals can compete fairly.

As a field, physical education, exercise science, and sport includes both disciplinary and professional dimensions. The discipline is the body of knowledge of the field. Scholars and researchers engage in activities designed to provide greater scientific understanding and insight. The professional dimension of the field focuses on providing services to people of all ages in many different settings. Professionals use the body of knowledge and specialized skills to meet the unique needs of people and help them improve their health and quality of life. The growth of knowledge in physical education led to specialized areas of study, such as sport and exercise psychology, sport sociology, sport pedagogy, sport philosophy, sport biomechanics, exercise physiology, motor development, motor learning, adapted physical activity, sport history, and sport management. Each practitioner should be knowledgeable about these specialized areas of study as well as appreciate their interrelatedness and their contribution to the discipline as a whole.

The field of physical education, exercise science, and sport is continuously changing. To grow as a professional, it is important to stay up-to-date with the latest research, both scientific and practitioner-based, and technological tools. Understanding research reports, learning about research findings, and utilizing the newest technology allow professionals the opportunity to provide best practices and instruction to students, clients, and athletes within physical education, exercise science, and sport programs.

DISCUSSION QUESTIONS

1. More and more individuals of all ages engage in physical activity, yet the number of overweight and obese individuals continues to rise. Discuss how professionals in physical education, exercise science, and sport can continue to educate and find ways to engage people in physical activity in an attempt to combat the obesity crisis.

2. In this text, physical education, exercise science, and sport are defined as one field. In today's society, should they be collectively considered one field or separately as multiple fields? Why? What factors can you use to support your stance?

3. Of the 12 subdisciplines, which subdiscipline most closely aligns with your desired profession? Why have you chosen to go into that profession?

SELF-ASSESSMENT ACTIVITIES

These activities are designed to help you determine if you have mastered the materials and competencies presented in this chapter.

1. Without consulting your text, describe the 12 subdisciplines of physical education, exercise science, and sport. Discuss how these areas are interrelated. Use examples to illustrate why it is important to be knowledgeable about the various specialized areas within the discipline.

2. Compare and contrast the definitions of exercise, physical activity, physical education, physical fitness, and sport. Describe how they are interrelated and whether one supersedes the others.

3. Refer to the 12 Steps to Understanding Research Reports box located on page 23. Search for a scientific or practitioner-based article that focuses on contemporary physical education, exercise science, and sport or one of the 12 subdisciplines. Complete Step 1. You need to use a different source from the references listed at the end of the chapter. You can choose to use this same article throughout the text as you continue to work on the 12 steps or you can select a different article that aligns with the content of each chapter. *Note:* If you do select a different article for a later chapter, it would be best to start with Step 1 for that article, because it is important that each step build on the previous ones.

4. The Get Connected box on page 3 lists newsletters for physical education, exercise science, and sport. Subscribe to one of these newsletters. Discuss the benefits the Internet offers to professionals in the field. For the semester, keep copies of your newsletters and summarize what you have learned at the end of the semester.

REFERENCES

1. The International Health, Racquet & Sportsclub Association: Industry Statistics, 2005, 2007 (http://cms.ihrsa.org).

2. Sporting Goods Manufacturers Association: Sporting Goods Industry, Press Release, April 6, 2010 (www.sgma.com/press).

3. National Federation of State High School Associations: 2008–2009 High School Athletics Participation Survey, 2009 (http://www.nfhs.org).

4. National Collegiate Athletic Association: 2008–2009 NCAA, 2010 Member Report (www.ncaa.org).

5. National Association of Intercollegiate Athletics: Member Services, 2010 (naia.cstv.com/member-services).

6. US Department of Health and Human Services: Healthy people 2010: understanding and improving health, ed 2, Washington, D.C., 2000, US Government Printing Office (www.healthypeople.gov/healthypeople).

7. US Department of Health and Human Services: The Surgeon General's Vision for a Healthy and Fit Nation, 2010 (www.surgeongeneral.gov).

8. US Department of Health and Human Services: Promoting better health for young people through physical activity and sports: A report to the president from the secretary of health and human services and the secretary of education, Washington, D.C., 2000, US Government Printing Office.

9. US Department of Health and Human Services: Citing "dangerous increase" in deaths, HHS launches new strategies against overweight epidemic, Press release, March 9, 2004 (http://archive.hhs.gov/news/press/2004pres/20040309.html).

10. US Department of Health and Human Services: Healthy people 2000: national health promotion and disease prevention objectives, Washington, D.C., 1996, US Government Printing Office.

11. US Department of Health and Human Services: Physical activity and health. A report of the Surgeon General, Atlanta, Ga., 1999, US Department of Health and Human Services, Centers for Disease Control and Prevention, National Center for Chronic Disease Prevention and Health Promotion.

12. Centers for Disease Control and Prevention: 2005 CDC Youth Risk Behavior Surveillance Survey, Washington, D.C., 2005 (www.cdc.gov).

13. National Center for Educational Statistics: Back to School Statistics Fast Facts 2009 (http://nces.ed.gov).

14. Ziegler EF: From one image to a sharper one!, Physical Educator 54(2):72–77, 1997.

15. Corbin C: The field of physical education—common goals, not common roles, JOPERD 64(1):79, 84–87, 1993.

16. Henry F: Physical education: an academic discipline, Journal of Health, Physical Education, and Recreation 37(7):32–33, 1964.

17. Siedentop D: Introduction to physical education, fitness, and sport, ed 3, Mountain View, Calif., 1998, Mayfield.

18. Freeman WH: Physical education and sport in a changing society, ed 5, Boston, Mass., 1997, Allyn & Bacon.

19. Charles JM: Scholarship reconceptualized: the connectedness of kinesiology, Quest 48: 152–164, 1996.

20. Lumpkin A: Introduction to physical education, exercise science, and sport studies, ed 6, New York, 2007, McGraw-Hill.

21. Denzin NK: Child's play and the construction of social order, Quest 26:48–55, 1976.

22. Rossman GB and Rallis SF: Learning in the field: an introduction to qualitative research, ed 2, Thousand Oaks, Calif., 2003, Sage.

23. Locke LF, Silverman SJ, and Spirduso WW: Reading and understanding research, ed 2, Thousand Oaks, Calif., 2004, Sage.

 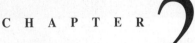

PHILOSOPHY, GOALS, AND OBJECTIVES

OBJECTIVES

After reading this chapter the student should be able to—

- Discuss key concepts of philosophy and their application to physical education, exercise science, and sport.
- Define sport philosophy and describe its historical development and areas of study.
- Begin to develop a professional philosophy.
- Discuss the goals and objectives of physical education, exercise science, and sport.
- Identify the characteristics of a physically educated person.
- Explain what is meant by the cognitive, affective, and psychomotor domains of behavior and how education contributes to development within these domains.
- Describe the purposes and the importance of assessment in physical education, exercise science, and sport.

Professionals in physical education, exercise science, and sport face the challenge of preparing children, youth, and adults—with a wide range of abilities and a multitude of needs, and from increasingly diverse backgrounds—to engage in a physically active and healthy lifestyle. To provide instruction and practice that can enhance the number of individuals that are physical movers for a lifetime, it is important for you to develop a professional philosophy that reflects your experiences and beliefs within your field.

Having a specific philosophy will guide your actions, improve your professional practice, and help you explain the value and contributions of physical education, exercise science, and sport programs to the lives of individuals and to society. Dramatic changes have occurred in the last five decades, and more exciting opportunities and challenges await us in this new millennium.

GET CONNECTED

Cooper Institute—information about the Fitnessgram and Activitygram assessments, fitness resources, and research.

http://www.cooperinstitute.org

International Association for the Philosophy of Sport—website for the organization offers access to resources related to the philosophy of sport, including a blog of current news.

http://www.iaps.net/ > Resources

National Association for Sport and Physical Education (NASPE)—NASPE, part of AAHPERD, offers information about national standards for physical education as well as coaches, codes of conduct for sport and physical education, and position papers related to philosophical issues such as fitness for physical activity professionals and the use of physical activity for punishment.

www.aahperd.org/NASPE >Standards & Position Statements

Your professional philosophy creates a framework (i.e., a way of thinking, a perspective) in which you formulate the goals and objectives of your program. As professionals, we must define the goals and objectives of our programs based on the context in which we work, whether in a corporate fitness center, cardiac rehabilitation program, or a community sports program. Clearly defined goals and objectives are essential if the potential of physical education, exercise science, and sport to foster optimal human development, enhance health, and enrich the quality of life is to be fulfilled.

This chapter discusses major philosophies, the philosophy of sport and physical activity, and the goals of physical education, exercise science, and sport. Learning in the cognitive, affective, and psychomotor domains within physical education, exercise science, and sport programs is discussed. Implementing assessment within instruction and practice is essential in determining whether our program participants have achieved the stated goals and objectives.

PHILOSOPHY

For some people the term *philosophy* conjures up visions of an individual sitting in the ivory towers of a university, pondering seemingly unanswerable questions. Or it may call up the image of an individual sitting atop a rock next to the bank of a stream, looking at the water rippling by and contemplating the meaning of life. Do you think of philosophy as too abstract in nature to have practical value? Maybe it would help you to appreciate the worth of philosophy if it were defined simply as a set of beliefs that guides one's actions and give direction to one's life.

What Is Philosophy?

Philosophy, derived from the Greek word *philosophia*, means "the love of wisdom."[1] Philosophers pursue the truth through the systematic investigation of reality, knowledge, meanings, and values. Philosophy can also be defined as a set of beliefs relating to a particular field, for example, a philosophy of sport, fitness, or physical education. Philosophy is a system of values by which one lives and works. Your system of beliefs and values guides your conduct in both your personal and your professional life. Philosophy helps individuals address the problems that confront them through the use of critical thinking, logical analysis, and reflective appraisal.

What does it mean to be a "good sport"?

Questions that reflect the concerns of philosophers include the following:

- What is the role of human beings on this earth?
- What are the origin and nature of the universe?
- What constitutes good and evil, right and wrong?
- What constitutes truth?
- Is there a God?
- Do human beings have souls, that is, some essence that exists yet cannot be seen?
- What is the function of education in society?
- What relationship exists between mind and matter?

Are there additional questions you have philosophized about that are not listed? What were they? What brought you to philosophize about such topics? Throughout the remainder of the

philosophy section, consider how these philosophies can relate to your personal life and future professional career.

Philosophy is conventionally divided into four domains or branches of study, providing a framework for the examination of philosophical concerns. Each branch contributes to our overall understanding of the world in which we live and offers us greater insight in our search for wisdom.

Branches of Philosophy

Philosophy's branches of study are generally divided into four domains: metaphysics, epistemology, logic, and axiology. *Metaphysics* seeks to address the ultimate nature of reality, that is, what is real and exists. Speculative in its approach, metaphysics may be used to understand the relationship between mind and body or the essential meaning of sport.

Epistemology is the branch of philosophy concerned with examining the nature of knowledge. It uses critical, analytical methods to examine the structure of knowledge, its origin, and its limits. This approach can help us define the nature of the discipline (i.e., body of knowledge) of physical education, exercise science, and sport.

Logic focuses on the examination of ideas in an orderly and systematic way. Logic uses a critical approach to study how ideas relate to each other, and applies sound and reasoned judgment to decision-making. Logic can help members of our field design sound research approaches or organize facts to document the contribution of physical activity to well-being.

Axiology examines the nature of values. Two extensions of axiology are ethics and aesthetics. *Ethics* is concerned with issues of right and wrong, responsibility, and standards of conduct. Speculative in nature, ethics examines moral values. Moral reasoning helps people determine what the right thing to do is in a given situation or circumstance. The development of character, the nature of fair play, and issues of justice are just a few of the ethical concerns of physical education, exercise science, and sport. *Aesthetics*

BRANCHES OF PHILOSOPHY

Branch	Focus	General Questions	Physical Education, Exercise Science, and Sport Questions
Metaphysics	Nature of reality	What is the meaning of existence? What is real?	What experiences in a physical education program will better enable the individual to meet the challenges of the real world?
Epistemology	Nature of knowledge and methods of obtaining knowledge	What is true?	What is the validity of the knowledge pertaining to physical activity and its influence on the development of the individual?
Logic	Systematic and orderly reasoning	What is the method of reasoning that will lead to the truth?	What process should a researcher use to determine the value of physical education to program participants?
Axiology	Aims and values of society	How do we determine what has value, and on what criteria is this judgment based?	What is the value of physical education programs to the individual?
Ethics	Issues of conduct, right and wrong	What is the highest standard of behavior each person should strive to attain?	How can sport be utilized to develop ethics?
Aesthetics	Nature of beauty and art	What is beauty?	Why are skilled performers' movements beautiful to view?

is the study of the nature of beauty and art. The beauty of skilled movement and artistic expression through dance enable us to see movement as an art form.

These branches represent different aspects of philosophy. In developing a comprehensive philosophy for a discipline, such as physical education, exercise science, and sport, each of these areas is addressed. The Branches of Philosophy box highlights the focus of each branch, provides a typical general question that may be posed, and shows how these questions may be framed within the context of physical education, exercise science, and sport.

Major Philosophies

The six major philosophies that have been typically described with respect to their impact on the field of contemporary physical education, exercise science, and sport are idealism, realism, pragmatism, naturalism, existentialism and humanism. These philosophies have particularly influenced educational goals, objectives, content, and methodology, as well as the roles and responsibilities of teachers and students. Although space precludes an extensive discussion of each philosophy, a brief overview of the basic tenets of each is provided, with suggestions of how they can potentially influence professionals in their work.

Idealism

As a philosophy, *idealism* emphasizes the mind as central to understanding and the critical role that reasoning plays in arriving at the truth. Under this philosophy, values and ideals are held in high regard and are considered to be universal and absolute. Values and ideals do not change, regardless of circumstances.

Professionals who follow the tenets of idealism would emphasize the development of character, the importance of values, and the application of reasoning in their work. A youth sport coach who espoused the philosophy of idealism would promote the development of character and the ideals of sportspersonship among the athletes on her team over winning. A fitness leader who believed in the philosophy of idealism would place a high value on serving as a role model to his clients. A cardiac rehabilitation specialist who followed the tenets of idealism would solicit from his cardiac patient, a former runner, the meaning running held for him, understand the patient's desire to return to running, and work with the patient to develop a realistic rehabilitation program to accomplish this goal.

Realism

The philosophy of *realism* emphasizes the use of the scientific method to arrive at the truth. Reasoning and understanding the natural laws of nature are features of this philosophy. The total development of the person is important, and physical activity has an important role in this endeavor.

An exercise physiologist who subscribed to the philosophy of realism would carefully evaluate the scientific evidence in order to better understand the contribution of different types of physical activity to health. Physical educators who

believed in realism would incorporate frequent assessment procedures into their classes, so that their students would have a means to monitor their progress toward attainment of their goals. In accordance with this philosophical approach, coaches would select training techniques based on the scientific evidence of their effectiveness, and would use a systematic, progressive approach in designing practices.

Pragmatism

According to the philosophy of *pragmatism*, experiences—not ideals or realities—are the basis of truth. Because individuals experience different situations, reality differs from person to person. Thus, within this philosophical approach, whatever works in a given situation at a given time is seen as successful. Although pragmatists see truth as variable and rightness as individually determined, they emphasize social responsibility. Pragmatists emphasize problem solving, consideration of individuals' needs and interests, development of individuals' social skills, and cooperation.

A pragmatist conducting a community fitness program for older adults would design the program to meet their needs and interests. A college recreational sports director would be sure to include a variety of different activities in the program offerings, so that the students would be able to choose activities that were personally meaningful and enjoyable. A corporate worksite

Philosophy influences athletes' attitudes toward winning and helps them interpret the meaning of success.

health promotion specialist who believed in the pragmatic approach may choose to incorporate Project Adventure problem-solving activities into a special program for middle managers; after the completion of the activities, she would ask them to share their perceptions of their experiences while she facilitated the discussion.

Naturalism

The belief that life is governed by the laws of nature is central to the philosophy of *naturalism*. Naturalism emphasizes the importance of considering each individual's level of growth and development in learning, and designing experiences that are congruent to the individual's needs. Self-direction, individualized learning, and competition against oneself are important in this approach. Play and outdoor activities provide beneficial opportunities for exploration and problem solving as a means of personal growth and learning.

Physical educators who believe in the philosophy of naturalism would use developmentally appropriate physical activities with their students at all levels of instruction, and individualized learning would be emphasized. Fitness leaders who adhere to the tenets of naturalism would encourage their program's participants to take advantage of opportunities to engage in outdoor pursuits during their leisure time as a means of incorporating physical activity into their lifestyle.

Existentialism

According to the *existentialist* philosophy, reality is determined by individuals' experiences. An individual's experiences and choices create a uniquely personal worldview and affect their perception of reality. Existentialism emphasizes the freedom of individuals to think as they choose and to make choices, but stresses that they must accept the consequences of their actions. Creativity, individuality, self-responsibility, and self-awareness are important aspects of this philosophy; learning experiences should reflect these attributes.

Under the existentialist philosophy, a sport psychologist would encourage an athlete to carefully reflect upon his experiences in order to identify the thoughts that led to poor performances. The sport psychologist would offer the athlete a variety of options to deal with these issues, allowing the athlete to choose among the alternatives. A coach who advocated an existentialist philosophy would emphasize the athlete's responsibility in adhering to the established code of conduct. The coach may allow some individuality in dress, but would emphasize the athlete's responsibility in adhering to training rules. A physical educator would allow students to select from a variety of activities within the program, promoting reflection and individual responsibility for learning.

Collectively, the beliefs and tenets of the traditional philosophies of idealism, realism, pragmatism, naturalism, existentialism, and humanism have influenced physical education, exercise science, and sport programs.

Humanism

A *humanistic* philosophy emphasizes the development of the full potential of each individual. Personal growth, self-actualization, and the development of values are central tenets of this philosophy. Treating students as individuals, valuing the dignity of each person, enhancing self-esteem, fostering personal and social development, and promoting self-responsibility are hallmarks of this approach. Within the realm of physical education, exercise science, and sport, humanism encourages a greater emphasis on meeting individual needs, and recognizes that one type of program is not suited for all individuals. The feelings, needs, goals, capabilities, and limitations of individuals should be carefully considered in conducting programs. For example, in corporate fitness, programs are designed to meet the needs of individual clients, assumption of responsibility for one's own health and fitness is stressed, and a holistic approach to health is emphasized.

Modern Educational Philosophy

Today's educational philosophy reflects several influences. Most schools today follow an

CENTRAL BELIEFS UNDERLYING TRADITIONAL PHILOSOPHIES

Idealism	The mind interprets events and creates reality; truth and values are absolute and universally shared.
Realism	The physical world is the real world and it is governed by nature; science reveals the truth.
Pragmatism	Reality is determined by an individual's life experiences; the individual learns the truth through experiences.
Naturalism	Reality and life are governed by the laws of nature; the individual is more important than society.
Existentialism	Reality is based on human existence; individual experiences determine what is true.
Humanism	Reality and life consider humans to be of primary importance; personal growth, self-actualization, and the development of values are emphasized.

educational philosophy based on many of the beliefs advocated by John Dewey. John Dewey is recognized as the leader of the progressive education movement, and his ideas were influential in shaping American education.

Dewey's ideas of *progressive education* reflect a pragmatic orientation. Progressives believed that education was the avenue to improving the social conditions of society. Dewey's approach of "learning by doing" significantly changed the nature of American education. This child-centered approach to learning emphasized children taking an active role in their learning, as opposed to being passive recipients of knowledge conveyed to them by the teacher.[2]

Dewey also believed in the unity of the mind and the body. Educational activities were viewed as contributing to the development of the total person, not just the mind. The tenets of progressive education lent support to the inclusion of physical education in the school curriculum. Physical activity developed the physical goals of education, as well as contributing to its intellectual and social goals. This philosophy of education through the physical was to become one of the most important influences on twentieth-century physical education.[2]

The Mind-Body Relationship

What is the relationship between the mind and the body? Are they separate, independent entities? Or are the mind and body a unified, interdependent, dynamic organism? Philosophers have long debated these questions, resulting in varying answers and perspectives.

The belief that the mind and the body are separate entities is termed *dualism*. Dualism views the mind and the body as independent, with either the mind or the body being superior. Usually, dualists emphasize the superiority of the mind over the body, relegating the body to an inferior role. The reduction or elimination of school physical education programs in order to increase time for more "academic" pursuits reflects the emphasis on development of the mind at the expense of development of the body. There are other times in physical education, exercise science, and sport programs when the emphasis is placed solely on the development of the body. When the development of the body is emphasized under this philosophical approach, this is referred to as *education of the physical*. Because the mind and the body are separate entities, educating or developing the body has no effect on the mind.

In contrast to the dualist approach, *monism* views the mind and the body as a fused, unified

Some sports, such as the martial arts, emphasize the development of the mind and spirit as well as the body.

entity. Because the mind and the body are viewed as a unified whole, neither one can be subservient to the other; physical activity is as important as intellectual activity. From this philosophic perspective, physical education is as important as the rest of the courses in the educational curriculum. When physical education, exercise science, and sport adopt this philosophical approach, physical activity is seen as a medium for the development of the total person. This approach of *education through the physical* is the most dominant force in contemporary physical education.

The monist, holistic approach is central to our mission of promoting lifespan participation in physical activity. Achievement of lifespan participation requires that professionals embrace the developmental approach to physical activity—that is, design physical activity programs to promote fitness and motor skills and to instill in participants an appreciation for the contribution of physical activity to one's total well-being.

Philosophy of Sport and Physical Activity

Sport philosophy emerged as a specialized area of study in the mid-1960s and 1970s. The definition, scope, historical development, and areas of study are discussed in this section.

Definition and Scope

Sport philosophy is the systematic and reflective study of the truth, meanings, and actions of sport. Sport philosophers use logic and reasoning to gain a broader understanding of how sport contributes to our lives, and to analyze the principles that guide our professional practices and actions. Sport philosophers study the values connected with sport, examine the relationship between the mind and body, and debate ethical dilemmas. They call upon us as professionals to critically reflect upon our beliefs and assumptions about sport and challenge us to use our insight and knowledge for the well-being of others.

Historical Development

Sport philosophy traces its roots to physical education. Kretchmar[3] describes the evolution of sport philosophy as a progression through three periods: the eclectic philosophy-of-education approach (1875–1950), the comparative systems approach (1950–1965), and the disciplinary approach (1965–present).

Historically, the period between the late 1800s and the 1950s was marked by educational reform. Progressive education advocates directed their efforts at reforming an educational system that stressed rote memorization, focused on the 3 Rs—reading, writing, and arithmetic—and emphasized order and conformity rather than meeting the individual needs of children. As schools changed in response to pressures for reform, more active, individualized learning experiences were provided for the students, and support for the inclusion of other subjects in the educational curriculum emerged. At this time, physical education's contribution to the physical development and health of children had been generally recognized. Yet there was little recognition of the potential of physical education and sport to contribute to the psychosocial development of children and to enrich their lives.

From 1950 to 1965 the systems approach was the dominant philosophical approach used by scholars in the field. The major tenets of the traditional philosophies of idealism, realism, pragmatism, naturalism, existentialism, and humanism were compared (e.g., naturalism versus realism) and applied to the goals, objectives, values, and conduct of educational programs. These comparisons were then extrapolated to physical education, and implications for practical concerns, such as program content and teaching methodology, were discussed. Physical education philosophers of this time focused their efforts largely on physical education and its effects on students. They gave limited attention to the critical analysis of sport and human movement outside of the educational setting.

In the mid-1960s and during the 1970s, as the physical education disciplinary movement grew and sport assumed an increasingly prominent role in our society, sport philosophy emerged as a specialized area of study. The sport philosophers of this era focused their efforts on critically analyzing the many complex dimensions of the sport experience and directed less attention to the study of physical education. They addressed such questions as the nature of sport, values achieved through participation, and the meaning of competition. Ethical issues such as cheating, intentional fouling, the use of performance-enhancing drugs, and the promotion of equity also captured scholars' attention. As sport philosophy expanded, sport was defined more broadly and more attention was given to the study of other forms of physical activity engaged in by people of all ages and abilities.

Scholars became interested in other types of physical activity as the subdiscipline matured. The philosophy of physical activity or human movement is much broader in its scope than sport philosophy is. The philosophy of physical activity encompasses the study of many dimensions of physical activity, such as games, dance, and active outdoor pursuits. Scholars are interested in studying the meaning of such experiences to the participants, the mind-body relationship and how it influences and is influenced by physical activity, the values promoted through engagement in physical activity, and ethical values associated with physical activity.

Areas of Study

As sport philosophy became more organized and sophisticated, philosophers undertook the investigation of a wider array of topics. Their work may now focus on the value of different types of physical activity or the relationship of the mind and the body. They also encourage the use of logic and analytical skills to address ethical issues, and make use of insight and knowledge to promote positive change. Some of the questions sport philosophers may investigate include:

• What is the meaning of competition for athletes with disabilities?

- What are the ethical implications of genetic engineering and its potential use in elite sport?
- What role does sportspersonship play in influencing the values derived from competition?
- How does culture influence the meaning derived from participating in sport?
- Why do some athletes risk permanent disability by continuing to participate in sport when injured?
- Why do adults persist in emphasizing winning in sport when children want to emphasize the fun elements associated with play?
- Does participation in sport develop character?
- Does a coach have the right to control the athlete's lifestyle choices (e.g., curfew, code of conduct)?
- What is the relationship between play, work, and sport?
- How does athletic ability influence the meaning of sport for the participant? Are the values derived from participation in sport different for athletes of different abilities?
- How can opportunities to participate in physical activity be made more just and equitable?

The philosophies of physical activity and sport help us understand the meaning of movement and involvement to participants. This knowledge can help professionals make decisions and develop guidelines that will lead to a more positive experience for those involved. Sport philosophy offers us a systematic, reasoned approach to examining our beliefs, exploring the connections and relationships between our personal values, critically reflecting on societal values, and aligning our actions according to the goals and aims to be achieved.

One of the challenges facing physical education, exercise science, and sport in the twenty-first century is eliminating disparities in physical activity. Philosophy offers us guidance in addressing inequities in physical activity opportunities experienced by underserved populations. Philosophy invites us to think critically about what we do, what we ought to do, and how we can change to

provide more inclusive, equitable opportunities in sport for all people.

Your Professional Philosophy

A professional philosophy is important for all physical educators, exercise scientists, and sport leaders. A professional philosophy will help you articulate the worth and value of the field and will influence the design and leadership of your programs. Your philosophy will be reflected in your actions as a professional, the manner in which you handle the responsibility of being a role model, and your behaviors toward and interactions with the people you serve.

Your professional philosophy can serve as a guide in making ethical decisions as you confront many issues and problems within the field. When confronted with ethical decisions, you can use your professional philosophy to reflect on how you ought to act, what is right and wrong in the given situation, and what is just and unjust. Many professional organizations, such as the National Athletic Trainers' Association, also have a code of conduct or ethics that, in conjunction with your professional philosophy, will be of assistance in guiding your professional endeavors. (See Chapter 11 for more information.)

A professional philosophy can help solidify your commitment to your profession and offer you a direction for your efforts. As you develop and reflect on your professional philosophy and become more aware of the depth and breadth of the field, you will be imbued with a greater sense of the value of the field and a stronger sense of the worth of your endeavors.

A professional philosophy will be helpful in addressing both societal and professional questions that may affect the conduct of your program, your actions as a professional, and the outcomes experienced by the people you are serving. Some general questions that a philosophy might help you address are:

- What has value in today's society?
- What is relevant to the needs of people today?

- What are some inequities in opportunity that must be addressed? And what is my commitment to social justice?

As a professional, you will be confronted with many questions that must be addressed. Some examples are:

- Should youth sport programs mandate equal playing time for all participants?
- Should intercollegiate athletes be required to maintain a certain grade point average to participate?
- How should athletic trainers handle the situation when an athlete confides in them that they are using illegal performance-enhancing drugs?
- Should employees be required to participate in a corporate fitness program in order to receive health benefits?
- Should certification be required of all health-and-fitness club employees? If so, what certification should be required?
- Does an athletic director have a right to mandate that no athletes have a Facebook or MySpace account?
- How far should the media go in scrutinizing the private lives of professional athletes?
- Should fitness instructors be role models and "practice what they preach"? If so, what standards should each instructor meet?

A well-developed professional philosophy gives you some guidance in resolving these and a multitude of other questions and issues you will face.

Developing your professional philosophy will be one of your major tasks as you continue your professional preparation. One of the most commonly asked questions of job candidates by employers is "What is your professional philosophy?" Your professional philosophy will likely change as you learn more about the field, acquire more professional experience, and mature as an individual. As you begin to develop your professional philosophy, it may be helpful to think about your personal philosophy and use those beliefs as a starting point.

Ask yourself, what is your philosophy of life? What are your most important values? Maybe your philosophy of life is succinctly captured by one of these often-heard adages:

- "Do unto others as you would have them do unto you."
- "The end justifies the means."
- "Look out for number one."
- "Be the best that you can be."
- "Honesty is the best policy."
- "Things work out for the best."
- "Keep your nose to the grindstone, your shoulder to the wheel."

These adages are only a few examples of the beliefs that guide some individuals' lives. Can you capture the essence of your philosophy of life in a single noteworthy expression? How is your philosophy represented by the manner in which you lead your life? Are your actions congruent with your beliefs?

Many readers of this textbook have participated in athletics at the youth, interscholastic, and/or intercollegiate levels. Critically reflect back on your experiences. What was your coach's philosophy? How did that philosophy translate into the conduct of practices and games? Was your coach's philosophy reflected in one of the statements below?

- "Winning is everything."
- "Play hard, play fair."
- "No pain, no gain."
- "Win at all costs."

How did your coach's philosophy contribute to your experience and the value you derived from participation?

As you continue your education and pursue a career in your chosen area, it is important that you have a philosophy to guide your actions and efforts. During your undergraduate professional preparation, you will be encouraged to think logically and analytically about your beliefs and develop your own philosophy. The guidelines presented in the Developing Your Professional Philosophy box will help you determine, define, and articulate your

DEVELOPING YOUR PROFESSIONAL PHILOSOPHY

Steps	Questions to Consider
1. Review your past experiences in physical education, exercise science, and sport.	What were some of your most outstanding experiences in this field? What were some of your most disheartening ones? Why? Is there a professional you particularly admire, one who served as a role model for you or even prompted your entry into this field? If so, what was his or her philosophy?
2. Read about the different philosophies.	What theories are compatible with your beliefs? What theories are at odds with them? How do these theories translate into practice? What are the characteristics of programs conducted from these philosophical perspectives?
3. Review the philosophies of leaders in physical education, exercise science, and sport.	After reviewing the philosophies of leaders in the field, which of their beliefs are compatible with yours and which are incompatible?
4. Take advantage of opportunities you have during your professional preparation to talk to various professors about their philosophies.	What beliefs are evident in their teaching? As you critically examine your experiences during your professional preparation, do you ask yourself why things are the way they are? How could things change? How would these changes influence the philosophy of the program? Would these changes align with your professors' beliefs and philosophies?
5. Review the codes of conduct and ethical standards of various professional organizations.	Many physical education, exercise science, and sport professional organizations have standards of conduct that serve as guidelines for their members. What are the standards of conduct expected of professionals entering your prospective field? What are the expectations for service to the profession and to others?
6. Express your philosophy.	What are your current perspectives and beliefs about your prospective field? If you have previously written a professional philosophy, how has your philosophy changed or evolved? What factors influenced these changes?

philosophy of physical education, exercise science, and sport.

Developing a professional philosophy is a dynamic process. Your professional philosophy will likely change as you mature and gain experience in the field. Reflect on your experiences in life, ask questions and challenge assumptions, and view the development of your professional philosophy as an ongoing process that accompanies your development as a professional in physical education, exercise science, and sport.

One of the primary purposes of developing a professional philosophy that reflects your experiences and beliefs is to provide a context in which you view your profession. Your perspective on the field has the potential to impact the goals and objectives you develop within your physical education, exercise science, and sport programs. Collectively, professional philosophies and program goals and objectives formulate the foundation of your instruction and practice. In the next section, goals and objectives within the field of physical

Each individual's level of development should be considered in planning activities.

education, exercise science, and sport will be discussed.

Goals and Objectives Defined

Before we discuss the goals and objectives of physical education, exercise science, and sport, we will first define these terms. *Goals* are statements of purposes, intents, and aims that reflect desired accomplishments. Goals are expressed as general statements and are very broad in their direction. They state long-term outcomes to be achieved by participants in the program. A goal of contemporary physical education, exercise science, and sport is helping people acquire the necessary knowledge, skills, and appreciations to participate in physical activity throughout their lifespan.

Objectives are derived from goals. Objectives describe learning, specifically what individuals should know, do, or feel as a result of instruction. Objectives are more specific than goals. They are short-term statements of specific outcomes that build cumulatively to reach a goal. Objectives can be stated in many different ways and vary in their degree of specificity. They can be stated with reference to general behavior or with reference to specific outcomes. For example, one goal of *Healthy People 2010* is to increase life expectancy.[4] A general objective that will contribute to this goal is increasing the number of people who engage in exercise to achieve cardiorespiratory fitness. A more specific objective related to physical activity is increasing from 15% to 30% the proportion of adults who engage regularly, preferably daily, in moderate physical activity for at least 30 minutes per day.

Well-constructed objectives can take on many different forms and can be stated in many different ways. Most importantly, whatever the format, objectives should describe the behavior the individual will demonstrate when the desired outcome is achieved. When objectives are stated in terms that are measurable, they provide a means to assess the individual's progress toward the achievement of the goal. (See the Examples of

Physical Education, Exercise Science, and Sport Objectives box.)

Objectives may be developed for different areas of learning, that is, intellectual development, physical development, or social-emotional development. Objectives guide the development of assessment procedures and instructional experiences. They help professionals focus their efforts on the subject content that is most important for participants to learn.

Quality programs have a clearly defined mission and well-articulated goals. Objectives relate to the goals and are relevant to society's and participants' needs, experiences, and interests. Instruction is designed to help participants achieve the desired objectives and, ultimately, attain stated goals. Ongoing assessment yields meaningful information about participants' progress toward achievement of the goals and has the potential to inform future instruction.

GOALS OF PHYSICAL EDUCATION, EXERCISE SCIENCE, AND SPORT

Physical education, exercise science, and sport leaders' primary goal is the improvement of the well-being and quality of life of individuals who participate in our programs. We can accomplish this by socializing individuals into the role of participants who will make a long-term commitment to participation in enjoyable and meaningful physical activity and sport experiences. Our main purpose is to provide people with the skills, knowledge, and attitudes to participate in regular physical activity throughout their lifespan.

Increasingly, a significant public health role for physical education has been embraced by many professionals in the field. Corbin states, "Physical Education has much to offer society and it is my belief that it can be an effective agent of change—especially in promoting the health of our nation."[5] He adds, "Our principal goal should be healthy lifestyle promotion with an emphasis on active living for a lifetime. Physical educators can help every child find some form of activity

EXAMPLES OF PHYSICAL EDUCATION, EXERCISE SCIENCE, AND SPORT OBJECTIVES

Regardless of the setting in which they are conducted, all physical education, exercise science, and sport programs should have objectives that are clearly defined and relevant to the needs and interests of the participants. Can you identify the program associated with these objectives? Are these objectives for students in a secondary school physical education program, employees in a corporate fitness program, clients enrolled in a commercial fitness club, or adults involved in a community fitness and recreation program?

PHYSICAL FITNESS DEVELOPMENT OBJECTIVE
- The participant will complete a 20-minute aerobic dance routine designed to improve cardiovascular fitness.

MOTOR SKILL DEVELOPMENT OBJECTIVE
- The participant will demonstrate the proper technique in executing the tennis forehand.

COGNITIVE DEVELOPMENT OBJECTIVE
- The participant will be able to explain the scoring system used in golf.

AFFECTIVE DEVELOPMENT OBJECTIVE
- The participant will demonstrate an appreciation for the contribution of exercise to his or her life by participating in an unsupervised program of vigorous physical activity three times a week.

that can be performed and enjoyed throughout life."[5]

Since virtually all children attend schools, effective school programs can have a significant impact on the nation's health and are, perhaps, our greatest chance to change society for the better. But teaching skills and developing fitness are not enough. Students need to learn to value and enjoy physical activity. Additionally, students need both the knowledge and the self-management skills that lead to lifetime adherence. Students need to know how to self-assess their fitness level and modify their activity accordingly; they need to know how to set goals and plan programs so they can adapt their activities to their changing needs as they move into adulthood. If we can agree that this is our common goal and we focus on the delivery of quality programs to people of all ages, physical education can be a significant force in our society.

As education programs continue to expand beyond the traditional school setting, contemporary physical education, exercise science, and sport programs, in both public and private settings, can contribute to the attainment of individuals' goals. In order for this to occur, physical education, exercise science, and sport leaders must be cognizant of the goals of education and carefully design their programs to contribute to these desired outcomes.

Historical Development

Physical education, exercise science, and sport programs today trace their goals and objectives to those of school-based physical education programs. Throughout the years, many leaders in the field have articulated the goals and objectives of physical education. When we trace the historical development of the goals and objectives of physical education, we see a shift from emphasizing education *of* the physical to a focus on education *through* the physical; that is, the focus has shifted from exercising the body to enhancing the development of the whole person. In the twentieth century, the developmental model—education through the physical—emerged as the dominant focus.[2]

The developmental model began to take shape in the late nineteenth and early twentieth century. A leading physical educator of that time, Thomas Wood, in 1883 stressed that physical education should contribute to the complete education of the individual. In 1910, Clark Hetherington, the acknowledged "father of modern physical

education," viewed physical education's contribution to the educational process as encompassing organic education, psychomotor education, intellectual education, and character education. These objectives of the "new" physical education greatly influenced the nature and conduct of programs in the nation's schools. Most of the objectives set forth by leaders of physical education and sport today can be encompassed within the four areas originally defined by Hetherington.

Over a half century later, in 1964, Charles Bucher[6] identified four developmental objectives for physical education. These objectives were physical (organic) development, motor and movement development, mental development, and social development. Achievement of the outcomes associated with each of these objectives contributes to the development of "well-rounded individuals who will become worthy members of society."

Collectively, the prominent emphasis on the physical education objectives throughout the years has been on the development of the whole person, not just the body. Although the leaders have disagreed on the number of objectives and their wording, the objectives of physical education can be encompassed within four main groups: physical fitness development, motor skill development, cognitive development, and affective development. These objectives have strongly influenced our contemporary physical education, exercise science, and sport programs.

Contemporary Goals and Objectives

Contemporary physical education, exercise science, and sport programs are growing in popularity. These programs are diverse in content and varied in setting, and serve people of all ages. What are the goals and objectives of these contemporary programs? What outcomes should participants in these programs achieve? These questions can be addressed by reflecting on and drawing parallels from the goals and objectives established for school-based physical education programs.

In 1995, the National Association of Sport and Physical Education (NASPE), an association of the

American Alliance for Health, Physical Education, Recreation, and Dance (AAHPERD), published *Moving into the Future: National Standards for Physical Education—A Guide to Content and Assessment.*[7] This document identified content standards for physical education, presented assessment guidelines, and offered teachers sample benchmarks to assist them in assessing student learning.

NASPE's effort reflects one of the primary goals of the national education reform movement—the clarification of important goals and the establishment of content standards for each area of the school curriculum. The development of national content standards for physical education parallels the development of national standards for each of the other areas of the school curriculum.

In 2004, NASPE published the revised standards for physical education in the second edition of the document *Moving into the Future.*[8] These revised standards (see the National Standards for Physical Education [2004] box) reflect what students should know and be able to achieve through participation in a quality physical education program.

Though developed in reference to school physical education, these significant goals and objectives are relevant to physical activity and sport programs in nonschool settings serving people of all ages. As Zeigler[9] states:

> The profession has a responsibility to function and serve through the entire lives of people, not just when they are children and young people in schools and colleges. This means we should serve both boys and girls and men and women of all ages who are "special," "normal," and "accelerated."
>
> This can be carried out throughout the lifespan by both public and private agencies, as well as by families and individuals in their own ways. To assume lifetime responsibility would permit us to enlarge the scope—the breadth and the depth—of our profession's outlook.

NASPE's initiatives offer professionals in both school and nonschool settings a common conceptual framework to guide their endeavors. This framework clearly identifies goals and outcomes associated with quality programs. Professionals in all settings can incorporate the assessment benchmarks, points of emphasis, criteria, and suggested assessment techniques into their programs. The assessment guidelines provide a means to both evaluate participants' achievements and, at the same time, enrich learning by incorporating assessment strategies into the instructional process.

The past 100 years have seen the emergence of a consensus about the primary objectives of physical education and, more recently, the characteristics of a physically educated person. In both traditional school and nonschool settings, quality physical education, exercise science, and sport programs can contribute to the development of the whole person. The four primary objectives of physical education and, by extension, exercise science and sport—physical fitness, motor skill development, cognitive development, and social-emotional development—and the goals and outcomes characteristic of a physically educated person relate to the three domains of learning. The three learning domains—cognitive, affective, and psychomotor—help us understand the needs of participants and the skills and abilities to be acquired. In education as well as within the field of physical education, exercise science, and sport, achievement of goals and objectives has traditionally been described with reference to learning in the three domains, as will be discussed in the next section.

LEARNING IN THE THREE DOMAINS

Objectives for learning can be classified into three domains or areas of behavior: cognitive (thinking), affective (feeling), and psychomotor (doing). The cognitive domain is concerned with the acquisition of knowledge and its application. The affective domain includes the promotion of values, the fostering of social skills, and the enhancement of emotional development. The psychomotor domain involves the development of motor skills and physical fitness.

It is critical that professionals consider all three domains when planning learning experiences

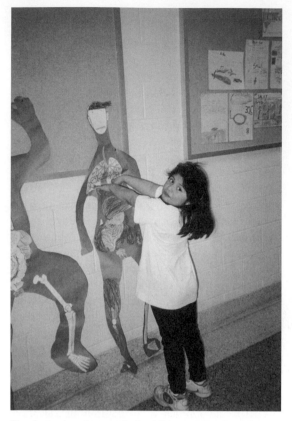

Physical education can help children understand the human body. This 8-year-old is pointing to the lungs, which she says "help you live and get air to run hard."

to meet individuals' needs. Separation of behaviors into domains simplifies the formulation of objectives. It enables us to more readily take into account individuals' levels of development in each domain as we design and conduct activities. However, these domains are interrelated and, as professionals, we must keep this at the forefront of our minds as we work with people in our programs.

Physical education, exercise science, and sport can contribute to learning in each of the three domains. The extent to which physical education, exercise science, and sport contribute to cognitive and affective development depends heavily on the degree to which this development is emphasized within the specific program.

Physical education's unique contribution to the educational curriculum is in the psychomotor domain. Development in this domain encompasses the objectives of motor skill development and physical fitness. While the psychomotor domain is our primary focus, there are many ways that we can accomplish our goals in this area while enhancing development in the other two domains.

Education is a process of learning that can take place in many different settings. In programs conducted outside the school setting, physical education, exercise science, and sport contribute to the cognitive, affective, and psychomotor development of program participants. These programs involve people of all ages, in a diversity of settings, and with many different goals. As we continue to expand our programs, we must actively seek to extend the opportunity for participation to all people, regardless of gender, race, ethnic and cultural background, and socioeconomic status.

Taxonomies

Taxonomies serve as a guide for professionals in planning for learning outcomes and achievement of the desired goals. A taxonomy organizes educational objectives in a progressive hierarchy, from low to high, using developmental theories as a basis for formulating those objectives. Behaviors at one level serve as the foundation and prerequisite for behaviors at a higher level. Stated more simply, lower-order objectives serve as stepping stones to the attainment of higher levels of achievement.

Taxonomies have been developed for each domain. Although these taxonomies are often described with reference to education and the school setting, they offer guidelines for professionals in all fields who work with people to enhance learning and promote human development. Quality physical education, exercise science, and sport programs contribute to the development in each domain.

Cognitive Domain

The cognitive domain is concerned with the acquisition of knowledge and the development of intellectual skills. Bloom and his colleagues developed a taxonomy of educational objectives for this domain in the 1950s.[10] These objectives reflect an increase in complexity at each level of development. Learning facts is the initial objective, and from this grows understanding and application of concepts, critical analysis, synthesis, and evaluation. (The Cognitive Domain box presents the objectives for this domain.)

Development of knowledge and understanding is an important objective for physical education, exercise science, and sport programs in all settings. Our programs are concerned with educating individuals about the many dimensions of human movement, including the knowledge within our discipline.

Physical education, exercise science, and sport contribute to knowledge of the human body, exercise, disease, and health. In the school setting, physical education is the sole area of the curriculum that teaches students about human movement and explores its many dimensions. Through the physical education program, individuals can gain a greater understanding of the various organ systems of the body (e.g., cardiorespiratory system), how they function, and how they can best be maintained. The relationship between exercise and physical activity, disease, and health is an important one for students to comprehend. Students who apply this knowledge to their own lives can enhance their health and reduce their chances for disease, enabling them to lead happier and more productive lives. In other settings, such as wellness clinics in hospitals or worksite health promotion programs, professionals help young adults learn how to incorporate physical activity into their daily lives so they can lead longer, healthier lives.

The learning of physical activities involves various cognitive processes. Learners must understand the techniques of the skill being taught and then be able to translate this information into an appropriate, coordinated movement. Related principles and concepts of movement should also be taught so that individuals can move more effectively. For example, children should know that a throw is more effective when one steps in the direction of the throw and follows through toward the intended target. Moreover, successful performance in many sport activities requires modifying movements to meet the demands of a changing situation (e.g., applying backspin to the tennis ball to catch one's opponent off guard). This requires individuals to learn from their experiences (e.g., which modifications of a skill lead to success). Cognitively, individuals must analyze

THE COGNITIVE DOMAIN

Category	Description	Application
1. Knowledge	Memory; ability to recall; bringing to mind appropriate information. Lowest level of learning outcomes in cognitive domain.	**PE**—What are the critical elements of the overhead clear in badminton? **Ex Sci**—What are the health-related components of fitness? **Sport**—What are the primary rules of basketball?
2. Comprehension	Grasping the meaning of material; understanding without perceiving implications; interpreting; translating; estimating; predicting. One step beyond memory; lower level of understanding.	**PE**—How do the critical elements of the overhead clear in badminton compare to those of the softball/baseball throw. **Ex Sci**—How are the health and motor components of fitness similar and different? **Sport**—How are the primary rules of basketball similar to those of soccer?
3. Application	Ability to use learned information in new situations; applying rules, methods, and concepts. Higher level of understanding.	**PE**—When is the best time to use the overhead clear in badminton? Why? **Ex Sci**—What exercises would you suggest to a 40-year-old woman who is just starting to workout? **Sport**—On offense, the point guard has picked up her dribble and you are being defended by an opponent. What movement(s) can you do to create opportunities to get open?
4. Analysis	Breaking down material into its component parts; clearly perceiving organization and relationships between parts; identifying; selecting; inferring. Higher intellectual level.	**PE**—In a game of badminton, your opponent consistently wins the point by landing the shuttle at the front of the court. How will you adjust your game play to improve your opportunities to score? **Ex Sci**—What target heart rate zone would you prescribe for cardiorespiratory exercises for a 55-year-old man who just had a minor heart attack? **Sport**—In a basketball game, most of your opponent's scoring is inside the key. How will you change your defense to prevent your opponent from scoring?
5. Synthesis	Ability to put parts together to form a new whole; producing new patterns, routines, or structures; addressing creative behaviors.	**PE**—After playing singles in badminton, you decide you want to play doubles. How is playing doubles different from playing singles, and how will you change your game play? **Ex Sci**—What workout would you create, using the FITT (Frequency, Intensity, Time, Type) principle, for a 25-year-old woman whose goals are to lose 5 pounds and increase muscular strength? **Sport**—Your team is up by two points with 1 minute left in the game. How will your team play out the last minute?

THE COGNITIVE DOMAIN (*Continued*)

Category	Description	Application
6. Evaluation	Ability to judge values of ideas and concepts, based on definitive criteria or standards. Contains elements of all other categories and judgments based on specific criteria; highest learning outcome.	**PE**—In a singles game of badminton, you lose by a score of 15–6. Reflecting upon your game play, how would you explain what tactics and strategies your opponent utilized to win the game? What skills, tactics, and strategies do you need to work on to improve your game performance? **Ex Sci**—How will you adjust your client's workout based on the following information from an assessment of the workout's results: a 20-pound increase in the client's one-rep max on the bench press, no improvement in flexibility, and lowering of the client's resting heart rate by two beats per minute? **Sport**—Throughout the season thus far, your team is averaging 20 turnovers per game. What drills can your team practice that have the potential to decrease the number of turnovers per game?

their performance, synthesize the information, and apply it to the new situation.

Professionals in all settings need to place more emphasis on the scientific principles and concepts underlying the performance of various activities. Physical activities are not performed in a vacuum. As such, instructors should continually provide appropriate knowledge and information for participants and encourage them to question what they are doing. "Why should I exercise regularly? How will this exercise contribute to the rehabilitation of my knee? Why is warming up before exercising important? How can I get more distance for my golf drive? What can I do to throw the ball farther? Why is it important to play by the rules?" Participants should be provided with more opportunities to think, to apply problem-solving skills to physical activity situations, and to experience situations that allow for creativity and individual expression.

Teachers can also use fitness activities to stimulate cognitive development. Students can self-analyze their fitness levels, identify areas of improvement, apply their knowledge to design

an individualized exercise program, and evaluate their progress regularly, adjusting their program as needed. These cognitive skills of analysis, identification, application, and evaluation contribute to the educational goal of preparing students to be lifelong learners. These activities also give students skills to modify their fitness programs during their adult lives as their needs change, a critical feature of lifespan involvement.

Technology is increasingly being used to enhance the teaching of concepts of physical activity. For example, a physical education teacher at Agassiz Middle School in Fargo, N.D., uses heart-rate monitors to help students understand important concepts related to physical activity.[11] Students learn about the Fitness Education Pyramid, which graphically depicts the different types of health benefits associated with varying levels of activity intensity. The heart rate monitors give students vivid feedback about the effects of activity on their hearts and enable them to monitor their efforts as they participate. This feedback enhances the students' understanding of important fitness concepts.

Knowing how to monitor your heart rate, calculate your training zone, and modify your fitness program to meet your individual needs are cognitive outcomes that can be achieved in programs.

Children at Agassiz Middle School, in Fargo, N.D., learn about the Fitness Education Pyramid.

Our programs can contribute to our understanding of sport, a major institution in our society and in many other cultures throughout the world. Sport affects a country's economy, politics, government, and educational system. Sport dominates the newspapers, magazines, radio, and television. Millions of people of all ages are involved as participants in sport, and millions more enjoy sport as spectators. Because sport is a part of our culture and others throughout the world, it should be understood from a sociological and psychological perspective. Of course, a body of sport knowledge also exists concerning such things as rules, strategy, safety measures, terminology, and etiquette.

Physical education, exercise science, and sport professionals can help people become wise consumers of goods and services that influence their health and fitness. The health and fitness industry is a multibillion-dollar industry. Unfortunately, it is an area in which goods and services of doubtful value find a ready market. Advertisements in popular magazines promise a quick weight loss or a rapid shape up. Infomercials promoting exercise equipment and nutritional supplements capture the attention of thousands of people. Professionals can help participants in their programs learn how to evaluate such pronouncements critically and be wise consumers in the burgeoning marketplace.

Within the school setting, physical education can contribute to cognitive development in many significant ways. Like other curricular areas, it can promote the development of critical thinking skills, and it can provide exciting opportunities for multidisciplinary study. Uniquely, physical education is the one area of the curriculum in which students can obtain knowledge about human movement, fitness, and sport to serve as a foundation for a lifetime of participation.

Affective Domain

Many factors influence individuals' learning, including their feelings about themselves, the learning experience, and the subject. Recognizing this, Krathwohl and his associates developed the taxonomy for the affective domain.[12] This taxonomy reflects the development of values, appreciations, attitudes, and character. As individuals progress through the levels within this domain, they move from a concern about themselves to a value structure that embraces concern for others. At the highest level, their internalized values directly influence their choices and actions. Affective development also encompasses social and emotional development. (The objectives are shown in the Affective Domain box.)

Quality physical education, exercise science, and sport programs conducted by qualified leaders can enrich development in the affective domain. These desirable outcomes should not be left to chance, but actively sought through carefully planned approaches designed to promote growth in this area.

All people have certain basic social needs. These include feelings of belonging, recognition, self-respect, and love. Fulfillment of these needs contributes to social development. Physical education, exercise science, and sport programs can help participants meet some of these social needs. For example, elderly participants who join an exercise program typically benefit not only physically but socially, deriving pleasure from meeting with their group regularly and forming new friendships. Such interactions help to diminish the feelings of isolation experienced by many elderly who live alone.

Social development is further encouraged by opportunities to interact with program participants. For example, in school physical education programs, students have more opportunities to interact with one another and work together than in any other area of the educational curriculum. Interscholastic sport programs have long extolled their value in promoting learning that teaches athletes how to work together as part of a team, compete fairly, accept responsibility, and respect the rights of others.

Promotion of a positive self-concept and enhancement of feelings of self-worth and self-respect are desired outcomes associated with this domain. One way that physical education, exercise science, and sport activities can contribute to these outcomes is to provide opportunities for individuals to develop competence in physical skills and to challenge themselves to attain new levels of achievement and realistic goals. Experiences should be structured to allow for meaningful success for all involved. Individuals who perceive themselves as competent and have confidence in themselves as movers are more likely to seek involvement in physical activities.

Valuing physical activity for enjoyment and challenge is an example of an affective outcome.

THE AFFECTIVE DOMAIN

Category	Description	Application
1. Receiving	Sensitivity to the existence of certain events or stimuli; awareness; willingness to receive or attend to phenomena.	**PE**—Students follow the teacher's directions. **Ex Sci**—A cardiologist listens to her patient describe their symptoms. **Sport**—Players choose to shake hands with the opposing team after a win or loss.
2. Responding	Active attention to stimuli; reacting to a situation beyond mere perception; responding overtly.	**PE**—Students choose to use rock-paper-scissors to decide whether the ball was in or out in a game instead of arguing the call. **Ex Sci**—A client questions the benefits and potential side effects of a new fad diet. **Sport**—A player practices hitting in the batting cages before and after the team's actual practice on a daily basis.
3. Valuing	Assigning worth to stimuli or phenomena; placing a value on events; characteristics of a belief or attitude; appreciation.	**PE**—Students voluntarily participate in physical activity outside of school. **Ex Sci**—Elderly participants create a walking club in their neighborhood for social and physical development. **Sport**—Players demonstrate fair play and good sportspersonship to their coaches, teammates, and opponents.
4. Organizing	Internalizing values and organizing them into a system; determining interrelationship among values; arranging values in hierarchical form; comparing, relating, and synthesizing values.	**PE**—Students accept responsibility for their own behavior. **Ex Sci**—Individuals accept a physical therapist's guidelines as to when they can return to competition. **Sport**—A player recognizes his or her own abilities, limitations, and values and develops realistic aspirations of how he or she can contribute to the team.
5. Characterizing by a value or complex	Acting in accordance with internalized values; behaving consistently with accepted values and integrating them into personality.	**PE**—Students appreciate and value the opportunity to collaborate and socialize with their classmates as they problem-solve how to accomplish a challenge or task successfully. **Ex Sci**—Individuals commit to 30 minutes of daily physical activity to enhance their health and decrease stress levels. **Sport**—Players choose to eat healthy and work hard to increase their performance instead of taking performance-enhancing drugs.

Helping young people develop a healthy self-esteem is important. Drug and alcohol abuse and a myriad of other social problems have been linked to low self-esteem. Programs that empower participants through opportunities for leadership, promotion of competence, and development of improved self-image through establishing and maintaining a high level of fitness enhance the self-esteem of participants.

The development of positive attitudes and appreciation for the contributions that engaging in regular physical activity makes to lifelong health and well-being are outcomes that physical education, exercise science, and sport professionals are increasingly emphasizing. Knowledge of the benefits of physical activity and the development of the skills to participate in various activities are not, in and of themselves, sufficient to promote lifespan involvement. If we are to achieve our goal of promoting regular physical activity, we must instill in participants the motivation to lead a healthy, active lifestyle. Our programs should help participants appreciate the contribution that physical activity can make to their health, performance, and rewarding use of leisure time.

Professionals should be concerned with helping individuals clarify and think through their value judgments. We must move beyond the lower-order objective of creating an interest in physical activity. Helping participants achieve the higher-order objective of internalizing values should be our focus. At this level, values directly influence what individuals choose to do and how they behave. Thus, we must help individuals develop values that will lead to a physically active lifestyle. Additionally, we must give attention to developing their decision-making and self-management skills, which will help them in translating their values into action.

Decision-making skills and self-management skills are particularly important for achieving wellness. Many lifestyle choices that individuals make have the potential to influence their health. Decisions that individuals make about eating, exercising, managing stress, and using leisure time can have a positive or negative impact on their health. Helping individuals clarify their values and make decisions congruent with their beliefs can enhance their quality of life.

Professionals can promote social responsibility, an important component of good citizenship. Hellison[13] developed a model to promote responsibility that has been successfully used with at-risk students in both school- and community-based programs. This model emphasizes personal growth through self-control, involvement, goal setting, and assisting others. Success, personal awareness, problem-solving, and self-reflection are also incorporated within this model. This approach and other thoughtfully designed instructional experiences can do much to promote the development of socially acceptable values.

Professionals must also give careful thought to the influence of their own behaviors, values, and actions on their program participants. How important is it for professionals to practice what they preach? Professionals who aspire to promote affective development must carefully weigh this question. As leaders, they serve as models for participants. Consideration for the needs and feelings of others, respect for each individual, and enthusiasm for physical activity are some behaviors physical educators, exercise science, and sport professionals should exhibit if they want to promote the same behaviors within their participants.

Physical education, exercise science, and sport also provide a venue to develop ethics and morals. In physical education classes and sport experiences, students and athletes have the opportunity to respond to codes of conduct, to decide what is right or wrong, and to make choices that have moral implications. Professionals can promote further development in this area by having students and athletes reflect on their decisions and behavior. Students can also be asked to assume officiating responsibilities in games or to make their own calls (e.g., calling one's own fouls in a game or calling the ball in or out in a tennis match). Discussion of students' and athletes' behaviors following these situations can help participants further clarify their values.

Our programs have long been extolled as a means through which character development can occur. However, character development can be either positive or negative in nature. As Docheff points out, "The outcome of character development is determined by a number of factors—that is, the character of those that support and drive the endeavor, including coaches, teachers, administrators, parents."[14] Professionals can exert a great influence on character development. However, as professionals, "we must take personal responsibility for the development of good character in others by the demonstration of good character in ourselves." Gough suggests that the most significant character-building challenge is "often more a matter of doing the good, than a matter of knowing the good, more a matter of having the strength of character to do that right thing than a matter of analyzing and resolving complicated moral dilemmas."[15] Helping individuals develop the habit of "doing good" is critical to our character-building endeavors.

Physical education, exercise science, and sport programs can contribute to an appreciation of beauty. The ancient Greeks stressed the "body beautiful" and did their exercises and athletic contests in the nude to display the fine contours of their bodies. When people move, whether it is to perform an everyday task or a sport skill, their movements can have a degree of elegance and beauty. Included in the performance of such acts as catching a football, making a basketball goal, executing a high jump, completing a two-and-one-half-somersault dive, or performing a complex dance can be rhythm, grace, poise, and ease of movement that are beauty in action.

Physical education, exercise science, and sport foster development in the affective domain. The enhancement of self-esteem, promotion of social responsibility, clarification of values, development of attitudes, and appreciation of beauty are just some contributions that physical education, exercise science, and sport can make to the development of the whole person.

Psychomotor Domain

Developed by Dave, the taxonomy of objectives in the psychomotor domain shows a progression

Acquisition of motor skills is one focus of the psychomotor domain.

of development that provides the foundation for programs of physical activities.[16] The lower-order objectives focus on the acquisition of basic movements and perceptual abilities. The higher-order objectives emphasize the development of fitness and highly skilled movements, as well as increased creativity in the use of these movements. (The Psychomotor Domain box lists the objectives of this domain.)

Development of fitness is also included within this domain. Corbin presents a taxonomy that moves in progression from exercising to achieving fitness and then to establishing personal exercise habits.[17] The higher-order objectives focus on learning how to evaluate one's own fitness level and resolve fitness problems.

The psychomotor domain is the main focus of our field. Psychomotor development of the individual is our primary contribution to the educational curriculum and exercise and sport programs. Although physical education can contribute in many meaningful ways to development in the other domains, psychomotor development in the schools is the unique responsibility of the physical educator. Psychomotor development is concerned with two primary objectives: motor skill development and physical fitness development.

Motor Skill Development

The development of motor skills is sometimes referred to as the development of neuromuscular or psychomotor skills, because effective movement depends on the harmonious working together of the muscular and nervous systems. The acquisition and refinement of motor skills essential for everyday activities such as posture and lifting and for movement in a variety of physical activities, such as dance, sports, aquatics, or outdoor pursuits, are important outcomes of motor skill development. The development of motor skills focuses on helping individuals learn how to move effectively to accomplish specific goals efficiently, that is, with as little expenditure of energy as possible.

Motor skill development is a sequential process that occurs throughout one's lifespan. Infants possess reflexive, involuntary movements that are replaced with voluntary movements as they mature. Fundamental movements, such as running and throwing, begin to develop in early childhood around the time the child can walk independently. These fundamental motor skills progress through various stages, such as imitation and manipulation, leading to the mature form of the skill. As children progress through these stages, they exhibit a greater degree of competency in their movements, the movements become more precise, and fewer errors occur.

Fundamental movements form the basis for the development of specialized motor and sport skills in the later childhood years. Fundamental movements such as running, kicking, trapping, and dodging now can be articulated and applied to a sport such as soccer. Movements such as running, striking, and sliding can be incorporated into a game of tennis. In these situations, increased demands are placed on the individual with respect to form, speed, accuracy, and complexity of skill performance. If we are to achieve our goal of lifespan participation in physical activity, careful attention must be paid to the development of each individual's motor skills. As our programs expand to meet the needs of people of all ages, from preschoolers to the elderly, we must be prepared to promote the acquisition and refinement of motor skills in diverse populations.

The development of individuals' motor skills to their fullest potential requires that individuals have the opportunity to be involved in structured movement experiences that are appropriate to their development level. These experiences should provide meaningful instruction, offer sufficient opportunity for skill practice, and encourage effort and continued practice outside the structured setting. Physical educators who work with young children play a critical role in achieving our goal of promoting lifelong participation. It is important that children acquire competency in the basic, fundamental motor skills so that they can adapt these skills to the more stringent demands of sports and other physical activities such as dance and recreational pursuits. Individuals who

THE PSYCHOMOTOR DOMAIN

Category	Description	Application
1. Imitation	Observing and patterning behavior after someone else, perhaps with low-quality performance.	**PE**—After the physical education teacher demonstrates the shooting technique in basketball, the students imitate her performance without a ball, then with a ball in self-space before they can shoot at the basket. **Ex Sci**—Members of a yoga class follow the instructor's directions as they move from a Downward Dog into a Warrior II pose. **Sport**—A volleyball coach demonstrates the approach to the spike then has his players repeatedly perform the same approach (without a ball) before they participate in a spiking drill.
2. Manipulation	Ability to perform certain actions by following instructions and practicing.	**PE**—In a basketball shooting drill, the students shoot from self-selected distances (marked by poly spots) without a defender for 10 minutes at the beginning of each class period. **Ex Sci**—Members of a yoga class make up their own warm-up pattern, which consists of four different poses, at the start of each class. **Sport**—A softball coach demonstrates a soft toss drill to the team so the players can work on their hand-eye coordination. The players get into six small groups and perform the same drill following the coach's instructions.
3. Precision	Refining; becoming more exact, with few apparent errors.	**PE**—Students repeatedly practice their gymnastics routine until it has seamless transitions and solid beginning and ending poses, and each movement has appropriate body alignment. **Ex Sci**—A client practices keeping her body straight and bending her elbows at a 90-degree angle as she attempts 10 traditional push-ups daily. **Sport**—A golfer reviews video clips of his putting technique. He adjusts the speed of his backswing as he hits golf balls from the same distance with the goal of getting 40 out of 50 into the cup.
4. Articulation	Coordinating a series of actions; achieving harmony and internal consistency.	**PE**—Students create a line dance that aligns to the beat of the music. **Ex Sci**—As a warm-up, a client jumps rope for 3 minutes consecutively without tripping over the rope or stopping due to fatigue. **Sport**—During a baseball game, the defensive team completes a perfect relay from right field to get the runner out at home.
5. Naturalization	Performing at a high level automatically, without needing to think much about it.	**PE**—During a soccer game, students move without the ball to create space and get open to receive a pass from their teammates. **Ex Sci**—A runner records negative splits over a 10-mile course without checking the time after each mile. **Sport**—A quarterback changes the offensive play call after noticing that the defense is setting up to blitz.

lack the prerequisite skills will have trouble meeting these demands. Learning experiences that provide for success while developing skill proficiency increase the probability that students will incorporate physical activity into their lifestyle.

Physical education is the only area within the school that helps students in developing their motor skills. Through a progressive curriculum, students move from competency in the basic movements to the performance of skilled movements, including sport skills. They are provided with opportunities to learn how to modify these movements to meet changing situational demands and unique personal needs. They also have the opportunity to explore movement as a medium of communication, as a vehicle for creativity, and as a means to understand other cultures. Though many current physical education curriculums emphasize fitness promotion, the development of motor skills should not be neglected. This is essential for lifespan participation. The likelihood of individuals engaging in physical activity regularly increases if they have the skills to participate successfully in activities that are enjoyable and personally satisfying.

School physical education programs should offer a balanced variety of activities that allow young people to develop competency in lifetime activities that are personally meaningful and enjoyable. A balance should exist in any physical education program among team, dual, and individual (lifetime) sports, along with dance, yoga, outdoor pursuits, gymnastics, and cooperative activities. Team sports such as basketball and soccer provide an opportunity for students to develop skills and to enjoy working and competing together as a team. However, in many school physical education programs, team sports dominate the curriculum at the expense of various individual and dual sports, such as tennis, swimming, badminton, and golf. In such cases, the students are deprived of the opportunity to develop skills in activities that they can participate in throughout their adult lives. Only through a balanced program of team, dual, and individual sports and dance, yoga, outdoor pursuits,

gymnastics, and cooperative activities is it possible to develop well-rounded individuals.

In adulthood, an individual's participation in sports and recreational activities is influenced by a number of factors. Past exposure, interests, abilities, enjoyment, motivation, opportunity, time, and financial considerations are just a few factors that influence the nature and level of adults' participation. If one primary purpose of physical education, exercise science, and sport is to promote a physically active lifestyle that will contribute to the optimal development and health of the individual, we must provide individuals of all ages with the necessary motor skills to do so. The skills individuals acquire will help determine how they spend their leisure time as well as what path they will choose to develop fitness. For example, a person who excels in swimming may spend much of his or her leisure time engaged in related activities, or choose to follow a fitness program based on swimming. If an individual excels in tennis, he or she may frequent the courts.

Professionals working outside the school setting with adults face special challenges in teaching motor skills. Adults may want to learn a new sport, yet lack proficiency in the prerequisite fundamental movement skills. They may, for example, exhibit poorly developed running or throwing skills. Professionals working with these adults must use instructional strategies to help them master the fundamental movements while incorporating instruction about the sport skills into the lesson to challenge the adults.

Sports, aquatics, and dance give individuals enjoyable activities for use during their free time. They offer a pleasurable means to relax after work and are popular recreational pursuits on the weekends. Development of motor skills for participation in sport and recreational activities is important for people of all ages, including those individuals with disabilities. Professionals in all settings must be prepared to teach individuals with a diversity of needs and to modify activities and instructional strategies to be appropriate to the abilities of the individuals with whom they are working. Challenging activities that lead to skill development and meaningful participation are essential to providing a positive learning experience for all individuals, including those with special needs.

Physical Fitness Development

The evidence supporting the contribution of physical activity and health-related fitness to well-being and quality of life is overwhelming. Development and maintenance of physical fitness has long been heralded as one of the most important outcomes of school physical education programs. Fitness promotion is the focus of many nonschool physical education, exercise science, and sport programs as well.

A progressive, systematic approach to the development of physical fitness should be used. First and foremost, the program should consider

Improving fitness is an important goal of many worksite health promotion programs.

the needs of the individual. Based on these needs, the program should be designed to accomplish the desired outcomes. Careful attention should be given to helping individuals identify and develop proficiency in activities that are enjoyable and meaningful to them while contributing to the attainment of fitness. This will encourage individuals to make these activities an integral part of their lifestyle.

If we are to accomplish our objectives related to physical fitness, a multifaceted approach is needed. Obviously, we must teach exercises and activities that promote fitness. However, this is not enough. Through our programs, individuals must acquire the knowledge to design and modify their fitness program to meet their changing needs. Moreover, our programs must instill within each individual the desire to make fitness a lifelong pursuit, the enjoyment of physical activity, and the appreciation of the value of leading a healthy, active lifestyle.

Contemporary physical education, exercise science, and sport support the development of physical fitness and physically active lifestyles for people of all ages. Unfortunately, the majority of our nation's people are not involved in physical activity on a regular basis and thus do not realize the concomitant health benefits. Minorities, people who are economically disadvantaged, women, older adults, and people with disabilities are disproportionately inactive. As professionals, we must increase our efforts to reach out and involve people from these populations in our programs.

Quality school-based physical education programs can contribute significantly to the education of the individual and enhance learning and development in all three domains: cognitive, affective, and psychomotor. For professionals working in settings outside the school, an understanding of the behavioral domains, taxonomies, and objectives helps them to more effectively structure their programs to achieve desired outcomes. Professionals in all settings must also assess the progress of their participants in achieving the desired outcomes. Assessment should be an integral part of all physical education, exercise science, and sport programs.

ASSESSMENT OF LEARNING

How do professionals determine whether the participants in their physical education, exercise science, and sport programs have achieved the stated objectives? How do we diagnose the needs of the individuals engaged in our programs? What is the best way to monitor participants' rates of progress? How do participants know when they have accomplished their goals? How can we motivate people to persist in their endeavors? What changes can we make in our programs to be more effective? How can we show the worth of our programs in this era of accountability? How can we, as professionals, enhance our own abilities to meet the needs of participants in our programs? Assessment enables us to answer these and many other important questions.

Assessment is a critical component of quality physical education, exercise science, and sport programs. Assessment should be a dynamic, ongoing process integrated into programs and viewed as an essential, crucial element of any program, be it conducted in a school or nonschool setting. The development of quality physical education, exercise science, and sport programs requires establishing clear goals, assessing participants' needs, setting specific objectives, planning learning experiences, providing effective instruction, and evaluating the outcomes.

Assessment can yield important information about participants' progress, program quality, instructional practices, and the effectiveness of professionals. Evaluation promotes accountability. Participants are accountable for their performance and professionals are accountable for participants' achievements. Today more than ever, demonstrating the worth and value of our programs is critical. Assessment is central to this purpose because it provides meaningful information about learning and achievement related to goals, objectives, and outcomes in the affective, cognitive, and psychomotor domains. Assessment links the content standards to the instructional process and to the participants' achievements. Assessment is a continual endeavor, one that is essential to the learning process.

Assessment Defined

Assessment is the process of gathering information to learn what participants know and are able to do, in order to determine their progress toward achievement of goals and objectives. Measurement and evaluation are closely related processes. *Measurement* is the process of gathering information or collecting data. *Evaluation* is the process of interpreting the information or data. Assessment is more encompassing in its scope than evaluation, including data collection, interpretation, and decision-making.

NASPE identifies "the primary goal of assessment as the enhancement of learning, rather than documentation of learning."[7] Assessment has a broader purpose than the assignment of a grade or the use of a checklist to denote progress. As a critical component of any program, assessment helps professionals make decisions and conduct programs that are in the best interests of the participants.

Assessment encompasses a variety of measurement, evaluation, and assessment techniques that have as their primary purpose the gathering and interpretation of information. This information is used to make decisions that will enhance the outcomes achieved and the experiences of participants in physical education, exercise science, and sport programs.

Purposes of Assessment

As an integral component of quality physical education, exercise science, and sport programs, assessment, when used correctly, can contribute in many ways to the achievement of learning and enhancement of development in the cognitive, affective, and psychomotor domains. The main purposes of assessment include diagnosis, placement, monitoring of progress, determination of achievement, motivation, program improvement, and evaluation of instructor effectiveness. (See the Assessment box for a definition and list of purposes of assessment.)

Diagnosis is one of the most important uses of assessment. Diagnostic procedures can be used to identify individuals' strengths and weaknesses, levels of abilities, and developmental status in the various domains. When working with children with disabilities, the adapted physical activity specialist may use the Denver Developmental Screening Test to identify motor, language, and personal-social skills of the children. A sport psychologist working with an intercollegiate athletic team to improve its performance uses several paper-and-pencil tests to find out athletes' satisfaction, perception of team climate, attentional styles, and leadership roles. Additional knowledge gleaned from interviews of the athletes and coaches and from personal observation of the team during practice and games helps the sport psychologist identify factors limiting the team's achievement.

Exercise and physical activity prescription uses diagnostic information to design programs to meet identified needs. A cardiac rehabilitation specialist uses the results of an exercise stress test to prescribe an exercise program for the postcardiac patient. A personal trainer reviews the various assessments of a client's fitness level, nutritional status, and lifestyle habits, and then designs an individualized wellness program for the client. Working with the athlete's physician, an athletic trainer plans a program of exercise to restore the full range of motion to an athlete who is recovering from a rotator cuff injury.

Classification, or placement of individuals into groups based on their abilities, is another purpose of assessment. For children with disabilities, assessment influences their educational placement and the type of services they receive. Sport activity instructors commonly assign people to ability groups for instruction, believing that same-ability grouping facilitates learning.

Determination of achievement is one of the primary purposes of assessment. Physical education, exercise science, and sport programs involve purposeful activity directed toward the attainment of certain goals. Have the program participants achieved the stated objectives? Does the senior citizen know how to modify his walking program as he increases his level of fitness? Are the children in a youth sport program mastering the basic skills of soccer? Do the physical fitness test results reveal that the student has achieved a satisfactory level of health-related fitness? Does the running log of a participant in the community fitness program reveal a commitment to exercising on a regular basis? Without assessment, how would we know whether our participants have achieved the desired objectives? Assessment can provide an indicator of achievement at the end of a program. When assessment is done at both the beginning and the end of the program, improvement can be seen. Incorporation of various assessment techniques throughout the program allows for the tracking of participants' progress.

Assessment can enhance the motivation of participants, encouraging them to improve further. Learning experiences that provide for frequent self-testing and incremental successes allow sixth-grade students to see that their volleyball skills are

---

ASSESSMENT

Assessment is the process of gathering information to learn what participants know and are able to do in order to determine their progress toward achievement of goals and objectives.

Purposes of Assessment
- Diagnosis
- Placement
- Monitoring of progress
- Determination of achievement
- Motivation
- Program improvement
- Evaluation of leadership effectiveness

Computerized fitness equipment is becoming increasingly common. This technology makes it easier for people to monitor their workout and self-assess their fitness status.

improving and that hard work yields results. An athlete is motivated to continue to rehabilitate her knee when she sees that the weight that she can lift with her injured leg increases each week. An employee in a corporate fitness program is motivated to continue to exercise each day at 6 A.M. when he sees a decrease in his time to complete a mile and perceives himself as having more energy to meet the demands of the day. Assessment is also motivating to professionals when they see that the time and effort they have invested in their programs have benefitted the program's participants.

Assessment affects participants in varied ways. Assessment influences participants' perceptions of themselves as learners and, more specifically, their perceptions of their competence as movers. It can enhance their confidence in their abilities and create positive attitudes toward participation. Participants can use assessment to focus their learning on relevant tasks, to guide their expenditure of time, to consolidate their learning, and to develop learning strategies for the future.

Another purpose of assessment is program evaluation. Assessment can provide evidence of the effectiveness of the program. Corporate fitness directors can document the progress and concomitant health gains made by employees enrolled in the program. This lets the employer know whether the program is beneficial to the employees and whether the investment in the program has yielded cost savings. This more global approach can also be used to improve the program. From this perspective, items such as program content, progression of instructional experiences, administration and organization, facilities and equipment, and time allocation are addressed as part of the overall program assessment. This enables professionals to make improvements in their programs to heighten their effectiveness.

Professionals who care deeply about their professional endeavors reflect upon all the information gathered via the assessment process to improve their own effectiveness. They might ask themselves, "Are there any changes that I can make in my presentation? Is the order of the instructional tasks the best sequence to enhance participants' developments? Do I need to give participants more guidance?" These and other questions can help professionals enhance their effectiveness and thus influence the outcomes of the participants in their programs.

There are different avenues professionals can use to assess the outcomes achieved by participants in their programs. The ability of assessment procedures to enhance learning by connecting assessment to instruction and to enrich the experience of program participants makes it critical that assessment is included as an integral part of physical education, exercise science, and sport programs.

The Role of Technology in Assessment

Technology is increasingly influencing the assessment processes. Computers help in maintaining records of test results or keeping a log of participants' involvement in the program.

One example of computerized record keeping is the Cooper Institute's Fitnessgram.[18] The Fitnessgram is used in many schools throughout the nation to provide students and their parents with information about the student's fitness profile. The program measures the health-related components of fitness—cardiorespiratory endurance, muscle strength and endurance, flexibility, and body composition. The Fitnessgram can be seen in Figure 2-1. The Fitnessgram provides a computerized report on the fitness status of each student. The profile is constructed from the individual's performance on the test items. When necessary, exercise recommendations are made, based on the test performance of the individual. The Fitnessgram also makes it easy for teachers, parents, and students to compare their performance on the current test to performances on previous tests. This makes it easy to note where improvements have been made and identifies fitness areas that require attention. The Fitnessgram helps teachers keep track of their students' fitness levels and determine whether the stated program objectives are being achieved.

Related to the Fitnessgram is the Activitygram, which is shown in Figure 2-2.[18] The Activitygram provides an assessment of the student's physical activity both on school and non-school days. This assessment was included in the Fitnessgram to help reinforce to students the importance of being physically active on a daily basis.[18] In order to maintain fitness, students must develop lifetime habits of regular physical activity. The Activitygram helps students become more aware of their physical activity patterns.

Computerized assessment and record-keeping systems are becoming increasingly popular. One system is the HealthFirst TriFit system. The HealthFirst TriFit system enables professionals to perform a complete fitness assessment and design personalized exercise and nutrition programs for their students or clients.[19] Assessment of cardiovascular function, body composition, flexibility, muscular strength, and a variety of biometric measures can be performed. The testing instruments, such as the bicycle ergometer used to assess cardiorespiratory endurance or the skinfold calipers used to help determine body composition, are directly interfaced with the computer. Additional information from other assessments can be entered into the computer by the professional. The HealthFirst software analyzes the results of the tests performed and creates a profile of the student's or client's health fitness status. Personalized fitness programs can then be created using the HealthFirst software. Progress reports can also be generated, allowing the tracking of fitness activities and assessments over a period of time. Additionally, there is an online learning center that students and clients can access to perform health risk appraisals or find out additional information on a multitude of topics pertaining to fitness and wellness.

Corporate fitness centers also use computers in their fitness programs. A computerized check-in system records employee participation. After exercising, employees use the computer to record the type of exercise they performed, the duration of the exercise period, and their weight. A record of each employee's progress toward his or her goals is easily maintained. This information is helpful to program managers in charting facility

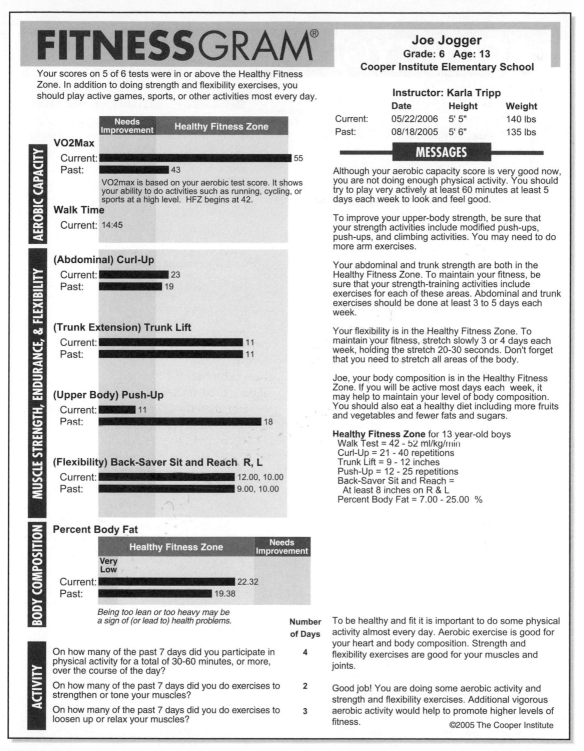

FITNESSGRAM®

Joe Jogger
Grade: 6 Age: 13
Cooper Institute Elementary School

Your scores on 5 of 6 tests were in or above the Healthy Fitness Zone. In addition to doing strength and flexibility exercises, you should play active games, sports, or other activities most every day.

Instructor: Karla Tripp

	Date	Height	Weight
Current:	05/22/2006	5' 5"	140 lbs
Past:	08/18/2005	5' 6"	135 lbs

AEROBIC CAPACITY

	Needs Improvement	Healthy Fitness Zone

VO2Max
Current: 55
Past: 43

VO2max is based on your aerobic test score. It shows your ability to do activities such as running, cycling, or sports at a high level. HFZ begins at 42.

Walk Time
Current: 14:45

MESSAGES

Although your aerobic capacity score is very good now, you are not doing enough physical activity. You should try to play very actively at least 60 minutes at least 5 days each week to look and feel good.

To improve your upper-body strength, be sure that your strength activities include modified push-ups, push-ups, and climbing activities. You may need to do more arm exercises.

Your abdominal and trunk strength are both in the Healthy Fitness Zone. To maintain your fitness, be sure that your strength-training activities include exercises for each of these areas. Abdominal and trunk exercises should be done at least 3 to 5 days each week.

Your flexibility is in the Healthy Fitness Zone. To maintain your fitness, stretch slowly 3 or 4 days each week, holding the stretch 20-30 seconds. Don't forget that you need to stretch all areas of the body.

Joe, your body composition is in the Healthy Fitness Zone. If you will be active most days each week, it may help to maintain your level of body composition. You should also eat a healthy diet including more fruits and vegetables and fewer fats and sugars.

MUSCLE STRENGTH, ENDURANCE, & FLEXIBILITY

(Abdominal) Curl-Up
Current: 23
Past: 19

(Trunk Extension) Trunk Lift
Current: 11
Past: 11

(Upper Body) Push-Up
Current: 11
Past: 18

(Flexibility) Back-Saver Sit and Reach R, L
Current: 12.00, 10.00
Past: 9.00, 10.00

Healthy Fitness Zone for 13 year-old boys
Walk Test = 42 - 52 ml/kg/min
Curl-Up = 21 - 40 repetitions
Trunk Lift = 9 - 12 inches
Push-Up = 12 - 25 repetitions
Back-Saver Sit and Reach =
   At least 8 inches on R & L
Percent Body Fat = 7.00 - 25.00 %

BODY COMPOSITION

Percent Body Fat

	Healthy Fitness Zone	Needs Improvement
	Very Low	

Current: 22.32
Past: 19.38

Being too lean or too heavy may be a sign of (or lead to) health problems.

ACTIVITY

	Number of Days
On how many of the past 7 days did you participate in physical activity for a total of 30-60 minutes, or more, over the course of the day?	4
On how many of the past 7 days did you do exercises to strengthen or tone your muscles?	2
On how many of the past 7 days did you do exercises to loosen up or relax your muscles?	3

To be healthy and fit it is important to do some physical activity almost every day. Aerobic exercise is good for your heart and body composition. Strength and flexibility exercises are good for your muscles and joints.

Good job! You are doing some aerobic activity and strength and flexibility exercises. Additional vigorous aerobic activity would help to promote higher levels of fitness.

©2005 The Cooper Institute

Figure 2-1   The Fitnessgram can be used by teachers to generate a computerized report of the physical fitness status of students.

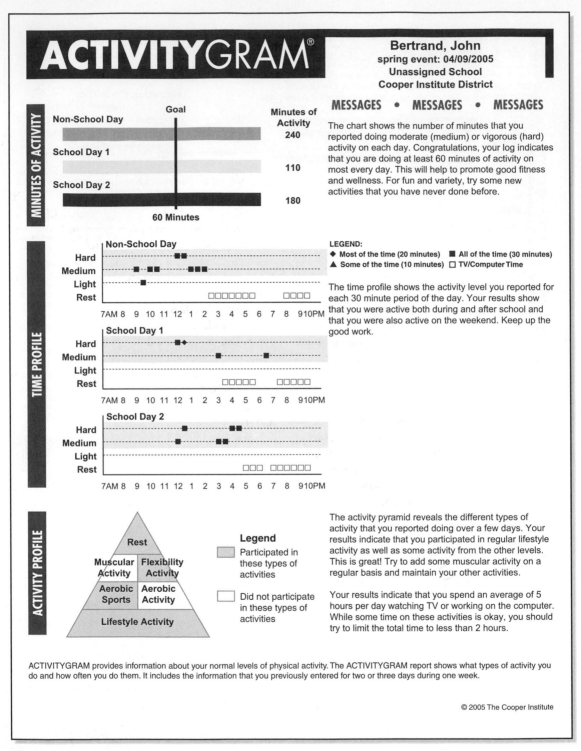

Figure 2-2 The Activitygram can be used to assess students' activity levels during both school and nonschool days.

usage, calculating the benefits of the programs, and documenting program effectiveness.

Heart rate monitors are valuable tools for teaching children and adults about fitness in both school and nonschool settings. These monitors, worn on the wrist, track heart rate and provide positive reinforcement to the wearers as they work to achieve their goals. They provide physical education teachers, exercise scientists, and sport leaders with valuable information that they can use to modify their teaching methods. A printout of the exercise session provides a permanent record of participants' work.

The impact of computer technology has been felt throughout the field of physical education, exercise science, and sport. Exercise physiologists use computers to regulate equipment during highly complex tests of cardiovascular function and to analyze the voluminous amounts of data generated. Athletic trainers assess the extent of an injury, carry out a course of treatment, and monitor the rehabilitation process. Computerized equipment, such as the Cybex, offers both the injured athlete and the athletic trainer continuous feedback on their weight training efforts during rehabilitation. Biomechanists use special computer programs to analyze motions and force production. Sport sociologists and sport psychologists use computers to conduct sophisticated data analysis. Fitness professionals rely on computers

for record keeping. Club members punch in their personal code on a computer console next to each piece of exercise equipment. As a digital display shows weight lifted and repetitions performed, the computer keeps track as well, providing the member and the professional with a continuous record of the member's progress.

There are many interactive websites on the Internet that allow individuals to complete a health risk appraisal and have ready access to information they can use to modify their lifestyles. Interactive logs enable individuals to keep track of their physical activity and dietary intake, making it easy for them to track and continually monitor their fitness program from any location worldwide.

Many handheld devices and smart mobile phones, such as the iTouch or BlackBerry, have great fitness and health applications available, many of them at little or no cost. These applications enable professionals to easily enter fitness data and then later upload the information they have collected to their desktop computer for further analysis and inclusion in their database.

As we move forward in the twenty-first century, technology will play an important role in helping physical education, exercise science, and sport professionals assess a multitude of outcome measures and monitor the progress of participants in their programs.

SUMMARY

Philosophy is critical to our endeavors. The major branches of philosophy include metaphysics, epistemology, logic, axiology, ethics, and aesthetics. Philosophies such as idealism, realism, pragmatism, naturalism, existentialism, and humanism have influenced the nature and practice of physical education, exercise science, and sport programs. Over the years, the philosophy of education through the physical has significantly influenced the design and conduct of our programs.

Sport philosophy emerged as a specialized area of study in the mid-1960s and 1970s. As this area grew,

emphasis shifted from philosophical issues associated with physical education in schools to the study of sport. Sport philosophers use logic and critical reasoning to study the meaning of physical activity and the mind-body relationship. As this subdiscipline matured, the philosophical study of physical activity broadened.

Each professional should develop his or her own philosophy. One's philosophy influences the goals and objectives or outcomes sought from one's programs and the methods by which these goals and objectives are attained. Goals are broad statements of aims that reflect desired accomplishments. Objectives are more specific statements of outcomes that build progressively to the achievement of the goals. Contemporary physical education, exercise science, and sport emphasizes the development of the whole person through participation in quality physical education, exercise science, and sport programs. The objectives of physical education, exercise science, and sport encompass four areas: fitness development, skill development, knowledge, and affective development.

The past decade has seen professional efforts devoted to identifying the qualities of a physically educated person. According to NASPE, a physically educated person has learned skills to perform a variety of physical activities, is physically fit, participates regularly in physical activities, knows the benefits of involvement in physical activity, and values the contribution of physical activity to a healthy lifestyle. NASPE developed content standards for physical education and guidelines for assessment. These standards and guidelines offer professionals in all settings a valuable framework to guide their efforts.

Human behavior is often described with reference to three domains: cognitive, affective, and psychomotor domains. Taxonomies organize the objectives associated with each domain into hierarchies. These taxonomies guide professionals in designing programs to meet the needs of their participants. Physical education, exercise science, and sport programs contribute in many ways to learning in these three domains.

Assessment of learning is critical in physical education, exercise science, and sport. Assessment is a continual process that serves many purposes. These include diagnosis, prescription, classification, determination of achievement, documentation of progress, enhancement of motivation, program improvement, and professional development. There are many types of assessment methods for professionals to utilize.

Technology is increasingly influencing the assessment process. Computers have been used for record keeping, regulation of testing equipment, and data analysis. Professionals in all settings have found technology to be of great value in their endeavors.

The next chapter will discuss the role of physical education, exercise science, and sport in our society.

DISCUSSION QUESTIONS

1. Of the six major philosophies, which one do you identify with the most? Why do you identify with this philosophy? How do you think your philosophical perspective can impact you as a future professional?

2. As a physical educator, exercise scientist, or sport leader, how do you develop goals and objectives for your program? How do these goals and objectives align with your professional philosophy?

3. Describe how assessment aligns with program goals and objectives. What assessments would you use to learn whether your students/clients/players have met the goals and objectives?

SELF-ASSESSMENT ACTIVITIES

These activities are designed to help you determine whether you have mastered the material and competencies presented in this chapter.

1. Compare the characteristics of physical education, exercise science, and sport programs guided by each of the major philosophies: idealism, realism, pragmatism, naturalism, existentialism, and humanism.

2. Using the Developing Your Professional Philosophy box, attempt to write your philosophy of physical education, exercise science, and sport. Reflect on your experiences, review various philosophies, and take time to talk with some of your professors about their philosophy.

3. Reflect on your experiences in youth, interscholastic, and intercollegiate sport. How did these experiences

contribute to your development in the cognitive, affective, and psychomotor domains? What changes could have been made in the programs to further enhance development in each of the domains?

4. Refer to the 12 Steps to Understanding Research Reports box located in Chapter 1. Answer the questions in Step 2 for the same article you selected in Chapter 1.

REFERENCES

1. Mechikoff RA and Estes SG: A history and philosophy of sport and physical education, ed 4, New York, 2006, McGraw-Hill.

2. Siedentop D: Introduction to physical education, fitness, and sport, ed 3, Mountain View, Calif., 2007, Mayfield.

3. Kretchmar RS: Philosophy of sport. In JD Massengale and RA Swanson, editors, The history of exercise and sport science, Champaign, Ill.,1997, Human Kinetics.

4. US Department of Health and Human Services: Healthy people 2010: understanding and improving health, Washington, D.C., 2000, US Government Printing Office.

5. Corbin CB: Physical education as an agent of change, Quest 54:182–195, 2002.

6. Bucher CA: Foundations of physical education, ed 4, St. Louis, 1964, Mosby.

7. National Association for Sport and Physical Education: Moving into the future: national standards for physical education—a guide to content and assessment, St. Louis, 1995, Mosby.

8. National Association for Sport and Physical Education, Moving into the future: national standards for physical education, ed 2, Reston, Va., 2004, AAHPERD.

9. Ziegler E: The professional's relationship to fitness for people of all ages, JOPERD 56(1):15, 1985.

10. Bloom BS, editor: Taxonomy of educational objectives: the classification of education goals, handbook I: cognitive domain, New York, 1956, David McKay.

11. Strand B, Mauch L, and Terbizan D: The fitness education pyramid—integrating the concepts with the technology, JOPERD 68(6):19–27, 1997.

12. Krathwohl DR, Bloom BS, and Masia BB: Taxonomy of educational objectives, handbook II: affective domain, New York, 1964, David McKay.

13. Hellison D: Teaching personal and social responsibility in physical education. In S Silverman and C Ennis, editors, Student learning in physical education: applying research to enhance instruction, Champaign, Ill., 1996, Human Kinetics.

14. Docheff D: Character in sport and physical education—summation, JOPERD 69(2):24, 1998.

15. Gough RW: Character development—a practical strategy for emphasizing character development in sport and physical education, JOPERD 69(2):18–20, 23, 1998.

16. Dave R: Psychomotor levels. In RJ Armstrong, editor, Developing and writing behavioral objectives, Tucson, Ariz. 1970, Educational Innovators Press.

17. Corbin CB: Becoming physically educated in the elementary school, Philadelphia, 1976, Lea & Febiger.

18. The Cooper Institute for Aerobics Research, The Fitnessgram, Dallas, Texas, 1999, The Cooper Institute for Aerobics Research.

19. HealthFirst USA, TriFit, Albuquerque, N.M., 2001, HealthFirst USA.

CHAPTER 3

ROLE IN SOCIETY

OBJECTIVES

After reading this chapter the student should be able to—

- Understand the changing demographics of the United States and their implications for physical education, exercise science, and sport.
- Interpret to colleagues and to the public the role of physical education, exercise science, and sport in the promotion of health and the attainment of wellness.
- Discuss the physical activity of people of all ages and the implications for physical education, exercise science, and sport.

Societal trends influence the role of physical education, exercise science, and sport in our society. One significant trend is the changing demographics of our population. Our society is more culturally diverse than at any other time in its history. This diversity will become even greater as we move farther into the twenty-first century. As professionals committed to enriching the lives of all people, we must, as DeSensi states, increase our "consciousness and appreciation of differences associated with heritage, characteristics, and values of people."[1]

Two other societal trends that hold implications for physical education, exercise science, and sport are the wellness movement and the fitness and physical activity movement. The wellness movement emphasizes the individual's responsibility to make informed choices that will lead to an optimal state of health. Disease prevention and health promotion are the cornerstones of this movement. In the fitness and physical activity movement, participation in physical activity by people of all ages are encouraged. There is substantial evidence to support the value of leading a physically active lifestyle across the lifespan.

CHANGING DEMOGRAPHICS

As we move into the second decade of the twenty-first century, the United States is in the midst of demographic changes that will profoundly influence our future as a nation and will greatly affect the nature and conduct of physical education, exercise science, and sport programs.[2–6,*] Racial and ethnic diversity grew dramatically in the United States during the last three decades of the twentieth century and will increase even more in the decades to come. Our growing diversity requires that we, as physical educators, exercise scientists, and sport leaders, be able to work effectively in cross-cultural situations. Changes within and among different population groups, such as children and older adults, determine the demand for education, health care, facilities, and other services that meet the needs of different segments of the population. This, in turn, will influence job opportunities, funding for services, and the nature and conduct of programs designed to serve these populations.

In the United States, we are currently living longer and healthier lives. Public health initiatives, advances in medical science, and improvements in standards of living have contributed to dramatic improvements in the longevity of the population. At the beginning of the twentieth century, the average life expectancy in the United States was 47.3 years. In 2006, life expectancy for the US population rose to 77.7 years, with whites and women outliving blacks and men by over 5 years.[7] US Health and Human Services Secretary Tommy G. Thompson said, "Americans on the average are living longer than ever before, and much of this is due to the progress we've made in fighting diseases that account for a majority of deaths in the country. But we can do even more by eating right, exercising regularly and taking other simple steps to promote good health and prevent serious illness and disease."[5]

Improvements in health have contributed to the growth of the older population during the last century. In 1900, about 4% of the population was 65 years and older. In 2000, an estimated 35 million people—or about 13% of the population—was

*Data compiled from US Department of Commerce, US Census Bureau, Census 2000 (www.census.gov); Centers for Disease Control and Prevention, National Center for Health Statistics (www.cdc.gov/nchs); National Center for Education Statistics (http://nces.ed.gov); Federal Interagency Forum on Child and Family Statistics (www.childstats.gov); United States Department of Health and Human Services (www.hhs.gov).

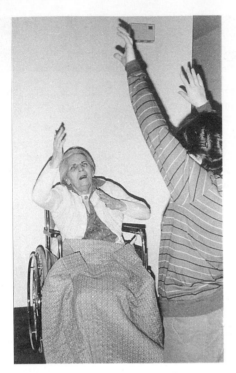

Participation in appropriate exercise can help elderly people increase their flexibility.

65 years and older. The number of older Americans is projected to grow rapidly in the first half of the twenty-first century. In 2011 the "baby boom" generation, born between 1946 and 1964, will begin to turn 65. By 2030, it is projected that one in five people, or 20% of the population, will be 65 and older. The most rapidly growing segment of the older population is the 85 and older group. In 2000, about 2% of the population was 85 and older. By 2050, it is projected that nearly 5% of the US population will be 85 and older.

The number of children in the United States influences the demand for schools and teachers, health care services and professionals, and facilities and services that serve children and their families. In 2000, there were 70.4 million children, or 26% of the population under the age of 18. This was a decline from the peak of 36% at the end of the "baby boom" in the twentieth century. The percentage of children in our population is projected to remain relatively stable and is estimated to comprise 24% of the population in 2020. School enrollment is projected to continue to increase slightly through 2010.

As a nation, our cultural diversity continues to grow. The surge in immigration increased our diversity tremendously. The 2000 census data revealed that 12.5% of the population was Hispanic, which can be people of any race, and 87.5% of the population was non-Hispanic. With respect to race, 75.2% of the population was white, 12.3% of the population was African American, 0.9% American Indian or Alaskan Native, 3.6% Asian, and 0.1% Native Hawaiian and other Pacific Islanders. About 2% of the population identified themselves as multiracial. By the year 2010, projections indicate that ethnic and racial minority groups will account for 32% of the population, compared to 20% of the population in 1980. The Hispanic population is the fastest-growing of any racial and ethnic group, and it is estimated that 25% of the population will be Hispanic by the year 2050. In 2008, minorities made up 48% of US children, compared to 37% in 1990.[8]

Changes in the racial and ethnic diversity of the United States are reflected in all age groups. For example, the elderly are becoming more racially and ethnically diverse. In 1994, only 1 person in 10 was a member of a minority, but this should climb to 2 people in every 10 by 2050. The proportion of the elderly who are Hispanic is expected to rise from 4% to 16% over the same period.

More dramatic changes are expected in the school-age population. In 2008, 44% of public school students were minorities, an increase from 22% in 1972. Black and Hispanic students accounted for 17% and 21%, respectively, of public school enrollment.[9] In 2050, it is projected that Hispanic children will comprise 31% of all children, compared to 43% and 16% for whites and African Americans, respectively.

The changes in the racial and ethnic composition of student enrollments have altered the diversity of language and culture in the nation's schools. In 2007, 10 million school-age children spoke a language other than English at home and had difficulty in speaking English; this is 10 times

RACE AND ETHNICITY IN THE UNITED STATES: CENSUS 2000

US Census Race and Ethnicity Category Definitions

White — People having origins in any of the original peoples of Europe, the Middle East, or North Africa

Black or **African American** — People having origins in any of the Black racial groups of Africa

American Indian and **Alaskan Native** — People having origins in any of the original peoples of North and South America (including Central America), and who maintain tribal affiliation or community attachment

Asian — People having origins in any of the original peoples of the Far East, Southeast Asia, or the Indian subcontinent

Native Hawaiian and **Other Pacific Islander** — People having origins in any of the original peoples of Hawaii, Guam, Samoa, or other Pacific Islands

Some other race — People who were unable to identify with the five categories

Hispanic or **Latino** — Persons of Cuban, Mexican, Puerto Rican, South or Central American, or other Spanish culture or origin regardless of race

Non-Hispanic — Persons who are not of Hispanic origin regardless of race

Population by Race and Hispanic Origin

Race and Hispanic Origin	Percent
RACE	
Total population	**100.0**
One Race	97.6
White	75.2
Black or African American	12.3
American Indian and Alaskan Native	0.9
Asian	3.6
Native Hawaiian and Other Pacific Islander	0.1
Some other race	5.5
Two Races	2.4
HISPANIC or LATINO	
Total population	**100.0**
Hispanic or Latino	12.5
Not Hispanic or Latino	87.5

Source: US Census Bureau. *Overview of Race and Hispanic Origin Census 2000 Brief.* Washington, D.C.: US Census Bureau, 2001.

the number in 1979.[10] There are several school systems in the United States where more than 100 languages are spoken by the students. The variety in culture and language enriches the learning environment while at the same time creating great challenges for the schools.

Socioeconomic status exerts a significant influence on many aspects of an individual's life, including health status, educational attainment, and future employment. Poverty is associated with poor health outcomes for all ages, including higher rates of mortality. Unfortunately, many adults and children live in poverty today, and poverty rates vary by age, sex, race, ethnicity, family composition, and employment. Poverty level differs by the size of the household. The 2008 poverty threshold was an annual income below $11,000 for a single person and below $22,100 for a family of four.[11]

In 2005, 12.5% of the population, or 37 million people, lived below the poverty level. The poverty rate for white non-Hispanics was 8.39%, for blacks 24.9%, for Hispanics 21.8%, and for Asians and Pacific Islanders 11.19%.[12] Poverty was greatest in the southern United States.

By the time you read this textbook, the population and cultural diversity statistics presented in this section will have changed based on the 2010 census (see http://www.census.gov). It is predicted that the 2010 census will demonstrate how our society continues to become more culturally diverse across all demographic groupings. This increase in cultural diversity will have implications on our physical education, exercise science, and sport programs. For the first time in over a century, our longevity may decrease, or at the very least stay the same. The change in life expectancy is in large part due to the increase in chronic and degenerative diseases, many of which are directly or indirectly caused by poor nutrition and lack of physical activity. The population of children will remain stable; however, our country as a whole will continue to get older, and poverty rates will certainly be affected by the poor economic state of our country over recent years. Over the next few decades our country will continue to see a shift in the demographics of our population due to the increase in cultural diversity.

Implications of Changing Demographics

The many demographic changes that are occurring in the twenty-first century present professionals with great challenges and with extraordinary opportunities. As we reflect on these demographic and societal changes, we must ask ourselves what we can do to provide opportunities for participation in physical activity for all people. How can we involve a greater number of older people in our programs? How can we design programs that are sensitive to the values and needs of different racial and ethnic populations? How can we provide access to our programs for individuals living in poverty? How do we reach underserved populations and, most importantly, what is our commitment to doing so? Attainment of our

goal of lifespan participation in physical activity for all people requires that we do much more than we are currently doing to reach people of all ages, socioeconomic backgrounds, and different population groups.

Our nation's increasing cultural diversity makes it imperative that physical education, exercise science, and sport professionals reflect carefully on their view of cultural diversity and their commitment to providing opportunities for lifelong involvement in physical activity for all people. DeSensi defines cultural diversity as the "differences associated with gender, race, national origin, ethnicity, social class, religion, age, and ability/disability, but it can also be extended to include differences in personality, sexual orientation, veteran status, physical appearance, marital status, and parental status."[1] DeSensi's broad definition embraces many different groups. As you reflect on this definition, do you feel prepared to work with culturally diverse populations, whether in a school, community, worksite, health care, or private setting? Are you culturally competent?

Culture plays a complex, significant role in the health and well-being of people of all ages. Culture influences an individual's health, beliefs, behaviors, activities, access to care, adherence to programs, and treatment outcomes. Communication between the professional and the client/patient/student is influenced by cultural norms, including norms related to language and usage, eye contact, personal space, expression of symptoms and concerns, openness or extent of disclosure, and degree of formality in the interaction. Because health is significantly influenced by cultural beliefs, cultural issues should be a major consideration in the design and implementation of health promotion and prevention services, including physical activity programs.

The US Department of Health and Human Services Office of Minority Health defines cultural and linguistic competence as "a set of congruent behaviors, attitudes and policies that come together in a system, agency or among professionals that enables effective work in cross-cultural situations. 'Culture' refers to integrated patterns of human behavior that include the language, thoughts, communications, actions, customs, beliefs, values, and institutions of racial, ethnic, religious or social groups. 'Competence' implies having the capacity to function effectively as an individual and an organization within the context of the cultural beliefs, behaviors and needs presented by consumers and their communities."[13]

How do you achieve cultural competency? The US Department of Health and Human Services Bureau of Primary Health Care's publication *Cultural Competency: A Journey* states that achieving cultural competency is a journey, an ongoing developmental process of personal reflection and growth.[14] The journey begins with an awareness of and reflection on your own cultural heritage, your values, beliefs, biases, and prejudices and how they may affect your perceptions and interactions with people of other cultures.

Cultural competency requires thoughtful examination of your own cultural heritage and the privileges and disadvantages associated with your culture. It necessitates understanding how power, privilege, oppression, discrimination, stereotypes, and prejudice influence opportunities for different cultural groups. Gaining knowledge of other cultural beliefs, values, and behaviors of other cultures, recognizing that people of different cultures have different ways of communicating and behaving, and learning another language are part of the journey toward cultural competency.

However, there is more to cultural competency than just being knowledgeable about different cultures or being able to speak a second language. The Administration on Aging guidebook *Achieving Cultural Competence* states:

> To achieve cultural competency, professionals must first have a sense of compassion and respect for people who are culturally different. Then, practitioners can learn behaviors that are congruent with cultural competence. Just learning the behavior is not enough. Underlying the behavior must be an attitudinal set of behavior skills and moral responsibility. It is not about the things one does. It is about fundamental attitudes. When a person has an inherent caring, appreciation, and

respect for others, they can display warmth, empathy, and genuineness. This then enables them to have culturally congruent behaviors and attitudes. When these three elements intersect, practitioners can exemplify cultural competence in a manner that recognizes, values, and affirms cultural differences among their clients.[15]

During the twenty-first century, professionals will assume a greater role in health promotion and disease prevention as the role of physical activity in improving health, preventing disease, and extending the length and enhancing the quality of life becomes even more widely accepted. The health disparities among different population groups, as reflected in life expectancy, are significant. The Bureau of Primary Health Care views cultural competence as an essential component of their program "100% Access, 0 Disparities," which seeks to eliminate health disparities among underserved populations by increasing access to quality treatment and health promotion programs.[16] Cultural competence is likewise critical to our efforts as professionals to promote lifespan involvement in physical activity for all people.

When professionals practice in a culturally competent way, they design and implement programs that appropriately serve people of diverse cultures in a manner that affirms participants' worth and dignity. Programs incorporate the values, traditions, and customs of the cultural group. Members of the cultural group are involved in meaningful ways in the creation and conduct of the health promotion or disease prevention program. Professionals respect individual rights, use effective communication skills that convey respect and sensitivity, and appreciate how diversity enriches our lives. When the culture of a specific population group or community is incorporated into programs, professionals are more likely to be effective in their efforts.

Racial and linguistic minorities are underrepresented in education, health promotion, and health care occupations, as well as in physical education, exercise science, and sport occupations. The majority of educators and health professionals are from the white Anglo culture, the dominant

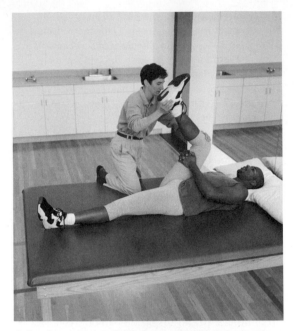

Cultural competency is important for athletic trainers because it can enhance treatment outcomes.

culture in our society. Are you sensitive to the fact that cultures different from the dominant culture may suffer oppression, discrimination, and lack of access to many of the opportunities enjoyed by the dominant culture? Are you willing to work toward social justice and elimination of inequalities?

As a professional in the field, you need to recognize how culture influences an individual's behavior and worldview. This recognition will help you work with individuals from different cultures. For example, minorities are under-represented in athletic training, an allied health profession. According to the National Collegiate Athletic Association (NCAA), only 5% of the Division I head athletic trainers are African Americans. Yet at the Division I level, 23% of athletes are African Americans.[17] It is likely that athletic trainers will be working with athletes from different cultures than their own. Ford writes, "Patients' cultures influence their perception of care, compliance, communication, and the injury or illness assessment and management process."[18] When cultural competence is an important part

of clinical practice, a patient's culture is considered in the assessment, delivery of treatment, and development of effective management plans. Ford emphasizes that optimal outcomes are achieved when athletic trainers respond with sensitivity to cultural issues.[18]

Within the school setting, there is a lot of diversity among students. However, there is significantly less diversity among faculty and staff. Currently, in the elementary and secondary schools, 43% of the students are minorities. Yet the majority of teachers are white; only 13% of teachers are minorities.[19] Given the diversity inherent in the school setting, it is important that physical educators have the opportunity to develop the skills to work successfully with students from different social, ethnic, and cultural backgrounds as well as students with different abilities.

According to Burden, Hodge, O'Bryant, and Harrison, physical education professional preparation programs have a "responsibility to implement diversity training such that novice teachers are trained and socialized with culturally relevant content knowledge, pedagogy and management skills and multiple experiences teaching culturally, linguistically, and ethnically diverse learners."[20] Such training is critical if we are to achieve our goal of eliminating disparities in physical activity levels, improve the health of participants in our programs, and socialize our learners into being physically active throughout their lifespan.

Cultural competency is essential to the achievement of lifespan involvement in physical activity for all people. The significant and complex role that culture plays in the health and well-being of people of all ages makes it important that professionals develop cultural competency. Understanding culture helps professionals appreciate cultural differences and utilize their knowledge of the strengths and beliefs of different groups to achieve positive health outcomes and avoid stereotypes and biases that limit services and further contribute to health disparities among different groups. When professionals practice in culturally competent ways, they recognize, value, and appreciate cultural differences.

WELLNESS MOVEMENT

Over the past 60 years, we have experienced tremendous changes in our approach to health, seen dramatic shifts in life expectancy, and acquired a greater understanding of the causes of diseases. Nationally, we have seen a growing emphasis on disease prevention and health promotion. These changes will be discussed throughout this section, as they have important implications for physical education, exercise science, and sport professionals and programs.

Wellness and Health

The wellness philosophy reflects a change from our traditional approach to health. Traditionally, good health was viewed as freedom from disease. From this perspective, if an individual was not ill, he or she was considered healthy. However, in 1947 the World Health Organization (WHO) defined health as a "state of complete physical, mental, and social well-being and not merely the absence of disease and infirmity."[21] The WHO definition offered a broader, multidimensional perspective of health than the traditional freedom-from-illness approach.

In the latter part of the twentieth century, the holistic approach to health grew in popularity. Holistic health focuses on the whole person and encompasses the intellectual and spiritual dimensions of health in addition to the physical, mental, and social dimensions included in the WHO definition. From the holistic point of view, individuals who are healthy have achieved a high level of wellness.

Wellness is a state of optimal health and well-being. It is living life to the fullest and striving to achieve one's potential as a person. It is a state of being in which the individual's physical, emotional, social, mental, spiritual, and environmental aspects of health are in balance. See Wellness Definitions box for definitions of each aspect of health. The physical aspect of health refers to how one's body functions and freedom from disease. Being active on a regular basis, following sound nutritional

practices, maintaining a healthy body weight, and getting sufficient sleep all contribute to physical well-being. Emotional well-being is enhanced through appropriate expression of a wide range of emotions and effective stress management.

WELLNESS DEFINITIONS

Physical	Refers to how one's body functions, freedom from disease, being active on a regular basis, following sound nutritional practices, maintaining a healthy body weight, and getting sufficient sleep.
Emotional	Enhances well-being through acceptance of one's feelings, appropriately expressing a wide range of emotions, and effectively managing stress.
Social	Emphasizes developing of interpersonal skills and healthy, fulfilling relationships as well as contributing to the welfare of others and one's community.
Mental	Is characterized by sound decision-making skills, intellectual growth, and high self-esteem.
Spiritual	Reflects a sense of purpose in life and living in accordance with one's beliefs and values.
Environmental	Encompasses where an individual lives and works, including amount of noise, level of pollution, availability of safe places to walk, and type of housing.

Social wellness emphasizes the development of interpersonal skills and healthy, fulfilling relationships. Mental wellness is characterized by sound decision-making skills, intellectual growth, and high self-esteem. Spiritual health reflects a sense of purpose in life and living in accordance with one's beliefs and values. For some, this dimension means practicing their religion. Lastly, the environment in which the individual lives and works affects one's health. Environmental wellness looks at the amount of noise, the level of pollution, the availability of safe places to walk, and type of housing, among other factors.

Wellness emphasizes individuals' taking personal responsibility for their health and understanding how the choices they make impact their well-being. Many lifestyle choices we make, whether smoking tobacco or working out on a regular basis, influence our health and well-being, both on a daily scale, and across our lifespan. However, while focusing on individual responsibility, the wellness approach to health recognizes that a multitude of forces—societal, genetic, environmental, and personal—interact to affect one's health. Living conditions, heredity, and societal conditions such as poverty, access to education, and discrimination exert a significant influence on one's well-being.

Epidemiologic Shift

In the twentieth century there was a gradual epidemiologic transition from infectious to chronic diseases as the leading causes of death. In 1900, the leading causes of death were influenza, pneumonia, tuberculosis, and gastrointestinal problems (e.g., diarrhea). Life expectancy was 47.3 years.

Half a century later, in 1950, life expectancy had drastically increased to 68 years due to the development of antibiotics, the availability of vaccines, and improvements in housing, sanitation, food and water supplies, and diet. In 2006, average life expectancy was 77.7 years. Currently, the leading causes of death are chronic diseases, specifically heart disease, cancer, and stroke.[22]

As this epidemiologic shift from infectious to chronic diseases occurred, the role of risk factors in disease occurrence and early mortality received greater attention, because those factors increase the likelihood of disease and health problems. Risk factors can be categorized as nonmodifiable or modifiable. Nonmodifiable risk factors are age, gender, race, ethnicity, and heredity. Modifiable risk factors include smoking, physical inactivity, diet, obesity, sun exposure, and alcohol use, to name a few. Modifiable risk factors are controllable. By the choices we make and the habits we develop, we can influence our health and longevity. More and more evidence shows that an individual's lifestyle influences the occurrence of chronic diseases such as heart disease, cancer, or diabetes.

Chronic Disease in the United States

In the United States, the Centers for Disease Control and Prevention (CDC) reports that "chronic diseases—such as cardiovascular disease (primarily heart disease and stroke), cancer, and diabetes—are among the most prevalent, costly, and preventable of all health problems.[22] Chronic diseases account for about 70% of all deaths [see Figure 3-1] and approximately 75% of health care costs each year." More than 1.7 million American deaths each year, or 7 out of every 10, are from chronic disease. Millions more people suffer due to disability and pain associated with chronic disease, which affects their quality of life. Additionally, 1 in every 10 Americans experiences major limitations in activity due to chronic disabling conditions.

Two of the most prevalent chronic diseases are cardiovascular disease and cancer, the number one and number two causes of death in the United States. Cardiovascular disease, which includes coronary and congestive heart disease, stroke, and hypertensive disease, is the number one killer of males and females in the United States. In 2004, over 870,000 people died from cardiovascular disease.[23] Physical inactivity, poor nutrition, obesity, and tobacco use contribute to cardiovascular disease.[24] Sedentary people have nearly twice the risk of cardiovascular disease as those who are active.[24]

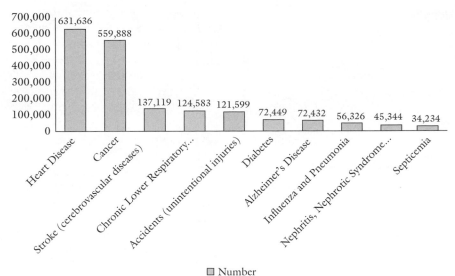

☐ Number

Figure 3-1   Leading causes of death in the US in 2006.
Source: Data from Centers for Disease Control and Prevention, Statistics for 2006

Smokers have twice as much risk of cardiovascular disease as nonsmokers.[24] Although the risk for inactivity and smoking are similar, the prevalence of inactivity in the nation is greater than the incidence of smoking. Cancer is the number two cause of death in the United States. According to the American Cancer Society, approximately one-third of the over 500,000 cancer deaths are related to poor nutrition, physical inactivity, overweight and obesity, and other lifestyle factors.[25] Addressing these modifiable risk factors will lead to improvement in the health of the nation.

The top modifiable causes of death in the United States are tobacco use, poor diet, and physical inactivity.[24] Tobacco use is the leading cause of death, its use implicated in 467,000 deaths per year.[26] Poor diet and physical inactivity, together, are responsible for at least 365,000 preventable deaths each year.[26] The CDC reported that deaths due to poor diet and physical inactivity rose by 33% over the last decade.[27] The director of the CDC, Dr. Julie Gerberding, stated, "The fact that more than a third of deaths in America each year are related to smoking, poor eating habits and physical inactivity is both tragic and unacceptable, because these are largely preventable behaviors."[27] The use of tobacco, poor dietary habits, and physical inactivity are modifiable risk factors that must be changed if the health of the nation is to improve.

Health Goals of the Nation

During the 1980s and 1990s, societal interest in promoting health and preventing disease increased. The accumulation of evidence supported the fact that changes in behavior could reduce individuals' risk of disease, increase their span of healthy life, and improve their quality of life. This evidence stimulated the growth of national disease prevention and health promotion initiatives.

These national initiatives set forth ambitious goals for improving the nation's health. The first document, *Healthy People: The Surgeon General's Report on Health Promotion and Disease Prevention*,[27] released in 1979, established goals to reduce premature deaths and preserve independence for older adults.[28] In 1980, *Promoting Health/ Preventing Disease: Objectives for the Nation*[29] set 226 public health objectives to be achieved by 1990. [27] In 1990, the US Department of Health and

Community fitness trails are popular with residents.

Human Services released *Healthy People 2000: National Health Promotion and Disease Prevention Objectives.*[30]

The latest report, *Healthy People 2010*,[31] stresses improvement of the health of the nation through a comprehensive approach that emphasizes health promotion and disease prevention. *Healthy People 2010* recognizes that "individual health is closely linked to community health—the health of the community in which individuals live, work, and play. Likewise, community health is profoundly affected by the collective beliefs, attitudes, and behaviors of everyone who lives in the community."[31] The underlying premise of *Healthy People 2010* is that the health of the individual is virtually inseparable from the health of the community and that the health of every community determines the overall health of the nation.[31] From this premise comes the vision for *Healthy People 2010*—"Healthy People in Healthy Communities."

Have these initiatives been successful? These past three decades have seen dramatic progress in improving the nation's health. Infant mortality rates significantly declined, childhood vaccinations rose to an all-time high, and death rates for coronary heart disease and stroke decreased.[31] Yet heart disease remains the nation's number one

killer. HIV/AIDS continues to be a serious health problem, and all too often mental health disorders go undiagnosed and untreated.[31] Too many people still smoke, obesity among children and adults continues to rise, and too few people eat a balanced diet and are physically active enough to gain health benefits. By the time you read this text, the new objectives for *Healthy People 2020* will lead the charge for promoting health and preventing disease throughout the next decade.

Healthy People 2010 is a blueprint for improving the health of individuals and the health status of the nation. Two overarching goals—increasing the quality and years of healthy life and eliminating health disparities—provide a focus for the nation's health promotion and disease prevention efforts. To accomplish these goals, 467 specific objectives were established, organized into 28 focus areas.

The first goal of *Healthy People 2010* focuses on helping people live longer and improving their quality of life. The focus of this goal is two-fold: increasing the years lived and increasing the years lived in good health, free from disability and activity restrictions. Enhancing the quality of life is essential as efforts to improve longevity yield results. Health-related quality of life "reflects a personal sense of physical and mental health and the ability to react to factors in the physical and social environment."[31]

The second goal of *Healthy People 2010* is to eliminate health disparities among different demographic groups in the United States. Health disparities are differences that occur by gender, race, ethnicity, education, income, disability, geographic location, or sexual orientation. (See the Health Disparities among Demographic Groups box for examples.) Health disparities are reflected in the overall health of the nation; if the health of the nation is to improve, disparities must be eliminated.

Achieving the *Healthy People 2010* overarching goals of increasing the quality and years of healthy life and eliminating health disparities represents a wide range of health challenges that must be addressed by individuals, communities, states, and the nation. Achievement of health equity requires a collaborative, multidisciplinary approach. According to *Healthy People 2010*, the "greatest opportunities for reducing health disparities are in empowering individuals to make informed health care decisions and in promoting community-wide safety, education, and access to health care."[31] The guiding principle of *Healthy People 2010* is that every person—regardless of age, gender, race, ethnicity, income, education, geographic location, disability, and sexual orientation—deserves equal access to comprehensive, culturally competent health care.[31]

The two overarching goals of *Healthy People 2010* establish the health agenda for the United States. To accomplish these goals, 28 focus areas, each with specific objectives, were identified.

HEALTH DISPARITIES AMONG DEMOGRAPHIC GROUPS

Gender	• Women have a longer life expectancy than men (80.4 years to 75.2). • 30% of the gap between men and about 40% of that between women is attributable to cardiovascular disease and its effects.[a]
Race and Ethnicity	• The death rate from heart disease for African Americans is more than 40% higher than it is for whites, and the death rate from cancer is more than 30% higher than it is for whites. • Hispanics have higher rates of blood pressure and are almost twice as likely to die from diabetes as non-Hispanic whites.
Education and Income	• Activity limitation caused by chronic disease occurs three times more frequently among people whose income is low than among people with higher incomes. • The overall death rate for adults with less than 12 years of education is more than twice the death rate for those with 13 or more years of education.
Disability	• People with disabilities have lower rates of vitality and physical activity, and higher rates of obesity compared to people without disabilities.[b]
Geographic Location	• Rural populations are less likely to exercise regularly, and experience higher rates of heart disease, cancer, diabetes, and injury-related deaths than people living in urban areas.[b]
Sexual Orientation	• Gay men experience health issues such as HIV/AIDS, substance abuse, depression, and suicide at a higher rate than their heterosexual peers.

For more information pertaining to disparities, see www.cdc.gov or www.healthypeople.gov.

HEALTHY PEOPLE 2010 OBJECTIVES FOR PHYSICAL ACTIVITY AND FITNESS

Goal: Improve health, fitness, and quality of life through daily physical activities

Number	Objective	Baseline Percentage	Target Percentage
22-1	Reduce the proportion of adults who engage in no leisure-time physical activity.	40	20
22-2	Increase the proportion of adults who engage regularly, preferably daily, in moderately physical activity for at least 30 minutes per day.	15	30
22-3	Increase the proportion of adults who engage in vigorous physical activity that promotes the development and maintenance of cardiorespiratory fitness 3 or more days per week for 20 or more minutes per occasion.	23	30
22-4	Increase the proportion of adults who perform physical activities that enhance and maintain muscular strength and endurance.	18	30
22-5	Increase the proportion of adults who perform physical activities that enhance and maintain flexibility.	30	43
22-6	Increase the proportion of adolescents who engage in vigorous physical activity for at least 30 minutes on 5 or more of every 7 days.	27	35
22-7	Increase the proportion of adolescents who engage in vigorous physical activity that promotes cardiorespiratory fitness 3 or more days per week for 20 or more minutes per occasion.	65	85
22-8	Increase the proportion of the nation's public and private schools that require daily physical education for all students.		
	a. Middle and junior high schools	17	25
	b. Senior high schools	2	5
22-9	Increase the proportion of adolescents who participate in daily school physical education.	29	50
22-10	Increase the proportion of adolescents who spend at least 50% of school physical education class time being physically active.	38	50
22-11	Increase the proportion of adolescents who view television 2 or fewer hours on a school day.	57	75
22-12	Increase the proportion of the nation's public and private schools that provide access to their physical activity spaces and facilities for all persons outside of normal school hours (that is, before and after the school day, on weekends, and during summer and other vacations).	Developmental. No data available	
22-13	Increase the proportion of worksites offering employer-sponsored physical activity and fitness programs.	46	75
22-14	Increase the proportion of trips made by walking—trips 1 mile or less.		
	a. Adults aged 18 years and older	17	25
	b. Children and adolescents aged 5 to 15 years	31	50
22-15	Increase the proportion of trips made by bicycling.		
	a. Adults aged 18 years and older—5 miles or less	0.6	2.0
	b. Children and adolescents aged 5 to 15 years—2 miles or less	2.4	5.0

Source: US Department of Health and Human Services. *Healthy People 2010: Understanding and Improving Health.* 2nd ed. Washington, D.C.: US Government Printing Office, 2000.

Fast foods and large portion sizes contribute to the increase in obesity in our society.

One of the focus areas was physical activity and fitness, and 15 specific objectives were identified for this area (see *Healthy People 2010* Objectives for Physical Activity and Fitness box). The selection of physical activity and fitness as a focus area affirms the significant benefits and critical contribution of physical activity and fitness to good health. Engaging in moderate-intensity physical activity for at least 30 minutes a day on most days of the week yields substantial health benefits. Additional health benefits can be gained through increasing the intensity or amount of physical activity. Promoting active lifestyles throughout the lifespan is important to the health of the nation.

The *Healthy People 2010* physical activity and fitness objectives for adults center on reducing the number of adults who participate in no physical activity during their leisure time and increasing the number of adults who engage in moderate to vigorous physical activity on a regular basis. Adults are encouraged to incorporate into their lives activities that enhance and maintain muscular strength, muscular endurance, and flexibility.

Adolescence is an important age for developing health habits that will persist into adulthood. Encouraging adolescents to incorporate moderate or vigorous regular physical activity into their lifestyles is important for their health, both now and in the future. *Healthy People 2010* calls for decreasing adolescents' sedentary behavior, such as television watching or computer usage, while promoting more active behavior, which will benefit their health. School physical education can play an important role in improving the nation's health by teaching students the skills, knowledge, and attitudes conducive to lifespan participation. School physical education classes also provide opportunities for students to be active during their day. Increasing the number of schools providing daily physical education for all their students and structuring physical education classes so students can be more active during the classes will contribute to the nation's health goals.

Healthy People 2010 recognizes that the places in which people live, work, and play—their communities—can significantly influence their ability to participate in physical activity. Access to facilities and safe places to walk, for example, can increase participation in physical activity by people who live within the community. Increasing the number of the nation's schools that provide access to their physical activity facilities and outdoor spaces outside of the normal school hours, such as on the weekends or in the summer, offers people within the community a place to go to work out, play sports, or engage in a variety of recreational pursuits. Encouraging people of all ages to increase the number of trips made by walking or biking provides a simple way to include physical activity within their lives. People are more likely to work out when the location is convenient and it is easy to fit their workout into their day. Worksite health promotion and fitness programs make sense; they are convenient for the millions of workers employed by the company, often free or low-cost, and frequently available before and after work. Further increasing the number of worksites that offer employee health promotion programs will increase the number who take advantage of them and work out on a regular basis.

Nutrition and overweight is another focus area of *Healthy People 2010*. Nutrition and diet are a significant factor in chronic disease and premature deaths. A diet high in sodium and saturated fats, devoid of fruits and vegetables, and unbalanced with respect to nutrients contributes to disease. An imbalance between food consumed and physical activity leads to overweight and obesity. Many chronic diseases are associated with overweight and obesity. Overweight and obesity increase individuals' risk for high blood pressure, type 2 diabetes, coronary heart disease, stroke, and some types of cancer. Adolescents who are overweight are at increased risk for being overweight as adults.

The *Healthy People 2010* objectives for nutrition and overweight focus on promoting health and reducing chronic disease associated with diet and weight. Among the objectives are increasing the number of adults who are at a healthy weight and reducing obesity and overweight among children, adolescents, and adults.

Currently, the United States is in the midst of an obesity epidemic. The National Health and

Nutrition Examination Survey (NHANES), conducted periodically since 1960, tracks the prevalence of overweight and obese youths and adults. The NHANES results indicate that overweight and obesity among adults have risen to an all-time high (see Figure 3-2). In 2005–2006, an estimated 67% of adults were overweight or obese (including about 34.3% considered obese) and about 6% considered extremely obese, which is a dramatic increase from the 1970s, when 47.7% of adults were overweight or obese, 14.6% of them obese.[32] These statistics signify the incline in overweight and obesity over the past 30 years, particularly the staggering increase in the proportion of obese adults, which has more than doubled.

Obesity among children and adolescents has also reached a record high, about 17% (see Figure 3-3). In 2005–2006, it was estimated that 10.4% of children aged 2 to 5, 19.6% of children aged 6 to 11, and 18.1% of adolescents aged 12 to 19 were obese.[33] The biggest and most concerning change that has occurred with children and adolescents' weight is that in 2003–2004 the results were based on *overweight*; however, the staggering numbers reported above demonstrate a significant increase in *obese* children and adolescents.

Overweight and obesity present serious health risks to individuals and have been linked to increased mortality. This is becoming more apparent as 80% of overweight and obese children and adolescents are becoming overweight and obese adults.[33] Attainment of the health goals of the nation requires that efforts be made to address the obesity epidemic. The National Institutes of Health states that even a small weight loss, of 5% to 15% of body weight, can improve health and quality of life. For a person who weighs 200 pounds, losing 10 to 30 pounds can decrease the chance of heart disease, reduce the risk of having a stroke, and lessen the likelihood of type 2 diabetes.[34]

As the rate of obesity continues to rise, so do the prevalence of chronic, degenerative, and hypokinetic diseases. Although it is very important to educate those individuals who are already overweight and obese, it is even more important to educate our nation in regard to health promotion and

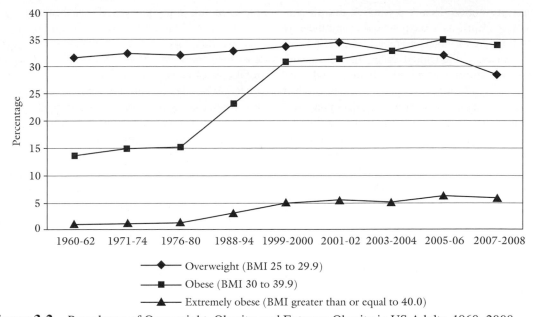

Figure 3-2   Prevalence of Overweight, Obesity, and Extreme Obesity in US Adults, 1960–2008.

Source: National Health and Nutrition Examination Survey (www.cdc.gov/nchs/nhanes.htm).

Flegal KL, Carroll MD, Ogden CL, and Curtis LR. "Prevalence and Trends in Obesity Among US Adults, 1999–2008." *JAMA,* 303(3), 235–241.

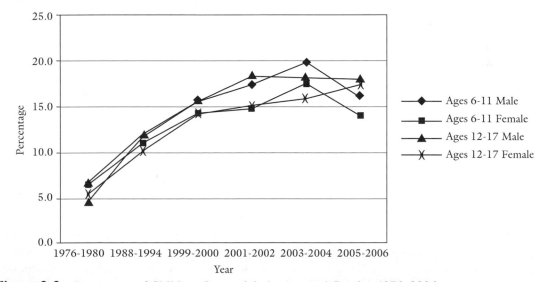

Figure 3-3   Percentage of Children Overweight by Age and Gender, 1976–2006.

Source: National Health and Nutrition Examination Survey (www.cdc.gov/nchs/nhanes.htm).

disease prevention. Health promotion and disease prevention efforts have the potential to significantly constrain the enormous and rapidly escalating cost of health care in the United States. In 1999, health care expenditures totaled $1.2 trillion and consumed over 13% of the US gross national product (GNP), more than any other industrialized nation.[35] In 2008, just 6 years later, costs had risen to $2.3 trillion, or 16.2% of the GNP.[35] Costs continue to rise at an astronomical rate and are projected to reach $4.5 trillion or 19.3% of the GNP in 2019.[36]

Poor health is costly, as are the choices individuals make regarding their lifestyles. Secretary of Health and Human Services Tommy G. Thompson stated, "The choices we make about diet, activity and tobacco affect not only our own lives, but also affect the economic health of our families, our businesses and even our nation as a whole."[37] Taking into account both direct and indirect costs of diseases and lifestyle choices helps you to see

Jumping rope is one way to develop fitness.

the economic consequences of poor health. For example, in 2004 the estimated cost of cardiovascular disease was $368.4 billion.[38] In 2003, the overall cost for cancer was $189.5 billion.[39] In 2000, the total cost of obesity in the United States was estimated to be $117 billion; the cost of inactivity was estimated to be $76 billion.[39] Addressing these conditions can significantly reduce health care costs and make dramatic improvements in the health of the nation, reducing premature death and disability and enhancing the quality of life.

Spiraling health care costs are a major concern of US businesses. Illness and premature employee death cost American industry billions of dollars a year. Poor health and fitness contribute to decreased productivity and increased absenteeism. Premiums for medical insurance continue to rise. The growing health care costs and the realization of the benefits to be gained through health promotion and fitness programs have led many corporations to establish programs for their employees. Corporations have found that medical costs and absenteeism drop and productivity increases after the introduction of a health promotion program.

In 2010, First Lady Michelle Obama, US Department of Health and Human Services Secretary Kathleen Sebelius, and US Surgeon General Regina Benjamin issued *The Surgeon General's Vision for a Healthy and Fit Nation* to help Americans lead healthier lives through better nutrition, regular physical activity, and improving communities to support healthy choices. Benjamin stated, "To stop the obesity epidemic in this country, we must remember that Americans will be more likely to change their behavior if they have a meaningful reward—something more than just reaching a certain weight or dress size. The real reward has to be something that people can feel and enjoy and celebrate. That reward is invigorating, energizing, joyous health. It is a level of health that allows people to embrace each day and live their lives to the fullest—without disease, disability, or lost productivity."[40] The report is primarily based on the obesity crisis within our nation. First Lady Obama responded alarmingly to the current crisis: "The surge in obesity in this

OBESITY AND PHYSICAL ACTIVITY—QUICK FACTS

PREVALENCE

- Obesity in the US has reached epidemic proportions. Approximately 67% of adults are overweight, and 34% are obese. During the last decade, obesity rates among adults have risen by more than 60%.
- Approximately 19% of children and adolescents aged 6 to 19 are considered to be overweight. Since 1980, overweight has doubled among children and tripled among adolescents.
- Over 50% of adults do not get enough physical activity to provide health benefits. Over 25% of adults participate in no physical activity during their leisure time.
- Approximately a third of high school students did not meet the physical activity recommendations for moderate or vigorous physical activity. Only 28% participate in daily high school physical education classes.

OBESITY, INACTIVITY, AND HEALTH

- Obesity is associated with increases in death from all causes.
- Physical inactivity and poor diet contribute to 400,000 preventable deaths a year; only tobacco contributes to more deaths per year (435,000).
- Physical inactivity and unhealthy eating contribute to obesity, cancer, cardiovascular disease, diabetes, osteoporosis, and arthritis.
- Overweight or obese individuals experience social stigmatization and discrimination in academic and employment situations.

ECONOMIC CONSEQUENCES

- In 2000, health care costs associated with obesity were $117 billion.
- In 2000, health care costs associated with inactivity were $76 billion.
- If only 10% of adults started a regular walking program, an estimated $5.6 billion in heart disease costs could be saved.

PHYSICAL ACTIVITY AND HEALTH BENEFITS

- Adults of all ages can realize benefits from regular, moderate physical activity, such as 30 minutes of brisk walking 5 or more times a week. Greater amounts of activity will yield additional health benefits.
- Children and adolescents can realize benefits from participation in at least 60 minutes of moderate to vigorous physical activity on most days of the week.

Source: Compiled from the Centers for Disease Control and Prevention, National Center for Health Statistics, and the President's Council on Physical Fitness and Sports.

country is nothing short of a public health crisis that is threatening our children, our families, and our future. In fact, the health consequences are so severe that medical experts have warned that our children could be on track to live shorter lives than their parents. The paper released today is an incredibly important step in directing the Nation's attention to solving the obesity epidemic and we do not have a moment to waste."[40] (See the Recommendations—*The Surgeon General's Vision for a Healthy and Fit Nation* box on page 97 later in this chapter for more information.)

A focused effort is needed if the *Healthy People 2010* objectives and *Surgeon General's*

Vision for a Healthy and Fit Nation recommendations are to be met. Americans show limited progress in achieving previous goals, objectives, and recommendations suggested by *Healthy People* and calls to action from the nation's administration. As you will see in the next section on physical activity and fitness, too many people of all ages are inactive, fail to achieve the recommended amount of regular physical activity, make unhealthy food choices, and are overweight or obese. This is cause for great concern as we begin the second decade in the twenty-first century.

The wellness movement encourages people to make lifestyle decisions that will enhance their health and well-being. An increased emphasis on health promotion and disease prevention has led to some improvements in the health of our nation. People are aware that the manner in which they live and their personal choices significantly impact their health and quality of life. Additionally, there is a greater understanding of how the environment, society, and economic status influence people's health and quality of life. Elimination of disparities in health and, ultimately, in lifespan is one of the nation's top health priorities.

Implications of the Wellness Movement

What role should physical education, exercise science, and sport take in promoting health and achieving national public health goals? The public health focus on health promotion and disease prevention presents a tremendous opportunity for professionals to increase their contributions to the health and welfare of all people. In 2001, the CDC's Task Force on Community Preventive Services released a report which identified interventions (see Task Force on Physical Activity Effective Interventions box) that were effective in increasing physical activity.[41] Although this report was released 10 years ago, knowledge of which interventions were most effective can continue to help policy makers and physical activity and health professionals use their community resources most effectively to reach national physical activity goals and objectives.

TASK FORCE ON PHYSICAL ACTIVITY EFFECTIVE INTERVENTIONS

- Information Approaches
- Community-wide campaigns
- Point-of-decision prompts
- Behavioral and Social Approaches
- School-based physical education
- Social support interventions in community settings
- Individually adapted health behavior change
- Environmental and Policy Approaches
- Access to places for physical activity

Physical education, exercise science, and sport programs in both school and nonschool settings provide an avenue for people of all ages to be active and to acquire the skills, knowledge, and values conducive to leading a physically active lifestyle. School physical education programs have a critical role to play in achieving a healthy and physically active lifestyle. If the health of the nation is to be improved, effective use must be made of school health and physical education programs. The schools provide an efficient means to reach over 50 million students a year. As professionals, we must be strong, passionate spokespeople on behalf of physical education and sport. The decline in the number of children participating in daily physical education must be reversed. Quality programs are critical to this effort. The inclusion of physical education as an integral component of a comprehensive school health program is another approach to increasing physical education programs. During these impressionable years, much can be done by schools and parents working together to lay the groundwork for healthy living as an adult.

School physical education programs should provide the foundation for participation in physical activities throughout one's lifespan. Physical education programs for young children should focus on attainment of proficiency in fundamental skills and movement concepts. In the upper elementary grades and middle-school years, students should be exposed to a variety of activities in the areas of sport, dance, aquatics, and outdoor pursuits. This exposure allows students to identify activities that are enjoyable and satisfying to them.

In high school, students should have the opportunity to develop competency in several activities that are personally meaningful. Fitness promotion is important. Teachers must provide a sequence of experiences that will give students a knowledge base of physical education and sport so that they can learn how to direct their own exercise programs, modify physical activities to suit their changing needs, and wisely select activities to participate in during their leisure time. Physical educators must also remember it is important to offer experiences that are challenging, meaningful, and personally satisfying to participants and are conducive to developing motivation for continued participation throughout life. The entire physical education program should be seen as developmental in nature, offering a series of planned learning experiences that focus on development of fitness, motor skills, knowledge, and values that will lead to lifespan participation.

The school setting also offers a means to reach adults. Over 5 million adults are employed by the schools, in both instructional and noninstructional positions. More schools are offering worksite health promotion programs, similar to those found in corporations, to their employees. These programs often encompass fitness promotion, skill development, and health education.

The use of the school as a community center has not reached its full potential. Although more schools are opening their doors to the community during evening hours, on the weekend, and during the summer, many schools remain unused and others underutilized. The use of the school as a community center would enable us to reach adults and offer a diversity of programs to meet their needs. Moreover, school-based adult programs offer a means to bring physical activity and sport experiences to adults who lack the financial resources to join a fitness club or do not have a program at their worksite. They provide an avenue to reach all people within the community. Programs can be designed

Physical education is an educational basic.

to focus on the needs of people of all ages, ranging from young adults to the older adults, at a minimal cost. Other programs can be started that foster family participation, emphasizing children and parents participating in activities together.

The growing number of older Americans makes it important to have physical activity programs to meet their many needs. Their needs are quite diverse. Millions of older Americans participate in sports. Other older Americans can benefit from physical activity programs that help them maintain the necessary health and vitality to live independently for as long as possible. In this manner, physical education, exercise science, and sport can increase the number of years of healthy life as well as make life more satisfying.

Worksite health promotion programs have grown tremendously. Many worksite programs have increased their scope of offerings from just a fitness program to include an array of different activities. Programs vary but may include fitness programs, recreation activities, and health promotion programs such as cancer and hypertension screening, nutritional counseling, and smoking cessation. Another change is that businesses have moved from viewing these programs as the perks of upper management to making these programs available to employees at all levels. This growth of programs has led to an increase in career opportunities in this sector.

Commercial fitness clubs and community agency programs, such as those at the YMCA, are growing. Additionally, they have expanded the populations served. Although these programs were initially targeted toward adults, they are now reaching out to the elderly and preschool children. These programs provide instruction in skills, encourage the development of fitness, offer education, and strive to promote regular participation.

As the United States becomes more diverse, the challenge of addressing disparities in health status and access to opportunities will become greater. Greater efforts must be made to reach racial and ethnic minorities, people with disabilities, and people with low incomes. As Siedentop states, professionals should understand inequities that may limit access to opportunities to participate in activity based on "irrelevant attributes such as race, gender, age, handicapping condition, or socioeconomic status. Individuals should value fair access to participation so much that they are willing to work at local, regional, and national levels to make that activity more available to more people."[42]

If physical education, exercise science, and sport professionals are to take on a public health role, they must be willing to work as part of a comprehensive team dedicated to the improvement of the nation's health status. Professionals must realize that physical activity is only a part of the means to achieving optimal health. Nutritionists, health educators, medical personnel, and others have a critical role to play in the wellness movement. It is important

Enjoyable physical activity is a good approach to developing health-fitness components.

that all professionals work cooperatively to achieve the realization of the nation's health goals and the attainment of optimal well-being for each individual.

FITNESS AND PHYSICAL ACTIVITY MOVEMENT

Enthusiasm for exercise and fitness is at an unprecedented level in the United States today, with millions of people spending countless hours and billions of dollars on exercise and sport. The fitness and physical activity movement, which began as a trend in the 1970s, has over four decades later grown to be an enduring feature of our society. Men and women of all ages are participating in fitness and sport activities to an extent not witnessed before in this country. It appears that being physically active is for many children and adults an ingrained part of American life.

However, when data about participation are closely examined, the widespread extent of physical activity and fitness in American society is not supported. As previously stated, available data show that many children and adults are leading sedentary lives.

In 1996, *Physical Activity and Health: The Surgeon General's Report* was released.[43] This landmark document convincingly set forth the contribution physical activity can make to the health and lives of all people. The contribution of physical activity to health—shown in the Benefits of Regular Physical Activity box—continues to be the primary focus of the most recent *Surgeon General's Vision for a Healthy and Fit Nation* (2010)[40] and the *Physical Activity Guidelines for Americans* (2008).[44]

Several key messages are presented in these documents:

- People of all ages can benefit from physical activity.
- People can improve their health by engaging in a moderate amount of physical activity on a regular basis.
- Greater health benefits can be achieved by increasing the amount of physical activity, through changing the duration, frequency, or intensity of effort.

The *Physical Activity Guidelines for Americans* and the American College of Sports Medicine's *Physical Activity and Public Health Guidelines*[44] recommend that children, adolescents, and adults engage in moderate to vigorous physical activity each week. Children and adolescents (aged 6 to 17) are recommended to engage in 60 minutes of moderate physical activity daily and vigorous physical activity three times a week. It is also recommended that they engage in muscle- and bone-strengthening activity 3 days a week. Adults (aged 18 to 64) are recommended to engage in moderate-intensity exercise (2 hours and 30 minutes a week), vigorous-intensity aerobic physical activity (75 minutes a week), or an equivalent combination of moderate- and vigorous-intensity aerobic physical activity each week. Aerobic activity, such as brisk walking or gardening, should be performed in episodes of at least 10 minutes, preferably spread throughout the week. Adults should also partake in muscle-strengthening activities twice a week.

The recommendation to include moderate-to-vigorous-intensity physical activity as part of one's daily schedule represents an effort to broaden the scope of physical activity recommendations. It is hoped that with additional opportunities to engage in beneficial physical activity, more people will participate. While participation in some cases is not of

THE BENEFITS OF REGULAR PHYSICAL ACTIVITY

Strong and moderate evidence suggests that regular physical activity improves health in the following ways:

- Reduces the risk of:
  - Early death.
  - Heart disease.
  - Stroke.
  - Type 2 diabetes.
  - High blood pressure.
  - Adverse blood lipid profile.
  - Metabolic syndrome.
  - Colon and breast cancers.
- Helps prevention of weight gain.
- Helps with weight loss when combined with a diet.
- Increases cardiorespiratory and muscular fitness.
- Prevents falls.
- Reduces depression.
- Improves cognitive function for older adults.
- Improves functional health for older adults.
- Helps to reduce abdominal obesity.

Source: US Department of Health and Human Services. *Physical Activity Guidelines for Americans.* Office of Disease Prevention and Health Promotion, 2008 (www .health.gov/paGuidelines).

sufficient intensity to develop cardiovascular fitness, being physically active does yield health benefits.

The emphasis on moderate-to-vigorous physical activity and the focus on integration of physical activity into one's lifestyle offer additional opportunities for sedentary individuals to improve their health through participation in physical activities that are enjoyable and personally meaningful, and fit more easily into their daily schedules. Healthy lifestyle patterns, including regular physical activity, should be developed when people are young. These lifestyle patterns can then be carried into adulthood, reducing the risk of disease. People who regularly participate in moderate amounts of physical activity can live longer, healthier lives.

Before reading a description of the fitness and physical activity status of children, youth, and adults, you may find it helpful to understand how the data are collected. Several different national surveys track physical activity, nutrition, and health status of people in many different age groups. Each survey strives to obtain a representative sample that includes different population groups—race, ethnicity, age, gender, etc. (See box on Health Surveys and Measurement of Obesity and Physical Activity.)

Estimating physical activity levels and healthy body weight for children, adolescents, and adults is a challenging task. Despite the variability in survey estimates for physical activity and overweight/obesity, and the limitations of the body mass index (BMI), it is clear that both the children and adults of this country need to be more active and to eat healthier.

Fitness and Physical Activity of Children and Youth

Are our nation's children and youth fit? Are they participating in sufficient physical activity to gain

Sit-ups are often used as part of a health fitness assessment.

HEALTH SURVEYS AND MEASUREMENT OF OBESITY AND PHYSICAL ACTIVITY

Surveys

Several national surveys help track the health status of children, youth, and adults. These surveys strive to obtain a representative sample that includes different population demographics—age, race, ethnicity, gender, geographic location, etc. These surveys were used to establish baseline measures for some of the *Healthy People 2010* objectives (and upcoming *Healthy People 2020*) and monitor progress toward their attainment.

- Behavioral Risk Factor Surveillance System (BRFSS) uses telephone surveys to collect data from over 200,000 people in all the states, the District of Columbia, and US territories. (http://www.cdc.gov/brfss)
- Youth Risk Behavior Surveillance System (YRBSS) is a school-based, written survey of about 14,000 students in grades 9–12. (http://www.cdc.gov/healthyyouth/yrbs)
- National Health Interview Survey (NHIS) uses personal interviews to collect data. About 40,000 households and 100,000 respondents are interviewed. (http://www.cdc.gov/nchs/nhis.htm)
- National Health and Nutrition Examination Survey (NHANES) incorporates a combination of personal interviews and direct physical examination to gather data on the health status of individuals. As part of the direct physical examination, each individual's height and weight are measured using standardized techniques. About 10,000 people are examined. (http://www.cdc.gov/nchs/nhanes.htm)

Note: On self-reported measures, such as interviews or written surveys, respondents tend to respond to questions in a way that provides a more positive profile of themselves. For example, individuals tend to underreport their weight, which leads to a lower prevalence of overweight and obesity; actual measurement of the weight leads to more accurate results.

Body Mass Index (BMI)

To determine whether an individual is at a healthy weight, BMI is often used because it can be calculated easily and rapidly from data collected from interviews, surveys, or direct measurement. BMI is calculated for the individual by dividing the weight in kilograms by the height in meters squared (BMI = weight kg/height m^2).

- Children and adolescents are considered *at risk for overweight* if their BMI is in at least the 85th percentile, and *overweight* if their is in at least the 95th percentile of the gender- and age-specific CDC Growth Charts for the United States.
- Adults are considered *overweight* if their BMI is 25 or more, *obese* if their BMI is 30 or more, and *extremely obese* if their BMI is 40 or more. A BMI of 30 indicates that a person is about 30 pounds overweight; 6-foot-tall person who is 221 pounds and a 5-foot-6-inch-tall person who is 186 pounds both have a BMI of 30. Extremely muscular individuals may have a high BMI yet not be at risk for poor health.

---

health benefits and reduce their risk for disease? The answers to these questions hold important implications for the achievement of our public health goals and for the health and future well-being of children and youth.

It is difficult to arrive at a clear picture of the fitness status and physical activity patterns of the nation's children and youth. The historical shift from performance-related to health-related fitness, the growing emphasis on the accrual of moderate

Since physical activity patterns are formed in childhood, children must be encouraged to spend less time watching TV and more time being active. Computer time should be limited as well.

to vigorous physical activity, and the variability in procedures involved in testing and sampling of subjects contribute to the difficulty. There has been no large-scale fitness testing of children and youth since the 1980s. However, there is sufficient information to help us understand that we, as physical education, exercise science, and sport professionals, need to do much more to help children and youth lead a more active lifestyle.

The 2007 Youth Risk Behavior Surveillance System (YRBSS) surveyed over 14,000 students to assess the presence of health risk factors.[45] The results offer us insight into the youths' physical activity patterns and their physical education experiences (see Figure 3-4). The students completed questions on their participation in physical activity during the 7 days preceding the survey. The YRBSS revealed:

- About one-third (34.7%) of the students were physically active for 60 minutes or more a day on 5 or more of the past 7 days, meeting the recommended physical activity guidelines for health. Males were more active than females, 43.7% versus 25.6%. White males were the most active (46.1%) and black females the least active (21%).

- One in 4 students (24.9%) did not participate in 60 or more minutes of physical activity on any day during the past 7 days. More females were inactive than males (31.8% versus 18%). Black students were the most inactive (32%); black females were more inactive than black males. Inactivity tended to increase as students' grade level in school increased.

- Being on the computer and watching television reduces the time to be active. Twenty-five percent of students played video or computer games and 35.4% watched television for 3 or more hours a day on an average school day. Females (20.6%) were on the computer less than males (29.1%). Black students played on the computer (30.5%) and watched television (62.7%) more than any other race or ethnicity.

YRBSS also gathered information on enrollment, daily participation, and activity time in physical education. Over half the students, 53.6%, attended physical education classes during the week. Overall, one-third of the students participated in daily physical education; this is a marked decrease from 41.6% in 1991. Accumulation of 60 minutes of physical activity a day is recommended for health benefits. Activity during physical education classes can contribute to this total. More than 80% of the students reported they actually exercised or played sports for more than 20 minutes during an average physical education class.

Overweight and obesity present a serious health risk for youth and adversely affects body composition, one of the health-fitness components. According to the YRBSS, 15.8% of the students were at risk for becoming overweight.[45] The prevalence was similiar for both male and female students. Risk for overweight was higher among black and Hispanic students than white students, 19% versus 18.1% versus 14.3%. More than 1 in 10 students were overweight.

In achieving and maintaining a healthy body weight it is important that healthy weight loss, weight gain, and dietary practices be followed. About 46% of students reported that they were trying to lose weight; females were twice as likely

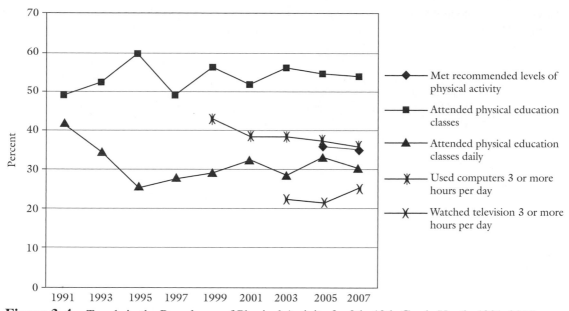

Figure 3-4   Trends in the Prevalence of Physical Activity for 9th–12th-Grade Youth, 1991–2007.
Source: Centers for Disease Control and Prevention. YRBSS: Youth Risk Behavior Surveillance System, National Trends in Risk Behaviors, 1991–2007 (www.cdc.gov/healthyyouth/yrbs).

Skills learned at an early age can provide the foundation for lifelong pursuits.

than males to try to lose weight. Sixty-one percent of the students reported they exercise to lose weight or to keep from gaining weight, and approximately 41% of the students tried to manage their weight by eating less food, consuming fewer calories, or selecting foods low in fat to eat. Twelve percent of the students reported that they went without eating for 24 hours to lose weight or to prevent weight gain. About 6% of the students took diet pills, powders, or liquids and about 1 in 20 students reported vomiting or taking laxatives to lose weight or prevent weight gain. Females were much more likely than males to engage in these various weight loss practices. Additionally, only about 1 in 5 students consumed the recommended five servings of fruits and vegetables daily.

The NHANES surveys provide us with additional information about the occurrence of overweight among children and adolescents. The results support previously mentioned statistics from the CDC that overweight among children and adolescents has reached a record high and its prevalence has increased from 30 years ago.

Collectively, the findings from the YRBSS and the NHANES indicate that too many of our nation's children and youth are inactive and overweight, particularly during their adolescent years, when they reduce their physical activity.

Quality physical education, exercise science, and sport programs are needed that focus on helping all young people get active and stay active. Special efforts must be made to address disparities in activity among population groups. Because females tend to be less active than males, special efforts must be made to encourage them to stay involved in physical activities.

Physical education, exercise science, and sport professionals should collaborate with policy makers, teachers, parents, and community members to develop and maintain quality physical activity programs in the schools and in the community. The emphasis should be on enjoyable participation in physical activity. A diverse range of noncompetitive and competitive activities appropriate for different ages and abilities should be offered, in both school and community settings.

Fitness is important for all people. These adults, in wheelchairs, are playing a game of volleyball at a local gymnasium.

Children and youth need opportunities to learn skills, knowledge, and attitudes to lead a physically active lifestyle. Special efforts must be made to encourage and sustain participation by underserved populations. Quality programs, however, are not enough; programs need to be accessible. Affordable programs remove socioeconomic barriers to participation, and when programs are offered where children and youth live, they invite participation on a regular basis. Lifespan involvement in physical activity begins with promoting a healthy, active lifestyle in children and youth.

Fitness and Physical Activity of Adults

How many adults are physically active on a regular basis? And what can be done to increase the number of adults who incorporate physical activity into their lifestyle? Information from national health surveys helps answer these questions. We can also gather information about the extent of adult physical activity by examining health club memberships and making inferences based on the purchases of sporting goods and exercise equipment.

The 2008 National Health Interview Survey reveals that participation in regular leisure-time physical activity sufficient to realize health benefits has held steady during the last decade. About 33% of adults engaged in regular physical activity during their leisure time—at either a moderate intensity level at least 5 times a week for a minimum of 30 minutes or a vigorous intensity level at least 3 times a week for 20 minutes a session.[46] Men engaged slightly more frequently in regular leisure-time physical activity than women, and younger adults were more active than older adults.[46]

Differences in leisure-time physical activity participation were associated with level of education, poverty, race, and ethnicity (see Figure 3-5). For example, higher levels of education and higher levels of income were associated with greater participation by adults, and non-Hispanic whites were more active than non-Hispanic blacks and Hispanics.[46] For specific statistics on these examples, see the National Health Interview Survey website (http://www.cdc.gov/nchs/nhis.htm).

Despite national and local initiatives to increase physical activity, the percentage of adults

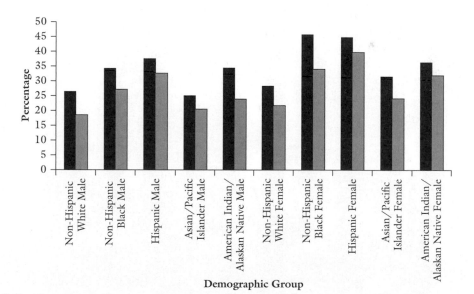

Figure 3-5 Prevalence of Leisure-Time Inactivity Among Adults by Race, Ethnicity, and Gender.
Source: National Center for Health Statistics. Health, United States, 2006 (www.cdc.gov/nchs).

who are inactive has remained fairly steady for the last 10 years. Even though there is a growing recognition of the contribution of physical activity to good health, an estimated 40% of adults engage in no physical activity during their leisure time.[47]

Physical activity plays an important role in maintaining a healthy body weight. As discussed previously, overweight and obesity among adults have reached record high levels. It is estimated that over 66 million adults, or 66%, are overweight or obese.[48] While the exact contribution of physical activity to the management of weight cannot be quantified, researchers do know that eating healthy and moving more are important. Addressing the obesity epidemic requires developing and sustaining healthy dietary practices and increasing physical activity. Increasing the number of adults who are physically active could help reverse the rising levels of overweight and obesity and improve the health of the nation.

Understanding the level of adult participation in our society is challenging. The picture of participation in our society is quite perplexing and often contradictory—health club memberships

are booming, fitness and sports participation appears to be growing, yet overweight and obesity have reached epidemic proportions.[49] Although many people are sedentary or overweight, millions of adults are active. Using information from the International Health, Racquet and Sportsclub Association (IHRSA) and the Sporting Goods Manufacturers Association (SGMA) helps us see a broader, different view of adult participation in physical activity.

Health club membership in both for-profit and nonprofit (e.g., YMCA) clubs increased steadily in the 1990s. Clubs offer members their choice of a wide range of activities, opportunities for group exercise, and the chance to work out under the supervision of a fitness professional. Personal training is the most popular service. (See the Health Club Memberships box for recent IHRSA data on health club membership.)

The SGMA reports expenditures for sport and exercise equipment as well as for sport apparel and athletic shoes. It also conducts periodic surveys pertaining to participation in physical

Health club membership continues to rise. Treadmills remain a popular means of working out.

HEALTH CLUB MEMBERSHIPS

Data from the International Health, Racquet and Sportsclub Association revealed the following information on health club memberships and members:

- 45.5 million people were members of a health club.
- 13.7 million health club members were aged 18 to 34.
- 14 million health club members were aged 35 to 54.
- 9.9 million health club members were aged 55 or older.
- Women represented more health club members than men (54% versus 46%).
- 51% of health club members had an annual household income greater than $75,000; 33% had an annual household income greater than $100,000.
- Only 9% of health club members had an annual household income of less than $25,000.

Source: The International Health, Racquet and Sportsclub Association. *Industry Statistics, 2005, 2007* (http:// cms. ihrsa.org).

SGMA EXPENDITURES AND PARTICIPATION

According to the Sporting Goods Manufacturers Association, the following data were reported in relation to sport, fitness, and recreation expenditure and participation:

- While more than 170 million Americans were active in a fitness, team sport, recreational, or outdoor endeavor, nearly 45 million were only casually active and more than 60 million were not active at all.
- The two fitness machine categories which generated the most sales are treadmills ($870 million) and elliptical machines ($687 million).
- Some of the top 10 fitness activities included walking (111 million Americans participating), bowling (57 million), treadmill (51.4 million), weight training (50+ million), running/jogging (44 million), fishing (41 million), bicycling (40.1 million), and stretching (36.3 million).
- The most popular team sports played were basketball (24 million), soccer (13.8 million), baseball (13.7 million), touch football (9 million), and slow-pitch softball (8.5 million).
- Sixty-three percent of all 6–17-year-olds played at least one team sport and two-thirds of them played team sports on a "frequent" basis.
- Among "core" participants (those who participate 50 days or more a year), nearly 30% of fitness participants were aged 55 or older.
- Fitness sales (wholesale) reached $71.8 billion in 2009, which included $28.2 billion for sport apparel, $12.3 billion for athletic footwear, over $20.2 billion for sporting goods equipment, $4.2 billion for exercise equipment, and $27.3 billion in recreational transport.
- The three largest sporting goods retailers are Dick's Sporting Goods, Sports Authority, and Hibbett Sports.

Source: Sporting Goods Manufacturers Association. *Industry Statistics, 2009, 2010* (www.sgma.com).

activities and sports. Both the expenditure and participation reports help us understand the nature and extent of participation by adults in sport, fitness, and recreational activities. (See the SGMA Expenditures and Participation box.)

The SGMA report indicates that many Americans are active on a regular basis. However, buying home exercise equipment does not guarantee use on a regular basis. Additionally, many people buy athletic footwear for fashion reasons, rather than for the purpose of working out or engaging in physical activity. Research shows that most Americans, over 80% of the population, realize that physical activity is good for their health even though only 20% of the population gets enough exercise.[50] Health club memberships and consumer spending on sports and fitness equipment show that American attitudes have changed over the past

Daily, moderate physical activity is important for all members of the family.

20 years,[50] but there is a wide gap between positive attitudes and actual fitness behavior.

Physical activity is beneficial for the health and well-being of people of all ages, including the older population. Even among the frail and very old adults, mobility and function can be maintained and improved through engagement in regular physical activity. *Healthy People 2010* reported that over 50% of adults aged 65 to 74 were sedentary, and that increased to 65% in the over- 75 age group.[31] As this segment of the population grows during the twenty-first century, it is critical that more of our efforts be directed toward helping older Americans stay active throughout their lifespan.

Adults of all ages need to increase their participation in moderate and vigorous physical activity. Although the percentage of adults that are active enough to receive health benefits and the percentage of adults that are leading sedentary lives vary from report to report, it is clear that too many adults are inactive. Inactivity, coupled with the rising increase in obesity, places too many adults at increased risk for chronic diseases. Most adults know that physical activity is good for them; however, the gap between knowing about physical activity and doing physical activity is quite large. Physical education, exercise science, and sport professionals have an important role to play in closing the gap between knowledge and action and helping all people adopt and maintain a program of moderate physical activity throughout their lifespan.

Implications of the Fitness and Physical Activity Movement

Although many Americans of all ages are not exercising vigorously with sufficient frequency, intensity, and duration to maintain an adequate level of health-related fitness, many people are making a commitment to incorporating moderate physical activity into their lifestyle. Furthermore, the increased documentation of the positive relationship between adequate levels of health-related fitness and wellness offers strong support for physical education, exercise science, and sport programs. It also emphasizes the need for fitness and physical activity programs to reach all ages of our society, regardless of gender, race, educational level, occupation, economic status, and community setting. As professionals, we must capitalize on the interest in fitness and its contribution to health to promote and secure funding for our programs.

Professionals must also become leaders in the fitness and physical activity movement and exert a significant influence on its direction. Corbin[51] points out that medical doctors, self-appointed experts, and movie stars are at the vanguard of the movement. Many of these people lack the qualifications, training, and expertise to direct this movement. Additionally, the proliferation of products and programs related to exercise and fitness has raised some concern about their validity. Professionals have the necessary knowledge and skill and must take over the leadership responsibilities within the movement. As Corbin[51] states, in assuming the burden of leadership, we must practice what we preach. Professionals should be role models and should reflect a commitment to a healthy lifestyle, with physical activity as an integral component of that lifestyle. Failure to practice what we preach damages our credibility.

Findings relative to the physical activity levels of the nation's youth show an urgent need for the fitness and physical activity movement to reach the children and youth of our nation. Schools should emphasize lifelong fitness, and this education should begin early in life. School-based programs must teach students the skills for lifetime participation and foster an appreciation for the value of fitness and physical activity in maintaining an optimal state of well-being. Fitness education should also be extended to parents. Parents' roles in shaping their children's physical activity habits should be recognized, and professionals should involve parents in creating positive physical activity patterns. Because much of children's and youth's physical activity takes place outside of the school setting, school and community physical activity programs should be closely coordinated so that the maximum benefits are derived from participation. The CDC and *The Surgeon General's Vision for a Healthy and Fit Nation* have developed guidelines for school and community programs to promote physical activity among the nation's

youth.[52] These guidelines make it clear that promoting lifelong physical activity requires a coordinated effort among the home, school, and community. (See the Recommendations—*The Surgeon General's Vision for a Healthy and Fit Nation* box.) Moreover, it emphasizes the inclusion of physical education as part of a comprehensive school-wide approach to promote well-being.

Many adults, when questioned about reasons for lack of participation in physical activity, cite lack of time. With the new recommendations on physical activity, more options are provided to incorporate physical activity into daily life. Furthermore, as the number of worksite programs continues to

---

RECOMMENDATIONS—*THE SURGEON GENERAL'S VISION FOR A HEALTHY AND FIT NATION*

Improving Our Communities	Neighborhoods and communities should become actively involved in creating healthier environments. Increasing the availability of supermarkets and outdoor recreational facilities and limiting advertisements for less-healthy foods and beverages are examples of ways to create a healthier living environment.
Healthy Choices and Healthy Home Environments	Change starts with the individual choices Americans make each day for themselves, their families, and those around them. Reducing the consumption of sodas and juices with added sugars; eating more fruits, vegetables, and whole grains; limiting television time; and being more physically active help us achieve and maintain a healthy lifestyle.
Creating Healthy Child Care Settings	It is estimated that more than 12 million children aged 6 and under receive some form of child care on a regular basis from someone other than their parents. Parents should talk with their child care providers about changes to promote their children's health.
Creating Healthy Schools	To help students develop lifelong health habits, schools should provide appealing healthy food options, including fresh fruit and vegetables, whole grains, water, and low-fat beverages. School systems should also require nutrition standards and daily physical education for students.
Creating Healthy Worksites	Employers can implement wellness programs that promote healthy eating in cafeterias, encourage physical activity through group classes, and create incentives for employees to participate.
Mobilizing Medical Communities	Medical care providers must make it a priority to teach their patients about the importance of good health. Doctors and other health care providers are often the most trusted source of health information and are powerful role models for healthy lifestyle habits.

Source: US Department of Health and Human Services. *The Surgeon General's Vision for a Healthy and Fit Nation.* (www.surgeongeneral.gov/library/obesityvision/index.html).

grow, greater opportunities for involvement will be available. Convenience is a factor that influences whether or not people will work out. Onsite opportunities with flexible hours will make it more convenient for adults to incorporate physical activity into their daily routine. Some corporations are also rewarding individuals who work out by reducing their out-of-pocket costs for insurance. The growth in sales of home exercise equipment is also a positive sign that people are meeting their need for exercise by placing equipment in their homes. Some adults have hired personal trainers to guide their home exercise programs.

Culturally competent professionals are needed to design and implement programs that are sensitive to the needs and values of different population groups, such as racial and ethnic minorities, females, and the aged. Health promotion and disease prevention programs are most effective when they incorporate the cultural beliefs and practices of the targeted population. Not only must we make a special effort to encourage underserved populations to be more active, but we must also recognize and address the barriers that serve to limit participation in physical activity.

Barriers such as cultural beliefs, financial constraints, physical limitations, and unsafe neighborhoods influence participation in physical activity. Prejudice and discrimination needlessly limit opportunities. Addressing disparities in participation and inequities in opportunities requires that professionals make a commitment to challenging the status quo and working to increase opportunities for underserved populations. Equity-oriented physical educators, exercise scientists, and sport leaders are needed if we are going to achieve our goal of lifespan involvement in physical activity for all people.

This is true for serving both children and adults. Family members are important role models for physical activity involvement. However, an increasing number of children in single-parent families, many of whom are at risk for poor school outcomes, may not have the parental support for involvement. Collingwood states that physical fitness programs for at-risk youths require strong

leadership, role modeling, and a focused, structured effort to achieve the desired outcomes.[53] Besides fitness promotion, structured physical fitness programs can affect many risk factors associated with the problems of at-risk youth. Properly designed and led by committed leaders, programs can increase well-being, enhance self-esteem, and teach important life skills such as goal setting, planning, and values development.[49]

Socioeconomic status is a significant influence on participation in physical activity. Individuals who come from affluent backgrounds have greater involvement than those from less affluent circumstances. They have more disposable income they can use to support their involvement in fitness and sports. Children, youths, and adults from lower economic strata have fewer resources available. Their limited resources—money, energy, and time—must be spent on securing the necessities of life: food, shelter, clothing, safety, and medical care. There is little left for the less crucial activities of life such as exercise and sports. Even access to physical activity programs that are affordable may be difficult for those living in low-income neighborhoods. The relatively poor health of people in lower socioeconomic groups may also limit their participation. Harris notes that these obstacles to physical activity are "outward manifestations of the relative lack of power that accompanies low socioeconomic status."[49] Compared to those who are wealthier, those who are poor have less control over their lives, encounter greater stress, receive less social support from others, and must deal with the realization that they are deprived. "In general, they encounter serious barriers to an immediate access to a high quality of life, to chances of attaining such a life in the future, . . . and have little power to bring about changes that might improve the situation."[49] As professionals, we must understand these inequities, the strong feelings they evoke, and the strategies that can be effectively employed to change this situation.

During the 1990s, there was enormous growth in private sector industries related to sport and fitness, such as gymnastics clubs and fitness clubs.

These industries provided greater opportunities for participation for those able to afford the fees. Historically, the most widely available opportunities for participation have been in the public sector in schools, community recreation programs such as youth soccer, and public facilities such as parks and swimming pools. As the shift toward private opportunities continues, efforts must be directed at expanding public sector opportunities and making them available to people of all socioeconomic classes. Offering low-cost programs and reduced fees for those unable to pay will allow individuals from low-income groups to participate. However, reducing fees may not be sufficient. For example, one city pool lowered its fees for children but found that did little to increase the number of participants

from lower-income families. When the city offered free bus transportation to the pool, participation increased in record numbers. Not only must opportunities be provided, but steps must be taken to ensure that people can access these opportunities. Even in the public sector, fees may limit participation.

A large segment of our population is over 50, and that segment is growing rapidly. Because of the remarkable increases in longevity and the growing awareness that some of the risks associated with disease and disability can be reduced, health promotion is emerging as a significant theme in geriatrics. Physical activity is a critical component of a healthy lifestyle and—according to the CDC—is essential to healthy aging (see http://www.cdc.gov/physicalactivity/everyone/guidelines/olderadults.html for specific health benefits and physical activity guidelines for older adults).

Professionals can contribute in many different ways to the promotion of physical activity by older adults. Exercise physiologists can take a leadership role in determining the amount of physical activity necessary for health benefits for different population groups. The impact of physical activity on disease, disability, and quality of life needs to be tracked over a period of time. Exercise physiologists have the qualifications to play a leading role in this effort.

Exercise physiologists and other professionals are needed to conduct high-quality programs for older adults in many different settings, such as community settings, retirement communities, worksites, schools, assisted living facilities, senior citizen centers, health and sport clubs, hospital wellness programs, and other settings easily accessible to the older population. A greater effort must be made to assist individuals in selecting physical activity options that match their interests, lifestyles, and functional abilities as well as identifying avenues to pursue them. Educating medical and other health care professionals about the value of physical activity and disseminating information about "best practices" programs that can be replicated in other settings is a role that professionals can capably undertake.

Regular moderate physical activity can yield important health benefits for people of all ages.

A concerted effort by professionals must be made to reach all segments of the population and to give them the necessary skills, knowledge, and attitudes to develop and maintain adequate levels of health-related fitness. We must sustain participation by that small segment of society, the individuals who exercise vigorously enough to maintain an adequate level of health-related fitness. We must encourage the people who engage in moderate physical activity to upgrade the intensity of their efforts to achieve the full benefits of appropriate vigorous exercise. Finally, we must reach out to those individuals who exercise irregularly, if at all, and help them begin to incorporate physical activity into their lives. Accomplishment of these goals requires committed, qualified professionals and a diversity of programs conducted in a variety of settings and targeted to all segments of the population.

FOCUS ON CAREER: Health and Aging

PROFESSIONAL ORGANIZATIONS

- American Association for Health Education (AAHE)
    http://www.aahperd.org/aahe
- American Association for Physical Activity and Recreation (AAPAR)
    http://www.aahperd.org/aapar
- American Public Health Association (APHA)
    http://www.apha.org
- Geronotological Society of America
    http://www.geron.org

PROFESSIONAL JOURNALS

- *American Journal of Health Education*
- *American Journal of Public Health*
- *The Gerontologist*
- *Journals of Gerontology*
    - Series A: *Biological Sciences and Medical Sciences*
    - Series B: *Psychological Sciences and Social Sciences*

SUMMARY

The role of physical education, exercise science, and sport in our society is influenced by societal trends. One significant trend is the changing demographics of our population. Our society is more culturally diverse than at any point in its history, and the diversity will increase as we move farther into the twenty-first century. We are living longer. Our society is becoming older; it is estimated that the number of people aged 65 and older will equate to 20% of the population by 2030. The number of people with disabilities continues to grow. The structure of the family is changing. Too many Americans live in poverty; poverty is associated with poor health and school outcomes. As physical educators, exercise scientists, and sport leaders, we must be committed to providing opportunities for lifelong involvement in physical activity for all people. Cultural competency is important in working with people from diverse population groups to adopt and maintain a physically active lifestyle. Cultural competency includes appreciating differences, valuing the uniqueness of individuals, and committing to addressing inequities in opportunities.

The wellness movement the fitness and physical activity movement also hold several implications for physical education and sport. The wellness movement emphasizes health promotion and disease prevention through lifestyle modification and individual responsibility for one's own health. Fitness and physical activity are integral parts of a healthy lifestyle. The evidence supporting the contribution of physical activity to health continues to mount. *Healthy People 2010*

and *The Surgeon General's Vision for a Healthy and Fit Nation* document the significant role physical activity plays in promoting well-being. Within the past few decades there has been a tremendous surge of interest in fitness and physical activity. However, when participation patterns are examined, too many children and adults lead a sedentary lifestyle. Professionals need to increase their efforts to involve people in physical activity. The wellness movement and the fitness and physical activity movement offer strong support for the development of nonschool physical education, exercise science, and sport programs to reach people of all ages.

DISCUSSION QUESTIONS

1. Today's society is more culturally diverse than ever before. Describe the benefits and barriers you may encounter as you educate diverse individuals across all populations. How does the cultural diversity in the United States influence the overall health and well-being of the entire population?

2. *Healthy People 2010* and *The Surgeon General's Vision for a Healthy and Fit Nation* have developed goals and objectives to decrease the number of chronic, degenerative, and hypokinetic diseases. What role(s) do physical education, exercise science, and sport professionals have in getting

students, clients, and players to meet these goals and objectives? How will we know if they have met the goals and objectives?

3. Do you consider yourself to be a physically educated person? Why or why not? How did you determine whether you are a physically educated person or not?

4. Many children, youth, adults, and older adults are inactive. How can you motivate individuals to engage in physical activity? How can professionals educate all individuals across the lifespan about the importance of physical activity and proper nutrition?

SELF-ASSESSMENT ACTIVITIES

These activities are designed to help you determine if you have mastered the material and competencies presented in this chapter.

1. You have been invited to speak to a community group on the role of physical activity in the promotion of health and the attainment of wellness. Prepare a short speech reflecting the contribution of physical education, exercise science, and sport to a healthy lifestyle. Use the information provided in the Get Connected box to locate current information about the value of physical activity.

2. For each of the *Healthy People 2010* objectives for physical activity and fitness, provide specific

examples of how school and nonschool physical education, exercise science, and sport programs can help in their attainment.

3. As can be seen from the information on changing demographics, our society is becoming more diverse. What specific steps can physical education, exercise science, and sport professionals take to reach underserved populations? Are you culturally competent to work with our nation's increasingly diverse populations?

4. Refer to the 12 Steps to Understanding Research Reports box in Chapter 1. Answer the questions in Step 3 for the same article you selected in Chapter 1.

REFERENCES

1. DeSensi JT: Understanding multiculturalism and valuing diversity: a theoretical perspective, Quest 47:34–43, 1995.

2. National Center for Health Statistics: Health United States 2001, Hyattsville, Md., 2001 (www.cdc.gov/nchs).

3. US Census Bureau. Census 2000, Washington, D.C., 2001 (www.census.gov).

4. US Department of Education: A back to school report on the baby boom echo: growing pains, US Department of Education, Washington, D.C., 2000 (www.ed.gov).

5. US Department of Health and Human Services: Life expectancy hits new high in 2000; mortality declines for several leading causes of death, Press release, October 10, 2001 (www.cdc.gov).

6. Federal Interagency Forum on Child and Family Statistics: America's children: key indicators of well-being, 2001. Washington, D.C., 2001, Federal Interagency Forum on Child and Family Statistics (www.childstats.gov).

7. National Vital Statistics Reports 57(14): 2009 (www.cdc.gov/nchs/fastats/lifexpec.htm).

8. Yen: Minority births soon to overtake white births. Experts: 2010 could be the tipping point. March 10, 2010 (www.recordpub.com/news/article/4785615).

9. National Center for Health Statistics: Public elementary and secondary school student enrollment and staff counts from the common core of data: school year 2007–2008. November 2009 (www.nces.edu/gov).

10. US Census Bureau. Washington, D.C., 2006 (www.census.gov/Press-Release/www/releases/archives/facts_for_features_special_editions/007108.html).

11. US Census Bureau. Washington, D.C., 2009 (www.census.gov/prod/2009pubs/p60–236.pdf).

12. Armas GC: National poverty rate rises for 2nd year in a row, September 27, 2003 (www.montanaforum.com/rednews/2003/09/27/build/economy/poverty2.php?nnn=6).

13. US Department of Health and Human Services Office of Minority Health: Revised CLAS standards from the office of minority health, Closing the Gap, February/March 2001 (www.omhrc.gov).

14. US Department of Health and Human Services Bureau of Primary Health Care: Cultural competence: a journey, Washington, D.C., 1998, Bureau of Primary Health Care.

15. US Department of Health and Human Services Administration on Aging: Achieving cultural competence: a guidebook for providers of services to older Americans and their families, Washington, D.C., 2001, Department of Health and Human Services (www.aoa.gov).

16. US Department of Health and Human Services Bureau of Primary Health: Moving Toward 100% Access and 0 Health Disparities. Washington, DC: US Department of Health and Human Services Bureau of Primary Care; 2002.

17. National College Athletic Association, 2001–2002 race demographics of NCAA member institutions' athletic personnel, 2003 (www.ncaa.org).

18. Ford MG: Working toward cultural competence in athletic training, Athletic Therapy Today, 8, 8: 60–66, 2003.

19. National Education Association, NEA and teacher recruitment: an overview, 2004 (www.nea.org).

20. Burden JW, Jr., Hodge SR, O'Bryant CP, and Harrison L, Jr.: From colorblindness to intercultural sensitivity: infusing diversity training in PETE programs, Quest 56:173–189, 2004.

21. World Health Organization: Constitution of the World Health Organization, chronicle of the World Health Organization, 1:29–43, 1947.

22. Centers for Disease Control and Prevention: Chronic disease overview, 2004 (www.cdc.gov/nccdphp/overview.htm).

23. National Center for Health Statistics: Deaths, 2004, March 30, 2007 (www.nchs.gov).

24. Mokdad AH, Marks JS, Stroup DF, and Gerberding JL: Actual causes of death in the

United States, 2000, JAMA 291:1238–1245, 2004.

25. American Cancer Society: Statistics for 2004 (www.cancer.org/docroot/STT/stt_0.asp).

26. Danaei G, Ding EL, Mozaffarian D, Taylor B, Rehm J, et al., The preventable causes of death in the United States: comparative risk assessment of dietary, lifestyle, and metabolic risk factors. PLoS Med 6(4):e1000058 (doi:10.1371/journal.pmed.1000058).

27. United States Department of Health and Human Services: Study shows poor diet, inactivity close to becoming leading preventable cause of death, March 9, 2004 (www.smallsstep.gov/sm_steps/news_updates.html).

28. US Department of Health, Education, and Welfare: Healthy people: the surgeon general's report on health promotion and disease prevention, Washington, D.C., 1979, US Government Printing Office.

29. US Department of Health and Human Services: Promoting health/preventing disease: objectives for the nation, Washington, D.C., 1980, US Government Printing Office.

30. US Department of Health and Human Services: Healthy people 2000: national health promotion and disease prevention objectives, Washington, D.C., 1996, US Government Printing Office.

31. US Department of Health and Human Services: Healthy people 2010: understanding and improving health, ed 2, Washington, D.C., 2000, US Government Printing Office (www.healthypeople.gov/healthypeople).

32. Centers for Disease Control and Prevention: NHANES 2005–2006, December 23, 2009 (www.cdc.gov/nchs/nhanes.htm).

33. Centers for Disease Control and Prevention: Childhood overweight and obesity, updated March 31, 2010 (www.cdc.gov/obesity/childhood/index.html).

34. United States Department of Agriculture: Big benefits from small loss, March 29, 2007. (www.nutrition.gov).

35. Centers for Medicare and Medicaid Services: Fact sheet—national health expenditures, 2008 (www.cms.gov).

36. Centers for Medicare and Medicaid Services: National health expenditure projections, 2009–2019 (www.cms.gov).

37. Centers for Medicare and Medicaid Services: Highlights—national health expenditures, 2002, 2004 (www.cms.gov).

38. US Department of Health and Human Services: HHS issues report on the impact of poor health on businesses, Press release, September 16, 2003 (archive.hhs.gov).

39. National Center for Chronic Disease Prevention and Health Promotion: Preventing obesity and chronic diseases through good nutrition and physical activity, August 2003 (www.cdc.gov/nccdphp/pe_factsheets/pe_pa.htm).

40. US Department of Health and Human Services: The surgeon general's vision for a healthy and fit nation, 2010 (www.surgeongeneral.gov).

41. Centers for Disease Control and Prevention: Increasing physical activity: a report on recommendations of the Task Force on Community Preventive Services, MMWR 50(RR-18), 2001.

42. Siedentop D: Valuing the physically active life: contemporary and future directions, Quest 48:266–274, 1996.

43. US Department of Health and Human Services: Physical activity and health: a report of the surgeon general, Atlanta, GA, 1996, US Department of Health and Human Services, Centers for Disease Control and Prevention, National Center for Chronic Disease.

44. US Department of Health and Human Services: Physical activity guidelines for Americans, 2008, Office of Disease Prevention and Health Promotion (www.health.gov/paguidelines).

45. Centers for Disease Control and Prevention: Youth risk behavior surveillance—United States, 2007 (www.cdc.gov/healthyyouth/yrbs).

46. National Center for Health Statistics: Summary health statistics for US adults: national health interview survey, 2008 (www.cdc.gov/nchs/data/series/sr_10/sr10_242.pdf).

47. National Center for Health Statistics: Health, United States, 2006 with chartbook on trends in the health of Americans (www.cdc.gov/nchs).

48. Centers for Disease Control and Prevention: NHANES 2003–2004, March 29, 2007 (www.cdc.gov/nchs/nhanes.htm).

49. Harris JC: Enhancing quality of life in low-income neighborhoods: developing equity oriented individuals, Quest 48:366–377, 1996.

50. American Sports Data, Inc.: Booming health clubs, slipping fitness participation, and healthier diets all coexist in the overweight society, Press release, August 28, 2000 (www.americansportsdata.com).

51. Corbin CB: Is the fitness bandwagon passing us by? Journal of Physical Education, Recreation and Dance 55(9):17, 1984.

52. Centers for Disease Control and Prevention: Guidelines for school and community programs to promote physical activity among young people, 1997, United States Public Health Service, US Department of Health and Human Services, Washington, D.C. (www.cdc.gov).

53. Collingwood TR: Providing physical fitness programs to at-risk youth, Quest 49:67–88, 1997.

PART

II

Foundations of Physical Education, Exercise Science, and Sport

In Part I, physical education, exercise science, and sport were defined and their philosophy and objectives discussed. Part II builds on that knowledge by discussing the foundations of physical education, exercise science, and sport. Trained physical education, exercise science, and sport professionals should understand the foundations of their field. Part II begins with a discussion of the historical foundations of physical education, exercise science, and sport in Chapter 4. Chapter 5 provides an overview of motor behavior. Chapters 6, 7, 8, and 9 present the biomechanical, physiological, sociological,

and psychological bases from which physical education, exercise science, and sport derive their principles and concepts. These areas of study are the major sciences or subdisciplines of physical education, exercise science, and sport—namely, exercise physiology, motor behavior, sport and exercise psychology, sport sociology, and biomechanics. The principles and concepts discussed in these chapters introduce the professional to the knowledge needed to plan and conduct meaningful programs in physical education, exercise science, and sport.

HISTORICAL FOUNDATIONS

OBJECTIVES

After reading this chapter the student should be able to—

- Identify events that served as catalysts for physical education, exercise science, and sport's growth.
- Identify some of the outstanding leaders in physical education, exercise science, and sport over the course of history and the contributions each made to the field.
- Discuss recent developments in physical education, exercise science, and sport.
- Draw implications from the discussion of history of principles that will guide the professional future of physical education, exercise science, and sport.

Contemporary physical education, exercise science, and sport in the United States is built on a rich heritage. Our programs today have been influenced by philosophies, practices, and sports from other cultures, but particularly the programs of ancient Greece, Rome, Great Britain, Sweden, and Germany. Events in the United States, such as colonialism, the expanding frontier, the Great Depression, the growth of public school education, urbanization, and technology, have affected the growth and direction of our field. Within the United States, dynamic, visionary leaders advanced the scope and status of physical education, exercise science, and sport. This chapter provides a brief overview of the history of physical education, exercise science, and sport from ancient times to recent developments. Space limitations preclude a more detailed approach. Additional information is provided at the Online Learning Center. Generally, the terms *physical education* and *sport* are used in reference to early historical developments, with *physical education* typically used to refer to school-based programs and *sport* used to refer to organized, competitive contests. It is only in the latter decades of the twentieth century that the term *exercise science* emerged.

History enlightens us—it enables us to understand how contemporary physical education, exercise science, and sport has been shaped by the leaders and events of the past. History guides us—it suggests future possibilities and courses of action that might be most effective in the years to come.

History is a scholarly field of study, focusing on the study of change over time. Historians engage in descriptive and interpretive research.

Descriptive research objectively describes, in as much detail as possible, what has happened in the past. According to Mechikoff and Estes, "descriptive history explores the who, what, when, and where of the past, and it tries to do so without transposing ideas, values, and judgments from the present onto the events of the past. Interpretive history seeks to explain the how and why of events that happened in the past. . . . Unlike descriptive history, the interpretive perspective introduces the historian's subjective bias into the interpretation, and history is no longer 'just the facts.'"[1] The interpretive perspective seeks to explain the significance of historical events within the historical and social context of the time. Mechikoff and Estes state that the interpretive approach "allows much of the fullness and richness of the history to come forth, and it makes the narrative much more open to discussion and understanding. In contrast, descriptive histories are no better or worse

than interpretive histories; they are merely different types of accountings of what occurred in the past."[1] History expands our understanding of society as well as physical education, exercise science, and sport.

SPORT HISTORY

Sport history emerged as a subdiscipline within the realm of physical education, exercise science, and sport in the late 1960s and early 1970s. Its definition, scope, historical development, and areas of study are discussed in this section.

Definition and Scope

Struna describes sport history as a "field of scholarly inquiry with multiple and often intersecting foci, including exercise, the body, play, games, athletics, sports, physical recreation, health, and leisure."[2] The term *sport* in this discussion is used broadly to incorporate the multiple foci of the field, as suggested by Struna. Sport historians

Women's basketball at Smith College, Northampton, Mass., 1904.

examine the historical development of sport. They describe and analyze the actions and behaviors of leaders, examine and interpret significant events, study the evolution of organizations, and explore the emergence of trends. It is difficult to appreciate the evolution of sport without understanding the practices, philosophies, and beliefs that were popular at the time. Sport historians are interested in how the past has shaped sport as we experience it today.

Historical Development

There has long been an interest in the history of sport. Early works on the history of sport typically were descriptive in nature, describing the development of a specific sport (e.g., baseball), chronicling the contributions of a leader to physical education (e.g., Dudley Sargent), or documenting certain events (e.g., the development of the forerunner to the American Alliance for Health, Physical Education, Recreation, and Dance). However, as interest in the history of sport grew, more interpretive analytical studies were undertaken. These interpretive studies, which incorporated information about the historical and

social context of the time, greatly enriched our understanding of sport. Through analytical studies of sport, we gain insight into the following:

- How games and sports came to be included in the school physical education curriculum.
- How Victorian-era conceptions of morality influenced sports participation by females.
- The impact of segregation on sports opportunities for blacks.
- How the "new physical education" developed and how the philosophy of "education through the physical" evolved.
- The conditions under which the exercise and sports sciences emerged.

Sport history is a dynamic field. Struna reports that prior to the 1960s, much of the research on sport history was produced by scholars in departments of history.[2] Physical educators who conducted historical studies were more narrow in their approach, focusing on activities and individuals who had a role in shaping physical education. By the 1980s, Struna found that this trend had reversed. Many of the leading sport historians were faculty in departments of exercise and sport science.[2] Additionally, scholars from other fields besides history and physical education, such as the humanities and anthropology, began to investigate sport. The scholars used different perspectives for their work, thus enhancing our understanding of the many different dimensions of sport.

As sport history grew as a fertile area of research, sport historians undertook a wider range of questions. Throughout the 1970s, historians focused primarily on describing and explaining organized, competitive sport, its evolution, and its programs. However, as the field grew, a wider range of questions were addressed, using more analytical approaches. As Struna points out, historians came to understand that "modern" sport—organized, competitive physical contests—needs to be interpreted in light of the context in which it was created. Historians need to understand that sport is constructed by a particular group of people during a particular time. This understanding has elicited a wider range of questions—not only about the history of sport, but about the context in which it developed. Struna notes that questions arise about "practices and conceptions of exercise and health, about multiple contexts in which games and exercise and physical training existed, and about the sources of variance in experiences over time."[2] This recognition that sport needs to be studied in the context of the time and society in which it was created has helped historians "to understand our past experiences on their own terms, rather than on ours, and to employ multiple frames to make sense of the many dimensions of past experiences."[2]

With the growth of interest in the history of sport, in 1973 the North American Society for Sport History (NASSH) held its first meeting. NASSH provides a central forum for sport history scholars from all disciplines to exchange ideas and share their work. NASSH's *Journal of Sport History* is recognized as one of the preeminent publications in the field and provides a means for scholars to disseminate their research.[2] Other journals that provide avenues for sport history research are the *Canadian Journal of History of Sport and Physical Education,* the *International Journal of Sport History, Sport History Review,* and the *Journal of Olympic History.*

Areas of Study

As sport history grew as a specialized area of study, sport historians sought to investigate a wider array of topics within the realm of sport, including physical education, dance, play, conceptions of the body, sport, and exercise. Sport historians also came to recognize that many groups—such as racial and ethnic minorities and females—have been overlooked in historical research on sport. Some of the questions sport historians may investigate include:

- How did urbanization influence the development of sports in America?
- How did the sport activities of Native Americans influence the recreational pursuits of the early colonists?
- What factors influenced the inclusion of physical education in the curriculum of the schools?
- How did youth sport develop and what is its impact on youth culture?
- How did segregation influence the participation of blacks in sports?
- What factors contributed to the establishment of the National Collegiate Athletic Association?

As Mechikoff and Estes point out, history often provides us with an illuminating perspective.[1] It helps us understand why we think and act the way we do and gives us some idea about what may happen in the future.[1] Sport history helps physical education, exercise science, and sport professionals gain a greater understanding of the events, forces, and leaders that shaped the field of today, and offers us guidance for our behaviors and actions in the future.

ANCIENT GREECE AND ROME

One profound influence on the development of physical education and sport was the civilization of ancient Greece (prehistoric times–338 B.C.). The city-states of ancient Greece, particularly Athens, placed a high value on physical activity, viewing sport, exercise, and fitness as integral to education and life. The Greek ideal stressed the unity of the mind, body, and spirit. Reflecting this principle,

Greek education encompassed both intellectual and physical development. The expression "a sound mind in a sound body" exemplifies this belief. Gymnasiums served as centers for intellectual discussions as well as sport instruction and physical training. Males received instruction in physical activities, such as wrestling, running, and jumping. Development of the body was valued, and the Greeks engaged in training to develop their physiques. The guiding principle of Athenian society, *arête*—the pursuit of excellence—encouraged individuals to push themselves to achieve to the highest extent possible.

In honor of the gods, Greeks held festivals, where sporting events gave Greek men the opportunity to demonstrate the beauty of their physique as well as their athletic abilities. The most renowned of these festivals was the Olympic Games, held in honor of Zeus, the chief god. Beginning around 776 B.C., the Olympic Games

were held every four years and featured music, feasting, and athletic contests spanning at least five days. The Olympic Games were so important that the frequently warring city-states declared a truce so that contestants from all city-states could safely travel and participate in the games.

During the ancient Roman period (500 B.C.– 27 B.C.), physical activity was also regarded with importance, although its role was different than in Greece. Being fit and having athletic prowess were important to Rome's military success. Males received training in many physical activities, such as archery, wrestling, riding, and fencing. Strength development was important so that the men could be successful in defending the state and waging war as Rome sought to expand its empire.

After Rome conquered Greece, Greek gymnastics were introduced to the population, but were not popular. Romans preferred professional sports, often blood sports such as gladiatorial contests, men fighting wild animals, and men fighting each other to the death. Spectators enjoyed these and other events, such as chariot races. Feasting and drinking bouts, in conjunction with little physical activity, led to the decline of the Roman population's fitness. Ultimately, the Roman Empire came to an end, with the poor physical condition of its citizens one of the contributing factors in its decline.

The programs of ancient Greece, in particular, influenced physical education programs in the United States. The Greek ideal of the unity of the mind and body is reflected in many contemporary physical education programs. The development of the body and the pursuit of excellence stand as the motive for many who welcome the challenge of competition at their own level and who value achievement over winning.

This Greek vase, called an *amphora,* was found in eastern Greece and dates to about 550 to 525 B.C.

EARLY MODERN EUROPEAN PROGRAMS

During the late 1700s and 1800s, early modern Europe experienced the rising tide of nationalism. Against this backdrop, physical education programs in Germany, Sweden, and Great Britain developed and expanded. During the 1800s, proponents of these programs introduced them to the United States.

Germany

During the early modern European period, physical education in Germany focused on the development of strong citizens through programs in the schools and community associations. Physical education leaders of the time, such as Johann Bernhard Basedow (1723–1790), Johann Christoph Friedrich Guts Muths (1759–1839), and Adolph Spiess (1810–1858), were instrumental in promoting school gymnastics. Their programs focused on exercises and instruction in activities such as gymnastics, games, marching, running, and wrestling. These leaders believed that physical education deserved a place in the school curriculum.

In 1779, Basedow founded the Philanthropinium, a school for boys located at Dessau. The curriculum of the school was guided by the philosophy of naturalism, and he designed his program to meet the individual needs of his students. Physical activity played an important part in the daily program of all students; three hours a day were devoted to sport instruction and recreation activities and two hours a day to manual labor such as gardening. This was the first school in modern Europe that admitted boys from all

Drawing of a *Turnplatz,* a German exercise ground that included equipment for jumping, vaulting, balancing, climbing, and running.

Associations of gymnasts called *Turnverein* were still popular in the 1920s. At left, a member practices his skills on an apparatus in the *Turnplatz*. At right, members of the Durlach Turnverein are shown.

classes and that included physical education as part of the educational curriculum.

Guts Muths was an instructor in physical education at the Schnepfenthal Educational Institute, founded by Christian Gotthilf Salzmann (1744–1811). The school's program was greatly influenced by Basedow's naturalistic philosophy and incorporated many of his physical activities into the curriculum. As an instructor there for 50 years, Guts Muths developed an extensive program of outdoor gymnastics, which included tumbling, vaulting, the horizontal bar, and rope ladders. Three to four hours a day were devoted to physical activity. Guts Muths' book *Gymnastics for the Young* described the Schnepfenthal program and articulated the value of physical education in the development and education of children. Because of his outstanding contributions, Guts Muths is often referred to as one of the founders of modern physical education in Germany.

Friedrich Ludwig Jahn (1778–1852) developed the *Turnverein* movement, associations of gymnasts, in an effort to strengthen the country's youth. During his lifetime, Napoleon overran Germany. In hopes of contributing to the effort to free Germany from Napoleonic control and reunify the country, Jahn designed a gymnastics program to improve the fitness of German boys. In 1811, near Berlin, the first *Turnplatz*, an outdoor exercise area, was established. The *Turnplatz* had equipment for jumping, vaulting, balancing, and climbing. Here the gymnasts, known as turners, practiced on the apparatus. Running, wrestling, and calisthenics helped the boys become strong and fit. Jahn emphasized nationalism, building strong youth for the defense of Germany.

Jahn's system of gymnastics expanded throughout Germany. *Turnvereins* were formed in many cities. His book *German Gymnastics* outlined his program. As Germans immigrated to the United States, they formed *Turnvereins* where they settled. Proponents of the German system of gymnastics promoted their system in the United States during the 1800s.

Adolph Spiess advocated for the inclusion of gymnastics within the school curriculum. In the 1840s, influenced by the teachings of Guts Muths and Jahn, Spiess developed a system of school gymnastics and persuaded German officials to incorporate gymnastics into schools' curriculum. He believed that schools should be interested in the total growth of the child, which included intellectual and physical development, and that gymnastics should receive the same consideration as other subjects such as math and language. Spiess developed progressions for different grades, different ability levels, and different genders. Sport, marching, and gymnastics accompanied by music were included in the curriculum. Discipline and obedience were emphasized.

Sweden

During the early 1800s, gymnastics in Sweden was influenced by nationalism. Per Henrik Ling (1776–1839) played a major role in the development of gymnastics during this time. In 1814, Ling assumed the directorship of the Royal Gymnastics Central Institute, in Stockholm. At the institute, he developed a training program for military men that emphasized exercises that stressed mass drills and movements from position to position on command and in a prescribed, progressive sequence. Ling developed exercise apparatus, including stall bars, vaulting boxes, and oblique ropes.

In addition to his program of military gymnastics, Ling is credited with the development of medical, educational, and aesthetics gymnastics. He used the sciences of anatomy and physiology to examine the effects of physical activity on the body; this emphasis on the scientific approach stands as one of Ling's greatest contributions to physical education. This understanding aided Ling in designing a program of medical and therapeutic exercises, with the goal of restoring health to injured parts of the body and helping the weak regain their strength. His program of educational gymnastics laid the foundation for physical education in the schools. His aesthetic gymnastics emphasized the expression of feelings and thoughts through movement. An advocate of teacher training, Ling believed instructors of gymnastics needed to know proper techniques and have an understanding of the effect of exercises on the body. Ling's gymnastics became known as the Swedish system. Although the Swedish system of gymnastics used apparatus and emphasized precise movements in response to commands, it was less formal and strenuous than the German and Danish systems.

Hjalmar Frederik Ling (1820–1886), Per Ling's son, is recognized for his significant role in developing educational gymnastics. In 1861, Hjalmar Ling was put in charge of the educational gymnastics program at the Royal Gymnastics Central Institute, where he directed the program for 18 years. Ling developed written curriculum guides for elementary and secondary school gymnastics programs for both girls and boys, which included exercises arranged in progression by difficulty. From these tables of exercises, teachers could select and sequence exercises according to the age, ability, and needs of their students. His father's systematic and progressive approach to exercise was reflected in the Day's Order, a series of daily exercises for schoolchildren that move in sequence from head to toe.

Denmark

In the early 1800s, Danish gymnastics was also influenced by nationalism. Franz Nachtegall (1777–1847) played a significant role in shaping physical education programs in Denmark and is regarded as the father of Danish physical education. In 1799, Nachtegall opened a private outdoor gymnasium in Copenhagen, the first to be devoted to physical training. His curriculum was influenced by the work of Guts Muths. In 1804, Nachtegall was appointed by the Danish king to serve as the director of a training school for teachers of gymnastics in the army. In 1809, Nachtegall began working with Danish public schools to incorporate physical education into their curriculum for boys, at the elementary and secondary levels. As the need for school instructors grew, prospective teachers were trained with the military instructors at the training school, with the program lasting 15 to 18 months. In 1821,

Nachtegall was appointed director of gymnastics for Denmark and given authority over both civilian and military gymnastics. Danish programs of gymnastics emphasized fitness and strength, with formalized exercises performed on command and little individual expression allowed. Danish gymnastics used hanging ropes and ladders, poles for climbing, beams for balancing, and wooden horses for vaulting.

Great Britain

Great Britain during the early 1800s took a different approach to physical education. While other European countries stressed organized programs of gymnastics, Great Britain emphasized programs of organized games and sports. Sports have a long, rich heritage in Great Britain. Swimming, rowing, archery, riding, hockey, quoits, tennis, golf, football (soccer), and cricket were played prior to the 1800s.

Sport and recreational pursuits in Great Britain during this time were clearly divided among class lines or by socioeconomic status. Sports that required little equipment, such as football (soccer) and boxing, were popular among the working class. Sports such as cricket and rugby found popularity among the upper-class men, many of whom had played such sports at their private boarding schools. In addition to their love of sports, amateurism and its emphasis on playing for the love of the game is a lasting British legacy.

One of the leaders of physical education in Great Britain was Archibald Maclaren (1820–1884). Maclaren had a background in both sports and medicine. He believed that it was important to treat physical training as a science. He wrote several books on training, including *Training in Theory and Practice* and *A System of Physical Education*. In his work, he stresses that the objectives of physical education should take into consideration that the promotion of health is more important than the development of strength. Maclaren recognized that physical action is an antidote for tension, nervousness, and fatigue from hard work. He noted that the recreational exercise found in games and sport is not enough in itself for growing boys and girls, and that physical exercise is essential to optimum growth and development.

Maclaren believed both physical training and intellectual development were important. The mind and body represent a "oneness" in human beings and sustain and support each other. Maclaren stated that exercises should be adapted to an individual's level of fitness and that exercises should be progressive in nature.

During the early and mid-1800s, the philosophy of muscular Christianity developed and grew in popularity. Following the Reformation in the sixteenth century, Protestant sects, including the Puritans, enacted rigid prohibitions against participation in many physical activities and sports. Participation was viewed as sinful. Muscular Christianity argued that sports activities provided a means to teach and reinforce moral values and virtues, thus serving to build character.

Proponents of muscular Christianity suggested that physical weakness reflected moral and spiritual weakness; thus, engaging in physical activities and sport to develop the body reflected one's commitment to developing desirable Christian qualities. Other advocates of muscular Christianity believed that the body was the soul's temple and, as Christians, individuals were obligated to care for their physical being. Muscular Christianity—engaging in sport to build moral character—helped reconcile sport and religion. The philosophy of muscular Christianity greatly influenced English educational institutions, which came to promote the inclusion of sport in schools as a means to develop fair play, honor, and self-discipline among students and to prepare students for life.

The contributions of Germany, Sweden, Denmark, and Great Britain to physical education and sport influenced the development of programs in the United States. As individuals trained in these programs or systems of gymnastics came to the United States, they took an active role in promoting their approach to physical education. Their leadership influenced the development of programs in the United States during the 1800s.

PHYSICAL EDUCATION AND SPORT IN THE UNITED STATES

The growth of physical education and sport in the United States was influenced by European ideals, systems of gymnastics (exercises), and philosophies. In more recent years, there has been a greater incorporation of activities and beliefs from ancient Asian cultures, such as yoga, the martial arts, and the beliefs about the relationship between the mind, body, and spirit.

Colonial Period (1607–1783)

Colonists coming from Europe to settle in the New World found Native Americans leading a very active existence. Native Americans hunted, fished, canoed, ran from place to place, and engaged in a multitude of physical activities as they sought food, built shelters, and communicated with other tribes. Young men had to successfully complete a series of challenging physical tests in order to become warriors. Various forms of physical activity were included within their rituals (i.e., burial services, fertility-based ceremonies, and medicinal rites), which were performed in an effort to influence the religious forces they believed directed their lives.[3] Sport, dance, and dramatic enactments were incorporated into Native American festive celebrations and engaged in as forms of relaxation. Ray reports that numerous tribes engaged in sport as a substitute for intervillage or intertribal warfare.[4] Prior to major competitions, there was a period of preparation of the mind, body, and spirit. According to Ray, games and sport played important roles in the lives of Native Americans; they promoted group identity, served as an outlet for creativity, and offered opportunities for individual recognition.[4]

Tribal differences in culture and lifestyle influenced the physical activity of Native Americans, although there were many similarities in the games and sports of tribes across North America. Men, women, and children participated in various sports and games, with some activities being relegated to certain age groups or genders,

EUROPEAN CONTRIBUTORS—PHYSICAL EDUCATION, 1700s–1800s

Johann Bernhard Basedow (1723–1790)	Germany	Naturalism guided his development of physical education curriculum; program designed to meet individual needs; activities included dancing, fencing, riding, running, jumping, wrestling, swimming, skating, games, gymnastics, and marching
Johann Christoph Friedrich Guts Muths (1759–1839)	Germany	Naturalism influenced design of program; extensive program of outdoor gymnastics, using exercises and apparatus; wrote *Gymnastics for the Young and Games;* founder of modern physical education in Germany
Friedrich Ludwig Jahn (1778–1852)	Germany	Nationalism motivated establishment of *Turnverein* associations; program of gymnastics designed to build strong and fit youth and men with the goal of reunification of Germany
Adolph Spiess (1810–1858)	Germany	Promoted gymnastics as part of the school's curriculum, as important as other school subjects for both girls and boys; required trained teachers; program emphasized discipline and included variety of activities—marching, free exercise, gymnastics to music
Per Henrik Ling (1776–1839)	Sweden	Gymnastics training program for military using directed drills and exercises; therapeutic gymnastics to restore health; massage; emphasized the educational and aesthetic aspects of gymnastics; teacher training
Hjalmar Fredrik Ling (1820–1886)	Sweden	Promoted educational gymnastics; incorporation of physical education in the curriculum of schools
Franz Nachtegall (1777–1847)	Denmark	Incorporated gymnastics into Danish schools; gymnastics teacher training for schools and for military
Archibald Maclaren (1820–1884)	Great Britain	Emphasis on role of physical activity in health; contribution of physical activity to growth and development; organized sports and games; outdoor activities

while others were enjoyed by both males and females or adults and children.[4]

Physical prowess, cunning, coordination, skill, speed, and endurance were valued. Baggataway (lacrosse) was popular, and rituals often surrounded the game. The game was also used as a means to settle disputes. Rules and playing equipment varied by tribe. Shinny, a game similar to field hockey, in which a stick was used to propel a ball into a goal, was played by both males and females. Footraces often extended over many miles and allowed members of the tribe to demonstrate their speed and endurance. Swimming, canoeing, archery, various types of ball games, and games of chance were other popular activities among Native Americans.

When the first colonists from Europe arrived in North America, they were confronted with harsh conditions and focused their efforts primarily on survival. When they were not working, they engaged in recreational activities that varied according to their heritage, their religious beliefs, and the area of the country in which they settled. In the New England area, religious beliefs led to prohibitions against many physical activities. The Puritans saw pleasurable physical activities, such as dance and many games, as leading to sin and eternal damnation. Hard work, stern discipline, austerity, and frugality were thought to be secrets to eternal life and blessedness.

People in other sections of the nation, however, brought the knowledge and desire for various types of sport with them from their native countries. The Dutch in New York liked to engage in sports such as skating, coasting, hunting, and fishing. However, the outstanding favorite was bowling. In Virginia, many kinds of sports were popular, such as running, boxing, wrestling, horse racing, cockfights, fox hunts, and later, cricket and football.

Education during this time period was limited. Children attended academies that focused their efforts on helping students attain some degree of proficiency in the basic subjects of reading, writing, and arithmetic. Although advanced educational institutions existed, few students continued their education beyond the elementary level. Physical education was not part of the school curriculum. Recreational games and sports provided a diversion from hard work and allowed opportunities for socializing.

National Period (1784–1861)

During the national period, interest in education grew, and more schools were established for both females and males. The growth of female seminaries (private schools) increased educational opportunities for women. During the 1800s, free public education began to slowly become available for girls and boys, although opportunities for secondary school education and college education were limited. In the 1820s and 1830s, physical education began to be incorporated into school curriculums.

During the 1820s, German gymnastics was introduced to the United States by German immigrants. In 1825, Charles Beck (1798–1866), a turner, introduced Jahn's gymnastic program of exercise and apparatus to his students at the Round Hill School in Northampton, Mass. Beck built an outdoor gymnasium and started the first school gymnastics program. In 1826, Charles Follen (1796–1840) organized exercise classes, based on the German system, for students at Harvard University.

Catharine Beecher (1800–1878) was the director of the Hartford Female Seminary in Connecticut, an institution of higher education for young women. In 1828, she developed and implemented a program of physical education within the educational curriculum of the school. The program consisted of calisthenics performed to music. These exercises included Swedish gymnastics and were designed to improve the health and vitality of her students and to prepare them more fully for their future role as homemakers and mothers. She was among the first to advocate for the inclusion of daily physical activities into the public schools.

In the 1840s, many Germans immigrated to the United States, fleeing from the unstable political situation in Germany. The Germans brought with them their customs, and within a short period of time, *Turnvereins* began to be established. In 1851, in Philadelphia, the first national Turnfest was held. Turners from New York, Boston, Cincinnati, Brooklyn, Utica, and Newark engaged in this competition. As Germans moved westward to settle, they established *Turnvereins* societies in their communities.

During the early to mid-1800s, more schools and colleges opened their doors to both males and females. Gymnasiums and swimming pools

Wand drills were an important part of physical education program activities in the 1890s.

were constructed, increasing opportunities for participation. Intercollegiate athletics began during this period of time. In 1852, the first intercollegiate competition occurred. A crew race between Harvard and Yale was held, with Harvard winning the race. Intercollegiate athletics would begin to assume an increasingly prominent role on college campuses.

Sports participation grew as settlers became more established and religious prohibitions relaxed. Horse racing and footraces were popular. Baseball, which had evolved from the English sport of rounders, was "invented" in 1839. Rowing was a popular, and competitive, pastime. One of the favorite activities, however, was gambling on sport events.

Civil War Period through 1900

Many outstanding leaders with new ideas influenced the development of physical education and sport during the Civil War period and the late 1800s. Physical education was increasingly included in the schools, and sports grew in popularity.

In 1860, Dioclesian Lewis (1823–1886) developed the Lewis system of "light" gymnastics and introduced it to men, women, and children living in Boston. Lewis's program of gymnastics was directed at improving the health and well-being of

his participants. Exercises to improve the cardiovascular system were performed to music. Posture and flexibility exercises and light apparatus, such as wands, Indian clubs, and beanbags, were incorporated into his program. Schools adopted his program of gymnastics, and Lewis recognized the need to train teachers to instruct children using his system. In 1861, he established the Normal Institute for Physical Education in Boston to prepare teachers. Courses in anatomy and physiology, hygiene, and gymnastics comprised the 10-week professional preparation program. This was the first teacher training program in the United States.

Edward Hitchcock (1828–1911) and Dudley Sargent (1849–1924), both of whom were physicians, were central figures in the development of college physical education programs. In 1861, Hitchcock was named the director of health and hygiene at Amherst College. In this position, Hitchcock was responsible for the physical development and health of the students. Physical education classes consisted of developmental exercises performed using horizontal bars, rings, ropes, ladders, Indian clubs, vaulting horses, and weights. Marching and calisthenics were included within the curriculum, as were some sports skills. To monitor the progress of his students, Hitchcock used anthropometric or bodily measurements (e.g., height, weight, chest girth, etc.), before and

Staff and students of the first physical education class at the Chautauqua School in New York in 1886.

then after the completion of training. Hitchcock is recognized for his pioneering work using the scientific approach in physical education.

In 1879, Sargent was appointed director of the new Hemenway Gymnasium at Harvard University. Students who elected to take physical education received a medical examination and underwent a battery of anthropometric tests as the basis for an individually prescribed conditioning program. Sargent developed specially designed exercise equipment, which the students used in conjunction with carefully selected German and Swedish gymnastic exercises to work out. Students were also encouraged to participate in sports, such as baseball, fencing, and rowing. In 1881, Sargent founded the Sanatory Gymnasium, a school to prepare physical education teachers to utilize his scientific and comprehensive approach to physical education. Later this school became the Sargent School for Physical Education, and today it is the Sargent College of Boston University.

Delphine Hanna (1854–1941) attended Sargent's school and received training in his approach to physical education. In 1885, Hanna accepted a teaching position at Oberlin College, where she taught until 1921. In 1903, Hanna was promoted to full professor, the first woman in the United States to be a full professor of physical education. Hanna's training program for prospective teachers eventually evolved into one of the first professional preparation programs for physical education. Among her students were future physical education leaders Thomas Wood and Luther Gulick.

Dr. George Fitz (1860–1934), a research physiologist at the Harvard Lawrence Scientific School, called for physical education programs to be based on scientific principles. Research was needed to determine the body's physiological responses to exercise so that the actual benefits of exercise could be determined. In 1892, Fitz established a physiology laboratory to conduct research on physical activity at Harvard University.

During the 1880s, the complete Swedish system of gymnastics was introduced in the United States and became popular in the eastern section of the country. Hartvig Nissen (1855–1924) pioneered this effort. In 1883, he began teaching Swedish gymnastics at the Swedish Health Institute in Washington, D.C., and later continued his teaching in Boston. In Boston he assumed a leadership role in directing physical training for the Boston public school system and promoted the adoption of Swedish gymnastics. Baron Nils Posse (1862–1895), graduate of the Royal Central Institute of Gymnastics, came to Boston in 1885 and began teaching Swedish gymnastics. Bostonian philanthropist Mary Hemenway became an advocate of the Swedish system and wanted to have schoolchildren reap the benefits of this program. To train teachers in Swedish gymnastics, Hemenway underwrote the establishment of the Boston Normal School of Gymnastics in 1889. Amy Morris Homans (1848–1933) assumed a leadership position in this school, and Posse served as an instructor. Homans played an influential role in getting the Boston public schools to adopt the Swedish system of physical education in 1890, a system that was later adopted by schools throughout the state of Massachusetts. The Swedish system soon eclipsed the German system in popularity in the East, but the German system remained more prevalent in the Midwest.

The late 1880s were marked by considerable debate among physical educators regarding which system of gymnastics should serve as the curriculum in American schools. This controversy is often referred to as the "Battle of the Systems." Advocates for each system—the German, Swedish, and various systems developed by Americans (e.g., Hitchcock, Sargent)—articulated the merits of their system and advanced reasons why that particular system should be the national curriculum of the schools. In 1889, a pivotal point occurred in the development of the American system of physical education—the Boston Conference on Physical Training.

Organized and led by Mary Hemenway, with the assistance of Amy Morris Homans, the Boston Conference brought together prominent leaders in physical education to discuss and evaluate the various systems. The conference was significant because it stimulated discussion about the purpose of American physical education and which program would best serve the needs of the American

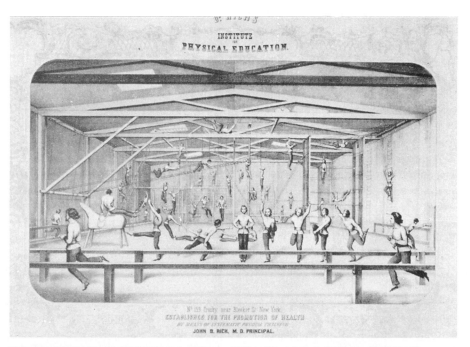

This graphic for Dr. Rich's Institute for Physical Education shows students engaging in a variety of physical education activities.

people. No consensus was reached about which system should be the national curriculum. Nils Posse suggested that what was needed was an American system designed for the American people.

The growth of physical education was encouraged by the efforts of the turners. The *Turnvereins* took an active role in promoting physical education, advocating for its inclusion in the schools. In order to prepare teachers for their system, the turners in 1866 established the North American Gymnastic Union in New York City. The curriculum of this 1-year program included physical education, anatomy, gymnastics instruction, and teaching methodology. This school eventually relocated to the Midwest and expanded to a 2-year training program in 1885. In 1907, the school moved to Indianapolis and eventually became associated with Indiana University.

Another stimulus to the growth of physical education during this time was the Young Men's Christian Association (YMCA), founded in London in 1844. The first YMCA opened in the United States in 1851. Because of the interest in gymnastics and other health-promoting activities, the YMCAs added physical education after the Civil War. To ensure qualified teachers for the association's programs, in 1885 the YMCA International Training School was founded in Springfield, Mass.; this school later became Springfield College. Luther Gulick (1865–1918) played an instrumental role in the YMCA Training School for over 15 years, serving first as an instructor and then as the superintendent. Gulick designed the YMCA logo, an equilateral triangle stressing the unity of the body, mind, and spirit and reflecting the importance of developing the whole person—physically, mentally, and spiritually. From 1903 to 1908, Gulick served as the director of physical training for the New York City public schools.

At the close of the century, there was greater recognition of the value of physical education to educational progress. Organized physical education programs began to appear as part of the curriculum in elementary and secondary schools in

the 1850s. California was the first state to require schools to offer physical education, in 1866, followed by Ohio in 1892. In 1881, the acceptance of physical education grew when the National Education Association recognized physical education as a curricular area.

A significant step in the development of physical education was the founding, in 1885, of the Association for the Advancement of Physical Education (AAPE). William Anderson (1860–1947), a teacher at Adelphi Academy in Brooklyn, was interested in learning more about how other physical education professionals were teaching and structuring their programs. He organized a meeting at Adelphi Academy and invited professionals in the field. Dr. Edward Hitchcock served as the first president of AAPE. When the group met again in 1886, they changed their name to the American Association for the Advancement of Physical Education (AAAPE). This organization was the forerunner of today's American Alliance for Health, Physical Education, Recreation, and Dance (AAHPERD). It should be noted that many professionals initially involved in AAPE were physicians and held M.D. degrees. They supported physical education because of the beneficial health effects it provided.

During the mid- to late 1800s, considerable progress occurred in the growth of organized sports. Tennis was introduced in 1874, and in 1880, the United States Lawn Tennis Association was organized. Golf was played in the United States in the late 1880s, and in 1894, the United States Golfing Association was formed. Bowling had been popular since the time of the early Dutch settlers in New York, but it was not until 1895 that the American Bowling Congress was organized. Basketball, one of the few sports originating in the United States, was invented by James Naismith in 1891. Some other sports that became popular during this period are wrestling, boxing, volleyball, skating, skiing, lacrosse, handball, archery, track, soccer, squash, football, and swimming. In 1879, the National Association of Amateur Athletics of America was developed, from which the American Athletic Union (AAU) was later formed.

The AAU has played an instrumental role in the participation of the United States in the Olympic Games. A pedagogist, Baron Pierre de Coubertin was attracted to the idea of using sport as a means to develop pride and honor among the youth of France.

During a visit to the United States, he met with Princeton history professor William Sloane, who shared with him information about the ancient Olympic Games. An idealist, Coubertin saw that the Olympics could embody the ideals to which he ascribed: amateurism, fair play, good competition, promotion of goodwill, and fostering of understanding among athletes of the world.

Upon returning to France in 1892, he proposed the reestablishment of the Olympic Games to the governing athletic organization. His proposal was not endorsed. Coubertin persisted and continued to work toward his goal. At an international meeting of amateur athletic associations in Paris in 1894, Coubertin was successful in establishing the modern Olympics; he nurtured their growth as the first president of the newly created International Olympic Committee.

The first modern Olympics were held in Athens in 1896. A small delegation of American athletes, organized by Professor Sloane, participated in the Athens Olympics. Participation was limited to males and to 28 events in 4 sports: track and field, gymnastics, target shooting, and fencing. From the first modern games in 1896, the Olympics grew in scope and popularity to become the event that they are today.

Intercollegiate athletics grew during this time period. With the first intercollegiate meet in the form of a crew race between Harvard and Yale in 1852, intercollegiate sports began to play a prominent role on college campuses. Williams and Amherst played the first intercollegiate baseball game in 1859, and Rutgers and Princeton the first football game in 1869. Other intercollegiate contests soon followed in tennis, swimming, basketball, squash, and soccer. Although mostly males participated in athletics, opportunities were available for women. For example, in 1896, the first intercollegiate women's basketball game was held,

with teams from the University of California and Stanford University competing.

Initially, intercollegiate athletics were organized and directed primarily by the students. Athletics were viewed by school administrators and faculty as extracurricular activities because they were not perceived as central to the educational mission of the university. However, as athletics grew in popularity and prominence, problems and abuses became more frequent. Faculty raised concerns about student athletes' academic performance, eligibility, commercialization, payment of athletes, and overemphasis on athletics at the expense of academics.

To address these and related concerns and to control its future growth, faculty and administrators became involved in the governance of athletics. Faculty athletic committees were formed on campus. Harvard University was the first to establish a committee, in 1892. The next step in assumption of faculty control was the development of university associations to govern athletics. In 1895, the Intercollegiate Conference of Faculty Representatives was formed. Comprising faculty representatives from seven Midwestern institutions, it established eligibility requirements for students pertaining to enrollment and academic performance, imposed limits on athletic financial aid, and developed guidelines for the employment and retention of coaches. This conference, which later became the Big Ten, was the forerunner of other conferences established throughout the country to govern intercollegiate athletics and to define its role in university life.

Opportunities for women to participate in sport were limited by the social constraints of the time. Women's sports consisted of those in which they could participate and continue to be ladylike; Victorian sensibilities and contemporary standards of morality led to women's participating in activities in which they could be fully dressed and not break out in a sweat. Individual sport activities, such as archery, were acceptable. As physical education programs grew in the schools, more women became interested in participating in a wider range of physical activities. Women's team

US LEADERS—PHYSICAL EDUCATION, 1800s–1900s

Charles Beck (1798–1866)	Introduced Jahn's program of gymnastics to students at Round Hill School, Mass. (1825–1830).
Charles Follen (1796–1840)	Organized exercise classes, based on the German system, for students at Harvard College (1826–1828).
Catharine Beecher (1800–1878)	Director of Hartford Female Seminary in Connecticut (1824); developed a program of calisthenics performed to music; physical activity important for women's health.
Dioclesian Lewis (1823–1886)	Developed system of "light" gymnastics using handheld apparatus; established Normal Institute for Physical Education in Boston to train teachers (1861); first teacher preparation program in the United States.
Edward Hitchcock (1828–1911)	Director of hygiene and physical education at Amherst College (1861–1911); pioneered the use of anthropometric measurements to evaluate effectiveness of training; first president of the Association for the Advancement of Physical Education (1885).
Dudley Sargent (1849–1924)	Director of Hemenway Gymnasium at Harvard College (1879); used anthropometric measurements to develop individualized conditioning programs for students; founded forerunner to Sargent College for Physical Education to prepare physical education teachers (1881).
Delphine Hanna (1854–1941)	Taught at Oberlin College (1885–1921); in 1903 promoted to full professor, the first woman full professor in physical education; developed anthropometric measurement tables for women; established a professional preparation program for physical education (1892).
George Fitz (1860–1934)	Stressed the importance of basing physical education programs on scientific principles, not assumptions; established physiological laboratory at Harvard University, where he and his students conducted research on physiological effects of physical activity (1892).
Hartvig Nissen (1855–1924)	A pioneer in the promotion of Swedish system of gymnastics in the United States; taught at Swedish Health Institute in Washington, D.C. (1883); served as assistant and later director of physical training for the Boston public school system, where he influenced the adoption of Swedish gymnastics (1891–1900).
Baron Nils Posse (1862–1895)	Leader in the promotion of Swedish system of gymnastics in the United States (1885); helped establish the Boston Normal School of Gymnastics to train teachers in Swedish system (1889).
Amy Morris Homans (1848–1933)	Director of the Boston Normal School of Gymnastics (1889); played an influential role in getting the Boston public school system to adopt the Swedish system of gymnastics (1890).
Luther Gulick (1865–1918)	Played a significant role in the development of the YMCA as an instructor and later superintendent of the YMCA International Training School in Springfield, Mass.; designed the YMCA logo, with the triangle representing unity of the mind, body, and spirit.
William Anderson (1860–1947)	Played an instrumental role in the founding of the Association for the Advancement of Physical Education (1885); had a interest in sharing information about teaching physical education and learning about different programs; director of physical training at Adelphi Academy in Brooklyn.

sports, such as basketball, became popular around the turn of the century; however, some schools and members of the public discouraged women's participation.

Around 1870, the high-wheeler bike, with a huge front wheel about 5 feet tall and a small rear wheel, became popular. However, the bike was rather unstable, and riders were prone to frequent accidents. Around 1886, the safety bicycle, the forerunner of today's bicycle, was invented, and both males and females began to ride in great numbers. The popularity of the bicycle led to changes in women's attire; women began dressing in ways that allowed for more freedom of movement and enabled greater participation in a wide variety of physical activities. (It is important to realize that during this time women had not yet gained the right to vote.)

Opportunities for blacks to participate in sports were also limited by societal constraints. After slaves were freed following the Civil War, they engaged in a variety of sports, with baseball,

boxing, and horse racing being the most popular. A rising tide of racism in the late 1800s led to the passage of "Jim Crow" laws that resulted in the segregation of blacks and whites in many areas of life, including schools, playgrounds, and sports. The banning of competition between blacks and whites led to the formation of separate sport leagues and college athletic conferences. This segregation continued through the 1900s, and integration in many sports did not occur until after World War II. Major league baseball remained segregated until 1946.

Early Twentieth Century

The early twentieth century marked a significant period of growth and development for both physical education and sport. From the 1900s to the 1940s, remarkable changes occurred in the philosophy, nature, and conduct of physical education programs. Physical education changed its focus from a narrow emphasis on systems of gymnastics,

Ina Gittings, a student at the University of Nebraska, pole vaulting in 1905.

exercise regimes, and calisthenics to a broader focus that encompassed games, sports, aquatics, dance, and outdoor activities. The "new physical education" developed, which emphasized a program of activities and the contribution of physical education to the total education of the individual. Physical education leaders debated whether physical education should emphasize education *of* the physical or education *through* the physical. Physical education teacher training programs grew in number, and graduate degrees in physical education began to be awarded with greater frequency.

Sport became increasingly organized during this time and grew tremendously in popularity. Extensive programs were established in schools and universities, and recreation programs flourished. Intercollegiate athletics were brought under more rigid academic control. Intramurals became more popular as the emphasis on sports for all gained momentum.

During the first decade of the twentieth century, Luther Gulick continued to promote play as important to the development of children. He played an instrumental role in the formation of the Playground Association of America in 1906, which sought to promote the development of urban and rural playgrounds, and served as its first president. By 1930, the Playground Association had evolved into the National Recreation Association.

Physical education began to change in scope. At the forefront of this change was Thomas Dennison Wood (1864–1951), who advocated the development of a new program of physical education that would enhance the development of the whole individual through participation in play, games, sports, and outdoor activities. Wood studied with Hanna at Oberlin College, served as the first director of the physical education department at Stanford University, and taught at the Teachers College of Columbia University from 1901 to 1932.

In an 1893 speech at the International Conference on Education, Wood presented his vision for a new physical education, one with an "aim as broad as education itself. . . . The great thought in physical education is not the education of physical nature, but the relationship of physical training to

Students participate in play day at the John Muir School in 1924.

completed education, and then the effort to make the physical contribute its full share to the life of the individual, in environment, training, and culture."[5] Wood called for a broader program of activities and a greater responsiveness to the needs of the individual. His program was first introduced under the title "natural gymnastics," but later became known as the "new physical education."

Robert Tait McKenzie (1867–1938), physician, physical educator, and noted artist-sculptor, was on the faculty of McGill University (Canada) from 1891 to 1904 and the University of Pennsylvania from 1904 to 1931. McKenzie worked to help develop physical education programs for individuals with disabilities.

World War I (1916–1919)

World War I started in 1914, and the United States' entry in 1918 had a critical impact on the nation and education. The Selective Service Act of 1917 called to service all men between the ages of 18 and 25.

Social forces were also at work during this period. The emancipation of women was furthered by passage of the Nineteenth Amendment. Women also began to show interest in sport and physical education, as well as in other fields formerly considered to be off-limits.

During World War I many physical educators, such as Dudley Sargent, Luther Gulick, and R. Tait McKenzie, contributed their services to the armed forces. The War Department's Commission on Training Camp Activities was created, and Raymond Fosdick was named its head. Joseph E. Raycroft of Princeton University and Walter Camp, the creator of "All-Americans," were named to head the athletic divisions of the army and the navy, respectively. Women physical educators were also active in conditioning programs in communities and industries at home.

When the war ended, the public had an opportunity to study the medical examiner's report for the men who had been called to military duty. One-third of the men were found physically unfit for armed service, and many more were physically inept.

Golden Twenties (1920–1929)

Many advances in physical education occurred during the Twenties that had a profound influence on physical education for decades to come. The "new physical education" began to take shape

Women playing field hockey at Smith College in Northampton, Mass., in 1904.

1851   1866

1910   1920

1927   *yesterday today tomorrow... the right costume for gymnasium, pool & dance*

Early physical education attire for American women.

objectives of physical education as organic development (fitness), psychomotor development (skill), character development (social), and intellectual development (mental). Hetherington, like Wood, believed that physical education had a broader purpose than the development of the physical aspects of the individual, which was the popular approach of the times. Hetherington is often credited with inventing the phrase "new physical education" to describe the changing emphasis of the field that was initially described by Wood.

Rosalind Cassidy (1895–1980) was also an advocate of "education through the physical"— the position that held that carefully designed programs of physical education could contribute to the development of the whole person. Cassidy's career as an educator spanned over 40 years. In 1927, she coauthored with Wood *The New Physical Education: A Program of Naturalized Activities for Education Toward Citizenship,* which described how physical education could contribute to the education of children through a well-planned program of physical education activities.

Jesse F. Williams (1886–1966) also advocated "education through the physical." He taught at the Teachers College of Columbia University for over 25 years, ending his tenure there in 1941. In 1927, Williams published *The Principles of Physical Education,* which set forth his beliefs that social responsibility and moral values can be developed through physical education. Williams's beliefs were based on the unity of mind and body. He argued that physical education should be included within the school curriculum because of its ability to contribute to the development of the whole child, and advocated for the idea that athletics could play a vital role in creating socially responsive citizens.

Jay B. Nash (1886–1965) strongly believed in the value of recreation and thought that through experiences such as camping, individuals would gain both an appreciation of nature and an understanding of the principles of democracy. In his view, the physical education curriculum should be designed to prepare students to use their leisure time in a worthy manner. Physical education

during this period, influenced by the leading progressive education theorists of the time, including John Dewey. Clark Hetherington's (1870–1942) philosophy of physical education was influenced by Wood's beliefs and his "natural gymnastics" approach. In 1910, Hetherington articulated the four should teach students recreational skills that they can use for enjoyable participation throughout their lifetime.

The 1920s and 1930s marked a time when an increasing emphasis was placed on defining the scientific basis of physical education. Measurement was used as a means of grouping students, assessing achievement, prescribing exercises, and motivating performance. Some leaders argued that it was important to be able to demonstrate outcomes and identify which programs of exercise yielded beneficial results. The growth of doctoral programs in physical education also stimulated an interest in research. In 1924, the Teachers College of Columbia University and New York University offered the first doctoral degrees in physical education, and other programs began to develop around the country as well. In 1930, the American Physical Education Association published the *Research Quarterly,* now called the *Research Quarterly for Exercise and Sport.*

Many problems arose in regard to college athletics. As a result, the Carnegie Foundation provided a grant, in 1923, for a study of intercollegiate athletics in certain institutions in the South by a committee of the Association of Colleges and Secondary Schools. Later, a study of athletic practices in American colleges and universities was conducted. The report of this study was published in 1929 under the title *American College Athletics.* The report denounced athletics as being professional rather than amateur in nature and as a means of public entertainment and commercialization. Problems such as recruiting and subsidizing athletes also were exposed.

During this period, intramural athletic programs increased in colleges and universities. Women's programs experienced an increase in the number of staff, hours required for student participation, activities offered, and physical education buildings in use.

Depression Years (1930–1939)

The 1929 stock market crash ushered in the Great Depression, which affected education.

Unemployment and poverty reigned. Health and physical education had a difficult time surviving in many communities.

During the period of economic depression in the United States, many gains achieved by physical education in the schools of the nation were lost. Budgets were cut back, and programs in many cases were either dropped or downgraded. Between 1932 and 1934, an estimated 40% of the physical education programs were dropped completely. Legislative moves were made in several states, such as Illinois and California, to do away with the physical education requirement.

Another development during the Depression years was that physical educators became more involved in recreation programs in the agencies and projects concerned with unemployed people. These later programs were being subsidized with special government assistance. The national association, recognizing the increased interest in recreation, voted to change its title to include the word *recreation*—the American Association for Health, Physical Education, and Recreation.

One of the leaders of this time was Charles McCloy (1886–1959). McCloy served as a YMCA instructor and director in China for more than 10 years and taught physical education at several colleges in the United States. He advocated "education of the physical," espousing the belief that school physical education's unique contribution to the education of the individual is organic and psychomotor development. According to McCloy, school physical education programs should focus their efforts on promoting fitness and teaching sports skills. Furthermore, McCloy recognized the importance of physical educators being able to document results and measure progress using scientific data. During and after World War II, McCloy served as a fitness consultant to the United States armed forces.

Interscholastic athletic programs continued to grow and in some situations dominated physical education programs and created many educational problems. The National Association of Intercollegiate Basketball was established in 1940 for the purpose of providing an association for the

Tennis at the turn of the century at Smith College in Northampton, Mass.

smaller colleges. It changed its name in 1952 to the National Association of Intercollegiate Athletics. In 1937, representatives of the Junior Colleges of California met for the purpose of forming the National Junior College Athletic Association.

Intramural athletics continued to grow in colleges and universities. Women's athletic associations also increased in number. The principles that guided such programs were established largely during the early years by the National Section of Women's Athletics.

Mid-Twentieth Century (1940–1970)

During the middle of the twentieth century, physical education and sport programs grew, in part, due to World War II (see the Mid-Twentieth

Century [1940–1970] box for significant events). Selective Service examinations of drafted men indicated that they were not in sound condition. This helped stimulate the development of physical training programs in branches of the armed forces, and President Franklin Roosevelt appointed John P. Kelly as the national director of physical training. The importance of fitness and its role in the national defense were highlighted by the establishment of a Division of Physical Fitness within the US Office of Defense Health and Welfare Services.

The war years had their impact on physical education programs in schools and colleges. At all levels, there was an emphasis on more formalized conditioning programs, with the goal of improving the fitness of children and youth. Girls and

MID-TWENTIETH CENTURY (1940–1970)

1942	The Division of Physical Fitness was established within the US Office of Defense Health and Welfare Services.
1950	The National Athletic Trainer's Association (NATA) was founded.
1953	President Eisenhower established the President's Council on Youth Fitness due to the low scores of American children on the Kraus-Weber Minimal Muscular Fitness Test. The council evolved into the current President's Council on Physical Fitness and Sports.
1953	The National Conference on Program Planning in Game and Sports for Boys and Girls of Elementary School Age brought professionals together to discuss the value of organized games and sport for children younger than high school age.
1954	The Federation of Sports Medicine was founded, which later became the American College of Sports Medicine (ACSM).
1956	The intramural movement at the collegiate level was supported by the National Conference on Intramural Sports for College Men and Women.
1964	The first National Institute on Girls' Sports was held.
1968	The Special Olympics was founded.

an article entitled "Muscular Fitness and Health." The article reported the results of the Kraus-Weber Minimal Muscular Fitness Tests given to European and American children. Nearly 60% of the American children had failed, compared with only 9% of the European children. The fitness test primarily measured flexibility and abdominal strength. Nevertheless, the condition of the American children was cause for concern. This concern eventually led President Eisenhower to establish the President's Council on Youth Fitness, the forerunner to the current President's Council on Physical Fitness and Sports.

A significant teacher shortage during and following the war led to an increase in professional preparation programs in colleges and universities. Early leaders in physical education were physicians, not physical educators. As the number of professional preparation programs in physical education grew, physical educators assumed many of the leadership roles. In 1954, a group of 11 physicians founded the Federation of Sports Medicine, which later became the American College of Sports Medicine (ACSM).

As sports programs expanded and participation increased, qualified individuals were needed to treat injured athletes and to design programs to prevent injuries. Physical educators, coaches, and other individuals stepped forward to fulfill these responsibilities, working as athletic trainers. In 1950, the National Athletic Trainers' Association (NATA) was founded.

Promoting participation of girls and women in competitive sports at both the high school and college levels was the result of several events during this time. In 1964, the first National Institute on Girls' Sports was held, with conference participants discussing ways to encourage more girls and women to participate in sports. The Division for Girls' and Women's Sports (DGWS) of AAHPERD played an important role in developing guidelines for girls' and women's participation. Another effort included becoming involved in the Olympic development movement as a means to promote more opportunities. These and many other efforts, as well as the societal changes of

women as well as boys and men were involved in their programs.

Another significant event occurred in December 1953, when the *Journal of Health, Physical Education, and Recreation* published

US LEADERS—PHYSICAL EDUCATION, 1900–1940

Thomas Dennison Wood (1864–1951)	Presented his vision for the "new education" at the International Conference on Education (1893); coauthored *The New Physical Education: A Program of Naturalized Activities for Education Toward Citizenship* with Cassidy (1927); his program of "natural gymnastics" came to be known as the "new physical education."
Robert Tait McKenzie (1867–1938)	Physician, physical educator, artist, and sculptor; worked to develop physical education programs for individuals with disabilities; wrote *Exercise in Education and Medicine* (1910); created hundreds of sculptures of athletes engaged in sporting events.
Clark Hetherington (1870–1942)	Articulated the four objectives of physical education as organic development, psychomotor development, character development, and intellectual development. Credited with the phase "new physical education" to describe the changing emphasis advocated by Wood.
Rosalind Cassidy (1895–1980)	A prolific writer, promoted the "new physical education" in *The New Physical Education: A Program of Naturalized Activities for Education Toward Citizenship,* coauthored with Wood; advocated for the "education through the physical" approach to teaching physical education.
Jesse F. Williams (1886–1966)	Advocate of "education through the physical" philosophy of physical education; stressed the development of social responsibility and moral values through physical education and athletics.
Jay B. Nash (1886–1965)	Believed physical education should give students the ability to use their leisure time in a worthy manner and should teach them recreational skills they can use for enjoyment throughout their lifetime.
Charles McCloy (1886–1959)	Was active in research and measurement, including anthropometry; advocated "education of the physical" philosophy; believed physical education's primary objectives are the development of organic vigor and skills.

those times, were all steps that led to a movement to increase opportunities in competitive sports by girls and women.

As sports became increasingly popular at various educational levels, renewed interest arose in providing sport competition for all students, not just for the skilled elite. At the college level, the intramural movement was spurred on by the 1956 National Conference on Intramural Sports for College Men and Women. The conference participants formulated principles and recommended administrative procedures that would lead to greater involvement by men and women in intramural sports.

Another significant development during this time was the increased emphasis placed on including sports within the physical education curriculum that could be played throughout a person's lifetime for enjoyment and fitness. The Lifetime Sports Foundation, begun in 1965, was instrumental in providing leadership in this area. School and college physical education programs changed to include a greater emphasis on teaching activities such as bowling, tennis, golf, and badminton.

While sports were being promoted at the high school and college levels, there was controversy regarding sports for children below the high

American physical education leaders William Anderson and Amy Morris Homans.

school level. The 1953 National Conference on Program Planning in Game and Sports for Boys and Girls of Elementary School Age brought together professionals in medicine, education, recreation, and other child-focus fields to discuss the value of organized games and sport for children that young. Two conference recommendations were that programs of games and sports be based on the developmental level of children, with no contact sports allowed for children under 12 years of age, and that competition be recognized as inherent in the growth and development of the child; whether it would be beneficial or harmful would depend on a multitude of factors.

During this time period, physical educators became more convinced that students with special needs, such as individuals who have physical or developmental disabilities, would benefit from participation in physical education and sport.

The growth of participation opportunities for individuals with disabilities increased during this time. One significant event was the founding of the Special Olympics in 1968. Since its inception, the Special Olympics has provided competitive sport opportunities for individuals with mental retardation. Adapted physical education received increased attention, with courses being included in the physical education professional preparation curriculum.

At the international level, leaders of physical education, health, and recreation began meeting with more frequency. These meetings provided leaders from different countries the chance to exchange ideas and communicate with one another. As part of the effort to bring leaders from different countries together, the International Council of Health, Physical Education, and Recreation (ICHPER) was formed in 1959.

LIFESPAN AND CULTURAL PERSPECTIVES: Sport History

- How did ancient Greek beliefs about the body influence the development of physical education?
- What role did sport play in the lives of the early Native Americans?
- How did Victorian conceptions of femininity influence women's participation in sports in the United States?
- What events have led to a greater emphasis on physical activity for older adults?
- How did segregation influence opportunities for blacks in sport?
- How did beliefs about the development of children influence the physical education curriculum in the 1800s?

Research in physical education continued to develop during this time. The Research Council of AAHPERD, established in 1952, focused on promoting research along strategic lines, providing assistance to researchers through dissemination of materials, and synthesizing research in professional areas. Research also became increasingly specialized. Studies were conducted in areas such as exercise physiology, motor learning, sociology of sport, and sport pedagogy.

SIGNIFICANT RECENT DEVELOPMENTS (1970–PRESENT)

Physical education, exercise science, and sport currently is in one of its most exciting eras. So many changes have occurred since 1970 that capturing them all in such a limited space is difficult. These changes include the disciplinary movement, the quest for identity, the emergence of the subdisciplines, new directions in professional preparation, and increased career opportunities in these dynamic fields. The national emphasis on disease prevention and health, promotion, and increasing evidence of the positive relationship between physical activity and health, have stimulated participation by people of all ages and created new opportunities within the realm of physical education, exercise science, and sport. Sport participation at

all levels and within all segments of the population has exploded. Legislation has increased opportunities for girls and women in sports and for people with disabilities. The Olympics have experienced a period of growth, withstood politicization, and emerged as a commercial venture of huge proportions. Technology has contributed in many ways to the continued growth of physical education, exercise science, and sport. Many of these recent developments are included within other chapters.

The Discipline

The disciplinary movement is generally acknowledged to have begun with Franklin Henry's 1964 clarion call for the study of the academic discipline of physical education.[6] It is only since the 1970s, however, that the body of knowledge composing the discipline of physical education, exercise science, and sport has grown rapidly. Expanded and rigorous research efforts by dedicated academicians, coupled with improvements in technology, have contributed to the explosion of knowledge. Specialized areas of study or subdisciplines such as exercise physiology, exercise and sport psychology, and motor learning have emerged (see Chapter 1).

The disciplinary movement that has been evolving since the 1970s led to considerable debate about the best name for our field of endeavor.

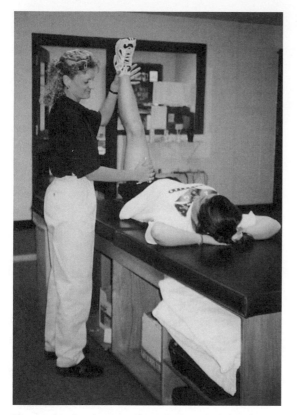

New professional preparation programs train students for nontraditional careers, such as athletic training.

nature of their work. In 1997, in the United States, there were more than 150 different names for departments in higher education.[8]

The growth of the discipline influenced professional preparation programs at colleges and universities. New courses were developed to embrace the knowledge within the subdisciplines. At the undergraduate level, these courses were initially incorporated into teacher preparation programs. Graduate programs were further developed to offer study within those areas of specialization. To this end, undergraduate programs in specialized areas such as exercise science, sport studies, and sport management were developed. The broadening of professional preparation programs within physical education, exercise science, and sport to encompass specialized areas of study has allowed students to prepare for a diversity of career opportunities within these expanding fields.

In the late 1960s and early 1970s, the proliferation of research and the desire to share findings with colleagues helped stimulate the formation of specialized scholarly organizations. For example, the North American Society for the Psychology of Sport and Physical Activity was founded in 1967, and the Philosophic Society for the Study of Sport was begun in 1972. Today there exist many professional organizations and journals focusing on specialized fields of study within physical education, exercise science, and sport, providing a plethora of outlets for the dissemination of research findings through presentations at conferences and professional journals.

Physical education, exercise science, and sport programs have expanded from serving school- and college-age populations to serving people of all ages—from preschoolers to the elderly. Expansion of programs from the traditional school setting to nonschool settings such as community centers and corporate fitness centers has occurred at an increasing rate. Private-sector programs in the health enhancement and leisure services industries have grown, creating a diversity of career opportunities for well-prepared individuals. The American College of Sports Medicine (ACSM), the National

The traditional name of physical education was perceived by some as too narrow and as failing to convey the expanding scholarly interest in sport. In 1989, the prestigious American Academy of Physical Education voted to change its name to the American Academy of Kinesiology and Physical Education and recommended *kinesiology* as the title of the discipline. Other popular names were physical education and sport, exercise science, and exercise and sport science. In 1994, Ziegler reported that *physical education and sport* was the most widely used title for the field worldwide.[7] As the disciplinary movement continued to grow in the 1970s and 1980s, departments of physical education in colleges and universities changed their name in an effort to more accurately convey the

Athletic Trainers' Association (NATA), the National Strength and Conditioning Association (NSCA), and the Aerobics and Fitness Association of America (AFAA) offer certification programs for professionals. (Professional preparation programs and career opportunities are discussed in Part III.)

One milestone in this period was the celebration in 1985 by the American Alliance for Health, Physical Education, Recreation and Dance (AAHPERD) of the one hundredth anniversary of its founding as the American Association for the Advancement of Physical Education.

Disease Prevention and Health Promotion

One of the most significant changes in society during these past decades is the increased emphasis on disease prevention and health promotion. As disease prevention and health promotion initiatives grew, greater attention was directed at helping individuals improve their health by incorporating health-enhancing behaviors into their lifestyle. At this time there was an emerging consensus of epidemiologists, experts in exercise science, and health professionals, as well as a growing body of evidence, that supported the contribution of physical activity to health and well-being. Four national health reports—*Healthy People* (1979),[9] *Promoting Health/Preventing Disease* (1980),[10] *Healthy People 2000* (1990),[11] and *Healthy People 2010* (2000)[12]—clearly identified the contribution that physical activity could make to well-being. These reports established specific objectives to be accomplished by physical education, exercise science, and sport, the attainment of which would lead to the improvement of the health of the nation.

The landmark 1996 report *Physical Activity and Health: A Report of the Surgeon General*[13] and, most recently, the 2010 *Surgeon General's Vision for a Healthy and Fit Nation*[14] affirmed the contribution of physical activity to the attainment and maintenance of health. These reports on physical activity and health emphasized that all Americans can substantially improve their health and quality of life by including moderate to vigorous physical activity in their daily lives. The goal of these national calls to action is to improve the health of the nation; this offers a tremendous challenge to all members of our field.

School Physical Education

Public health initiatives since 1970 have emphasized the critical role that school physical education programs can play in helping children acquire the skills, knowledge, and habits to be active throughout their lives. These decades have been marked by efforts to promote physical education and advocacy on behalf of quality physical education in the schools.

In 1971, the Physical Education Public Information Project (PEPI) was begun to inform the public, educators, and policy makers about the value of physical education. PEPI emphasized that "physical education is health insurance."[15] In 1986, the National Association of Sport and Physical Education (NASPE), an association of AAHPERD, defined the characteristics of a "physically educated person" (see Chapter 2).[16] In 1995 and again in 2004, NASPE published *Moving into the Future: National Standards for Physical Education—A Guide to Content and Assessment.*[17,18] For the first time in the United States, this document offered physical educators a national framework to guide the development of their physical education curriculums.

Periodic surveys such as AAHPERD's Shape of the Nation and the CDC's Youth Risk Behavior Surveillance System (YRBSS) provide information about the status of physical education in the nation's schools. The first Shape of the Nation survey, conducted in 1987,[19] revealed that only one state, Illinois, required daily physical education for kindergarten through 12th grade—which is still true today. Only 17 states require physical education to be included in students' grade point average, and 29 states allow exemptions and waivers that permit the substitution of other activities for physical education.[20]

The national standards and health reports such as *Healthy People 2010* called for increasing daily quality physical education for all students. School physical education is regarded as a key setting in which to increase the physical activity of children and youth as well as lay the foundation for a lifetime of physical activity. Yet despite the recognition that physical education can make a significant contribution to students' health, physical educators are facing tremendous pressures to justify their programs. Increasing pressures for academic reform have led to efforts to make more time in the curriculum for educational basics and to reduction in the time for "frills" such as art, music, and physical education (see Chapters 2 and 10). Furthermore, physical educators have reported tremendous pressure to justify their programs due to fiscal constraints.

As the twenty-first century progresses, greater efforts must be directed at promoting physical education as an educational basic, an integral part of the school curriculum for children and youth in all grades.

Physical Fitness and Participation in Physical Activity

The fitness movement began as a trend in the 1970s and has continued to expand. Many people of all ages lead an active lifestyle, engaging in activities such as jogging, biking, walking, and weight training to an extent never before seen. While it may appear that America is an active nation, studies report that too many adults engage in no physical activity during their leisure time (see Chapter 3). Recent studies have also raised alarms regarding the growing percentage of children, youth, and adults who are overweight and obese. While more individuals of all ages are participating in physical activities, much more needs to be done to encourage people to be active and to eat healthy.

Starting in the 1970s, there was a gradual shift from an emphasis on performance-related fitness to one on health-related fitness. During the 1970s and 1980s, as the emphasis on disease prevention and health promotion grew, the contribution of fitness to health gained increased

Sales of sports equipment have increased dramatically in the last decade, creating many new career opportunities in sports retailing.

recognition. Physical inactivity was linked to disease. To improve health, it was recommended that people engage in fitness activities on a regular basis.

At this time, there was a similar shift in fitness development and testing in the schools. In 1980, AAHPERD inaugurated the Health-Related Physical Fitness Test.[21] This test was designed to measure the fitness components associated with health. In 1988, AAHPERD introduced a new fitness test and educational program entitled Physical Best.[22] Physical Best emphasized not only the physical dimension of fitness but the cognitive and affective dimensions as well. The educational component was designed to help teachers assist students in attaining desirable fitness habits through individualized goal setting, motivational techniques, and encouragement of participation in physical activities outside the school setting. In 1994, AAHPERD and the Cooper Institute for Aerobic Research (CIAR) announced an agreement to collaborate on youth fitness testing and education. AAHPERD agreed to adopt CIAR's Prudential Fitnessgram system for testing and assessment of youth fitness. CIAR agreed to use AAHPERD's Physical Best educational materials to promote healthy lifestyles for all children and youth.

As researchers continued to investigate the relationship among fitness, physical activity, and health, they found that health-related benefits could be obtained at more moderate-intensity levels of activity than previously realized. In 1995, guidelines for physical activity reflecting this finding were issued by the CDC, the ACSM, and the National Institutes of Health (NIH) Consensus Development Conference on Physical Activity and Cardiovascular Health, recommending that all population groups should accumulate at least 30 minutes a day of moderate-intensity physical activity.[13] The new recommendations also emphasized that greater benefits would accrue by engaging in moderate-intensity activities for a greater period of time or participating in more vigorous physical activity.[13]

The fitness movement and the recognition of the importance of leading a healthy, active lifestyle were significant features of the past four decades. The shift from performance- to health-related fitness reflects the recognition by professionals in the field of the important role physical activity plays in promoting the health and well-being of people of all ages.

The Growth of Sports

Participation in sport has experienced phenomenal growth at all levels since the 1970s. Participation by children and youth involved in organized sport activities outside the school setting, under the guidance of public or private agencies, has grown tremendously. It is estimated that children and youth sports involve millions of children and adult volunteer coaches. Additionally, thousands of paid coaches work primarily in private sports clubs with elite performers.

Participation in interscholastic sports has grown from 3,960,932 boys and girls in 1971 to over 7,536,753 in 2008–2009.[23] More than 50% of students played on a sports team in a given year. There is an increased trend toward specialization in a specific sport at an early age. A youth may play on the school soccer team in the fall, participate in recreational league indoor soccer in the winter, play spring soccer, and then attend soccer camp in the summer. Some school districts, facing budgetary difficulties, have instituted "pay-to-play" plans in which athletes are charged fees to participate. Considerable concern has been raised that these fees will limit participation and disproportionately affect students from lower socioeconomic groups. The National Federation of State High School Associations opposes this practice, stating that sports have educational value and therefore students should have access to them as part of their educational experience.

At the collegiate level, participation in sports has increased as well. The National Collegiate Athletic Association (NCAA) reported that during the 1989–1990 academic year, 266,268 collegians participated in intercollegiate athletics; in 2008–2009, over 3.7 million collegians participated.[24] Thousands more collegiate athletes participate at the over 300 schools that are members of the National Association of Intercollegiate Athletes (NAIA)[25] and at the over 460 community colleges that are governed by the National Junior College Athletic Association (NJCAA).[26] Moreover, during this time, sport has emerged as big business in NCAA Division I schools. Media revenues for televising football and basketball games and tournaments have reached millions of dollars. For example, the major NCAA Division I-A football schools shared more than $100 million in revenue for the bowl games.

Participation in recreational leagues (e.g., softball, soccer, volleyball) and road races by adults has increased enormously as well. Master's programs in swimming and track and field, the National Senior Games, the National Olympic Festival, and state games such as the Empire State Games engage people of all ages in various levels of competition in a multitude of sports.

Professional sports have also increased during this time. Since the 1970s, expansion has resulted in the addition of many professional hockey, football, and baseball teams. Salaries of professionals have increased dramatically; multimillion dollar contracts have become increasingly common.

The past decade has seen the growth of professional basketball opportunities for women. The Women's National Basketball Association (WNBA), backed by the National Basketball Association, began its inaugural season in 1997. The Women's United Soccer Association (WUSA), the women's professional soccer league, played its first season in 2001. Unfortunately, due to financial issues, the league suspended its operations in 2003, but there is an effort to revive the league and continue play in the future. The number of women participating in professional sports, such as the Ladies Professional Golf Association (LPGA), has grown tremendously. Male and female athletes in both tennis and golf now compete for prizes worth millions of dollars; in golf, the winnings are equal for men and women.

Girls and Women in Sports

Since the 1970s, participation by girls and women in sports has grown rapidly. The dramatic increase in participation was enhanced by the changing attitudes toward women in society and by the passage of Title IX of the Education Amendments of 1972. The Title IX law specifically states, "No person in the United States shall on the basis of sex be excluded from participation in, be denied the benefits of, or be subjected to discrimination under any educational program or activity receiving Federal financial assistance." Over the past 38 years, this educational law has had wide-ranging effects on physical education and athletic programs in the United States.

One major reason Title IX came into existence was to ensure that girls and women receive the same (i.e., equal) rights as boys and men. Testimony before congressional committees prior to the enactment of this legislation showed that girls and women were being discriminated against in many educational programs, including physical education and athletics.

Participation in sports by girls and women has risen dramatically since the enactment of Title IX. According to the National Federation of State High School Associations, during 1971, the year before Title IX legislation, 3,366,000 boys and 294,000 girls competed in interscholastic sports in the United States. In 2008–2009, the federation reported that 4,422,662 boys and 3,114,091 girls took part in interscholastic sports.[23] This is an all-time high for participation by girls. Participation by women at the intercollegiate level also showed substantial increases. For example, according to the NCAA, 32,000 women competed in intercollegiate sports in 1972, whereas in 2004–2005, more than 160,000 women competed. (These figures include only NCAA-sponsored championship sports; thus the number of participants is greater than reported here.)

Title IX mandates certain provisions for physical education and athletic programs. With respect to physical education, no discrimination can occur in program offerings, quality of teachers, and availability and quality of facilities and equipment. Physical education classes must be organized on a coeducational basis. However, classes may be separated by sex for contact sports such as wrestling, basketball, and football. Also, within classes, students may be grouped by ability or on another basis except sex, although such groupings may result in single-sex or predominately single-sex groupings.

Title IX also caused changes in the conduct of athletic programs. Separate teams for men and women or a coeducational team must be provided in schools and colleges. For example, if only one team is organized in a particular school for a sport, such as swimming, then students of both sexes must be permitted to try out for the team.

TITLE IX—SELECTED HISTORICAL DEVELOPMENTS

"No person in the United States shall, on the basis of sex, be excluded from participation in, be denied the benefits of, or be subjected to discrimination under any education program or activity receiving Federal financial assistance."

1972	Title IX of the Education Amendments of 1972 prohibits sex discrimination in any educational program or activity receiving federal financial assistance, including employment, admission to college programs (e.g., science, math, medicine, law), and standardized testing; prohibits sexual harassment. This changes conduct of physical education classes and opens up opportunities for girls and women in intercollegiate and interscholastic sports.
1975	US Department of Health, Education, and Welfare clarifies policies relative to intercollegiate athletics. Three areas are identified for compliance: accommodation of students' interests and abilities, financial aid, and programmatic support.
1980	US Department of Education gives oversight for Title IX to the Office of Civil Rights (OCR).
1984	Supreme Court, in *Grove City College v. Bell*, rules that Title IX is program specific. Only programs or activities that receive direct federal funding need to comply with Title IX; narrow interpretation of Title IX.
1988	Civil Rights Restoration Act supersedes 1984 Supreme Court ruling in *Grove City College v. Bell*. All educational institutions receiving federal financial assistance, whether direct or indirect, must comply with Title IX; broad interpretation of Title IX.
1992	Supreme Court, in *Franklin v. Gwinnett County Public Schools*, rules that plaintiffs may receive monetary damages when an educational institution intentionally violates Title IX.
1992	National Collegiate Athletic Association (NCAA) publishes its first Gender Equity Study; annual reports required.
1994	Equity in Athletics Disclosure Act requires all higher education institutions to disclose information on participation and budgets for men's and women's intercollegiate sports; annual report available to the public.
1996	OCR issues clarifications about how institutions can demonstrate accommodating interests and needs of underrepresented gender; three-prong test—proportionality, history of progress, and accommodation of interests.
2002	US Secretary of Education establishes 15-member Commission on Opportunities in Athletics (COA) charged with reviewing Title IX to ensure that both males and females have equal opportunities to participate in athletics.
2003	OCR provides further clarification regarding compliance, including the use of proportionality as part of the three-prong test for assessing participation opportunities; COA issues report.
2005	Supreme Court, in *Jackson v. Birmingham Board of Education*, accords individuals who suffer retaliation as a result of reporting Title IX violations the right to sue the institution; protects "whistle-blowers."
2010	OCR overturns the policy that allowed colleges and universities to use a survey to demonstrate that they were meeting the athletic interests and abilities of women on campus. The policy allowed institutions to equate lack of response with a lack of interest in athletics; policy change will require educational institutions to use other data sources, in addition to the surveys, to learn students' athletic interests.

Sources: Women's Sports Foundation (www.womenssportsfoundation.org); Curtis M and Grant CHB. Gender Equity in Sports. Updated February 23, 2006 (http://bailiwick.lib.uiowa.edu/ge); Thomas K. "Rule Change Takes Aim at Loophole in Title IX."

New York Times, April 19, 2010 (www.nytimes.com/2010/04/20/sports/20titleix.html); Dougherty J. "Biden Announces Change in Title IX Women's Sports Policy."

Cable News Network (CNN), April 20, 2010 (http://edition.cnn.com/2010/POLITICS/04/20/biden.title.ix/index.html?hpt=Sbin).

Competitors in wheelchair archery take aim at the 2004 Paralympic Games in Athens.

Both sexes in educational institutions must be provided with equal opportunities for equipment and supplies, use of facilities for practice and games, medical and training services, coaching and academic tutoring, travel allowances, housing and dining facilities, compensation of coaches, financial assistance, and publicity. Equal aggregate expenditures are not required; however, equal opportunities for men and women are mandated.

There have also been changes since 1972 in the governance of women's intercollegiate sports. The Association of Intercollegiate Athletics for Women (AIAW), founded in 1972, initially was the governing body for women's intercollegiate sports. The AIAW established policies and procedures governing competition and conducted national championships for women's intercollegiate sports. The NCAA used its vast financial resources to entice teams to leave the AIAW; over a period of time, this led to the demise of the AIAW. In 1982, the NCAA and the NAIA assumed the governance of intercollegiate sports for women at all NCAA and NAIA institutions.

Throughout its history, many challenges to Title IX have been heard by the courts. In 1984, the United States Supreme Court ruled 6–3 in *Grove City College v. Bell* that Title IX should be regarded as program specific. In essence, this narrow interpretation of Title IX held that only programs directly receiving federal aid were required to comply with Title IX, not the institution as a whole. Before this ruling, Title IX was interpreted broadly; that is, institutions receiving any federal funds were required to comply with Title IX in all institution activities. Since athletic programs typically receive little, if any, direct federal funding, the threat of losing funding for noncompliance and nonsupport of women's athletics is without substance. While some institutions remained deeply committed to women's athletics, the fear existed that some institutions, without the threat of penalties for noncompliance, would allow women's athletics to stagnate or even to become victims of budgetary cutbacks.

In 1988, the Civil Rights Restoration Act superseded the 1984 Supreme Court ruling. Once again, Title IX was interpreted broadly and its applicability to athletics was reinstated. In 1991, the Office of Civil Rights announced that investigation of Title IX athletic complaints would be one of the office's priorities.

Title IX has led to dramatic changes in the conduct of physical education and athletic programs and to significant increases in participation by girls and women within these programs. (See the Title IX—Selected Historical Developments.) However, the impact of Title IX has been limited by several factors, including gender biases, limited budgets, inadequate facilities, lack of qualified leadership (i.e., coaches), and resistance to change.

Although equal opportunity is mandated by law and great strides have occurred within the last decades, much still needs to be accomplished within both physical education and athletic programs to achieve equity.

Programs for Individuals with Disabilities

In recent years, many judicial decisions and legislative acts have supported the rights of individuals with disabilities to have the same opportunities as other individuals. These mandates have resulted in significant changes in the conduct of physical education and athletic programs for individuals with disabilities. The rights of people with disabilities in programs for which schools and other sponsoring organizations receive federal funds were guaranteed by Section 504 of the Rehabilitation Act of 1973.

The most widely known and important law related to education for people with disabilities is the Education of All Handicapped Children Act of 1975. This law provided for a free and appropriate education for children aged 3 to 21. Section 121a.307 of the regulations stated that physical education services were to be made available to every child with a disability. All educational services are to be provided for students with disabilities in the least restrictive environment. In essence,

this means that a child with a disability is placed in a special class, or mainstreamed into a regular class, or moved between the two environments as dictated by his or her abilities and capabilities. Furthermore, the school assumes the responsibility of providing the necessary adjunct services to ensure that students with disabilities perform to their optimum capacity, whether they are integrated into a regular program or left in a special class. Each child with disabilities must have an individualized educational plan, or IEP.

In 1990, the Individuals with Disabilities Education Act (IDEA) was passed. Among its mandates was a requirement that all references to "handicapped children" be changed to "children with disabilities." It mandated that transitional services be provided to students as early as 14 and no later than 16 years of age. Transitional services are a coordinated set of activities designed to help students with disabilities make the transition from school to post-school life in the community. For example, if fitness development was part of the IEP, then linkages need to be created between the school and local fitness programs. IDEA also provides more opportunities for children with disabilities to receive assistive technologies to improve their abilities. For example, students can get racing wheelchairs or other specialized equipment that would enhance their ability to participate. Children

Wheelchair basketball at the 2004 Paralympic Games in Athens.

A man who is an amputee gets ready to race in the cycling competition at the 2004 Paralympic Games in Athens.

with disabilities must have the opportunity to participate in extracurricular activities and services, such as athletics, intramurals, and the art club.

IDEA stated that physical education and sport must be available to every child who is receiving a free and appropriate education. Each student with a disability must be afforded the opportunity to participate in a regular physical education program with children who do not have a disability unless the child is enrolled full-time in a separate facility or needs a specially designed physical education program. The philosophy, known as inclusion, is based on the rights of children with disabilities, regardless of severity, to attend their home schools and participate in the regular educational setting rather than be isolated from their peers in special programs. An alternative approach is the use of the least restrictive environment. The least restrictive environment places a child in the educational setting that is most appropriate for his or her abilities and developmental level. The environment can range from full inclusion in the regular setting to special programs in a self-contained setting. Regardless of the approach, it is important that children with disabilities have individualized programs that are appropriate for their developmental levels and that optimize their potential.

Federal legislation directed toward improving conditions for people with disabilities and meeting their educational needs has caused many changes. Schools are now required to provide physical education, intramurals, recreational programs, and athletic programs for students with disabilities. Adapted physical education programs have expanded. Teachers have had to learn different strategies to enhance learning opportunities for students with disabilities participating in regular physical education classes. Facilities have been altered and modified to meet the needs of the disabled.

In 1990, a landmark law, the Americans with Disabilities Act (ADA), was passed. This law seeks to end discrimination against individuals of all ages with disabilities and to remove barriers to their integration into the economic and social mainstream of American life. Five areas are addressed by the law: employment, public accommodations, public services, transportation, and telecommunications. The ADA mandates that all facilities, including recreational and sport facilities, must provide equal access and equal services to individuals with disabilities. This law opens playgrounds, swimming pools, gymnasiums, and health spas, for example, to individuals with disabilities, increasing their opportunities to participate in fitness and sport activities. In 1998, professional golfer Casey Martin sued the Professional Golfers' Association under the ADA for the right to ride a motorized cart in competition. Martin has Klippel-Trénaunay-Weber syndrome, a painful ailment that affects the circulation in his lower right leg and limits his ability to walk the golf course. It was ruled that the PGA Tour must accommodate Martin. This ruling was appealed, but in 2001 the US Supreme Court upheld this decision.

Since the 1970s, the number of individuals with disabilities participating in competitive sports has increased. The Amateur Sports Act of 1978 charged the United States Olympic Committee (USOC) to encourage provisions for sporting opportunities for the disabled, specifically to expand participation by individuals with disabilities in programs of athletic competition for able-bodied

SIGNIFICANT LEGISLATION FOR INDIVIDUALS WITH DISABILITIES IMPACTING PHYSICAL EDUCATION AND SPORTS

1973	Rehabilitation Act of 1973—Section 504	Prohibits discrimination against individuals with disabilities. Mandates equal opportunities and access to programs receiving federal assistance. Includes physical education, intramurals, and athletics in the school setting.
1975	Education of All Handicapped Children Act	Requires that children aged 3 to 21 who have disabilities receive a free and appropriate education in the least restrictive environment. Includes provision for physical education.
1978	Amateur Sports Act	Charges the United States Olympic Committee to provide assistance to amateur athletic programs and to expand opportunities for meaningful competition for individuals with disabilities.
1986	Education for All Handicapped Children Amendments	Mandates educational services for infants (up to 2 years old) with special needs and expanded services for 3- to 5-year-olds with special needs. Includes physical education.
1990	Individuals with Disabilities Education Act	Mandates that all references to "handicapped children" be changed to "children with disabilities." Students with disabilities have the right to free and appropriate education; must have opportunity to participate in general school curriculum and extracurricular activities, such as athletics. Requires transitional services for adolescents to help them transition from school to life after school, for example, forging linkages from physical education program to community physical activity programs.
1990	Americans with Disabilities Act	Seeks to end discrimination against people of all ages who have disabilities and to involve them in the mainstream of society. Addresses employment, public accommodations, public services, transportation, and telecommunications. Increases access to recreational and sport opportunities.
1998	Olympic and Amateur Sports Act	Affiliates Paralympics with United States Olympic Committee; Paralympics governed in similar fashion as other Olympic sports.

individuals. This charge served as the impetus for the formation of the Committee on Sports for the Disabled in 1983. In 1998, the Olympic and Amateur Sports Act was passed, amending the Amateur Sports Act. The new act strengthened the rights of athletes to compete, encouraged the growth of disabled sports, and provided for the Paralympics to be affiliated with the USOC, similar in fashion to other sport governing agencies.

Participation in national and international competitions and games by athletes with specific disabilities continues to rise. Competitions include the Paralympics, Special Olympics, World Games for the Deaf, and World Wheelchair Games, to name a few.

Olympics

In 1996, the centennial Olympic Games were held in Atlanta, Ga. In the 100 years since their rebirth in 1896, the Olympics had evolved into an event of global magnitude. In the 1896 Olympics held in

MODERN OLYMPIC SUMMER GAMES

Year	Location	Countries	Athletes	Sports	Events
1896	Athens, Greece	12	176	9	43
1900	Paris, France	29	1,224	20	95
1920	Antwerp, Belgium	29	2,675	25	160
1932	Los Angeles, United States	41	1,876	18	126
1948	London, Great Britain	59	4,369	21	149
1964	Tokyo, Japan	93	5,136	21	163
1972	Munich, West Germany	121	7,113	23	195
1988	Seoul, South Korea	159	8,453	27	237
1996	Atlanta, United States	197	10,329	31	271
2004	Athens, Greece	201	10,558	34	301
2008	Beijing, China	204	10,902	34	303

Source: Data from Sports Reference, LLC (www.sports-reference.com/olympics/summer/)

Athens, 311 athletes from 11 nations competed. In Atlanta, 10,750 athletes from 197 nations competed.

The modern Olympic Games, organized originally with the idealistic goal of fostering understanding among the people of the world, have become an instrument for political goals. Ideological differences have exerted a profound influence on the conduct of the games. The 1936 Olympic Summer Games, held in Berlin, were used by Adolf Hitler to further the Nazi ideology of Aryan supremacy. The Germans invested considerable resources in order to stage the most spectacular Olympics in history and to train the German athletes, all of whom typified the Nazi Aryan ideal. The German athletes won 89 medals, more than any other country in the games. The United States won 66 medals, 4 by the African American athlete Jesse Owens, who set 3 world and Olympic records. Owens's phenomenal performance refuted the Nazi theory of Aryan supremacy.

The 1972 Munich Olympics were marked by terrorism. Eight armed Arab guerrillas entered the Olympic Village complex occupied by the Israelis; a day later, 11 Israelis, 5 terrorists, and one German policeman were dead. Millions of people around the world mourned the slain athletes. After a memorial ceremony, the Munich Olympics continued.

Social and political issues led to boycotts at the 1976 Summer Olympics in Montreal over the issue of representation of China and the issue of apartheid. The United States led a boycott of the 1980 Summer Olympics in Moscow in protest of the Soviet Union's invasion of Afghanistan. The Soviet Union, in turn, led a boycott of the 1984 Summer Olympics in Los Angeles, claiming that the United States had to adhere to the Olympic ideals. The 1988 Summer Olympics in Seoul, Korea, saw Americans and Soviets competing. The International Olympic Committee took a strong position against drug "doping." Canadian sprinter Ben Johnson tested positive for steroid use after winning the 100 meters, and American Carl Lewis was then awarded the gold medal.

Several monumental events in the early 1990s, such as the collapses of the Berlin Wall and the Soviet Union, had a significant impact on the world and the Olympics. In 1992, the Germans competed in Barcelona as a unified team, and athletes from the former Soviet Union competed as

FOCUS ON CAREER: Sport History

PROFESSIONAL ORGANIZATIONS	• Sport History, Philosophy, and Sociology www.aahperd.org → About → Leaders → Research Academy • International Society for the History of Physical Education and Sport www.ishpes.org • North American Society for Sport History (NASSH) www.nassh.org
PROFESSIONAL JOURNALS	• *Canadian Journal of History of Sport and Physical Education* • *The International Journal of the History of Sport* • *Journal of Olympic History* • *Journal of Sport History* • *Sport History Review*

part of the Commonwealth of Independent States. South Africa competed for the first time in decades, and the Baltic states participated as independent countries for the first time since World War II. As more countries began to be more open about paying their athletes for their performances, the issue of amateurism became a moot point. Professional athletes began to participate in the games in increased numbers. Public attention was focused on the United States's basketball "Dream Team," which largely comprised professionals such as Michael Jordan, David Robinson, and Larry Bird. Growing commercialism and concern about the use of drugs continued.

The Winter Games also flourished during this time, mirroring the changes seen in the Summer Games. In the early 1990s, the International Olympic Committee voted to stagger the Winter and Summer Games in a 2-year rotation instead of a 4-year rotation. This started with the 1994 Winter Games in Lillehammer, Norway. It was believed that, given the high degree of public interest in the Olympics, the public would embrace this change. There would also be an economic benefit to the International Olympic Committee if the games were held every 2 years rather than every 4.

Over the past 100-plus years, the Olympic Games have developed into athletic contests that represent hundreds of nations and thousands of athletes from all over the world (see the Modern Olympic Summer Games box). New events have been added to the Summer and Winter Games, such as shot put, women's wrestling and ice hockey, beach volleyball, and mogul skiing. The US broadcasting rights currently exceed $1 billion, and an estimated 4 billion viewers watch the Olympic Games worldwide.

The Winter Games also flourished during this time and mirrored the changes seen in the Summer Games. In the early 1990s, the International Olympic Committee voted to stagger the Winter and Summer Games in a 2-year rotation instead of a 4-year rotation. This started with the 1994 Winter Games in Lillihammer, Norway. It was believed that, given the high degree of public interest in the Olympics, the public would embrace this change. There would also be an economic benefit to the International Olympic Committee if the games were held every 2 years rather than every 4.

Participation by women has increased during these past decades. Women's softball in 1996, and women's ice hockey in 1998, are just two of the new sports added to the Games. In 1998, following the Winter Games in Nagano, Japan, the International Olympic Committee stated that no new events would be added to the competition unless a comparable event could be added for women.

The Paralympics are an international Olympic competition for people with disabilities. The disability categories are amputee, cerebral palsy, intellectual disability, *les autres,* vision-impaired, and wheelchair. In the early 1990s, the International Olympic Committee mandated that the Paralympics would be the responsibility of the same country that hosted the Olympic Games. The same venues would be used, and the Paralympics would take place immediately following the closing of the Olympic Games. The 2008 Paralympics in Beijing involved 4,000 athletes and 2,500 team officials representing 146 countries. The athletes participated in 20 sports.[27]

In recent years the Olympics have been used as a means to further political ideologies. The line between amateurism and professionalism has disappeared. Commercialization has reached new heights and continues to grow. The Olympics have become an embedded component of our global culture.

SUMMARY

History provides the foundation for the field of physical education, exercise science, and sport. Many of our programs and activities today have been shaped by our heritage. Studying history also provides an appreciation for other cultures and the role of physical activity in these societies.

An adage states that "history tends to repeat itself." Recurring themes are apparent throughout the history of physical education, exercise science, and sport. For example, wars frequently served as the impetus for societies to intensify their physical education program or to justify its existence. Physical fitness was promoted among the populace to prepare for these war efforts.

However, studying history allows us to understand more fully many of the changes that have occurred in our field. The impact of different philosophies on the content and structure of physical education, exercise science, and sport programs, and changes in the nature and importance of objectives, can be discerned throughout the years. It is important to be aware of the events that served as catalysts and deterrents to the growth of physical education, exercise science, and sport.

The recent history of physical education, exercise science, and sport reveals many changes. Since the 1970s, the growth of the discipline, the emphasis on disease prevention and health promotion, changes in school physical education, the fitness movement and emphasis on physical activity, and the phenomenal growth of sports have contributed greatly to our field. By understanding the history of physical education, exercise science, and sport, a professional can better understand the nature of the field, appreciate the significant developments of today, and project trends for the future.

DISCUSSION QUESTIONS

1. How has physical education changed and developed over the past 250 years?
2. During each time period discussed in the chapter, how did societal movements and events influence sport, fitness, and physical education?
3. How have the Olympics and Paralympics changed and developed over time? What factors influenced the changes?
4. How has Title IX influenced the participation of girls and women in physical education and sport? Has the intent of the law, to provide equal opportunities for men and women, been upheld?

SELF-ASSESSMENT ACTIVITIES

These activities are designed to help you determine if you have mastered the materials and competencies presented in this chapter.

1. Describe events that served as catalysts for the growth of physical education, exercise science, and sport, and events that served as deterrents to the growth of physical education, exercise science, and sport throughout history.

2. Using the information provided in the Get Connected box, explore the history of the Olympic Games or other sports.

3. Project future developments for physical education, exercise science, and sport based on historical events, including events from both early and recent times.

4. Refer to the 12 Steps to Understanding Research Reports box in Chapter 1. Complete Step 4 for the same article you selected in Chapter 1.

REFERENCES

1. Mechikoff RA and Estes SG: A history and philosophy of physical education and sport: from ancient civilizations to the modern world, ed 2, New York, 2002, WCB/McGraw-Hill.

2. Struna NL: Sport history. In JD Massengale and RA Swanson, editors, The history of exercise and sport science, Champaign, Ill., 1997, Human Kinetics.

3. Salter M: Play in ritual. An ethnohistorical overview of native North America, Stadion 3(2):230–243, 1977.

4. Ray HL: Let's have a friendly game of war, Quest 14 June, 14:28–41, 1970.

5. Davenport J: Thomas Denison Wood: physical educator and father of health education, JOPERD 55(8):63–64, 68, 1984.

6. Henry F: Physical education: an academic discipline, Journal of Health, Physical Education, and Recreation 37(7):32–33, 1964.

7. Ziegler EF: Physical education and kinesiology in North America: professional and scholarly foundations, Champaign, Ill., 1994, Stipes.

8. Ziegler EF: From one image to a sharper one!, Physical Educator 54(2):72–77, 1997.

9. US Department of Health, Education, and Welfare: Healthy people: the surgeon general's report on health promotion and disease prevention, Washington, D.C., 1979, US Government Printing Office.

10. US Department of Health and Human Services: Promoting health/preventing disease: objectives for the nation, Washington, D.C., 1980, US Government Printing Office.

11. US Department of Health and Human Services: Healthy people 2000: national health promotion and disease prevention objectives, Washington, D.C., 1990, US Government Printing Office.

12. US Department of Health and Human Services: Healthy people 2010: understanding and improving health, ed 2, Washington, D.C., 2000, US Government Printing Office (www.healthypeople.gov/healthypeople).

13. US Department of Health and Human Services: Physical activity and health: a report of the surgeon general, Atlanta, Ga., 1996, US Department of Health and Human Services, Centers for Disease Control and Prevention, National Center for Chronic Disease Prevention and Health Promotion, and the President's Council on Physical Fitness and Sports.

14. US Department of Health and Human Services: The surgeon general's vision for a healthy and fit nation, 2010 (www.surgeongeneral.gov).

15. Biles F: The physical education public information project, JOHPER 41(7):53–55, 1971.

16. National Association for Sport and Physical Education: Definition of a physically educated person: outcomes of quality physical education programs, Reston, Va., 1990, AAHPERD.

17. National Association for Sport and Physical Education: Moving into the future: national standards for physical education—a guide to content and assessment, St. Louis, Mo., 1995, Mosby.

18. National Association for Sport and Physical Education: Moving into the future: national standards for physical education, ed 2, Reston, Va., 2004, AAHPERD.

19. National Association for Sport and Physical Education: Shape of the nation 1993, Reston, Va., 1993, AAHPERD.

20. National Association for Sport and Physical Education. Shape of the national report: status of physical education in the USA, Reston, Va., 2010, AAHPERD.

21. American Alliance for Health, Physical Education, Recreation and Dance: Health-related fitness test, Reston, Va., 1980, AAHPERD.

22. American Alliance for Health, Physical Education, Recreation and Dance: Physical best, Reston, Va., 1988, AAHPERD.

23. National Federation of State High School Associations: 2008–2009 high school athletics participation survey, 2009 (www.nfhs.org).

24. National Collegiate Athletic Association: 2008–2009 member report (catalog.proemags.com/publication/cc5da338#/cc5da338/1).

25. National Association of Intercollegiate Athletes, Member Services, 2010 (http://naia.cstv.com/member-services/).

26. National Junior College Athletic Association: 2010 (www.njcaa.org)

27. International Paralympic Committee: Paralympic Games 2010 (www.paralympic.org/Paralympic_Games).

MOTOR BEHAVIOR

O B J E C T I V E S

After reading this chapter the student should be able to—

■ Define motor behavior, motor development, motor control, and motor learning and understand the influence of readiness, motor development, motivation, reinforcement, and individual differences on the learning of motor skills.

■ Understand selected models of motor learning and the stages of learning and be able to draw implications for instruction in physical education, exercise science, and sport.

■ Apply to the teaching of physical education, exercise science, and sport basic concepts of motor learning such as feedback, design of practice, and transfer.

■ Describe the fundamental movements and the phases of motor development.

Motor behavior is a broad umbrella term used to encompass the areas of motor control, motor learning, and motor development. Motor control and motor learning trace their roots to experimental psychology, whereas motor development traces its roots to developmental psychology.

During the last 30 years, the study of motor behavior has grown tremendously and has become increasingly specialized. This chapter provides a short introduction to motor behavior. In this chapter, the terms *teacher* and *learner* are used in their broadest sense to encompass physical education, exercise science, and sport professionals who provide instruction to people of all ages in a diversity of settings.

MOTOR BEHAVIOR

One of the primary concerns of physical education, exercise science, and sport professionals is the learning and refinement of motor skills. *Learning* is defined as a relatively permanent change in behavior or performance as a result of practice or experience. Motor behavior is concerned with the learning or acquisition of skills across the lifespan and encompasses three areas: motor learning, motor control, and motor development. Thomas and Thomas identify three goals of motor behavior: first, "to understand how motor skills

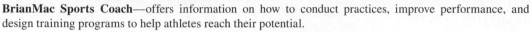

are learned"; second, "to understand how motor skills are controlled"; and third, "to understand how learning and control of motor skills changes across the life span."[1] All of these areas, although highly specialized, are interrelated. Although researchers in these areas focus on slightly different questions, a more highly integrated approach to research is seen today.

As motor behavior expanded as a field of study, scholars sought avenues to disseminate their research and opportunities to exchange ideas. In 1969, the *Journal of Motor Behavior* was founded by Richard Schmidt, and it continues to serve as one of the major outlets for researchers in the field. Additionally, the *Research Quarterly for Exercise and Sport* also publishes research on motor behavior. Motor learning, motor development, and sport psychology emerged as subdisciplines of physical education at relatively similar times and for a while their interests were aligned. In 1967, researchers in these fields founded the North American Society for the Psychology of Sport and Physical Activity (NASPSPA). Today, NASPSPA continues to provide a forum for motor behavior and sport and exercise psychologists, although

both groups have their own interests and focus within the organization. Researchers also present papers at the American Alliance for Health, Physical Education, Recreation and Dance (AAHPERD) convention. The National Association of Sport and Physical Education's (NASPE) Motor Development and Learning Academy, which was founded in 1979, also provides a forum for discussion and exchange of ideas through its

MOTOR BEHAVIOR

Motor Learning—the study of the acquisition of motor skills as a result of practice and experience.

Motor Control—the study of the neurophysiological and behavioral processes affecting the control of skilled movements.

Motor Development—the study of the origins of and changes in movement behavior throughout the lifespan.

program at the AAHPERD national convention and its newsletter.

MOTOR LEARNING AND MOTOR CONTROL

Motor learning and motor control are interrelated. The definition and scope of these specialized areas of study, historical development, and areas of study are briefly described in this section.

Definition and Scope

Motor learning is the study of the acquisition of motor skills as a result of practice and experience. Learning is inferred from changes in performance. For example, an instructor determines whether an individual has learned a tennis serve by observing and assessing the individual's performance. As the individual receives instruction and practices, performance of the tennis serve should improve—that is, become more consistent, effective, and efficient.

You would then infer from the individual's performance that learning had occurred. Motor skills range in scope from simple skills, such as learning to walk, to highly complex skills, such as those of an elite gymnast performing intricate tumbling passes as part of a floor exercise routine. Motor learning focuses on studying the cognitive aspects of motor skill acquisition. According to Thomas and Thomas, the goals of motor learning are "understanding the influence of feedback, practice, and individual differences, especially how they relate to the retention and transfer of motor skill."[1]

Intimately related to the area of motor learning is motor control. Motor control is the study of the neurophysiological and behavioral processes affecting the control of skilled movements. Thomas and Thomas summarize the goals of motor control as understanding "how the muscles and joints are coordinated during movement, how a sequence of movements is controlled, and how to use environmental information to plan and adjust movements."[1] Researchers in motor control are interested in the processes underlying the

With practice, motor performance becomes more efficient, effective, and consistent.

learning and performance of motor skills, such as how the nervous system works with the muscular system to produce and coordinate movement and how cognitive processes are involved in the learning and execution of motor skills.

Historical Development

The history of motor learning and motor control can be divided into three eras: the early period (1880–1940), the middle period (1940–1970), and the present period (1970–today).[2]

During the early period, although researchers investigated the acquisition of motor skills, their research focused on trying to understand how the mind worked rather than seeking to understand how skilled movements were produced.[2] One significant development was Thorndike's research on learning in 1927, which became known as the Law of Effect. Thorndike found that when responses to a situation were rewarded, they were strengthened and used more frequently, and hence became learned behaviors. Thorndike's work influenced subsequent work on the impact of feedback on motor skill acquisition.[2] Adams reports that it was during this early period that the basis for research in five major areas of motor learning was laid: knowledge of results, distribution of practice, transfer of training, retention, and individual differences.[3] Motor control research also began during this time, with some of the early work focusing on the qualities of muscle. The discovery that the brain produces electrical activity stimulated interest in the relationship between brain electrical activity and movement, which helped further researchers' understanding of how the nervous system controls muscles and movement.

The start of the middle period was marked by a surge of interest in motor learning. World War II had stimulated an interest in pilot selection and training. Motor learning research focused more on application, investigating such areas as transfer of training (e.g., what factors would enable a pilot to easily and successfully switch from flying one type of aircraft to another aircraft that was of a different size, with controls positioned differently?).

In the late 1940s, Craik advanced his ideas about the similarities between the human brain and the computer, which gave new insight into how the brain processes and uses information to determine the motor response.

In the 1960s, Franklin Henry published his landmark paper on the memory drum theory, which discussed the role of cognitive activity in motor learning.[2] Often considered the father of motor behavior, Henry—with his contemporaries, Fitz Hubbard, Jack Adams, Arthur Slater-Hammel, and John Lawther—helped set the stage for the emergence of the subdiscipline in the 1970s.[2] In 1968, Robert N. Singer published *Motor Learning and Human Performance,* the first book in the subdiscipline.

The 1970s marked the emergence of motor learning and motor control within physical education programs. As the subdiscipline emerged and evolved, motor behavior scholars began to move from the application of theories from psychology to explain motor skills to the development and use of their own theories and models to explain motor skill acquisition. In 1971, Adams' closed loop theory explained how feedback, following the performance of slow and discrete movements, is used to update the cognitive representation of the movement and improve subsequent performances of the motor skill.[3] In 1975, Schmidt's schema theory proposed the idea of a generalized motor program, that is, the idea that movement patterns such as kicking or throwing could be generalized to a variety of sports and settings. More recently, the dynamical systems theory, developed by Scott Kelso and other researchers, suggests that the neuromuscular system plays a prominent role in the selection of movements. According to Thomas and Thomas, the "information-processing view of motor behavior (motor programs or schema) based on the role of cognition and a central processing mechanism, has dominated the research literature in motor behavior for over 30 years. However, the dynamical systems view (movements organized by environmental constraints) has provided an alternative explanation and challenged information processing as the dominant theory in recent years."[1]

Areas of Study

Since the 1970s, many topics have captured the interest of researchers. Researchers have investigated the effectiveness of various types of practice, the impact of different types of feedback on motor performance, the use of cognitive strategies to improve performance, reaction time, and transfer of learning—how skills learned in one setting can enhance or hinder learning in another setting. Some researchers have focused their efforts on understanding motor problems in special populations—such as postural and coordination control in the aging.

Motor control also grew as a specialized area of study during this modern period. Motor control researchers have tried to determine how movements are coordinated, how the sequence of our behaviors is controlled, and how information obtained from the environment is used to plan and modify movements.

Researchers in motor learning and motor control may address questions such as these:

- How do the type and frequency of feedback impact skill acquisition?
- How does the structure of practice influence the retention of skills?
- How does skill performance change as beginners move from novice to advanced levels of performance?
- How does the aging process affect motor control? How do specific diseases, such as Parkinson's disease, affect an individual's ability to perform motor skills?
- When teaching a skill such as serving in tennis or pitching, should you first emphasize speed or accuracy?
- How do differences in individuals' learning styles influence their ability to learn motor skills?

As we begin the twenty-first century, advances in technology and a greater emphasis on cross-disciplinary research will further our understanding of how motor skills are learned and controlled.

Motor Learning Models

Many theories have been advanced to explain the process by which motor skills are learned and controlled. These theories help researchers formulate models to illustrate how learning occurs. Models developed from these theories serve as frameworks for professionals. They help professionals design and implement learning experiences for participants in their programs based on theoretical models of learning. The information processing model and the dynamical systems model are two models that have been used to describe motor skill acquisition and performance.

Information Processing Model

In its simplest form, the information processing theory explains motor learning in terms of cognition and the processing of information. Based on this theory, the information processing model consists of four components or processes: input, decision making, output, and feedback. This model is illustrated in Figure 5-1.

Input is the process of obtaining information from the environment. This information is obtained through the senses. Visual, auditory, kinesthetic, and other sensory information is transmitted through the nervous system to the brain where the process of *decision making* occurs.

During this procedure the input is processed; that is, it is sifted, evaluated, and interpreted. Relevant environmental cues are identified. Using this current information and relevant past experiences stored in memory, the individual selects an appropriate response. A decision is reached about what movement to make. The response is

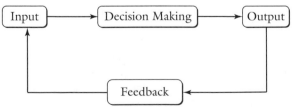

Figure 5-1   Information processing model

Fencing is a sport that requires rapid processing of information as well as split-second decision making skills.

organized; a "motor program" that will control the response is retrieved from memory. The muscles are directed to contract in proper order, with the proper amount of force and with the correct timing to produce the desired movement. The response and its execution are the *output*.

Feedback is information about the performance of the movement and its quality, appropriateness, or outcome. This information can be used to provide input for making ongoing adjustments in performance or to modify the next skill attempt. The knowledge gained from feedback can be used to improve the decision making process as well as the succeeding output. As an individual becomes more adept at performing the skill, often he or she also becomes more skilled at using the feedback to improve performance.

Teachers should be familiar with the manner in which individuals learn skills as well as the factors that influence their performance. This understanding will help them design practices that facilitate an individual's opportunity to learn through appropriate structuring of the learning environment. The teacher must give learners appropriate input through the careful selection of teaching methods, materials, and procedures.

The teacher must help the learner understand the goal of the movement and then distinguish between relevant and irrelevant information or cues with respect to that goal, drawing the learner's attention to cues essential for the decision making process and teaching the learner to disregard the irrelevant ones.

Next, the teacher must help the learner to become a wise decision maker. This can be accomplished by helping the learner evaluate his or her past experiences, by explaining the "why" of underlying skills and strategies, by instructing the learner on how to use the available feedback, and by making sure that the learner is attending to the right cues and interpreting the information correctly. The teacher can facilitate the learner's development of the desired skill using proper progressions and by giving the learner appropriate and sufficient practice opportunities.

Finally, the teacher can help the learner by providing feedback about the learner's performance and communicating this information to the learner in an understandable manner. Additionally, the teacher must draw the learner's attention to the feedback available during the execution of the skill as well as the information regarding the outcome of the performance. This information can provide the basis for adjustments in the learner's movements.

As you can see from the information processing model, the senses play a critical role in motor learning and performance. Vision is one of the most important senses for gathering information or input from the environment to use for decision making. An area of study that is gaining increasing emphasis is sports vision training. *Sports vision training* combines vision science, motor learning, biomechanics, sport psychology, and neuroanatomy to help individuals improve their performance.[4]

Dynamical Systems Model

The dynamical systems theory has gained increased acceptance during the past 20 years. This theory explains human movement as the result of the interaction between three systems: the individual or the organism, the environment, and the task. Characteristics of each system interact to influence movement.[5,6] Based on this theory, the dynamical systems model is shown in Figure 5-2.

Individual characteristics encompass the anatomical and physiological systems, heredity, height, weight, previous experiences, fitness status, motivation, and a host of other characteristics

such as perceptual skills and attention.[5,6] These are the individual differences that professionals take into account in designing movement experiences to learn new skills or improve performance.

The environment reflects the context in which the learning or performing is taking place. This could include physical characteristics such as the weather or space, or sociocultural characteristics such as competition or peer pressure.[5,6] The teacher is an important part of the environment and can exert a tremendous influence on learning.[5] Teachers' skill in presenting the task, structuring the progressions, creating a positive learning environment, directing learners' attention to relevant cues, and providing feedback to learners are just a few of the characteristics that interact with individual differences and the task to influence learning.[6]

The characteristics of the task must also be considered as part of the dynamical system interaction. Task characteristics reflect the demands of the task; for example, does the skill place a premium on speed, accuracy, or both?[6] The task difficulty needs to be considered as well. Another factor is the nature of the task. Does the skill require making adjustments to individuals in the environment, as in dribbling a ball down the field in soccer, or is the environment stable, as in archery? The rules of

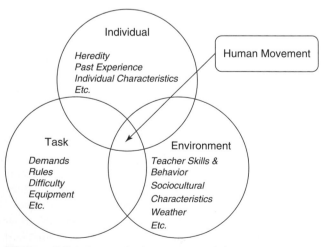

Figure 5-2   Dynamical systems model

a sport or game and the boundaries in which it is conducted are also task characteristics that must be considered.[5]

Professionals involved in the teaching of human movement skills need to consider the interaction of all three systems—individual, environment, and task—in designing learning experiences to develop skills. The environment and task systems are the most easily manipulated by the teacher to facilitate the acquisition and development of motor skills.[5] Additionally, failure to consider the characteristics of one of the systems, such as the maturity or fitness level of the individual, can hinder the acquisition of skills and limit performance. As a professional, it is important to realize the dynamic nature of this interaction and consider aspects of all systems in planning for learning.

As you can see from these brief descriptions of the information processing model and the dynamical systems model, human movement is an exceedingly complex phenomenon. Theories and the models developed from them give us some insight into understanding human movement and offer professionals guidance for developing and improving a wide variety of movements and skills. Advances in technology, increasingly sophisticated research methodology, and interdisciplinary approaches hold great promise for enhancing our understanding of motor skill acquisition and control.

An understanding of the manner in which individuals learn skills can help professionals make the learning process more effective and more enjoyable—that is, less frustrating for learners. Professionals must also be aware that skill learning occurs in stages.

Stages of Learning

As an individual learns motor skills and makes the transition from unskilled to skilled performer, he or she progresses through several stages. Fitts and Posner identified three stages of learning: the cognitive stage, the associative stage, and the autonomous stage.[7] The teacher must be cognizant of the characteristics of the learner at each stage to plan for instruction. Different instructional

strategies and techniques are required at each stage to make practice more effective. (See Table 5-1.)

Cognitive Stage

The first stage of learning is the cognitive stage. During this stage the learner is endeavoring to understand the nature goal of the activity to be learned. During this stage the learner might be concerned with such questions as "How do I stand?" "How do I hold the tennis racquet?" "How do you score in this game?" "What is the sequence of actions in this swimming stroke?" The learner also needs to pay close attention to the information provided by the instructor; this includes verbal directions as well as visual information, perhaps from demonstration of a skill or a videotape of a performer executing this skill. After analyzing this information, the learner formulates a plan of action based on his or her understanding of the task and the specific directions provided by the instructor. Formulating a plan of action is referred to as establishing a motor plan or an executive plan. A high level of concentration on the task is required as the learner tries to put together the various parts of the skill in the correct sequence.

As the learner makes initial attempts at performing the skill, the performance is characterized by a large number of errors, usually gross in nature, and a great deal of variability. Although the learner may have an idea about what he or she is doing incorrectly, the learner may not know how to correct it. To improve skill performance, the learner needs specific feedback from the instructor, communicated in understandable terms. For example, someone just learning the tennis forehand must concentrate on moving to the correct position on the court, the grip of the racquet, the stance, turning the body, keeping an eye on the ball, making contact with the ball with the head of the racquet so that it goes over the net, shifting the body's weight, following through, and returning to ready position. The beginner at times will hit the ball over the net; with the next attempt the learner might hit the ball into the net or out of the court or miss the ball entirely. The learner's actions, although performed in the correct sequence,

TABLE 5-1	Characteristics Associated with Stages of Learning		
Cognitive	**Associative**	**Autonomous**	
Learner's focus			
Cognitive understanding of the goal of the skill	Concentration on temporal aspects or timing of movements	Concentration on use of the skill in performance situations, use of strategies	
Concentration on spatial aspects or sequence of skill components			
Performance characteristics			
Lacking smoothness, inefficient, variable, large number of gross errors	Smoother, less variable, more efficient, reduction of extraneous movements, fewer and reduced range of errors	Smooth, efficient, highly refined and well organized spatially and temporally, adaptable to environmental demands	
Teacher's focus			
Provide overview of nature of skill and goal, feedback on intent of skill, information and demonstration of skill, cognitive understanding	Direct learner's attention to critical cues and feedback available; provide numerous practice opportunities; accommodate individual differences	Focus on refinement of response, consistency for closed skills and flexibility for open skills, use of skill in performance situations, feedback for refinement of movements	

may lack the smooth, polished look and the consistency of a highly skilled performer.

Associative Stage

The second stage is the associative stage. At this point the basics of the skill have been learned and the learner concentrates on refining the skill. During this stage the learner works on mastering the timing needed for the skill; the learner's performance looks smoother. Fewer errors are committed, and the same type of error tends to recur. The learner is also aware of some of the more obvious errors he or she is making in executing the task and can use this information to adjust subsequent performance. The tennis player learning the forehand may notice more success in getting the ball over the net and inside the boundaries of the court, although he or she cannot place the ball with any

assurance. The player may notice a frequent failure to follow through after contacting the ball, but he or she is not aware that the angle of the racquet face needs adjustment. The instructor can provide the learner with additional instruction focusing on specific actions and point out relevant cues.

Autonomous Stage

The third stage is the autonomous stage. This stage of learning is reached after much practice. The learner can perform the skill consistently with few errors. The skill is well coordinated and may appear to be performed effortlessly. During this stage the skill has become almost automatic. The learner does not have to pay attention to every aspect of the skill; he or she can perform the skill without consciously thinking about it at all. The tennis player no longer has to concentrate on the

Highly skilled performers exemplify the autonomous stage of learning.

fundamentals of the skill; instead, his or her focus can be directed to placing the ball in the court, varying the speed of the shot, placing spin on the ball, or executing game tactics. The learner also becomes more skilled at detecting errors and making adjustments, in a sense becoming his or her own teacher.

Individuals do not proceed through these stages at the same rate. It may also be difficult at times to identify what stage an individual is in. To plan practices to promote effective learning, however, the professional must be cognizant of the characteristics and the needs of the learner in the various stages. The professional also needs to be aware of the forces that influence learning.

Forces Influencing Learning

Learning implies a change in a person—a change in the method of both practicing and performing a skill or a change in an attitude toward a particular thing. Learning implies a progressive change of behavior in an individual, although some changes are rapid, such as when one gains insight into a problem. It implies a change that occurs as a result of experience or practice. It results in the modification of behavior as a consequence of training or environment. It involves such aspects as obtaining knowledge, improving skill in an activity, solving a problem, and making an adjustment to a new situation. It implies that a person has acquired knowledge or skill through instruction or personal study. Learning continues throughout life.

To create an effective learning situation, teachers must be cognizant of the forces influencing learning. Four of these forces—readiness, motivation, reinforcement, and individual differences—will be discussed.

Readiness

Successful acquisition of new information or skills depends on the individual's level of readiness. *Readiness* can be defined in terms of physiological and psychological factors influencing an individual's ability and willingness to learn. Physiological readiness in children is the development of the necessary strength, flexibility, and endurance, as well as development of the various organ systems, to such a degree that children can control their bodies in physical activities. Psychological readiness refers to the learner's state of mind. One's feeling or attitude toward learning a particular skill—in other words, the desire and willingness to learn— will affect one's acquisition of that particular skill. To create an effective learning environment, the teacher must keep in mind the individual's physiological and psychological readiness.

Teachers planning learning activities must be cognizant of the individual's cognitive, affective, and physical characteristics as well as the individual's past experiences. This knowledge will help the teacher plan an atmosphere conducive to

Learning experiences should be appropriate for the participant's abilities.

learning. The teacher should structure the learning experience so that the individual experiences success rather than the frustration that may come from trying to learn a task that is too difficult or beyond the individual's ability at that time. The teacher may need to modify the task to make it either easier or more challenging. For example, many Little League baseball teams have started letting the younger children hit the ball off a batting tee rather than hit a pitched ball. This adjustment was made because it was realized that the younger children were having difficulty tracking and successfully hitting a moving object. In being allowed to hit the ball while it was stationary— sitting atop a batting tee—the children were able to practice the skill of striking an object, or batting, and experience success in their endeavors.

Certainly hitting the ball from the tee was more satisfying to the children than swinging at the pitched ball and missing. Adjusting the learning task to the individual's ability requires consideration of the individual's physiological readiness. Planning learning experiences that promote success enhances the individual's psychological readiness to learn.

Motivation

Motivation is a basic factor in learning. The term *motivation* refers to a condition within an individual that initiates activity directed toward a goal. The study of motivation focuses on the causes of behavior, specifically those factors that influence the initiation, maintenance, and intensity of behavior.

Needs and drives form the basic framework for motivation. When individuals sense an unfulfilled need, they are moved to do something about it. This desire prompts people to seek a solution to the recognized need through an appropriate line of action. This line of action may require practice, effort, mastery of knowledge, or other behavior to be successful. For example, an individual who is hungry becomes motivated to seek food, whereas at the cognitive level, the individual who wants to pass a certification desires to acquire the necessary knowledge.

Motivation refers to an individual's general arousal to action. It might be thought of as the desire or drive a person must have to achieve a goal to satisfy a particular need. The term *need* refers to an internalized deficiency of the organism. The need might be physiological or psychological. The term *drive* refers to the concept of the stimulus for action. Motivation, for example, might be associated with the drive to exercise to satisfy the need to keep the body healthy. The motivating factor might be internal, resulting from the individual's own desire to be fit, or it might be the result of some outside force, such as peer pressure to be thin.

Although motives are internal in nature, they may be affected by external influences. However, it is common to describe an individual's motives as being either internal or external. Motives such as the desire to develop one's body, to have fun, or to test one's limits are examples of internal motives for learning. The desire to win awards, to appease parental pressures for participation, or to win money are examples of external motives for participation. An employee may decide to participate in an employee fitness program because of the desire to enhance his or her health status (internal motivation); on the other hand, the employee may participate because he or she was pressured to do so by the boss (external motivation). Internal motivation is more conducive to positive learning and performance and sustained participation than external motivation. The worth of the activity should be the inducement for learning and participation rather than rewards, punishments, or grades. In physical education, exercise science, and sport programs, motives such as the desire to develop one's body, the desire to learn basic movement skills and eventually develop more advanced skills for specialized games, and the desire to do one's best are all valid and should be encouraged.

The professional should be aware of the motives for the individual's participation in physical education, exercise science, and sport programs. Individuals' motives for learning and participation may differ considerably, so consideration of individual differences is important. For example, as previously mentioned, some participants in an employee fitness program may be internally motivated to join, while others, whose presence was suggested by their employer, may be externally motivated and perhaps even reluctant to participate in the activities. During the course of the program, however, the externally motivated participants may develop an internal motivation. The change could result because the professional made the program challenging, meaningful, and satisfying to the employee. As a consequence, the once reluctant employee may become an enthusiastic participant in the program.

The actions of the teacher can often have a positive effect on the individual's motivation. In a physical education and sport program, not all individuals will be motivated to the same extent to learn new skills; in fact, some individuals may not be motivated to learn at all. The teacher can enhance an individual's motivation for learning through goal setting, that is, establishing challenging, albeit attainable, goals for the individual. Motivation can also be enhanced by structuring the learning environment for success and by making the learning experience positive and enjoyable. An individual's level of motivation may also be enhanced through reinforcement.

Reinforcement

Physical education, exercise science, and sport professionals should be alert to the need to reinforce the learning of skills and other behaviors of those under their supervision when the desired performance takes place. *Reinforcement* is using events, actions, and behaviors to increase the likelihood of a certain response (e.g., a skill or a behavior) recurring. Reinforcement may be positive or negative. Reinforcement is considered positive when it is given following the desired response, and it is deemed negative when it is withheld following a desired response. Providing encouragement, praise, commendation, or a pat on the back following successful execution of a skill is an example of positive reinforcement. Such an acknowledgment of an individual's success not only will serve to reinforce correct skill performance but will also likely motivate the individual to continue in his or her efforts to master the skill. If a teacher belittles an individual's unsuccessful effort to perform a skill and discontinues this behavior when the individual successfully executes the skill, the teacher is using negative reinforcement.

Two types of reinforcers are tangible and intangible. Tangible reinforcers are material items such as a medal or money. Intangible reinforcers include verbal praise, a pat on the back, or a nod of approval.

Research suggests that reinforcement is more effective when given immediately after a response than when it is delayed. Random reinforcement tends to be more effective than continual reinforcement. For reinforcement to be effective it must be meaningful to, important to, or desired by the recipient.

Physical educators must accommodate individual differences among learners. These elementary school students are working with objects of different shapes as part of a perceptual-motor program.

Reinforcement, motivation, readiness, and development are important forces in learning. Another important consideration in planning for learning is individual differences.

Individual Differences

In any learning situation, be it with children or adults, the teacher must provide for individual differences among the learners. The importance of considering individual differences in readiness, motivation, and reinforcement has already been discussed. The teacher also should consider other differences when planning for learning.

Differences in social and economic backgrounds should be considered—some individuals come from middle-class families while others are economically disadvantaged. These factors can greatly influence the prior experiences these individuals bring to the learning situation. Differences in physical abilities among individuals in the learning situation may be pronounced. Differences in intelligence and preferred learning styles

hold implications for the manner in which the skills are to be taught. Personality differences must also be considered. Some individuals are outgoing, whereas others are shy and withdrawn. Some individuals are eager to try new skills, while others are reluctant or intimidated by the prospect of learning something new.

Designing learning experiences to accommodate individual differences requires careful planning and commitment on the part of the teachers. It is not an easy task to design learning experiences for a diversity of abilities, but it is not impossible. Physical education, exercise science, and sport professionals should strive to help each person to be the best he or she can be.

Motor Learning Concepts

In planning for motor learning, the professional must consider a learner's level of readiness, development, individual characteristics, motivation, and need for reinforcement. At this point it will be helpful to consider additional concepts, factors, and conditions that promote the learning of motor skills and improve performance.

1. *Practice sessions should be structured to promote optimal conditions for learning.* The manner in which practice sessions are organized can have a critical impact on the amount of learning that occurs. Practices should be organized so that distracting elements are eliminated from the setting. The instructor should ensure that the proper mental set has been established in the mind of the learner, the proper facilities and equipment are available, the learner has the proper background to understand and appreciate the material being presented, and conditions are such that a challenging learning situation exists.

Much research has been done on the organization of practice with reference to the relationship between practice periods and rest periods. (In the literature this is referred to as massed versus distributed practice.) Schmidt, after reviewing the research, states that "we should recognize that a single, optimal distribution of practice and rest periods does not exist."[8] The design of practice should consider the nature of the task to be learned, the characteristics of the learner, the energy costs of the tasks, and safety. Magill stresses that practice sessions should be structured to maximize the number of opportunities the learner has to try the task.[9] Siedentop emphasizes the need to maximize the amount of time the learner is practicing a task (time-on-task) and the need for the task to be appropriate for the level of the learner.[10]

2. *Learners must understand the task to be learned.* Helping the learner acquire a cognitive understanding of the nature of the task to be learned is one of the first steps in the learning process. As previously discussed in the stages of learning, the learner must establish an executive or motor plan for action; this involves understanding the nature of the task, analyzing the task, demands, and devising techniques to achieve the task goal. This conception of the task, or image, serves as a guide for the learner's initial attempts.

Typically, learners have been helped to establish an image of the task or skill through verbal instructions provided by the teacher. However, the teacher may overuse instructions when faced with the task of describing a complex movement. Too many instructions may overwhelm learners, and in an effort to cope with the avalanche of information about what to do and when to do it, learners may disregard much of the information. Instructions should focus on key elements of the task.

Succinct, accurate instructions in conjunction with other techniques such as demonstrations may be more useful than instructions alone in helping the learner understand the task. Demonstrations of the skill allow the learner to form an image of the task. The teacher can use instructions to call the learner's attention to the critical components of the skill. During the learner's initial performances of the task, the learner can model the performance exhibited. Children frequently learn skills on their own by imitating or modeling the performance of others. Teachers may also use films or videotapes of skilled performers to provide a model for performance.

3. *The nature of the skill or task to be learned should be considered when designing practice.* Skills can be classified in a variety of ways. To facilitate learning, practices should be appropriate to the type of skill to be learned.

One popular skill classification continuum, closed/open, is based on the predictability of the environment in which the skill is performed and the extent to which the performer can control the performance situation. The continuum ranges from predictable to unpredictable. (See Figure 5-3.)

Skills performed in a predictable, stable environment are classified as closed skills. The environment remains the same during the skill performance. The performer is self-paced; he or she chooses when to initiate the skill in the relatively stable environment. Driving a golf ball off a tee, executing a forward 2½ somersault dive from the 3-meter springboard, performing an uneven bars or parallel bars routine in gymnastics, and shooting a foul shot in basketball are examples of closed skills. Open skills are skills that are performed in an unpredictable environment. The environment is variable. The performer must continually modify

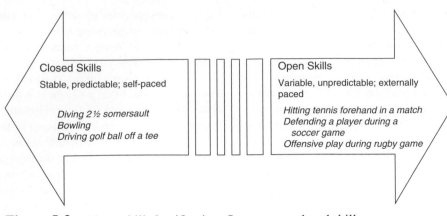

Figure 5-3   Motor skill classification: Open versus closed skills

and adapt his or her responses to the ever-changing environment. The performer must consider external conditions and adapt his or her skill to them. Shooting a goal during a soccer game, hitting a tennis backhand during a match, and dribbling down the basketball court to execute a layup are examples of open skills. Since this classification falls on a continuum, some skills may be placed more toward the middle of the continuum rather than at either end. For example, archery is a self-paced sport, with the archer shooting at a target a set distance away. However, in order to be successful the archer must take into account environmental conditions, such as the wind, and make modifications to his or her performance accordingly.

The teacher's design of practice should reflect the nature of the skill and the conditions under which the skill will eventually be performed. In practicing closed skills, where the environment remains relatively stable during the performance of the skill, the teacher should emphasize achieving consistency of movement. With open skills, the changing environment requires that the performer make alterations in performance to adjust to the changing conditions (e.g., movements of opponents and teammates, speed and direction of the ball, etc.). Thus, practice should be variable, with the student exposed to a variety of situations similar to those he or she will actually encounter when performing the skill.

During the initial stages of teaching an open skill, the teacher may structure the environment to be stable (closed) to make learning easier for the beginner. For instance, in learning to bat a pitched ball, the teacher may start the performer out hitting a ball off a batting tee; then the teacher may use a pitching machine set to pitch a ball at a certain speed and height. Finally, the performer is given the opportunity to hit balls thrown by a pitcher and must then learn how to adjust his or her swing to the varying speeds and heights of the ball. Thus, while open skills may be practiced under closed conditions initially, once the performer is ready, open conditions should prevail. In teaching open skills, the teacher must help the performer identify relevant cues in the environment that signify the need to change his or her response. Unlike with closed skills, in which attainment of response consistency is emphasized, achieving response flexibility and diversity is stressed in open skills. Providing the performer with variable practice conditions is important in learning open skills.

Other motor skill classifications are fine versus gross, discrete versus continuous, and self-paced versus externally paced. Further information on these skills may be found in the suggested readings at the end of this chapter.

4. *The nature of the task and the background of the learner should be considered in deciding whether to teach the skill by the whole or the part*

method.   The instructor must decide whether to teach a skill as a whole or to break it down into its component parts. For example, do you teach a skill such as the front crawl stroke as a whole, or do you break the stroke down and teach it by parts—arm action, leg action, and breathing? What about the jump shot in basketball? Or the tennis serve? If the learner is highly skilled and has had previous experience in the sport, is the whole or the part method better?

This area has been much researched, but the findings are somewhat confusing. At the risk of generalizing, the instructor should teach a highly complex task as parts. Parts should consist of individual, discrete skills. Tasks in which the skill components are highly interrelated, such as the jump shot in basketball, should be taught as a whole. Highly skilled learners with previous experience in the sport will probably be able to learn effectively if the whole method is used. Low-skilled learners or individuals with short attention spans, such as young children, may find it easier to learn if taught by the part method. It appears that all learners benefit from seeing a demonstration of the whole skill; this may enhance the organization of the information provided to the learner and the learner's understanding of the goal of the skill.

If the teacher were to teach the high jump by the part method, the learners would be taught the approach (run to the bar); then they would be taught the jump; next, they would be taught the landing. After all components had been taught, the learners would practice the total skill.

Another option is to use the progressive part method, which consists of initially teaching the first two parts of the skill, combining these two parts into a whole, teaching a third part, then connecting this to the first two parts, and so on. For example, the first two sequences in a dance routine would be taught and practiced, then the third sequence taught; then the third sequence would be added to the first two sequences, and all three sequences practiced together. This process of progressively adding parts of a skill is continued until the entire skill is learned.

In summary, the structure of the task—both its complexity and organization—and the characteristics of the learner must be considered in selecting methods of instruction.

5. *Whether speed or accuracy should be emphasized in learning a skill depends on the requirements of the skill.*   Teachers are often required to make a judgment as to whether speed or accuracy should be emphasized in the initial stages of learning a skill. For example, a highly skilled tennis player endeavors to serve the ball with as much velocity as possible into the service court. When teaching the tennis serve, should the teacher emphasize speed, accuracy, or both speed and accuracy? When teaching pitching, should the teacher emphasize throwing the ball as fast as possible, getting the ball into the strike zone all the time, or pitching the ball into the strike zone

Teachers must decide whether to emphasize speed or accuracy when teaching a skill that requires both elements.

as fast and as often as possible? This dilemma—whether to emphasize speed or accuracy—is often referred to as a speed-accuracy trade-off. In essence, to perform the skill as accurately as possible means that the performer will have to sacrifice some speed and perform the skill more slowly. Attainment of maximum speed or velocity in performing a skill is at the expense of accuracy. When both speed and accuracy are desired, both qualities will decrease.

Different sport skills have different speed and accuracy requirements. Pitching a ball or performing a tennis serve requires a high degree of both speed and accuracy. In throwing the javelin, speed is more important than accuracy, whereas in the tennis drop shot, accuracy in terms of court placement is more important than speed. The teacher must understand the requirements of the task and design practices accordingly.

The research seems to suggest that skills should be practiced as they are to be performed. This advice is relatively straightforward when the skill emphasizes either speed or accuracy. For example, based on the research findings, speed should be emphasized in teaching the javelin throw, and accuracy emphasized in the tennis drop shot. However, what about skills that place a premium on being both fast and accurate, such as pitching a ball or executing a tennis serve? One approach is to have the learner execute the skill as fast as possible and work on accuracy and control after speed has been attained. Another approach is to have the learner focus on being as accurate as possible by reducing the speed of the movements; then, once accuracy is attained, increasing the speed of the movements would be stressed. Emphasizing both speed and accuracy is another approach. The research suggests that when both speed and accuracy are of paramount concern, both variables should receive equal and simultaneous emphasis. The rationale is that mastery is sacrificed when an individual practices a motor skill at slower speed than is needed in the game situation, because the person must readjust to the faster situation. The teacher should understand the speed and accuracy demands of a skill and structure practices so that the learner can practice the skill as it is to be ultimately performed.

6. *Transfer of learning can facilitate the learning of motor skills.* The influence of a previously learned skill on the learning or performance of a new skill is called transfer of learning. The influence exerted may be positive or negative. When a previous experience or skill aids in the learning of a new skill, positive transfer occurs. For example, the student who knows how to play tennis readily learns how to play badminton because both skills require similar strokes and the use of the racquet. Most researchers agree that positive transfer most likely occurs when two tasks have similar part-whole relationships. Again, to use the example of racquet games, since many racquet games such as platform tennis, squash, tennis, racquetball, and badminton have similar part-whole relationships, it is believed that some transfer takes place. Transfer, however, is not automatic. The more meaningful and purposeful the experience, the greater is the likelihood of transfer. Transfer of training occurs to a greater degree under the following conditions: with more intelligent participants, in situations that are similar, where an attitude exists and an effort is made by the learner to effect transfer, when the principles or procedures that are foundational to the initial task are understood, and in situations where one teaches for transfer.

Teachers must also be aware of negative transfer. Negative transfer occurs when a previously learned skill interferes with the learning of a new skill. For example, an individual being introduced to the game of golf for the first time experiences difficulty in swinging the club because of his or her previous experience in another skill such as softball or baseball. In such cases the expression often heard is "You're swinging the golf club like a baseball bat."

Physical educators and coaches have become interested in transferring skills learned in practice sessions to actual game situations. To this end, they strive to make their drills as much like a game as possible, or they make an effort in the practice environment to familiarize their team with situations it may encounter in the game.

For example, during practice sessions before a basketball game, coaches may have their substitutes imitate the actions of the opponents so that the varsity team is familiar with the opponents' style of play on the night of the game.

Transfer may either facilitate or hinder the acquisition of a skill. Physical educators need to be aware of the principles of transfer so they can use positive transfer to promote skill learning and enhance performance and can readily counteract the effects of negative transfer.

7. *Feedback is essential for learning.* One of the most critical factors affecting learning is feedback. Feedback is information about an individual's performance. Feedback can serve several functions. It provides the learner with information about his or her performance. Using this information, the learner can make adjustments in the response prior to the next attempt. Second, feedback can serve to reinforce the learner's efforts, strengthening the correct response. Finally, feedback may also serve to motivate the learner by providing information about his or her progress.

Feedback may be classified in many ways. Feedback for error correction may focus on the outcome of the movement or the movement itself. Knowledge of results provides information about the effects of the movement on the environment, information that tells the learner whether or not the goal of the movement was achieved. Knowledge of performance provides information about the movement itself. The learner's awareness and feelings about how correctly the movement was executed in relation to the intended movement is knowledge of performance. For example, in shooting a foul shot in basketball, the player can readily see if the goal of the movement—putting the ball in the basket—was attained. This is knowledge of results. However, the player may know even before the ball goes in the basket that the shot will be good because the movement "felt right." This is knowledge of performance. Knowledge of performance depends on the learner being sensitive to the "feelings" associated with correct and incorrect performance;

in other words, the learner becomes aware of what feels right and what feels wrong. Changes in performance occur as the learner compares information about the outcome with the desired outcome and information about performance with his or her intended movement. The learner then adjusts his or her performance accordingly until the correct response is achieved.

Feedback may also be classified according to its source or according to when it is presented to the learner. Feedback may be described as intrinsic when the source of the information is the outcome of the task or skill itself.[11] Scoring an ace with a tennis serve, having the shot go slightly wide of the goal in soccer, and scoring on a foul shot in basketball are examples of intrinsic feedback. Information from external sources such as an instructor, friend, or videotape is classified as extrinsic or augmented feedback.[11] When the learner receives information during the performance of the skill, this feedback is referred to as concurrent. Feedback given after the performance is completed is called terminal feedback. Often feedback is a combination of information from various sources. For example, comments from the teacher during the learner's performance provide the learner with extrinsic concurrent feedback. A soccer player seeing the kicked ball go in the goal receives intrinsic terminal feedback.

How can professionals use feedback effectively? Docheff states that the most effective use of feedback includes both general and specific information.[12] One simple method to guide physical education, exercise science, and sport professionals in giving feedback is the use of a "feedback sandwich." The feedback sandwich combines all three functions of feedback: reinforcement, information, and motivation. For example, "Good job, Bob. With your elbow in line, you will always have good alignment when shooting the basketball. Keep up the good work." Physical education, exercise science, and sport professionals should plan for specific feedback. Feedback should be positive and relate to teaching cues. The feedback sandwich offers professionals a guide to increase the meaningfulness and effectiveness of their feedback.

The importance of feedback in the learning of skills is well recognized. Feedback is especially critical during the initial stages of learning a skill. It appears that knowledge of results is more helpful to the individual performing an open skill and that knowledge of performance is more valuable to the individual executing a closed skill. With highly skilled performers, whether they are performing a closed or an open skill, knowledge of performance is more helpful. Feedback should be communicated to the learner in a meaningful manner. The teacher should help the learner become aware of the available feedback and teach the learner how to use this information to improve his or her performance.

8. *Learners may experience plateaus in performance.*   The extent to which an individual has learned a skill may be inferred from his or her performance. When learning a new skill, an individual may initially demonstrate a sharp improvement in performance. This may be followed by a plateau, or a period in which little or no progress is made. Finally, additional practice results in further improvements in performance.

The plateau may occur for a variety of reasons, such as loss of interest and lack of motivation, failure to grasp a clear concept of the goal to be attained, lack of attention to the proper cues or attention to irrelevant cues, preparation for a transition from fundamental skills to more complex skills in the learning process, or poor learning conditions. Teachers should be cognizant of the plateaus and the conditions under which learners make little or no apparent progress in the activity. They should be especially careful not to introduce certain concepts or skills too rapidly, without allowing sufficient time for their mastery. They should also watch for certain physical deterrents to progress, such as fatigue or lack of strength. Some individuals cannot go beyond a given point because of physiological limits with respect to speed, endurance, or other physical characteristics. Often, however, it is not physiological limits but rather psychological limits that must be overcome. By implementing techniques to enhance the learner's interest and enthusiasm, these limits can be overcome.

GUIDELINES FOR PHYSICAL ACTIVITY INSTRUCTION

1. Use models of motor learning to assist in the planning of learning experiences.
2. Match the type of instruction to the individual's stage of learning.
3. Consider the individual's level of readiness when teaching new skills and information.
4. Plan instructional experiences that take into account the individual's level of development in all three domains—cognitive, affective, and psychomotor.
5. Use the powerful influence of motivation to facilitate learning.
6. Provide positive reinforcement to strengthen desirable responses.
7. Take individual differences into account when teaching by selecting approaches that accommodate a diversity of abilities and needs.
8. Structure practice sessions to promote optimal conditions for learning.
9. Help individuals gain an understanding of the task to be learned and its requirements.
10. Consider the nature of the skill or task when designing practice sessions.
11. Evaluate the task demands and assess the learner's background in deciding whether to use the whole or part method to teach a skill.
12. Study the requirements of the skill to determine whether speed or accuracy should be emphasized in teaching.
13. Facilitate learning by using positive transfer.
14. Incorporate appropriate meaningful feedback to help individuals correct their performance, motivate them, and reinforce their efforts.
15. Be prepared to deal with plateaus in performance.
16. Assist individuals in developing self-analysis skills.
17. Provide strong leadership that contributes to the attainment of the desired objectives.

9. *Self-analysis should be developed.* During the early periods of instruction when the basic techniques of the skill are being learned, learners need frequent instruction and help from the teacher. However, as the skill is mastered, the learner should rely less on the teacher's help and more on internal resources. A good teacher will help the learner to be his or her own teacher. This involves providing the learner with opportunities for self-criticism and analysis. The learner should be taught how to detect errors and how to correct them. By helping the student become aware of his or her performance and techniques by which it can be improved, the teacher is promoting lifelong learning.

10. *The leadership provided determines to a great degree how much learning will take place.* The teacher should make sure that the learner has a clear idea of the objective to be accomplished. Practices should be designed to maximize the learner's opportunities to perform the skill and minimize unproductive activities such as waiting. The teacher should be continually alert to detect correct and incorrect responses and encourage correct performance. The learner's motivation can be enhanced by providing him or her with opportunities to experience success and by presenting meaningful activities. The teacher should present material appropriate to the learner's level of understanding and be cognizant of individual differences. The teacher should use his or her leadership to promote participants' learning. The Guidelines for Physical Activity Instruction box summarizes motor learning concepts that will improve performance.

MOTOR DEVELOPMENT

Motor development is also encompassed within the broad area of motor behavior. The definition and scope of motor development, its background and emergence as a subdiscipline of physical education, and areas of study are briefly described in this section.

Definition and Scope

Motor development is the study of the origins of and changes in movement behavior throughout the lifespan. Motor development encompasses the study of biological (hereditary) and environmental influences on motor behavior from infancy to old age.[13] It involves understanding how motor behavior is influenced by the integration of psychological, sociological, cognitive, biological, and mechanical factors.[14]

According to Gallahue and Ozmun, the study of motor development uses both a process and a product approach. "As a process, motor development involves the underlying biological, environmental, and task demands influencing both motor performance and movement abilities of individuals from infancy through older adulthood. As a product, motor development may be regarded as descriptive or normative and is typically viewed in stages (infancy, childhood, adolescence, and adulthood) that reflect the particular interest of the researcher."[14]

Historical Development

Motor development traces its roots to developmental psychology. Gallahue and Ozmun[14] describe the history of motor development as moving through three periods of growth, based on the explanations used to describe the developmental process: the maturational period (1928–1946), the normative/descriptive period (1946 through the 1970s), and the process-oriented period (1980s to the present).

The maturational period marked the beginning of the growth of motor development as an area of study within physical education. During this time, researchers were interested in studying the underlying biological processes governing maturation. Early researchers such as Arnold Gesell (1928), Mary Shirley (1931), Myrtle McGraw (1935), and Nancy Bayley (1935) studied the sequences of motor development in young children, beginning in infancy. Their work led to a better understanding about the sequence of normal development, moving from the acquisition of early rudimentary movements to the attainment of mature movement patterns. The researchers found that although the rate at which children acquired motor skills varied, the sequence in which the children learned was relatively the same. Wild's 1938 study of throwing behavior in school-age children was the first research to focus on the development of fundamental movements in children rather than infants. Wild classified children's overhand throwing patterns into stages; her work later served as a model for classifying developmental movement patterns in children and influenced work in the field for years to come.

The normative/descriptive period focused on describing the motor performance of children, rather than the motor development of infants. Much of the work was undertaken by physical educators; Anna Espenschade, Ruth Glassow, and G. Lawrence Rarick were leading contributors of this era. These leaders were interested in children's acquisition of skills and how growth and maturation affect performance. Their research efforts and leadership in the establishment of doctoral programs in motor development during the 1950s and 1960s contributed to the emergence of motor development as a field of study within physical education.

Another area of research during this time was perceptual-motor development. When performing motor skills, sensory information, especially visual information, often guides performance.

As Gallahue and Ozmun describe, incoming sensory information is integrated with past information in memory to guide the movement response.[14] Sensory feedback from the movement itself is also an important aspect of perceptual-motor development.[14]

Motor development, motor learning, and motor control emerged as subdisciplines within the growing academic discipline of physical education during the late 1960s and early 1970s. As research expanded, the work of the previous period was extended and new areas of research developed. Researchers during the 1960s through the 1980s, such as Rarick and Robert Malina, concentrated their efforts on understanding the influence of growth and maturation on motor performance. Ralph Wickstrom's work on fundamental movement abilities helped us more fully understand these critical motor skills. Lolas Halverson, Mary Ann Roberton, Vern Seefeldt, and John Haubenstricker focused their efforts on understanding the development of fundamental motor skills, that is, the levels or stages that children passed through as they acquired skills.

In the 1970s, researchers became increasingly interested in exploring the processes underlying the development of motor skills across the lifespan. Kevin Connolly's edited book *Mechanisms of Motor Skill Development* set the foundation for further research into the cognitive processes associated with motor skill development.[2] Jerry Thomas was one of the leaders in researching how cognitive factors influence children's motor

LIFESPAN AND CULTURAL PERSPECTIVES: Motor Behavior

- How does aging affect the control of movements?
- How does early sensory stimulation affect the development of motor skills?
- How does socioeconomic status affect the development of motor skills?
- How does a deficit in auditory or visual processing affect the learning of specific motor skills?
- At what age can children safely engage in resistance training?

skill acquisition. David Gallahue and Kathleen Hayward contributed much to our understanding of lifespan motor development. Other researchers such as Esther Thelen, Scott Kelso, and Jane Clark developed theoretical frameworks to study motor development based on dynamical systems theory. The emphasis on understanding the processes involved in motor development plays an important role in research today.

Areas of Study

Many broad areas of study fall within motor development, including the influence of age on the acquisition of skills and the development of theories to serve as a framework for our understanding of how movements are developed and controlled. Specialists in motor development may investigate questions such as these:

- What are the hereditary and environmental factors most significantly associated with obesity?
- At what age can children safely engage in resistance training?
- How does socioeconomic status affect the development of motor skills?
- What are the developmental stages individuals go through as they acquire fundamental motor skills? What factors affect the rate of development?
- How does early sensory stimulation affect the development of motor skills?
- What are the changes in motor skill development experienced across the lifespan?

Since physical education, exercise science, and sport professionals are concerned with helping individuals of all ages acquire and improve their motor skills, motor development, from both its theoretical and applied perspectives, is important to professionals in our fields.

Phases of Motor Development

The study of motor development today emphasizes consideration of a multitude of factors that influence all aspects of development across the lifespan. Development is a highly interrelated process. According to Gallahue, the study of motor development must "encompass both the biological and environmental aspects of cognitive and affective behavior that impact on motor development, and it must look across various age periods of development. If it is to be of any real value to the practitioner, the study of motor development must not only focus on the skilled performer . . . but must instead analyze and document what individuals of all ages can do. . . ."[14]

Gallahue developed an hourglass model (see Figure 5-4) to illustrate how development is a continuous process, beginning at conception and continuing throughout the lifespan, ceasing at death.[13] In our hourglass is the "stuff of life: 'sand.'" He views sand entering our hourglass from two containers, which symbolize the hereditary and environmental contributions to the process of development. The heredity container has a lid, reflecting that at conception our genetic makeup is determined; thus the amount of sand in that container is fixed. The second container, the environment, has no lid; thus, more sand can be added to it from the environment and sand poured into our hourglass.

During the early reflexive (in utero to about 1 year of age) and rudimentary movement (birth to about 2 years of age) phases of motor development, the sand pours into the hourglass primarily from the heredity container. During the first two years of life, the sequential progression of motor development is quite rigid and invariable. For example, with the rudimentary movements, children learn to sit before they stand and stand before they walk. However, there is considerable variability in the rates at which children acquire these rudimentary skills. This variability in motor skill acquisition occurs throughout life. Motor skill acquisition is enhanced when individuals—infants, children, adolescents, and adults—receive additional opportunities for practice, encouragement, and instruction in an environment conducive to learning. When these opportunities are absent, acquisition of motor skills is inhibited. The rate of acquisition is also influenced by the nature and the requirements of the task.

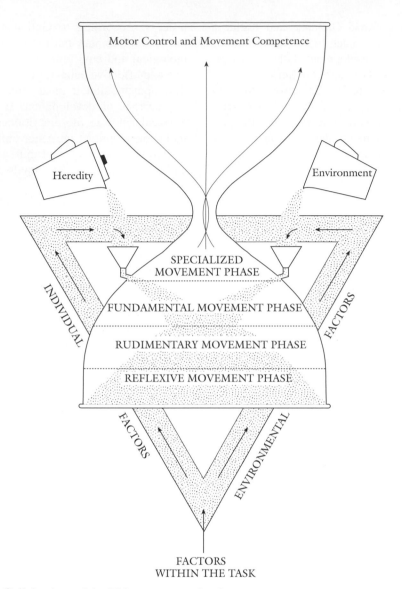

Figure 5-4 Gallahue's model of lifespan motor development
Source: Gallahue DL and Ozmun JC. *Understanding Motor Development: Infants, Children, Adolescents, Adults* (5th ed.).
New York: McGraw-Hill, 2002.

During the fundamental movement phase (ages 2 to 7), children begin to develop the fundamental movement skills, such as running, jumping, throwing, catching, and kicking. Gallahue divides the acquisition of these fundamental movement skills into three separate, but somewhat overlapping, stages: initial, elementary,

and mature (these are briefly described later).[13] Encouragement, instruction, and plentiful opportunities for practice are crucial for children to move through these stages.

Acquisition of specialized movement skills, from about ages 7 to 10 and older, is influenced by the attainment of mature, fundamental skills.

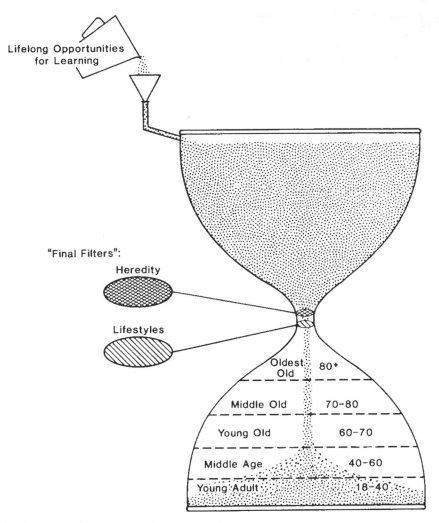

Figure 5-5 Emptying the overturned hourglass of life
Source: Gallahue DL and Ozmun JC. *Understanding Motor Development: Infants, Children, Adolescents, Adults* (5th ed.).
New York: McGraw-Hill, 2002.

Specialized motor skills are developed, refined, and combined; these skills are used for activities of daily living, recreational activities, and sports. These skills have improved form, greater accuracy, and better control than the fundamental motor skills.

After showing how our movements are developed, Gallahue then portrays the hourglass as turning over at some point in our lives; sand begins

to pour out, typically in our late teens and early 20s.[13] (See Figure 5-5.) The time for the "turnover" is quite variable and influenced more by social and cultural factors than by physical factors. Sand falls through two filters—the heredity filter and the lifestyles filter. Filters can be dense, allowing sand to go through slowly, or very porous, in which case sand will pass through rapidly.

FUNDAMENTAL MOTOR SKILLS

Locomotor Skills	Nonlocomotor Skills	Manipulative Skills
Walk	Bend and	Throw
Run	stretch	Catch
Jump and	Twist and turn	Strike
land	Push and pull	Dribble
Hop	Swing and	Kick
Leap	sway	Volley
Slide		
Gallop		
Skip		
Dodge		

The heredity filter represents our inherited predispositions, whether they are toward longevity or coronary heart disease. Sand also passes through the lifestyles filter, which is environmentally based and over which we have some degree of control. Physical fitness, nutritional status, physical activity, stress resistance, and spiritual well-being influence the density and, hence, the rate at which sand falls through this filter. Although we cannot stop the sand from flowing through the hourglass—that is, the aging process—we can control the rate at which it falls by as much as 40%. Gallahue describes the wonderful opportunities that we as professionals in these fields have to help people add more sand to their hourglass and to develop "lifestyles filters" that will slow the rate at which sand falls through the hourglass.[13] He points out that even when the hourglass is overturned and sand is flowing through to the bottom, we can still take advantage of many opportunities for continued development and activity, thereby adding more sand to our hourglass and increasing our longevity.[13]

Selected Fundamental Motor Skills

Fundamental motor skills encompass a broad range of skills that form the foundation for successful participation in games, sports, dance, and fitness activities. These skills can be categorized into locomotor, nonlocomotor, and manipulative skills. Locomotor skills are those in which the body moves through space, including running, jumping, and sliding. Nonlocomotor skills, or axial movements, are typically done from a relatively stationary position, using a stable base of support. Generally performed in place, nonlocomotor skills include bending, stretching, and pushing. Manipulative skills are skills used in handling objects; throwing, catching, striking, and kicking are examples of manipulative skills.

Fundamental motor skills are combined to create the specialized movement necessary in many activities. For example, the softball throw requires a combination of sliding (locomotor skill) and throwing (manipulative skills) and twisting (nonlocomotor skill). The triple jump in track is a combination of a hop, step, and jump. Other specialized sport skills require more complex combinations of movements.

The next section contains a brief analysis of selected locomotor, nonlocomotor, and manipulative motor skills. As children learn the skills, they should also acquire knowledge of the critical elements important to skill performance. This knowledge increases children's understanding of the technique and forms the foundation for future learning.

Locomotor Movements

The following locomotor skills are discussed: walking, running, jumping (for distance and height), hopping, leaping, skipping, sliding, and galloping. These are the skills most commonly used by elementary schoolchildren. Opportunities for students to explore and use these skills by themselves and in combination with nonlocomotor movements create a sufficient foundation for more complex movement skills.

Walking　Walking involves the transfer of weight from one foot to the other while moving. The weight of the body is transferred in a forward

Fundamantal motor skills are the foundation for skills used in many different sports activites.

direction from the heel to the ball of the foot and then to the toes. The feet should move parallel to each other, with the toes pointing straight ahead. One foot is in contact with the ground at all times; this is the support foot. The body is erect, with the head up. The arm action is coordinated with leg action; the opposite arm and leg move in the same direction. These movements should be rhythmical and natural.

Running   Running is similar to walking in several ways. However, some critical differences exist. In running, the movement is faster. The stride is longer, the flexion and extension of the legs are greater, and there is a momentary period of flight when the body is not supported at all. The body leans slightly forward to place the center of gravity above the front foot in the stride. The arms swing forward and back, opposing the legs, and contribute power to the movement.

Jumping   Jumping varies according to the goal of the task. Jumping for distance and jumping for height are common skills. The standing long jump, for example, is done by bending the knees and lowering the upper body into a crouched position. As the body rocks back on the feet, the arms are brought down and beyond the hips. At takeoff, the forward and upward swing of the arms is coordinated with the powerful extension of both the feet and legs. The body is propelled forward as if reaching for an object in front of the body. The knees bend in midair so that the feet do not touch the ground prematurely. The landing is on the feet, with the knees bending to absorb the impact and the body falling forward.

Hopping   Hopping involves forcefully pushing off the ground from one foot, a brief suspension in the air, and landing on the same foot. The push-off from the ground is made from the toes and the ball of the foot (supporting foot), with the knee of the opposite foot bent and that foot off the ground (nonsupporting foot). The arms are thrust upward to aid in body lift. The landing is on the toes, ball, and heel of the foot in that order. The knee is bent slightly to help absorb the shock of the landing. To aid in balance, the arms and nonsupporting foot are used. Hopping should be practiced with both feet.

Leaping   Similar to the run, a leap is a long step forward to cover distance or to go over an obstacle. It is an exaggerated running step, with the stride longer and the body projected higher in the air. In the leap, the toes of the takeoff foot leave the floor last, and the landing is on the ball of the opposite foot. The arms should be extended upward and forward to give added lift to the body during the leap. Often the legs are extended in the air. Before the execution of the leap, usually a short run is taken to gain momentum for the leap itself.

Skipping   A skip is a combination of a step and a hop, with feet alternating after each step-hop. A long step is taken on one foot, followed by a hop on the same foot, and then a step with the opposite foot, again followed by a hop. Balance is aided by swinging the arms in opposition to the legs.

Sliding   A slide is a sideways movement in which the weight of the body is shifted in the direction of the slide. In a slide to the right, the right foot steps sideways (leading foot); then the left foot (trailing foot) is quickly drawn close to the right foot. Weight is shifted from the leading foot to the trailing foot. The same foot continues to lead in sliding movements. The body maintains an upright posture and the arms are used for balance. The legs should not be crossed. The slide should be practiced in both directions.

Galloping   Galloping is similar to sliding, but the movement is performed in a forward direction. One foot leads in the forward direction (leading foot). After a step by the leading foot, the rear or trailing foot is brought quickly forward and close to the lead foot. The stepping leg is always the lead leg. Opportunities to lead with the right foot and with the left foot should be included in practicing the gallop.

Nonlocomotor Movements

Nonlocomotor movements are generally performed using a stable base of support. The nonlocomotor movement skills discussed are bending, stretching, twisting, turning, pushing, pulling, and swinging. Generally, they are performed in place and can be done from a variety of body positions (e.g., standing or sitting). They can also be combined with locomotor movements.

Bending and Stretching   Bending is a movement occurring at the joints of the body in which body parts are brought closer together. For example, by bending the body at the hips to touch the toes, a person is decreasing the angle between the upper and lower body at the hip joint. This is called flexion. Bending movements may be in several directions: for example, forward, backward, sideways, or in a circular motion. The range of bending movements is determined by the type of joint at which the movement occurs. Ball-and-socket joints permit the greatest movement. Hip joints and shoulder joints are examples of ball-and-socket joints. Hinge joints permit only backward and forward movements. The knee joint is a hinge joint.

A stretch is an extension or hyperextension at the joints of the body. Stretching is the opposite of bending. Most movements require complete extension only where the body parts adjacent to the joints are at a straight angle (180 degrees). However, in movements such as the wrist cock before a throw, hyperextension is needed to give added impetus to the throw.

Bending and stretching are necessary to maintain flexibility—the full range of movement about a joint. Bending and stretching are common to most of the activities of daily life (e.g., dressing and bathing), and they are very important to physical education activities. Teachers should provide daily activities in which these skills can be practiced and refined.

Twisting and Turning Twisting is a rotation of the body or a body part around its axis while maintaining a fixed base of support. Twisting movements can take place at the neck, shoulders, spine, hips, ankles, and wrist. The body can be in different positions, for example, standing or lying down. As in bending and stretching movements, the range of a twisting movement is determined by the type of joint.

Turning generally refers to a rotation of the body around in space. When the body is turned, the base of support is shifted from one position to another. Jumping up and landing facing the opposite direction and pivoting are examples of turns. A twisting action is typically used to initiate a turn. Turns should be practiced in both directions, left and right or clockwise and counterclockwise.

Pushing and Pulling Pushing is a forceful action directed toward increasing the distance between the body and an object. A push can be used to move an object away from the body or the body away from an object. Pushing an opponent away in a wrestling match and a box across the floor are two examples of pushing. Proper body position enhances the effectiveness of a push. A forward stride position enlarges the body's base of support, and bending the knees lowers the center of gravity and increases the body's stability. Proper body alignment helps prevent back injuries.

Pulling is a forceful action designed to decrease the distance between the body and an object. A pull brings the body and the object closer together. As in pushing, widening the base of support and lowering the center of gravity increase effectiveness. In a tug-of-war, participants widen their base of support and dig their heels in as they try to pull their opponents across the dividing line. Partner resistance exercises and rowing use both pushing and pulling. Steady, controlled movements are recommended for both pulling and pushing.

Swinging A swing is a circular or pendular movement of a body part or of the entire body around a stationary center point. The center point may be a joint, such as the shoulder in swinging the arm, or an outside axis, such as the swing on a high bar. When the force necessary to hold a body stationary is released, the force of gravity will cause that body part to swing. In most body movements, the force of muscular contractions is necessary to maintain body swing. Swinging movements should be continuous, rhythmical, and free flowing.

Manipulative Skills

Manipulative skills involve the propulsion and control of objects. The body is used to apply force to an object and to absorb force when receiving or controlling an object. The manipulative skills of throwing, catching, kicking, and striking are briefly described.

Throwing Throwing an object may involve the use of the underhand, sidearm, or overhand pattern. Since the overhand throwing pattern is most frequently employed by children and adults, this movement will be described.

When throwing, the ball is held in the fingers of the throwing hand. As the throwing action is initiated, the ball is brought back and the body rotates so the opposite side is toward the target. Weight is transferred back to the foot on the same side as the throwing hand. The arm is bent at the elbow, and the elbow leads slightly as the arm is brought forward for the throw. As the arm accelerates, a step forward onto the opposite foot is taken and the hips rotate forward. The arm quickly extends, the wrist snaps, and the ball is released. The arm follows in the direction of the throw, coming down and across the body.

Catching Catching involves the use of hands to stop and gain control of an object. As the object approaches, the individual makes a judgment about where it can be intercepted and moves to a location directly in line with the object, placing the hands in a position for effective reception. The eyes follow the flight of the object, and both hands reach out toward it. The object is grasped by the hands and pulled in by the arms and hands toward the body to absorb the object's force.

Kicking　Kicking is imparting force to an object by the foot and the leg. The kicking of a stationary object is the foundation for the kicking of a moving object and for punting.

In kicking, the supporting foot is placed alongside the object. The kicking leg, knee bent, moving freely from the hip, swings through an arc toward the object. As the foot contacts the object, the knee is extended and the body leans back for balance. The kicking leg follows through, continuing its movement toward the direction of the flight of the object. The arms, relaxed, move in opposition to the legs. The eyes focus on the object throughout the kick.

Striking　Striking involves using a body part (e.g., hand) or an implement (e.g., paddle, racquet, bat) to apply force to a stationary or moving object. The length, size, and weight of the implement as well as characteristics of the object being struck influence the nature of the movement pattern. Kicking, described earlier, is also considered a striking task.

For the striking action typically seen in batting, the body is positioned perpendicular to the line of flight of the oncoming ball. The feet are placed in a forward-backward stride position, approximately shoulder width apart. The trunk is rotated back, the weight is shifted to the rear foot, and a backswing is taken. The flight of the ball is followed by the eyes until just before making contact. Body weight is shifted onto the forward foot in the direction of the intended flight of the ball. With the hips leading, the hips and trunk are rotated in the same direction as the weight shift. Arms move forward into contact, and the follow-through action occurs in the direction of the line of flight.

Fundamental motor skills are the foundation for the development of specialized game, sport, dance, and fitness activities. These skills are the building blocks for the future. Acquisition of skills for lifetime participation begins with the mastery of these fundamental motor skills. All children, the skilled and the unskilled, need sufficient opportunities and a variety of experiences to master these important movement basics. (See references for more information on the development of motor skills.)

Development of Fundamental Motor Skills

Motor development specialists also investigate the sequential and overlapping stages children proceed through as they acquire skills. To illustrate the changes that occur as skills are developed, a brief overview of the stages associated with the acquisition of fundamental motor skills is presented. In acquiring fundamental motor skills, children pass through three stages: initial, elementary, and mature. Table 5-2 and Figure 5-6 show the three stages of the development of the overhand throwing pattern.

The initial stage reflects the child's early attempts at performing the skill. Poor spatial and temporal integration of the movements comprising the skill characterize this stage. The movements exhibit improper sequencing of parts of the skill, little body rotation, often exaggerated use of the body, poor rhythm, and difficulties in coordination. This stage is generally seen in 2-year-olds.

The elementary stage reflects greater control and rhythmical coordination of the movements. The temporal and spatial elements of the movement are better synchronized, and the movement is better coordinated. The movements are still restricted or exaggerated, and mechanical principles are not consistently applied to the performance. Typical 3- or 4-year-olds are at this stage. Gallahue and Ozmun[14] note that many individuals fail to move beyond the elementary stage in some of their movements. If you've watched adults using the overhand throw, you may observe an adult throwing with an elementary stage pattern, for example, stepping forward with the foot on the same side as the throwing arm rather than stepping forward with the opposite foot.

TABLE 5-2	Developmental Sequence for Overhand Throwing

I. Throwing
  A. Initial stage
    1. Action is mainly from elbow
    2. Elbow of throwing arm remains in front of body; action resembles a push
    3. Fingers spread at release
    4. Follow-through is forward and downward
    5. Trunk remains perpendicular to target
    6. Little rotary action during throw
    7. Body weight shifts slightly rearward to maintain balance
    8. Feet remain stationary
    9. There is often purposeless shifting of feet during preparation for throw
  B. Elementary stage
    1. In preparation, arm is swung upward, sideward, and backward to a position of elbow flexion
    2. Ball is held behind head
    3. Arm is swung forward, high over shoulder
    4. Trunk rotates toward throwing side during preparatory action
    5. Shoulders rotate toward throwing side
    6. Trunk flexes forward with forward motion of arm
    7. Body weight shifts forward definitely
    8. Leg on same side as throwing arm steps forward
  C. Mature stage
    1. Arm is swung backward in preparation
    2. Opposite elbow is raised for balance as a preparatory action in the throwing arm
    3. Throwing elbow moves forward horizontally as it extends
    4. Forearm rotates and thumb points downward
    5. Trunk markedly rotates to throwing side during preparatory action
    6. Throwing shoulder drops slightly
    7. Hips, legs, spine, and shoulders rotate definitely during throw
    8. Weight during preparatory movement is on rear foot
    9. As weight is shifted, there is a step with opposite foot
II. Developmental Difficulties
  A. Forward movement of foot on same side as throwing arm
  B. Inhibited backswing
  C. Failure to rotate hips as throwing arm is brought forward
  D. Failure to step out on leg opposite the throwing arm
  E. Poor rhythmical coordination of arm movement with body movement
  F. Inability to release ball at desired trajectory
  G. Loss of balance while throwing
  H. Upward rotation of arm

Source: Gallahue DL and Ozmun JC. *Understanding Motor Development: Infants, Children, Adolescents, Adults* (5th ed.). New York: McGraw-Hill, 2002.

The mature stage is marked by increased efficiency, enhanced coordination, and improved control of movements. Increases in size and strength contribute to greater force production. According to Gallahue and Ozmun, most children should be at the mature stage by age 5 or 6.[14] However, some skills may develop later, particularly manipulative skills that require tracking and intercepting moving objects, such as catching or striking. The greater visual-motor requirements

INITIAL

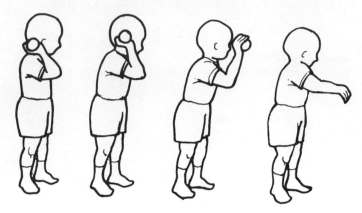

ELEMENTARY

MATURE

Figure 5-6   Stages of the overhand throwing pattern

Source: Gallahue DL and Ozmun JC. *Understanding Motor Development: Infants, Children, Adolescents, Adults* (5th ed.). New York: McGraw-Hill, 2002.

of these tasks contribute to their later development. Greater range of motion, increased accuracy, and better adaptation to environmental conditions characterize this stage. Development of the mature form of the skills is enhanced when plentiful opportunities for practice are provided, along with instruction and encouragement—opportunities that would be available through a developmentally appropriate quality elementary physical education program. Failure to acquire the mature form of the skill adversely impacts the development of more specialized skills in the later years.

Clark points out that poorly developed motor skills serve as a "proficiency barrier" to the development of more sport-specific skills in the later years, be it adolescence or adulthood.[15] A strong motor skills foundation provides for new movement opportunities later in life, whether sport or recreational in nature, such as skiing, rock climbing, and tennis. Another, perhaps unintended, consequence of poorly developed motor skills is that children and youth may lack self-efficacy regarding their motor performance. The lack of confidence in themselves as movers may make it less likely that they will participate in physical activity when older.[15] Professionals working with adults in the area of sport

instruction, recreation activities, or fitness who find that those adults exhibit poorly developed motor skills must be prepared to help the adults improve and refine their skills. Attention must also be paid to helping adults with poor self-efficacy increase their confidence as movers.

This chapter is designed to provide the reader with a brief overview of some of the concepts and concerns in the realm of motor behavior. An understanding of how individuals learn motor skills will help physical education, exercise science, and sport professionals design experiences to promote effective learning. Promoting effective learning is a concern of professionals working in both school and nonschool settings. In the school setting, for example, elementary school physical educators are concerned with helping children master fundamental motor skills, high school teachers focus their efforts on assisting students in acquiring skills in a variety of lifetime sports, and coaches spend countless hours helping their athletes refine the skills necessary for high-level performance. In the nonschool setting, athletic trainers may help injured athletes regain efficient motor patterns, while exercise leaders in a corporate or community program may help adults attain proficiency in such lifetime sports

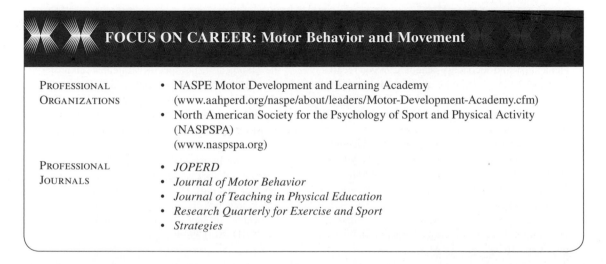

FOCUS ON CAREER: Motor Behavior and Movement

PROFESSIONAL ORGANIZATIONS	• NASPE Motor Development and Learning Academy (www.aahperd.org/naspe/about/leaders/Motor-Development-Academy.cfm) • North American Society for the Psychology of Sport and Physical Activity (NASPSPA) (www.naspspa.org)
PROFESSIONAL JOURNALS	• *JOPERD* • *Journal of Motor Behavior* • *Journal of Teaching in Physical Education* • *Research Quarterly for Exercise and Sport* • *Strategies*

as golf or tennis. Thus, understanding how learning occurs and can be facilitated is important foundational knowledge for professionals to possess. The manner in which individuals control their movements (motor control) and the impact of development (motor development) on learning are also important considerations in designing learning experiences.

SUMMARY

Motor behavior—specifically motor control, motor learning, and motor development—traces its roots to psychology. These fields emerged in the mid-1960s and 1970s from the parent discipline of psychology and developed identities as subdisciplines in the growing academic discipline of physical education, now referred to as physical education, exercise science, and sport.

Motor behavior is a broad term, encompassing motor control, motor learning, and motor development. Motor control is the study of the neural mechanisms and processes by which movements are learned and controlled. Motor learning is the acquisition of motor skills as a consequence of practice and experience. Motor development is the study of the origins and changes in movement behavior throughout the lifespan.

Many theories and models have been advanced to describe learning. One theory is the information processing model. According to this model, learning and performance of skills can be described as a series of information processing tasks consisting of input, decision making, output, and feedback. Another theory is the dynamical systems model. This model explains the learning and performance of motor skills as the interaction between the individual, the environment, and the task. Individuals pass through three stages when learning a motor skill: cognitive, associative, and autonomic. Learning is influenced by readiness, motivation, reinforcement, and individual differences. To facilitate motor learning, physical education, exercise science, and sport professionals should incorporate concepts from motor learning into the design of their practices.

Fundamental motor skills form the foundation for learning more complex skills. In developing these fundamental skills, individuals move through three stages: initial, elementary, and mature. Professionals should understand how motor skills develop so they can design learning experiences to facilitate their acquisition.

DISCUSSION QUESTIONS

1. Reflect on your physical education classes in elementary and secondary school. Can you recall a student who exhibited poor motor skills? Can you think of a student who possessed well-developed motor skills? Based on what you recall, how does motor skill ability influence participation in physical education? Try to think about social and emotional consequences of being poorly or highly skilled as well as the effects on participation.

2. How is individuals' failure to achieve mature forms of fundamental motor skill a proficiency barrier for the learning of more advanced sports skills? How might this affect their participation in lifespan physical activity?

3. Reflect on Gallahue's hourglass model of motor development. What specific strategies can professionals use to help individuals add more "sand" to their hourglass, thereby prolonging the time those individuals can enjoy being physically active?

4. Clark, in an article on the importance of motor literacy, suggests that children who do not possess motor literacy are "left behind" just as children who do not possess reading or math literacy are "left behind." Do you agree or disagree with this statement? (For more information, see Clark JE: On the problem of motor skill development, JOPERD 78(5):39–40, 2007.)

SELF-ASSESSMENT ACTIVITIES

These activities are designed to help you determine if you have mastered the material and competencies presented in this chapter.

1. You are a teacher in the school setting, a sport instructor in a community setting working with senior citizens, or a fitness leader in a corporate fitness program working with adults. How would you incorporate each of the following concepts into your program: readiness, reinforcement, motivation, and individual differences?

2. Explain how you would use either the information processing model of learning or the dynamical systems model to enhance an individual's acquisition of a skill. You may find the following readings helpful to you as you complete this task:

   Garcia C and Garcia L: A motor-development and motor-learning perspective, JOPERD 77(8):31–34, 2006.

   Rukavina PB and Foxworth KR: Using motor-learning theory to design more effective instruction, JOPERD 80(3):17–23, 27, 2009.

3. Review the list of motor learning concepts that promote the learning of motor skills and improve performance. Select five of those concepts and illustrate how you would apply them to the teaching of a fundamental skill or sports skill.

4. Refer to the 12 Steps to Understanding Research Reports box in Chapter 1. Complete Step 5 for the same article you selected in Chapter 1.

REFERENCES

1. Thomas JR and Thomas KT: Motor behavior. In SJ Hoffman and JC Harris, editors, Introduction to kinesiology: studying physical activity, ed 3 Champaign, Ill., 2009, Human Kinetics.

2. Thomas JR: Motor behavior. In JD Massengale and RA Swanson, editors, The history of exercise and sport science, Champaign, Ill., 1997, Human Kinetics.

3. Adams, JA: Historical review and appraisal of research on the learning, retention, and transfer of human motor skills, Psychological Bulletin 101:41–74, 1987.

4. Knudson D and Kluka DA: The impact of vision and vision training on sport performance, JOPERD 68(4):17–24, 1997.

5. Garcia C and Garcia L: A motor-development and motor-learning perspective, JOPERD 77(8):31–34, 2006.

6. Rukavina PB and Foxworth KR: Using motor-learning theory to design more effective instruction, JOPERD 80(3):17–23, 27, 2009.

7. Fitts PM and Posner MJ: Human performance, Belmont, Calif., 1967, Brooks/Cole.

8. Schmidt RA: Motor control and learning, ed 4, Champaign, Ill., 2005, Human Kinetics.

9. Magill RA: Motor learning and control: concepts and applications, ed 8, New York, 2006, McGraw-Hill.

10. Siedentop D and Tannehill D: Developing teaching skills in physical education, ed 4, Mountain View, Calif., 2000, Mayfield [McGraw-Hill].

11. Rink JE: Teaching physical education for learning, ed 6, New York, 2010, McGraw-Hill.

12. Docheff DM: The feedback sandwich, JOPERD 61(9):17–18, 1990.

13. Gallahue DL: Understanding motor development: infants, children, adolescents, adults Indianapolis, 1989, Benchmark.

14. Gallahue DL and Ozmun JC: Understanding motor development: infants, children, and adolescents, ed 6, New York, 2006, McGraw-Hill.

15. Clark JE: On the problem of motor skill development, JOPERD 78(5):39–40, 2007.

C H A P T E R **6**

BIOMECHANICAL FOUNDATIONS

O B J E C T I V E S

After reading this chapter the student should be able to—

- Define the term *biomechanics* and articulate its relationship to kinesiology.
- Identify the value of biomechanics for physical education, exercise science, and sport professionals.
- Understand some of the terminology associated with the subdiscipline of biomechanics.
- Explain the meaning of mechanical principles and concepts that relate to stability, motion, leverage, and force. Illustrate the application of these principles to physical skills and sport techniques.
- Describe some of the techniques used to analyze motion.

Understanding the factors that govern human movement is essential for physical education, exercise science, and sport professionals. Physical educators, exercise scientists, and sport leaders are concerned with helping individuals learn how to move efficiently and effectively. In elementary physical education classes, the teacher is concerned with helping students learn fundamental motor skills such as throwing and running, which provide a foundation for learning more advanced sport skills. In competitive athletics, where the difference between winning and losing may be one-hundredth of a second or a fraction of a centimeter, a coach may use scientific methods such as high-speed photography and computer simulation to fine-tune an athlete's form. The weekend golfer, seeking to break par, requests the assistance of the golf pro to eliminate a troublesome slice from his or her swing. The golf pro may then videotape the golfer's performance to determine the source of error and to illustrate to the golfer the needed changes. The athletic trainer rehabilitating an athlete recovering from shoulder surgery uses knowledge of the range of motion of this joint to help develop an effective rehabilitation program. The adapted physical educator analyzes the gait of a child with cerebral palsy in order to prescribe physical activities to improve it. The exercise instructor closely monitors a client working on a Cybex machine to ensure the exercise is being performed properly through the range of motion. These examples show how physical education, exercise science, and sport professionals use the scientific knowledge of human motion from the realms of kinesiology and biomechanics to help individuals move efficiently and effectively.

KINESIOLOGY AND BIOMECHANICS

The study of human movement is the focus of kinesiology and biomechanics. *Kinesiology* is the scientific study of human movement. The term *kinesiology* is derived from the Greek *kinesi,* meaning "motion." Defined more broadly, kinesiology is used by some professionals as an umbrella term to encompass the subdisciplines that emerged from physical education in the 1970s. In this chapter, the term *kinesiology* will be used in a more narrow, traditional sense to refer to the anatomical and physiological study of human movement. To understand human movement fully, one needs an understanding of body movement, or kinesiology.

Kinesiology involves the study of the skeletal framework, the structure of muscles and their functions, the action of the joints, and the neuromuscular basis of movement. Kinesiology helps us appreciate the intricacies and wonder of human motion. Hamilton and Luttgens write,

> One who gives it any thought whatever cannot help being impressed not only by the beauty of human motion but also by its apparently infinite possibilities, its meaningfulness, its orderliness, its adaptability to the surrounding environment. Nothing is haphazard; nothing is left to chance. Every study that participates in the movement of the body does so according to physical and physiological principles.[1]

Kinesiology helps us see human motion through new eyes and gain a greater appreciation for human movement.

Students of physical education, exercise science, and sport study kinesiology in order to learn how to improve performance by analyzing the movements of the body and applying the principles of movement to their work. Hamilton and Luttgens identify three important purposes for the study of kinesiology.[1] Physical education,

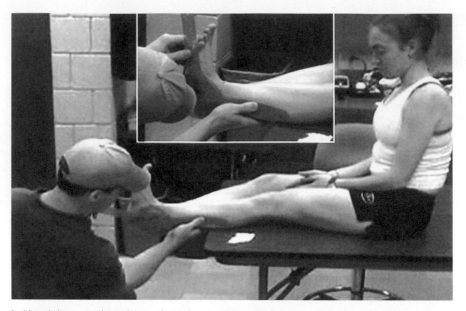

In kinesiology, students learn about the structure and function of the musculoskeletal system in relationship to human movement. Here, two students practice measuring ankle range of motion using a goniometer. Students also learn to take anthropometric measurements, perform manual muscle testing, and break down sport skills into individual joint motions and muscle actions.

exercise science, and sport professionals can use their knowledge of kinesiology to help the people with whom they work perform with optimum safety, optimum effectiveness, and optimum efficiency. Safety is of paramount concern for all professionals. We design and conduct movement experiences for participants in our programs so that participants avoid doing harm to their bodies. Professionals and participants work together to set goals for effective performance. Typically, the effectiveness of a performance is judged by success or failure in meeting those goals. Our programs should be designed to enable our participants to achieve their goals. Professionals and participants strive to achieve their stated goals as efficiently as possible—that is, with the least expenditure of effort. Thus, according to Hamilton and Luttgens, safety, effectiveness, and efficiency are the underlying aims of using kinesiology in physical education, exercise science, and sport.[1]

Kinesiology helps prepare physical education, exercise science, and sport professionals to teach fundamental motor skills and specialized sport skills to people of all ages, as a means of optimizing performance. Kinesiology offers professionals a background from which to evaluate exercises and activities and how they affect the body.

Definition and Scope

Biomechanics, as a subdiscipline of physical education, exercise science, and sport, focuses on the application of the scientific principles of mechanics to understand movements and actions of human bodies and sport implements (e.g., a tennis racquet). The term *biomechanics* can be better understood by examining the derivation of the word. *Bio* is from Greek and refers to life or living things, and *mechanics* refers to the field of Newtonian mechanics and the forces that act on bodies in

In biomechanics, students study the movements of athletes to improve performance and reduce injury. Here, three students are measuring the electrical activity of the calf muscle during walking using surface electromyography. They also have reflective markers on the joints of the lower extremity to measure motions of the ankle and knee during walking. Reflective markers are often used when doing motion capture or video analysis of human movement.

motion. Biomechanists study how various forces affect human motion and how movements can be improved in terms of efficiency and effectiveness.

Kinesiology and biomechanics are integrally related. An understanding of how the body moves, including the function and actions of the joints, muscles, and bony structure, is essential to the understanding of biomechanics. In order to effectively study the influences of forces on motion—biomechanics—one must be knowledgeable about the actions of the joints and the muscles that cause these forces; this is the realm of kinesiology. Both kinesiology and biomechanics are fundamental to understanding human movement and to helping individuals attain their fullest potential.

The principles of biomechanics can be applied in many fields of study outside of physical education, exercise science, and sport. These include biology, physiology, engineering, aerospace engineering, physical and occupational therapy, and medicine.

Historical Development

While biomechanics, as it is known today, emerged as a specialized field of study in the mid–1960s to 1970s, Aristotle (384–322 B.C.) is thought to have been one of the first scholars to study the muscles and motions of the human body, which he described in his book *De Moto Animalium On the Movement of Animals.*[2] Many other Greek and Roman scholars were fascinated by the structure and function of the human body and continued to make contributions to the understanding of the mechanics of human motion. Giovanni Borelli (1608–1679) is credited as the first scholar to apply the principles of levers to the function of the human body, to determine the forces acting on the joints of the body, and to estimate the location of the center of mass of a person. Borelli wrote the second *De Moto Animalium,* which was published after his death; Borelli is considered by many to be the father of modern biomechanics.[2]

In the United States, starting in the late 1800s, the term *kinesiology* was used to refer to the science of applying mechanics to the study of movement. Until recently, the terms kinesiology and biomechanics were used interchangeably. Wilkerson chronicles the growth of biomechanics through three stages: the early foundations (referred to as the kinesiology era), the organization of the subdiscipline (the biomechanics era), and the development of biomechanics.[3]

The kinesiology era spanned the late 1800s and the first six decades of the twentieth century, and represented the infancy of biomechanics. During this time frame, the term *kinesiology* was used to refer to the application of mechanics to the study of movement. Atwater credits Nils Posse as the first to use the term *kinesiology.*[4] Posse wrote *The Special Kinesiology of Educational Gymnastics,* published in 1894.

Scholars of the early to the mid-twentieth century contributed to the growth of kinesiology/biomechanics through their teaching, research, and writing. Arthur Steindler, Charles McCloy,

Ruth Glassow, Thomas Cureton, M. Gladys Scott, Katharine Wells, Marion Broer, and John M. Cooper were some of the early kinesiologists who led the way in developing and promoting the application of mechanical principles to the study of human movement. In 1935, Steindler, a physician and professor at the University of Iowa where he taught kinesiology classes, became the first person to use the term *biomechanics* in the physical education literature. These early kinesiologists laid the foundations of biomechanics.

Wilkerson describes the 1960s as the beginning of a new era in the development and growth of biomechanics—the emergence from physical education of biomechanics as a subdiscipline within the evolving exercise and sport sciences.[3] During this time the term *biomechanics* started to slowly replace the term *kinesiology* and was used more frequently to describe the scientific application of mechanics to the study of human movement. There was a greater emphasis on the study of both the anatomical and mechanical aspects of human movement. Advances in technology, instrumentation, and methodology contributed to the proliferation of research during this time.

Courses in kinesiology/biomechanics increased at both the undergraduate and graduate levels. At the graduate level, biomechanics began to emerge as an area of specialization. In 1977, the first national symposium on teaching kinesiology/biomechanics was held, during which there was considerable discussion about the differences between the terms *kinesiology* and *biomechanics*. Additionally, this meeting served as the impetus for the development of guidelines for teaching undergraduate kinesiology/biomechanics; *Guidelines and Standards for Undergraduate Biomechanics/Kinesiology* was first published in 1980, and revised in 1992.[5] According to the guidelines, biomechanics/kinesiology at the undergraduate level should provide students with "(1) an understanding of how the human body and external forces create human movement, (2) the knowledge necessary to undertake a systematic approach to the analysis of motor skills activities and exercise

programs, and (3) the experience of applying that knowledge to the execution and evaluation of both the performer and the performance in a clinical or educational milieu."[5] These guidelines influenced the learning experiences of countless physical educators, exercise scientists, and sport leaders as well as other future professionals concerned with the study of human movement.

The development of the biomechanics era was marked, according to Wilkerson, by the formation of scholarly societies, the organization of academic workshops and seminars, and the creation of scholarly journals; these provided a forum for the exchange of ideas, dissemination of research findings, and communication within the field.[3] In 1963, a kinesiology interest was formed within the American Association for Health, Physical Education, Recreation, and Dance (AAHPERD), and in 1965, it officially became the Kinesiology Section of AAHPERD. In 1974, the Kinesiology Section became the Kinesiology Academy, and in 1993, it changed its name to the Biomechanics Academy.

Several scholarly societies were formed by those interested in biomechanics and, more specifically, the biomechanics of sports. In 1973, the International Society of Biomechanics was founded, and in 1976, the American Society of Biomechanics was formed. These societies are very broad in their focus, including professionals from physical education, medicine, ergonomics, biology, and engineering. The growing interest in biomechanics in sports and the desire to help bridge the gap between biomechanics research and the teaching and coaching of sports led to the establishment, in 1982, of the International Society for Biomechanics in Sports (ISBS).

During this time, several journals were created to serve as outlets for research and the exchange of ideas. In 1968, the first issue of the *Journal of Biomechanics* was published. The *International Journal of Sport Biomechanics* first appeared in 1985 and was later renamed the *Journal of Applied Biomechanics*. Most recently, in 2002, ISBS published its new journal, *Sports Biomechanics*.

Cyclists have benefited greatly from improvements in equipment design and research designed to help them streamline and refine their body position to improve performance.

The growth of biomechanics has been remarkable. As biomechanics emerged and flourished, specialized areas of interest have developed within the subdiscipline. Biomechanists may specialize in a particular sport, such as swimming, or focus their research on a specific topic, such as footwear. Other biomechanists choose to direct their attention to more clinical concerns, such as rehabilitation. Other areas of interest in the broad and ever-expanding field include gait and posture analysis and computer simulation.

Biomechanics enables physical education, exercise science, and sport professionals to analyze human movement scientifically, increasing their ability to help individuals move safely, efficiently, and effectively to achieve their movement goals. There is a growing trend within the fields of exercise and sport sciences to refer to biomechanics as *sport biomechanics*. Additionally, as we move toward the future, there is a greater interest in using biomechanics to work not only with elite athletes, but with people of all abilities, and to strengthen and improve their performance of a diversity of movement tasks.

Reasons for Studying Biomechanics

Biomechanics is recognized as a subdiscipline of physical education, exercise science, and sport. As a result of reading this chapter, prospective professionals will have a better understanding of the parameters of this field of study and will recognize the value it has for them in future careers. In some cases, perhaps, it will motivate further study and specialization in this field of endeavor.

Many professionals can profit from the study of biomechanics. To be effective as practitioners, physical educators, exercise science, and sport professionals should have an understanding of the principles of biomechanics. Knowledge of biomechanics will provide the professional with a better understanding of the human body and the various internal and external forces that affect human movement, as well as the forces that act on object motion. This in turn will enable professionals to be better instructors, coaches, and leaders of the many physical activities and skills within physical education, exercise science, and sport.

Coaches who want to be expert in their field need a sound foundation in the area of biomechanics. Biomechanics offers important scientific knowledge that can improve performance, and the best coaches are taking advantage of this knowledge. Coaches of athletes today who are involved in many areas of high school, college, and Olympic sport find competition very intense. Therefore, coaches of athletes who wish to excel must use all this knowledge and the best techniques available. Biomechanics can be used to improve sport techniques and equipment, thus enhancing athletes' performance while assuring their safety.

Biomechanics is often at the forefront of changes in technique and technology. A great example is in the sport of swimming. In the late 1960s and early 1970s, James Counsilman, author of *The Science of Swimming,* worked with biomechanists to study the forces involved in propulsion in swimming.[6] In 1971, Brown and Counsilman filmed swimmers wearing lights on their hands as they swam in a darkened pool.[7] This allowed the pattern of the swimmers' hands to be identified and their actions carefully studied. It was found that the traditional technique of a straight arm pull was not as efficient as a curved arm pull technique that created lift forces.[7]

LIFESPAN AND CULTURAL PERSPECTIVES: Biomechanics

- How can shoes be better designed to reduce the chances of people with diabetes experiencing ulcerations on their feet?
- Which type of exercise would be most effective in reducing falls in individuals over the age of 70?
- What is the optimum design of a snowboard?
- How does an individual's posture when using exercise equipment (stepper, weights, etc.) influence gains achieved from exercise?
- How do the performance patterns of elite divers differ from the 3-meter board to the 10-meter platform?
- How can a sport biomechanist use computer-enhanced images to improve the performance of an age group swimmer?
- How does an individual's gait change when using a brace for a torn anterior cruciate ligament? Which type of brace is most effective?

At the time of this research, it was thought that the lift forces created by the curved arm pull were essential for creating propulsion and optimizing swim technique. As research in swimming continued, further studies revealed that a curved arm pull is advantageous, but that the optimization of drag forces during the pull due to the curved path is more important than the creation of lift forces for creating propulsion.[8] Currently scientists are studying the creation of vortices in the water by elite swimmers and how the timing, shape, and placement of these vortices are indicative of efficient swimming strokes.[8] Exciting new advances in swimming technique and technology are inevitable as scientists and coaches continue to increase their understanding of propulsion in swimming.

Innovations by athletes have also advanced biomechanics research. Athletes have created new techniques that have led to higher levels of performance, for example, in high jumping and tennis. Until the late 1960s, high jumpers approached the bar from an angle, thrust an arm and a leg up and over, then executed a kick, and the body "rolled" over the bar. In 1968, high jumper Dick Fosbury, utilizing his unorthodox flop style of jumping, won the gold medal at the Olympic Games in Mexico. The "Fosbury Flop" style of jumping used a curved approach to the bar with the jumper

going over backward in a twisting lay-back of the body. Within 10 years, the traditional, long-used roll style of jumping was replaced by the flop style and records soared to new heights. Similarly, as a young tennis player, Chris Evert used a two-handed backhand drive to return the ball over the net. Now it is common to see players use this stroke, which gives greater control and speed than the traditional one-handed backhand stroke.

Some other professionals within the field of physical education, physical science, and sport who use the principles of biomechanics to improve an individual's movements and skill performance are adapted physical educators, athletic trainers, and exercise leaders. Knowledge of kinesiology and biomechanics helps these professionals design and conduct programs to enhance individual movement skills.

There are many specialized areas of study within biomechanics. Developmental biomechanics focuses on studying movement patterns and how they change across the lifespan, from infancy to old age and with people with disabilities. Especially with the aged, an understanding of the biomechanical principles involved in activities of daily living, such as walking, climbing stairs, lifting, and carrying, is important in designing activities to enable individuals to remain independent and able to care for their needs. For example, researchers are studying individuals with osteoarthritis to identify risk factors for developing this degenerative disease, which affects over 21 million Americans, predominantly those over the age of 65. Results from current research suggest that individuals with knee osteoarthritis often have altered gait biomechanics.[9–12] It is not yet known if the atypical gait patterns predispose individuals to knee osteoarthritis or if these patterns develop over the course of the disease, but researchers continue to make progress toward understanding the cause and developing preventative guidelines for this debilitating disease.[10–12]

The biomechanics of exercise is another specialized area of study. Exercise should be based on both physiological and biomechanical principles. An understanding of the biomechanics of exercise can help maximize the benefits of exercise and reduce the chances of injury. Physical educators, exercise scientists, and sport leaders can use biomechanical principles of exercise to make sure individuals are performing the exercise correctly and achieving maximum benefits. For example, to reduce the load on the knee, people are commonly taught to keep their shins vertical and not let the knees go in front of the toes when performing squats. While keeping the shins vertical does reduce the torque on the knee by about 25%, as compared with unrestricted motion during a squat, the torque on the hip has been shown to increase almost tenfold when the shins are kept vertical.[13] This transfer of torque to the hips from the knees may place unsafe forces on the hip and low back region.[13] Physical educators, exercise scientists, and sport leaders should stay abreast of current research in strength training techniques to prevent unnecessary injuries and optimize training benefits.

Rehabilitation biomechanics is the study of the movement patterns of people who are injured or who have a disability. This helps professionals understand how the injury or disability has altered the normal movement pattern of individuals. This information is then used to design programs to help individuals move optimally within their constraints and to restore normal function when possible. Athletes recovering from anterior cruciate ligament (ACL) repair surgery have benefited from biomechanical research on the effectiveness of closed versus open chain exercises during ACL rehabilitation. Open chain exercises are typically non-weight-bearing exercises where the hand or foot is free to move. An example is a leg curl. Closed chain exercises are usually weight-bearing exercises in which the hand or foot is fixed and remains in contact with the resistance, such as the ground. An example is a squat. Over the last decade rehabilitation exercises for ACL repair have utilized predominantly closed chain exercises due to less stress on the ACL graft.[14] Recent studies have suggested that implementing open chain exercises can improve knee stability and improve an athlete's chances of returning to competition without imposing dangerous loads on the ACL graft during rehabilitation.[15]

Equipment design is a growing area of biomechanics. Changes in equipment can lead to dramatic increases in performance. The speed skating event at the 1998 Nagano Olympics served as a showcase for new technology: the clap skate. The Dutch-invented clap skate, with its hinged blade, redefined record times. With conventional skates, the skater uses the quadriceps, not the calf muscles, and pushes through the back side of the skate. The clap skates use a hinge-and-spring mechanism to attach the front of the skate boot to the blade. The heel is not attached to the blade; thus when the foot is raised above the ice, the blade snaps back to the heel, making the characteristic clapping noise. The clap skate allows the skater to use the calf muscles, making the push more powerful. The blade also remains on the ice for a longer time, allowing for a longer stride and greater speed.

Biomechanists are also involved in the testing of new fabrics, evaluating them in terms of their potential to contribute to performance. New fabrics, developed after years of testing, help competitors in several different sports decrease their times by reducing water or air resistance. In the 2000 Olympic Games in Sydney, swimmers wore new bodysuits created out of a special material that offered less resistance through the water than human

Physical education, exercise science, and sport professionals, when helping individuals perform exercises, should make sure that each movement is performed correctly and conforms to accepted biomechanical principles. This is important for safety reasons as well as to help ensure that the individual achieves the desired benefits.

skin. Modeled on a shark's skin, Speedo's Fastskin material helped competitors shave seconds off their times, critical in a sport where the difference between winning and finishing second can be as little as one-hundredth of a second.[16] In the 2002 Winter Olympic Games, similar "speed suits" were worn by speed skaters. Nike's Swift Skin and Descente Vortex suits, along with the accompanying hoods, gloves, and skate covers, allowed skaters to cover their body from head to foot in a material designed to decrease air resistance.[16] Extensive testing went into the development of these fabrics, designed to decrease friction and, consequently, improve performance. Biomechanists and other sport scientists continually work to modify textiles and designs in hopes of greater performances. Prior to the 2008 Olympics in Beijing, Speedo introduced the LZRRacer suit, which was even more technologically sophisticated than the Fastskin suit. Constructed from elastane and nylon with polyurethane panels, the suit repels water, and its tight fit compresses the swimmer's body.[17] The suit uses core stabilization technology to help swimmers maintain a more hydrodynamic body position even while fatigued and allows better oxygen flow to the muscles.[18] Its design reduces drag significantly, helping LZR-clad swimmers achieve better times. Twenty-nine of the 32 Olympic gold medal winners wore the LZR suit.[18] Swimmers broke 25 world records at the Olympics; 23 of them were broken by swimmers competing in the LZR suit.[19] Critics termed these new suits and others like them "technological doping," and swimming's international governing body, FINA, issued new regulations in 2010 regarding swimsuit manufacturing.[19]

Biomechanists working in the area of equipment design have also contributed to great changes in sport techniques, higher levels of performance, reduction of injury, and increased safety. The design of running shoes has changed radically since the early 1970s. More cushioning, greater attention given to injury prevention, establishment of a greater variety of sizes, and designs to fit specific purposes (e.g., running, cross-training, basketball) are reflected in athletic shoes today. Athletic shoes are designed today to accommodate users' special needs, such as pronation, and to enhance comfort and performance. Greater attention has also been given to the needs of women. The sporting goods industry since the mid-1980s has been building equipment, such as skis and running shoes, specifically for women, as opposed to simply manufacturing scaled-down versions of the men's models. An understanding of the way the body works, knowledge of the demands of the sport, and the ability to apply biomechanical principles are important in equipment design.

The application of biomechanical principles is not limited to the realm of physical education, exercise science, and sport. Biomechanists working in industry use this information to ensure safe working conditions for and efficient performance from the workers. In medicine, knowledge from biomechanics can be used by orthopedists to evaluate how pathological conditions affect movement or to assess the suitability of prosthetic devices for patients. As the field of biomechanics continues to expand, its contribution to our understanding of human movement will become even more significant.

Major Areas of Study

Biomechanics is concerned with two major areas of study. The first area is biological in nature, as implied in the term *biomechanics.* Motion or movement involves biological aspects of the human body, including the skeletal and muscular systems. For example, bones, muscles, and nerves work together in producing motion. A muscle receives

a signal from a nerve, causing a contraction. The muscle contraction creates force which acts on a bone. The bone works as a lever, amplifying motion and allowing us to perform motions such as walking, throwing, and jumping. It is not possible to understand motor skill development without first knowing about biological aspects underlying human movement, such as joint action, anatomical structures, and muscular forces.

The second major area of study in biomechanics relates to mechanics. This area of study is important because it utilizes the laws and principles of Newtonian mechanics and applies them to human motion and movement. Biomechanics is also concerned with object motion. The study of mechanics includes *statics,* or the study of factors relating to nonmoving systems, such as those that contribute to stability and balance. It also includes *dynamics,* or the study of mechanical factors that relate to systems in motion. In turn, dynamics can involve a *kinematic* or *kinetic* approach. Kinematics is concerned with describing motion and includes the study of time and space factors in motion such as velocity and acceleration. Kinetics is concerned with understanding the cause of motion and includes the study of forces such as gravity and muscles that act on a system.

Research in biomechanics is concerned with studying movement and factors that influence performance. The kinds of questions that may be studied are listed below:

- How do running motions change as children develop?
- How do forces summate to produce maximum power in the tennis serve?
- What are the movement patterns of world-class hurdlers?
- How can athletic shoes be designed to reduce injuries on artificial turf?
- What is the wrist action of elite wheelchair marathon athletes?
- What is the optimal design of the javelin?
- What are the critical performance elements of throwing? Of various fundamental motor skills?

Of various sport skills? What are the common errors associated with the performance of these skills, and how can they best be remediated? How do the mechanics of these fundamental motor skills change with age?

- Which techniques are best for increasing the range of motion after reconstructive surgery of the shoulder?
- What is the best body position for swimming the butterfly stroke?
- Is a specific brand of rowing ergometer safe to use? Can individuals of all fitness levels effectively use this piece of fitness equipment? Are the benefits claimed by the manufacturer for its use accurate?

These are only a few of the questions that can be addressed through biomechanical research techniques. In answering these questions, researchers measure such factors as joint angles and muscle activity, force production, and linear and angular acceleration. The next section presents selected biomechanical terms.

SELECTED BIOMECHANICAL TERMS RELATED TO HUMAN MOTION

The field of biomechanics has a specialized scientific vocabulary that describes the relationship between force and motion. As previously defined, kinematics is concerned with understanding the spatial and temporal characteristics of human movement, that is, the direction of the motion and the time involved in executing the motion. Important terms related to kinematics include *velocity, acceleration, angular velocity,* and *angular acceleration.* Understanding the relationship between linear and angular motions is also a very important part of kinematics. Kinetics is concerned with the forces that cause, modify, or inhibit motion. Terms related to kinetics are *mass, force, pressure, gravity, friction, work, power, energy,* and *torque.* (See Table 6-1.)

Velocity refers to the speed and direction of a body and involves the change of position of a body per unit of time. Because bodies in motion are continually changing position, the degree to

TABLE 6-1	**Selected Biomechanical Terms**

Kinematics—study of space and time factors in motion, such as velocity and acceleration
Kinetics—study of forces that act on a system, such as gravity and muscles
Velocity—change in the speed or direction of a body per unit of time
Acceleration—change in velocity
Angular velocity—angle that is rotated in a given unit of time
Angular acceleration—change in angular velocity for a given unit of time
Mass—amount of matter possessed by an object
Force—any action that changes or tends to change the motion of an object; described in terms of magnitude and direction
Pressure—ratio of force to the area over which the force is applied
Gravity—force that accelerates all objects vertically toward the center of the earth
Center of gravity—point at which all of an object's mass is balanced at a specific moment
Friction—force that occurs when surfaces come in contact with each other
Work—force that is applied to a body through a distance and in the direction of the force
Power—amount of work accomplished in one unit of time
Energy—capacity of a body to perform work
Torque—twisting, turning, or rotary force applied to the production of angular acceleration

which the body's position changes within a definite time span is measured to determine its velocity. For example, the velocity of a baseball from the time it leaves the pitcher's hand to the time it arrives in the catcher's glove can be measured in this manner.

Acceleration refers to the change in velocity involving speed or direction of a moving body. An individual playing basketball, for example, can add positive acceleration when dribbling toward the basket on a fast break, or the player can change pace and slow down (decelerate) to permit another player to screen for him or her.

Angular velocity is the angle that is rotated in a given unit of time. *Angular acceleration* refers to the change of angular velocity for a unit of time. For example, when a bowling ball is rolled down a lane, its angular velocity can be computed mathematically in terms of revolutions per second. The angular acceleration, on the other hand, occurs after the bowling ball is released and the ball actually starts rolling, instead of sliding, which occurs immediately on release.

The relationship between linear and angular motions of body parts should be understood. Northrip, Logan, and McKinney cite the following examples: (1) a throwing motion involves angular velocity of the wrist joint, which helps to determine throwing speed; (2) kicking a football involves the angular velocity of the kicker's ankle joint, which helps to determine kicking performance.[20] The final linear velocity that results in both cases is achieved as the sum of many angular motions at the body joints. Because most body movements are rotational movements at the body's joints, to achieve the best results in skill performance, it is necessary to integrate linear and angular motions.

Mass is the amount of matter possessed by an object. Mass is a measure of the object's inertia, that is, the resistance of the object to efforts made to move it and, once it has begun to move, to change its motion. The mass of an object influences the amount of force needed to produce acceleration. The greater the mass, the larger the force needed. For example, in track and field, a larger force would be needed to accelerate a 16-pound shot (mass = 7.27 kilograms) than a 12-pound shot (mass = 5.45 kilograms).

Force is any action that changes or tends to change the motion of an object. Forces have both a magnitude (i.e., size) and a direction. Forces on the body can occur internally, such as when a muscle contracts and exerts forces on the bone to which it is attached. External forces such as gravity also can act on the body.

Pressure refers to the ratio of force to the area over which the force is applied. For example, 16-ounce boxing gloves will distribute a given force over a larger surface area than 12-ounce boxing gloves, thus reducing pressure. In this case, distributing the pressure will ensure less chance of injury from blows when the 16-ounce gloves are used.

Gravity is a natural force that pulls all objects toward the center of the earth. An important feature of gravitational pull is that it always occurs through the center of mass of an object. In the human body, the center of mass is known as the *center of gravity*. The center of gravity is the point at which all of the body's mass seems to be located and the point about which an object would balance. The position of the center of gravity is constantly changing during movement. It can be either within or outside the body, depending on the shape of the body. It always shifts in the direction of movement or the additional weight. When human beings stand erect with their hands at their sides, the center of gravity is located at the level of the hips. Athletes can use their knowledge about the center of gravity to better their skills. For example, the basketball player during a jump ball swings both arms forward and upward to assist in gaining height. Once in the air, the player allows one arm to drop to his or her side and strives to get maximum reach with the other arm. By dropping one arm to the side, the player can reach farther beyond the center of gravity than with two arms overhead.

Friction is a force that occurs when surfaces come in contact and results when the surfaces move past each other. The roughness of the surfaces and the amount of force pressing them together influence the amount of friction. The rougher the surface and the greater the force, the greater the magnitude of friction. Friction plays an important role in traction. Traction is important to athletes. The ability of athletes to make quick turns, change direction rapidly, stop, and propel themselves forward without losing footing depends on having the right amount of traction.[20] Shoe manufacturers design shoes to provide athletes with the right amount of traction for the specific sport, playing surface, and weather conditions.[20] Reduction of friction is important in sports such as skating and skiing, where the ability to glide over ice and snow is critical to performance.[20]

Understanding the principles of biomechanics can assist gymnasts in improving their performance.

Work refers to the force that is applied to a body through a distance and in the direction of the force. An individual who bench-presses 240 pounds through 2 feet is doing work. The direction of the motion is the same as the direction of the force, and therefore the total amount of work is figured by multiplying 240 pounds by 2 feet, which equals 480 foot-pounds of work for each repetition.

Power is the amount of work accomplished in one unit of time. For example, a person performs a certain task, such as running, and exerts a certain amount of horsepower to perform the task in a given amount of time. In order to exert twice as much horsepower, the runner would have to perform the same task and accomplish the same amount of work (i.e., run the same distance) in half the amount of time.

Energy relates to the capacity of a body to perform work. Two types of energy used in biomechanics are (1) kinetic energy, the energy a body has because it is moving (such as a skier whose weight and velocity determine kinetic energy); and (2) potential energy, the energy that accrues as a result of the position that a body occupies relative to the earth's surface. The weight of the body and its height above the surface are used to determine potential energy. For example, a diver at the peak of a dive has the capacity to do work because of his or her position relative to the earth's surface. When he or she falls toward the water, the weight of the body does work equal to its magnitude times the distance the body moves in the direction of force.

Torque represents a twisting, turning, or rotary force related to the production of angular acceleration and is contrasted with the force necessary to produce linear acceleration. Torque can also be produced as a result of the rotation of a body or body part. For example, supination and pronation of the radioulnar joint can produce torque. The production of torque is essential in gymnastics because of the many movements required in routines that use apparatus such as the high bar, parallel bars, uneven parallel bars, and rings.

MECHANICAL PRINCIPLES AND CONCEPTS RELATED TO MOVEMENT

Movements are governed by mechanical principles. Biomechanists use these principles in the analysis of movement. To illustrate some mechanical principles, selected principles and concepts relating to stability, motion, leverage, and force are presented in this section.

Stability

Stability is an important factor in all movement skills. It is related to equilibrium and balance. When all the forces acting on the body are counterbalanced by equal and opposite forces so that the sum of the forces equals zero, equilibrium is maintained. A state of equilibrium occurs when the body's center of gravity is over its base of support and the line of gravity (a line drawn from the center of the gravity to the center of the earth) falls within the base. The base of support of the body is the area outlined when all the points in contact with the ground are connected. The greater the body surface in contact with the ground, the larger the base of support. Thus, a sitting position has a larger base of support than a standing position. A stance that places four points of the body in contact with the ground, rather than just two points as in standing, typically increases the base of support.

Stability is the body's ability to return to a position of equilibrium after it has been displaced. The greater the body's stability, the more difficult it is to affect its equilibrium.

Static equilibrium occurs when the center of gravity is in a stable position (e.g., when one is sitting or performing a handstand in gymnastics). Dynamic equilibrium is a state in which the center of gravity is in motion (e.g., when one is running or performing a cartwheel in gymnastics). In sport and movement terminology, stability is often referred to as balance. The body's ability to maintain stability or balance is governed by three primary principles.

Principle

The lower the center of gravity is to the base of support, the greater the stability. When performing activities that require stability, individuals should lower their center of gravity. In running, for example, individuals can stop more efficiently and quickly if they bend their knees, thereby lowering the center of gravity, and place their feet in a forward stride position. Other examples include a wrestler taking a semicrouched position and a football lineman assuming a three-point stance.

Principle

The nearer the center of gravity is to the center of the base of support, the more stable the body. When the center of gravity extends beyond the boundaries of the base of support, balance is lost. Keeping the body's weight centered over the base of support helps promote stability. However, in activities where the objective is to move quickly in one direction, shifting the weight in the direction of the movement can aid performance. For example, in starting a sprint race, the runners will lean forward to get out of the starting blocks quickly.

Tai Chi has been found to improve balance in the elderly. The wide base of support offers the instructor stability as she leads the class through the movement.

Some activities, such as walking on a balance beam, require a small base of support. It is very easy to lose one's balance in these types of activities. When balance is lost while performing on the balance beam, the arm or leg on the opposite side from which the person is leaning is raised to shift the center of gravity back toward the base of support.

Principle

The wider the base of support is, the greater the stability.   Widening the base of support helps achieve greater stability. When standing, for example, spreading the feet in the direction of movement adds stability. For activities in which a stance is required, using both hands and feet will create the widest base.

To increase stability in situations when receiving or applying force, the direction of the force must be considered. When receiving either a fast-moving object or a heavy force, widen the base of support in the direction from which the force is coming. When applying a force, widen the base in the direction from which the force is to be applied.

Motion

Motion implies movement. Motion can be classified as linear or rotary; the human body usually employs a combination of both. The rotary action of the legs used to propel the body in a linear direction is an example.

DID YOU KNOW?

1. Softball batters generally have about two one-hundredths of a second less to decide to swing at a fast ball than baseball players. Top pitch speeds (in mph) in softball reach the low 70s, while top speeds in baseball are in the high 90s. However, since the distance to the plate is shorter in softball, at these speeds softball batters have about 0.417 seconds before the ball reaches the plate, while baseball players have about 0.437 seconds.
2. The title of fastest man or woman in the world goes to the world record holder in the 100-meter dash. Currently, for men, Usain Bolt holds that honor with a time of 9.57 seconds and an average speed of 23.8 mph. Florence Griffith Joyner holds the women's title at 10.49 seconds, running an average speed of 21.3 mph. These are just their average speeds; sprinters reach top speeds above 25 mph.
3. The fastest recorded spin in figure skating is 240 rpm, done by Ronald Robertson. That is four revolutions per second. Nathalie Krieg holds the record for longest spin, spinning for 3 minutes and 20 seconds.
4. The current record holder in heavy weight lifting, Hossein Rezazadeh, lifted 263 kilograms (579 pounds) in the clean and jerk. He is 6 feet 1 and weighs 345 pounds. While that is truly impressive, Halil Mutlu, known as the "Little Dynamo" and coming in at 123 pounds and 4 feet 1 inch tall, holds the world record in the 56-kilogram class with a clean and jerk of 168 kilograms (370 pounds). He lifted three times his body weight!
5. Ski jumpers reach speeds in excess of 60 mph before they leave the ramp and fly through the air for 5 seconds. On a "large hill" a ski jumper will start on top of a ramp which is typically over 33 meters (436 feet) above the landing area at the bottom of the hill. The skier glides down this 100 meters (320 ft) ramp before taking off and flying over 145 meters (475 feet) in the air—farther than the length of a football field.

Linear Motion

Linear motion refers to movement in a straight line and from one point to another. In running, for example, the body should be kept on a straight line from start to finish. Also, the foot and arm movements should be back and forth in straight lines rather than from side to side across the body.

Rotary Motion

Rotary motion consists of movement of a body about a center of rotation, called the axis. In most human movements, rotary motion is converted into linear motion. Rotary motion is increased when the radius of rotation is shortened. Conversely, rotary motion is decreased when the radius of rotation is increased. Examples include tucking the head when performing tumbling stunts, to increase the rotation of the body, and holding the arms out when executing a turn on the toes on ice, to slow the body.

To have motion, the equilibrium of a body must be destroyed or upset. Equilibrium is upset when the forces acting on a body become unbalanced. A force is required to start a body in motion, to slow it down, to stop it, to change the direction of its motion, or to make it move faster. Everything that moves is governed by the laws of motion formulated by Sir Isaac Newton. These laws describe how things move and make it possible to predict the motion of an object.

Newton's First Law

The law of inertia states that a body at rest will remain at rest and a body in motion will remain in motion at the same speed and in the same direction unless acted on by some outside force.

For a movement to occur, a force must act on a body sufficiently to overcome that object's inertia. If the applied force is less than the resistance offered by the object, motion will not occur.

Concepts

1. Once an object is in motion, it will take less force to maintain its speed and direction (i.e., momentum). For example, it takes an individual more effort to start pedaling a bicycle to get it under way than it does to maintain speed once the bicycle is moving.

2. The heavier the object and the faster it is moving, the more force that is required to overcome its moving inertia or to absorb its momentum. In football, an opponent will have to exert more force to stop a massive, fast-moving lineman than to stop the lighter-weight and slower-moving quarterback.

Newton's Second Law

The law of acceleration states that a change in velocity (i.e., acceleration) of an object is directly proportional to the force producing it and inversely proportional to the object's mass.

If two unequal forces are applied to objects of equal mass, the object that has the greater force applied will move faster. Conversely, if two equal forces are applied to objects of different masses, the smaller mass will travel at the faster speed.

For example, in shot putting, the athlete who is stronger and thus able to expend more force will toss the 12-pound shot farther than an athlete who possesses less strength. Also, an athlete will find more force is needed to propel a 16-pound shot than a 12-pound shot.

Concepts

1. The heavier the object, the more force needed to speed it up (positive acceleration) or slow it down (negative acceleration).

2. An increase in speed is proportional to the amount of force that is applied; the greater the amount of force that is imparted to an object, the greater the speed with which that object will travel.

3. Momentum is a measure of both speed and mass. If the same amount of force is exerted for the same length of time on two bodies of different mass, greater acceleration will be produced in the less massive object. If the two objects are propelled at the same speed, the more massive object will have greater momentum once inertia is overcome and will exert a greater force than the less massive object on something that it contacts.

Newton's Third Law

The law of action and reaction states that for every action there is an equal and opposite reaction.

Bouncing on a trampoline and springing from a diving board are examples of the law of action and reaction. The more force one exerts on the downward bounce, the higher the bounce or spring into the air. The thrust against the water in swimming is another example of an equal and opposite reaction—the water pushes the swimmer forward with a force equal to the force exerted by the swimmer on the backward thrust of the strokes.

Concept

1. Whenever one object moves, another object moves too and in the opposite direction. When you push something, it pushes back; when you pull on something, it pulls back.

Leverage

Efficient body movement is made possible through a system of levers. A lever is a mechanical device used to produce a turning motion about a fixed point, called an *axis*. A lever consists of a fulcrum (the center or axis of rotation), a force arm (the distance from the fulcrum to the point of application of force), and a weight or resistance arm (the distance from the fulcrum to the weight on which the force is acting). The bones of the body act as levers, the joints act as the fulcrums, and the force to move the bone or lever about the joint or fulcrum is produced by the contraction of the muscles.

Three types of levers are determined by the relationship of the fulcrum (axis), the weight, and the point of application of force. In a *first-class lever* the fulcrum is located between the weight and point of application of force. In a *second-class lever* the weight is between the fulcrum and the force. In a *third-class lever* the force is between the fulcrum and the weight. (See Figure 6-1.)

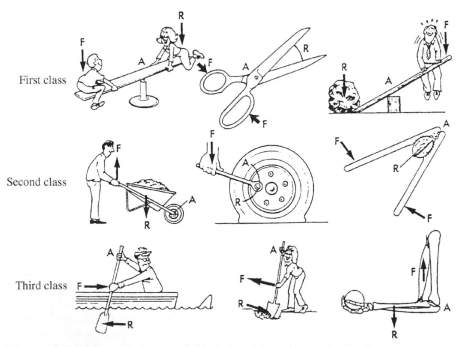

Figure 6-1   First-, second-, and third-class levers (A = axis, F = force, R = resistance).

Levers enable one to gain a mechanical advantage by producing either strength or range of motion and speed. First-class levers may produce both strength and speed, unless the fulcrum is in the middle of the force and weight, which produces a balanced condition. Second-class levers produce force, and third-class levers favor range of motion and speed. The movements of the body are produced mostly through third-class levers. In third-class levers, the point of application of the force (produced by the muscles) is located between the fulcrum (the joint) and the resistance (the object to be moved).

The length of the force arm is the key to producing either force or range of motion and speed. If great force is desired, the force arm should be as long as possible. If range of motion and great speed are desired, the force arm should be shortened. The internal levers of the body cannot be controlled in regard to the length of the force arm. However, when using implements such as bats and racquets, long force arms can be created by holding the implement near the end, thereby producing greater force. If a person were interested in achieving greater speed to swing a bat, he or she would "choke up" on the bat to reduce the force arm. When using an implement to produce greater force or speed, the size and the length of the implement must match the strength of the person who is handling the implement.

Concepts

1. Levers are used to gain a mechanical advantage by producing either speed or force.
2. Greater speed is produced by lengthening the resistance arm, and greater force is produced by lengthening the force arm.

Force

Force is the effect that one body has on another. It is invisible, but it is always present when motion occurs. It should be pointed out, however, that there can be force without motion. An example of a force in which no motion is evident is the push against a wall by a person. The wall does

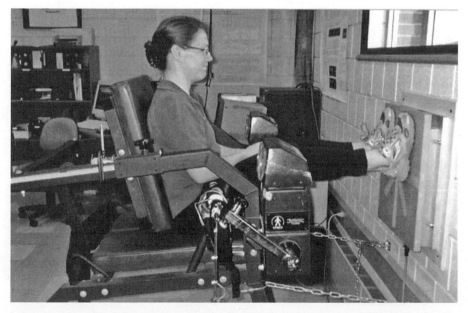

Leg press strength is being measured with a force plate attached to a wall. The force plate is connected to a computer where peak force and rate of force developed are displayed.

not move, although great force might be exerted. Another example occurs when two arm wrestlers are pushing against each other with equal force and their arms remain relatively motionless.

Professionals should be aware of the principles relating to the production, application, and absorption of force when they teach movement activities.

Production of Force

Body force is produced by the actions of muscles. The stronger the muscles, the more force the body is capable of producing. However, the force of the muscle group or groups must be applied in the same direction and in proper sequence to realize the greatest force. In the high jump, for example, the body should be lowered on the last step before the jump. This lowering of the body will enable the jumper to contract the muscles of the thigh, which are the strongest of the body. The upward movement of the arms will give added force to the jump when coordinated with the upward push of the legs. It should be remembered that the principles of stability and the laws of motion, must be observed in the performance of the high jump if the greatest height is to be attained.

Force also must be generated to propel objects. The same principles apply as mentioned above. In the swing of a softball bat, the application of force is possible because of the production of force by different muscle groups in a coordinated manner. For maximum force, the body should be rotated at the hips, shoulders, arms, and hands in a sequential order. The summation of these forces will produce the greatest momentum. A follow-through is necessary both to avoid jerky movements, decelerating prior to contact, and to reduce the possibility of injury to the muscles or tendons.

Application of Force

The force of an object is most effective when it is applied in the direction that the object is to travel. Many activities in sport involve the projection of the body or another type of object into the air. To project an object or the body forward most efficiently, the force should be applied through the center of mass of the object and in a forward direction. To move the body upward, the body should

Absorption of force is important in catching objects. The catcher's mitt, which distributes the force over a greater area, and the action of giving with the catch help absorb the force of the pitched ball.

Force production is a critical component in many sports. such as shot putting.

be rigid and all the force directed upward through the center of the body. The example of the vertical jump will illustrate this principle. Force from the legs must be applied to the ground such that the upward reaction force from the ground is directed through the center of the body. If the jumper leans forward or sideways when pushing off from the ground, the force will cause rotation and forward or sideways motion instead of purely vertical motion, and the jumper will not jump as high.

When someone throws an object, the following three main factors are of concern: (1) the speed of the throw, (2) the distance of the throw, and (3) the direction that the object will travel.

The speed of the throw depends on the speed of the hand at the moment of release of the object. The speed of the arm can be increased by lengthening it to its fullest, rotating the body, shifting the weight properly, and taking a step in the direction of the throw. These movements must be done in a continuous motion to maintain momentum. If an implement such as a bat or paddle is used, it becomes an extension of the arm; therefore, the same principle applies. The implement should be held as close to the handle end as possible to create a longer arm. This will enable the person to generate more speed.

The distance of the throw will be affected by the pull of gravity and air resistance. The distance that an object will travel, therefore, depends on the angle of release in addition to the force imparted in the throw. The pull of gravity and air resistance will affect thrown objects less if they are released at an angle of approximately 45 degrees. This represents a compromise between releasing an object at a large angle and having it remain in the air but not go very far because of wind resistance, and releasing the object at a smaller angle where the pull of gravity will keep it from traveling very far.

The direction or accuracy of the throw depends on the point of release of the object. The release must be a point in the arc of the arm at which the object is tangent to the target. To better achieve the desired angle of release, the throwing arm should be moved in a flatter arc at the time of release. In making the overhand throw in softball, for example, the hand should travel in the straightest line possible toward the target, on both the backswing and the follow-through.

In addition to gravity and air resistance, the flight of thrown and batted objects is also affected by the spin of the object. The object will travel in the direction of the spin.

Absorption of Force

Many instances occur when persons must receive or absorb force. Examples include absorbing the force of a thrown object, as in catching a football or softball, landing after a jump, and heading a soccer ball. The impact of the force should be gradually reduced, and it should be spread over as large an area as possible. Therefore, when someone catches a ball, the arms should be extended to meet the ball. On contact, the hand and arms should give with the catch. When landing from a jump, the person should bend the hips, knees, and ankles to gradually reduce the kinetic energy of the jump, thereby reducing the momentum. The feet must also be spread slightly to create a larger area of impact (base).

Concepts

1. The more muscles that are used, the greater the force that is produced (provided, of course, that they are the same size muscles).
2. The more elasticity or stretch a muscle is capable of, the more force it can supply. Each working muscle should be stretched fully to produce the greatest force.
3. When objects are moved, the weight of the objects should be pushed or pulled through the center and in the direction that they are to be moved.
4. When heavy objects are moved or thrown, the force of the muscles should be used in a sequential manner. For example, the order in throwing should be trunk rotation, shoulder, upper arm, lower arm, hand, and fingers.
5. When body parts (arms and legs) or implements such as bats and paddles are used, they should be extended completely when making contact with an object to be propelled.

This creates a long movement arm, thereby creating the greatest force; the implements should be gripped at the end.

6. When receiving or absorbing the force of a thrown object (as in catching a ball), a fall, or a kick, the largest possible area should be used to absorb the force. For example, the student should use two hands to catch a hard-thrown ball; more area will be available to absorb the force of the ball.

7. The absorption of force should be spread out as long as possible by recoiling or giving at the joints involved in the movement.

To analyze an individual's motor performance, physical education, exercise science, and sport professionals need to be cognizant of the principles governing movement. Selected principles pertaining to stability, motion, leverage, and force were discussed in this section. Professionals are also concerned with such concepts as friction, aerodynamics, hydrodynamics, and ball spin and rebound in the evaluation of performance. An understanding of both biomechanics and kinesiology provides the professional with a foundation for understanding and analyzing human movement.

BIOMECHANICAL ANALYSIS

Various instruments and techniques are used by biomechanists to study and analyze motion. During the past 15 years, improvements in instrumentation coupled with advances in computers and microchip technology have greatly assisted biomechanists in their endeavors. Additionally, the development of better and more creative methods of using these instruments has greatly enhanced the understanding of human movement and the ability to improve performance.[21] These tools include computers, anthropometry, timing devices, cinematography, videography, electrogoniometry, electromyography, dynamography, telemetry, and stroboscopy. Sometimes researchers use wind tunnels. These tools, as well as visual observation, can be used to perform quantitative and qualitative analysis of human movement.

Instruments and Techniques

Computers play an important role in biomechanical research. Biomechanical analysis requires dealing with prodigious amounts of data. The use of computers in dealing with such data is a necessity. Additionally, much of the instrumentation used in biomechanical research is linked to a computer. Much of the analysis of information can be performed online so that the results can be available almost instantly.

Computers can also be used to simulate movements. Simulation requires the use of mathematical formulas to develop models of a specific movement. Then, this computer model can be used to assist biomechanists in determining the effects of certain modifications in the movement or certain variables on performance. For example, simulation can address such questions as, What is the effect of altering the takeoff position of a dive on the subsequent performance? Or, How does air resistance affect a skier's performance? This approach helps researchers determine how a performance can be improved. Comparisons of the optimal or ideal performance and an individual's actual performance are enhanced through the use of computer technology. The computer is used to generate graphic representations of the ideal performance and the actual performance. The drawing of the actual performance is compiled from analysis of the films of the performer. These graphic representations of the ideal performance and an individual's actual performance can then be compared. This helps to detect errors and identify strategies to improve performance. Computers offer biomechanists tremendous assistance in understanding human movements.

Motion capture and high-speed imaging are two of the basic tools employed in biomechanical research. Sophisticated cameras are used to capture an individual's performance on a computer. These high-speed cameras capture details of movements that may escape the unaided eye of the professional observing the performer's movements. It is possible to measure such things as the speed, angle, range, and sequence of moving

COACHES TURN TO TECHNOLOGY

In the digital era, as video cameras have become smaller, cheaper, and easier to use, many coaches and trainers are adding digital video to their coaching methods. Using any digital camcorder (though camcorders that have a manual shutter and at least a 10x zoom are best for sports), coaches can take video clips of their athletes and break down the skill in slow motion, view the skill side by side with another athlete, or even compare different views of a skill, all using readily available sports analysis software. Coaches can also add audio or text comments and highlight specific techniques using drawing tools. Many of the software packages are available for less than $500, making this an affordable tool that requires no special training. For information on some of the different sports analysis software programs, try the following websites: www.analysisprogram.com, www.dartfish.com, www.elitesportsanalysis.com, www.sportscad.com, www.motioncoach.com, and www.sportsmotion.com.

Below is an example analysis of a golf swing using an off-the-shelf camcorder and simple sports analysis software program. At set up (picture A), the position of the golfer's head and body is highlighted. Notice that the golfer sets up with the ball more toward his front foot. During the backswing (picture B), the golfer's hips move backward as he rotates his upper body back. At the top of the backswing (picture C), the hips have already started moving forward and the club is cocked to about 90 degrees. During the downswing (picture D), the golfer's hips continue to move forward; the head stays down and ends up right at the setup position. In this swing the golfer's wrist starts to break a little early. Just prior to contact (picture E), the golfer has continued to drive his hips forward, but the head and shoulders remain in the same position as setup.

segments. Motion capture provides graphic representations of the movement which can be completed in real time, while the performance is taking place, or postcapture via computer processing. Completion of mathematical calculations based on information provided from the computer model is an essential part of movement analysis. This process is greatly speeded and simplified through the use of computers. Motion capture is used not only for biomechanical analysis but also by the motion picture and video game industries

for computer animation. High-speed imaging utilizes sophisticated cameras to capture performances either on digital media such as DVDs and memory cards or directly to a computer hard drive. Immediate feedback is available to the performer, coach, or practitioner via a computer or video monitor with slow: motion and stop-action capabilities to aid in the study of the performance.

Stroboscopy is a an older photographic technique that can still be used today to study human movement. This technique allows filming to take place against a darkened background, with light flashed onto the subject being filmed. The total movement is recorded on a single frame of film as a sequence of images. For example, with this technique it is possible to take a picture of the total forehand stroke in tennis, which shows the path of the various body segments in the total execution of the stroke. This facilitates the analysis of the individual's movements. With this technique, one person's execution of a movement skill (e.g., the forehand tennis stroke or the wrist action used) can be compared with that of another person or the ideal performance.

Videography is the use of video systems to record an individual's performance. Video systems consist of a video camera, recorder, and playback unit. Over the last decade almost all video equipment has become digital, which has greatly increased the ease of using video for performance evaluation. Unlike motion capture systems, video systems are relatively inexpensive, easy to use, and readily available to practitioners. The ability to directly play back what has been recorded allows for immediate viewing by the analyst and prompt

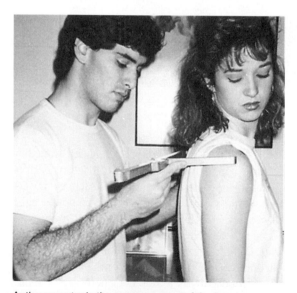

Anthropometry is the measurement of the human body. Various devices are used to provide information about the body and its segments.

feedback to the performer. This is one of the most inexpensive high-technology systems for the analysis of movement. Advances in technology have led to better-quality cameras, sophisticated playback capabilities that yield greater clarity of still and stop-action images, and user-friendly software packages for simple and inexpensive video analysis of human movement.

Anthropometry is concerned with the measurement of the human body. The length, width, diameter, circumference (girth), and surface area of the body and its segments are measured. Correct identification of anatomical landmarks is crucial to obtaining accurate measurements. Information about the structure of the human body is used to calculate the forces acting on the joints of the body and the forces produced by movement. Information about the structure of an individual's body is important in developing computer models of performance.

Timing devices or chronoscopes are used to record speeds of body movements. Some types of timing devices are stopwatches, digital timers, counters, switch mats, photoelectric cells, and real-time computer clocks. The chronoscope is started at a preselected point in time, typically the initiation of a movement, and then stopped at a preselected time, such as the completion of a movement. The speed of movement is then calculated. Radar guns can also be used to provide instantaneous information about speed.

Electrogoniometry is a technique that can be used to provide information about the angles of the joint as part of a total motion pattern. Another term for an electrogoniometer is an elgon. An elgon works like a goniometer (see Chapter 7 for information about the use of goniometers to measure flexibility) but uses electrical devices such as potentiometers to measure the degrees of movement at a joint. This information can be transferred directly to a computer, recording paper, or oscilloscope. For example, this instrument would permit the study of the knee-joint action when a particular skill, such as walking or running, is executed. It can also measure range of motion, angular velocity, and acceleration. Electrogoniometry may be particularly useful when combined with electromyography.

Electromyography (EMG) is used to measure the electrical activity produced by a muscle or muscle group. When properly processed, this measurement serves as an approximate indicator of the amount of force being developed by a muscle. This provides a means to observe the involvement of a particular muscle or muscle group in a movement. Surface electrodes are placed over the muscle or muscle group, or fine wire electrodes are inserted into the muscle to be observed. Electrical impulses from muscle activity are then processed, recorded, and displayed on an oscilloscope, recording paper, or computer. EMG can be used to record the muscle activity associated with a particular performance; when EMG is done during various periods of time, a record of progress can be made. Certain rhythms of muscle

activity are associated with a performance. An athlete who is not performing well or is in a slump may display a different EMG rhythm than normal. This information can be used to assist the athlete in correcting errors and regaining the desired form. EMG is often used in conjunction with electrogoniometry. Researchers may also make recordings of brain wave activity using the electroencephalograph (EEG) concurrently with EMG; this provides the researcher with information on how the brain influences motor activity (this is studied within the realm of motor control).

Dynamography is a technique used to measure the forces produced during a movement. To measure strength, particularly static strength, spring devices and cable tensiometers are used. Strain gauges are devices that are also used to measure strength. They have been incorporated into equipment such as athletic footwear insoles,

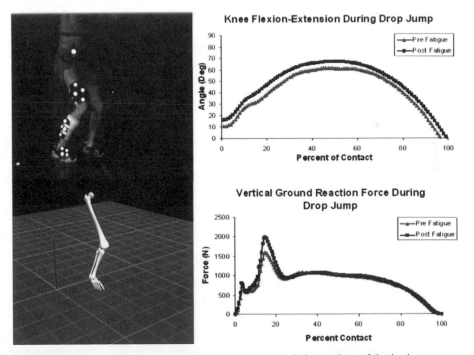

Reflective markers are often used in motion capture to track the motions of the body and create computer models which are used to do a biomechanical analysis of the motion. In this example, knee motion and ground reaction forces were measured during a drop jump before and after fatigue.

bicycle pedals, and uneven parallel bars to measure the force produced by the performers using this equipment. Another device that is used to measure force is the force platform. Force platforms can be built into the floor to measure forces such as those associated with a foot striking the floor during walking. They can also be designed to measure force production by athletes during sprint starts, pole vaulting, and gymnastics.

Telemetry involves the wireless recording of various aspects of movement. Telemetry systems consist of specialized electrodes that are attached to the individual and a transmitter that sends the information to the receiver that records it. Telemetry systems can be used to transmit information about heart rate or joint angles (electrogoniometry) during a performance. A distinct advantage of this technique is that it permits movement data to be recorded without encumbering the performer with wires and other equipment that can hinder performance. With improvements in technology, many companies are making data logging systems that enable data from sensors to be stored on memory cards used in small data recording and storage units worn by the performer. These units are often as small as cell phones. This technology has greatly increased the mobility of performers during data collection as well as the number of activities that can be studied.

Wind tunnels are used in many ways to improve athletes' performance. Nike used a wind tunnel to measure air resistance during the development of their Swift Skin,[16] and Speedo used one for the development of the LZR Racer suit.[17] Wind tunnels are used to determine whether equipment design can be improved: for example, whether the shape of a new helmet for cycling or a change in the composition of a bike wheel actually reduces air resistance. Reducing air resistance helps athletes achieve better times in their sports.

Skiers and sliders (such as bobsledders or lugers) use the wind tunnel to refine their movements for optimum efficiency and speed. These athletes experiment with various body positions inside the wind tunnel. Researchers, including biomechanists, analyze the video of the athletes to provide information about the aerodynamics of each position. Sometimes special force measuring devices are used to provide additional information to assist in the identification of the optimum body position. Working together, researchers, coaches, and athletes use this information to assist athletes in making form adjustments that will lead to optimum performance.

Advances in computers and instrumentation as well as the manner in which they are used have contributed much to the understanding of human movement. For example, the intersection of biomechanics and biofeedback has stimulated the development of new devices to improve sport. *Biofeedback* is the provision of information about a physiological parameter, such as muscle tension, to an individual. The individual then uses this information to modify his or her response. The Swing Trainer and the Cycle Trainer developed by Innovative Sports Training can be used in rehabilitation or as an aid to improve performance. The Swing Trainer provides complete real-time 3-D golf swing analysis and biofeedback training. Using sensors that easily attach to the body, the Swing Trainer captures the full range of the golf swing and provides precise information on all aspects of it. Audio and visual biofeedback ensures optimal body positioning. When the individual is out of position, a tone alerts the individual, and a video displays the proper position. The Cycle Trainer works in a similar fashion; it measures critical orthopedic angles, body positions, pulse, and power output during cycling.

Analysis

Quantitative and qualitative methods can be used to analyze human movement. *Quantitative analysis* uses many of the techniques described previously to provide specific numerical information about the movement being studied. Specific information, for example, about the joint angles during movement, the force generated, and the speed of movement is provided.

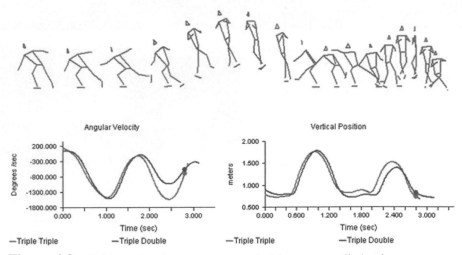

Figure 6-2 In biomechanics, movements of athletes are studied to improve performance as well as reduce the occurrence of injury. Here, a computer model of a triple lutz–triple toe loop in figure skating is displayed, while the jump height and angular velocity of the triple lutz–triple toe loop are compared to those of a triple lutz–double toe loop.

Quantitative analyses are used predominantly in research efforts and are increasingly incorporated in clinical diagnoses, treatment, and rehabilitation, and as part of the overall training program of elite athletes to help them optimize their performance (e.g., biomechanists work with elite athletes at the US Olympic Training Center in Colorado Springs, Colo.).

Qualitative analysis also provides important information about the movement being studied. Qualitative analysis relies most commonly on visual evaluation of the movement. The movement can be described in such terms as successful or unsuccessful or performed with difficulty or with ease. An individual's performance also can be compared with another individual's performance or against a standardized model. Videography, which can be used for quantitative analysis, can also be used effectively for qualitative analysis. Instead of using the video to calculate various kinematic and kinetic measures, the video of an individual's movement can be studied to identify performance errors and to determine effective corrections.

Qualitative analysis is most commonly used by practitioners. It offers practitioners who may not have access to sophisticated equipment or have the background to employ advanced techniques a method to effectively analyze an individual's movements. Biomechanical analysis can be used by athletic trainers in designing a rehabilitation program, by physical educators in conducting an evaluation of fundamental motor skills, and by exercise leaders in ensuring that clients perform each exercise correctly.

Teachers and coaches can use biomechanical analysis to improve students' and athletes' performance of sport skills. Additionally, teachers and coaches are often faced with the task of evaluating several performers of diverse skill levels in a short period of time. The use of video and slow-motion/stop-action playback can be useful to the practitioner in assessing an individual's performance.

USING SCIENCE TO IMPROVE TRAINING

To be competitive, athletes in many sports are turning to sports science to give them an extra edge. In biomechanics, this often involves vertical jump testing. This is not your typical vertical jump, though. Athletes perform three specific types of jumps while the forces they create against the ground during the jump are measured. Scientists then examine these forces, looking at variables such as peak force produced, rate of force developed, and peak power. These variables help the sports scientists diagnose the lower extremity strength and power status of the athletes, helping fine-tune the athletes', training programs for the future.

Squat jumps reflect concentric force producing capabilities of the lower extremity. Countermovement jumps add an eccentric/stretch-shortening cycle to jump performance at moderate speed. Lastly, drop jumps reflect reactive and ballistic characteristics of strength and power at very high speeds. Each of these areas of strength and power is trained with different exercise regimens, such as exercises with heavy loads, exercises using moderate resistance moved as quickly as possible, and plyometric exercises. Athletes in sports including gymnastics, weight lifting, bobsledding, track and field, and figure skating use the results of this testing to fine-tune their training programs. This type of testing is frequently done by biomechanists at the US Olympic Training Center for Olympic hopefuls.

Here is an example of a force tracing for a countermovement jump. In a countermovement jump,

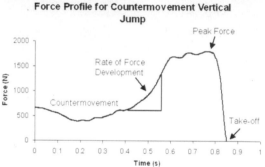

Force Profile for Countermovement Vertical Jump

the athlete starts standing and then bends the knees and swings the arms back before exploding upward. In a squat jump, the athlete starts with a 90-degree knee bend and explodes straight upward. In a drop jump, the athlete steps off a box then explodes upward upon landing.

Video equipment has become increasingly available in school and community settings.

If video equipment is not available, then the professional must rely directly on his or her observations of the individual's performance. Whether the professional is using video or directly observing the individual's performance, the professional should keep in mind relevant biomechanical principles, have a mental image of the ideal performance of the skill being observed, and thoroughly understand the nature of the skill being performed. As an observer, the professional should be objective and proceed in a systematic fashion.

Adrian and Cooper[21] and Brown[22] offer several suggestions to physical education, exercise science, and sport professionals using visual evaluation techniques to assess skill performance. These suggestions, which can be incorporated into the practitioner's observation plan, are:

- Observe the skill from a correct vantage point. Being in the correct position is essential to observing the critical components of the skill. When possible, view the skill from at least two perspectives.
- Observe the individual performing the skill several times before offering suggestions for improvement. This will permit the identification of consistent performance problems that may not be evident during a single performance attempt.
- Use the whole-part-whole method for the observation. After observing the total movement, focus on the movement of the body parts (e.g., legs, trunk). Observe the sequencing and timing of these parts. Observe the range of motion and look for unnecessary or extraneous movements. Then, again observe the whole body and focus on the coordination and sequencing of the movements of various body parts with respect to each other.

- If the performer is using an implement such as a racquet, or imparting force to another object such as a discus or ball, it is also important to focus on the action of the implement or object.
- The overall effectiveness of the movement should be evaluated.
- A performance checklist can be used to guide the observation and to ensure that critical performance elements are viewed and not overlooked.

Once the observation is completed, practitioners should identify the errors in performance and give the performer accurate and relevant feedback about his or her performance. (See Chapter 5 for a discussion of feedback.)

Knudson suggests that professionals use a comprehensive approach when performing qualitative analysis of motor skills in order to intervene to improve performance.[23] Rather than focusing solely on error detection and provision of corrections, or limiting themselves to biomechanical factors, professionals should take a more holistic

At the US Olympic Training Center in Colorado Springs, Colo., biomechanists work with elite athletes to refine their skills and optimize their performance.

and interdisciplinary approach, using many of the exercise and sport sciences as they design an intervention to improve performance. Knudson's four-step approach includes preparation, observation, evaluation/diagnosis, and intervention.[23] Accuracy and consistency are important in conducting qualitative assessment.

During preparation, physical education, exercise science, and sport professionals must gather information about the movement to be analyzed and about the performer. What are the critical features of the movement? What are the abilities of the performer? Knudson encourages professionals to strive to increase their knowledge of human movement by being students of movement, studying movements and factors that influence the performance.[23]

Analysis of the kinematics of movement must be combined with observational experiences to accurately perceive critical features of movement. It is important to correctly select the critical features of the movement that are necessary for optimal performance. These critical features determine whether a movement is safe, efficient, and effective. Knowledge of biomechanics helps professionals determine which are the critical features of a skill.

Professionals benefit from a systematic approach to observation. The traditional approach emphasizes observing critical features based on the temporal phases of a skill—preparation, action, and follow-through.[23] Other professionals prefer a more holistic approach, watching several trials of a skill in order to form an overall impression of performance and then focusing on critical features.[22]

Accurate diagnosis requires determining the underlying strengths and weaknesses of the performance. Here the movement is analyzed relative to the predefined critical features.

In the intervention phase, the professional focuses the performer's attention on one critical feature of the movement, rather than overwhelming the performer with multiple corrections. Knudson suggests that the professional identify the intervention that would create the most improvement in performance and is the least difficult for the performer to implement.[23] Interventions are more likely to be successful when the diagnosis is accurate.

Consistency is another important aspect of qualitative analysis. According to Knudson, multiple observations of the performer improve the consistency and reliability of the analysis.[23] Consistency is further enhanced when the critical features have been precisely and clearly defined. Lastly, a simple approach to classifying critical features can improve consistency.

Hudson offers a method of analysis based on 10 core biomechanical concepts that is appropriate for professionals in an instructional setting. Six of the concepts pertain to essentially all human movements: range of motion, speed of motion, number of segments, nature of the segments (plane of movement), balance, and coordination.[24] Four of the concepts more commonly apply when projectiles are used: extension at release/contact, compactness, path of projection, and spin.[24] When observing an individual's performance, a professional can assess each

---

CORE BIOMECHANICAL CONCEPTS

Range of motion
Speed of motion
Number of segments
Nature of segments
Balance
Coordination
Compactness
Extension at release/contact
Path of projection
Spin

Source: Hudson JL. "Applied Biomechanics in an Instructional Setting." JOPERD 77(8), 25–27, 2006.

relevant concept using a qualitative or quantitative approach. Multiple observations are useful in assessing performance.

Hudson notes that the key to this observational strategy is deciding which core concept is the best point for intervention.[24] Does the individual need to increase or decrease the range of motion when executing a football pass? Does the coordination of certain body segments need to be simultaneous or sequential when the individual is performing the triple jump? Does the javelin thrower need to change the angle of release to increase the length of the throw? Using core concepts as the basis of observation helps professionals make decisions about how to best intervene to improve performance.

Physical education, exercise science, and sport professionals use qualitative analysis in many different ways to help participants in their programs move safely, efficiently, and effectively. Developing skills in qualitative analysis requires an understanding of biomechanical principles and the ability to accurately and consistently observe, assess, and prescribe strategies to improve the performer's movement, whether the movement is a sport skill, a specific exercise, or a task of daily living.

The Future

Technology will continue to drive the advancement of knowledge. Adrian and Cooper state, "With today's sophisticated technology, we have been able to learn more about human movement in the past ten years than in any previous decade."[21] To answer future questions, Adrian and Cooper assert that "we must use basic concepts about what is known to pose the questions of the future and create more effective, safe, and rewarding human movement."[21]

Adrian and Cooper state that mathematical modeling of the anatomical characteristics of individuals, coupled with computer simulation techniques, enables biomechanists to make predictions of performance as well as to develop new and advanced performance techniques.[21] Expertise in mathematics, anatomy, physiology, physics, and computers is necessary to take advantage of these approaches. Data collected via the tools of motion capture, high-speed imaging, dynamography, electrogoniometry, electromyography, and accelerometry forms the foundation for modeling and is entered into the computer, where it is analyzed using various software packages. Simulations allow movements to be varied with respect to speed, timing, range of motion, and environment. Through simulations, these changes in movement variables can be explored and determinations can be made about the optimization of performance and its safety. Computer-assisted drawing and design programs can expedite the design of equipment.

Advances in the analysis of human movement continue to be made at a rapid pace. The increased availability of technology at a decreased cost will make sophisticated analyses readily available to teachers, coaches, athletic trainers, athletes, fitness participants, and practitioners. The use of multidisciplinary teams, composed of sport scientists from the various subdisciplines, will facilitate the integration of data from multiple sources, enhancing our comprehension and enabling physical education and sport professionals to work more effectively with students, athletes, and individuals of all ages seeking to move more efficiently and effectively. The integration of biomechanics with motor development can increase our understanding of movement across the lifespan and enable us to more readily design solutions to remediate problems and safely advance the motor performance of people of all ages and abilities.

Expert profiling and simulations advance the frontier of knowledge and lead to improvements in performance. The United States Olympic Committee Sports Science and Technology Committee has funded several projects, including simulations of bobsled runs and modeling and simulation of paddles and oar blades for rowing and canoeing.

FOCUS ON CAREER: BIOMECHANICS

PROFESSIONAL ORGANIZATIONS	• American Society of Biomechanics (www.asbweb.org) • International Society of Biomechanics (www.isbweb.org) • International Society of Biomechanics in Sports (www.csuchico.edu/isbs/) • International Sports Engineering Association (www.sportsengineering.co.uk)
PROFESSIONAL JOURNALS	• *Clinical Biomechanics* • *Journal of Applied Biomechanics* • *Journal of Biomechanics* • *Research Quarterly for Exercise and Sport* • *Sports Biomechanics* • *Sports Engineering*

Worldwide databases make data available to interested researchers throughout the world. These databases allow for diagnosis of movement problems, profiling, and collaborative research ventures.

The World Wide Web offers a wealth of information to individuals interested in biomechanics. For example, one site—*Biomechanics World Wide* (see Get Connected box)—offers links to profiles of different biomechanists, laboratories worldwide, and even a place to trade or sell equipment. Specialized areas of study are represented, including gait and locomotion, sport and exercise biomechanics, muscle, motor control, computer simulations, ergonomics, orthopedics, prosthetics, and biomedical engineering. Also included on the site is information on biomechanics societies, career opportunities, and professional journals. This site and other related sites offer access to current information and a venue to share ideas and stimulate collaborative endeavors.

As we move further into the twenty-first century, another exciting trend is the shift in the population that biomechanists study and with whom they work.[3] Wilkerson suggests that in the future we will see a great emphasis on research on women and the elderly, two populations that were not studied in the past.[3] Additionally, there will be a shift toward studying people with a wider range of abilities and in a greater array of settings; our research will expand from a focus on the elite athlete to a broader focus on people not only participating in sports but carrying out their tasks of daily living.

Strohmeyer points out that there has been little biomechanical research focused on individuals who are overweight or obese.[25] Given that this population is rapidly growing at all age levels, there is a fertile area for research. Physical activity plays an important role in attaining and maintaining a healthy body composition. Understanding how being overweight or obese affects movement efficiency, effectiveness, and safety is critical if we as professionals are to help this population become more active.

SUMMARY

Understanding the factors that govern human movement is essential for physical education, exercise science, and sport professionals. Physical education, exercise science, and sport professionals are concerned with helping individuals optimize their movements. To accomplish this task, they need to thoroughly understand the mechanical principles that regulate movement. The analysis of human movement and sport object movement using the principles of physics and mechanics is called biomechanics. In recent years the study of biomechanics has grown tremendously in the United States, and it is commonly recognized as a subdiscipline of physical education, exercise science, and sport.

Biomechanics is concerned with two major areas of study. The first area focuses on the anatomical aspects of movement while the second area concerns itself with the mechanical aspects of movement. Needless to say, these areas are closely related. Biomechanists have a specialized scientific vocabulary to describe their area of study. The terms *power, acceleration, velocity, mass, pressure, friction, work, energy, angular velocity* and *acceleration, torque,* and *gravity* are defined in this chapter. Selected biomechanical principles and concepts pertaining to stability, motion, leverage, and force are explained and illustrated.

Within the last 15 years, improvements in instrumentation and its application have been numerous, which has greatly expanded the knowledge base. Although the practitioner may not have access to much of the specialized equipment used by the biomechanist researcher, the practitioner can use available equipment, such as video equipment, or direct observation to analyze performance. Understanding the principles of biomechanics is essential in improving individuals' performance.

DISCUSSION QUESTIONS

1. How are kinesiology and biomechanics different and integrally related? Do professionals *have* to have knowledge and understanding of both kinesiology and biomechanics? How can each subdiscipline impact the movement of athletes, clients, and students?

2. In small groups, discuss experiences you have had (as a professional or as an athlete, client, or student) with biomechanics of exercise or rehabilitation biomechanics. What assessments or techniques were conducted? How did the analyses of these assessments or techniques transfer into improved movement or performance?

3. As an athlete and physical mover, how has your motion in your sport changed since you were a child (e.g., running, throwing a football, swimming, driving a golf ball)? What contributed to these changes?

SELF-ASSESSMENT ACTIVITIES

These activities are designed to help you determine if you have mastered the materials and competencies presented in this chapter.

1. Write a short essay of 250 words on the worth of biomechanical knowledge to the practitioner in physical education, exercise science, and sport. Write the essay from the perspective of a practitioner, in a career that you are considering for the future, that is, teacher, coach, athletic trainer, exercise physiologist, or sports broadcaster.

2. Explain and illustrate the meaning of each of the following terms: power, acceleration, velocity, mass, pressure, friction, work, energy, torque, and center of gravity.

3. Using a sport with which you are familiar, illustrate principles and concepts relating to stability, motion, leverage, and force.

4. Using the information provided in the Get Connected box, access *BioMechanics* magazine or CoachesInfo. Select an article of interest and write a short summary of the article and its application to your future career.

5. Using the information provided in the Get Connected box, access Exploratorium Staff Picks: Sports Science. Find one activity that is of interest to you and write a short description of that activity to present to the class.

6. Using the information provided in the Get Connected box, access CoachesInfo. Select one article related to sports, strength and conditioning, or recreational pursuits to read and critique. In writing your critique, summarize the article, identify five key points that would be helpful to professionals in the field, and then critique the article.

7. Refer to the 12 Steps to Understanding Research Reports box in Chapter 1. Complete Step 6 for the same article you selected in Chapter 1.

REFERENCES

1. Hamilton N and Luttgens K: Kinesiology, ed 10, New York, 2002, McGraw-Hill.

2. Martin RB: A genealogy of biomechanics, Lecture, annual conference of the American Society of Biomechanics, University of Pittsburgh, Pittsburgh, Penn., October 23, 1999 (www.asbweb.org).

3. Wilkerson JD: Biomechanics. In JD Massengale and RA Swanson, editors, The history of exercise and sport science, Champaign, Ill., 1997, Human Kinetics.

4. Atwater AE: Kinesiology/biomechanics: perspectives and trends, Research Quarterly for Exercise and Sport 51:193–218, 1980.

5. Biomechanics Academy, National Association for Sport and Physical Education, AAHPERD: Guidelines and standards for undergraduate biomechanics/kinesiology, Reston, Va., 1992, AAHPERD.

6. Counsilman JE: The science of swimming, Englewood Cliffs, N.J., 1968, Prentice Hall.

7. Brown RM and Counsilman JE: The role of lift in propelling swimmers. In J Cooper, editor, Biomechanics, Chicago, 1971, Athletic Institute.

8. McCabe C and Sanders R: Propulsion in swimming, CoachesInfo, 2004 (www.coachesinfo.com).

9. Lynn SK, Reid SM, and Costigan PA: The influence of gait pattern on signs and symptoms of knee osteoarthritis in older adults over a 5–11 year follow-up period: a case study analysis, The Knee 14:22–28, 2007.

10. Hurwitz DE, Sumner DR, Adriacchi TP, and Sugar DA: Dynamic knee loads during gait predict proximal tibial bone distribution, Journal of Biomechanics 31:423–430, 1998.

11. Miyazaki T, Wada M, Kawahara H, Sata M, Baba H, and Simada S: Dynamic loads at baseline can predict radiographic disease progression in medial compartment knee osteoarthritis, Annals of the Rheumatic Diseases 61:617–622, 2002.

12. Weidenhielm L, Svennson OK, and Brotsom LA: Change of adduction moment about the hip, knee and ankle joints after high tibial osteotomy in osteoarthritis of the knee, Clinical Biomechanics 7:177–180, 1992.

13. Fry AC, Smith JC, and Schilling BK: Effect of knee position on hip and knee torques during the barbell squat, Journal of Strength and Conditioning Research 17:629–633, 2002.

14. Mikkelsen C, Werner S, and Eriksson E: Knee surgery, sports traumatology, arthroscopy, Official Journal of the ESSKA 8:337–342, 2000.

15. Fleming BC, Oksendahl H, and Beynnon BD: Open- or closed-kinetic chain exercises after anterior cruciate ligament reconstruction? Exercise and Sport Sciences Reviews 33:134–140, 2005.

16. Boyle A: The high-tech race for Olympic gold, February 1, 2002 (www.msnbd.msn.com/id/3079010).

17. Naughton K: Making a splash, Newsweek, June 20, 2008 (www.newsweek.com/2008/06/20/making-a-splash.html).

18. Kessel A: Born slippery, Observer, November 23, 2008 (www.guardian.co.uk/sport/2008/nov/23/swimming-olympics2008).

19. Charette R: FINA proposes banning high-tech swim suits, IIEEE Spectrum: The Risk Factor, July 27, 2009, (spectrum.ieee.org/riskfactor/computing/it/fina-proposes-banning-hightech-swim-suits).

20. Northrip JW, Logan GA, and McKinney W: Introduction to biomechanical analysis of sport, ed 2, Dubuque, Iowa, 1979, William C. Brown.

21. Adrian MJ and Cooper JM: The biomechanics of human movement, Dubuque, Iowa, 1987, Benchmark Press.

22. Brown EW: Visual evaluation techniques for skill analysis, Journal of Physical Education, Recreation and Dance 53(1):21–26, 1982.

23. Knudson D: What can professionals qualitatively analyze? JOPERD 71(2):19–23, 2000.

24. Hudson JL: Applied biomechanics in an instructional setting, JOPERD 77(8):25–27, 2006.

25. Strohmeyer S: The biomechanical implications of obesity in K–12 learners, JOPERD 78(8):40–41, 2007.

CHAPTER 7

EXERCISE PHYSIOLOGY AND FITNESS

OBJECTIVES

After reading this chapter the student should be able to—

- Define exercise physiology and understand the importance of exercise physiology to the practitioner.
- Understand components of health- and performance-related fitness.
- Understand and appreciate the role of physical activity in health.
- Explain the principles and guidelines for designing fitness programs.
- Use the FITT formula to design a fitness program.
- Describe other factors related to fitness and performance.

Exercise physiology is the study of the body's responses and its adaptation to the stress of exercise. Exercise physiologists are concerned with investigating both the immediate (acute) and the long-term (chronic) effects of exercise on all aspects of body functioning. These effects include the responses of the muscular system, the action of the nervous system during physical activity, the adjustments of the respiratory system, and the dynamics of the cardiovascular system. Improving the body's response to exercise also is an important area of study. The effects of exercise are examined at different levels, ranging from the subcellular to the systemic level. One major area of study for exercise physiologists is the description and explanation of the myriad of functional changes caused by exercise sessions of variable frequency, intensity, and duration.

The field of exercise physiology offers professionals a strong foundation of knowledge about the effects of exercise on the body. Professionals, whether teachers in a school or nonschool setting, coaches, fitness leaders employed in a commercial club, or exercise physiologists working in a corporate fitness setting or a hospital, must understand the body's responses to exercise. Knowledge of the principles governing different types of training programs and the guidelines to be followed in constructing an exercise prescription enables professionals to design programs to meet each individual's physical activity needs and goals.

Exercise physiology has become increasingly sophisticated. New research procedures and measurement techniques, coupled with advances in equipment, computer technology, and other related disciplines, such as biochemistry, have contributed to rapid expansion of the knowledge base. While fitness and elite performers long have been a key concern of exercise physiologists, interest in recent years has encompassed virtually all aspects of human performance and people of all skill abilities and all ages, from the very young to the elderly, including individuals with disabilities.

EXERCISE PHYSIOLOGY: AN OVERVIEW

Exercise physiology is one of the most rapidly growing areas of specialization within the field of physical education, exercise science, and sport. The definition, historical development, and areas of study and scope are discussed in this section.

Definition

Exercise physiology is the study of the effects of exercise on the body. Specifically, exercise physiology is concerned with the body's responses and adaptations to exercise, ranging from the system level to the subcellular level. These modifications can be short-term—that is, lasting only for the duration of the activity—or long-term—present as long as the activity is continued on a regular basis.

As a subdiscipline, exercise physiology is one of the largest and most popular areas of study within the realm of physical education, exercise science, and sport. Today the depth and breadth of knowledge in exercise physiology is growing rapidly because of the proliferation of research, which is facilitated by increasingly sophisticated technology and by the widespread interest of professionals in this field.

Historical Development

Exercise physiology emerged as a specialized area of study in the mid-1960s and 1970s. Exercise

LIFESPAN AND CULTURAL PERSPECTIVES: Exercise Physiology

- What is the recommendation for physical activity needed to yield health benefits in people over the age of 65?
- How does the cardiovascular system respond to prolonged weightlessness, such as that experienced in space?
- At what age should children begin weight training? What type of weight training program is best for children?
- How do individual differences in age, sex, ethnicity, prior health status, and family background influence a person's response to physical activity?
- How does age affect aerobic capacity?
- What is the relationship between childhood physical activity levels and fitness and adult physical activity levels and fitness?

physiology traces its roots to the mid-1800s and early 1900s. Then, as now, the discipline of physiology influenced the ongoing work in exercise physiology.

Edward Hitchcock, Dudley Sargent, Thomas D. Wood, Robert Tait McKenzie, and George Fitz were instrumental in laying the early foundations of exercise physiology and promoting the scientific basis of physical education.[1] While at Amherst College in the 1860s, Edward Hitchcock used anthropometric techniques to measure changes in his students' development after they participated in his physical training program. At Harvard University in 1879, Dudley Sargent used anthropometry in his physical education classes to investigate the effects of exercise on the body. In the 1890s, Thomas D. Wood helped promote the scientific basis of physical education. During his tenure at Stanford University, Wood developed a 4-year degree program leading to an undergraduate degree in physical training and hygiene.

Physiologist Dr. George Fitz established the first formal exercise physiology laboratory at Harvard University in 1892. At a time in physical education's history when the merits of various systems were being debated, Fitz advocated using a scientific approach to evaluate each system, so that the actual benefits of each system could be

determined. Noted physician, physical educator, and sculptor R. Tait McKenzie advocated investigating the effects of exercise on various systems of the body and helped promote the idea of preventive medicine.[1]

One of the seminal events in the growth of exercise physiology was the founding of the Harvard Fatigue Laboratory in 1927. Lawrence J. Henderson and G. E. Mayo established the lab, and David Bruce Dill served as its director until it closed in 1946. The lab attracted many notable researchers who conducted groundbreaking research on exercise and environmental physiology.[1] Many of these researchers established research laboratories throughout the country, for which the Fatigue Lab served as a model.

In the mid-1960s and early 1970s, the growth of exercise physiology as a specialized area of study was stimulated by university and physical education leaders' calls for more stringent teacher training and a greater emphasis on scholarship and academic rigor in graduate programs in physical education. Thus, undergraduate areas of specialization evolved and undergraduate majors were developed, such as exercise science, adult fitness, and cardiac rehabilitation.

In 1968, Dr. Kenneth H. Cooper published his first book, *Aerobics*, followed by its sequel,

The New Aerobics, in 1970. Dr. Cooper's work popularized the term *aerobics*. He was a pioneer in promoting aerobic exercise, such as running, swimming, walking, and cycling, and stressing its contribution to health. Dr. Cooper was an early leader in disease prevention and today he heads the Cooper Institute and the Cooper Aerobics Center in Dallas, Texas, where research and educational efforts contribute to our understanding of the role of physical activity in health.

During the 1970s, the American Physiological Society (APS) accorded greater recognition to the rapidly expanding field of exercise physiology. Exercise physiology was officially included as part of one of the APS's specialty sections.

The 1980s and 1990s marked an era when there was greater understanding of the significant relationship between physical activity and health. In 1996, the first Surgeon General's Report on *physical activity and health* was released.[2] National health reports, such as *Healthy People 2010,*[3] secured greater public recognition of the role of physical activity and well-being.

As research in the realm of exercise physiology continued to grow, more scholarly journals and professional organizations were established to serve as outlets for the dissemination of scientific work. Some of the early researchers' works were published in the *American Journal of Physiology* (founded in 1898), *the Journal of Applied Physiology* (1948), and the *Research Quarterly* (1930), which became the *Research Quarterly for Exercise and Sport.* Researchers also presented papers and conducted workshops at meetings of the American Alliance for Health, Physical Education, Recreation, and Dance (AAHPERD).

In 1954, physicians, physiologists, and physical educators came together to establish the American College of Sports Medicine (ACSM). In 1969, *Medicine and Science in Sports* began its publication, and in 1980, this periodical was renamed *Medicine and Science in Sports and Exercise.* In 1974, ACSM published its first edition of *Guidelines for Graded Exercise Testing and Prescription* and in 1975, it conducted the first certification exams in exercise leadership and cardiac

rehabilitation. In 1997, ACSM published its first issue of *Health and Fitness Journal.* More recently, ACSM developed a clinical exercise physiology registry and in 2000 offered its first certification exam for clinical exercise physiologists.

As exercise physiology grew, other journals were founded and offered additional outlets for scholars to share their research; these include *The Physician and Sports Medicine, Exercise and Sport Science Reviews, American Journal of Sports Medicine,* and *International Journal of Sports Medicine.*

Areas of Study

Exercise physiology encompasses a broad range of topics. Examples of some areas of study are:

- Effects of various exercise programs on the systems of the body, including circulatory, respiratory, nervous, skeletal, muscle, and endocrine systems.
- Relationship of energy metabolism to performance.
- Effects of various environmental factors, such as temperature, humidity, altitude, pollutants, and different environments (e.g., in space or undersea), on physiological responses to exercise and performance.
- Effects of individual differences such as age, sex, initial level of fitness, or disability on fitness development and performance.
- Effectiveness of various rehabilitation programs on the recovery of injured athletes, on diseased individuals, and on individuals with disabilities.
- Effects of ergogenic aids such as drugs or music on performance.
- Health and therapeutic benefits to be gained from engaging in appropriate levels of physical activity.

Exercise physiologists can work in many different settings. They can be involved in conducting research in a laboratory setting, teaching exercise science courses at a college or university, or engaged in a variety of clinical activities, such as guiding an elite athlete through a graded

EXERCISE PHYSIOLOGY—EMERGING FIELDS OF STUDY

Cardiac rehabilitation	Focuses on the assessments of cardiovascular functioning and on the effectiveness of various exercise programs in preventing cardiovascular disease and rehabilitating individuals suffering from the disease.
Exercise biochemistry	Examines the effects of exercise at the cellular level, specifically within the muscle cell.
Exercise epidemiology	Studies the relationship between physical activity and mortality.
Pediatric exercise	Studies the response of the body to exercise during childhood, including the effects of growth and maturation and how responses differ between children and adults.

exercise test on a treadmill, directing a cardiac rehabilitation program at a hospital, or administering a worksite health promotion program.

Historically, performance and fitness are the two areas of research that have dominated exercise physiology. Much attention has been directed by researchers to the area of cardiovascular exercise physiology, which examines how oxygen is used by the cardiovascular system during exercise. Researchers have also focused a great deal of effort on the study of exercise metabolism, investigating the metabolic responses to exercise and training conducted under a variety of conditions. Four areas of study that are emerging and increasing in popularity are cardiac rehabilitation, exercise biochemistry, exercise epidemiology, and pediatric exercise (see the Exercise Physiology— Emerging Fields of Study box for definitions).

The application of knowledge from the realm of exercise physiology appears to focus predominantly on studying the effects of physical activity and exercise on the body. Two primary areas of application can be discerned: first, the enhancement of fitness, promotion of health, and prevention of disease; and second, the improvement and refinement of motor performance, especially in sport. The principles of exercise physiology can be used to improve and maintain both health-related and motor-skill-related fitness. As in the other subdisciplines of physical education, exercise science, and sport, there is a growing emphasis on research and application across the lifespan, from the very young to the aged.

Knowledge of and skills associated with exercise physiology are used in many different ways by professionals. Physical education teachers help children set and attain fitness goals, both in physical education class and through participation in physical activity outside the school. Coaches typically use training guidelines to help their athletes achieve high levels of fitness essential for performance in specific sports. Cardiac rehabilitation specialists work in hospitals, clinics, worksites, or community settings, enhancing the fitness of post–heart attack patients, performing fitness evaluations, and leading preventive programs. Fitness professionals in private clubs, community programs, and corporate settings design, conduct, and evaluate fitness programs for people of all ages. Strength training specialists work with professional, intercollegiate, and interscholastic athletes and in rehabilitation. Athletic trainers develop preventative and rehabilitation programs for injured athletes.

The current tremendous interest in health, fitness, and physical activity by the public and the expansion of the knowledge base of this field also have enhanced professional opportunities. An increasing number of young people are undertaking undergraduate and graduate study in exercise physiology and preparing to pursue careers in adult fitness, cardiac rehabilitation, and strength development. (Career opportunities in these areas are discussed in Chapter 13.)

Exercise physiology is an exceptionally broad area of study, with a long, rich history. Exercise physiology incorporates knowledge from many scientific disciplines, such as biology, chemistry, physiology, and anatomy. Additionally, given the depth and breadth of the discipline, it is difficult within the limitations of this chapter to provide a worthy introduction to the area. Therefore, it was decided to focus on one area of exercise physiology—fitness—and approach it from an applied perspective. It is hoped that this approach will allow students enrolled in this introductory course to gain insight into the field of exercise physiology and be able to relate the information they are learning to their own experiences with exercise, fitness, and performance. As students continue their undergraduate preparation, they will have the opportunity to study exercise physiology more extensively.

Physical Fitness

Physical fitness is the ability of the body's systems to function efficiently and effectively. Individuals who are physically fit have the ability to "carry out daily tasks with vigor and alertness, without undue fatigue, and with ample energy to enjoy leisure-time pursuits and to meet unforeseen emergencies."[4]

Contemporary professionals commonly view physical fitness as a quality comprising 11 different components, each with specific requirements for its development and maintenance. Fitness components

DEFINITIONS OF PHYSICAL FITNESS COMPONENTS

Fitness Component	Definition
Health-Related Components	
Body composition	Amount of body fat relative to fat-free content, expressed as a percentage
Cardiorespiratory endurance	Maximum functional capacity of the cardiorespiratory system to sustain work or physical activity involving large muscle groups over an extended period
Flexibility	Range of movement possible at a joint or joints
Muscular endurance	Ability of a muscle or muscle group to repeat muscular contractions against a force or to sustain a contraction over time
Muscular strength	Maximum amount of force that can be exerted by a muscle or muscle group against a resistance during a single contraction
Skill-Related Components	
Agility	Ability to change direction rapidly with control
Balance	Ability to maintain equilibrium while stationary or moving
Coordination	Ability to execute movements smoothly and efficiently
Power	Ability to produce force at a fast speed; a combination of strength and speed usually applied during a short period
Reaction time	Time elapsed between the administration of a stimulus and the body's response to the stimulus
Speed	Ability to move the body quickly

typically are classified into two categories: health and motor skill performance.[4] The Definitions of Physical Fitness Components box identifies and defines the health and skill performance components.

Health fitness is important for all individuals throughout their lifespan. The achievement and maintenance of those qualities necessary for an individual to function efficiently and to enhance his or her health through the prevention and remediation of disease are the central focus of health fitness.

Performance-related or *skill-related physical fitness* emphasizes the development of those qualities that enhance the performance of physical activities such as sport. Whereas health fitness is concerned with living better, performance-related fitness is concerned with performing sport-related skills better and more efficiently. Moreover, performance-related fitness is specific to the sport or activity in which the individual engages. Different degrees of performance-related fitness components are needed, depending on the specific motor activity. For example, the degree of power, agility, and speed needed by a football player are different from those required by a tennis player, though both individuals need these qualities to perform at an optimal level.

Fitness, be it health- or performance-related, must be viewed in relation to an individual's characteristics (e.g., age, health status, occupation, preferences), needs, and goals, and the tasks that must be performed. All individuals possess certain levels of each of the health- and performance-related fitness components. The extent to which each quality is developed depends on the individual. A weekend tennis player needs a different level of physical fitness than a competitive wheelchair marathoner; a 70-year-old grandparent requires a different level of fitness than the 10-year-old grandchild. Professionals charged with the responsibility of designing and conducting fitness programs should ask the program participants, "Fitness for what?" Does the participant desire physical fitness that will contribute to general health or to outstanding performance in a particular sport? All people should seek to achieve and maintain an optimal level of physical fitness with respect to their individual needs.

Because exercise physiology is concerned with both the body's immediate and long-term responses to exercise, the development and conduct of fitness programs to meet an individual's specific fitness needs should be guided by knowledge from this field. Elite athletes preparing for competition, healthy adults wanting to work out on a regular basis, patients recovering from heart disease, youth sport athletes training for competition, injured participants rehabilitating from injury, elderly citizens aspiring to live independent lives, and individuals with disabilities who are striving to meet the challenges of life can all benefit from participation in a well-designed physical fitness program based on the principles of exercise physiology.

Physical Activity, Physical Fitness, and Health

Today, the effects of physical activity and fitness on the health status of the individual are a major area of research in exercise physiology. A major threat to the health and well-being of Americans is chronic diseases, many of which can be categorized as hypokinetic diseases. *Hypokinetic diseases* are caused by insufficient physical activity, often in conjunction with inappropriate dietary practices. Coronary heart disease, hypertension, osteoporosis, noninsulin-dependent diabetes, chronic back pain, and obesity are examples of hypokinetic diseases.

Health Risk Factors

Researchers have identified risk factors that contribute to chronic diseases, such as heart disease and cancer—the major causes of death in the United States today. The causes of these diseases are a complex interaction of biological, environmental, and behavioral factors. Inherited and biological factors, such as gender, race, age, and inherited susceptibility to disease, cannot be changed. However, other risk factors associated with the environment and behavior may be amenable to change, reducing the individual's risk for disease.

Environmental factors, which include physical (e.g., air quality) and socioeconomic (e.g., poverty) factors, are associated with poor health outcomes. While they can be changed, people may face obstacles in doing so. For example, it is difficult to move above the poverty line, especially in troubled economic times; however, people can take an active role in their community to bring about change. They can speak out for clean air, support community-based health initiatives, and reduce their interactions with environments that are unhealthy.

Behavioral factors, such as smoking, inactivity, and poor nutrition, reflect individual behavior choices. These factors can be changed by individuals taking personal responsibility for their health and reducing the presence of chronic disease factors in their lifestyle. Taking responsibility for eating healthy, incorporating physical activity into one's lifestyle, and using alcohol only in moderation are steps individuals can take to reduce their risk factors and enhance their overall level of health.

Physical inactivity has been identified as a risk factor for several diseases. Individuals who lead a sedentary—that is, physically inactive—life have increased risk of morbidity and mortality from a number of chronic diseases.[2,3,5] One striking example is the relationship between physical activity and coronary heart disease, the leading cause of death in the United States. Individuals who are inactive have almost twice the risk of coronary heart disease as those who are active.[2,3] The degree of risk is similar to those better known risk factors of cigarette smoking, hypertension, and obesity.

Dose-Response Debate

The compelling evidence that physical activity can have substantial health benefits, such as increasing longevity and decreasing the risk of many chronic diseases, has led to an ongoing debate about the amount of physical activity necessary to achieve these desired health outcomes. The *dose-response* debate centers on questions such as: "What kind of activity should be performed? How long does the workout need

to be? How much effort or intensity should the activity require? How frequently should physical activity be performed to achieve health benefits?" The *dose* refers to the total amount of energy expended in physical activity; the *response* refers to the changes that occur as a result of being physically active.

The consensus of the Centers for Disease Control and Prevention (CDC),[6,7] the ACSM,[8] and the US Department of Health and Human Services (HHS)[9] is that regular engagement in physical activity can yield substantial health benefits, reducing morbidity and mortality rates. Based on evidence gathered, it is recommended that adults engage in 150 minutes per week of moderate-intensity physical activity or 75 minutes of vigorous physical activity.[6–9] Moderate-intensity physical activity means you are working hard enough to raise your heart rate and break a sweat, yet still are able to carry on a conversation in activities such as biking (less than 10 mph), walking briskly, or ballroom dancing. In vigorous physical activity, such as running, swimming laps, or hiking uphill, you will not be able to say more than a few words without pausing for a breath. In addition to aerobic activity, the CDC,[6,7] ACSM,[8] and HHS[9] recommend that you engage in muscle strengthening exercises on 2 or more days a week that work all the major muscle groups. Individuals who incorporate this dose, or level of physical activity, into their lifestyle will reap substantial health benefits and reduce their risk for disease. Additional health benefits can be gained through greater amounts of physical activity than the recommended dose.[5,10]

For those individuals who have difficulty fitting 30 minutes of continuous physical activity in their busy daily schedule, they can satisfy the guidelines by accumulating 30 minutes of physical activity during the course of the day. Bouts of three 10-minute or two 15-minute sessions of physical activity throughout the day are sufficient to meet the guidelines. Individuals should also strive to incorporate more physical activity into their lives throughout the day, by taking the steps rather than the elevator or parking a bit farther away and walking to their destination.

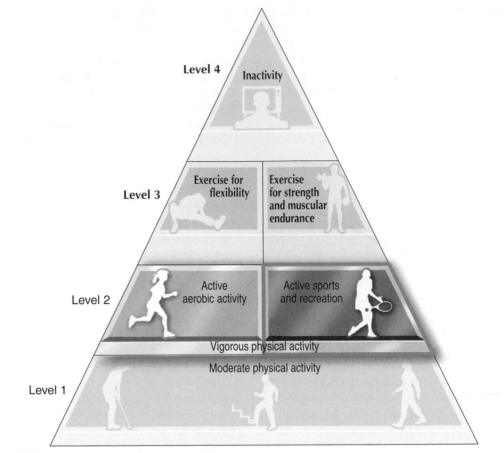

Figure 7-1   The physical activity pyramid

Source: Corbin, Welk, Corbin, Welk—*Concepts of Fitness and Wellness: A Comprehensive Lifestyle Approach* (ed 8) 2009, McGraw-Hill. Reproduced with permission of The McGraw-Hill Companies.

Moderate-intensity physical activities should be incorporated into individuals' daily routine and become an integral part of their lifestyle. The National Association for Sport and Physical Education's Council on Physical Education for Children and the CDC recommend that children aged 2 and up should be physically active at least 60 minutes a day and up to several hours a day, broken up into several sessions.[11] Intermittent moderate-to-vigorous physical activity should be encouraged and long periods of inactivity discouraged.

The physical activity pyramid (see Figure 7-1) is helpful in understanding the different types of physical activities and their benefits.[12] The first level of the pyramid reflects lifetime physical activity that is associated with health benefits, chronic disease reduction, and reduced risk of premature death. Levels 2 and 3 reflect guidelines for development of cardiovascular fitness, flexibility, and muscle fitness. Level 4 indicates that some rest and inactivity are important, but too much inactivity results in low levels of fitness and poor health.

Many health benefits can be achieved by regular participation in lifestyle physical activities. Sedentary people will benefit the most from changing from inactive to active; by incorporating moderate-intensity physical activities into their lifestyle, they substantially decrease their risk for disease and premature death. Individuals can

Spinning classes are a popular fitness offering at employee fitness centers, community programs, and fitness clubs.

accrue greater health benefits by increasing the time they engage in moderate-intensity physical activity or by participating in more vigorous physical activity associated with health fitness.

Health Benefits

The relationship between physical activity and health gives professionals the opportunity to make a significant contribution to the health of the nation and to the lives of individuals with whom they work. Physical activity has been associated with a myriad of health benefits. Physical activity can increase longevity; a significant 20–30% reduction in all-cause mortality is associated with adherence to recommended physical activity guidelines for health.[13]

Enhanced cardiovascular function is one health benefit of physical activity. This helps reduce the risk of heart disease. Benefits accrued include a more efficient level of cardiovascular function, stronger heart muscles, lower heart rate, reduced blood pressure, increased oxygen-carrying capacity of the blood, and improved coronary and peripheral circulation. Resistance to atherosclerosis is improved as desirable serum cholesterol levels are maintained, low-density lipids are reduced, and protective high-density lipids are increased. Thus, the risk of a heart attack is lessened, and the chances of surviving a heart attack are increased. Physical activity can also help reduce other risk factors associated with cardiovascular disease such as obesity and hypertension.

Physical activity can help maintain a desirable body composition. Excessive body fat is hazardous to one's health and can shorten one's life. Elevated serum cholesterol levels, diabetes, hypertension, gallbladder disease, cardiovascular disease, osteoarthritis of the weight-bearing joints, and some types of cancer are all associated with being overweight. Additionally, many adults and children who are obese experience psychological stress and self-concept problems. Being physically active on a regular basis helps maintain a healthy body composition by using excess calories and by preventing the addition of undesirable weight, thus reducing susceptibility to disease. Physical activity also can contribute to improved physical appearance and self-image.

Muscular strength, muscular endurance, and flexibility also are important to good health. Millions of Americans suffer from problems with low-back pain. Many of these problems can be attributed to muscular weakness and imbalance, which in turn can be attributed to inactivity or participation in inappropriate activities. Millions of elderly and individuals with disabilities may have trouble performing tasks of daily living because of insufficient development of these fitness components. Regular and appropriate physical activity can help these individuals achieve functional independence. Reduced risk of muscle and joint injury is also a positive outcome of regular and appropriate activity.

The value of physical activity is not limited only to the body; it also contributes to sound mental health. It may help alleviate mental illness and reduce susceptibility to depression and anxiety. Being active can help individuals withstand and manage stress more effectively. Many people find that exercising provides a release from tensions and makes them feel better. Regular participation in physical activity can contribute to the development of a positive self-concept and greater self-esteem. It enhances self-confidence, emotional stability, assertiveness, independence, and self-control.

Socialization is another benefit of participation in exercise and physical activities. Sports, recreational activities, and exercise groups offer opportunities to fulfill the desire to belong to a group as well as the desire for recognition. These are important psychosocial needs.

Besides enhancing health, health fitness can contribute to increased work efficiency. Individuals who are fit have more energy, which contributes to greater productivity and efficiency of both physical and mental tasks. More energy is available for recreational activities and leisure-time pursuits. Fit individuals can also better withstand fatigue. Physical exercise can improve one's sleeping patterns.

Health fitness can improve overall general motor performance. Physical activities associated with daily living as well as sport skills can be performed more efficiently by individuals who are fit. Additionally, fit individuals recover more quickly from vigorous exercise and work than do unfit individuals. Physical activity enhances one's appearance and posture through the development of proper muscle tone, greater flexibility, and an enhanced sense of well-being.

Regular exercise can help mitigate the debilitating effects of old age. To be most effective in mitigating the effects of aging, the integration of regular physical activity into one's lifestyle should begin early in life. Individuals who remain active and physically fit throughout their life will retain a more desirable level of cardiovascular health, muscular strength, muscular endurance, and body composition.

Individuals who exercise regularly are likely to engage in other positive forms of health-promoting behavior. Because they do not want to negate the benefits accrued from exercise, they may also strive to eat properly, get sufficient rest and relaxation, and manage the stress in their lives. Personal health and well-being become an important personal priority.

Regular and appropriate physical activity has many benefits. However, to realize these benefits, a person must be active all year. To function properly and at a high level, the human organism needs exercise as an essential ingredient on a regular basis, just as it demands nutritious food every day. Being active throughout one's life is essential for continued good health.

FITNESS DEVELOPMENT

In order to plan a fitness program, professionals must have a knowledge of how energy is produced for physical activity. Understanding energy demands helps in structuring the fitness program to achieve desired results. Principles of fitness training offer guidance for program planning. In developing fitness programs, the frequency, intensity, time, and type of physical activity must be specified.

Energy Production for Physical Activity

Energy is necessary for the performance of physical activity, whether it is physical activity associated with the activities of daily living, moderate-intensity activity to improve health, exercise to improve fitness, participation in sports for recreation, or involvement in highly competitive athletics. Muscles must produce energy to move. Metabolism is the sum of all chemical reactions in the body, including energy production and energy utilization.

Energy for muscular contraction is produced from the breakdown of food we eat; food serves as a fuel source for the body. Protein, carbohydrates, and fat, macronutrients from food, are broken down via a series of processes to three main molecules—amino acids, glucose, and fatty acids. These molecules, in turn, are delivered via the bloodstream to the cells. In the cells, through a series of chemical reactions, *adenosine triphosphate,* or *ATP,* is created. ATP is used as energy to perform muscular activity.

TABLE 7-1	Energy Systems Used	
Energy System	**Length of Time**	**Type of Activity**
Anaerobic	6–60 seconds	Any type of sprint (running, swimming, cycling) Short-duration, explosive activities
Combined systems	1–3 minutes	Medium-distance activities (400 and 800 meters) Intermittent sports activities
Aerobic	More than 3 minutes	Long-distance events Long-duration intermittent sport activities

Source: Prentice W. *Fitness and wellness for life* (6th ed.). New York: McGraw-Hill, 1999.

There are two major ways that energy, specifically ATP, is generated for activity: the anaerobic system and the aerobic system. *Anaerobic* means without oxygen; *aerobic* means with oxygen. The type of task performed, specifically the duration of the activity and its intensity (or the rate at which energy is expended), determines which energy system will contribute the majority of the energy required. (see Table 7-1).

The anaerobic system provides energy for tasks that demand a high rate of energy expenditure for a short period—for example, the 100-yard dash, 50-yard freestyle swim sprint, or shot put— or in events where power—that is, quick, explosive movements—is necessary, such as gymnastics or football.[14] This system produces energy quickly to meet immediate demands. It uses ATP and other necessary molecules for the chemical reactions that are stored in the muscle cells. When these small stores of ATP are used up, the body then uses stored glycogen as an energy source. Glycogen is broken down to glucose, which is then metabolized within the muscle cells to generate ATP for muscle contraction. Because body fuels can be metabolized to produce small amounts of ATP for energy without the use of oxygen, this is referred to as anaerobic metabolism. However, the amount of work that can be performed anaerobically is limited. The anaerobic system can support high-intensity exercise for only about 1 minute. One product of anaerobic energy production is lactic acid, which accumulates in the muscles and contributes to fatigue.

When exercise continues for a prolonged time, the aerobic system provides the energy for physical activity. Physical activities requiring a lower rate of energy expenditure over a longer time, such as jogging 5 miles, cross-country skiing 10 kilometers, or engaging in a basketball game, use aerobic metabolism to supply the energy.[11] For performing aerobic activities, a constant supply of oxygen is required by the muscles performing the work. Oxygen is used as part of a more complex process to generate ATP from carbohydrates and fats. The aerobic system is tremendously efficient at extracting ATP from the food nutrient molecules and without producing fatiguing by-products such as lactic acid.

In many activities, these systems function simultaneously. For example, many physical activities that would be considered aerobic in nature, such as basketball, soccer, racquetball, and long-distance races, include an anaerobic component. These activities require periodic bursts of speed or power, such as sprinting up the court for a long pass, accelerating past an opponent to an open space, and sprinting towards the finish line.

The anaerobic and aerobic systems of the body can be improved through training. Anaerobic training typically involves alternating high-intensity activity with rest periods of varying lengths; the number of repetitions in this cycle depends on the goal of the training. Anaerobic training increases the ability to do anaerobic work, tolerance for lactic acid, and muscle size. In contrast, aerobic training generally involves exercising at a lower intensity for a longer amount of time. Aerobic training improves the capacity of the body to transport and use oxygen, to generate ATP aerobically, and to utilize carbohydrates and stored fats for energy production. Aerobic training improves the function of the cardiovascular system. Understanding the different energy systems is important in developing, implementing, and evaluating training programs to improve fitness.

Principles of Fitness Training

Knowledge from the field of exercise physiology offers guidelines for professionals to use when planning and conducting programs to improve fitness. These principles should be followed whether the exercise program is being designed by an elementary school physical educator to improve students' health fitness, by a coach to improve athletes' performance, by an exercise leader to enhance adults' fitness, or by an exercise specialist as part of a patient's cardiac rehabilitation program. Several physiological and behavioral factors must be taken into account if the sought-after benefits—improvement and maintenance of fitness—are to be realized.

1. **Principle of overload.** To gain improvements in health and fitness, an individual must perform more than his or her normal amount of exercise. An increased demand or workload (i.e., overload) must be placed on the body for benefits to occur. The body's adaptation to this increased workload leads to changes in fitness levels. For example, if improvement in muscular strength is the goal, the muscles must be exercised with a greater weight than normal.

2. **Principle of specificity.** The specificity principle indicates the need for an individual to perform a specific type of exercise to improve each fitness component or improve fitness of a specific body part.[15] Simply put, training must occur with the specific muscle or body part the person is attempting to improve.[16] Therefore, training programs should be designed and overload applied with specific goals in mind. For example, stretching exercises will have little impact on cardiorespiratory fitness, and weight training

exercises such as squats and lunges build fitness in the legs, not in the arms. Professionals must understand individuals' fitness goals and sport demands to design fitness programs specifically to achieve these aims.

3. **Principle of progression.** Overload should be applied gradually and steadily increased (i.e., progressed) for best results. As the body adapts to the overload, the overload should be systematically increased by altering the frequency, duration, or intensity of the exercise. An individual training to gain cardiorespiratory endurance may begin an exercise program by jogging 2 miles at a moderate intensity. The next week the individual would increase the distance to 2½ miles while still working at the same level of intensity. Week after week, the overload would be adjusted until the desired level of fitness were attained. Programs should be carefully monitored so that the individual is challenged by the workout but not overwhelmed.

4. **Principle of diminishing returns.** According to the dose-response relationship, as the dose or amount of physical activity increases, the gains accrued increase accordingly. As individuals become fitter, the benefits they receive from working out may not be as great as when they initially started. For example, sedentary individuals or those just beginning a fitness program tend to record the greatest magnitude of changes for small doses of physical activity. However, as these individuals become fitter, the gains achieved become less and less, even though physical activity is increased. This occurs as individuals approach their limits of adaptability. When improvements become less, or even diminish, maintenance of fitness becomes important.

5. **Principle of variation.** There are many different ways to achieve desired fitness goals. Including variation into a training program maintains individuals' interest and provides a change of pace while still making progress toward desired goals. Variation helps alleviate boredom and overcome plateaus or

periods where there seems to be little progress. Manipulating the intensity of exercise, its duration, or its type can introduce variability into the program. Alternating hard workouts with easier workouts and running in different locations within the community are some ways to introduce variability into the individual's fitness program.

6. **Principle of reversibility.** The phrase "use it or lose it" sums up this important principle. Inactivity or disuse leads to a gradual erosion of the benefits achieved through overload. Gains in fitness begin to erode in as little as 2 weeks after cessation of training. Cardiorespiratory gains deteriorate most quickly and can disappear within 5–10 weeks of inactivity.[14] Strength gains erode more slowly; some strength gains remain for six months to one year after cessation of training.[14] To retain current fitness levels, individuals must continue to be active. However, less physical activity is needed to maintain fitness than was required to achieve it. Therefore, individuals can reduce their level of physical activity through modifications in the frequency, intensity, or duration of exercise.

7. **Principle of individuality.** Individuals respond differently to exercise. Individuals will differ in their rates of improvement and their potential levels of achievement. Heredity exerts a strong influence on fitness attainment. Heart and lung size, muscle fiber types, and physique are all influenced by heredity. Age, maturation, motivation, nutrition, and initial level of fitness also influence individuals' response to training. Individuals' activity preferences exert an important influence on their continued engagement in physical activity. Consideration of individual differences and tailoring the exercise program to these needs contributes to individuals' adherence to their fitness program.

8. **Principle of recovery.** The body needs time to adapt to the demands placed on it. Incorporating time for rest into the fitness program aids the body in this effort. Many individuals integrate recovery into their training by alternating the types of activities performed or by varying the muscle groups being trained. For example, an individual may work one day on improving upper body strength and devote the next day's training to working lower body strength. Researchers have also found that working out seven days of the week increases the risk of injury.

9. **Principle of safety.** Safety is of paramount concern in designing a fitness program. Before starting a program, individuals should have a thorough medical screening. This is particularly critical when special conditions exist, such as beginning an exercise program after a long period of inactivity or

Many adults exercise with sufficient intensity, duration, and frequency to realize health benefits.

for rehabilitation after a heart attack. Special medical conditions, such as diabetes, require careful monitoring to ensure the safety of the individual. Additionally, individuals should be warned of the proper precautions to take when exercising in special weather conditions, such as intense heat, high humidity, or extreme cold. Finally, individuals should learn how to monitor carefully their responses to exercise and report any unusual occurrences (e.g., excessive breathlessness) to the professional conducting the program or to a physician.

Professionals must be aware of fitness principles when designing an exercise program. These principles offer guidelines to professionals and help ensure that individuals in their programs will achieve their fitness goals. In designing a program, professionals should include a warm-up and a cooldown. Last, professionals need to consider a host of other factors, such as goal setting and adherence, in designing and conducting fitness programs.

FITT Formula

To achieve and maintain fitness, individuals must exercise on a regular basis. They must exercise sufficiently to cross the threshold of training; to achieve optimal results, they must exercise within the fitness target zone. When professionals prescribe an exercise program for an individual, they must specify the frequency, intensity, time, and type of exercise. These variables are used in constructing an exercise prescription or program for an individual.

Each fitness component has a specific threshold of training that must be achieved. The *threshold of training* is the minimum level of exercise needed to achieve desired benefits.[12] The *target zone* begins at the threshold of training and defines the upper limits of training and the optimal level of exercise.[12] Exercise beyond the upper limit may be counterproductive.

Frequency refers to the number of exercise sessions per week—for example, three to five times per week. Achieving and maintaining health fitness requires that the individual exercise on a regular basis.

Intensity is the degree of effort or exertion put forth by the individual during exercise. It is how hard a person works. For example, the intensity of effort put forth by a runner can be described as 80% of his or her maximum effort, and the effort put forth during strength training can be described as weight lifted—for example, 80 pounds. Intensity is often viewed as the most important of the exercise variables.

Time is the duration of the length of the activity, such as 40 minutes of exercise. Time is how long an exercise must be performed to be effective.

GENERAL TRAINING PRINCIPLES

FITT Formula and Training Load	Principles
• Frequency—exercise sessions per week • Intensity—degree of effort or exertion • Time—duration of activity • Type—type of activity • Threshold of training—minimum level of activity needed to achieve desired benefits • Target zone—amount of physical activity needed to achieved desired benefits; range defined by the threshold of training and the upper limit of training	• Overload • Specificity • Progression • Diminishing returns • Variation • Reversibility • Individuality • Recovery • Safety

Type is the mode of exercise being performed. Since fitness development is specific, different types of activities build different components of fitness. Activities such as jogging, rowing, bicycling, stretching, and weight training are types of exercise that can be used to realize specific fitness gains. The selection of the type of exercise should be guided by the fitness goal to be achieved.

The acronym FITT can be used to help remember these prescriptive variables. These exercise variables are interrelated and can be manipulated to produce an exercise program appropriate to an individual's needs and to the outcomes wanted.

For example, cardiovascular improvement can be realized by jogging (type) at 70% effort (intensity) for 40 minutes (time) five times a week (frequency) or at 85% intensity for 20 minutes four times a week. Individuals who are just starting a program to improve their fitness may be more successful if they exercise at a lower intensity for a longer session. Individuals who are obese may find it beneficial to exercise for shorter periods (duration) but more often during the week (frequency).

(See the Guidelines for Developing Health-Related Fitness box for specific criteria of the FITT principle.)

GUIDELINES FOR DEVELOPING HEALTH-RELATED FITNESS

Cardiorespiratory endurance

- Frequency: 3–5 days per week
- Intensity: 55%/65–90% of maximal heart rate or 40%/50–85% of heart rate reserve*
- Time: 20–60 minutes
- Type: Aerobic activity

Muscular strength and endurance

- Frequency: 3 days per week
- Intensity: Strength requires high resistance, 6–8 repetitions

  Endurance requires low resistance, 12–20 repetitions
- Time: 1–3 sets
- Type: Isotonic or progressive resistance exercises; can also use isometric and isokinetic exercises

Flexibility

- Frequency: 2–3 days per week
- Intensity: Stretch past the normal length until resistance is felt
- Time: Hold the stretch 5–10 seconds initially, building to 30–45 seconds
- Type: Static or contract-relax techniques

Body composition

- Maintain present level of physical activity and reduce caloric intake
- Maintain present level of caloric intake and increase level of physical activity
- Reduce caloric intake and increase level of physical activity
- Eat a diet low in fat

*ACSM guidelines[17] state that lower intensity values—that is, 55–64% of maximal heart rate or 40–49% of heart rate reserve—may be appropriate for those individuals who are unfit.

Triathletes train to develop high levels of fitness and skill in several sports.

HEALTH FITNESS COMPONENTS

Health fitness can help prevent hypokinetic diseases, which are caused by insufficient physical activity. People who have hypokinetic diseases frequently experience loss of flexibility, cardiovascular degeneration, bone and muscle weakness, and bladder and bowel malfunctions. One risk factor that contributes to premature susceptibility to heart disease and stroke is lack of physical activity. Moreover, it is believed that hypertension and obesity, which are also risk factors associated with heart disease, can be helped by participation in regular physical activity.

The components of health fitness include cardiorespiratory endurance, body composition, muscular strength and endurance, and flexibility. In this section, each fitness component is defined, its relationship to health delineated, methods to improve the fitness component discussed, and techniques to measure the component identified.

Cardiorespiratory Endurance

Cardiorespiratory endurance is the body's ability to deliver oxygen effectively to the working muscles so that an individual can perform physical activity. Efficient functioning of the cardiovascular system (i.e., heart and blood vessels) and the respiratory system (i.e., lungs) is essential for the distribution of oxygen and nutrients and removal of wastes from the body.

The performance of sustained vigorous physical activities is influenced by the efficiency of the cardiorespiratory system. The more efficient the system, the greater the amount of physical activity an individual can perform before fatigue and exhaustion occur. Performance diminishes greatly when sufficient oxygen cannot be provided by the cardiorespiratory system to the working muscles.

Cardiorespiratory endurance is regarded as the most important component of health fitness. Because of the benefits derived from improved cardiorespiratory function—such as the potential for reducing the risk of cardiovascular disease, improving work capacity, and providing greater resistance to fatigue—this component, if properly developed, can make a major contribution to an individual's health.

Cardiorespiratory endurance is concerned with the aerobic efficiency of the body. Aerobic efficiency is the body's ability to supply fuel and oxygen to the muscles. One of the major factors influencing aerobic efficiency is the capacity of the heart to pump blood. A well-conditioned heart is able to exert greater force with each heartbeat; consequently, a larger volume of blood is pumped through the arteries and throughout the body.

Another important factor in cardiorespiratory endurance is the efficiency of the lungs. The amount of oxygen that can be supplied to working muscles is a limiting factor in performance. When demands for oxygen increase, such as during strenuous exercise, the body's ability to take in and provide oxygen to the working muscles is an important determinant of the amount of work that can be performed. The greater the body's ability to take in and deliver oxygen, the longer a person can exercise before fatigue and exhaustion occur. Thus, individuals who have well-developed circulatory and respiratory systems can deliver more oxygen and therefore can exercise for a longer period.

Many benefits have been attributed to aerobic exercise. Aerobic exercise is activity that can be sustained for an extended period without building an oxygen debt in the muscles. Bicycling, jogging, skipping rope, rowing, walking, cross-country skiing, and swimming are some examples of aerobic activities.

The benefits of aerobic exercise include the ability to use more oxygen during strenuous exercise, a lower heart rate at work, the production of less lactic acid, and greater endurance. Aerobic exercise improves the efficiency of the heart and reduces blood pressure.

Cardiorespiratory endurance is important for the performance of many sport activities. In sport activities that require an individual to perform for an extended period, such as a 500-yard swim or a soccer game, cardiorespiratory endurance can have a profound impact on performance.

Individuals who have trained and developed a high level of cardiorespiratory endurance can work at a higher level of intensity without fatigue than individuals who are unfit. Additionally, fit individuals can perform more work before reaching exhaustion. Furthermore, following exercise, fit individuals recover faster than unfit individuals.

Cardiorespiratory fitness can be improved and maintained through a well-planned program of exercise that follows the FITT formula. Physical activity of an appropriate frequency, intensity, duration, and type can enhance cardiorespiratory fitness.

Frequency. The ACSM recommends three to five exercise sessions per week for minimal improvement in cardiovascular fitness. Many individuals choose to work out more often; however, the body must have time to recover from the effects of exercise. Exercising every other day and following a strenuous workout day with a less strenuous recovery day are strategies individuals can implement to allow the body to recover.

Intensity. For development of cardiorespiratory fitness, physical activities must be of sufficient intensity. During exercise, heart rate changes in proportion to the energy requirements of the task. As the energy requirements increase, there is a corresponding increase in heart rate. Thus, heart rate can be used to monitor the intensity of exercise. (See the Measuring Your Heart Rate box). Because heart rate slows within 1 minute following exercise, it is often recommended that

the pulse be monitored for 10 seconds and then multiplied by 6 (or monitored for 6 seconds and multiplied by 10) to determine beats per minute. For an accurate reading, the heart rate should be monitored within 15 seconds of the cessation of exercise.

Exercising at the proper intensity is essential for a safe and effective workout. Intensity can be controlled by speeding or slowing the pace of exercise. To realize training benefits, the intensity of the exercise must be regulated so that the heart rate is elevated to a predetermined level and maintained within a certain range. This level is called the threshold of training and the range is called the target heart rate zone.

The ACSM recommends that individuals who desire to develop and maintain cardiorespiratory fitness should exercise at one of the following intensity levels:

- 55/65%–90% of maximal heart rate (HR_{max})
- 40%/50%–85% of heart rate reserve (HRR)
- Maximum oxygen uptake reserve (VO_2R)

The lower intensities, 55–64% of HR_{max} and 40–49% of HRR, are most appropriate for individuals who have a low level of fitness.[17]

Maximal heart rate (HR_{max}) for both males and females is estimated to be 220 beats per minute. Maximal heart rate is related to age; as individuals age, their maximal heart rate decreases. HR_{max} is calculated by the following formula:

$$HR_{max} = 220 - age$$

Heart rate reserve (HRR) is the difference or range between resting heart rate (RHR) and maximal heart rate (HR_{max}). HRR is calculated by the following formula:

$$HRR = HR_{max} - RHR$$

There are several formulas that can be used to calculate a target heart rate (THR) to monitor the intensity of exercise. One way is to calculate a percentage of HR_{max}. This can be done by using the following quick and simple formula:

$$THR = (Target\ Intensity)(HR_{max}).$$

Another method to calculate target heart rate is to use a formula based on HRR. This method, commonly called the Karvonen Equation, takes into account the individual's resting heart rate and provides a more accurate estimation than the HRmax formula. This formula is

$$THR = (Target\ Intensity)(HR_{max} - RHR) + RHR.$$

Examples of these calculations are shown in the Examples for Calculations of Heart Rate for Training Zone Using HR_{max} and HRR Methods box.

Target heart rates allow individuals to easily monitor their exercise and reach sufficient intensity to cross the threshold of training and be in the target heart rate zone. Individuals should select an intensity that takes into account their current level of fitness and their fitness goals. Intensity can be progressively increased as conditions warrant.

Time. The ACSM recommends 20–60 minutes of continuous aerobic activity. This amount can be accumulated during one or more sessions throughout the day. The exercise sessions should be a minimum of 10 minutes in duration.[17]

The intensity and duration of the activity are critical to achieving and maintaining fitness. Generally, as the intensity of the activity increases, its duration decreases; conversely, as intensity decreases, the duration of the activity increases. Typically, for the development of health-related cardiorespiratory endurance, lower intensities and longer durations are recommended. It is important to remember, however, that both the intensity and

MEASURING YOUR HEART RATE

You can determine your heart rate by counting the frequency with which your heart contracts in a period of time and converting this to the standard measure in beats per minute. Make sure you press just firmly enough to feel the pulse. If you press too hard it may interfere with the rhythm.

You can detect your pulse by placing a finger or fingers on your lower arm near the base of the thumb.

Your pulse can also be easily detected over the carotid artery in the front of the neck.

Students at Agassiz Middle School in Fargo, N.D., use heart rate monitors to measure the intensity of their efforts.

heart rate is maintained at an elevated level for an extended period. These activities typically involve vigorous and repetitive whole-body or large muscle movements that are sustained for an extended period. Popular aerobic activities include jogging, running, walking, swimming, cycling, rowing, aerobic dance, and cross-country skiing. Because these activities are somewhat continuous in nature, the intensity of the workload can be easily regulated by controlling the pace. Intermittent activities such as racquetball, basketball, and tennis involve various intensities of effort during the course of the activity. Thus, it is more difficult to regulate the degree of effort expended during these activities. However, these activities can contribute to the improvement of cardiorespiratory endurance if they are of sufficient intensity.

In summary, to develop and maintain cardiorespiratory fitness, it is recommended that the individual exercise three to five times a week, with an intensity sufficient to elevate and sustain the heart rate in the target zone for at least 20 minutes. Exercise should involve aerobic activities that are continuous, vigorous, and,

duration of the activity must meet minimum requirements for fitness development to occur.

Type. Aerobic activities should be used to develop cardiorespiratory endurance. Aerobic activities are those in which a sufficient amount of oxygen is available to meet the body's demands. During the performance of these activities, the

Examples for Calculations of Heart Rate for Training Zone Using HR_{max} and HRR Methods

A 20-year-old has a resting heart rate (RHR) of 70 beats per minute (bpm). Calculate the training zone—the threshold and upper limits for training. If the person wants to train at an intensity of 65%, calculate the target heart rate (THR).

	Maximal Heart Rate (HR_{max})	Heart Rate Reserve (HRR)
Formula	THR = (Target Intensity)(HR_{max})	THR = (Target Intensity)(HR_{max} − RHR) + RHR
HR_{max}	HR_{max} = (220−age) = 200 bpm	HR_{max} = (220−age) = 200 bpm
Threshold of Training	THR = (55%)(200) = 110 bpm	THR = (40%)(200−70) + 70 = 122 bpm
Upper Limit Target Zone	THR = (90%)(200) = 180 bpm	THR = (85%)(200−70) + 70 = 181 bpm
Training at 65% Intensity	THR = (65%)(200) = 130 bpm	THR = (65%)(200−70) + 70 = 155 bpm

Practice calculating training heart rates using different ages, intensities, and resting heart rates. What patterns do you notice?

most important, enjoyable to the individual. Individuals who stop exercising tend to lose their fitness gains within 5 to 10 weeks. Achieving and maintaining a high level of this critical fitness component requires a long-term commitment and the incorporation of exercise into one's lifestyle.

Cardiorespiratory fitness can be measured. The best method to determine the level of cardiovascular functioning is to measure maximum oxygen consumption. The more oxygen the body is able to deliver and use, the more work the body is able to perform before becoming fatigued. Maximum oxygen consumption is the greatest rate at which the oxygen is processed and used by the body.

Measurement of maximum oxygen consumption requires a sophisticated laboratory setting and well-trained personnel to monitor carefully

A grade exercise test on the treadmill can be used to determine maximum oxygen consumption.

Source: Wilson, G.—Exploring Exercise Science 2010, McGraw-Hill. Reproduced with permission of The McGraw-Hill Companies.

the performance of the individual during the test. This testing is usually done on an individual basis. Following prescribed test protocols, the individual exercises on a treadmill or bicycle ergometer and breathes through a specially designed mouthpiece. Various physiological and metabolic parameters are monitored, such as heart rate, respiration rate, and rate of oxygen consumption. The exercise task is made progressively more difficult until no further increase in oxygen consumption is noted; this point is considered to be the maximum oxygen intake for the task. Although this test yields highly accurate information, it is expensive and time consuming, and requires sophisticated equipment and highly trained personnel.

There are a variety of other methods that can be used to provide a good estimate of cardiorespiratory endurance. These tests measure the maximum amount of work that can be performed over a specified period. The most commonly used tests are the 12-minute or the 9-minute run/walk, the timed $1\frac{1}{2}$- or 1-mile run/walk, and the Harvard step test. These tests are most often used in school and community fitness programs. When these tests are properly conducted, results can be used to accurately estimate maximum oxygen consumption and provide an indicator of cardiorespiratory fitness.

Body Composition

Body composition is a description of the body in terms of muscle, bone, fat, and other elements. With respect to health fitness, it refers to the percentage of body weight composed of fat as compared with fat-free or lean tissue. Having a high percentage of body fat is a serious deterrent to fitness and health.

Height and weight tables traditionally have been used to determine desirable body weight. Individuals whose body weight exceeds set standards for their sex, age, and physical stature by 10% to 20% are considered overweight.[14] People overweight by 20% of their optimum weight are obese, and those who are overweight by more than 50% of their optimum weight are considered morbidly obese or superobese.[14]

It should be noted that being overweight can be attributed to having an excess of either fatty or lean tissue. For example, certain athletes, such as football players, could be classified as overweight. However, when their body composition is examined, the excess weight is attributable to muscular development and their overall percentage of body fat is quite low (e.g., a professional football player can weigh 250 pounds or more, yet have only 12% body fat or less). The important consideration with respect to health fitness, therefore, is not weight but proportion of fat to lean tissue.

The average percentage of body fat is 18% for men and 23% for women. (For different ranges of body fat, see the Body Fat Percentage Norms for Men and Women box.) The percentage of body fat should not be less than 5% in men and 12% in women (the higher percentage for women is necessary for protection of the reproductive organs).[14] Extremely low percentages of body fat are hazardous to one's health. It is highly important that professionals and the public realize that a certain amount of adipose tissue or fat is essential for the body to function. Body fat also serves to protect internal organs. *The goal of fitness programs is not eliminating body fat, but helping individuals attain desirable levels of body fat.*

Body composition can also be assessed using the body mass index (BMI). The National Institutes of Health (NIH) has adopted the use of the BMI to determine if an individual is at risk for poor health outcomes due to overweight or obesity.[18] BMI is calculated by dividing the weight of the individual in kilograms by the height in meters squared (for an estimate, multiply the individual's weight in pounds by 703 and then divide by the height in inches squared). For most people, BMI more closely correlates with total body fat than the traditional height-weight tables and provides a clearer indication of disease risk.[18] However, one limitation of BMI is that it overestimates the degree of fatness of very muscular individuals.

According to the NIH Clinical Guidelines, for adults, overweight is defined as a BMI between 25 kg/m² and 29.9 kg/m² and obesity is defined

BODY FAT PERCENTAGE NORMS FOR MEN AND WOMEN

Description	Women	Men
Essential Fat	10–13%	2–5%
Athletes	14–20%	6–13%
Fitness	21–24%	14–17%
Acceptable Range	25–31%	18–24%
Obesity	>32%	>25%

Source: *ACE Lifestyle & Weight Management Consultant Manual*

as a BMI of 30 kg/m² or greater.[18] A person who has a BMI of 30 kg/m² is about 30 pounds overweight; a person who weighs 221 pounds and is 6 feet tall and person who is 5 feet 6 inches tall and weighs 186 pounds both have a BMI of about 30 kg/m².[18] For children and adolescents, overweight is defined as a BMI at or above the 95th percentile for age and sex, based on the revised CDC growth charts.[19]

The health consequences of overweight and obesity are enormous. Approximately 400,000 deaths per year are associated with overweight and obesity.[19] Epidemiological studies show that people who are obese have a 50% to 100% increased risk of premature death from all causes compared to those persons with a BMI of 20 to 25 kg/m².

Overweight and obesity are associated with increased risk for coronary heart disease, type 2 diabetes, certain types of cancer, low-back pain, respiratory problems, and musculoskeletal disorders such as knee osteoarthritis. For example, a weight gain of 10 to 20 pounds presents an increased risk of coronary heart disease (nonfatal myocardial infarction and death) of 1.25 times in women and 1.6 times in men.[19,20] Greater weight gains—22 pounds in men and 44 pounds in women—result in an increased coronary heart disease risk of 1.75 and 2.65, respectively.[19–21] Additionally, overweight and obese individuals may experience social stigmatization, discrimination, and poor body image.[18]

Body composition is influenced by nutrition and physical activity. Although body composition is genetically related to body type, the nature and amount of food consumed and the extent of participation in physical activity exert a profound influence on body composition. Poor nutritional practices contribute to an unfavorable body composition. Eating more calories than needed and consuming a high-fat diet lead to high percentages of body fat.

Dietary guidelines suggest that individuals reduce their consumption of fat. The average American derives 34% of his or her calories from fat, compared with the recommended 25% to 30% with no more than 10% from saturated fats.[22] Sedentary individuals have lower levels of caloric expenditure. Leading a physically active lifestyle can contribute to a favorable body composition.

Energy balance is important to achieving a favorable body composition. The relationship between food intake and energy expenditure is critical. This relationship is often referred to as energy or caloric balance:

Energy or caloric balance	=	Number of calories taken into the body as food	−	Number of calories expended

Energy is expended through three processes: (1) basal metabolism, or maintenance of essential life functions; (2) work, which is any activity requiring more energy than sleeping and includes exercise; and (3) excretion of body wastes.

A neutral balance occurs when the caloric intake is equal to the caloric expenditure. Under these circumstances, body weight is maintained. When a positive balance exists—that is, when more calories are consumed than expended—the excess is stored as fat and body weight increases. A negative balance occurs when more calories are expended than consumed; this results in weight loss. Weight control requires maintaining the appropriate energy or caloric balance.

Caloric tables are useful in monitoring the number of calories consumed. Energy expenditure

tables are helpful in monitoring energy expended. (See the Caloric Expenditures for Common Physical Activities box.) These tables provide information about the calories expended both during the performance of daily living tasks such as house cleaning and during participation in physical activities such as bicycling.

Body composition can be improved. Individuals who have an unhealthy percentage of body fat can reduce it by modifying their lifestyle. Fat loss can be accomplished by several means: (1) consuming fewer calories through dieting, (2) increasing caloric expenditure by increasing the amount of exercise, and (3) combining a moderate decrease in caloric consumption with a moderate increase in exercise or caloric expenditure.

Exercise increasingly is being recognized as a critical component of fat loss. Often those desiring to lose fat focus on counting the number of calories consumed and neglect the exercise component. Exercise can aid in fat loss in several ways: (1) it can increase caloric expenditures (a 180-pound person walking 4 miles in an hour will expend approximately 400 calories); (2) it can suppress appetite and thereby contribute to reduction in caloric intake; (3) it can increase the metabolic rate for some time after vigorous exercise, thereby permitting extra calories to be burned; and (4) it can contribute to health fitness. Also, because sedentary living contributes to poor body composition, incorporation of regular appropriate exercise into one's lifestyle helps to successfully manage one's body composition.

Note that individuals who desire to gain weight should focus on increasing lean body mass (muscle) rather than body fat. This can be accomplished by following a sound muscle training program in conjunction with an appropriate increase in caloric intake to realize a gain of 1 to 2 pounds per week. Failure to incorporate muscle training as part of a total fitness program will result in excess calories being converted to fat. Thus, even though the weight gain is achieved, the percentage of body fat may be less than optimal. Therefore, a weight gaining program should combine a reasonable increase in caloric intake and a well-planned

CALORIC EXPENDITURES FOR COMMON PHYSICAL ACTIVITIES

Moderate Physical Activity	Calories/ Hour	Vigorous Physical Activity	Calories/ Hour
Hiking	370	Running/jogging (5 mph)	590
Light gardening/yard work	330	Bicycling (>10 mph)	590
Dancing	330	Swimming (slow freestyle laps)	510
Golf (walking and carrying clubs)	330	Aerobics	480
Bicycling (<10 mph)	290	Walking (4.5 mph)	460
Walking (3.5 mph)	280	Heavy yard work (chopping wood)	440
Weight lifting (general light workout)	220	Weight lifting (vigorous effort)	440
Stretching	180	Basketball (vigorous)	440

Note: Approximate calories per hour for a 154-pound person. Calories burned per hour will be higher for people who weigh more than 154 pounds (70 kilograms) and lower for people who weigh less.

Source: Adapted from the 2005 *Dietary Guidelines Advisory Committee Report,* United States Department of Agriculture.

http://www.health.gov/DietaryGuidelines/dga2005/document/html/chapter3.htm

muscle training program to achieve an optimal body composition.

Sound practices should be followed in losing fat. Experts suggest the following guidelines regarding fat loss:

1. Prolonged fasting and diets that severely restrict calories are medically dangerous. These programs result in loss of large amounts of water, electrolytes, minerals, glycogen stores, and other fat-free tissue, with a minimal amount of fat loss.

2. Moderate caloric restriction is desirable, such as consuming 500 calories less than the usual daily intake. It is important that the minimum caloric intake not go below 1,200 calories per day for a woman and 1,400 calories per day for a man, and that sound nutritional practices are followed.

3. Appropriate regular exercise of the large muscles assists in the maintenance of fat-free tissue, including muscle mass and bone density, and results in the loss of weight, primarily in the form of fat.

4. A sound program should be comprehensive in nature. It should include a nutritionally sound, low-fat diet with mild caloric restriction, regular and appropriate exercise to increase caloric expenditure, and behavior modification. Weight loss should not exceed 2 pounds per week.

5. Maintenance of proper weight and desirable body composition requires a lifetime commitment to proper eating habits and regular physical activity.

A word of caution: Some individuals become obsessed with weight loss, dieting, and exercise. This obsession can, in conjunction with a host of other factors, contribute to the development of an eating disorder. Two common eating disorders are anorexia nervosa and bulimia.

Anorexia nervosa is a disease in which a person develops a psychological aversion to food, resulting in a pathologic weight loss. Bulimia involves recurrent episodes of binge eating and subsequent purging by self-induced vomiting, use of laxatives, and/or excessive exercising. Both disorders have a higher prevalence among young women, although men do suffer from these conditions as well. These disorders pose a severe threat to health and require professional treatment.

Body composition can be measured. Several methods can be used to determine the percentage of body fat. One of the most accurate methods is hydrostatic weighing. This involves weighing an individual on land and then in an underwater tank. Body density is then determined, and this information is used to calculate the percentage of lean body weight and body fat. This technique is used most often in exercise physiology laboratories and hospitals. It requires expensive equipment and is time consuming, thus is not practical for use with large groups of people.

Air displacement plethysmography, also known as the Bod Pod, offers another means of assessment of body composition. Similar to hydrostatic weighing, the Bod Pod uses air instead of water. A person sits in the enclosed chamber (pod) and computerized sensors measure the amount of air displaced by the person's body. This approach offers similar accuracy to underwater weighing without requiring a person be submerged in water. It is easy to use, but its cost limits its availability. This technique is used most often in exercise physiology laboratories or clinical settings.

Dual-energy X-ray absorptiometry (DXA) is an extremely accurate way to assess body composition. This technique requires that the individual lie on a table while a machine, using two energy sources, scans alongside the body. This procedure yields an estimate of the body's density as well as information about the amounts of fat stored in different parts of the body. DXA is now considered the gold standard for measurement of body composition. Because it is extremely accurate,

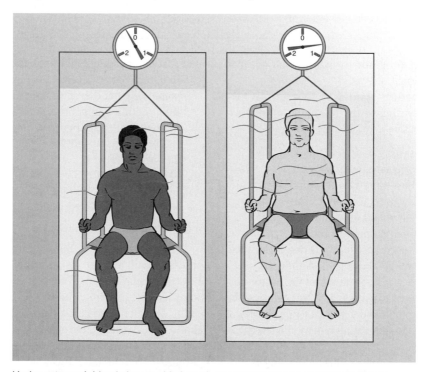

Underwater weighing is is a sophisticated, accurate technique used to determine body composition. In this illustration, the underwater weighing technique demonstrates two individuals with the same height and weight, but different body composition.

Source: Powers, S. K., Howley, E. T. (2009). Exercise Physiology: Theory and Application to Fitness and Performance (ed 7), McGraw-Hill. Reproduced with permission of The McGraw-Hill Companies.

DXA estimates of body composition can serve as a criterrion by which other techniques, such as skinfolds, can be compared. Assessment of body composition with this technique is typically performed in exercise physiology research laboratories or in clinical settings.

Bioelectrical impedance analysis is an increasingly popular way to assess body composition. Electrodes are attached to an individual's body at the wrist and ankle, and a low-level electrical current is sent through the body. The resistance to the flow of the current as it passes through the body is measured. Because muscle tissue has a greater water content than fat tissue, it conducts electricity better and offers less resistance to the current. The resistance to the current is greater when there is a high percentage of body fat. The resistance to the current and body size are used to estimate the percentage of body fat. Assessments of individuals who are dehydrated or have eaten within three to four hours of the measurements may yield inaccurate results. There are also scales that incorporate the same principles to provide estimates of body fatness; the individual stands on a metal plate atop the scale and the resistance to the flow of the current is measured. Bioelectrical

impedance analysis can be performed relatively quickly, making it easy to use in field-based settings or to screen large groups of people.

Of the alternative approaches to measurement, the most common is the use of skinfold measurements. Skinfold measurements are taken from several selected sites, such as the triceps, subscapular, and thigh, with skinfold calipers. Formulas are then used to calculate the percentage of body fat. This method is relatively inexpensive, can be used with large groups of people, and produces accurate information when performed by well-trained individuals.

Professionals need to be cognizant of the limitations associated with the various measures of body composition. It is important to recognize circumstances under which results may be misleading, such as when the body composition values are affected by an individual's hydration status or when an individual is overweight due to having a high muscle mass rather than being overfat. Errors such as these may result in individuals being classified as obese or unfit, when they are actually healthy and fit. Professionals should make sure they know how to administer the assessment correctly and can interpret the results accurately.

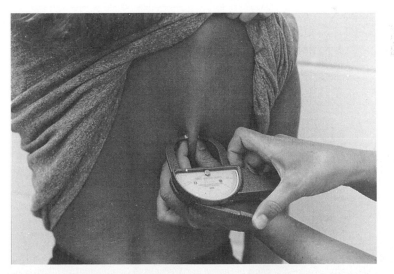

Skinfold measurements can be used to calculate a person's percentage of body fat.

Muscular Strength and Endurance

Muscular strength is the ability of a muscle or muscle group to exert force against a resistance. Specifically, it is the maximum amount of force that a muscle or muscle group can apply against a resistance in a single effort.

The ability of a muscle or muscle group to exert force repeatedly is known as muscular endurance. Muscular endurance also refers to the capacity of a muscle or muscle group to sustain a contractive state over a period of time.

Different muscles in the body can have different levels of strength and endurance. Moreover, muscles used more frequently are stronger and have greater endurance than muscles used less frequently. When muscles are not used, strength and endurance decrease.

Many people perceive muscular strength and endurance as important only for athletes or those engaged in occupations that require heavy work, for example, construction. Although muscular strength and endurance are necessary for these people to perform their responsibilities effectively, these fitness components are also important for all people. Strength and endurance are necessary for performing everyday tasks, maintaining proper posture, and resisting fatigue. As individuals age, maintaining adequate levels of strength and endurance is particularly important, because these fitness components play a critical role in the maintenance of functional independence. Additionally, the development of adequate strength and endurance is an important objective of many rehabilitation programs.

Muscular strength and endurance are important to good health. They contribute to the maintenance of proper posture and the improvement of personal appearance. Because strong muscles provide better protection for body joints, the risk of joint injuries is decreased. Millions of Americans suffer from low-back pain. Weak abdominal muscles and poor flexibility contribute to this problem. Strengthening the appropriate muscles and developing increased flexibility can help alleviate this condition.

High levels of muscular strength and endurance are important for athletes. Strength is a critical element of sport performance. Strength training for sport must be specifically related to the particular characteristics required for performance of the sport. Thus, the strength training of a sprinter will differ markedly from that of a shot

Three types of muscle fitness exercises: (A) isotonic, (B) isometric, and (C) isokinetic.

Source: Corbin, Welk, Corbin, Welk—*Concepts of Fitness and Wellness: A Comprehensive Lifestyle Approach* (ed 8) 2009, McGraw-Hill. Reproduced with permission of The McGraw-Hill Companies.

putter, which will be different from that of a gymnast. For effective performance, each athlete requires the development of a high level of strength in specific muscles or muscle groups.

Strength combines with other physical elements to enhance the quality of performance. For example, power, which is strength combined with speed, is an important motor skill fitness component. Power is the quality that permits a basketball player to jump high and to snare rebounds off the backboard, a golfer to drive a golf ball 250 yards down the fairway, or a gymnast to execute a double back somersault. Many movements in sport require an explosive effort during execution. When force is generated quickly, the movement is known as a *power movement*. Power is critical to successful performance in many sports today, and proper strength training can enhance this component.

Isometric, isotonic, and isokinetic exercises can be used to develop muscular strength and endurance. Body movements depend on the contraction of muscles. As a muscle contracts, tension is created within the muscle and the muscle shortens, lengthens, or remains the same.

Isometric exercises. A muscle contracts isometrically when it exerts force against an immovable resistance. Although tension develops within the muscle, the length of the muscle remains relatively constant and there is little to no movement on the joint. This is referred to as a *static contraction*. For example, stand in a doorway and place the palms of your hands at shoulder height against the frame. Push with all your might and feel the tension develop in your muscles. Even if you grunt and groan as you contract your muscles to their maximum, it is impossible for you to move the resistance, in this case, the door frame.

Another approach to performing isometric contractions is to contract one muscle against another muscle, applying an equal and opposite force; in this case, the opposing muscle serves as a resistance. For example, raise your arms to shoulder height and place your palms together. Push against your palms as you contract your muscles. There should be no movement as your muscles work against one another.

When one is performing isometric exercises, it is suggested that the muscle generate a maximum force for 5 seconds, with the contraction repeated five to ten times each day. Isometrics offer the advantage of not requiring any equipment; any immovable object or your own body serves as the resistance. One frequently cited disadvantage of isometric exercise is that strength is developed at only a specific joint angle, not through the entire range of motion. Isometric exercises are most often used to develop strength at a specific joint angle to enhance a particular movement or for injury rehabilitation.

Isotonic exercises. Isotonic contractions occur when force is generated while the muscle is changing in length. For example, to lift a weight from its starting point when performing a biceps curl, the biceps muscle must contract and shorten in length. This is called a *concentric contraction*. To control the weight as it is lowered back to the starting position, the biceps muscle continues to contract while gradually lengthening. This is referred to as an *eccentric contraction*. When exercising isotonically, it is essential to use both concentric and eccentric contractions for the greatest improvement to occur and also to exercise through the range of motion.

One problem associated with isotonic training is that the force applied to the weight varies throughout the range of motion. This is attributable to the effects of gravity and the system of levers within the body. Once the initial resistance is overcome, lifting the weight can be easy or difficult, depending on the position of the weight relative to the body. Thus, the muscles are not working at or near their maximum effort throughout the range of motion.

Common forms of isotonic exercise equipment are free weights, barbells, dumbbells, and various machines. Some isotonic exercise machines have been designed specifically to vary the resistance throughout the range of motion. This permits the muscles to exert their maximum effort throughout the entire range of motion.

Isotonic exercises are probably the most popular means of developing strength and endurance.

Millions of people use this approach to achieve and maintain desired levels of muscular development.

Isokinetic exercises. When one is performing isokinetic exercises, the length of the muscle changes while the contraction is performed at a constant velocity. Isokinetic devices such as the Cybex are designed so that the resistance can be moved only at a certain speed, regardless of the amount of force applied. The speed at which the resistance can be moved is the key to this exercise approach. Because isokinetic machines can be expensive, they are most often used in the diagnosis and treatment of various injuries.

Muscular strength and endurance can be improved. Many different methods of training can be effective to develop these fitness components. Although weight training is not necessary to realize gains in muscular strength and endurance, this approach is popular with many people. The term *progressive resistance exercise* is commonly used to denote weight training programs that involve working out against a resistance that is progressively increased as the muscle adapts to the workload or resistance.

Although all principles of training should be incorporated into a weight training program, the principle of overload is of critical importance. Improvements in strength and endurance occur only when a muscle or muscle group is worked at a higher level than that to which it is accustomed—it must be overloaded. As muscle development increases, the body adapts to the level of resistance. To further improve, the workload must be progressively increased. Once the desired level of fitness is achieved, maintenance of this level requires continued training at the current resistance.

When planning a training program, one must consider the weight used per lift, the number of repetitions per set, the number of sets per workout, and the number of workouts per week. (For more information, see the Definitions for Muscular Strength and Endurance Training box.) Because there are so many weight training programs available, only general guidelines with respect to frequency, intensity, and duration will be presented.

Frequency. The training program must include time for the muscles to rest and recover from the workout while adapting to a higher physiological level. The same muscle group should not be worked on successive days. Recommended frequency plans are a full-body workout every other day; alternate lower- and upper-body workouts; and working each muscle group 1 or 2 days per week.

Intensity. The intensity of the workout refers to the extent to which the muscles are overloaded. Overload can be accomplished by any combination of the following: increasing the resistance or weight lifted, increasing the number of repetitions per set, increasing the number of sets per workout, increasing or decreasing the speed at which the repetition is performed, and decreasing the time of rest between sets.

Programs can be designed to develop strength, endurance, or both, depending on the number of repetitions and the amount of resistance selected.

Time. The duration of the training program depends on the person's level of fitness, fitness goals, equipment available, and time available to work out. One to three sets are often completed of each exercise. The amount of rest between each set varies according to the individual's program. It is recommended to change a strength and endurance program every 8 to 12 weeks to provide variability to the muscles and continue to apply overload.

Muscular strength and endurance can be measured. Because muscular strength and endurance are specific to each muscle or muscle group, the level of development can vary among the various muscles or muscle groups. Therefore, the strength and endurance of each muscle or muscle group must be measured.

Strength can be measured isometrically by using a dynamometer. As muscle contraction occurs, the force is transmitted to the instrument and can be recorded (e.g., the hand dynamometer can be used to determine grip strength). Strength can be measured isotonically by determining the maximum amount of weight that can be moved

DEFINITIONS FOR MUSCULAR STRENGTH AND ENDURANCE TRAINING

Resistance	Workload or weight being moved.
Repetition maximum (RM)	Maximum force that can be exerted or maximum weight of resistance lifted in a single effort; the intensity of the workout can be expressed as a percentage of 1 RM (e.g., if a person can bench-press 200 pounds, 80% of 1 RM would be 160 pounds).
Repetition	Performance of a designated movement or exercise pattern through the full range of motion.
Set	Number of repetitions performed without a rest.

once through the designated range of motion (e.g., bench press); this is 1 repetition maximum or 1 RM.

Endurance can be measured by determining the number of repetitions of a particular movement that can be performed continuously (e.g., the number of repetitions of the bench press that can be performed with a designated resistance) or the number of repetitions performed within a specified period of time (e.g., the number of sit-ups that can be performed in 1 minute). Endurance also can be determined by measuring the time a specific contraction can be sustained (e.g., how long a static push-up can be held).

Flexibility

Flexibility can be defined as the maximum range of motion possible at a joint—that is, the extent

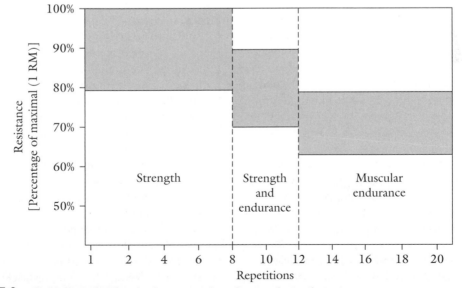

Figure 7-2   Guidelines for developing strength and muscular endurance

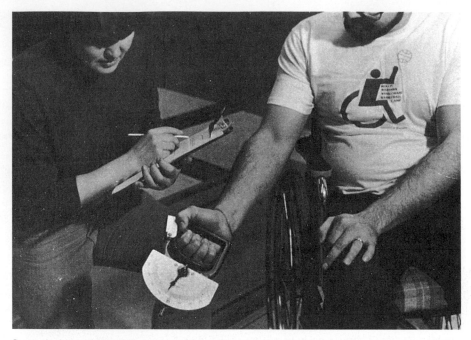

Some devices are specially designed to assess grip strength, such as this hand dynamometer.

of movement possible about a joint without undue strain. Although it is one of the most important fitness components, it is often overlooked, and consequently its development is neglected.

The extent of movement possible at a joint is influenced by the structure of the joint. For example, the elbow and the knee are hinge joints, allowing movement in one direction only; flexion (bending) and extension (straightening) are the only movements possible. In contrast, the shoulder and hip are ball-and-socket joints; this joint structure allows movement in many directions, usually with a greater range than the hinge joint. Soft tissues such as muscles, tendons, and ligaments greatly influence the range of movement possible at a joint. Flexibility is affected by the length that a muscle can stretch (i.e., its elasticity). When muscles are not used, they tend to become shorter and tighter, thus reducing the joint's range of motion.

Flexibility is essential to performing everyday tasks and is also a critical component in the performance of many sport activities. Activities such as gymnastics, yoga, swimming, karate, and dance place a premium on flexibility. Limited flexibility decreases the efficiency with which everyday and sport activities can be performed. Thus, the development of flexibility should be addressed in designing a fitness program.

Flexibility is important to good health. Flexibility is important for maintaining good posture. Poor postural alignment can cause pain and limit one's ability to move freely.

Flexibility can help prevent low-back pain. Nearly 85 million Americans suffer from episodes of low-back pain each year. This condition is caused by poor muscle development and poor flexibility. Improving muscle development and flexibility in conjunction with using proper care in sitting, standing, and lifting objects can help alleviate this condition.

Flexibility is also important for preventing muscle injuries. Poor flexibility can contribute to uncoordinated and awkward movements, thus increasing the potential for injury. Muscle soreness and body stiffness following vigorous physical activity can be alleviated by using a good stretching program to develop flexibility both before and after an activity session.

Flexibility is important for the performance of physical activities. Flexibility is important to the performance of even the simplest everyday activities. Imagine how difficult it would be to get dressed without adequate flexibility. Developing and maintaining flexibility are critical to helping elderly people be functionally independent. Some physical conditions, such as arthritis or cerebral palsy, severely restrict flexibility. Improving flexibility to the greatest degree possible, given one's capabilities, can have a significant impact on one's quality of life—even to the extent of allowing a dependent individual to become functionally independent.

Athletes recognize the importance of flexibility in sport performance. Adequate flexibility can enhance performance capabilities by allowing the athlete to stretch and reach further, to generate more force when kicking or throwing an object, and to change positions more quickly and efficiently. Poor flexibility can adversely affect performance. For example, a sprinter may have a shorter stride length and less speed because tight hamstring muscles can adversely affect his or her ability to flex the hip joint. Because certain sports require an extremely high degree of flexibility for successful performance, stretching exercises to enhance flexibility are typically included as part of an athlete's warm-up and cooldown activities. These activities enhance the elasticity of the muscles and thus help reduce the likelihood of injury and muscle soreness.

Decreased flexibility can be caused by many factors. People who are active tend to have better flexibility than those who are sedentary. When muscles are not used, they tend to become shorter, tighter, and less elastic. Consequently, flexibility decreases. Age is another factor that influences the extent of flexibility. It is important to encourage people to remain active as they grow older so that the effects of aging on fitness will be minimized.

Excessive amounts of body fat impede movement and flexibility. Consider the difficulty of

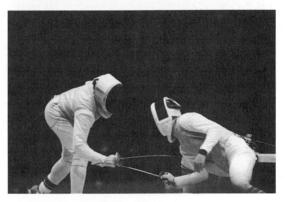

To be successful, athletes must develop the fitness components required by their sports.

severely obese people when they are trying to tie their shoelaces: The fat deposits serve as a wedge between the parts of the body, thereby restricting movement.

Muscle tension can affect flexibility. Individuals who experience prolonged stress often respond by bracing or tensing the muscles in their neck, shoulders, and upper back. This tightens the muscles for long periods, thus reducing flexibility. Muscle imbalance also can restrict flexibility. When weight training, for example, if an individual strengthens one group of muscles around a joint while neglecting the development of the opposing group (e.g., the quadriceps muscle group in the front of the thigh is strengthened but the hamstring muscle group in the back of the thigh is not), flexibility will be decreased. Therefore, to ensure maximal flexibility when weight training, it is important to perform each exercise correctly, through the full range of motion, and develop opposing muscle groups.

Flexibility can be improved. Participating in some physical activities can promote flexibility. Swimming, for example, can improve the flexibility of several joints. Also, because the activity is non-weight-bearing, swimming in a warm pool is often recommended for people with arthritic conditions.

Flexibility also can be improved through a stretching program. Because flexibility is specific to each joint, improvement and maintenance of flexibility requires a program that incorporates specific exercises for the major joints of the body. Flexibility exercises can be performed using ballistic, static, or contract-relax stretching techniques.

Ballistic stretching. This dynamic method uses the momentum generated from repeated bouncing movements to stretch the muscle. Although it is effective, most experts do not recommend this technique because it may overstretch the muscle and cause soreness or injury.

Static stretching. An extremely popular and effective technique, static stretching involves gently and slowly moving into the stretch position and holding it for a certain period of time. Movement should take place through the full range of motion until a little tension or tightness is felt in the muscle or muscle group. As the muscle relaxes,

Maintaining flexibility helps elderly people continue to function independently.

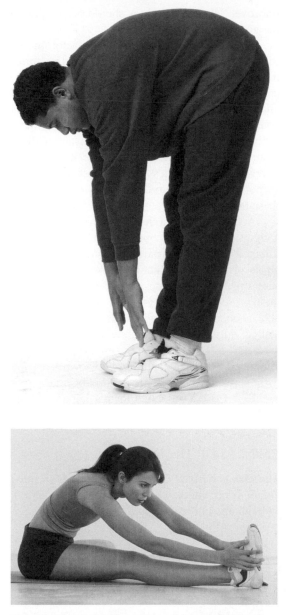

The standing straight-leg toe touch is an example of a ballistic exercise, which is not recommended by experts. The sitting hamstring stretch is safer and can be performed using static stretching or the contract-relax technique.

the stretch should be extended and held again. Stretching should not be painful. Care must be taken not to force the joint to move too far, which could cause an injury. Stretches should be held from 10 to 30 seconds and a minimum of five repetitions performed for each exercise. Flexibility exercises should be performed at least three to five times a week. If flexibility at a particular joint is extremely poor, a daily stretching program can be recommended. Flexibility exercises also should be performed at the start and end of a workout.

Contract-relax technique. When one is performing stretching exercises, it is important that the muscles involved are relaxed. The contract-relax technique facilitates the relaxation of muscles. Muscles are arranged in pairs; when one contracts, the opposing muscle in the pair relaxes (e.g., when the quadriceps muscles contract, the hamstring muscles relax). When one uses this technique to develop flexibility, the muscle opposite the one to be stretched is contracted for at least 5 seconds. This relaxes the muscle to be stretched. To apply this technique to the development of hamstring flexibility, an individual would contract the quadriceps muscles, thus relaxing the hamstrings. This technique allows the stretch to be performed through a greater range of motion.

Because flexibility is specific, a program for improvement and maintenance of flexibility must include exercises for each movement at the joint for which flexibility is being developed.

Flexibility can be measured. Because flexibility is joint specific, there is no one test that can be used to provide an overall measure of an individual's flexibility. The goniometer, a large protractor with movable arms, provides a measurement of the range of movement in terms of degrees.

There also are a number of other tests that have been developed to measure movement at certain joints and require little equipment to perform. For example, the sit-and-reach test is used to assess the flexibility of the lower back and hamstring muscles.

A goniometer can be used to measure hip flexion.

DESIGNING AN EXERCISE PROGRAM

The interactive nature of the exercise components allows for the design of exercise programs to meet individuals' needs. Personal characteristics such as fitness status, medical status, and age must be considered when prescribing exercise. Medical conditions such as heart disease, diabetes, and asthma must be taken into account when designing an exercise program. Appropriate modifications must be made to selected exercises to ensure participants' safety.

The next consideration in planning an exercise program is the participant's fitness needs and goals. The program must be designed to provide opportunities for the development of the fitness component the participant desires to improve. Selected activities should be specific to the goal.

Enjoyment is another critical factor in the selection of exercises. Adherence to the training program is enhanced when the participant enjoys the prescribed exercise. Activities should allow participants to achieve the desired fitness goals while maintaining interest and enjoyment. Individuals who find an activity enjoyable will be more likely to continue the exercise long enough to realize desired fitness improvements and to incorporate exercise into their lifestyle to maintain these improvements.

Achievement of a desirable level of fitness is a significant concern, but attention also must be directed to educating participants about the principles of designing a personal exercise program, assessing their own fitness, and resolving personal fitness problems. Development of a knowledgeable, independent fitness and health consumer— an individual who can achieve and maintain fitness for a lifetime—is an important priority. People need to take charge of their own lives and assume responsibility for their level of fitness. See Figure 7-3 for a guideline for participants to develop their own exercise plan.

EFFECTS OF TRAINING

The results derived from regular periods of muscular work or exercise are many and varied. Individuals who participate regularly in exercise

Figure 7-3   MyPyramid—Daily Food Recommendations
Source: United States Department of Agriculture. MyPyramid, http://mypyramid.gov. (February 25, 2007)

adapted to their needs and thereby attain a state of physical fitness may be called *trained*. Individuals who allow their muscles to get soft and flabby and are in poor physical condition can be referred to as *untrained*.

A trained individual is in a better state of physical fitness than a person whose life is sedentary and inactive. When two people, one trained and one untrained, of approximately the same build are performing the same amount of moderate muscular work, evidence indicates that the trained individual has lower oxygen consumption, lower pulse rate, larger stroke volume per heart-beat, less rise in blood pressure, greater red and white blood cell counts, slower rate of breathing, lower rate of lactic acid formation, and a faster return to normal blood pressure and heart rate. The heart becomes more efficient and is able to circulate more blood while beating less frequently. Furthermore, in strenuous work that cannot be performed for a long period of time, the trained individual has greater endurance, a capacity for higher oxygen consumption, and a faster return to normal heart rate and blood pressure.

Training results in a more efficient organism. Since improved efficiency of heart action

DESIGNING AN EXERCISE PROGRAM

STEP 1: Set goals that are realistic (are they attainable?) and measurable (can they be assessed?).

- General goals (e.g., lose weight, run a 5K)
- Specific goals (based on health-related or motor performance components of fitness)

STEP 2: Establish a timeline to accomplish general and specific goals (include start and end dates).

STEP 3: Develop a physical activity program based on goals.

FITT Guidelines	Cardiorespiratory Endurance	Flexibility	Muscular Strength	Muscular Endurance	Other
Frequency					
Intensity					
Time					
Type					
Location					

Number of Overall Minutes Participating in Physical Activity

Monday	Tuesday	Wednesday	Thursday	Friday	Saturday	Sunday	Weekly Total

enables a greater flow of blood to reach the muscles and thus ensure an increased supply of fuel and oxygen, more work is performed at less cost; improvements in strength, power, neuromuscular coordination, and endurance occur; coordination and timing of movements are better; and an improved state of physical fitness results.

SPECIAL CONSIDERATIONS FOR FITNESS

There are many different factors that should be considered in conducting fitness programs, such as environmental conditions, nutrition, and ergogenic aids. These factors will be discussed in this section.

Environmental Conditions and Fitness

Participants' safety should always be the primary concern of professionals conducting fitness programs. Exercising in an exceptionally hot, humid environment or in extreme cold requires both short- and long-term physiological adaptations by the body. Professionals and participants should be aware of the risk these conditions impose and how fitness programs need to be modified for safe participation.

Extreme caution must be used when exercising in hot, humid weather. The body's normal temperature is 98.6 degrees Fahrenheit. During exercise, as the body's temperature rises, several methods are used by the body to cool itself. The main method of cooling is evaporation. As you exercise, you perspire or sweat, and the evaporation of the sweat keeps the body temperature within normal limits. When it is hot and humidity reaches 65%, heat loss through evaporation is less effective, and the body's ability to dissipate heat is impaired.[23] Additionally, excessive sweating and lack of fluid replacement can lead to dehydration. A person who is dehydrated stops sweating, and evaporation no longer cools the body. Heat-related problems such as heat cramps, heat exhaustion, and heat stroke can occur under hot and humid conditions.

Heat cramps are muscle cramps, typically in the muscles most used in exercise. Heat exhaustion is characterized by muscle cramps, weakness, dizziness, disorientation, nausea, elevated temperature, profuse sweating, rapid pulse, and

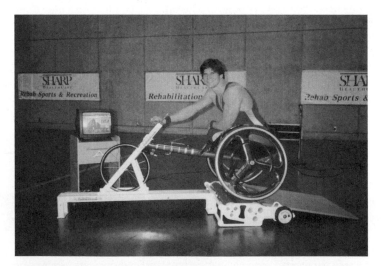

Specialized fitness equipment has been developed to meet the needs of athletes in wheelchairs. This resistance trainer, created by D & J Development, has an interactive computer that simulates road racing conditions.

collapse. Heat stroke is a life-threatening emergency. The symptoms include a sudden collapse, unconsciousness, rapid pulse, relatively dry skin from lack of sweating, and a core body temperature of 106 degrees Fahrenheit or higher. In heat stroke, the sweating mechanism breaks down and the body is unable to dissipate heat by sweating. If heat stroke occurs, immediate action is necessary to reduce the temperature of the body and access medical care.

To prevent heat-related problems, use caution when exercising in hot, humid weather. Be sure to drink plenty of fluids before, during, and after exercise to replace fluids lost through evaporation. Water and commercial sport drinks such as Gatorade and Powerade are good for replenishing fluids. Exercise in the coolest part of the day, either early in the morning or in the evening. On extremely hot and humid days, participants should consider decreasing the intensity of their workout to reduce heat stress. Other considerations may involve canceling the workout or exercising indoors in a cool environment. It is also important to take time to acclimatize the body to the hot and humid weather. Acclimatization occurs usually in 5 to 7 days.[23] Exercise should be reduced from the normal level as the body adjusts to the stress of heat.

Cold weather also requires precautions during exercise. Conserving heat is a major concern when exercising in cold weather. Hypothermia, the breakdown of the body's ability to produce heat, can occur when the weather is between 50 and 60 degrees Fahrenheit and it is damp and windy. Hypothermia occurs when the body temperature drops below 95 degrees Fahrenheit. Shivering and loss of coordination initially occur. As the body's temperature drops further, shivering stops, muscles stiffen, and unconsciousness occurs. This is a medical emergency, and first aid efforts should focus on raising the body's temperature and seeking immediate medical attention.

Extreme cold can also lead to frostbite. To prevent cold-related problems, participants should be aware of the conditions that contribute to hypothermia. Before exercising, individuals should check both the temperature and wind chill to determine whether it would be dangerous to exercise. Dress properly for exercise in cold weather. Hats should be worn to reduce the loss of body heat through the head. Several light layers of clothing should be worn so that the body temperature can be more easily regulated. Try to avoid getting wet in cold weather, which increases the risk for hypothermia. To prevent frostbite, wear a mask, gloves, and a hat. Be sure to take time to gradually acclimatize to exercising in the cold. In extreme conditions, consider canceling or limiting workouts or moving to an activity that can be performed indoors.

Environmental conditions pose challenges to individuals seeking to work out on a regular basis. It is important to be aware of the current weather conditions, the risks they pose, and the adaptations necessary to exercise safely. Maintaining the core body temperature, taking time to gradually acclimatize to conditions, following safety precautions, and using common sense can help reduce the health risks associated with exercising under conditions of extreme heat, humidity, or cold.

Nutrition and Fitness

Nutrition plays an important role in enhancing fitness and health. The central focus of nutrition is the study of food requirements for the production of energy and the regulation of bodily processes.

"You are what you eat" is an adage that captures the critical contribution of nutrition to our health and well-being. What we eat can affect our health, growth and development, and ability to perform various activities that fill our lives. In terms of health fitness, the foods we consume directly affect our body composition and the energy we have available to engage in physical activity. The energy derived from food is measured in kilocalories, which are commonly referred to as calories. Regulating one's energy balance by carefully monitoring caloric consumption and expenditure is important in achieving a desirable level of health fitness. Individuals must also consume sufficient calories so that they have the energy necessary for work and to lead a physically active lifestyle.

A nutrient is a basic substance that is used by the body to sustain vital processes such as the repair and regulation of cellular functions and the production of energy. The six major categories of nutrients are carbohydrates, fats, proteins, vitamins, minerals, and water. Carbohydrates, proteins, and fats—the three macronutrients—provide the energy required for muscular work. They also have a critical role in the maintenance of body tissues and the regulation of their functions.

Vitamins and minerals have no caloric value. Although they are required only in small amounts, they are essential to body functioning. Vitamins are needed for normal growth and development. Vitamins do not provide energy directly, but play a critical role in releasing energy from the foods that are consumed. Minerals are essential to the regulation and performance of such body functions as the maintenance of water balance and skeletal muscle contraction.

Water is the most basic of all the nutrients— it is necessary to sustain life. The most abundant of all the nutrients in the body, water accounts for approximately 60% of the body's weight. Water is necessary for all of the chemical processes performed by the body. It is essential for such functions as energy production, digestion, temperature regulation, and elimination of the by-products of metabolism.

Maintaining a proper water balance is crucial. Insufficient water causes dehydration; severe dehydration can lead to death. People who are physically active should carefully monitor their water intake to ensure that an adequate fluid balance is maintained. This is particularly critical for individuals who exercise in a hot, humid environment. Exercising under these conditions typically causes excessive sweating and subsequently large losses of water. Sufficient water should be drunk to ensure that proper fluid balance is maintained.

Individuals should also be aware of their consumption of carbohydrates, fats, and proteins. The United States Department of Agriculture (USDA)

recommends that carbohydrates be the primary source of calories, followed by fats and proteins.[12] Carbohydrates should constitute 55–60% of an individual's calories, and protein about 10–15%. No more than 30% of calories should come from fat, with no more than 10% coming from saturated fat.[12]

The USDA *Dietary Guidelines for Americans,* published in 2005, provides advice to Americans on making healthful food choices.[24] The *Dietary Guidelines* organizes its recommendations into nine areas, as shown in the *Dietary Guidelines for Americans, 2005* Key Recommendations box. (Note: The USDA updates its guidelines every 5 years. At the time this book was written, these guidelines were current; however, the 2010 key recommendations are currently available at http://www.mypyramid.gov/guidelines/index.html.[25]) The guidelines highlight the importance of consuming adequate nutrients within caloric needs, maintaining a healthy weight, and being active for at least 30 minutes a day on most days of the week. According to the guidelines, a healthful diet emphasizes fruits, vegetables, whole grains, and fat-free or low-fat milk and milk products. Lean meats, poultry, fish, beans, eggs, and nuts should be included within the diet. The diet is low in saturated fats, trans fats, cholesterol, salt (sodium), and added sugars. The guidelines also stress the importance of including fiber in one's diet and limiting the consumption of sodium while consuming potassium-rich foods. Alcohol should be consumed only in moderation. Additionally, the guidelines include recommendations specific ethnic groups and for special populations, such as pregnant and lactating women, children, and adults with hypertension.

In reviewing the *Dietary Guidelines* it is important to recognize that the USDA has recommended physical activity as integral to good health, and its inclusion reflects the intimate relationship between caloric intake and caloric expenditure. To reduce the risk of chronic disease in adulthood, the guidelines recommend that individuals engage in 30 minutes of moderate-intensity physical activity on most days of the week, above usual activity, and indicate that greater health benefits can be attained by engaging in more vigorous

DIETARY GUIDELINES FOR AMERICANS, 2005
KEY RECOMMENDATIONS

Adequate nutrients within caloric needs	• Consume a variety of nutrient-dense foods and beverages, choosing foods that limit the intake of saturated and trans fats, cholesterol, added sugars, salt, and alcohol. • Meet recommended intakes within energy needs by adopting a balanced eating pattern, such as the MyPyramid.
Weight management	• To maintain body weight in a healthy range, balance calories from foods and beverages with calories expended. • To prevent gradual weight gain over time, make small decreases in food and beverage categories and increase physical activity.

Physical activity	• Engage in regular physical activity and reduce sedentary activities to promote health, psychological well-being, and a healthy body weight.
	  • To reduce the risk of chronic disease in adulthood: Engage in at least 30 minutes of moderate-intensity physical activity, above usual activity, at work or home on most days of the week.
	  • Greater health benefits can be obtained by engaging in physical activity of a more vigorous intensity on most days of the week.
	  • To help manage body weight: Engage in approximately 60 minutes of moderate-to-vigorous-intensity activity on most days of the week while not exceeding caloric intake requirements.
	  • To sustain weight loss in adulthood: Participate in at least 60 to 90 minutes of daily moderate-intensity physical activity while not exceeding caloric requirements.
	• Achieve physical fitness by including cardiovascular conditioning, stretching exercises for flexibility, and resistance exercises or calisthenics for muscle strength and endurance.

Food groups to encourage	• Consume a sufficient amount of fruits and vegetables. • Eat a variety of fruits and vegetables each day. Select vegetables from all groups (e.g., dark green, orange, legumes). • Consume at least half of your grains from whole grains. • Consume three cups per day of fat-free or low-fat milk or equivalent milk products.
Fats	• Consume less than 10% of calories from saturated fatty acids and less than 300 milligrams per day of cholesterol, and keep trans-fatty acid consumption as low as possible. • Keep total fat intake between 20% and 35% of calories.
Carbohydrates	• Choose fiber-rich fruits, vegetables, and whole grains often. • Choose and prepare foods and beverages with little added sugars or caloric sweeteners.
Sodium and potassium	• Consume less than 2,300 milligrams (approximately 1 teaspoon of salt) of sodium per day. • Consume potassium-rich foods, such as fruits and vegetables.
Alcoholic beverages	• Drink alcoholic beverages in moderation—one drink per day for women and up to two drinks per day for men.
Food safety	• Avoid microbial food-borne illness through careful food preparation, cooking, processing, and refrigeration.

Source: United States Department of Agriculture. *Dietary Guidelines for Americans 2005,* www.health.gov/dietaryguidelines/dga2005.htm

physical activity. The guidelines also promote the development of health-related fitness, with an emphasis on cardiovascular conditioning, stretching exercises for flexibility, and progressive resistance exercises or calisthenics for muscle strength and endurance.

For individuals interested in managing their body weight, the guidelines recommend 60 minutes of moderate-to-vigorous-intensity physical activity on most days of the week, while not exceeding caloric intake requirements. For those adults who have lost weight and want to sustain their weight loss, it is recommended they engage in at least 60–90 minutes of daily moderate-intensity physical activity and not exceed caloric requirements.

The *Dietary Guidelines* also suggests that individuals use the USDA MyPyramid and the DASH (Dietary Approaches to Stop Hypertension) Eating Plan to help them integrate dietary recommendations into their lifestyle. MyPyramid (see Figure 7-3) provides a personalized approach to healthy eating and physical activity. The pyramid comprises six bands, representing the five food groups (grains, vegetables, fruits, milk, and meat and beans) and oils needed each day for good health.[25] The different widths of the bands suggest how much food a person should choose from each group every day. [25] The specific amount that should be consumed depends on the individual's age, sex, and level of physical activity.[25] Moderation is represented by the narrowing of the bands of each food group as they come together at the apex of the pyramid.[25] At the base are foods with little or no solid fats or added sugars, whereas the narrow bands at the top are foods containing more added sugars and solid fats.[25] The foods at the base should be selected more than foods at the top. Physical activity is integral to good health and is represented by the steps and the person climbing them. Physical activity should be performed on a daily basis. MyPyramid strives to offer a personalized approach to healthful eating, providing a wide array of options for individuals to incorporate into their life.

Ergogenic Aids

Athletes at all levels seek different means to improve their performance. One way to improve performance is through the use of ergogenic aids. According to Powers and Howley,[26] ergogenic aids are work-producing substances or phenomena believed to increase performance.[26]. Athletes use ergogenic aids to enhance energy use, production, or recovery in their quest for improved performance.

Ergogenic aids take many different forms and are used by many athletes to enhance their performance. There are mechanical aids (weight belts and breathing strips), psychological aids (stress management and hypnosis), pharmaceutical aids such as legal drugs (caffeine) and illegal drugs (anabolic steroids), physiological aids (blood doping and oxygen supplementation), and nutritional aids (carbohydrate supplementation and creatine).

Exercise physiologists study the effects of ergogenic aids on an individual's physiologic state as well as the individual's performance. For example, they investigate the effects of different amounts or doses of the substance, the impact on both short- and long-term performance, and whether the effect is different for trained or untrained individuals.[26] They also consider whether the ergogenic aid works better for power or endurance tasks and whether it has an impact on fine or gross motor tasks.[25] Researchers have found that for some of the ergogenic aids, the weight of the evidence does not support the claims for improved performance, increased muscle size and strength, or quicker recovery.[25] However, oftentimes athletes, convinced that their chosen approach works, may use it despite evidence not supporting the sought-after benefits.

Caffeine

Caffeine, a stimulant, is found in a variety of foods, drinks, and over-the-counter products. The International Olympic Committee (IOC) classifies caffeine as a restricted drug, allowing its use up to a urine level of 12 micrograms per milliliter, which is about six to eight cups of coffee. Caffeine is absorbed rapidly from the gastrointestinal tract, rising to a significant level in the blood about 15 minutes after consumption, with the peak concentration about 45–60 minutes after ingestion. Given this, an athlete wanting a boost in performance from caffeine needs to consume it about an hour before the event. Ingestion of the equivalent of about two cups of coffee has been shown to have an ergogenic effect.

Caffeine enhances the function of skeletal muscle, increasing tension development. It stimulates the sympathetic nervous system, which typically leads to increased alertness and decreased perception of fatigue. Research suggests that caffeine can increase endurance performance. However, the ergogenic effect on performance is variable and is influenced by the dose and the amount of caffeine the athlete typically consumes. Athletes who do not regularly consume products with caffeine typically see more pronounced ergogenic effects than athletes who are regular consumers of caffeine. Additionally, athletes who abstain from caffeine for a period of days prior to its use have more pronounced effects.

Some side effects associated with the use of caffeine include very rapid heart rate, diuresis, insomnia, nervousness, diarrhea, and anxiety. Athletes who choose to use this ergogenic aid should be careful to monitor their dosage, modify the dose to take into account their pattern of caffeine consumption, and be cognizant of the side effects.

Carbohydrate Loading

Carbohydrate loading, or glycogenic supercompensation, is a practice followed by athletes who compete in endurance events lasting 60 to 90 minutes or longer. Carbohydrates perform a critical role in the production of energy in the body. They are converted to glycogen and are stored in the liver and muscles. Blood glucose, a by-product of the breakdown of carbohydrates, also is important to energy production. Muscle glycogen stores are used for muscle energy metabolism, and the liver's store of glycogen is used to replace blood glucose. During prolonged exercise, the stores of glycogen decline to very low levels, contributing to muscle fatigue, performance decrement, and exhaustion.

In an effort to maximize performance, endurance athletes practice carbohydrate loading before an event. By modifying their diet to eat more complex carbohydrates than normal, athletes hope to store additional glycogen in their muscles and liver, sometimes up to four times the usual level. During competition, athletes draw on these additional stores to delay fatigue and to maintain their race pace for a longer time. In addition to modifying their diet, athletes also change their training regimen to ensure that their glycogen stores are at capacity.

There are several approaches to carbohydrate loading. One approach, termed the classical approach, requires athletes to begin the process of carbohydrate loading seven days prior to competition. Both athletes' training and diet are modified. Seven days prior to competition, athletes deplete their muscle glycogen stores by training to exhaustion. Hard training continues for the next three days, followed by three days of rest prior to competition. In addition to altering their training schedule, athletes modify their diet. Typically, on the first day when training to exhaustion occurs, athletes consume a diet consisting of about 50% carbohydrates. During the other three hard training days, a diet high in fat and protein is eaten. The three days before competition, on the rest days, athletes consume a diet consisting of about 90% carbohydrates. On the day of the event, athletes eat a high-carbohydrate meal, typically consuming complex carbohydrates such as grains, pasta, rice, or bagels. Not all athletes find this approach to be beneficial. Some athletes have difficulty handling the extremes in diet. Other athletes are uncomfortable stopping their training three days before their competition.

Researchers determined that another approach, referred to as the modified approach, could be successfully used to maximize glycogen stores.[26] This approach does not require athletes to exercise to exhaustion in order to deplete their glycogen stores, nor does it require athletes to eat extremely low or extremely high amounts of carbohydrates. Instead, athletes gradually reduce the intensity and duration of their workouts on the days preceding competition while modifying their diet to increase their carbohydrates to 70%. For example, five days before the event, athletes would decrease their workout time from 90 minutes to 40 minutes, while eating a 50% carbohydrate diet. After two days, workout time again is reduced, this time from 40 minutes to 20 minutes, while carbohydrate consumption is increased to 70%. The day prior to competition, athletes rest and continue to consume the 70% carbohydrate diet. This approach has been found to be effective in increasing glycogen stores and enhancing performance. Some athletes tolerate this approach better than the classical approach.

During the meal prior to the event, it is recommended that athletes consume between 1 and 5 grams of carbohydrate per kilogram of body weight.[26] Athletes should eat from 1 to 4 hours before exercise.[26] The meal should be easily digestible carbohydrate, but, if it is taken 1 hour before exercise, it should be in liquid form. Prior to trying carbohydrate loading before a competition, the athlete should test the procedure during practice. It should also be noted that following strenuous exercise, athletes can hasten their recovery by consuming carbohydrates.

Hydration, Energy, and Sports Drinks

During exercise, heat is dissipated by the body to minimize the increase in body core temperature. The primary mechanism through which this occurs is the evaporation of sweat. As exercise intensity increases, so does the evaporation of sweat. Exercising in hot and humid environments increases the evaporation of sweat even more. Researchers have found that in hot weather as much as 2.8 liters per hour can be lost in sweat.[25] In events of long duration, such as a marathon, some runners can lose as much as 8%

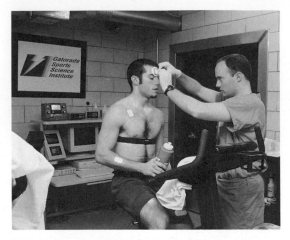

To determine the effects of a sports drink on performance, companies test athletes under various performance conditions. Here an athlete is being prepared for testing at the Gatorade Sports Science Institute.

of their body weight.[25] In addition to loss of water, electrolytes that are critical to the normal function of the body are lost. Levels of electrolytes such as sodium, calcium, chloride, and potassium decrease. The loss of fluid and electrolytes adversely affects cellular functions. If these fluids and electrolytes are not replaced, significant health problems could arise, such as heat stroke, and performance decrement will occur.

Exercise physiologists investigate the optimal way to replace lost water and electrolytes. Fluid replacement during exercise is associated with lower heart rate, body core temperature, and levels of perceived exertion. The ease of fluid replacement depends on the activity. During intermittent activities such as soccer or football, it is easier for an athlete to replace lost fluid and electrolytes. During prolonged activities, such as marathon running, fluid replacement typically occurs on the go.

Water is often regarded as the natural choice for fluid replacement. It is readily available and inexpensive. It is generally recommended that 4–6 ounces of water be consumed for every 15–20 minutes of exercise, especially during prolonged exercise and conditions of high heat and humidity.[25] One problem associated with using water to rehydrate is that oftentimes athletes do not drink enough water to adequately replace the fluids. To some athletes, it is not as palatable as some of the other fluid-replacement beverages, so they drink an insufficient quantity. Another problem with drinking water to rehydrate is that is does not contain electrolytes or carbohydrates.

Sports drinks are popular for maintaining hydration. They are formulated to maximize fluid absorption. Sports drinks are designed to enhance performance through replacement of lost electrolytes and supplying of additional carbohydrates to replenish glucose stores. Researchers have found that sports drinks containing 6–8% carbohydrates are well tolerated by athletes and provide extra energy to enhance performance.[25] Because of the variety of flavors offered, athletes find drinking sports drinks more appealing than drinking water.

Fluid replacement during exercise reduces athletes' heart rate and body temperature as well as athletes' perception of exertion. The greater the rate of fluid intake, the lower the athletes' responses.[26] Additionally, Powers and Howley report that drink temperature influences absorption rate; cold drinks are absorbed more rapidly than warm drinks.[26] For exercise lasting less than 60 minutes, replacement of fluids using water is adequate. However, when exercise lasts longer than an hour, drinks should contain sodium, chloride, and carbohydrates.

In planning for fluid replacement, the athletes' state of fitness and the intensity and duration of the event must be taken into account. Additionally, attention must be paid to environmental conditions, such as excessive heat and humidity, extreme cold, and high altitude, as they require increased fluid intake to avoid dehydration.

Creatine

Many individuals use nutritional supplements in hopes of enhancing their athletic performance. One popular supplement used to improve performance in events placing a premium on strength or power is creatine commonly known as phosphocreatine.

Phosphocreatine in skeletal muscle is important to the production of ATP, a critical source of energy in high-intensity brief exercise lasting less than five seconds. Sprinting 50 meters in track, explosive events such as high jumping, short bursts of speed in soccer, and rapid weight lifting movements rely on this energy source. During these intense efforts, phosphocreatine is depleted, reducing the rate of ATP production.

Phosphocreatine is a limiting factor in short-term, high-intensity events. In an effort to increase stores of muscle phosphocreatine and have more fuel available to support short, high-intensity activity, many athletes have used creatine supplementation. Additionally, many athletes use creatine supplementation in conjunction with a resistance training program to maximize their muscular strength and increase their fat-free mass.

Compared to other supplements, there has been much research on the efficacy of creatine as an ergogenic aid.[27] Research findings have been varied, with some supporting creatine's effectiveness as an ergogenic aid in brief, high-intensity events, while other studies find less evidence to support anecdotal claims.[27] There is also less evidence that creatine supplementation can enhance performance in events lasting more than 90 seconds.[27] The ACSM's position is that creatine supplementation enhances exercise performance in events involving short periods of extremely powerful activity, especially during repeated efforts.[27] Additionally, research has shown individual variability in the supplement's effects, with some individuals benefiting more than others from its use.[27]

Typically, athletes go through a loading phase in which they try to maximize the amount of phosphocreatine in their muscles. They load their muscles by ingesting 5 grams of creatine four to six times a day for 5 days. This phase is sufficient to saturate the muscles and maximize the amount of phosphocreatine available for ATP production. However, in addition to using creatine supplementation prior to an event to improve performance, athletes use it to maximize the effects of their training, often in the off-season. Many athletes continue

Development of strength is one reason athletes use ergogenic aids.

supplementation for weeks or months, ingesting several grams of creatine a day. During this phase, they engage in intense training to increase muscle strength, muscle size, and body mass.[27] Creatine supplementation allows athletes to train at higher workloads, enabling them to perform more repetitions per set of a given exercise and to recover more quickly between exercise sets.[27]

Little research has been conducted on the short- and long-term effects of oral creatine supplementation. Some athletes have experienced muscle cramping, excessive water retention, and gastrointestinal disturbances from supplementation. However, overall, it appears that creatine supplementation for up to 8 weeks does not produce major health risks.[25] More research is needed on the long-term effects of supplementation.

Anabolic-Androgenic Steroids

Anabolic-androgenic steroids are synthetic forms of testosterone, the primary male sex hormone. Testosterone secreted by the testes is responsible for the development of masculine characteristics seen in adolescents and continued into adulthood. Testosterone functions both androgenically—stimulating the growth of male characteristics—and anabolically—promoting the growth of tissue, muscle mass, weight, and bone.[25]

Synthetic forms of testosterone were developed by scientists who sought to maximize the anabolic effects and minimize the androgenic effects.[25] Originally, these synthetic forms were developed to help promote the growth of tissue in patients suffering from certain debilitating diseases. The ability of steroids to develop muscle mass and strength soon attracted the attention of athletes. Athletes began to take steroids and use heavy resistance-training programs in an effort to acquire significant strength gains.

Numerous research studies were conducted to investigate the mechanism of strength gains and various performance claims. There was considerable variation in the results of the studies. Additionally, due to ethical constraints of testing on human subjects, the dosages used in studies were the recommended therapeutic dosage. Athletes seeking to improve their performance typically self-administer 10 to 100 times the recommended dosage.[26] Many athletes did accrue significant strength gains. As the number of athletes using steroids increased, many sports governing bodies, including the IOC, banned them.

Even though illegal, steroid use by athletes continues. Athletes and others, including adolescents, use anabolic steroids to enhance performance and improve physical appearance. Anabolic steroids are taken orally or injected. Typically, dosages are taken daily in cycles of weeks or months, then stopped, for a period of time, and then resumed. Sometimes, in an effort to obtain maximum gains while minimizing the negative effects, users combine several different types of steroids, a process referred to as stacking.

Steroid abuse is most prevalent in sports where the premium is placed on strength. Power lifting, throwing events in track and field, American football, and baseball are sports in which athletes may seek to gain an advantage through the use of steroids.

Many serious side effects, some irreversible, are associated with steroid use. For both males and females, adverse side effects associated with chronic steroid use include increased risk of heart disease, liver tumors and cancer, increased cholesterol, and hypertension. Psychological effects of use include mood swings and aggressive behavior. In males, side effects include male-pattern baldness, acne, and voice deepening. Males also experience a decrease in testicular function, including a decrease in sperm production, and gynecomastia—breast development. Females taking steroids experience irreversible voice deepening and enlarged clitoris. Increased facial hair, decreased breast size, increased libido, increased appetite, and menstrual irregularities are also outcomes of chronic steroid use in females. Adolescent users risk a decrease in their ultimate height. Adolescents' long bones are still growing, and if they abuse steroids, the growth plates of these bones may cease growing prematurely.

The use of ergogenic aids can take many forms, be it mechanical, psychological, physiological, or pharmacological. Some ergogenic aids have been shown to be beneficial through research while others gain popularity through anecdotal evidence. Users of ergogenic aids need to be careful to understand the correct manner of usage, whether it is legal or not, and the associated health consequences.

FOCUS ON CAREER: Exercise Physiology

PROFESSIONAL ORGANIZATIONS

- American College of Sports Medicine (www.acsm.org)
- American Physiological Society (www.the-aps.org)
- Exercise Physiology Academy (www.aahperd.org/naspe/about/leaders/Exercise-Physiology-Academy.cfm
- National Strength and Conditioning Association (http://www.nsca-lift.org)

PROFESSIONAL JOURNALS

- *American Journal of Physiology*
- *Clinical Exercise Physiology*
- *Exercise and Sport Sciences Reviews*
- *International Journal of Sport Nutrition and Exercise Metabolism*
- *Journal of Aging and Physical Activity*
- *Journal of Applied Physiology*
- *Journal of Strength and Conditioning Research*
- *Medicine and Science in Sports and Exercise*
- *The Physician and Sports Medicine*
- *Research Quarterly for Exercise and Sport*
- *Strength and Conditioning Journal*

SUMMARY

Exercise physiology is the study of the effects of exercise on the body, ranging from the level of the system (e.g., cardiovascular system) to the subcellular (e.g., production of ATP for energy) level. Exercise physiologists are interested in both the acute and chronic adaptations of the body to exercise. Professionals in physical education, exercise science, and sport build on this foundational knowledge in many different ways. Knowledge from exercise physiology is used to design effective fitness programs for people of all ages, to guide the development and implementation of cardiac rehabilitation programs, to plan programs to help children and youths incorporate physical activity into their life, to conduct training programs for elite athletes, and to structure rehabilitation programs for injured athletes and exercise enthusiasts.

A major concern of the exercise physiologist is fitness development, maintenance, evaluation, and outcomes. Within the profession, interest has increased in health-related fitness as opposed to performance-related fitness. The components of health-related and performance-related fitness are different, and the extent to which these components are developed depends on individuals' goals. The health-fitness components are cardiovascular function, body composition, muscular strength and endurance, and flexibility. Attainment of desirable levels of these components can enhance one's health and well-being. Individuals who are unfit are at increased risk for disease.

Many health benefits are derived from physical fitness and the incorporation of physical activity into one's lifestyle. Physical education, exercise science, and sport professionals should follow medical guidelines and sound training principles in developing and implementing physical fitness programs. Professionals should be aware of contributors to fitness, such as sound nutritional practices. Physical education, exercise science, and sport professionals must take an active role in educating the American public about proper fitness and nutritional practices.

Another area of study for exercise physiologists is ergogenic aids. Ergogenic aids, such as caffeine, creatine, sports drinks, carbohydrate loading, and steroids, are used in an attempt to improve performance.

DISCUSSION QUESTIONS

1. How would the dose-response debate and FITT principle influence the design of an exercise program for a 35-year-old man who is inactive and wants to lose 10 pounds?

2. How do you assess individuals' health-related components of fitness? Why is it important to assess their levels of fitness? What should professionals do based on the results?

3. How do individuals who want to (a) maintain weight, (b) lose weight, or (c) gain weight need to adjust their nutrition and exercise programs?

4. Should anabolic steroids remain illegal and banned from all sports governing bodies? Why or why not?

SELF-ASSESSMENT ACTIVITIES

These activities are designed to help you determine if you have mastered the material and competencies presented in this chapter.

1. Define exercise physiology and discuss its importance to professionals in physical education, exercise science, and sport. Investigate one of the areas of study in exercise physiology and write a short paper on a selected topic of interest to you.

2. Using the information provided in the Get Connected box, access the ACSM site and review one of the position papers. What new insights did you gain? How can you use this information as a

professional? Or access the President's Council on Fitness, Sports, and Nutrition site and read the latest *Research Digest*. What are the implications of this research for professionals?

3. In a short paper, discuss how an individual's lifestyle and habits may be a deterrent to a state of fitness and health. What rationale would you use to persuade a friend or a relative who was tired all the time, feeling overwhelmed by stress, and overweight to start a physical fitness program? What excuses may be offered for not being active? How could you counter these excuses?

4. Research information on the variety of ergogenic aids available to individuals aspiring to improve their performance. Prepare a short presentation on a selected aid, including mechanism of effect,

claims for use, research on efficacy, legality of the aid, and other related areas.

5. Using the Internet, research the calories contained in fast food meals. Create various combinations of meals, seeing how the calories and fat in each meal change with the choice of items and their size. Create a healthful fast food meal as well. Summarize your findings relative to calories and fat in fast food. Again, using the Internet, find a caloric expenditure table and determine how much physical activity you would need to expend these calories. Write a short paper discussing what you have learned.

6. Refer to the 12 Steps to Understanding Research Reports box in Chapter 1. Complete Step 7 for the same article you selected in Chapter 1.

REFERENCES

1. Buskirk ER: Exercise physiology, part I: early history in the United States. In JD Massengale and RA Swanson, editors, The history of exercise and sport science, Champaign, Ill., 1997, Human Kinetics.

2. US Department of Health and Human Services: Physical activity and health: a report of the surgeon general, Atlanta, Ga., 1996, US Department of Health and Human Services, Centers for Disease Control and Prevention, National Center for Chronic Disease Prevention and Health Promotion.

3. US Department of Health and Human Services: improving health, Washington, D.C., 2000, US Government Printing Office.

4. President's Council on Physical Fitness and Sport: Definitions: health, fitness, and physical activity, Research Digest, March 2000.

5. Blair SN, LaMonte MJ, and Nichaman MZ: The evolution of physical activity recommendations: how much is enough?, American Journal of Clinical Nutrition, 79(suppl.):913S–920S, 2004.

6. Centers for Disease Control and Prevention: Measuring physical activity intensity, updated May 10, 2010 (www.cdc.gov/physicalactivity/everyone/measuring/index.html).

7. Centers for Disease Control and Prevention: How much physical activity do adults need?, Updated

May 10, 2010 (www.cdc.gov/physicalactivity/everyone/guidelines/adults.html).

8. American College of Sports Medicine. Physical activity and public health guidelines, 2007 (www.acsm.org/AM/Template.cfm?Section=Home_Page&TEMPLATE=CM/HTMLDisplay.cfm&CONTENTID=7764#Under_65).

9. US Department of Health and Human Services: 2008 physical activity guidelines for Americans, 2008, Office of Disease Prevention and Health Promotion (www.health.gov/paguidelines).

10. President's Council on Physical Fitness and Sports: Making sense of multiple physical activity recommendations, Research Digest, 3(19), 2002.

11. National Association for Sport and Physical Education: Physical activity for children: A statement of guidelines for children ages 5–12, ed 2, Reston, Va., NASPE.

12. Corbin CB, Welk GJ, Corbin WR, and Welk KA: Concepts of fitness and wellness: a comprehensive lifestyle approach, ed 6, New York, 2006, McGraw-Hill.

13. Lee I and Skerrett PJ: Physical activity and all-cause mortality: what is the dose response relationship, Medicine and Science in Sports and Exercise, 33(6 June Supplement 2001):S459–S471, 2001.

14. Prentice W: Get fit, Stay fit, ed 5, New York, 2009, McGraw-Hill.

15. Corbin CB, Welk G, Corbin WR, and Welk KA: Concepts of fitness and wellness: a comprehensive lifestyle approach, ed 8, New York, 2009, McGraw-Hill.

16. Hoeger WWK and Hoeger SA: Principles and labs for fitness and wellness, ed 9, 2009, Thomson Wadsworth.

17. Pollock ML, Gaesser GA, Butcher JD, Després J, Dishman RK, Franklin BA, and Garber CE: ACSM position stand: the recommended quantity and quality of exercise for developing and maintaining cardiorespiratory and muscular fitness, and flexibility in healthy adults, Medicine and Science in Sport and Exercise, 30:975–991, 1998 (www.acsm.org).

18. National Institutes of Health, National Heart, Lung, and Blood Institute: Clinical guidelines on the identification, evaluation, and treatment of overweight and obesity in adults. HHS, Public Health Service (PHS), 1998. National Heart, Lung, and Blood Institute, Bethesda, MD 20824-0105.

19. US Department of Health and Human Services: The surgeon general's call to action to prevent and decrease overweight and obesity, Rockville, Md., 2001, US Department of Health and Human Services, Public Health Service, Office of the Surgeon General. (www.surgeongeneral.gov/library).

20. Willett WC, Manson FE, and Stampfer MJ, Colditz GA, Rosner D, Speizer FE, and Hennekens CH: Weight, weight change, and coronary heart disease in women. Risk within the "normal" weight range, JAMA, 273(6):461–465, 1995.

21. Galanis DJ, Harris T, Sharp DS, and Petrovitch H: Relative weight, weight change, and risk of coronary heart disease in the Honolulu Heart Program, American Journal of Epidemiology, 147(4):379–386, 1998.

22. US Department of Agriculture Center for Nutrition Policy and Promotion: Is total fat consumption really decreasing, Nutrition Insights, no. 5, April 1998 (www.usda.gov/cnpp).

23. Prentice WE: Fitness and wellness for life, ed 6, New York, 1999, McGraw-Hill.

24. United States Department of Health and Human Services and United States Department of Agriculture, Dietary guidelines for Americans 2005 (www.health.gov/dietaryguidelines/dga2005/document/default.htm

25. United States Department of Agriculture: MyPyramid, retrieved 25 February 2007 (www.mypyramid.gov).

26. Powers SK and Howley ET: Exercise physiology: theory and application to fitness and performance. St. Louis, Mo., 2004, McGraw-Hill.

27. Rawson ES and Clarkson PM: Scientifically debatable: is creatine worth its weight?, Sport Science Exchange 91, 16(4), 2002 (www.gssiweb.com).

SOCIOLOGICAL FOUNDATIONS

OBJECTIVES

After reading this chapter the student should be able to—

- Show how sport is a socializing force in American culture.
- Discuss the nature and scope of sport.
- Trace the growth of sport in educational institutions in the United States and the attitude of educators toward this growth.
- Know the dimensions of concerns in sport today, including girls and women, children, minorities, violence, and the use of performance-enhancing substances.

Sport is an important part of this nation's culture and other cultures throughout the world. It captures newspaper headlines, holds television viewers' attention, produces millions of dollars a year in revenuc for entrepreneurs, and even impacts international affairs.

Sport exerts a strong influence on many aspects of the American lifestyle. Millions of Americans are glued to their chairs when featured baseball, football, basketball, and golf contests are scheduled to be televised. Advertisers target large percentages of their promotional budgets to buy airtime during sporting events to sell their wares. For example, a 30-second advertisement during the 2010 Super Bowl sold for over $2.6 million. This rate is in sharp contrast to the $42,500 (CBS) and $37,500 (NBC) charged to advertise during Super Bowl I in 1967.[1] Professional sports teams attract millions of spectators each year. Professional teams spend astronomical sums to obtain the best talent to sustain spectator support and interest and to ensure a profitable year for management. Newspaper coverage devoted to sports occupies more space than all the arts combined, and sports symbols and jargon infiltrate American language, art, and politics.

The big business of sport has also influenced the nature of college and secondary school sport. Schools and colleges, in an effort to field the best teams, may compromise their academic standards. It is not uncommon for

GET CONNECTED

University of Central Florida Institute for Diversity and Ethics in Sport—provides access to issues pertaining to race and gender within amateur, collegiate, and professional sports; current Race and Gender Report Cards for various sports; and information about the academic progress of collegiate athletes, including those who are participating in football bowl games or men's and women's NCAA Division I basketball championships.

www.tidesport.org

Institute for the Study of Youth Sports—offers information for parents, coaches, researchers, and youth on various aspects of youth sports, including the Bill of Rights for Young Athletes, coaching certification, and a coaches' code of conduct.

www.educ.msu.edu/ysi

National Alliance for Youth Sports—gives access to information about youth sports, links, and information for players, parents, coaches, and administrators.

www.nays.org

National Collegiate Athletic Association—provides information on many different aspects of collegiate sport, including current news. Click on Key Issues to access information on gender equity, participation rates, drug testing, and a multitude of other topics.

www.ncaa.org

Women's Sports Foundation—provides information on current issues, career opportunities, upcoming events, and links to research and topics of interest, including Title IX.

www.womenssportsfoundation.org

academically outstanding colleges to be more widely recognized for the feats of their athletic teams.

Within the last 10 years, the number of sport participants in our society has increased dramatically. Millions of people of all ages and abilities participate in a diversity of sport activities. Because of the social, political, legal, and educational influence of sport on cultures, it is important to examine this phenomenon.

SOCIOLOGY OF SPORT

The social significance of sport in America is unparalleled. As Leonard states, "Sport permeates virtually every social institution in society."[2] Sport influences and is influenced by social institutions such as economics, family, education, politics, religion, mass media, and popular culture. (See the Lifespan and Cultural Perspectives box.) "The ubiquity of sport is evidenced by news coverage, sports equipment sales, financial expenditures, the number of participants and spectators, and its penetration into popular culture (movies, books, leisure, comic strips, and everyday conversation)."[2] Coakley notes that sport, as a social phenomenon, has "meanings that go far beyond score and performance statistics. Sports are related to the social and cultural contexts in which we live."[3] The prominence and pervasiveness of sport in American culture and its institutional nature led to its study from a sociological perspective. The definition, scope, historical development, and areas of study are discussed in this section.

LIFESPAN AND CULTURAL PERSPECTIVES: Sociology of Sport

- Why do so few minorities and women hold coaching and administrative positions in intercollegiate and professional sports? What can be done to increase their opportunities?
- How does social class influence sport participation?
- How does disabled sport affect our perceptions of people with disabilities?
- How does sport influence our view of masculinity and femininity?
- How are children socialized into sport, and what can be done to sustain their involvement in sport?
- Do the Olympics contribute to international understanding?
- How does the use of Native American imagery in sport influence participants' and spectators' beliefs about Native Americans?
- What societal factors have contributed to parental violence in youth sports?

Definition and Scope

Sociology is concerned with the study of people, groups, institutions, and human activities in terms of social behavior and social order within society. It is a science interested in such institutions of society as religion, family, government, education, and leisure. Sociologists are also concerned with the influence of social institutions on the individual, the social behavior and human relations that occur within a group or an institution and how they influence the behavior of the individual, and the interrelationships between the various institutions within a society, such as sport and education or religion and government.

As a medium that permeates nearly every important aspect of life, sport has led some professionals to believe that it should receive intensive study, particularly as it affects the behavior of human beings and institutions as they form the total social and cultural context of society. Sport sociology focuses on examining the relationship between sport and society. Coakley[4] lists the major goals of sport sociology to be an understanding of the following:

- The factors underlying the creation and organization of sports.
- The relationship between sport and other aspects of society, such as family, education, politics, the economy, the media, and religion.

- The influence of sport and sport participation on individuals' beliefs about equity, gender, race, ethnicity, disability, and other societal issues.
- The social dynamics within the sport setting, such as organizational structure, group actions, and interaction patterns.
- The influence of cultural, structural, and situational factors on the nature of sport and the sport experience.
- The social processes associated with sport, including competition, socialization, conflict, and change.

Sport sociologists challenge us to critically examine our common and perhaps sacrosanct assumptions about sport, to scrutinize sport from different perspectives, and to understand social problems and social issues associated with sport (e.g., relationship between wealth and opportunity in sport). Sport sociologists examine societal forces that lead to change in sport (e.g., increased opportunities for women and changing conceptions of gender roles). Increasingly, sport sociologists seek to take a more active role in changing the status quo; they identify problems in sport and encourage changes that would transform sport and lead to equitable opportunities and promote human well-being (e.g., inequalities

The emphasis on being number one is so strong in the United States that oftentimes other values derived from participation in sport get forgotten.

of opportunities experienced by racial and ethnic groups).

Historical Development

Sport sociology emerged as a distinct field of inquiry in the late 1960s. The foundation for the emergence of sport sociology, however, can be traced back to the mid- to late 1800s. During this time, social scientists studied the nature and social functions of play, games, and sport—how these activities contributed to the development and building of character and reflected the culture of the times. In 1899, Thorstein Veblen wrote *The Theory of the Leisure Class,* in which he argued that sport represented a return to the days of

barbarism.[5] Sports were a way for the upper class to show that they were rich enough to avoid work and had the time to enjoy sport in their leisure.[6] A few sociologists of this period undertook the task of writing about sport as a social phenomenon, describing the relationships between sport and social behavior. The topics of this time included an ethnographic study of Native American games, the effect of sport participation on academic performance, and the role of sport in school.[5,6] However, as Sage notes, research was sporadic and often embedded in studies of play and games.[5]

The 1950s and 1960s marked a growth of interest in the sociology of sport. In 1953, physical educators Frederick Cozens and Florence Stumpf published *Sports in American Life,* which, according to noted sport sociologist George Sage, must be considered a pioneer effort to examine the role of sport in American society.[5] Noteworthy publications and presentations occurred during this time frame that described the need for and the importance of the field. This research included Johan Huizinga's *Homo Ludens* (1955), Roger Caillois's *Man, Play, and Games* (1961), Gerald Kenyon and John Loy's *Toward a Sociology of Sport* (1965), and Kenyon's *A Sociology of Sport: On Becoming a Sub-discipline* (1969).

The growth of interest and the desire to discuss ideas and to share research led to the development of scholarly organizations and journals. In 1964, Europeans and North Americans founded the International Committee of Sport Sociology (ICSS), which, in 1994, became the International Sociology of Sport Association (ISSA). ISSA is affiliated with UNESCO and is a subcommittee of the International Sociological Association (ISA) and the International Council of Sport Science and Physical Education (ICSSPE). In 1976, AAHPER (now AAHPERD) founded the Sociology of Sport Academy, whose mission was to promote the study of sport sociology. In 1980, the North American Society of Sport (NASS) was established, providing another forum for discussion and dissemination of research in sport sociology.

As research grew, scholarly journals focusing on sport sociology were developed. In 1966, ICSS began publication of the *International Review of Sport Sociology,* which, in 1984, became the *International Review for the Sociology of Sport.* In 1977, the inaugural issue of the *Journal of Sport and Social Issues* appeared. The first issue of the NASS publication *Sociology of Sport Journal* debuted in 1984 under the editorship of noted sport sociologist Jay Coakley. Additionally, *Quest* and the *Research Quarterly for Exercise and Sport* sometimes included articles on sport sociology.

The 1970s and 1980s were marked by an increased focus on socioeconomic and gender inequalities in sport and exercise and societal conceptions of the body.[6] In the 1990s, scholars increasingly directed their attention to racial and ethnic inequalities, particularly those faced by African Americans. The globalization of sport, the impact of the media, economics, and politics of sport in different cultures were also focuses in the 1990s.[6] All of the social inequalities researched over the past 40 years continue to receive considerable attention today.

Sport sociologists used a variety of different methods to collect quantitative and qualitative data for their research. As sport sociology emerged, expanded, and evolved, research moved from describing and analyzing sport to interpreting sport using a multitude of theoretical and methodological approaches. Today, many sport sociologists have taken a more active role—using a critical inquiry approach, they examine and interpret sport as well as make suggestions on how to solve problems in sport and transform sport to be more equitable.[3,6]

Areas of Study

Sport sociologists use sociological research strategies to study the behavior of individuals and groups within the sport milieu. Some questions sport sociologists might address are:

- Does participation in sport build character? Does it prepare individuals for life?
- Does sport help minorities, including women, become more fully integrated into society? How

does participation in sport affect the social and economic status of minorities?
- How do the mass media affect sport?
- What are the effects of youth sport programs on the lives of participants and their families?
- How are politics and sport related? Religion and sport? The economic status of the community or the country and sport?
- How does interscholastic and intercollegiate sport influence the academic achievement of its participants?
- How do coaches influence the lives of their athletes?

To address these and other questions, sport sociologists may examine historical circumstances, social conditions, economic factors, political climate, and relationships among the people involved.

As a field of study, the sociology of sport will likely continue to grow, expanding both in depth and breadth. However, many challenges face the field. For example, Coakley[4] points out that there is a need for further research leading to the development of theories about sport and its relationship to society and social life. Furthermore, he suggests that there is a need to focus additional attention on female participants in sport and on participation in sport throughout the lifespan (currently only childhood and early adulthood participation are highlighted).[4] Before a discussion of several areas of concern to sport sociologists, it may be helpful to define sport and discuss its nature and scope.

SPORT: A DEFINITION

In order to study sport in a systematic manner, it is necessary to develop a specific definition of sport. Such a definition has traditionally, by its very nature, been limiting and restrictive. Yet it provides a focus and a shared perspective by which to understand the relationship of sport to society.

Coakley defines sports as follows:

> Sports are well-established, officially governed competitive activities in which participants are motivated by internal and external rewards.[3]

Sport is said to be institutionalized when there are standardization and enforcement of the rules, emphasis on organization, and a formal approach to skill development.

This definition refers to what is popularly known as organized sport activities. On the basis of this definition, three often-asked questions can be addressed: (1) What kinds of activities can be classified as sport? (2) Under what circumstances can participation in activities be considered sport? (3) What characterizes the involvement of participants in sport?

Sport Activities

What physical activities can be considered sport? Jogging? Chess? Auto racing? Weight lifting? Are participants in a pickup baseball game engaged in sport even though their activity is different in nature from the game professionals play?

Sport requires that participants use relatively complex physical skills and physical prowess or vigorous physical exertion. Because these terms can be conceptualized as part of a continuum, at times it is difficult to make the distinction between physical and nonphysical skills, between complex and simple motor requirements, and between vigorous and nonvigorous activities. Because these terms are not quantified, determining what is complex physical activity and what is not can be a difficult task. Furthermore, not all physical activities involving complex physical skills or vigorous physical exertion are classified as sport. The circumstances and conditions under which these physical activities take place must be considered when classifying a physical activity as sport.

Conditions

The circumstances or context in which participation in physical activities occurs can be designated as ranging from informal and unstructured to formal and structured. For instance, compare the nature of a playground pickup game of basketball with a scheduled game between two professional teams. The individuals involved in both situations are playing basketball, but the nature and consequences of these games are different. Thus, the question is: Are both groups of individuals engaged in sport?

When sport sociologists discuss sport, they most often are referring to physical activity that involves competition conducted under formal and organized conditions. Given this perspective, friends engaged in an informal game of basketball are not participating in sport, whereas athletes participating on the professional teams are participating in sport. From the sociological point of view, sport involves competitive physical activity that is institutionalized.

According to sociologists, *institutionalization* is a standardized pattern or set of behaviors sustained over a period of time and from one situation to another. Thus, competitive physical activity can be considered sport when it becomes institutionalized. Institutionalization occurs when there is standardization and enforcement of the rules governing the activity, emphasis on organization and the technical aspects of the activity (e.g., training, use of strategies, specialization and definition of the roles of players and coaches), and a formalized approach to skill development (e.g., use of experts to provide instruction).

Participation Motives

Sport depends on maintaining a balance between intrinsic and extrinsic motivations. When the intrinsic satisfaction of being involved coexists with extrinsic concern for external rewards (e.g., money, medals, approval from parents or a coach), sport occurs. The balance does not have to be 50-50, but when one source of motivation begins to greatly outweigh the other, changes occur in the nature of the activity and the experience of the participants. When participants' intrinsic motives prevail, the organization and structure of physical activity become one of play. When participants' extrinsic motives such as medals or money prevail, physical activity changes from sport to what is often referred to as spectacle or work. It should be noted that during the course of a single sport event, participants may shift back and forth from intrinsic to extrinsic sources of motivation. At times, participants may be absorbed in the flow of the action and revel in the satisfaction of being involved. Moments later, they may be motivated by the desire to win a medal or receive the adulation of the crowd; the play spirit becomes replaced with the desire to reap external rewards.

According to Coakley, an alternative approach to defining sports strives to understand sports within the social and cultural contexts of particular societies. Two key questions guide this approach: "What activities do people in a particular group or society identify as sports? Whose sports count the most in a group or society when it comes to obtaining support and resources?"[3] This approach serves as a focal point for sport sociologists to scientifically examine the role of sports in people's lives and within a particular society.

As a field of study, the sociology of sport has grown tremendously over the past four decades. Due to space limitations, an overview of only a few topics can be presented in this chapter. The topics selected were chosen to enable students to relate to them based on past experience and the contemporary nature of the topics. This chapter includes interscholastic and intercollegiate sport, girls and women in sport, minorities in sport, children and youth sport, violence in sport, and performance-enhancing substances in sport.

SPORT IN EDUCATIONAL INSTITUTIONS

In the United States, organized sports are accepted as an integral part of the extracurricular offerings of schools and colleges. Since the initial inclusion of athletics in educational institutions in the late 1800s, concerns were raised about the educational worth of athletics and its relevancy to the educational mission of the schools.

Despite some criticism about the educational merits of interscholastic and intercollegiate athletics, they continue to grow in popularity. The National Federation of State High School Associations (NFHS) Athletic Participation report for 2008–2009 revealed that participation in high school athletics reached an all-time high of 7,536,753, including record highs for girls (3,114,091) and boys (4,422,662).[7] (See Figure 8-1.) Opportunities for students with disabilities to participate in adapted sports continue to slowly increase. More schools offer adapted sports such as basketball, bowling, floor hockey, softball, soccer, and track and field. However, school offerings and participation numbers are low—about 3,000 athletes.[4] Efforts need to be made to increase the opportunities for individuals with disabilities to participate in sport.

A review of NFHS athletic participation data revealed some trends regarding participation in sports. For boys' sports, the greatest gains in participants were found in 11-player football, outdoor track and field, baseball, and wrestling.[7] Girls' participation increased the most in competitive spirit squads, outdoor track and field, indoor track and field, and cross country.[7] It is also interesting to note the growth of sports traditionally associated with the opposite gender. For example, in 1995–1996, no boys played field hockey, traditionally a female sport; however, 716 boys participated in 2005–2006, which unfortunately declined to 174 in 2008–2009.[7] Girls' participation has also increased in traditionally male sports, such as wrestling, football, and baseball. Fifteen years ago, over 1,100 girls wrestled;

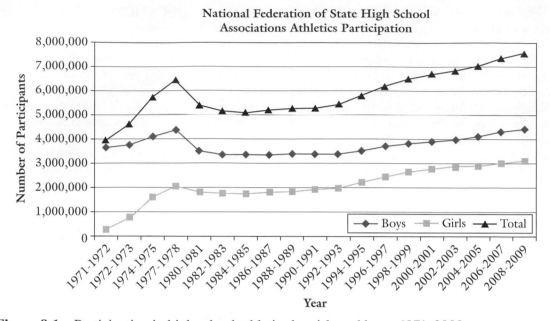

Figure 8-1   Participation in high school athletics by girls and boys, 1971–2009.

Source: Data from National Federation of State High School Athletic Associations. High School Athletics Participation Survey, 2008–2009.

however, in 2008–2009, over 6,000 girls from 1,034 schools wrestled, 700 played football, and 1,100 played baseball.[7]

Participation at the collegiate level has also experienced strong growth. In 2008–2009, the National Collegiate Athletic Association (NCAA), the largest governing body of athletics, reported that 423,325 athletes participated in intercollegiate athletics, 240,822 men and 182,503 women.[8] This is an increase of over 133,000 athletes from 1994–1995, 80,000 of them women. Note that these NCAA participation figures represent only those athletes who participate in sports in which the NCAA sponsors championships. Thus, many more participate in nonchampionship NCAA sports and many more men and women engage in sports in community college and non-NCAA member institutions.

Interscholastic and intercollegiate sports play an important role in our American culture, a role not limited to the participants or coaches involved in the experience. Because athletics plays such an important role in our society, it is interesting to examine some of the sociological implications of the phenomenon.

Interscholastic Sport

Interscholastic sport is viewed by many, including the National Federation of State High School Associations, as an integral part of the educational experience for high school students and, increasingly, junior high and middle school students as well.

While there is widespread support for interscholastic athletics, there has also been much criticism of these programs. Proponents of interscholastic athletics cite their valuable contributions to the educational mission of the schools. Critics take the position that sport interferes with the attainment of educational goals. (See the Popular Arguments For and Against Interscholastic Sport box.)

Participation in interscholastic sport can benefit students in several ways. Participation in sport can help students develop a high level of physical

Since the advent of Title IX in 1972, girls' and women's sports have grown in popularity. The University of Connecticut basketball players autograph photos for their fans prior to their 2004 NCAA championship appearance.

fitness and attain a high degree of proficiency in selected sport skills and knowledge of various aspects of the game. Other benefits of participation include the development of sportspersonship, cooperation, leadership, and loyalty. Sport can provide opportunities for personal growth, pave the way for the development of friendships, develop decision making and critical thinking skills, teach self-discipline and commitment, enhance self-esteem and personal status, and promote the acceptance of others regardless of race or ethnic origins.

However, whether participation in sport enhances academic achievement is a very complex and debatable question. When viewed as a group, high school athletes generally have better grade point averages and express more interest in higher education than their nonathletic peers.[3] It is important to note, however, that such differences are typically small. It is also difficult to isolate the influence of sport participation from other factors known to influence academic achievement, such as family background, economic status, support and encouragement from significant others, and individual characteristics.

Interscholastic sport can also heighten school spirit and engender parental support. In many locales across the country, interscholastic athletics provides a focal point for the community.

Whether or not interscholastic sport programs help participants attain desirable educational goals, as well as provide a positive experience for those students involved, depends a great deal on the manner in which the programs are conducted. These desired outcomes do not accrue automatically as a result of participation in the program. They can, however, be realized when school administrators and coaches make a concerted and thoughtful effort to structure sport programs to provide experiences that will lead to the attainment of educational goals and fulfillment of students' needs.

Interscholastic sport programs are an integral part of the educational experience for millions of US high school students, and enjoy widespread support. Nevertheless, in many schools across the country, interscholastic sport programs are in serious need of reform. Some programs have little relevancy to the education process. Critics of interscholastic sport also denounce the overemphasis on winning, restriction of opportunities for students, and eligibility requirements for participation. Concern has also been voiced pertaining to drug abuse, soaring costs, pressures from parents and community supporters, and coaches' behavior.

Overemphasis on winning is one of the most frequently voiced criticisms of interscholastic sport. This disproportionate emphasis is reflected in the increased specialization in one sport by athletes, the participation of injured athletes, the subversion of the educational process, and the dependence of coaches' jobs on their win-loss records.

Compared with just 10 years ago, more high school athletes are foregoing multisport competition and specializing in one sport.[9] Whereas in the past, athletes would compete in fall, winter, and spring sports, there is a trend toward competing in only one sport a year. Increasingly, athletes engage in conditioning programs and informal practices for their chosen sport in the off-season and

POPULAR ARGUMENTS FOR AND AGAINST INTERSCHOLASTIC SPORT

Arguments For

1. Involves students in school activities and increases interest in academic activities.
2. Builds self-esteem, responsibility, achievement orientation, and teamwork skills required for occupational success today.
3. Fosters fitness and stimulates interest in physical activities among students.
4. Generates spirit and unity and maintains the school as a viable organization.
5. Promotes parental, alumni, and community support for school programs.
6. Gives students opportunities to develop and display skills in activities valued in society, and to be recognized for their competence.

Arguments Against

1. Distracts students from academic activities and distorts values in school culture.
2. Perpetuates dependence, conformity, and a power and performance orientation that is no longer useful in society.
3. Turns most students into passive spectators and causes too many serious injuries to athletes.
4. Creates a superficial, transitory spirit that is unrelated to educational goals.
5. Deprives educational programs of resources, facilities, staff, and community support.
6. Creates pressure on athletes and supports a hierarchal status system in which athletes are unfairly privileged over other students.

Source: Coakley J. *Sport in Society: Issues and Controversies* (10th ed.). New York: McGraw-Hill, 2009.

attend specialized sport camps and play in community leagues during the summer. Proponents of sport specialization stress that such an emphasis is needed to develop proficiency in advanced skills, refine strategies, remain competitive with other teams, and increase an athlete's chances of receiving college grants-in-aid. Critics argue that specialization limits athletes' development, denying them opportunities to develop skills in other activities, participate with other athletes, and learn from other coaches. Athletes who specialize may be exploited by coaches seeking to win, they are subjected to overuse injuries, are at risk for athletic burnout (i.e., are tired and emotionally exhausted from participating), and may drop out of the sport, often near the point of reaching their fullest potential.

In an effort to win, coaches may resort to undesirable behaviors. They may pressure athletes to practice and play when injured. In an effort

to maintain player eligibility, coaches may steer athletes toward easier courses, pressure teachers to pass athletes or, in some cases, alter athletes' grades.

Winning is overemphasized when teachers are hired or fired based on their coaching win-loss records rather than their abilities as teachers. Good teachers have been fired because of poor coaching records, and poor teachers have been retained because of their outstanding coaching accomplishments.

If interscholastic sport is to realize its educational potential, it is important that winning be kept in perspective. The educational goals of learning and development should be emphasized, not the win-loss record.

The restricted number of opportunities for participation is another criticism of interscholastic sports. Schools typically have both a varsity and a junior varsity team in a variety of sports, although larger schools also may have freshman and reserve teams. Thus, when a given school offers both a varsity and a junior varsity basketball team for boys and for girls, perhaps as few as 48 students will have the opportunity to participate. Many students who are less skilled are excluded, despite their love of the game, and often no other scholastic sport opportunities are provided for them. Furthermore, in addition to consuming a great deal of the time and energy of physical education teachers, interscholastic sport teams utilize monies, facilities, equipment, and other resources that could be used for general participation (e.g., intramurals). In addition, even though federal legislation has mandated that boys and girls must have equal opportunities, often the informal support and commitment so necessary to develop and maintain quality programs for females is lacking. (This is discussed elsewhere in this chapter.)

Academic requirements for eligibility are also a controversial issue. Most high schools require that students meet certain academic standards to be eligible to participate in extracurricular activities, including sports. These standards often exceed the criteria required to stay in school. Many states have adopted "no pass, no play" policies, setting forth even more stringent requirements for athletes to maintain their eligibility. These requirements vary, but typically the policy bars participation of those individuals who do not pass all of their courses or who fail to maintain a certain grade point average during a marking period.

Advocates of this policy believe that establishing stringent standards for participation in sport programs will have a positive effect on athletes' academic performance. In order to maintain their eligibility, athletes will be motivated to pursue their studies. Critics of this policy point out that students who stay in school mainly to play sports now find themselves ineligible and may drop out of school.

The central issue of the no pass, no play controversy is, according to Siedentop, the educational importance of interscholastic sport.[9] Eligibility standards may be appropriate if sport is an extracurricular activity and participation is a privilege to be earned. If, however, sport is an integral part of the educational experience—if it has educational value—then is it appropriate to deny this experience to any student? If participation in interscholastic athletics contributes to educational goals, if the experience can promote learning and foster personal development, why should any student be denied this opportunity? Siedentop also relates this argument to the exclusionary nature of interscholastic sport discussed previously.[9] If participation in sport is an important developmental experience for adolescents, it should be more widely available so that more students, both boys and girls, can benefit.

One of the most serious problems in the schools is drug abuse. Much media attention has been focused on the use of performance-enhancing drugs, such as anabolic steroids, in professional, international, and intercollegiate sports. However, such drug use is a concern in interscholastic sports as well. It is estimated that many adolescents use anabolic steroids illegally, with girls accounting for approximately one-third of the users.[10] When taken in amounts far exceeding the recommended dosage (megadoses) and coupled with intense physical workouts, anabolic steroids can build muscle and enhance performance. The side effects associated with such large dosages are serious and lead to irreparable damage. The American Academy of Pediatrics states that the use of steroids poses a special danger to adolescents: "High school and middle school students and athletes need to be aware of the effect steroids have on growth. Anabolic steroids, even in small doses, have been shown to stop growth too soon. Adolescents also may be at risk for becoming dependent on steroids. Adolescents who use steroids are also more likely to use other addictive drugs and alcohol."[11] Coaches also must be prepared to address the use of supplements, such as creatine, and other serious issues, including the use of tobacco, alcohol, and illegal drugs such as marijuana, amphetamines, and cocaine.

Soaring costs are increasingly becoming a concern in interscholastic athletics. Rising costs for injury and liability insurance as well as costs associated with providing programs for girls and for students with disabilities have caused some schools to reduce the scope of their athletic programs or require athletes to pay in order to participate. A "pay-to-play" policy requires students who desire to participate in sports to pay for the opportunity. Critics have decried this policy because it discriminates against students who cannot afford to pay. Some schools and communities, in response, have made provisions so that economically disadvantaged students can participate in the athletic program. However, few of these students choose to participate.

Many pressures exert an insidious influence on interscholastic sport programs. When school administrators, community members, and parents pressure coaches to win; when the expectations of parents exert too much pressure on their children to excel; and when coaches place undue pressure on their athletes to perform, the quality of the sport experience can deteriorate rapidly. Sport becomes unrewarding and less enjoyable than it should be, and harmful to the participants. The educational experience becomes subverted and educational outcomes unrealized.

When high school coaches exert undue pressure on athletes to perform, when they excessively control the lives of their athletes, and when they physically or verbally abuse their athletes to set an example for the rest of the team, then the educational goals of interscholastic sport will go unfulfilled. There are coaches who equate obedience with self-discipline, demand single-minded dedication to sport, and provide no opportunity for athlete involvement in decision making (such as in setting team goals or planning game strategies). These coaches may win games, but they are failing to further the aims of education. Coaches who foster personal development of their athletes by guiding them, by allowing them to make decisions and to live with the consequences of those decisions, and by enhancing the worth and dignity of each athlete will help interscholastic sport fulfill its educational mission.

Intercollegiate Sport

Given the tremendous diversity of intercollegiate sport programs, it is easy to understand how the nature of the intercollegiate sport experience for participants can vary greatly from school to school, and within each program. The number of sports offered by a school can range from as few as 10 teams to as many as 25 different teams for men and women.[12] In smaller institutions, the athletic program may be part of and funded by the physical education department, the coaches may have faculty teaching status, and one individual may serve as the coach for two or more teams. In contrast, at larger institutions, separate athletic departments exist; athletics has its own budget and generates substantial revenue from gate receipts and contributions; coaches have no teaching status; and an individual coaches only one sport. Program philosophies vary as well; in some institutions the educational nature of intercollegiate sport is emphasized, while in other institutions sport is seen as big business.

Financial assistance for athletes varies and may be directly influenced by the skill of the athlete. Some schools offer no athletic scholarships; financial assistance is based solely on financial need. Other schools offer athletes a full scholarship that covers all expenses for tuition, room, board, fees, and books. Still other schools may offer partial assistance to athletes, such as providing only a tuition waiver. Given the tremendous diversity of intercollegiate sport programs, it is reasonable to believe that the nature of the intercollegiate sport experience for participants varies widely throughout the United States.

Intercollegiate sport is regulated by three primary governing bodies: the National Collegiate Athletic Association (NCAA), the National Association of Intercollegiate Athletics (NAIA), and the National Junior College Athletic Association (NJCAA). These associations attempt to administer intercollegiate athletic programs in accordance with educational principles.

The NCAA is the largest, most powerful governing body in intercollegiate athletics. In 2009, the NCAA had 1,055 active member institutions, divided into five divisions based on the characteristics of their athletic program.[13] Division I includes 331 schools and is divided into three divisions. Division I-FBS (Football Bowl Subdivision, formerly Division I-A) consists of 119 schools with 'big-money, high-profile' football teams. Division I-FCS (NCAA Football Championship Subdivision, formerly Division I-AA) comprises 119 schools with smaller football programs, and Division I-AAA includes 93 teams with no football programs. Division I "big-time" programs typically highlight football or men's basketball, because of their potential to generate revenue, often in the millions of dollars for successful programs. Divisions II and III are composed of 291 and 431 schools, respectively.

Athletes who participate in the big Division I programs generally possess a higher level of athletic talent, face a greater time commitment to their sport, receive full athletic scholarships, experience a greater amount of travel, and benefit from greater media exposure. Pressures to have a winning program are often immense, and the consequences of winning and losing are usually much greater. Economic survival for these programs frequently depends on their ability to generate revenue through gate receipts, contributions, and, increasingly, television contracts. Winning teams generate interest among fans, which increases gate receipts, which in turn provides more money to hire coaches with proven winning records to raise the athletic program to even greater heights. Commercialism and entertainment dominate; educational goals are de-emphasized and often subverted, and athletics is transformed into a business and entertainment venture.

As with interscholastic sport, overemphasis on winning can lead to the subordination of educational goals. Such goals as sportspersonship, character development, and social development may be abandoned when winning becomes the most important objective. Desire and pressure to win may lead to the subversion or violation of rules in an effort to recruit the best athletes and maintain their eligibility.

The academic achievement of intercollegiate athletes is a major concern. There are many student-athletes who exemplify the true meaning of the word—they have combined sports and academics successfully. A prominent example is former US Senator Bill Bradley, who played basketball for Princeton University, was named a Rhodes scholar, and had an outstanding professional basketball career before entering government service. In many colleges and universities, the academic achievements of athletes are comparable to those of their nonathlete peers. Studies have shown that the academic performance of athletes on women's teams, NCAA Division III teams, and other non-revenue-generating teams is comparable to other college students.

There are, however, many instances in which the term *student-athlete* is truly a misnomer; in these cases athletics is given a much higher priority than academics. This is particularly true of student-athletes in the big-time programs. Athletes in these programs, especially those in revenue-generating sports such as football and basketball, face considerable demands on their time and energy that can interfere with their academic work.

Some athletes in big-time programs can successfully balance the time-consuming demands of athletics with the rigorous demands of academics and excel in both areas. However, sometimes the pressures on coaches to win translate into pressure to keep athletes eligible. Focusing attention on eligibility rather than on learning can lead to many abuses. Coaches may recruit athletes who lack the academic preparation needed to succeed at the challenges of college. They counsel athletes into taking easy courses, pressure professors to give them good grades, and encourage athletes to enroll in majors that require little academic effort. Unfortunately, progress toward a degree is not monitored as closely as is maintenance of athletic eligibility. Additionally, because many black athletes are from rural and inner-city schools, where quality education programs are often lacking, a higher proportion of black athletes are affected.

In 1990, the US Congress passed a law requiring all colleges and universities to make public the

TABLE 8-1   Federal Graduation Rates for Division I Student-Athletes Entering in 2003 (Percentages)

	General Student Body			Student-Athletes		
	Male	Female	Total	Male	Female	Total
Black	38	49	44	49	63	53
Hispanic	51	58	55	47	70	58
White	62	67	65	60	74	68
Total	60	65	62	57	72	64

Source: Data from NCAA. *2009 NCAA Graduation Rates Report* (www.ncaa.org).

Graduation Success Rates (GSR) for Division I Student-Athletes Entering in 2003 (Percentages)

	Overall	Male	Female	Football	Men's Basketball	Women's Basketball
Black	63	57	76	58	56	75
Hispanic	73	66	83	63	62	87
White	84	79	90	79	81	89
Total	79	72	88	67	64	83

Source: Data from NCAA. *2009 NCAA Graduation Rates Report* (www.ncaa.org).

graduation rates of their athletes, starting in 1991. However, even the availability of this information makes it difficult to get a true picture of the graduation rates of athletes. Additionally, the formula used by the US government, often referred to as the federal formula, is often criticized for failing to take into account students who transfer to another institution or who leave school to play on a professional team.

The 2009 NCAA Division I graduation rates, based on the federal formula, are shown in Table 8-1. The graduation rates are based on individuals who received an athletic scholarship and who graduated within 6 years of initial college entry. The data show that Division I athletes with athletic grants graduate at a similar rate to the collective student body; the graduation rate for female athletes is higher than for male athletes and other female students; black male and female athletes graduate at a higher rate than the overall black student body, yet at a lower rate than white athletes; graduation rates are lowest in the revenue-producing sports of football and basketball; and black athletes are more likely to leave school with a grade point average lower than 2.0.[14]

To address the shortcomings in the calculation of the federal graduation rate, the NCAA developed the graduation success rate (GSR). The GSR takes into account students who have transferred or not returned for a variety of reasons (e.g., financial circumstances or going professional), but left the institution in good academic standing (note that this does not mean they were on track for their degree). This is thought by the NCAA to be a more accurate reflection of the academic success of their athletes. Unlike the federal rate, rates are not calculated for the general student body, so no comparisons can be made of the student-athletes' academic performance to that of the general student body.

As you review the data in Table 8-1, what types of patterns do you see? How do you believe the graduation rate of the general student body would be affected if the GSR were used to calculate their success? What do you believe are the various sociological factors that contribute to these patterns? If you participate in intercollegiate athletics, how does your participation impact your academic success?

Trying to make sense out of the graduation rates of student-athletes is a complex process. Neither the federal rate nor the GSR takes into account students' majors or their courses. Concern has been raised that some student-athletes are guided into certain majors by athletic departments, interested more in keeping the athlete eligible than in academically preparing the athlete for the future. In a similar vein, athletes may be overrepresented in certain courses, perhaps because they are easy to fit into their heavy workload or because they do not interfere with practices and team meetings.

Another effort to address the academic concerns associated with big-time revenue-producing sports is the establishment of a minimum academic progress rate (APR). This rule, passed in 2004, applies to more than 5,700 Division I teams. APR is based on academic eligibility, retention, and academic success (GSR) of student-athletes and is calculated each semester.[15] A team receives 1 point for every athlete who is academically eligible and 1 point for each athlete who remains enrolled in school.[15] A complex formula adjusts for different team sizes. The highest APR score is 1,000 points.[15] Teams that fail to achieve a minimum score of 925 can lose one or more of their allocated scholarships, depending on how far below 925 they score.[15] A score of 925 reflects a graduation rate of about 50 percent.[15]

In 2006, the Institute for Diversity and Ethics in Sport reported that 24 of the 64 football teams playing in bowls failed to meet the NCAA APR standard, scoring lower than the 925 points.[16] Four of the teams were penalized, having to cut 10% of the scholarships they would be allowed to award during the upcoming academic year.[16] Only 4 years later, in 2010, there was a dramatic increase when 61 of the 67 football teams (i.e., 91%) met the APR standard. Although this increase in academic success should be applauded, the achievement gap between black and white athletes continues to be an issue. Lapchick addresses

this issue when he states, "In spite of the good news, the study showed that the disturbing gap between white and African-American football student-athletes remains a major issue; 21 teams or 31 percent of the bowl-bound schools graduated less than half of their African-American football student-athletes, while only two schools graduated less than half of their white football student-athletes."[16]

Another effort by the NCAA to improve the academic performance of athletes in Division I and II teams focuses on player eligibility, both initially as a freshman and then as a continuing student. Starting in 1983, the NCAA adopted a set of academic standards that freshmen had to meet in order to be eligible to play, practice, and receive financial aid their first year. Currently, in 2007, to compete as a freshman, a student must have graduated from high school, completed a minimum of 14 core courses (math, English, science, etc.) with a minimum grade point average (GPA) in each of the courses, and earned a qualifying score on either the ACT or SAT test.[17] Students' GPA and standardized test score requirements are based on a sliding scale; the higher a student's core GPA, the lower the minimum standardized test score requirements.[17] For example, a high school student with a core GPA of 3.5 needs a combined verbal and math score on the SAT of 420 in order to be eligible as a freshman. On the other hand, a high school student with a core GPA of 2.0 must achieve a combined verbal and math score on the SAT of 1010 for freshman eligibility. High school students who aspire to play in Division II must have a core GPA of 2.0.[17] The minimum standardized test scores are 820 on the SAT (verbal and math only) or an ACT sum score of 68.[17]

By setting initial eligibility standards, the NCAA hoped to send a strong message to high school administrators, coaches, and athletes that academic achievement was a prerequisite for participation in Division I and II athletics. It was further hoped that initial eligibility rules would help colleges and universities break the habit of recruiting athletes who had neither the academic background nor the potential to graduate within a 5-year period. It also provides first-year athletes who need a year to strengthen their academic abilities without the added pressures and time commitments associated with participation in sports.

The initial eligibility rules are controversial. Critics charge that they discriminate against economically disadvantaged students who were not fortunate enough to receive a strong high school preparation for college and those who do not have the resources to pay for commercial test preparation courses or to retake the standardized tests.

The overall ineligibility rate in 2001 was 6.8%.[18] The ineligibility rate for black student-athletes was 20.6%, compared to 9.2% and 3.7% for Hispanic and white student-athletes, respectively.[18] The ineligibility rate for student-athletes whose family income was less than $30,000 was 16.7%, compared to 2.1% for student-athletes whose family income was $80,000 or more a year.[18] Concerns were also raised about the cultural bias of the standardized tests, in particular the SAT. According to critics, the SAT discriminates against blacks and women. The average SAT scores for most minority groups are lower than for white students, and females' scores are significantly lower than males'.[19] For both the SAT and the ACT, average scores increase as family income increases.[18] These disparities are of concern because they reflect limited opportunities for minorities and females.

Continuing eligibility requires the student-athletes to make progress toward graduation. The NCAA's 40-60-80 rule requires steady progress toward completion of graduation requirements and the attainment of a specified GPA to remain eligible to compete. By the end of their second year, athletes must complete 40 percent of their graduation requirements with a GPA of at least 1.8.[15] At the conclusion of their third year, athletes must have completed 60 percent of the requirements with a GPA of at least 2.0.[15] Eighty percent of the requirements must be completed with a GPA of at least 2.0 by the end of the fourth year for athletes to remain eligible to compete.[15]

The long-term effectiveness of these academic reform measures remains to be seen. It is hoped that they will lead to an increased emphasis on academic achievement for athletes at both the high school and college levels. It appears that these measures are steps toward restoring much-needed academic integrity to intercollegiate athletic programs.

Several other problems beset big-time intercollegiate sport, including the fact that sport has become big business. This commercialism has led to financial concerns receiving a greater priority than the education and personal development of the athletes. Television contracts increase the pressure to have a winning program in order to reap greater financial benefits. Media coverage of sport continues to grow. The NCAA's recent contract with CBS—$10.8 billion for 14 years, from 2011 to 2024—for the Division I men's basketball championship, reflects the tremendous interest in the commercial value of intercollegiate sport.[20] Almost 80% of the NCAA's revenue comes from television rights.

There is increasing concern about the exploitation of athletes. Some intercollegiate athletes can generate millions of dollars for their institution, but the only compensation permitted under NCAA rules is tuition, room, board, books, and fees. Even at the most expensive institutions, when the total cost of the athletic scholarship is divided by the number of hours athletes are required to devote to their sport, the pay per hour is low.[10] Although critics say it is difficult to place a value on the benefits of a college education, oftentimes athletes are strongly encouraged to focus their energies and efforts on sports instead of academics. All too often, athletic departments are concerned with athletes' academic status only until their 3 or 4 years of eligibility are used up; after this period, their concern about the academic progress of athletes is minimal. Most adversely affected by this practice are athletes from lower socioeconomic backgrounds and those who have received poor preparation for college from their high schools. These athletes often do not have the financial resources to pay for the extra semesters needed to graduate. Furthermore, because much of their efforts had previously been devoted to sport rather than academics, they may find it difficult to cope with the academic demands without the extra assistance (e.g., tutors) previously available to them as members of sport teams.

Several other issues in intercollegiate sport must be addressed. The media have increased the public's awareness of violations of recruiting regulations. Illegal recruiting practices, such as cash payments to prospective athletes, must be stopped. Drug abuse also is a problem. Athletes, in an effort to enhance their performance, may abuse such drugs as amphetamines and anabolic steroids. Although drug testing policies and procedures have become more stringent, methods to mask the use of drugs have become more clever. The effect of win-loss records on the retention of coaches, the role of coaches within institutions of higher education, and the role of alumni and other influential supporters in the hiring and firing of coaches must be carefully evaluated and monitored.

The 1980s and early 1990s were marked by calls for the reform of intercollegiate athletics. Abuses have become so serious and so widespread that the academic integrity of educational institutions sponsoring these programs is challenged. In 1990, the US Congress called for monitoring athletes' graduation rates. In 1991, the Knight Foundation Commission on Intercollegiate Athletics released a report calling for the reform of intercollegiate athletics. University presidents were called upon to exercise greater control over their sport programs, in terms of both fiscal responsibility and academic integrity.[21] Greater attention must be focused on containing the spiraling costs of intercollegiate athletics. Equally important, careful attention must be given to enhancing the academic performance of student-athletes. The NCAA has passed legislation that focuses on providing opportunities and conditions that foster better academic achievements by student-athletes. Among these rulings are the elimination of athletic dormitories, reductions in the number of hours practiced per week and in the length of the season, and more stringent monitoring of the student-athlete's academic progress toward a degree.

In 2001, 10 years after it issued its landmark 1991 report, the Knight Foundation Commission on Intercollegiate Athletics released another report, entitled *A Call to Action: Reconnecting College Sports and Higher Education.*[22] The report states, "While the NCAA and individual schools have made considerable progress . . . the problems of big-time college sports have grown, rather than diminished. The most glaring problems—academic transgressions, a financial arms race, and commercialization—are all evidence of the widening chasm between higher education's ideals and big-time college sports."[22]

In examining the widening chasm between the goals of education and big-time athletics, the Knight Commission noted the following:

- Big-time athletic programs operate with little interest in scholastic matters beyond the maintenance of athlete eligibility. The graduation rates for football players and men's basketball players are dismally low.
- The ever-growing "arms race" of spending has led to rapidly rising expenditures. Only about 15% of athletic programs at all levels operate in the black. Deficits are growing each year. Some programs have sought to control expenses by dropping minor sports. Many big-time programs are refurbishing or building new stadiums and arenas; in some cases, they are naming them after corporate sponsors. Over 30 college football and men's basketball coaches are paid a million dollars or more a year—more than anyone in the college or university, including the president.
- Big-time college sports resembles the professional model of sports. Commercialization of college sports has led to vastly larger television and athletic shoe contracts and to more and more space in the stadiums and arenas being sold to advertisers. Corporate trademarks and sponsors' logos appear on athletes' uniforms and equipment.

After reviewing the academic performance of student-athletes, the escalating spending on athletics, and the growing commercialization of intercollegiate sport, the Knight Commission recommended a "one-plus-three" model to reform collegiate athletics. The "one" was the establishment of a coalition of presidents who would work in concert with such groups as the American Council on Education to restore athletics as an integral part of the educational enterprise. The coalition would address the "three"—academic reform, de-escalation of the athletics arms race, and de-emphasis of the commercialization of intercollegiate athletics. In terms of academic reform, the key point is that "students who participate in athletics deserve the same rights and responsibilities as all other students."[22] Some of the recommendations to accomplish this goal are:

- Tie championships and postseason opportunities to graduation rates. By 2007, teams that graduate less than 50% of their players were ineligible for conference championships or postseason play.
- Hold athletes accountable, the same as other students, with respect to criteria for admission, academic support services, choice of major, and satisfactory progress toward a degree.
- Reduce the length of the season and postseason competition and lessen practice time commitments to allow athletes a reasonable chance to complete their degree.
- Encourage the NBA and the NFL to develop minor leagues to provide another route to professional careers.

The second key point is that to keep expenditures under control, the coalition should insist that "athletic departments' budgets be subject to the same institutional oversight and direct control as other university departments."[22] Among the recommendations to the coalition to accomplish this goal are:

- Reduce expenditures associated with big-time football and basketball, including reducing the number of scholarships awarded in Division I football.
- Ensure that compliance with Title IX and support of women's programs does not become an excuse for soaring costs, while expenses in big-time sports continue unchecked.

- Bring coaches' compensations in line with existing compensation norms across the institution.
- Distribute television revenue from the NCAA Division I Final Four based on an institution's improving academic performance, enhancing the athletes' collegiate experience, and achieving gender equity.

Last, with respect to commercialization, the fundamental issue is that "colleges and universities must take control of athletics programs back from television and other corporate interests."[22] With respect to this goal, the coalition should:

- Insist that institutions alone determine when games will be played and how they will be broadcast, rather than allowing television to dictate terms.
- Prohibit athletes from wearing corporate trademarks or sponsors' logos on their uniforms.
- Actively work to ban gambling on collegiate athletics.

Like interscholastic sport, intercollegiate sport has the potential to contribute to the educational goals of the institutions that sponsor it. Whether these educational goals are attained depends on the leadership. When winning is overemphasized, commercialism is rampant, and athletes are exploited, the educational relevance of these programs is called into question. When winning is placed in perspective, when academic achievement is strongly supported, and when athletes are encouraged and given opportunities to develop to their fullest potential, then the educational mission of intercollegiate athletics will be fulfilled.

GIRLS AND WOMEN IN SPORT

Prior to the 1970s, opportunities for girls and women to compete in sports were limited. Over the past 38 years, there has been a dramatic increase in girls' and women's participation in sports. This increase is visible at all levels of competition—the Olympics, professional and amateur sports, intercollegiate and interscholastic sports, and youth sports.

The relatively recent increase in participation by girls and women in the United States can be attributed to several factors. These include federal legislation, the women's movement, the fitness movement, and an increased public awareness of female athletes.

Federal legislation, specifically Title IX of the Education Amendments of 1972, was one of the most influential factors, because it mandated equal treatment for women and men in programs receiving federal assistance. Because Title IX is politically controversial and the guidelines are complex, implementation and enforcement of this law are difficult. After its implementation, access to sport opportunities for women increased. However, it should be noted that only programs directly receiving federal aid are required to comply with the Title IX regulations, not whole institutions. Because athletic programs typically receive little if any direct federal funding, the threat of losing funding for noncompliance and nonsupport of women's athletics is not a substantial one.

In 2005, over 30 years after Title IX was passed, Donna Lopiano, executive director of the Women's Sports Foundation, estimated that more than 80% of colleges and universities were not in compliance with Title IX.[23] The Office of Civil Rights has a three-pronged test to determine if an institution is in compliance. A school must meet one of these three tests to be within the law:

1. *Proportionality.* Are the opportunities for males and females substantially proportionate to the school's full-time undergraduate enrollment? Recent court decisions indicate that being within five percentage points is acceptable and within the law. Thus, if 49% of the enrollment is female, between 44% and 54% of the athletes should be female.

2. *History and continued practice.* Even though a school has a disproportionate number of male athletes, as long as the school is adding more women's sports and has added one recently, generally within the last 3 years, the school would probably be considered in compliance.

3. *Accommodation of interests and abilities.* If a school can demonstrate that its women do not have enough ability or interest to sustain additional teams, the school would be considered in compliance. However, if there are club teams playing sports, this could indicate to the court that there is sufficient interest to support another team.

Great strides have been made toward equity. Much more needs to be done to create additional opportunities for participation in sports at all levels.

The impact of Title IX has resulted in noticeable increases in participation of girls and women at both the interscholastic and intercollegiate levels. The growth of participation by girls in interscholastic sport following the passage of Title IX can be seen in Figure 8-1. At the intercollegiate level, there has been an increase in the number of teams for women, the hiring of qualified coaches, and the offering of athletic scholarships to outstanding high school women athletes. In 1972, 32,000 women competed in intercollegiate sports; the NCAA reported that nearly 175,994 women participated in its athletic programs in 2007–2008.[24] Spectator interest in women's sports has grown as well, which has resulted in increased attendance at games. For example, NCAA women's basketball attendance for the 2009–2010 season surpassed 11 million for the

Since Title IX, sports opportunities for girls and women have increased. Sports are no longer just for fathers and sons.

third straight year and was the second highest total in history.[25] Connecticut and Tennessee both had a season attendance of over 200,000. Television coverage of women's sports has increased; the NCAA championships in swimming and diving, basketball, gymnastics, volleyball, and track and field have been televised in recent years. Even coverage of regular-season events has expanded.

The women's movement has encouraged increased participation in athletics by women. It has helped redefine societal, occupational, and family roles for women and has given women more control over their lives. For example, women athletes were once perceived by many as unfeminine or were stigmatized for engaging in high levels of competition; but athletic participation by women is now regarded as acceptable. Ideas about what is masculine and what is feminine are based on societal definitions and may be needlessly restrictive, creating barriers to participation.[3] In the future, as society's attitudes continue to change, more people may come to perceive sport not as a masculine activity but rather as a human activity.

Playing sports can be an empowering experience for girls and women by changing their perceptions of themselves. Sports can foster feelings of competence, promote confidence, and help girls and women see themselves as more in control of their lives. This is important because quite often in our society, girls and women are portrayed as weak, dependent, and powerless. The President's Council on Physical Fitness report *Physical Activity and Sport in the Lives of Girls,* released in 1997, uses an interdisciplinary approach to examine the impact of physical activity and sport on the lives of girls.[26] The report emphasizes the contributions physical activity and sport can make to the "complete girl"—her social, physical, emotional, and cultural environment—rather than to just one aspect of her life. Some of its conclusions are:

- Exercise and sport participation can be used as a therapeutic and preventive intervention to enhance the physical and mental health of adolescent girls.

- Exercise and sport participation enhance mental health by offering adolescent girls opportunities to develop positive feelings about their bodies, improved self-esteem, tangible experiences of competency and success, and enhanced self-confidence.
- Sport contributes to educational goals. Compared to their nonathletic peers, high school female athletes have higher grades and lower dropout rates, and are more likely to go to college.
- Poverty substantially limits many girls' access to physical activity and sport. This is particularly true for minorities, who are overrepresented in lower socioeconomic groups.
- The potential for girls to derive positive experiences from physical activity and sport is limited by lack of opportunity and stereotypes.

The benefits of participation are great. Physical education and sport professionals must create greater opportunities for participation and work to remove barriers that limit participation.

Since the 1970s, the fitness movement has encouraged many women to participate in physical activities, including sport. Many women started engaging in jogging, walking, aerobics, and swimming to realize the associated benefits of fitness, particularly to feel good and look better. Although there is still an emphasis on engaging in physical activities to look better and to preserve one's youthfulness, there is also a growing emphasis on the physical development of the body. Additionally, many women have moved from engaging in fitness activities to engaging in competitive athletics; joggers have gone on to participate in road races, marathons, and even triathlons. Interest in fitness has also led to an increase in the number of women participating in community sport programs in such sports as softball, volleyball, and basketball.

As participation by girls and women increases, there will be more women athlete role models. The increased coverage and publicity given to women athletes have allowed girls and women to read about the achievements and watch the performance of women athletes in a wider range of sports than ever before. The accomplishments of Olympic gold-medal American female athletes in softball, soccer, swimming, track and field, gymnastics, basketball, skiing, and other sports may encourage many girls to participate in sports and pursue their athletic ambitions.

Professional opportunities for women are also increasing. In 1996, two professional women's basketball leagues—the American Basketball League and the Women's National Basketball Association (WNBA)—were organized, offering elite women athletes the opportunity to continue to participate in their sport. The American Basketball League folded after the 1998–1999 season. The WNBA has grown rapidly. Its 13 teams, organized into two conferences, attracted 1.77 million spectators during the 2009 season.[27]

Women had the opportunity to play professional soccer in the United States. In 2001, the Women's United Soccer Association (WUSA) launched its inaugural season. The eight-team league featured players from the US Women's World Cup championship team and many top international players. The 87 games drew over 700,000 fans, with an average attendance of 8,295.[28] Twenty-two games were nationally televised on TNT and CNN/SI.[28] Over 5 million viewers tuned in to these broadcasts. Unfortunately, in 2004, due to financial issues, the league ceased operation. Although professional opportunities for women are increasing, they are still limited.

Legislation, the women's movement, the fitness movement, and increased visibility accorded female athletes have done much to expand opportunities for women in sport. However, while opportunities for girls and women in athletics have increased tremendously over the past four decades, whether participation rates will continue to grow for women depends to a great extent on the expansion of opportunities for involvement and the support and encouragement of female athletic endeavors.

Financial considerations may serve to limit opportunities for participation by girls and women. When school, collegiate, and community athletic programs are threatened with cutbacks, programs for girls and women are most at risk for losing financial support. Because these programs are newer and not as established as similar programs for men and boys, they have had less time to gather administrative and community backing and may not be able to elicit sufficient support to survive cutbacks. Participation opportunities for females also may be adversely affected because the establishment and development of new programs generally requires greater financial support and resources than do established programs. Because many programs for females are new or in the process of development, successful growth of these programs requires financial commitment. Yet despite the need, programs for females tend to be funded at lower levels than programs for males. This lack of funding hampers program growth and adversely affects opportunities for participation and quality competition.

In spite of the passage of Title IX and improvements in opportunities, sex discrimination is still a feature of many athletic programs. New laws are often met with resistance and questions about how to implement them. Additionally, people tend to be reluctant to change the status quo. Individuals with a vested interest in maintaining the status quo may use their power and control of financial resources to thwart the progress of women's programs. Women across the nation at all levels of competition are still denied fair treatment. Such discrimination can be as blatant as the refusal to fund a program. But inequality often occurs in less noticeable forms, such as the provision of quality equipment, supplies, and uniforms; the assignment of games and practice time; the use of facilities and locker rooms; the allocation of equal funds for travel and the availability of travel opportunities; the access to quality coaches, size of coaching staff, and compensation of coaches; the opportunity to receive support services such as academic tutoring; the administration of medical and training services; and the publicity accorded to individual athletes and the team.

Despite Title IX prohibitions against discrimination, women still do not receive equitable treatment in sport. Furthermore, violations of Title IX are often not prosecuted vigorously. Commitment, time, and effort are needed to ensure compliance with the law and ensure that the spirit of the law becomes an integral part of athletic programs at all levels.

Today there are fewer female coaches for women's sports than in the years following the passage of Title IX. Despite the fact that women's sport programs have increased, the proportion of women in coaching and athletic administrative positions has declined. For example, at the intercollegiate level, Acosta and Carpenter[29] report that the percentage of female coaches of women's sport programs decreased from 90% in 1970 to 58% in 1978 to 42.4% in 2006.[29] This is one of the lowest percentages of head coaches that has been reported to date. As you can see from tracking the percentages across the years, head coaching opportunities for women are decreasing. And, although men serve as head coaches for 57.6% of women's teams, only 2% of the head coaches of men's teams are women.[29] In 1972, 90% of women's intercollegiate athletic programs were headed by female athletic administrators. The NCAA report reveals that 18% of director of athletics positions are held by women; about one-third of the associate director and assistant director positions are held by women. Peg Bradley-Doppes, a past president of the National Association of Collegiate Women Athletics Administrators, in a speech before the Knight Commission in 2000 asked that the commission "reaffirm the policies that will reinforce principles related to gender equity, diversity, ethics, and integrity in educational sport environments."[30]

Reasons for the underrepresentation of women in these positions have been debated widely, and the results of the research are confusing. However, one reason that is frequently cited is the lack of well-qualified women coaches and administrators. Recently, several programs have been implemented in the United States to recruit and train more women coaches. It is also important to note that the lack of visibility of women coaches and administrators within the sport structure provides few role models for females who aspire to careers in these areas. Other reasons include the persistence of traditional stereotypes of women and resistance of those in power, predominantly men, to providing opportunities for women.

One of the concerns raised by some opponents to the implementation of Title IX was that compliance with Title IX, specifically the expansion of sport opportunities for girls and women, would substantially reduce opportunities for boys and men. In 2001, the United States General Accounting Office (GAO) released its report on gender equity entitled *Intercollegiate Athletics: Four-Year Colleges' Experiences Adding and Discontinuing Teams*.[31] This report monitored changes in athletic programs for the two largest intercollegiate athletic associations, the NCAA and the NAIA, for a period covering 18 years, from 1981–1982 through 1998–1999. Several of its findings are:

- The number of women participating in intercollegiate athletics increased substantially, from 90,000 to 163,000—an 81% increase. Men's athletic participation experienced a modest 5% increase, from 220,000 to 230,000.
- Women's teams increased from 5,695 to 9,479, an increase of 3,784 teams. Men's teams increased by 36 teams, from 9,113 to 9,149 teams. Although women have more teams than men, they still have fewer participants because of the large number of men participating in team sports with large squad sizes, such as football.
- Both men's and women's sports added teams. The sport added most frequently for both men and women was soccer. Women's soccer increased from 80 teams to 926. Men's soccer increased by 135 teams, from 744 teams to 879.
- Both men's and women's teams were discontinued. Among women's sports, gymnastics was most often dropped, decreasing from 190 teams to 90 teams. Fencing teams also decreased for women, from 76 teams to 45 teams. For men's sports, wrestling experienced the largest decrease, from 428 teams to 257 teams. Men's gymnastics also decreased from 82 teams to

26 teams and men's tennis dropped from 952 teams to 868 teams.

- Over the report's time period, 962 institutions added teams and 307 discontinued teams. Most schools, 72%, were able to add teams—usually women's teams—without discontinuing any teams. Schools added nearly three times as many women's teams as men's teams—1,919 teams for women compared to 702 teams for men. Schools discontinued more than twice as many men's teams; 386 men's teams were discontinued compared to 150 teams for women.

- Among the institutions that added teams, the two most often-cited factors that influenced the decision were the need to address student interest in a particular sport and the need to meet gender equity goals and requirements. Overall, 52% of the schools cited student interest as a great factor and 47% of the schools indicated the need to meet gender equity goals and requirements as the reason for adding women's teams. Reasons for adding a women's team varied by the size of the institution. For example, at the NCAA Division I-A level, 82% of the schools cited gender equity considerations, compared to 35% of the schools at the Division III level.

- Of the schools that discontinued a men's team, 33% cited a lack of student interest as a factor, 31% cited gender equity concerns, and 30% reported a need to reallocate the athletic budget to other sports as factors influencing their decision.

- Major factors associated with discontinuing men's sports varied by the size of the institution. Fifty-four percent of NCAA Division I-A schools reported that meeting gender equity goals and requirements influenced their decision, whereas 44% of Division III schools most often cited absence of sufficient student interest as influencing a decision to discontinue a team.

Schools that expanded their athletic options for women by adding teams and not discontinuing men's teams used a variety of strategies to accomplish this task. Most often, the schools obtained additional revenue for the program expansion rather than containing costs and reallocating revenue. Division I-A schools tended to rely on generating revenue from other sports and from outside sources.[31] At smaller schools, such as Division III and NAIA schools, additional monies from the institution's general fund and reallocation of existing resources provided the funds to support the growth of athletic opportunities for women.[31]

Although some schools have been successful in increasing opportunities for women and men, there is concern that, as Bradley-Doppes states, "schools are choosing to cut programs rather than ask all teams to operate on smaller pieces of the financial pie. In fact, schools are spending more money on men's sports than ever. . . . The 1999 NCAA Revenue and Expenses of Division I and II Intercollegiate Athletics Programs study revealed that in Division I-A institutions the average total operating expenses for women's sports were $3,741,000, while average total operating expenses for men's sports were $9,544,000."[30] The Women's Sports Foundation reported that in 2003–2004, while females represented 44% of all college athletes, they received only 37% of sports operating dollars.[23]

More opportunities for both men and women to participate in sports can be achieved by reducing excessive funding of sports rather than denying opportunities to participate. This could be achieved in many different ways, such as holding the line on spending in men's sports, generating new revenue sources to support women's sports, and decreasing excessive spending by limiting squad sizes, decreasing the number of scholarships, or trimming excesses from existing budgets, such as teams spending the night in hotels before a home game. Remember that Title IX prohibits discrimination on the basis of sex, and that federal regulations require that both men and women be provided with equitable opportunities, including opportunities to participate in intercollegiate athletics.

Although women's participation in sport has increased dramatically during the last 38 years, the accomplishments of female athletes are often trivialized and ridiculed by both men and women. For example, women often have to suffer with team names and mascots that belittle physical competence and minimize the achievement of female athletes. To illustrate, at one university, the men's teams are referred to as the Bears and the women's teams as the Teddy Bears; other examples are the Blue Hawks and Blue Chicks, the Rams and Rambelles, and the Tigers and the Tigerettes. Were the men's and women's teams at your high school or college referred to by different nicknames? If so, what messages do these names send to the public about the abilities of the athletes and the seriousness of their endeavors?

Discrimination is also noticeable in sports outside the school setting. At the international level, for example, where efforts to bring about changes have not been supported by legislation, women typically have fewer events in which to participate and are less likely to be rewarded for their efforts than men. Even though changes have occurred, women are still underrepresented in international sport.

Other factors that have contributed to the inequities experienced by women in sport are myths about the consequences of athletic participation and the physical, social, and psychological characteristics of women. Examples of these myths include the belief that strenuous participation in sport can lead to problems in childbearing (it has been shown that athletes who are in excellent physical condition have shorter and easier deliveries and experience fewer problems such as backache after the birth of a child)[4] and the belief that the fragile bone structure of women makes them more likely to experience injuries than men (when both men and women athletes experience similar training regimens and care and practice under the leadership of qualified coaches, injury rates are similar for both genders in any given sport). Other myths perpetuate the belief that participating in sports can threaten one's femininity (women athletes typically do not see their involvement as a threat to their image). Although research and education have done much to dispel these myths, they still persist and serve to needlessly limit participation by women.

Events of the past 38 years have served to increase opportunities for participation by women in sport at all levels. Federal legislation, the women's movement, the fitness movement, and increased visibility and recognition of the achievements of women athletes have helped females of all ages to benefit from opportunities to participate in sports. However, while progress has been made, continued increases in participation by women will depend on eliminating barriers to involvement such as financial constraints, less-than-full compliance with Title IX, lack of women coaches and administrators, minimization of women's accomplishments, and unfounded beliefs or myths. Coakley notes that gender equity is a complex issue and suggests that the following guideline from the 1993 NCAA Gender Equity Panel may be helpful in thinking about this issue: "An athletics program is gender equitable when either the men's or women's sports program would be pleased to accept as its own the overall program of the other gender."[4] Qualified and committed leadership is needed to change the structure of sport programs in order to reduce inequities and to further eliminate barriers to participation so that all individuals, regardless of gender, can enjoy the benefits of sport.

MINORITIES IN SPORT

Sport is often extolled as an avenue by which to transcend differences in race and cultural backgrounds. It has been said, for example, that "sport is color-blind"—that on the playing field a person is recognized for ability alone, and rewards are given without regard to race and class. The widely televised performances of black and Hispanic male athletes in such sports as baseball, basketball, track and field, boxing, and football suggest to millions of viewers that sport is relatively free of the prejudice and discrimination often found in other areas of society. Despite a commonly held belief that sport allows individuals to accept one another on the basis of their physical competence, close scrutiny of the sport phenomena reveals that sport organizations are typically characterized by the same patterns of prejudice and discrimination found in the surrounding society.

Historically, sport in the United States has been characterized by racism and prejudice. While blacks and other minorities have a rich history of sport participation, prior to the 1950s, minorities were rarely given access to mainstream sport competition in the professional leagues, colleges and universities, and schools. Members of minorities organized their own leagues and competed within them; for example, blacks had their own basketball and baseball leagues. The integration of professional sport did not occur until 1946, when Jackie Robinson "broke the color barrier" by playing for the then Brooklyn Dodgers. Integration of intercollegiate sports occurred later and was particularly slow to occur in the South. The US Supreme Court's decision in *Brown v. Board of Education* in 1954, as well as the civil rights movement of the 1970s, slowly led to the integration of schools and the opening of doors to sports for minorities.

Currently, the participation of black athletes remains concentrated in a few sports. Black athletes are overrepresented in certain sports such as football, and basketball. These sports typically require no expensive equipment or training, have coaches readily available through the public schools, and offer visible role models to aspiring athletes. Black athletes are underrepresented in such sports as volleyball, swimming, hockey, gymnastics, soccer, golf, and tennis. The expenses increasingly required for many of these sports, such as private lessons and elite coaching, expensive equipment, funds for travel, and club memberships, as well as the virtual lack of role models in these sports, discourage minority participation. Participation by black women has been very limited, and accomplishments of black women athletes are typically accorded little attention.

Minority men and women are significantly underrepresented in coaching and managerial positions in sports at all levels. For nearly

20 years, Dr. Richard Lapchick has authored a Racial and Gender Report Card (RGRC) that provides comprehensive analysis of opportunities for women and minorities in sports. College and professional sports organizations are assigned a grade, ranging from A+ to F, based on their hiring practices. Grades are given for gender, race, and both combined. Professional sports studied include the National Football League (NFL), National Basketball Association (NBA), Women's National Basketball Association (WNBA), Major League Baseball (MLB), and Major League Soccer (MLS). (See Table 8-2 for 2009 RGRC findings for professional sport teams.) The 2008–2009 Racial and Gender Report Card for college sport (see Table 8-3) showed that college sport received a C+ for race and a B for gender, giving it a combined C+ overall.[32]

Collectively, findings indicate that professional and collegiate sport teams are making some strides in hiring minorities and women. There have been more, but not many, opportunities for minorities and women to occupy powerful, decision making positions within the sports. White men continue to occupy positions of power, at both coaching and administrative levels, within professional and collegiate sports. While there has been some progress in providing opportunities for women and minorities in intercollegiate sport, it is evident that much more needs to be accomplished.

The impact of societal beliefs about different racial and ethnic groups can be seen in the pattern of positions and roles played by athletes from different racial and ethnic backgrounds. Coakley uses the term *race ideology* to refer to a "web of ideas and beliefs that people use to give meaning to skin color and evaluate people and forms of social organization in terms of racial classifications."[3]

In some team sports, such as baseball, football, and women's volleyball, players from certain racial or ethnic groups are disproportionately represented at certain positions, in a phenomenon known as *stacking*. For example, in professional baseball, black players are most heavily concentrated in the outfield positions, whereas

TABLE 8-2 2009 Racial and Gender Report Card for Professional Sports

League	Race	Gender	Combined	Statistical Highlights
NFL	A–	C	B	• The percentage of white players remained constant at 31% while the percentage of African American players increased slightly from 66% to 67%. • In the NFL office, 25% of the professionals were African American, Latino, Asian, Native American, and "other." Over 27% of the professionals were women. • No person of color has ever held majority ownership of an NFL team.
NBA	A+	A–/B+	A	• In the NBA, almost 82% of the players were people of color, increasing from the previous year's 80%. The percentage of African American players increased to 77%; Latinos remained constant at 3%; Asians increased to 1%; and international players remained constant at 18%. • Women held 43% of the professional positions in the NBA league office, an increase of two percentage points from the previous Report Card and a higher percentage than for any other men's professional league in any previous Report Card. • There were one Asian and 11 African American head coaches at the beginning of the 2008–2009 NBA season. The NBA still continues to have the highest percentage of head coaches of color in all pro sports, at 40% of the total.
WNBA	A+	A+	A+	• The number of white players decreased by 14 percentage points. • Donna Orender remains the only woman president of a professional sports league. • There were five African American head coaches at the start of both the 2008 and 2009 WNBA seasons, an increase of two coaches from the 2007 season. • There were five women head coaches at the start of the 2008 season and six women head coaches during the 2009 season, increasing from 31% in 2007 to 36% in 2008 and 46% in 2009.
MLB	A	B	B+	• The total population of players of color (39.6%) was composed of Latino (27%), African American (10.2%), and Asian (2.4%) players. • At the directorial and managerial level, 26% of the 91 employees were people of color, while women occupied 34% of the front-office positions at the MLB central office. • People of color held 33.4% of coaching positions in MLB (up 2.4 percentage points from 2007). African Americans held 12% (down one percentage point) and Latinos held 21% (up four percentage points).
MLS	A	B	B+	• There were four minority head coaches in the 2008 season. Of the MLS assistant coaches, 9.5% were minorities, down from 17%. • There were three CEOs and team presidents in the 2009 season who were Latino or Asian. MLS has had the highest percentage of minorities as CEOs or presidents of any professional sport. • The percentage of women as team senior administrators increased from 20.4% to 24.8% in 2008, while the percentage of minorities decreased by 1.6 percentage points to 18.9%.

Source: Data from Lapchick RE. *2009 Racial and Gender Report Card.* Institute for Diversity and Ethics in Sport, 2010 (www.tidesport.org) UCF College of Business Administration.

TABLE 8-3   2008–09 Racial and Gender Report Card for Intercollegiate Sports

Student-Athletes

- In Division I football, African Americans accounted for 46.4% percent of the athletes and whites, 46.6%, indicating that the levels of participation between these two races were as close to equal as they have ever been for a given year since this data was first recorded.
- In Division I basketball, African Americans accounted for 60.4% of the athletes and whites, 32.6%, representing the highest percentage of whites since 1999–2000.
- People of color had 21.5% of the softball positions while having only 15.6% of the men's baseball positions.
- The percentage of white male student-athletes in Division I, II, and III combined was 72.2%—18.5% for African Americans, 4.2% for Latinos, 1.5% for Asians, and 0.4% for American Indians/Alaska Natives.
- The percentage of white female student-athletes in Division I, II, and III combined was 78.9%—11.3% for African Americans, 3.8% for Latinas, 2% for Asians, and 0.4% for American Indians/Alaska Natives.

Coaching

- Whites dominated the head coaching ranks on men's teams, holding 89.2%, 88.7%, and 92.5% of all head coaching positions in Divisions I, II, and III, respectively.
- African Americans held 7.2%, 5.3%, and 4% of the men's head coaching positions in the three NCAA divisions, respectively.
- Likewise on the women's teams, whites held 87.7%, 88.9%, and 91.9% of all head coaching positions in Divisions I, II, and III, respectively.
- African Americans held 7%, 5.1%, and 4.4% of the women's head coaching positions in the three NCAA divisions, respectively.
- Almost 40 years after the passage of Title IX, women still do not represent the majority of coaches in the women's game. This year's numbers show no progress in women coaching women's sports in most sports. Women head coaches in Division I basketball stayed virtually the same (64.7% in 2007–2008, 64.3% in 2005–2006). Division I track/cross-country, which combines the head coaches of cross-country, indoor track, and outdoor track, saw a slight decrease in female head coaches, from 20.8% in 2005–2006 to 20.2% in 2007–2008. In all other sports, men led 57.4% of the women's teams while women were head coaches in only 42.1% of the programs.

Administration

- Whites held the overwhelming percentage of athletic director positions in all three divisions, at 90%, 92%, and 97% in Divisions I, II, and III, respectively. This compares to 93.1%, 92.3%, and 96.1% in 2005–2006 respectively.
- African Americans held 7.2%, 3.8%, and 1.8% of athletic director positions, respectively, in Divisions I, II, and III. This compares to 5.5%, 3.8%, and 1.9% in 2005–2006, respectively.
- Women lost ground as athletics director in Divisions II and III and remained static in Division I since the last Report Card in 2006. In Division I, 7.8% of athletic directors were women, which matches 2006. In Division II, there was a decrease from 18.7% to 15.6%, and in Division III there was a slight decrease from 27.3% to 27.1%.

Source: Data from Lapchick RE. *2009 Racial and Gender Report Card: College Sport.* Institute for Diversity and Ethics in Sport, 2010 (www.tidesport.org). UCF College of Business Administration

As college football teams changed their offensive strategies so that quarterbacks became more like running backs, more African Americans were recruited for the position.

white players are concentrated at the positions of pitcher and catcher and in the infield. Whites are disproportionately represented in positions requiring leadership, dependability, and decision making skills, while black players are overrepresented in positions requiring speed, agility, and quick reactions.[3] In women's intercollegiate volleyball, blacks are disproportionately represented at spiker, while whites are overrepresented at setter and bumper.[3]

Stacking patterns are widespread and occur in other sports and in countries throughout the world (e.g., in British soccer, black West Indians

and Africans are overrepresented in the wide forward position, while white players are overrepresented at the goalie and midfielder positions).[3]

Stacking reflects stereotypical beliefs about different racial and ethnic groups—for example, that blacks are better jumpers, while whites are better leaders. Although stacking is one of the most studied topics in sociology of sport, there are serious disagreements about why stacking patterns exist. But even though a consensus is lacking about the causes of stacking, it is important to recognize that stacking perpetuates patterns of prejudice and discrimination in sport.

Native Americans have long participated in sports, often uniting physical activities with cultural rituals and ceremonies.[33] Although many Native Americans have achieved success in sport, little recognition has been given to their accomplishments. Public acclaim most often has focused on the few Native Americans, such as Jim Thorpe, who were outstanding athletes on segregated government-sponsored reservation school football and baseball teams. On the whole, participation by Native Americans in most sports has been and continues to be limited.

Poverty, poor health, lack of equipment, and a dearth of programs are factors that often serve to limit Native American sport participation. Concern about loss of cultural identity, prejudice, lack of understanding, and insensitivity by others toward Native Americans act in concert with the other factors previously mentioned to curb sport involvement.

One example of this lack of sensitivity is the use of school names and mascots that perpetuate white stereotypes of Native Americans. Team names such as Indians or Redskins and a team mascot dressed up as a savage running around waving a tomahawk threatening to behead an opponent reflect distorted beliefs about Native Americans. Such inappropriate or distorted caricatures of Native Americans who, as school mascots, are painted on gymnasium walls and floors, do little to increase student and public awareness of the richness and diversity of Native American culture. It is even more ironic that this occurs in institutions that by definition exist to educate people about the different cultures within the world in which they live. These stereotypes are often accepted as valid depictions of native people and serve to demean the cultural heritage and history of Native Americans.

Concerned American Indian Parents is a group committed to the elimination of Native American stereotypes in advertising and sport. The poster shown in Figure 8-2 is one example of this group's efforts to heighten public awareness of the racism experienced by Native Americans that has become an accepted aspect of sport in the United States. As Coakley writes:

> The use of the name Redskins cannot be justified under any conditions. To many Native Americans, redskin is as derogatory as "nigger" is for black Americans. It is symbolic of such racism that the capitol city of the government that once put bounties on the lives of native peoples has a football team named the Redskins. It symbolizes a continuing lack of understanding of the complex and diverse cultures and the heritage of native peoples and is offensive to anyone aware of the history of native peoples in North America.[4]

In 2001, the United States Commission on Civil Rights issued a statement on the use of Native American images and nicknames as sports symbols. The commission called for an end of the use of Native American images and team names by non-Native schools. The commission believes that:

> the use of Native American mascots and their performances, logos, images and nicknames by schools are [*sic*] both disrespectful and insensitive to American Indians and others who object to such stereotyping. The stereotyping of any racial, ethnic, religious or other groups, when promoted by our public educational institutions, teaches all students that stereotyping of minority groups is acceptable—a dangerous lesson in a diverse society. Schools have a responsibility to educate their students; they should not use their influence to perpetuate misrepresentations of any culture or people.[34]

In addressing the contentions of schools that continue to use Native American imagery under the claim that their use stimulates interest in Native American culture and is a form of honoring Native Americans, the commission points out that these schools have failed to listen to Native American groups and civil rights organizations that oppose the symbols. Furthermore,

> these false portrayals prevent non-Native Americans from understanding the true historical and cultural experiences of American Indians. Sadly, they also encourage biases and prejudices that have a negative effect on contemporary Indian people. These references

Figure 8-2 A poster used by Concerned American Indian Parents to increase the public's awareness of racism toward Native Americans

may encourage interest in mythical "Indians" created by the dominant culture, but they block genuine understanding of contemporary Native people as fellow Americans.[34]

Many state education departments have issued directives urging schools to ban the use of Native American imagery for mascots, team names, and logos. The commission does not see this as a trivial matter. The use of the imagery is offensive and must stop. Finally, the commission states,

> The Commission has a firm understanding of the problems of poverty, education, housing, and health care that face many Native Americans. The fight to eliminate Indian nicknames and images in sport is one front of the larger battle to eliminate obstacles that confront American Indians. The elimination of Native American nicknames and images as sports mascots will benefit not only Native Americans, but all Americans. The elimination of stereotypes will make room for education about real Indian people, current Native American issues, and the rich variety of American Indians in our country.[34]

In 2003, the NCAA recommended that institutions using Native American mascots, including nicknames and logos, review their use. The NCAA found the use of Native American stereotypes and caricatures at odds with the NCAA's commitment to cultural diversity. In 2005, 19 colleges and universities whose use of the Native American imagery was deemed "hostile and abusive" were informed by the NCAA that they could not host postseason championships unless they changed their nicknames, mascots, and logos. Additionally, when teams from these institutions participated in postseason play at other institutions, they could not use their Native American mascots or imagery. Postseason play is a lucrative event for many institutions, and many coaches relish the home court/field advantage, particularly in the play-offs. The ban on hosting postseason play was seen as added incentive for institutions to change and comply with the NCAA's recommendation.

Some institutions, such as Florida State University, home of the Seminoles, and the University of Utah, home of the "Running Utes," appealed the ruling, citing in their cases that the local tribes supported their use of the nicknames, mascots, and imagery. After consideration, the NCAA exempted Florida and Utah from the ruling. However, the University of Illinois was not successful in its request for an exemption. The university wanted to retain its "Fighting Illini" and "Illini" nicknames. It also wanted to keep Chief Illiniwek, its mascot since 1920. Chief Illiniwek, dressed as an Indian brave in buckskin and a headdress, wearing "war" paint and carrying a feathered tomahawk, would mimic a war dance on the field and court to incite the crowds at university sport events. Unlike with Florida and Utah, the local Native American tribes did not support the retention of the chief. In response to the university's appeal, the NCAA allowed Illinois to keep its nicknames because they were deemed to reflect the origin of the name of the state. However, the appeal to retain Chief Illiniwek and associated imagery was denied.

For some, the NCAA's actions were controversial. The critics believed that the NCAA had exceeded its jurisdiction, making policy for institutions rather than limiting its efforts to intercollegiate athletics. Still others thought raising awareness of the issue was enough, and that institutions should be responsible for deciding whether to change their Native American mascots. Other critics were concerned that the NCAA in effect backed down from its ruling by allowing exemptions for Florida and Utah. Myles Brand, a former president of the NCAA and Indiana University, saw the NCAA taking on an important role in confronting this issue, stimulating serious discussion, and helping move the issue forward. Brand saw the mascot issue as an example of how intercollegiate athletics can play a "catalytic role in social change. Decades from now, I predict, we will look back and wonder why we ever tolerated such behaviors."[35] Brand further stated, "We should not underestimate the potential of athletics to contribute to social change, nor should we shy away from that responsibility."[35]

Stereotypes are the foundation of prejudice and racism. Attitudes change slowly. This is particularly true concerning prejudicial beliefs about different racial and ethnic groups. As discussed in Chapter 3, cultural competency is important in the field of physical education, exercise science, and sport. Understanding and respecting cultures' worldviews is critical to addressing issues of opportunity and equity. In an era when our society is becoming increasingly multicultural and diverse, it is important that we, as physical education, exercise science, and sport professionals, step up and take a leadership role in this issue. As Staurowsky points out, "Professionals from the allied fields of sport science and physical education are perhaps positioned better than anyone else to provide leadership on this issue, given the integral role we play in facilitating athletic opportunities for students. By calling for elimination of stereotypes in the form of American Indian images, we can contribute positively to the education of all of our children, Indian and non-Indian alike."[36]

SPORT FOR CHILDREN AND YOUTH

For many Americans, participation in youth sport activities is an integral part of growing up. It is estimated that over 20 million boys and girls participate each year in youth sport, that is, organized sport activities that take place outside the school setting.[37] Furthermore, it is estimated that over 3 million volunteer coaches are involved with these programs. Youth sport ventures are organized around such sports as football, baseball, softball, tennis, ice hockey, golf, gymnastics, soccer, and swimming.[38] An increasing number of opportunities for girls to participate in these programs at all levels is being offered, and it appears that many more children are beginning to compete in these programs at younger ages.

While participation in youth sport has grown tremendously over the past decade, there is widespread concern about the nature and outcomes associated with these programs. Even though these programs are extremely popular, considerable criticism is voiced about the manner in which they are conducted. As you read about the benefits, harmful effects, and criticisms of youth sport programs, it may be helpful to keep in mind your own experiences and those of your friends in youth sport. Consider the following questions:

- What did you like most and least about your experiences?
- What did you learn from participating in youth sport?
- How did your parents influence your participation and what was the extent of their involvement with the program?
- How would you characterize the nature and effectiveness of the coaching you received or observed?
- How did you, your teammates, parents, and coaches respond to your successes and failures?
- At what age did you discontinue your participation in youth sport and what were the reasons for stopping?
- What changes would you make in the organization of the program to make the experience a more positive one for all involved?

As with school sport, many benefits have been ascribed to participation in youth sport programs. Proponents of youth sport emphasize that it promotes physical fitness, emotional development, social adjustment, a competitive attitude, and self-confidence. In addition, youth sport programs provide opportunities for the development of physical skills, encourage the achievement of a greater level of skill, give children additional opportunities to play, and offer a safer experience than participation in unsupervised programs.

As with school sport, one of the greatest criticisms of youth sport is its overemphasis on winning. Critics also voice concerns that children's bodies may be underdeveloped for such vigorous activities, that there is too great an emotional strain and pressure on the participant, and that the players are too psychologically immature to compete in such a setting. Youth sport programs are cited as being too selective and excluding too

Too often, our attention is focused on the game or winning, leading us to overlook important messages from the athlete.

is, they should be organized and conducted in such a way as to enhance the physical, cognitive, and affective development of each child and youth participant. This development is particularly critical during the child's younger years. The fun of playing (rather than victory over an opponent) should be stressed, participation opportunities for many children of all abilities should be provided (rather than limiting participation to the gifted few), and the development of skills within the sport and in other sports should be stressed (rather than specialization).

Specialization is another frequently voiced concern. During their early years, children should be given an opportunity to develop proficiency in fundamental motor skills and be exposed to a variety of sports. Some children are guided at an early age into a specific sport, such as soccer, or into a specific position within a sport, such as a pitcher. This early specialization deprives children of an opportunity to develop an interest and skills in a variety of sports.

Concern about specialization has further increased within the last decade. During this time there has been a growth of private sport leagues and clubs that emphasize the development of skills in a particular sport. This often leads to beginning high-level sport instruction and competition at an early age; children may begin as early as 3 years of age in such sports as swimming, gymnastics, skating, and soccer.[10] Training is serious and often occurs on a year-round basis. Physically, children may be at risk for the development of overuse injuries because they are often involved in practicing on a daily basis for several hours at a time. Psychologically, these participants may experience burnout from doing the same thing year after year. They may drop out before reaching their optimal level of performance, even after many years of successful participation.

Some professionals in the field of physical education, exercise science, and sport take the position that competitive sport for youth is not inherently bad or good. Instead, they point out that sport is what one makes it. Under sound leadership, if the welfare of the child is the primary consideration,

many children who would like to participate, and as promoting specialization at too early an age. Additional criticisms are directed toward overenthusiastic coaches and parents who take winning too seriously, who pressure children to achieve, and who place their needs before the needs of the child.

Overemphasis on winning has led to many of the abuses found within youth sport programs. The desire to win has led coaches to employ such behaviors as conniving to get the best players in the league on their team, holding lengthy practice sessions and endless drills to perfect skills, and berating children for their mistakes.

Many professionals decry the overemphasis on winning. They believe that youth sport programs should be developmental in nature—that

The quality of leadership exerts a significant influence on the outcomes experienced by youth sports participants.

if the environment is warm and supportive, and if the sport is administered in light of the needs and characteristics of the participants, much good can be accomplished. However, if poor leadership is provided, harmful effects will accrue.

Many recommendations have been set forth by professionals to improve youth sport. Professionals suggest that programs be structured so that children can experience success and satisfaction while continuing to develop their abilities. This may mean modification of the rules, equipment, and playing area to promote success and participation rather than failure and elimination. For example, simplified and fewer rules, smaller balls, smaller fields, bigger goals, batting tees rather than pitchers, rule changes to facilitate scoring, and a requirement of equal playing time for all participants are some of the ways that youth sport programs can be changed to make the experiences more positive for all participants.

Programs should be structured to include elements that children find enjoyable within their own informal games. Plenty of action, opportunity for involvement, close scores to keep the game exciting and interesting, and friendship are important to children; these elements should be infused into youth sport programming.[7] Children also should be given opportunities to be involved in decision making, such as deciding what strategies to use or planning a practice session. They can also be given the responsibility for self-enforcement of rules during the game.

As previously mentioned, the quality of leadership can exert a significant influence on the outcomes children derive from participating in youth sport. Coaches within youth sport programs are typically volunteers, often parents, who have received little if any training on how to coach children. Recognizing this, professionals within the field have directed increased attention toward the development of coaching education programs. These programs emphasize understanding the growth characteristics and developmental needs of children, modifying existing programs to meet these needs, incorporating proper training techniques into the design of the program, and supporting the efforts of children while providing developmentally appropriate opportunities to help them become better players. Enhancing children's self-esteem, recognizing their accomplishments, and praising their efforts are more appropriate than ridiculing, shaming, and belittling their achievements and attempts.

The key to successful youth sport programs is putting the needs of the child first. Programs should be designed to meet the children's needs, not those of adults. Youth sport programs should be organized on a developmental model, not a professional model. Programs should focus on fostering children's physical, cognitive, and affective development. The whole child as a moving, thinking, feeling human being should be considered when designing and conducting youth sport programs.

VIOLENCE IN SPORT

Violence is one of the major problems facing sport today. It is particularly noticeable in professional contact sports such as football and hockey. Physical and psychological intimidation of one's opponent is considered an essential part of professional basketball. Yet do such forms of intimidation lead to violence? Have coaches gone too far in psyching up their teams to go out and "kill" their opponents? In some contact sports, such as hockey, some players are even designated as "enforcers"—charged with protecting their own players and aggressively intimidating their opponents. However, violence is not limited to contact sports; bench-clearing brawls occur with greater frequency in even noncontact sports such as baseball. Has violence gotten out of control?

The media has done much to bring incidences of sport violence to the public's attention. Newspapers and sport periodicals give readers glowing, blow-by-blow accounts. Television glamorizes such events, often replaying them in slow motion. Special videos and YouTube clips are being produced that show incident after incident of players using violence and force in pursuit of victory.

Some experts have expressed concern that the popularity and visibility of professional athletes lead athletes at lower levels of competition to imitate their actions, including their violent behavior. Other athletes, including those at the high school and even the youth sport level, may emulate the playing style of sport professionals. Thus, violence permeates other levels of sport and its impact on the nature of the game grows.

Spectator violence is also a concern, as media coverage of violent behavior at sport events throughout the world verifies. At some events, fans have stampeded the field and, in the process, trampled other fans to death. Outbreaks of fights among fans are reported. Experts have found that spectator violence is related to the actions of the players during the contests. In essence, player violence tends to increase the likelihood of violence by fans during and following the game. The media's promotion of games for their potential for violence tends to encourage spectator violence. The potential for violence also increases when fans believe that their team was robbed of a score or a victory by incompetent or unfair officiating. Crowd dynamics also influence the occurrence of spectator violence, including the amount of alcohol consumed, the importance of the contest, the demographics of the crowd, crowd size, and seating arrangements.

Violence between players and spectators is a concern as well. One distressing incidence of violence between professional players and fans occurred on November 19, 2004. During a Detroit Pistons versus Indiana Pacers game at the Palace of Auburn Hills in Detroit, a brawl erupted. A hard foul to Pistons center Ben Wallace by Pacers forward Ron Artest led to Ben Wallace's retaliating with a hard shove to Artest's neck. Events escalated from there, with opposing players shoving each other and fans heckling the players and throwing objects onto the court. Artest, hit by a drink thrown by a fan, ran into the stands to confront the individual he believed had thrown it. More players followed into the stands, and fans spilled onto the court. Punches, shoves, and kicks were exchanged between players and fans in the ensuing violent brawl that lasted over 10 minutes. NBA Commissioner David Stern acted quickly, suspending five Pacers and four Pistons for over 140 games. Artest was suspended for the remainder of the season, one of the harshest suspensions in NBA history. By his actions, Commissioner Stern sent a strong message that such behavior was not only inappropriate, but unacceptable. According to Stern, "The line is drawn, and my guess is that it won't happen again—certainly not to anybody who wants to be associated with our league."[39] Additionally, in the days following what some have deemed the worst brawl in the history of the NBA, criminal charges were filed against players and fans involved. The charges typically were for assault and battery.

Parental violence during youth sport events appears to be occurring with distressing frequency. Increasingly, the media carry stories about parents attacking the coach, beating the umpire, or engaging in fights with parents of the opposing team. One of the most shocking incidents occurred in 2000, when a parent, Thomas Junta, fought another parent, Michael Costin, who was supervising the youth ice hockey practice in which the sons of both men participated. The argument was over rough play on the ice. Unconscious after the beating, Costin was hospitalized and died the next day. After a jury trial, Junta was found guilty of involuntary manslaughter, and on January 25, 2002, he was sentenced to 6 to 10 years in state prison. What impact did this tragedy, which received national attention, have on parental violence in youth sport? Unbelievably, 2 days after the sentencing, a brawl broke out among 30 parents during a match at a youth hockey game in Colorado. Four parents, including an off-duty police officer, were charged with disorderly conduct. Strong leadership is needed to eliminate parental violence in youth sports, and

parents need to be held accountable for their actions. Policies must be established that will serve the best interests of the youth who are participating in these programs.

It is important to note that the environment in which the contest takes place contributes to its potential for violence. As Coakley points out, spectators bring issues and ideologies that are reflective of events within their communities to sport events.[4] When conflict and violence are an integral part of a community, the likelihood of spectator violence at a local sporting event increases. For example, highly publicized contests between rival high schools where high levels of racial and ethnic tension exist in the communities have led to violence. In some communities, efforts to prevent violence at school sport events have led to the banning of all spectators from the events or the playing of events at neutral sites.

The question of how to deal with the problem of violence in sport has no single, simple solution. Experts are in agreement, however, that some type of control must be instituted, and it must start with people who love sport and want to protect it from intrusions that will lower its value. They point out that violence is to be abhorred, particularly because it interferes with proper play, detracts from excellent athlete performance, and is barbaric in nature. Most spectators, it is suggested, do not want to see players hurt or crippled. They want to see clean, hard tackles and body checks. This is the essence of the game and sport itself.

It has been suggested that to reduce violence, stricter penalties should be imposed at all levels of sport. Indeed, athletes in some sports and at some levels of competition are being penalized more severely for violent acts. However, the real and best solution to the problem of violence is a change in attitude on the part of all people concerned. If subscribed to by professional and amateur players, coaches, spectators, sport entrepreneurs, and the public in general, the ideals of playing within the spirit and the letter of the rules, defeating one's opponent when at one's best, and having respect for other players will reduce the violence marring the playing fields and sport arenas today.

The potential for spectator violence can be reduced when some forethought is given to the factors that contribute to violence and thoughtful planning results in steps to minimize the occurrence of these factors. Reducing violence among contestants, decreasing the media hype that portrays the contest as a confrontation among hostile opponents, using competent officials to control the flow of the game, and taking preventive crowd control measures can decrease spectator violence. Violence can also be decreased by formulating better relations between the teams and the community and by athletes' taking steps to become actively involved in the communities in which they play and live.

PERFORMANCE-ENHANCING SUBSTANCES IN SPORT

Citius, altius, fortius—the Olympic motto of "swifter, higher, stronger"—embodies the quest for excellence for many athletes. At the elite level, where races are won by a thousandth of a second, a gold medal by a tenth of a point, and fame by a fraction of a centimeter, athletes are constantly experimenting with new ways to enhance their performance. Today, being swifter, higher, and stronger than one's competitors may lead athletes to seek "better performance through chemistry" and use or abuse performance-enhancing substances. Unfortunately, the use and abuse of performance-enhancing substances is not just a problem at the elite level, but one that has filtered down to athletes at the collegiate and high school levels.

Professional leagues, sporting bodies, the International Olympic Committee, and the NCAA are among the organizations that have antidoping policies, with accompanying long lists of banned substances. Among those substances are anabolic steroids, human growth hormone, and amphetamines, as well as their derivatives. Athletes take these and other substances, often at many times the recommended doses, in an effort to gain strength, increase power, work harder during training, or enhance endurance. The ultimate goal is to improve one's performance.

Sport sociologists study the use of these performance-enhancing substances by athletes. They seek to answer such questions as "If sports build character, why do athletes cheat and use banned substances?" or "Why do some athletes seek an unfair advantage by using banned substances?" Coakley, in a discussion of deviance in sport, invites us to look at the use of performance-enhancing substances in sport as a form of deviance associated with overconformity to the high power and performance sport ethic.[40]

Coakley defines the sport ethic as a "set of norms that many people in power and performance sports have accepted as the dominant criteria for defining what it means to be an athlete and to successfully claim an identity as an athlete."[40] The four norms associated with the sport ethic are making sacrifices, striving for distinction, taking risks and playing through the pain, and accepting no limits in pursuit of the dream.

When athletes embrace the sport ethic, they give sport priority over all aspects of their life. They pressure themselves to live up to their own expectations as well as those of their coaches and their teammates. They make the necessary sacrifices and are willing to pay the price to play. Athletes strive to achieve distinction, constantly seeking to improve and achieve at the highest level. Athletes take risks; they do not back down from a challenge. Courage enables them to overcome fear and accept risk of failure. It is courage that enables athletes to play in pain. Lastly, athletes pursue their dream with dedication, believing success is possible for those willing to work hard to achieve it.

When athletes go to the extreme to conform to the sport ethic, this overconformity carries with it significant risks to their health and well-being. Examples of overconformity that present health risks to athletes include severely restricting food and prolonged exercising in rubber suits to make weight in wrestling, running an excessive number of miles in training for cross-country, and using huge doses of pain killers to play when injured. Why do athletes, often unquestioning, take such risks?

According to Coakley, one reason for over-conformity is that athletes will do anything to stay involved in sport because the sport experience is so exhilarating.[40] Second, athletes perceive that their chances of staying involved and competing at higher and higher levels are enhanced when they overconform to the sport ethic.[40] Coaches want dedicated, committed athletes, willing to sacrifice all for the love of sport. Lastly, continued involvement where normative boundaries are exceeded infuses drama and excitement into athletes' lives.[40] This increases their commitment and investment in sport as well as bonding them to other athletes. Overconformity to the sport ethic is to many athletes not deviant behavior but an affirmation of their athletic identity.[3]

The use of banned performance-enhancing substances falls within the range of deviant over-conformity to the sport ethic. It is not, as some would suggest, because athletes are not disciplined enough to achieve gains through hard work. Nor is it really a desire to cheat. Athletes view performance-enhancing substances as a means to gain an edge. Some see the use of such substances

as the avenue to being able to play at the highest possible level, an opportunity to stay involved in a sport they love. Athletes who are deeply committed to their sport often will do whatever it takes to achieve distinction.

How widespread the use of banned performance-enhancing substances is among athletes is difficult to determine. One way the sport world has sought to cope with the use of illegal performance-enhancing is through drug testing. Two of the many drug testing agencies are the World Anti-Doping Agency and the United States Anti-Doping Agency. They conduct drug testing for athletes involved in Olympic sports.

Drug testing is controversial. Critics consider drug testing a violation of privacy rights, and in some societies it violates cultural norms. Additionally, as rapidly as new tests are developed for banned substances, athletes switch to an undetectable drug or use masking drugs to obscure test results. Drug testing is also costly, and paying for testing draws on funds that could be used to provide health programs for athletes. Proponents of drug testing see it as necessary in

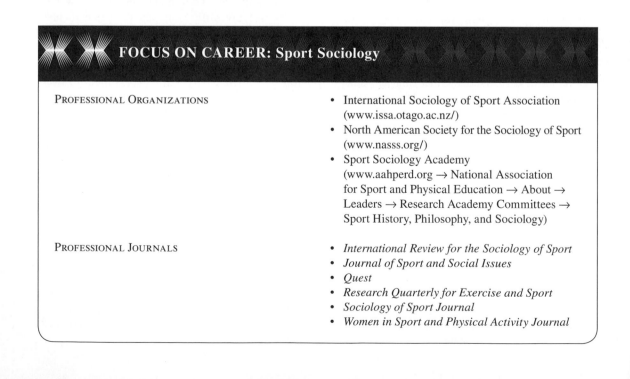

FOCUS ON CAREER: Sport Sociology

PROFESSIONAL ORGANIZATIONS

- International Sociology of Sport Association (www.issa.otago.ac.nz/)
- North American Society for the Sociology of Sport (www.nasss.org/)
- Sport Sociology Academy (www.aahperd.org → National Association for Sport and Physical Education → About → Leaders → Research Academy Committees → Sport History, Philosophy, and Sociology)

PROFESSIONAL JOURNALS

- *International Review for the Sociology of Sport*
- *Journal of Sport and Social Issues*
- *Quest*
- *Research Quarterly for Exercise and Sport*
- *Sociology of Sport Journal*
- *Women in Sport and Physical Activity Journal*

order to protect the health of athletes. Testing is also necessary to guarantee a level playing field, where the winners are those who have toiled diligently to develop their skills rather than those athletes who have access to performance-enhancing substances.

Educational programs and treatment approaches have been used to try to stem the use of illegal performance-enhancing substances. Strong punishment for violators, such as a lifetime suspension or a 2-year ban from competition, stands as a powerful deterrent to the use of illegal performance-enhancing substances. Despite these and other approaches, news headlines continue to report stories of track stars, football players, baseball standouts, elite cyclists, and other athletes found to be using illegal drugs to gain a performance edge.

In order to transform sport and deal with current and future challenges, all those involved in sport should think critically about the meaning, purpose, and organization of sport and take an active role in addressing these challenges in order to maintain the integrity of sport performance.

SUMMARY

Sport is an important part of American culture. As a social institution, sport influences and is influenced by other institutions in our society, such as politics, education, family, religion, and the media. Its pervasiveness has led to the study of sport from a sociological perspective.

Sport has a significant role in educational institutions. Over 7 million youths play sports at the high school level. At the collegiate level, thousands of men and women compete. Sport can have both a positive and negative influence on the lives of its participants. Among the problems associated with sport in educational institutions are an overemphasis on winning, athletic goals overshadowing academic goals, soaring expenditures, continued growth of big-time sport, and inequities in opportunities for women and minorities.

Sport sociologists are interested in transforming sport, changing the nature of sport so that it is more equitable and beneficial for those involved. Racism, including the use of Native American imagery, is one of the topics studied by sport sociologists. Among other topics studied are gender issues, opportunities for girls and women in sports, sport for people with disabilities, violence in sport, and the use of performance-enhancing substances.

It is important for physical education, exercise science, and sport professionals to understand the significant role of sport as an institution in our society. In the future, it is hoped that as a professional in this field you will take a more active role in creating greater opportunities for all people in sport.

DISCUSSION QUESTIONS

1. What is the role of sport in American culture and its impact on various institutions in society, such as economics, education, family, and the media?

2. What are the sociological implications of educational sport? What are the benefits and possible disadvantages of participating in educational sport? Reflect carefully on your personal experiences in sport. How did they contribute to your personal development and educational goals?

3. Consider the information provided in this chapter on Title IX. Is your high school, college, or university meeting one or more prongs of the three-pronged test used to determine compliance? Describe how it is or is not in compliance. What implications could the results have on male and female sport participation?

4. What you perceive will be the nature of the sport experience—for players, coaches, and spectators—over the next 10 to 20 years?

SELF-ASSESSMENT ACTIVITIES

These activities are designed to help you determine if you have mastered the materials and competencies presented in this chapter.

1. Use the information provided in the Get Connected box to explore more deeply the extent of participation by girls and women in sport. What are the benefits of participation? How can participation be increased further, especially among underrepresented population groups such as minorities and girls and women from low socioeconomic backgrounds? What can be done to increase the number of women in coaching and athletic administration?

2. Using the information in the Get Connected box, access the University of Central Florida's Institute for Diversity and Ethics in Sport. Browse through the reports provided on gender equity, racial diversity, and academic progress of collegiate athletes. Select one report to read and summarize. Use

PowerPoint to make a presentation on your topic to your class or group. Be sure to include statistics to support your points.

3. Interview two college students who played high school sports, one of whom plays on an intercollegiate team, about their experiences as students and as athletes, and how their experiences of being athletes changed their experiences of being students. Using the information provided in the chapter, create specific questions in relation to race, gender, sexuality , opportunity, discrimination, GPA, standardized exams, and other topics you deem pertinent to the player's story. Write a reflective paper synthesizing the students' experiences and relate it back to the data in the chapter.

4. Refer to the 12 Steps to Understanding Research Reports box in Chapter 1. Complete Step 8 for the same article you selected in Chapter 1.

REFERENCES

1. MSNBC: Cost of a Super Bowl ad through the years U.S. business, updated (www.msnbc.msn .com/id/16874732/ns/business-us_business).

2. Leonard II WM: A sociological perspective of sport, ed 5, Boston, 1998, Allyn and Bacon.

3. Coakley J: Sport in society: issues and controversies, ed 10, New York, 2009, McGraw-Hill.

4. Coakley J: Sport in society: issues and controversies, ed 6, Dubuque, Iowa, 1998, WCB/McGraw-Hill.

5. Sage GH: Sport sociology. In JD Massengale and RA Swanson, editors, The history of exercise and sport science, Champaign, Ill., 1997, Human Kinetics.

6. Harris JC: Sociology of physical activity. In SJ Hoffman and JC Harris, editors, Introduction to kinesiology: studying physical activity, Champaign, Ill., 2000, Human Kinetics.

7. National Federation of State High School Associations: 2008–2009 High School Participation Survey (www.nfhs.org).

8. National Collegiate Athletic Association: 1981–1982—2008–2009 NCAA sports sponsorship and participation rates report, Indianapolis, Ind., 2010, NCAA (www .ncaapublications.com).

9. Siedentop D: Introduction to physical education, fitness, and sport, ed 7, Mountain View, Calif., 2009, Mayfield.

10. American Academy of Pediatrics, Organized Sports for Children and Preadolescents. Pediatrics Vol. 107, No. 6 June 2001, pp. 1459–1462.

11. American Academy of Pediatrics: Steroids: play safe, play fair. 2002. (www.aap.org/family/ steroids.htm)

12. National Collegiate Athletic Association: 2006 Fact Sheet (www.ncaa.org)

13. National Collegiate Athletic Association: 2008– 2009 member report (catalog.proemags.com/ publication/cc5da338#/cc5da338/1).

14. National Collegiate Athletic Association: 2009 NCAA graduation rates report (www.ncaa.com). Retrieved 26 May 2010.

15. National Collegiate Athletic Association: History of academic reform, 2009. (www.ncaa.org). Retrieved 26 May 2010.

16. Lapchick R: Keeping score when it counts: assessing the 2009–2010 bowl_bound college football teams—academic performance improves but race still matters, 2010.

17. National Collegiate Athletic Association: Initial eligibility requirements for prospective student-athletes, 2010. (www.ncaa.org). Retrieved 27 May 2010.

18. National Collegiate Athletic Association: Initial eligibility (www.ncaa.org).

19. National Center for Fair and Open Testing: What's wrong with the NCAA's test score requirements? (www.fairtest.org).

20. National Collegiate Athletic Association, 2010 News: NCAA signs new 14-year TV deal for DI men's basketball CBS and Turner join forces to pay $10.8 billion for tournament rights fee (www.ncaa.org).

21. Knight Foundation: Report of the Knight Foundation Commission on Intercollegiate Athletics, 1991. Available from the National Collegiate Athletic Association.

22. John S. and James L. Knight Foundation: A call to action: reconnecting college sports and higher education, [Place], 2001, Knight Commission. (www.knightfdn.org).

23. Women's Sport Foundation: Title IX, 2006 (www.womenssportsfoundation.org). Retrieved 6 March 2007.

24. National Collegiate Athletic Association: 1981–1982—2007–2008 NCAA sports sponsorship and participation rates report, Indianapolis, Ind., 2008, NCAA (www.ncaa.org).

25. National Collegiate Athletic Association: NCAA news—women's basketball attendance, updated May 27, 2010 (www.ncaa.org).

26. The President's Council on Physical Fitness and Sports: Physical activity and sport in the lives of girls, Washington, D.C., 1997, President's Council on Physical Fitness and Sports.

27. Women's National Basketball Association (www.wnba.com).

28. Women's Pro Soccer (www.womensprosoccer.org).

29. Acosta RV and Carpenter LJ: Women in intercollegiate sport: a longitudinal study—nineteen year update, 1977–2004. Available at www.womensportfoundation.org

30. National Association of Collegiate Women Athletics Administrators: A time of opportunity, challenge, change and transformation in intercollegiate athletics, 2000, retrieved 6 March 2007 (www.ncawaa.org).

31. United States General Accounting Office: Intercollegiate athletics: four-year colleges' experiences adding and discontinuing teams, Washington, D.C., 2001, United States General Accounting Office.

32. Lapchick RE: 2009 Racial and Gender Report Card, 2010, Institute for Diversity and Ethics in Sport. UCF College of Business Administration.

33. Oxedine JB: American Indian sports heritage, Champaign, Ill., 1988, Human Kinetics.

34. United States Commission on Civil Rights: Commission statement on the use of Native American images and nicknames as sports symbols, Washington, D.C., 2001, United States Commission on Civil Rights (www.usccr.gov).

35. Brand M: NCAA correctly positioned as a catalyst for social change, The NCAA News, October 24, 2005, 5–6.

36. Staurowsky EJ: American Indian imagery and the miseducation of America, Quest 51:382–392, 1999.

37. Patel DR, Greydanus DE, and Pratt HD: Youth sports: more than just sprains and strain, Contemporary Pediatrics, March 2001, 18(3):45

38. Martens R: Youth sport in the USA. In M Weiss and D Gould, editors, Sport for children and youth, Champaign, Ill., 1986, Human Kinetics.

39. Lapchick RE: Rough play is out of bounds, ESPN. Com, Page 2. November 24, 2001.

40. Coakley J: Sport in society: issues and controversies, ed 8, New York, 2004, McGraw-Hill.

CHAPTER 9

SPORT AND EXERCISE PSYCHOLOGY

OBJECTIVES

After reading this chapter the student should be able to—

■ Describe the psychological benefits of participation in sport and physical activities.

■ Understand the different theories of behavior and their potential application to exercise adherence.

■ Discuss the roles of anxiety and arousal in the performance of motor skills and the application of intervention strategies to enhance performance.

■ Understand motivation, goal setting, self-talk, and imagery and how they can be effectively used in physical education, exercise, and sport.

Sport and exercise psychology has its legacy in psychology. In the 1970s, as the academic scope of physical education grew, sport psychology emerged as a subdiscipline. Initially, sport psychologists focused on competitive sport and the elite athlete. As the subdiscipline grew, sport psychologists became interested in studying participation in exercise and other facets of physical activity. Additionally, their focus broadened from working with elite competitors to include people of all ages and abilities. The name of the subdiscipline today, sport and exercise psychology, reflects this expanded focus.

This chapter provides a short introduction to sport and exercise psychology. It includes a brief overview of the development of the subdiscipline. Selected topics within sport and exercise psychology are briefly discussed; space limitations preclude the inclusion of more topics and limit the depth of discussion. Given that caveat, this chapter presents information on motivation, the psychological benefits of physical activity, exercise adherence, personality, anxiety and arousal, imagery, goal setting, self-talk, and various intervention strategies. It is hoped that this brief glimpse will stimulate your interest in this area and encourage further study.

SPORT AND EXERCISE PSYCHOLOGY

Sport and exercise psychology is a rapidly growing subdiscipline of physical education, exercise science, and sport. Initially, this subdiscipline was closely aligned with motor learning; however, during the last two decades it has evolved as a distinct field of study. The definition and scope, historical development, and areas of study within sport and exercise psychology are described briefly in this section.

Definition and Scope

Sport and exercise psychology is defined by Vealey as "the systematic scholarly study of the behavior, feelings, and thoughts of people engaged in sport, exercise, and physical activity."[1] According to the Association for the Advancement of Applied Sport Psychology, sport and exercise psychology focuses on the psychological and mental aspects of participation in sport and exercise, seeking to understand how psychological processes influence and are influenced by participation.[2] The International Society of Sport Psychology states that "this dynamic field can enhance the experience of men, women, and children of all ages who participate in physical activity, ranking from those who do so for personal enjoyment to those who pursue a specific activity at the elite level."[3]

The scope of sport and exercise psychology is quite broad, encompassing both theoretical and applied approaches and reflecting close ties to the discipline of psychology. The initial work in the subdisicpline focused on sport and elite athletes. Today, the focus has expanded and includes the psychological dimensions of competitive sport participation and engagement in fitness, exercise, and physical activity. Sport and exercise psychology seeks to understand, influence, and improve the experiences of people of all ages and abilities, ranging from the youth sport participant to the elite Olympic performer and from the elderly individual engaging in an exercise rehabilitation program following a heart attack to the healthy adult who enjoys lifting weights on a regular basis.

Historical Development

The early history of sport and exercise psychology is closely related to motor learning. As these areas of study grew in the 1970s in the United States,

Paralympians mentally rehearse their performances before the competition begins.

they began to emerge as separate subdisciplines of the academic discipline of physical education; however, in Europe today, these areas remain closely aligned under the umbrella of sport psychology.

In the late 1890s and early 1900s, physical educators and psychologists began to write about the psychological aspects of physical education and sport. The most notable of these early researchers was Norman Triplett, who, in 1898, studied the effects of the presence of other people on the performance of motor skills.[1] The influence of the presence of other people—that is, an audience—on motor performance later developed into an area of research known as social facilitation.[1]

In 1918, Coleman Griffith, commonly recognized as the father of sport psychology, began his groundbreaking work in sport psychology as a doctoral student at the University of Illinois.[4] Later,

as director of the Athletic Research Laboratory at Illinois, Griffith engaged in research on motor learning and on the psychological aspects of sport. Additionally, he taught sport psychology classes, published numerous research articles, and authored two books considered classics in the field—*Psychology of Coaching* (1926) and *Psychology of Athletics* (1928). Like the applied sport psychologists of today, Griffith's research extended outside of the laboratory setting; he observed and interviewed outstanding athletes and coaches of the time, such as Red Grange and Knute Rockne, regarding motivation and the psychology of coaching.[4] In 1938, Griffith was hired by Philip Wrigley as the Chicago Cubs baseball team's sport psychologist. In this capacity, Griffith worked with players and researched ways to enhance motivation and develop self-confidence.

From 1940 to 1965, Gill characterizes the research in sport psychology as sporadic.[4] Following World War II, colleges and universities established motor behavior research programs. As previously mentioned in the chapter on motor learning and control, Henry, Slater-Hammel, Hubbard, and Lawther were instrumental in developing research programs focusing on motor learning and performance. These research programs included some work on topics currently within the realm of sport psychology today. Another important contribution of this time was Warren Johnson's study, in 1949, of pregame emotion in football, which served as the basis for later research on emotions associated with competition.[4] Lawther's publication, in 1951, of *The Psychology of Coaching* reflected an applied sport psychology orientation to coaching athletes.

In the 1960s, several texts were published that included information about the psychological aspects of sport and learning. These books introduced both undergraduate and graduate physical education students to both motor learning and sport psychology.[4] Bryant Cratty, who became one of the most prolific authors in the field, published *Movement Behavior and Motor Learning* in 1964 and *Psychology and Physical Activity* in 1967.[4] In 1968, Robert Singer's textbook *Motor Learning*

> ◢◣◢◣ **LIFESPAN AND CULTURAL PERSPECTIVES: Sport and Exercise Psychology**
>
> - How do sociocultural factors influence participants' adherence to an exercise program?
> - Does age influence the psychological benefits derived from participation in physical activity?
> - Do personality traits and psychological dispositions of elite athletes vary by ethnicity or gender?
> - How can self-efficacy be developed in children with low skill ability?
> - What interventions are most effective in mediating the effects of anxiety in Senior Games competitors?

and Human Performance was published.[4] Another book published during this era caused considerable controversy—Bruce Ogilvie and Thomas Tutko's book *Problem Athletes and How to Handle Them* (1966). Gill notes that this book was criticized by scholars intent on advancing the scientific nature of sport psychology for its clinical approach and lack of a scientific framework.[4] However, the book was popular among coaches and helped set the stage for applied sport psychology in the 1980s.[4]

The late 1960s and the 1970s marked the emergence of sport psychology as a subdiscipline of physical education. Courses were developed for inclusion within the graduate and undergraduate physical education curriculums, graduate programs were inaugurated and research programs established, professional societies were organized, and specialized sport psychology journals were created. Scholars such as Rainer Martens, Dorothy Harris, Daniel Landers, and William Morgan helped shape the direction of the field.[1,4]

As the amount of research grew and interest in sport psychology developed, outlets for dissemination of research and forums for the exchange of ideas were needed. In 1965, the International Society of Sport Psychology was founded. Two years later, in 1967, professionals interested in motor learning and sport psychology formed the North American Society for the Psychology of Sport and Physical Activity (NASPSPA). In 1975, the Sport Psychology Academy was organized as part of NASPE, a substructure of AAHPERD. *Research Quarterly* and journals in the parent field of psychology served as the major outlets for

publication of research until the *Journal of Sport Psychology* began publication in 1979.

However, during this time sport psychology was still aligned with motor learning and drew heavily on the parent discipline of psychology for theories. Much of the work was conducted in laboratory settings, rather than within sport, and offered little help to teachers, coaches, and participants.[4] In 1979, Martens called for a greater emphasis on applied issues within sport psychology, including a focus on more relevant issues, a greater emphasis on field-based rather than laboratory-based research, and the development of sport-specific conceptual models.[4] This shift in focus was reflected in the work of sport psychologists in the 1980s.

The 1980s marked a period of tremendous expansion for sport psychology. Many scholars embraced a more applied approach to sport psychology. More field-based research with sport participants was conducted, and a greater emphasis was placed on the application of research to real-world sports events. In 1986, the Association for the Advancement of Applied Sport Psychology (AAASP) was organized; it comprises three interrelated focus areas: intervention and performance enhancement, health psychology, and social psychology. In 1987, the inaugural volume of *The Sport Psychologist* was published, providing another outlet for scholarly work with an applied focus.

Another factor that helped shape the field was the growing interest of more clinically trained psychologists in sport psychology.[4] One noteworthy contribution during this time frame was that of Richard Suinn, a clinical psychologist whose work with the US Olympic ski team did much to bring sport psychology to public attention.[4] Another significant step in the growth of sport psychology occurred in 1986, when Division 47, Exercise and Sport Psychology, became a formal division within the American Psychological Association.

It was during the 1980s that exercise psychology evolved as a specialized area of study. Researchers became interested in understanding the psychological aspects of fitness, exercise, health, and wellness, including psychological factors that influence participation and the influence of participation on those involved. Attention was also directed toward enhancing the experience for those participants involved in health-related physical activity. This growth of interest occurred at a time when more and more research and public attention was being directed toward the significant contribution of physical activity to health. To reflect the expanding scope of the subdiscipline, in 1988, the *Journal of Sport Psychology* was renamed the *Journal of Sport and Exercise Psychology.*

Sport and exercise psychology during the 1990s and today reflects the rich diversity of this subdiscipline, both in research and practice. As Gill writes,

> Some researchers emphasize theory-based basic research with tight controls, and search for underlying physiological mechanisms; others shun traditional research, using interpretive approaches and searching for experiential knowledge. Some are not concerned with research at all, but seek information on strategies and techniques to educate, consult, or clinically treat sport and exercise participants.[4]

Some researchers seek to focus exclusively on sport psychology; others on exercise psychology. As sport and exercise psychology continues to grow and evolve in the twenty-first century, Gill suggests that it is likely that more sport- and exercise-specific approaches will develop and that

there will be a greater appreciation "of the richer understanding that can be gained through collaborative research across specializations, such as exercise physiology and motor learning."[4]

Areas of Study

Sport and exercise psychology includes many different areas of study. Sport and exercise psychologists are interested in understanding factors that influence participation in sport and exercise. For example, why do some athletes "choke" under pressure? Why do some postcardiac patients fail to complete their rehabilitation program? Sport and exercise psychology also studies the psychological outcomes derived from participation. For instance, does participation in an exercise program reduce stress and alleviate depression? Does participation in youth sport build character?

Sport and exercise psychology can also help physical educators, exercise scientists, and sport leaders make modifications to sport and exercise programs to enrich the experience for the participants involved. This could include helping athletes learn techniques to regulate their level of arousal to achieve optimal performance, teaching coaches how to promote self-confidence or to motivate their athletes, or building more social support into exercise programs to promote adherence and provide greater enjoyment for the participants.

Areas of study within sport and exercise psychology include attentional focus, personality, aggression and violence, self-confidence and self-efficacy, self-talk, arousal, social reinforcement, adherence, team building, commitment, and level of aspiration. Researchers design and assess the effectiveness of various interventions to enhance performance and participation, such as cognitive restructuring, mental rehearsal, and social support. Researchers are also interested in factors that cause people to become involved in sport and exercise and those factors that lead to peoples dropping out or discontinuing participation.

The amount of research produced by scholars in sport and exercise psychology has grown tremendously over the past decade. Examples of questions that may be investigated by researchers include:

- Is the personality profile of the outstanding or elite athlete different from that of the average athlete or nonathlete?
- How does participation in an exercise program influence one's body image? Or one's feelings of self-efficacy and control?
- What are the psychological benefits derived from participation in physical activity? What is the dose-response relationship between physical activity and psychological effects?
- Does one's personality change as a result of participation in sport or an exercise program? If so, what is the nature of the change?
- In what way does anxiety influence performance in various types of sports?
- How can an athlete deal most effectively with the stress of competition? What strategy would be most helpful for an athlete to use to deal with the pressure of competition?
- What factors influence an individual's adherence to an exercise or rehabilitation program?
- Does participation in sport empower athletes with disabilities?
- How does an individual's self-confidence affect his or her performance? How can self-confidence be developed most effectively and then used to maximize performance?
- How can self-efficacy in adolescents be increased to promote the establishment of beneficial physical activity patterns?

These are only a sample of the type of questions that may be addressed by researchers in sport and exercise psychology.

Sport psychologists today work with both male and female athletes to help them perform at their optimal level. Sport psychologists work with professional sport teams, national sport teams (US Olympic teams in various sports), and intercollegiate teams. Some professional athletes or athletes that compete at an elite level, such as in figure skating, may engage the services of a sport psychologist to help them achieve their goals.

Knowledge of sport psychology is important to coaches at all levels. It can help coaches more fully understand the psychological impact of their coaching behaviors and decisions on the athletes. Coaches can incorporate information from sport psychology into their preparation of athletes for competition and use information during competition to help their teams perform at their highest possible level. Additionally, coaches may find it beneficial to understand the factors that contribute to athletes' continuing commitment to a sport and the factors that predispose athletes to discontinue sport participation.

Specialists in exercise psychology focus their efforts on individuals participating in exercise and rehabilitation programs. Researchers have sought to identify the psychological determinants of participation in physical activity and the factors that influence the completion of rehabilitation regimens. Given the documented evidence supporting the contribution of regular physical activity to health, understanding the psychological dimensions of participation is of critical importance to physical education, exercise science, and sport professionals working in these areas. Such an understanding can help practitioners design programs and structure experiences to enhance the probability that program participants will engage in physical activity to the extent necessary to realize health benefits and incorporate physical activity into their lifestyle.

Sport and exercise psychologists can provide educational or clinical services, depending on their credentials. Clinical sport psychologists have extensive training in psychology and are licensed by state boards to treat people with psychopathology. Clinical sports psychologists may treat participants with personality disorders, eating disorders, or chemical dependency. They supplement their training in psychology with additional training in sport and exercise psychology.

Educational sport and exercise psychologists often have a background in physical education, exercise science, and sport, with extensive training in sport and exercise psychology. They are not licensed psychologists. The AAASP offers a certification program for applied sport psychology that recognizes attainment of professional knowledge in sport psychology, including health and exercise psychology, intervention and performance enhancement, and social psychology. Upon meeting the requirements for certification, an individual is conferred the title of Certified Consultant, Association for the Advancement of Applied Sport Psychology.

Certified consultants engage in educational activities focused on the "development and understanding of cognitive, behavioral, and affective skills in participants of all ages and at all skill levels."[2] Examples of educational activities include informing individuals and groups about the role of psychological factors in exercise, physical activity, and sport and teaching participants specific psychological skills such as imagery or coping skills that they can use to enhance their participation.[2] Another activity is the education of organizations and groups in areas such as development of team cohesion, strategies to promote exercise adherence, and modification of youth sport programs to enhance the experience for the young athletes. As the AAASP notes, "Although some individuals may possess coaching expertise and/or knowledge of the analysis and treatment of psychopathology, these two areas are excluded from the role definition association with AAASP certification."[2]

Sport and exercise psychology encompasses many areas of study. The next section will provide a brief overview of some topics within this subdiscipline. First, the psychological benefits of physical activity are presented, followed by information on motivation and exercise adherence. Personality, anxiety and arousal, goal setting, self-talk, and mental imagery are addressed. A short discussion of various psychological intervention techniques concludes the chapter.

PSYCHOLOGICAL BENEFITS OF PHYSICAL ACTIVITY

The role of physical activity in enhancing well-being is receiving increased professional and public recognition. The physiological effects of engaging in physical activity on a regular basis are well documented. There is also a growing body of evidence supporting the psychological benefits of physical activity.[5,6] Psychological benefits have been noted for both aerobic and resistance exercise. It appears that moderate-intensity exercise has the best psychological benefits.

Benefits

The psychological benefits of participating in physical activity include

- Improved health-related quality of life, by enhancing both psychological and physical well-being.
- Improved mood. Mood states influence our outlook on life, emotions, thought processes, and behaviors.
- Apparently allieviated symptoms associated with mild depression. Physical activity may be a valuable adjunct to therapy in cases of chronic, severe depression.
- Reduced state anxiety—that is, feelings of tension, apprehension, and fear associated with various situations.
- Effective stress management. Physical activity can serve as a buffer against stress as well as provide a healthful means of stress reduction.
- Contribution to the development of the self. Physical activity enhances self-concept and improves self-esteem or feelings of worth. It also promotes greater self-efficacy and self-confidence.
- Affiliation with other human beings, an important psychological need.
- Opportunities to experience peak moments. Peak moments are characterized by feelings of being lost or absorbed in the activity, feelings of "flow," or feelings of powerfulness or being able to do no wrong. Participants have reported feelings of euphoria, such as the runner's high.
- Recreation and a change of pace from long hours of work or study. Individuals return to their daily routine feeling refreshed, both mentally and physically.
- Challenges that, when successfully met, provide a sense of achievement. Some physical activities include certain elements of risk, such as mountain climbing, that provide excitement and opportunities for mastery.

PSYCHOLOGICAL BENEFITS OF PHYSICAL ACTIVITY

- Improves health-related quality of life
- Enhances mood
- Alleviates symptoms of mild depression
- Reduces state and trait anxiety
- Serves as a buffer against stress and means of stress reduction
- Enhances self-efficacy, self-confidence, self-esteem
- Offers a means of affiliation with others
- Improves cognitive functioning
- Provides opportunities to refresh and reenergize
- Presents challenges that can lead to sense of achievement
- Gives means for nonverbal expression of emotion
- Provides opportunities for creative and aesthetic expression

- Aesthetic and creative experiences. Activities such as dance allow individuals to express their emotions in a nonverbal manner and provide opportunities for individual interpretation.

The psychological benefits of physical activity are being increasingly understood and offer exciting possibilities for research.

Mechanism of Effect

Researchers have advanced several hypotheses to explain the effects of exercise on mental health. Hypotheses have been developed that explain the mechanism of effect from a psychological or a physiological perspective. Among the psychological hypotheses offered are the cognitive behavioral hypothesis and the distraction hypothesis. One physiological hypothesis that has received considerable attention is the endorphin hypothesis.

According to the *cognitive behavior hypothesis*, participation in exercise promotes positive thoughts and feelings.[7] These serve to counteract negative thoughts and feelings as well as mood states associated with depression and anxiety.[7] Nonexercisers who begin and adhere to an exercise program, a task many nonexercisers perceive as difficult, experience enhanced feelings of competence and an increase in self-efficacy.[7] Increased

self-efficacy is also associated with effort and persistence, factors that will help individuals continue to participate in exercise and reap the psychological benefits.[7]

The *distraction hypothesis* proposes that the psychological benefits of exercise accrue because engaging in exercise distracts individuals from their cares, worries, and frustrations.[8] Exercise provides individuals with a "time out" from events and issues in their life that are associated with feelings of anxiety or depression.

The *endorphin hypothesis* explains that psychological benefits associated with exercise are due to the increased secretion of endorphins. Endorphins are chemicals produced in the brain in response to a stimuli, including stressors. As a stressor, exercise elicits the production of endorphins. Elevated levels of endorphins are associated with improved mood and enhanced sense of well-being. Endorphins are also associated with a reduction in pain. The general well-being produced by endorphins reduces levels of depression, anxiety, and other negative mood states.[8] The popular press often refers to the improved mood associated with prolonged exercise as the "runner's high." Although there is agreement that the body does produce endorphins in response to prolonged exercise, the research on the mechanism of positive effects has been equivocal.

Although many hypotheses have been advanced, the mechanism by which exercise promotes psychological benefits is not clear at this point in time. Research investigating these and other hypotheses yields conflicting results. What is known, however, is that there is a positive relationship between exercise and various psychological states. Before starting an exercise program, individuals should consult with their physician.

The value of physical activity as a therapeutic modality is increasing, and new avenues are being explored. However, Fontaine points out that several important questions need to be addressed about the therapeutic value of physical activity (PA). These questions include:

1. How and under what circumstances should PA be incorporated into therapy for patients with mental health disorders?
2. What are the long-term effects of PA on mental health disorders?
3. Does regular PA protect against developing mental health disorders?
4. What is the optimal PA prescription for various mental health disorders?[9]

Fontaine notes that despite these questions, it appears that physical activity can play an important role in the treatment of mental health disorders.[9]

Dance therapy and recreation therapy (see Chapter 13) utilize physical activity as part of therapeutic and rehabilitation processes. The role of physical activity in improving mental health and psychological well-being offers exciting possibilities in treatment and prevention.

MOTIVATION

Motivation is a critical factor in learning, performance, and participation in sport and physical activity. It influences the initiation, maintenance, and intensity of behavior. Motivation directs and energizes us; it determines whether or not we will practice with a high level of intensity or get up at 6 A.M. to workout before work. Motivation influences whether we will continue an activity or choose to discontinue participation. As previously discussed in Chapter 5, motivation can be influenced by internal and external factors.

Individuals are intrinsically motivated when the motive for starting or engaging in a behavior is derived from the individual's own desires, enjoyment, needs, and aspirations. For example, a soccer player who engages in the sport because she loves the "beautiful game" and has a passion for it that drives her to participate and an adult who desires to be healthy and joins a water aerobics program are intrinsically motivated. Intrinsic motives drive a person who is quadriplegic and seeks to challenge himself by playing quad rugby; he relishes the competition associated with the sport as well as the camaraderie gained from being part of a team.

On the other hand, individuals are extrinsically motivated when they engage in an activity in hopes of gaining external rewards. An employee who signs up for a worksite fitness program to gain the $1,000 bonus promised by the employer for participation is extrinsically motivated. A young gymnast who competes to gain trophies and the approval of her parents is participating for the external rewards.

Intrinsic motivation is more conductive to long-term commitment and engagement in sport and physical activity. As professionals, it is important for us to realize the importance of intrinsic motivation in sustaining involvement by participants in our programs. There are many theories explaining motivation. However, as Vealey points out, "the key to understanding motivation is realizing that all humans, regardless of their individual goals, are motivated to feel competent, worthy, and self-determining."[1] The question, then, for us as professionals is, what can we do to help individuals develop or increase their intrinsic motivation?[1] This answer is complex and reflects an intersection of a multitude of factors, but simply stated, we can create opportunities to help individuals develop competence and promote feelings of self-efficacy. We can promote feelings of personal accomplishment, recognize hard work, engender self-confidence, and offer support as individuals pursue their goals. It is important that we recognize that participants' motives for participation in our pro-grams vary, and we need to respect their motives. However, if we want to sustain participation, we must focus on promoting intrinsic motivation.

Motivation is critical to achievement. Whether it is achievement in the athletic arena or as a participant in lifelong physical activity, motivation plays an important role in determining whether or not an individual will persist until a goal is achieved. Goal setting is a critical facet of motivation. Having both short- and long-term goals helps individuals focus their behavior and mobilize their energies in the right direction. Physical education, exercise science, and sport professionals can help individuals achieve their goals by assisting them in developing realistic goals, creating positive expectations for success, providing encouragement, offering appropriate feedback, assisting them to redefine their goals when necessary, and developing new goals as

desired goals are achieved. Goal setting is discussed more later in the chapter.

Motivation is critical to the initiation, persistence, or maintenance of the desired behavior, whether it is related to participation in competitive sport or engagement in physical activity for health, enjoyment, or recreation. What motivates an individual to begin a new sport or to start a fitness routine? Equally important, once the new behavior is initiated, what contributes to an individual's continuing the behavior? And what motivates an individual to work hard to achieve desired goals? Sustaining engagement in physical activity is important to the realization of the physiological and psychological benefits associated with participation in regular physical activity. Research on exercise adherence has helped us determine factors that contribute to individuals' continuing to work-out and incorporating physical activity into their lives. This is discussed later in the chapter.

As professionals, we must develop effective behavioral strategies to help sedentary individuals adopt a healthy, active lifestyle.

EXERCISE ADHERENCE

An expanding area of research is investigation of exercise adherence. Researchers have found that patients' adherence to prescribed medical regimens is a great concern. Although figures vary, authorities estimate that half of all patients fail to comply with their medical treatment.[10] The past decade has brought greater recognition of the value of exercise as a therapeutic modality. Exercise is increasingly being prescribed as part of an overall treatment approach to several diseases, including cardiovascular diseases and diabetes. Unfortunately, the compliance rates for participants in exercise programs are similar to those in other medical regimens. Adherence to supervised exercise programs ranges from about 50% to 80% in the first 6 months.[10] Other researchers report that only 30% of individuals who begin an exercise program will be exercising at the end of 3 years.[11]

Knowledge that a particular behavior has either good or harmful influences on our health does not consistently affect our behavior. Most individuals are aware of the behaviors that detract from wellness—smoking, high-fat diet, sedentary lifestyle, and so on—yet continue to engage in these behaviors despite the health consequences. Why aren't more people active? Despite the known benefits, why are there so few participants? And what can be done about it?

Understanding Behavior Change

How do you get people to begin to lead a more active lifestyle? How do you promote behavior change? Many theories and models of human behavior have been used to guide interventions to promote a more physically active lifestyle and encourage health-promoting behaviors. Among the models are the classic learning theories, the health belief model, social cognitive theory, the transtheoretical model, and the ecological perspective.

The *classic learning theories* emphasizes that learning a new complex pattern of behavior, such as moving from a sedentary to an active lifestyle,

is achieved by altering many of the small behaviors that compose the overall behavior. This suggests that a targeted behavior, such as walking continuously for 30 minutes a day, is best learned by breaking down the behavior into smaller goals to be achieved, such as walking for 10 minutes daily. Incremental increases, such as adding 5 minutes to daily walking a week, are then made as the behavior is gradually shaped toward the targeted goal. Rewards and incentives, both immediate and long-range, serve as reinforcement and motivation for the individual to achieve and maintain the targeted behavior. Looking better, receiving a T-shirt for participation, and experiencing a feeling of accomplishment all strengthen and sustain the behavior change.

The *health belief model* emphasizes that the adoption of a health behavior depends on the person's perception of four factors: the severity of the potential illness, the person's susceptibility to that illness, the benefits of taking action, and the barriers to action. Incorporation of cues to action, such as listing walking on your daily to-do list, is important in eliciting and sustaining the desired behavior. *Self-efficacy*, a person's confidence in his or her capability to perform the desired behavior, is included as an important component of this model.

Social cognitive theory states that behavior change is influenced by environmental factors, personal factors, and attributes of the behavior itself. Self-efficacy is central to this model. A person must believe in his or her ability to perform the behavior (self-efficacy) and must perceive an incentive for changing his or her behavior. The outcomes derived from the behavior must be valued by the person. These benefits can be immediate in nature, such as feelings of satisfaction or enjoyment from engaging in the behavior, or long-term, such as improved health from being physically active on a regular basis.

The *theory of reasoned action* is based on the idea that the most important determinant of an individual's behavior is the intention to perform that behavior. The intention to perform a behavior is influenced by two factors: the individual's attitude

SELECTED THEORIES AND MODELS OF HEALTH BEHAVIOR CHANGE

Classic learning theory | New behaviors are learned.

- Achievement of smaller goals leads to attainment of overall goals
- Reinforcement and motivation are critical

Health belief model | Adoption of a health behavior depends on the person's perception of four factors:

- Severity of the potential illness
- Susceptibility to that illness
- Benefits of taking action
- Barriers to action

Self-efficacy plays an important role.

Social cognitive theory | Behavior change is influenced by environmental and personal factors and attributes of the behavior itself.

- Self-efficacy is a critical component
- Requires a perceived incentive for changing behavior
- Outcomes must be valued by the person.

Theory of reasoned action and theory of planned behavior | Behavior change is strongly influenced by intention to change, which depends on:

- Individual's attitude toward the behavior
- Opinions of relevant others regarding the change
- Perceived control over behavior

Transtheoretical model | Behavior change proceeds through stages:

- Precontemplation
- Contemplation
- Preparation
- Action
- Maintenance
- Termination

Decisional balance and self-efficacy play an important role in the adoption of new behaviors.

Ecological approach | Health behavior change is affected by:

- Individual factors
- Sociocultural context
- Environmental influences

TRANSTHEORETICAL MODEL AND ITS APPLICATION TO PROMOTION OF PHYSICAL ACTIVITY

Stage of Change	Behaviors	Suggested Approaches by Professional
Precontemplation	No intention to change behavior in next 6 months	Educate the individual and deliver a clear message about the importance of physical activity to health
Contemplation	Awareness of the problem, the pros and cons of change; intention to take action within next 6 months	Highlight the benefits of change and try to shift the decisional balance
Preparation	Taking small steps or developing a specific plan of action to begin physical activity program (e.g., checking out walking routes or joining a fitness club)	Help the individual identify the best time to walk and safe walking route; teach the individual warm-up and cooldown stretches; assist the individual in developing a progressive walking plan (20 minutes at a moderate pace three times a week progressing to 30 minutes of brisk walking most days of the week)
Action	Making modifications in lifestyle and engaging in physical activity (e.g., getting up an hour earlier to fit walking into day); commitment to exercise	Encourage and support the individual in becoming active; help the individual monitor physical activity; discuss modifications in program as situation changes
Maintenance	Sustaining the change in behavior for at least 6 months; becoming increasingly confident in ability to sustain change (e.g., continuing to walk on daily basis); exercise becomes routine	Support the individual in remaining active; explore ideas with the individual for continuing to be active even when the schedule changes and the individual can't walk at the usual time, etc.
Termination	Behavior is fully integrated into lifestyle (e.g., walking is planned for as part of the day's activities); exercise patterns are integral part of life	The individual walks as part of the daily routine; offer to be available as a resource
Relapse	Move to previous stage	Remind the individual that relapse gives the opportunity to rethink physical activity strategy—what worked and what should be changed; encourage the individual to recommence physical activity at an appropriate level

Source: Adapted from Duffy FD and Schnirring L. "How to Counsel Patients about Exercise: An Office-Friendly Approach." *The Physician and Sportsmedicine*, 28(10), 53–54, 2000.

toward the behavior and the influence of relevant others in the environment. The individual's attitude reflects beliefs about the outcomes of the behavior and the values gained from changing the behavior. If the individual sees the outcome of changing a behavior as positive, this increases the likelihood of change. If relevant others support changing behavior, and the individual is strongly motivated by the opinions of others, this also supports behavior change. *The theory of planned action* incorporates the tenets of the theory of reasoned action and adds another concept—perceived control. *Perceived control* is similar to the concept of self-efficacy and reflects the individual's beliefs about his or her ability to perform the behavior. Individuals who intend to become more active are more likely to do so if they see being active as having a positive benefit, receive support from others for being active, and perceive themselves as being successful in being physically active.

The *transtheoretical model* of health behavior uses the concept of stages of change to integrate the processes and principles of change relating to health behavior.[12] (See the Transtheoretical Model and Its Application to Promotion of Physical Activity box.) The transtheoretical model views behavioral change as a spiraling continuum that begins at a "firm conviction to maintain the status quo by never changing, and proceeds through the conditions of someday, soon, now, and forever."[13] The stages of change are:

- Precontemplation is the stage at which people have no intention to change behavior within the foreseeable future, usually the next 6 months.
- Contemplation is the stage at which people are intending to take action sometime in the next 6 months.
- Preparation is the stage at which people take small or inconsistent steps toward change.
- Action is the point at which individuals have made modifications in their lifestyle. They are engaging in the health-promoting behavior.
- Maintenance is sustaining the change in behavior for at least 6 months. During this time, people become increasingly confident that they can maintain their changes.
- Termination is the stage in which the behavior is fully integrated into the lifestyle. People in this stage have a high degree of self-confidence that, despite temptations to relapse, they will continue the behavior.[12,13]

In this approach, a relapse or discontinuation of the behavior, such as ceasing to exercise, is seen as a return from the action or maintenance stage to an earlier stage. Relapse should be dealt with in a positive way so that the person does not see it as a failure and become demoralized, but rather perceives it as part of the process of change. Relapse presents individuals with an opportunity to learn which behavior strategies worked and which ones did not.[14]

Decisional balance and self-efficacy are important aspects of the transtheoretical model. *Decisional balance* involves weighing the relative pros and cons of the behavioral change, that is, perceived benefits, drawbacks, and barriers to change.[15] Self-efficacy is a person's confidence about his or her competence or abilities in a specific situation. In the context of behavioral change, self-efficacy is a person's belief that he or she can maintain a healthy behavior, such as exercising, or abstain from an unhealthy behavior, such as smoking.

The transtheoretical model has most frequently been applied to the cessation of unhealthy, addictive behaviors and more recently to the acquisition of healthy behaviors such as exercise. This model has been used to predict the use of sport psychology consultations by collegiate athletes.[16] It offers physical education, exercise science, and sport professionals great insight into the process of change and guidelines for developing intervention programs.

Another model that has increased in popularity in the last decade is the ecological approach. One criticism of many theories and models for changing health behavior is that they emphasize individual behavior change while paying little attention to the sociocultural and environmental influences on behavior. The *ecological approach* emphasizes a comprehensive approach to health, including developing individual skills and creating supportive, health-promoting environments. Creating longer-lasting changes and maintaining health-promoting habits can be enhanced by addressing environmental and societal barriers to change, such as limitations imposed by poverty on access to services or the difficulty in jogging or walking if one lives in an unsafe neighborhood. These interventions can take place in the family,

PROMOTING EXERCISE ADHERENCE

- Structure program to optimize social support to participants
- Offer programs at convenient times and locations
- Utilize goal setting, on both a short- and long-term basis
- Provide frequent assessment of progress
- Use qualified and enthusiastic leaders
- Foster communication between leader and participants
- Develop rapport among leader and participants
- Involve a variety of enjoyable activities
- Give participants a choice of activities
- Tailor frequency, intensity, and duration of activities to individuals' needs
- Incorporate reinforcement and rewards

school, worksite, community, and health institutions. Societal and environmental influences on health behavior must be considered by physical education, exercise science, and sport professionals.

Promoting Adherence

What are factors that promote adherence, encourage persistence, and prevent dropping out? Researchers have identified several factors that predispose individuals to drop out of exercise programs. In general, the researchers found that low self-motivation, depression, and low self-efficacy were related to decisions to quit the program, as was denial of the seriousness of one's cardiac condition.[10,17,18] Higher dropout rates were found among smokers, blue-collar workers, and individuals who either are obese, exhibit the type A behavior pattern, perceive that exercise has few health benefits, lead physically inactive lifestyles, or work in sedentary occupations. Lack of social support from significant others, family problems, and job-related responsibilities that interfered with the exercise program were also identified as factors associated with quitting. Social support from other participants was important to individuals who continued in the program. Group exercise programs usually had lower dropout rates than individually designed programs. Programs that were inconvenient to attend and that

involved high-intensity exercise were associated with higher dropout rates than programs that were conveniently located and offered exercise of a less-intense nature.

Knowing the factors associated with exercise program dropout enables practitioners to target intervention strategies to those individuals at greatest risk of discontinuing their participation. Intervention strategies to improve adherence include educational approaches and behavioral approaches. Educational approaches provide participants with information to increase their knowledge and understanding. Behavioral approaches focus on increasing individual involvement in the program and creating more healthful behavior patterns. These methods use such strategies as reinforcement, contracting, self-monitoring, goal setting, tailoring programs to meet individuals' lifestyles, and enhancement of self-efficacy. Behavioral approaches have been found to be more effective than educational approaches in promoting adherence.

Exercise adherence also can be enhanced through careful program design. One approach is structuring the program to increase the social support available to participants. Successful strategies include forming exercise groups rather than having the individual exercise alone and involving significant others, such as family members or friends, in encouraging the participant to exercise. Offering programs at times and locations convenient to the participant is important in maintaining involvement. The use of goal setting combined with periodic assessment of progress, use of qualified and enthusiastic leaders, establishment of ongoing leader and participant communication and rapport, and inclusion of a variety of enjoyable activities to meet individual needs are some techniques that can promote exercise adherence and reduce dropout rates.

The issue of adherence to treatment is also beginning to be addressed in the realm of sports medicine. Many of the psychosocial factors that contribute to exercise adherence are also critical to the success of rehabilitation programs. There is increased recognition that sports medicine specialists' and athletic trainers' knowledge of injury mechanisms and treatment protocols is not enough to ensure successful completion of the rehabilitation program. Researchers have found that rehabilitation adherence can be enhanced through the use of such strategies as goal setting, establishing effective communication, tailoring the program to individual needs, monitoring progress, and building a collaborative relationship to achieve the goals of therapy.[19] Social support has also been linked to rehabilitation adherence.

Social support is a complex, multidimensional construct and has been found to be related in many ways to health outcomes. With respect to rehabilitation, social support has been found to relieve distress, enhance coping, and help an injured athlete remain motivated throughout the recovery.[20] It has also been found to strengthen relationships between the injured athlete and team members, coaches, and providers of health care.[20] Understanding the significant role social support plays in exercise and rehabilitation adherence can assist physical education, exercise science, and sport professionals in developing psychosocial rehabilitation interventions.

Young professionals aspiring to work in fitness and rehabilitation fields, such as corporate fitness, athletic training, and cardiac rehabilitation, will find knowledge from the subdiscipline of sport and exercise psychology very valuable in their work.

PERSONALITY

Researchers have long been interested in personality types in sport. Some researchers sought to address the question of whether sport influences personality; other researchers have investigated whether there were personality differences between athletes and nonathletes. Still other researchers undertook the task of identifying the psychological differences between elite athletes and their less successful counterparts. One of the questions was whether it would be possible to predict the success of an athlete based on his or her personality characteristics.

Nature of Personality

Vealey describes *personality* as "the unique blend of the psychological characteristics and behavioral tendencies that make individuals different from and similar to each other."[1] Anshel describes personality as traits possessed by an individual that are enduring and stable.[21] Because traits are enduring and stable, they predispose an individual to consistently act in certain ways in most, but not all, situations; thus, there is a degree of predictability to an individual's actions. Anshel suggests that psychological dispositions (i.e., broad, pervasive ways of relating to people and situations) may be more helpful in studying athletes' psychological characteristics.[21] Personality traits are linked to predispositions. The personality traits of dominance, trait anxiety, and internal locus of control are linked to the type A disposition.

Personality and Sport

The early research focused on the relationship between personality traits and sport performance. Researchers addressed questions such as:

- Do athletes differ from nonathletes?
- Can athletes in certain sports be distinguished from athletes in other sports on the basis of their personality?
- Do individuals participate in certain sports because of their personality characteristics?

- Do highly skilled athletes have different personality profiles than less skilled athletes in the same sport?
- Are there certain personality traits that can predict an athlete's success in a sport?[22]

Researchers' findings have revealed contradictory answers to each of these questions. In many instances, problems in research design have contributed to these contradictory results. Cox, after an extensive review of the research on personality and sport, offers the following generalizations about men and women athletes relative to the questions posed above:

- Athletes and nonathletes differ with respect to personality characteristics. Various researchers have reported that athletes are more independent, objective, self-confident, competitive, and outgoing or extroverted, and less anxious than nonathletes.
- Sport participation has an effect on the personality development of young athletes during their formative years. Thus, youth sport experience can positively or negatively affect the development of personality.
- Athletes in one sport can be differentiated from athletes in another sport based on their personality characteristics. Perhaps the clearest example occurs between individual sport athletes and team sport athletes. It has been shown that individual sport athletes are less extroverted, more independent, and less anxious than team sport participants.
- World-class athletes can be correctly differentiated from less-skilled athletes by their psychological profile 70% of the time. Personality profiles that include situational measures of psychological states have been shown to be the most accurate in predicting level of athletic performance.[22]

While Cox has advanced some generalizations based on an overview of research in the area, much of the research is still inconclusive.[22]

Despite the controversies and the limitations of personality trait research, there is some agreement about the psychological characteristics of highly skilled athletes. Anshel reports:

> Highly skilled athletes score relatively low in neuroticism, tension, depression, anger, fatigue, and confusion. They tend to score very high in self-confidence, self-concept, self-esteem, vigor, need achievement, dominance, aggression, intelligence, self-sufficiency, mental toughness, independence (autonomy), sociability, creativity, stability, and extroversion. A composite of the psychological profiles of elite athletes reveals a person who is mentally healthy, physically and psychological mature, and committed to excellence.[21]

Anshel points out that these characteristics serve as a model of the elite athlete, but the value of applying these characteristics as the basis for athletic selection, promotion, or elimination is questionable.[21]

As interest in personality in sport grew, different approaches began to be utilized to study personality and psychological characteristics of athletes. The interactionist approach views behavior as being influenced by both the traits of the individual and situational and environmental factors. The study of personality states is another approach that has been undertaken by researchers to study athletes. Unlike traits, which are relatively stable, states fluctuate and are a manifestation of the individual's behaviors and feelings at a particular moment, reflecting the interaction of traits and situational factors. For example, anxiety has both a trait dimension (how you typically respond to situations) and a state dimension (how you feel at this moment or at particular point in time, such as before the start of the competition).

The emergence of cognitive psychology offers another perspective to understand the behaviors, feelings, and thoughts of athletes. According to this theory, individuals continuously process information from the environment, interpret the information, and then behave based on their appraisal of the situation. Cognitive psychology recognizes that individuals' thoughts about themselves and the situation influence their actions. Vealey reports that researchers using the cognitive approach were able to distinguish between successful and less-successful athletes.[1] Compared to less-successful athletes, successful athletes:

- possess more self-confidence,
- employ more effective coping strategies to maintain their optimal competitive focus despite obstacles and distractions,
- more efficiently regulate their level of activation to be appropriate for the task at hand,
- tend to be more positively preoccupied with their sport, and
- have a high level of determination and commitment to excellence.[21]

Anshel discusses psychological predispositions of highly successful athletes.[21] These athletes are characterized by risk taking. Risk taking involves engaging in actions that can lead to bodily harm and psychological harm, such as failure. Elite athletes take greater and more frequent performance risks than their less-successful competitors and enjoy that challenge of competitive sport. Highly competitive, they strive for success and measure their success by performing at their personal best rather than by just winning alone. Elite athletes are highly self-confident and possess a high degree of self-efficacy, a conviction that they can successfully perform the skills to yield the desired outcome. High expectations for success contribute to their achievement. However, they also have the ability to cope with failure and learn from their mistakes. They are able to shift their attention to the critical cues in the environment as the situation demands. Additionally, elite athletes can effectively manage their stress through the use of appropriate coping techniques and intervention strategies (e.g., self-talk, relaxation).

The research on personality and psychological characteristics of athletes, while at times presenting conflicting results, does offer us some insights into the psychological characteristics and thoughts of athletes. Differences in traits, predispositions, and cognitions influence athletes' behaviors and experiences in sport. What can be said with some degree of assurance is that each athlete must be treated as an individual.

ANXIETY AND AROUSAL

The goal of coaches, teachers, and sport psychologists is to optimize an individual's performance. To achieve this goal they must consider the effect of anxiety and arousal on performance.

Nature of Anxiety and Arousal

Anxiety, as defined by Levitt, is a subjective feeling of apprehension accompanied by a heightened level of physiological arousal.[23] *Physiological arousal* is an autonomic response that results in the excitation of various organs of the body. Examples of this phenomenon seen in athletes are

---

SIGNS OF ELEVATED AROUSAL AND HEIGHTENED ANXIETY

- Sweaty hands
- Frequent urge to urinate
- Increased respiration rate
- Elevated heart rate
- Deterioration in coordination
- Inappropriate narrowing of attention
- Distractibility
- Negative self-talk

Optimal arousal is important for superior performance. The level of optimal arousal varies according to the individual and the sport.

sweaty hands, frequent urge to urinate, increased respiration rate, increased muscle tension, and elevated heart rate.

Anxiety is commonly classified in two ways. Trait anxiety is an integral part of an individual's personality. It refers to the individual's tendency to classify environmental events as either threatening or nonthreatening. State anxiety is an emotional response to a specific situation that results in feelings of fear, tension, or apprehension (e.g., apprehension about an upcoming competition). The effects of both state and trait anxiety on motor performance have been studied by sport psychologists.

Anxiety, Arousal, and Performance

Coaches and teachers continually attempt to find the optimal level of arousal that allows individuals to perform their best. An arousal level that is too low or too high can have a negative impact on performance. A low level of arousal in an individual is associated with such behaviors as low motivation, inattention, and inappropriate and slow movement choices. A high level of arousal in an individual can cause deterioration in coordination, inappropriate narrowing of attention, distractibility, and a lack of flexibility in movement responses. It is important for each individual to find his or her optimal level of arousal for a given activity. However, no one knows for sure exactly how to consistently reach this ideal state. A variety of approaches have been employed by physical education, exercise science, and sport professionals in pursuit of this goal. These techniques include pep talks, motivational slogans and bulletin boards, relaxation training, imagery, and in some cases the professional services of a sport psychologist.

Sport psychologists and researchers have studied the relationships among anxiety, arousal, and sport performance. Cox, after a review of the research in this area, offered the following ideas:

- Athletes who feel threatened by fear of failure experience a high level of anxiety. Fear of failure can be reduced by defining success in individual terms and keeping winning in perspective.

- Athletes who possess high levels of trait anxiety tend to experience high levels of state anxiety when confronted with competition. Coaches who are aware of their athletes' levels of trait anxiety can better understand how they are likely to respond in a competitive situation. This knowledge will help coaches select appropriate strategies to adjust athletes' levels of state anxiety and arousal to an optimal level.

- Athletes' perceptions of a given situation influence their level of state anxiety. Not all athletes react to the competitive situation in the same manner. Each athlete perceives the same situation in a different way. Coaches must be aware that when placed in the same competitive situation, athletes experience different levels of anxiety. That is why "psych" talks may be an effective means of regulating the arousal level of some athletes and ineffective with other athletes. Techniques must be tailored to the individual athlete and the situation.

- An optimal level of arousal is essential for peak performance. The individual characteristics of the athlete, the nature of the skill to be performed, and the competitive situation influence the level of arousal needed.

- As the arousal level increases, athletes tend to exhibit the dominant or habitual response. Under the stress of competition, they tend to revert to skills they are most comfortable performing. Thus, if a volleyball player has been recently trained to pass the ball in a low trajectory to the setter, under the stress of competition, the player may revert to the safer, easier-to-perform high-trajectory pass.[22]

Research in sport psychology suggests several ways that coaches can help their athletes achieve their optimal performance, whether that means decreasing their level of arousal and anxiety or increasing it. One way to determine whether an athlete is "feeling up" as opposed to "uptight" is to help athletes accurately identify their feelings, encourage them to monitor their feelings and arousal levels before, during, and after competition, and help them learn and use appropriate strategies to enable them to reach their optimal state.

Anshel identifies several different approaches that can serve to reduce anxiety and arousal. These approaches include:

- Use physical activity to release stress and anxiety. A warm-up can provide an effective means to reduce stress; however, be careful that it is not so emotionally or physically intense that it leads to the depletion of the athletes' energy.
- To reduce the anxiety associated with the performance of new tasks and activities, develop, teach, and practice a precompetition routine so that it is comfortable and familiar to the athletes.
- Simulate games in practice to allow athletes to rehearse skills and strategies until they are mastered.
- Tailor preparation for the competition to the individual athlete. Athletes prepare for competition in different ways. Some athletes prefer to sit quietly before the competition, relax in their own way, and reflect on what they need to do in the upcoming events. Other athletes thrive on an exciting, noisy locker-room atmosphere and a high-emotion pep talk from the coach. Whenever possible, individualize athletes' preparation.
- Focus on building self-confidence and high but realistic expectations. Personal insecurities, self-doubts, low self-esteem, and fears about the competition heighten anxiety. Highlighting the athletes' strengths, reviewing game strategies, and expressing confidence in the athletes' abilities and efforts help promote positive thoughts, alleviate doubt, and decrease negative thinking.
- Assist athletes in coping with errors by keeping errors in perspective. Help the athletes to stay focused on present and future events when an error occurs, rather than dwelling on past events. Emphasize the opportunity to learn from mistakes, and help athletes avoid negative self-statements, which tend to exacerbate anxiety and disrupt performance.[21]

There are a host of additional strategies that coaches can use to help athletes manage their anxiety and arousal. Once again, coaches must be prepared to work with athletes as individuals and determine which approach best suits each athlete.

What can coaches do to "psych up" a team? Increasing the team's and athletes' levels of arousal is sometimes necessary. Anshel suggests that coaches take into account each athlete's ability level, age, psychological needs, and skills to be performed.[21] Remember that athletes respond differently to various techniques and need different levels of arousal to perform different tasks.[21] Coaches can also use a multitude of different strategies to increase arousal, including increasing the intensity of their voice, using loud and fast-paced music, setting specific performance goals, and using the warm-up to help athletes adjust their level of arousal.[21] Some coaches show video of the opponents, whereas other coaches may show highlights of the athletes' successful performances.[21]

Managing anxiety and arousal is a challenging task. Coaches must recognize that athletes' perceptions of a situation influence their anxiety and arousal. Individual differences in athletes' physical and psychological states require that techniques to help athletes achieve their optimal performance must be individualized. Anxiety can affect other factors that influence an athlete's performance, such as attention.

REDUCING ANXIETY AND AROUSAL TO ENHANCE PERFORMANCE

- Use appropriate physical activity, such as warm-ups
- Develop and use a precompetition routine
- Design practice situations to simulate competition
- Tailor preparation to the individual
- Build self-confidence and high, realistic expectations
- Help athletes keep errors in perspective
- Keep athletes' focus on the present event, not on past events
- Promote the use of positive self-talk
- Incorporate relaxation training as necessary

Psychological skills help athletes perform at their maximum level.

GOAL SETTING

Goal setting is important in many of the different environments in which physical education, exercise scientists, and sport leaders work. Goal setting can be used to help students in school physical education, athletes on sports teams, clients rehabilitating an injury, or adults involved in fitness programs. Goal setting is important both as a motivational strategy and as a strategy to change behavior or enhance performance. It is also used as an intervention strategy to rectify problems or to redirect efforts.

Types of Goals

According to Weinberg, a *goal* can be defined as "that which an individual is trying to accomplish; it is the object or aim of an action."[24] Goal setting focuses on specifying a specific level of proficiency to be attained within a certain period of time.[25] Goals can be categorized as outcome goals, performance goals, and process goals.

Outcome goals typically focus on interpersonal comparisons and the end result of an event. An example of an outcome goal is winning first place at the Senior Games regional track meet at the end of the season. Whether an outcome goal is achieved or not is influenced in part by the ability and play of the opponent.

Performance goals refer to the individual's actual performance in relation to personal levels of achievement. Striving to increase ground balls won in lacrosse from five to ten, decreasing the time to walk a mile from 20 minutes to 15 minutes, increasing the amount of weight that can be lifted following knee reconstruction, and improving one's free-throw percentage from 35% to 50% are examples of performance goals.

Lastly, *process goals* focus on how a particular skill is performed. For example, increasing axial rotation in swimming the backstroke and following through on the tennis backhand are two examples of process goals that focus on the improvement of technique. As technique improves, improvements in performance are likely to follow.

How Goal Setting Works

Goal setting leads to improved performance. Locke, Shaw, Saari, and Latham identify four distinct ways in which goal setting influences performance. It focuses attention, mobilizes effort, nurtures persistence, and leads to the development of new learning strategies.[26]

Goal setting leads to the focusing of attention on the task at hand and on the achievement of the goal related to that task. When there are no specific goals, attention has a tendency to wander, drifting from one item to the next without any particular attention or intent. When specific goals are set, individuals can direct their attention to that task and its accomplishments. For example, a volleyball player who has a goal of getting 15 kills in a match can then focus his efforts on the specific elements of the skill that will help accomplish this goal.

Once a goal is determined, to achieve the goal, individuals must direct their efforts toward its attainment. This mobilization of effort, in and of itself, can lead to improved performance. Knowing what you want to accomplish and having specific strategies to achieve it influence motivation and increase effort.

Not only does goal setting focus one's attention and mobilize one's efforts, but it encourages persistence. Persistence is critical. Often the attainment of goals involves a concentrated effort over an extended period of time. There may be periods of frustration and failure as individuals learn new strategies or challenge themselves to higher levels of achievement. Individuals need to persist in pursuit of their goals.

Development of relevant learning strategies is an essential aspect of goal setting. Strategies can include learning new techniques and changing the manner in which a skill is practiced. Strategies can also include developing a plan by which incremental changes in performance or behavior can be attained. For example, an individual desiring to lose 30 pounds through a combination of healthy dieting and increased physical activity may need to learn strategies to select healthier foods, to develop and modify a walking program, and to learn how to continue to maintain the weight loss once it is accomplished.

Properly implemented, goal setting can lead to improvements in performance and changes in behavior. Goals can be outcome, process, or performance oriented. Goal setting improves performance by directing attention, mobilizing effort, encouraging persistence, and introducing new strategies. Goal setting requires careful planning if it is to be effective as a motivational strategy or intervention strategy.

Principles of Effective Goal Setting

Several principles provide guidance for physical educators, exercise scientists, and sport leaders involved in goal setting. It is important that the goal setting program be structured and implemented correctly, because a decrement in performance can actually occur from improper goal setting. To help you get started with goal setting, think "SMART." SMART is an acronym suggested by Weinberg and Gould to help professionals remember the critical characteristics of effective goals.[27] Goals should be specific, measurable, action oriented, realistic, and timely.

Specific goals have been linked to higher levels of performance than no goals or general do-your-best-type goals. While do-your-best goals may be motivating and encouraging, they do not have as powerful an impact on performance as having specific goals. Furthermore, general goals such as "I want to be a better swimmer" or "I want to be healthier" are not as effective as specific goals. It is hard to monitor general goals or to know what types of changes need to be made to achieve them. A specific goal, such as a swimmer stating, "I want to reduce my time in the 200 freestyle to 1 minute 56 seconds from 2 minutes 5 seconds by the championships," is more likely to result in improvements in performance.

Additionally, measurable goals allow progress to be more easily monitored. Measurable goals provide individuals with feedback, which helps motivate them and sustain involvement. An individual who sets a goal of walking 30 minutes a day for 5 days a week at a brisk pace of 12 minutes a mile or less can easily monitor whether progress is being made toward goal attainment. Action goals, also referred to as observable goals, are goals that can be assessed through observation

---

SMART GOAL SETTING

- Specific—set specific versus general goals
- Measurable—design measurable goals to facilitate monitoring of progress
- Action-oriented—assess goal attainment by viewing person's actions
- Realistic—make goals challenging but achievable with effort, persistence, and hard work
- Timely—establish time frame for achievement

---

of a person's actions. By viewing the person's actions, you can determine whether or not the individual is exhibiting the desired goal or behavior.

Identification of the time frame for achievement is a critical part of goal setting. Will the goal be accomplished by the end of the season? Or within 1 month? The time frame should be long enough so that it gives a reasonable time to accomplish the goal. If the time frame is too short, it appears unrealistic, which may cause the individual to give up prematurely. If the time frame is too long, there is a tendency to procrastinate.

Goals that individuals establish should be moderately difficult so that the individuals feel challenged and have to extend themselves to achieve the goals. Goals must be perceived by individuals to be realistic and achievable with effort, persistence, and hard work.

Both Weinberg[24] and Cox,[7] noted sport psychologists, suggest several other principles that should be incorporated into goal setting in addition to the SMART goal characteristics. These include writing goals down, incorporating different types of goals into the program, setting short-term and long-term goals, providing individual goals within the group context, determining goals for both practice and competition, ensuring that goals are internalized by the individuals, regularly evaluating progress, and providing for individual differences.

Goals should be written down and monitored regularly to determine if progress is being made.

Some swimmers religiously chart each practice, writing down times for each set of repeats in a swim diary. Other swimmers may only chart their meet performances. What's important is that the individual knows his or her goal, writes it down, and tracks its progress consistently.

A variety of goals should be integrated into the goal setting plan. A combination of outcome, performance, and process goals is recommended. When individuals set goals based on their own performance, they feel more in control. Goals based on outcome measures, such as winning and losing, can lead to a loss of motivation and higher levels of anxiety.[7] The reason is that there are many aspects of an outcome goal that individuals cannot control, such as their opponents' ability. Furthermore, using a combination of different types of goals presents individuals with additional opportunities for success. For example, a swimmer can finish third and fail to achieve an outcome goal of finishing first in the event, but feel successful by posting a personal best time for the event, a performance goal.

Setting a long-term goal provides a direction for individuals' efforts. In addition to long-term goals, short-term goals should be established. Short-term goals play an important role in goal achievement. They serve as stepping stones to the long-term goal. Short-term goals provide individuals with benchmarks by which to judge their progress. This form of feedback serves to keep motivation and performance high. It allows individuals to focus on improvement in smaller increments and helps make the long-term goal task seem less overwhelming.

Goals should be set for different circumstances. Goals are important for both practice and competition. What happens in practice is reflected during performance in competition. Daily practices are a critical component of competitive success. If a tennis player wants to improve his first-serve percentage during competition, this goal should be given attention during practice. Practices also provide the opportunity to work on other goals that contribute to team success, such as working hard or communicating more with teammates.

Setting goals is the first step toward achievement. Participants in the Tenneco Health and Fitness program record their progress.

Goals can also be set for teams. Team goals provide a focus for practice goals. For example, if the lacrosse team's goal is to be ranked number one in the conference on winning ground balls, practice time should be allocated to the achievement of that goal. Additionally, individual performance goals that contribute to the achievement of the team goal, such as working on skills to increase the percentage of ground balls won, should receive attention.

Social support is acknowledged as an important factor in goal achievement. Social support has been found to be critical in achieving rehabilitation goals as well as health goals. For example, in cardiac rehabilitation programs, where individuals set goals related to fitness and nutrition, eliciting the support of a spouse or significant other increases the likelihood that individuals will achieve their goals. Expressions of social support, such as genuine concern and encouragement, also help individuals remain motivated and committed when they are discouraged or frustrated or hit a performance plateau.

Acceptance and internalization of goals by the individual is one of the most critical aspects of goal setting. Individuals must commit to the goals and invest themselves in their attainment. Allowing individuals to set their own goals increases their commitment to their achievement. Goals set by others, such as a personal trainer or a coach, may cause individuals not to feel ownership of the goals. Ownership can be enhanced by using a collaborative approach to goal setting. If goals are not determined by the individual, but are assigned by others, professionals should make sure that the individual commits to the assigned goal.

Provision for frequent evaluation needs to be incorporated into the goal setting plan. Evaluative feedback helps individuals assess the effectiveness of their goals and whether or not their goal achievement strategies are working. Additionally, goal setting is a dynamic process. Frequent evaluation allows both short- and long-term goals to be adjusted to reflect progress, the changing circumstances of the individuals, or the effectiveness of learning strategies.

Individual differences need to be taken into account when setting goals. Some individuals thrive on challenges and welcome goals whose achievement, although attainable, will be difficult. Other individuals require a boost in self-confidence and may benefit from a goal setting approach that uses many short-term goals, the achievement of which enhances their feelings of competence. Individual circumstances should be reflected in goal setting.

Physical education, exercise science, and sport professionals may find goal setting to be an integral part of their work. Goal setting can be used effectively in many different ways to help individuals improve their performance or change their behaviors relative to physical activity.

ENHANCING PERFORMANCE THROUGH SELF-TALK

What thoughts run through your head before an athletic performance? As you sit and wait to give a 10-minute speech in front of a class, what are you thinking? As you set out on your daily 3-mile jog, what conversations do you have with yourself in your head? What did you say to yourself as you took a test for this course? Cognitive approaches in sport and exercise psychology focus on understanding the relationship between

individuals' thoughts, feelings, and behavior or performance.

Nature of Self-Talk

What individuals say to themselves during performance can be positive or negative. These thoughts and associated feelings can influence self-confidence, which, in turn, impacts performance. Who would you rather have take a penalty kick in soccer—a soccer player who steps up to take the shot and thinks, "I consistently make this shot in practice; I can do it" or a player who steps up to take the shot and thinks, "What if I miss?" Which player's self-talk is more conducive to successful performance? Understanding and modifying individuals' self-talk is one focus of cognitive sport and exercise psychology.

According to Williams and Leffingwell, "Self-talk occurs whenever an individual thinks, whether making statements internally or externally."[28] *Self-talk* is thoughts that occupy individuals' mind or spoken words, and they can be positive or negative in nature. Positive self-talk

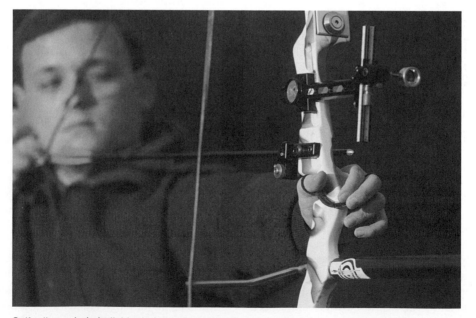

Self-talk can help individuals focus their attention and concentrate on relevant cues.

does not guarantee an outstanding performance, but it does enhance factors associated with better performance, such as self-confidence and a task-relevant focus of attention.[28] Sport and exercise psychologists use a variety of strategies to promote positive self-talk and to counteract the effects of negative self-talk.

Types of Self-Talk

There are several different types of self-talk. Task-relevant statements reinforce technique. For example, a volleyball setter may use the cue "diamond" to remind himself of the correct hand position. Positive self-statements refer to talk that encourages effort or persistence or reinforces feelings of confidence. A cross-country runner, facing an uphill stretch during the last kilometer, may say to herself, "I can do it" as a way of encouraging herself to push through to the finish. A third form of self-talk is mood words—words designed to elicit an increase in intensity or arousal. "Turn it on," a swimmer says to himself as he completes the last 50 yards of a 1,500-yard freestyle race.

Application of Self-Talk

There are several uses of self-talk. Self-talk can be effective in enhancing skill acquisition, focusing attention, modifying activation, and promoting self-confidence.[28] Self-talk is not only for athletes, but is also useful for individuals engaging in a variety of physical activities.

Self-talk can be useful when learning a new skill or modifying a previously learned skill or habit. Self-talk can range from rehearsing key words of the steps involved in a skill to the use of a cue word such as "step" to serve as a reminder of what to do. It is important that the self-talk focus on the desirable movement, versus what not to do. For example, if a tennis player wants to toss the ball higher in preparation for the serve, appropriate self-talk would be "High toss," not "Don't toss the ball so low."

Focusing attention is another effective use for self-talk. During practices or competition, athletes' attention may wander or be directed inappropriately. Cue words such as "focus" help athletes regain their concentration. Self-statements can also be used to help athletes focus on relevant task cues such as "mark up" or "adjust position relative to the ball."

The right intensity at the right time is critical in performance. Self-talk can be used by athletes to modify their intensity or arousal so that it is at an optimal level. Self-statements may be helpful in decreasing activation ("relax") or increasing it ("get psyched").

Promoting self-confidence is an effective use of self-talk. Self-confidence is influenced by a variety of factors, such as performance outcomes and skill ability. Self-confidence is also influenced by self-talk. Individuals' self-talk affects their self-confidence, either positively or negatively. Self-confidence is undermined with negative self-talk and feelings of doubt. Although self-criticism can provide an important source of feedback to improve later performances, it is important that it not be overgeneralized ("My shot went wide because of the direction of my follow-through" versus "I'm a terrible player"). Positive self-talk enhances feelings of competence. Self-statements prior to and during competition should be positive in nature and engender high levels of motivation and effort.

Modifying Self-Talk

Some individuals may not even be aware of their self-talk or its potential to impact performance. Sport and exercise psychologists work with individuals to help them use self-talk effectively. For individuals who have negative self-talk, steps can be taken to help them make changes. Williams and Leffingwell identify several approaches to modifying self-talk: thought stopping, changing negative thoughts to positive thoughts, countering, and reframing.[28]

Thought stopping uses a trigger or cue to immediately interrupt unwanted thoughts when they occur. An athlete who hears herself begin to say "I can't..." can interrupt this negative thought by saying to herself or out loud the word "Stop," or by visualizing a red traffic stop sign. Interrupting the negative thought before it leads to negative feelings and adversely influences behavior can have a beneficial effect on performance. With consistent use of thought-stopping, the frequency of unwanted negative self talk can be decreased.

Replacing negative thoughts with positive thoughts is another approach. With this approach, negative self-statements are immediately followed by positive self-statements. For example, a basketball player who misses a foul shot may make the negative statement "I never am good from the foul line." The player can replace that negative statement with "I made five of my eight shots tonight. With more practice, I can increase that percentage." Compared to thought stopping, this approach encourages individuals to replace a negative thought with a positive one, rather than simply stopping the negative thought.

Countering focuses on challenging individuals' beliefs that lead them to accept negative statements as being the truth. Countering uses facts, reason, and rational thinking to refute negative thoughts. Once these negative thoughts are refuted, individuals are more accepting of positive self-statements. For example, an athlete may perceive herself as someone who chokes under pressure can counter that belief by examining her past performances in pressure situations. When the evidence is reviewed, it shows that the athlete actually performs well under pressure, especially in critical games. Now she is helped to replace the negative thought with "I know I can come through under pressure."

The technique of *reframing* focuses on altering individuals' view of the world or changing their perspective. Through this approach, negative statements are changed to positive statements by interpreting the situation differently. An athlete who is nervous and perceives his pounding heart as reflecting his anxiety can reinterpret this as "I'm geared up and ready to go." Athletes fearful of competition and the associated stress of winning and losing can be helped to reinterpret competition as a challenge and an opportunity to test themselves while providing the additional benefit of identifying areas of improvement.

Changing the self-talk of individuals presents a challenge to sport and exercise psychologists.

First, individuals may not be aware of their negative self talk. Before modifying self-talk, sport and exercise psychologists need to help individuals realize that self-talk can be self-defeating and adversely influence performance. Exploring the underlying beliefs that perpetuate negative self-talk, such as low self-esteem, is also an important part of the process. In some cases, dealing with the underlying cause of the negative self-talk will require additional interventions. Another challenge is that thought patterns are deeply ingrained and changing them, just like changing any other habit, requires motivation, new skills, practice, and patience.

For greatest effectiveness in modifying negative self-talk, Williams and Leffingwell suggest using a combination of thought stoppage, changing negative thoughts to positive thoughts, reframing and countering.[28] Self-talk is only one cognitive approach that can be used to enhance the performance of individuals as well as their personal development.

The use of self-talk is not limited to the realm of athletics. Students in physical education classes can be taught to use cognitive strategies, such as self-talk, to enhance their feelings of competence as movers. When starting a new activity unit, some students might engage in self-talk such as "I'm no good at this." This negative statement and others like them result in loss of motivation and lack of effort. Instead, students can be helped to reframe their self-talk and to see that the new unit presents them with an opportunity to improve their skills or learn new ones.

Self-talk can play a critical role in the adoption of a physically active lifestyle. Middle-aged individuals just beginning an exercise program after two decades of inactivity may experience self-defeating thoughts that ultimately may lead to their discontinuing participation. "I can't do this—I was never athletic anyway" may precipitate participant dropout. Self-talk may also affect participation in rehabilitation programs. For example, a gymnast rehabilitating a shoulder after rotator cuff surgery may be beset with self-doubts about whether he will be able to return to competition. Negative self-talk such as "This is a waste of time" may lead to less than full effort being expended during the performance of the rehabilitation exercises. As a professional, you need to recognize that such negative self-talk can have an adverse impact on achievements by participants in your programs. With training, physical educators, exercise scientists, and sport professionals can learn how to effectively modify self-talk to enhance the experiences of participants in their programs.

MENTAL IMAGERY TO ENHANCE PERFORMANCE

Imagery is an important mental training tool found to be effective in improving the performance of athletes. Recreational marathoners, Olympic platform divers, and professional golfers are among the thousands of athletes that use imagery to improve their performance. Imagery develops a blueprint for performance, enabling athletes to improve their physical skills and psychological functioning during competition. Imagery can assist athletes in attaining their goals.

Vealey and Greenleaf define *imagery* as the "process of using all the senses to re-create or create an experience in the mind."[28] Anderson explains that "mental imagery occurs when a person images an experience. The person 'sees' the image, 'feels' the movements and/or the environment in which it takes place, and 'hears' the sounds of the movement—the crowd, the water, the starting gun."[29] In contrast to daydreaming, imagery is a systematic process that is consciously controlled by the person, who takes an active role in creating and manipulating the images and structuring the experience. Imagery does not involve overt physical movements. Imagery in conjunction with physical practice can improve performance.

Nature of Imagery

There are two types of imagery: external imagery and internal imagery. Athletes who engage in *external imagery* see themselves performing as if they were watching a video of their performance. For instance, when a golfer observes herself completing a putt for par on a sunny day or a quarterback watches himself successfully throw a pass through the hands of a defender to the outstretched hands of his receiver, they are using external imagery.

Internal imagery is when athletes construct the image of the performance from the perspective of their own eyes, as if they were inside their body when executing the skill. From this perspective, athletes' images are formed from what they would actually see, feel, and hear in the situation if they were actually there. Using internal imagery, a surfer would feel her muscles tense and relax as she balances and moves up and down the board, adjusting her body position to ride the wave; she would see the sun beating down on the ocean, the waves forming, and her feet's position on the board. She would notice the sparkling water droplets from the ocean on her body, and hear the sound of the surf. Athletes using internal imagery see the experience from within themselves.

Athletes who are skilled at the use of imagery can use both the internal and external perspectives effectively. Some sport psychologists suggest that internal imagery is most effective for rehearsing skills and refining performance, and external imagery may be most helpful in assisting athletes to correct critical aspects of their performance.[28]

Vividness is a critical feature of imagery. *Vividness* refers to the clarity and detail of the mental image constructed by the athletes. Vividness is enhanced through the use of color, incorporation of multiple senses, and integration of emotion within the imagery.[28] Imagery goes beyond just the visualization or seeing of an event. The incorporation of other senses, such as kinesthetic (sensations of the body as it moves into different positions), gustatory (taste), olfactory (smell), auditory (hearing), and tactile (touch) senses, adds much to the vividness of the image.

The use of multiple senses enriches the detail of the image. If you compare the two descriptions of the images that follow, it is easy to see how the use of multiple senses enhances the image. One swimmer uses only vision in constructing a visualization of his event—the 400-yard individual medley. The swimmer images swimming and seeing the wall coming closer and closer with each stroke as he approaches the turn. Another swimmer also visualizes the wall coming closer and closer with each stroke. But he adds information from his other senses to increase the richness of the image. The swimmer images feeling the undulations of his body in the butterfly stroke, smelling the familiar odor of the chlorine in the pool, maintaining the pressure on the palms of his hands and soles of his feet with each stroke, and hearing the roar of the crowd as he sprints home with his freestyle, closing in on a record time.

Adding emotions to imagery further enhances its vividness. The swimmer can enhance his image by adding the feelings associated with the anxiety he experiences as he walks out on deck to the event, waiting behind the starting block to be introduced. As he hears himself being introduced and the roar of the crowd, he can feel the excitement of the race and the challenge it presents, and replace anxiety with the confidence he has gained from months of hard work. As he completes the race and looks up to the scoreboard to see his time, he can image feeling jubilant and excited at achieving a personal best. In experiencing these emotions, athletes should tune into the associated physiological responses, such as their heart rate or sweaty palms, and recognize the positive and negative thoughts associated with the various emotions. Emotions coupled with multisensory input enhance the effectiveness of imagery.

Controllability is an essential feature of effective imagery. Vealey and Greenleaf define *controllability* as "the ability of athletes to imagine exactly what they intend to imagine, and also the ability to manipulate aspects of the images that they wish to change."[25] Athletes must be able to control their images so that they can manipulate the image in certain ways to focus on critical aspects of performance. The ability to control images allows athletes to re-create experiences and view them from different perspectives. It also allows athletes to place themselves in situations that have not occurred previously and rehearse different ways to effectively deal with these situations. If the situation occurs, athletes can respond to it competently and confidently because they have imagined their response. Being able to control the content and perspective of the image is critical to its effectiveness.

Uses of Imagery

Imagery is a versatile mental training technique and can be used in many different ways by athletes to enhance their performance. Vealey and Greenleaf identify seven uses for imagery: developing sport skills, correcting errors, rehearsing performance strategies, creating an optimal mental focus for competition, developing preperformance routines, learning and enhancing mental skills, and facilitating recovery from injuries and return to competition.[25]

Learning and practicing sport skills is one way that imagery can enhance athletes' performances. Athletes should select one or two skills to rehearse in their mind. They should rehearse these skills, focusing their imagery on executing the skill perfectly; this practice will help create a mental blueprint of the response. Athletes should incorporate as much relevant sensory information as they can. Athletes who are just beginning to learn a skill may benefit from viewing video of correctly performed skills. Coaches can also demonstrate the correct performance as well as provide verbal cues that will assist the athlete in correctly sequencing the skill's components or

---

IMAGERY USES

- Learn and practice sport skills
- Correct errors
- Rehearse performance strategies
- Optimize mental focus
- Enhance preperformance routines
- Strengthen mental skills
- Facilitate recovery from injury

mastering its timing. Athletes can perform the imagery on their own or the coach can incorporate imagery into the regular practice.

Error correction is another use for imagery. Athletes frequently receive feedback from their coaches suggesting corrections in skill execution or adjustments in execution of strategies. To enhance the effectiveness of this feedback, athletes can use imagery. After receiving feedback from the coach, athletes should image their performance with the corrections integrated into the image. Imagery allows athletes to experience how the skill or play looks and feels when performed correctly.

Learning and practicing performance strategies is another way that imagery can be used effectively by athletes. This allows athletes to rehearse what they would do in specific situations. For example, after a coach reviews set plays on a corner kick, soccer players can image themselves moving through the plays. This approach can also be used after the coach reviews a scouting report on an opponent. Using imagery, players can rehearse the strategies they will use against the opponent. For example, basketball players can rehearse the strategies they will use to counter the opponents' full-court press.

Imagery is also a useful tool for athletes seeking to optimize their mental focus. They can rehearse creating and maintaining a strong mental focus during competition. Vealey and Greenleaf suggest that coaches can assist athletes with this aspect of imagery by posing and helping answer two questions: "What will it be like?" and "How will I respond?"[28] Helping athletes understand the distractions, crowd noise and booing, and challenges in the competitive environment, such as poor officiating, allows them to imagine themselves effectively dealing with these situations. This advance preparation helps athletes to respond with greater confidence and composure, not react. Imagery allows athletes to gain experience in responding to a diversity of competitive challenges, whether expected or not.

Imagery is often incorporated into preperformance routines. Many athletes have a set routine they use prior to the performance of a skill, and imagery is a part of this routine. For example, a basketball player taking a free throw carefully positions her feet a certain way at the line, bounces the ball a set number of times, spins the ball in her hands, places her hands for the shot, and then takes a deep breath and exhales before shooting. Before releasing the ball, the player visualizes it leaving her hand, spinning, and entering the basket without touching a rim. Preperformance routines have beneficial effects on athletes' performance. These routines are practiced until they are automatic, essentially becoming part of the skill sequence.

Imagery can be used to strengthen a variety of mental skills critical to athletes' performance. It can enhance self-confidence and engender feelings of competence. This can be done by having athletes mentally re-create past successful performances, focusing on their accomplishments and the feelings associated with them. They can also rehearse via imagery coping confidently with performance errors, effectively managing their emotions in the heat of competition, and assertively meeting unexpected challenges during performance. The regulation of arousal is another way imagery can be used by athletes. Athletes can use imagery to psych up for a competition or to decrease their arousal if too high.

Facilitating recovery from injury and return to competition is another way that athletes can use imagery. When athletes cannot participate in practices because they are injured, they can attend practices and mentally image rehearsing skills and strategies. They can imagine themselves engaging in practices, performing drills, and scrimmaging, just as if they were participating. Imagery can also be used by athletes to enhance their recovery by setting rehabilitation goals and imaging their attainment.

Imagery can be used in many different ways to enhance athletes' performance. It can facilitate the learning of skills and correction of mistakes, and provide opportunities to rehearse and experiment with different performance strategies and tactics. Imagery can be used to strengthen athletes' mental skills and to aid in returning to

---

FOCUS ON CAREER: Exercise and Sport Psychology

PROFESSIONAL
ORGANIZATIONS

- American Psychological Association—Division 47: Exercise and Sport Psychology
  (www.apa47.org)
- Association for the Advancement of Applied Sport Psychology
  (www.aaasponline.org)
- North American Society for the Psychology of Sport and Physical Activity
  (www.naspspa.org)

PROFESSIONAL
JOURNALS

- *Journal of Applied Sport Psychology*
- *Journal of Sport and Exercise Psychology*
- *Research Quarterly for Exercise and Sport*
- *The Sport Psychologist*

---

competition following injury. Athletes use imagery during their training, immediately prior to and during a competitive event, and following competition. When using imagery, it is important that the skill or situation be visualized correctly. If the skill is imaged incorrectly, performance decrement could occur. As imagery is learned and practiced, users should be encouraged to be accurate and precise in their imagery in order to gain maximum benefit.

Imagery is an important mental skill. Even though imagery was discussed in relation to athletes, it can be used in a variety of performance situations, such as public speaking or taking the National Athletic Trainers' Association certification exam. Imagery, goal setting, and self-talk are important mental skills that can enhance the learning and performance of people in a variety of situations.

INTERVENTION STRATEGIES

In recent years, coaches, teachers, and sport psychologists have turned to a variety of intervention strategies to help athletes achieve their optimal performance. As discussed earlier, anxiety and arousal can have harmful effects on athletes'

performance. Athletes' performance can also suffer due to lack of motivation, poor level of self-confidence, and, because of the intimate relationship between the mind and the body, negative thoughts and feelings about themselves and their capabilities. With the help of appropriate intervention techniques, athletes learn skills and strategies to regulate their physiological and psychological state to achieve optimum performance.

Sometimes athletes experience excessive anxiety and arousal, which causes a deterioration in their performance. Intervention strategies focusing on reducing this level would benefit these athletes. One way to deal with elevated levels of arousal is through the use of a variety of relaxation techniques. These techniques teach the individual to scan the body for tension (arousal is manifested in increased muscular tension) and, after identifying a higher-than-optimal level of tension, to reduce the tension to the appropriate level by relaxing. Once specific relaxation techniques are learned, this process should take only a few minutes. Types of relaxation training include progressive relaxation, autogenic training, transcendental meditation, and biofeedback. A note of caution is in order here, however. Athletes should be careful not to relax or reduce their level of arousal too much, because this will have a harmful influence on their performance.

In recent years, the use of cognitive strategies to facilitate optimum performance has gained increased acceptance. Cognitive strategies teach athletes psychological skills that they can employ in their mental preparation for competition. In addition to focusing on alleviating the harmful effects of anxiety and arousal, these cognitive strategies can also be used to enhance motivation and self-confidence and to improve performance consistency. These approaches include cognitive restructuring, thought stopping, self-talk, hypnosis and self-hypnosis, goal setting, and mental imagery.

Some cognitive intervention techniques focus on changing athletes' thoughts and perceptions. Self-talk, previously discussed, is an example of a cognitive intervention technique. Cognitive strategies can also be used to alter athletes' perceptions of events, thus reducing anxiety. Affirmation of athletes' ability to succeed in an upcoming competition is another cognitive strategy frequently used to promote optimal performance.

Imagery is the visualization of a situation. This technique has been used in a variety of ways to enhance performance. It can be used to mentally practice skills or to review outstanding previous performances. By remembering the kinesthetic sensations associated with the ideal performance, the athlete hopes to replicate or improve performance. Imagery has also been used as an anxiety reduction technique. The athlete visualizes anxiety-producing situations and then sees himself or herself successfully coping with the experience, thus increasing confidence to perform successfully in similar situations.

Intervention strategies have proved useful in helping athletes maximize their performance. These strategies are not only for athletes but also have implications for all participants in physical activities and sport. For example, the beginning jogger may derive as much benefit from goal setting as the high-level performer. The practitioner using these strategies must be cognizant of individual differences; otherwise, performance may be affected adversely.

The growth of sport and exercise psychology has provided physical education, exercise science, and sport professionals with a clearer understanding of various psychological factors that may affect an individual's performance. Sport and exercise psychologists have been able to enhance individual performance through the use of a diversity of intervention strategies. Although much of the work done in the area of sport psychology has been with athletes, many of the findings and techniques are applicable to participants in a variety of physical activity settings such as school, community, and corporate fitness programs. As the field of sport and exercise psychology continues to expand, practitioners will gain further insight into how to enhance the performance of all individuals.

SUMMARY

Sport and exercise psychology is concerned with the application of psychological theories and concepts to sport and physical activity. Although the physiological benefits of physical activity are well documented, physical education, exercise science, and sport professionals also need to be familiar with the psychological benefits of engaging in physical activity on a regular basis. Unfortunately, too many adults are inactive, and many adults who start a physical activity program drop out. Motivation influences the initiation, maintenance, and intensity of behavior. Exercise adherence focuses on understanding the factors that influence initiation and continuation of physical activity programs. Several theories have been used in research on physical activity participation and health behavior change, including classic learning theories, the belief model, the transtheoretical model, social cognitive theory, and the ecological perspective.

Sport psychologists have studied many different areas relative to athletic performance, including personality, anxiety, and arousal. Goal setting, imagery, and self-talk are three approaches used to help individuals improve their performance. To help athletes perform at their best, sport psychologists assist athletes in learning and using a variety of intervention strategies. Some of the findings, methodology, and intervention strategies of sport psychologists can also be used in other physical activity settings to help us better understand and enhance the experiences of participants in our physical activity programs.

DISCUSSION QUESTIONS

1. Motivation affects our initiation, persistence, and intensity of behavior. Reflect back on your participation in athletics or consider your commitment to being physically active on a daily basis. What motivated you to begin participating in your sport or to start working out? If you ended your participation, what were the reasons for discontinuing? Were you more intrinsically or extrinsically motivated?

2. Many different models have been developed to provide a framework to understand and promote behavior change. Which model do you believe has the greatest potential to encourage adults to change from a sedentary lifestyle to a more active one? Explain your choice. What commonalities do you find between the models and how can you use this information to help participants engaged in physical activity programs?

3. Think carefully about your experiences in organized sport. What strategies did coaches use to motivate the team and psych them up for competition? Which strategies were the most effective and which were least effective? Why? How did coaches account for individual differences among athletes in their motivational strategies?

4. Self-talk can have an impact on performance, either facilitating or hindering achievement. Think back to a recent performance situation, in either sport or another aspect of your life, perhaps like giving a speech. What was your self-talk before, during, and after the event? Did it help, hurt, or not impact your performance?

SELF-ASSESSMENT ACTIVITIES

These activities are designed to help you determine if you have mastered the materials and competencies presented in this chapter.

1. Justify the claim that participation in physical activity can have positive psychological benefits. Develop a 500-word essay to substantiate your claim.

2. Using the information provided in the Get Connected box, access the MindTools or Athletic Insight site and read about one of the topics in sport and exercise psychology. Choose a topic that interests you. Then write one to two pages summarizing what you have learned and discussing how you can apply that information in your professional career.

3. Too many people are inactive on a regular basis. Furthermore, many people who begin an exercise program drop out. Using the information on exercise adherence, create a brochure that highlights both the physiological and psychological benefits of regular physical activity. Then include in your brochure information that would encourage people to begin and stay involved in a program (e.g., small groups with individually designed exercise programs). Be sure to include images and pictures highlighting physical activity and a catchy title.

4. In recent years, the field of sport psychology has expanded tremendously. As a practitioner, whether a teacher, coach, adapted physical educator, athletic trainer, or exercise physiologist, you are concerned with optimizing individuals' performance. Discuss the roles of anxiety, arousal, attention, self-talk, and goal setting in the performance of motor skills and the use of intervention strategies to enhance performance.

REFERENCES

1. Vealey RS: Psychology of sport and exercise. In SJ Hoffman and JC Harris, editors, Introduction to kinesiology: studying physical activity, Champaign, Ill., 2000, Human Kinetics.

2. Association for Applied Sport Psychology (www.appliedpsychonline.org).

3. International Society of Sport Psychology (www.issponline.org).

4. Gill D: Sport and exercise psychology. In JD Massengale and RA Swanson, editors, The history of exercise and sport science, Champaign, Ill., 1997, Human Kinetics.

5. US Department of Health and Human Services: Physical activity and health: a report of the surgeon general, Atlanta, Ga., 1996, US Department of Health and Human Services, Centers for Disease Control and Prevention, National Center for Chronic Disease Prevention and Health Promotion.

6. Berger BG: Psychological benefits of an active lifestyle: what we know and what we need to know, Quest 48:330–353, 1996.

7. Cox RH: Sport psychology: concepts and applications, ed 5, New York, 2002, McGraw-Hill.

8. Petruzzello SJ: Exercise and sports psychology. In SB Brown, Introduction to exercise science, Philadelphia, 2001, Lippincott Williams & Wilkins.

9. Fontaine KR: Physical activity improves mental health, The Physician and Sportsmedicine 28(10):83–84, 2000.

10. Brannon L and Feist J: Health psychology: an introduction to behavior and health, ed 2, Belmont, Calif., 1992, Wadsworth.

11. Dishman RK and Sallis JF: Determinants and interventions for physical activity and exercise. In C Brochard, RJ Shephard, and T Stephens, editors, Physical activity and health, fitness, and health: international proceedings and consensus statement, Champaign, Ill., 1994, Human Kinetics.

12. Prochaska JO and Velicer WF: The transtheoretical model of health behavior change, American Journal of Health Promotion 12:38–48, 1997.

13. Samuelson M: Commentary: changing unhealthy lifestyle: who's ready . . . who's not?: an argument in support of the stages of change component of the transtheoretical model, American Journal of Health Promotion 12:13–14, 1997.

14. Duffy FD, with Schnirring L: How to counsel patients about exercise—An office-friendly approach, The Physician and Sportsmedicine 28(10):53–54, 2000.

15. Herrick AB, Stone WJ, and Mettler MM: Stages of change, decisional balance, and self-efficacy across four health behaviors in a worksite environment, Journal of Health Promotion 12:49–56, 1997.

16. Leffingwell TR, Rider SP, and Williams JM: Application of the transtheoretical model to psychological skills training, The Sport Psychologist, 15:168–187, 2001.

17. King AC, Blair SN, Bild DE, Dishman RK, Dubbert PK, Marcus BH, Oldridge NB, Paffenbarge RS, Jr., Powell KE, and Yaeger KK: Determinants of physical activity and intervention in adults, Medicine and Science in Sports and Exercise Supplement 24(6):S221–S236, 1992.

18. Nieman, DC: Fitness and sports medicine: an introduction, Palo Alto, Calif., 1990, Bull.

19. Fisher AC, Scriber KC, Matheny ML, Alderman MH, and Bitting LA: Enhancing athletic injury rehabilitation adherence, Journal of Athletic Training 28(4):312–318, 1993.

20. Bianco T and Eklund RC: Conceptual considerations for social support research and exercise settings: the case of sport injury, Journal of Sport and Exercise Psychology, 23:85–107, 2001.

21. Anshel MH: Sport psychology from theory to practice, Scottsdale, Ariz., 1997, Gorsuch Scarisbrick.

22. Cox RH: Sport psychology concepts and applications, ed 6, New York, 2007, McGraw-Hill.

23. Levitt EE: The psychology of anxiety, Hillsdale, N.J., 1980, Earlbaum.

24. Weinberg RS: Goal setting in sport and exercise: research to practice. In JL Van Raalte and BW

Brewer, Exploring sport and exercise psychology, ed 2, Washington, D.C., 2002, American Psychological Association.

25. Vealey RS and Greenleaf CA: Seeing is believing: understanding and using imagery in sport. In JM Williams, Applied sport psychology: personal growth to peak performance, ed 5, New York, 2006, McGraw-Hill.

26. Locke EA, Shaw KN, Saari LM, and Latham GP: Goal-setting and task performance, Psychological Bulletin 90:125–152, 1981.

27. Weinberg RS and Gould D: Foundations of sport and exercise psychology, Champaign, Ill., 1999, Human Kinetics.

28. Williams JM and Leffingwell TR: Cognitive strategies in sport and exercise psychology. In JL Van Raalte and BW Brewer, Exploring sport and exercise psychology, ed 2, Washington, D.C., 2002, American Psychological Association.

29. Anderson A: Learning strategies in physical education: self-talk, imagery, and goal-setting, JOPERD 68(1):30–35, 1997.

SPORT PEDAGOGY

OBJECTIVES

After reading this chapter the student should be able to—

- Define physical education, sport pedagogy, curriculum, instruction, and assessment.
- Understand how the standards-based movement has influenced physical education programs in relation to curricular development, instructional processes, and assessment.
- Describe factors that influence curriculum development and know the goal, purpose, and characteristics of different curriculum models implemented in physical education.
- Describe the role of assessment in physical education programs and apply different types of assessments within instruction.
- Discuss how to be an effective physical education teacher.
- Discuss how the hidden curriculum, differences, and diversity influence students' experiences in physical education.

What can be done to increase quality daily physical education for all students in our schools? Physical education, exercise science, and sport professionals must take a leadership role in advocating for physical education. As advocates, we must be able to articulate the benefits of quality physical education and be knowledgeable about the role of physical activity in advancing the nation's health goals. As professionals, we must conduct quality programs, incorporate the physical education content standards, and assess student learning on a regular basis. Professionals must forge collaborative relationships with policy makers, community and school leaders, parents, and youths to increase physical education in the schools and expand opportunities for involvement in physical activity within the community. Although sport pedagogy most closely aligns with physical education teachers, exercise scientists and sport leaders have an important role in promoting physical activity outside of the school setting. Conducting quality programs, advocating for increased opportunities for physical activity, including daily physical education, and becoming actively involved in working for change are just some ways that professionals in physical education, exercise science, and sport can contribute to increasing physical activity opportunities for all people.

GET CONNECTED

PELinks4U—offers information on a variety of topics related to physical education, coaching, and adapted physical education, interdisciplinary efforts, and teaching in physical education.

www.pelinks4u.org

National Association for Sport and Physical Education—includes valuable information for physical educators to enhance their professional practice and their support for physical education, sport, and physical activity programs.

www.aahperd.org/naspe/

TPSR Alliance—provides information on teaching responsibility through physical activity, which includes news, events, current projects, and additional publications and links.

www.tpsr-alliance.org

PE Central—offers information on how teachers can incorporate assessment into their programs, including the purpose and importance of assessment, examples and ideas, and additional resources.

www.pecentral.org/assessment/assessment.html

SPORT PEDAGOGY: AN OVERVIEW

At a time when obesity rates continue to rise and physical activity levels decrease, sport pedagogy has become more important than ever before. Sport pedagogy continues to develop and evolve within the standards-based movement educational era. The emphasis on standards, assessment, and student learning has brought credibility and accountability to physical education. Although there is a dire need for students to be engaged in physical education and physical activity within and outside of school, sport pedagogy continues to face challenges within educational institutions. The definition and scope, historical development, and areas of study are discussed in this section.

Definition and Scope

Sport pedagogy is concerned with the study of teaching and learning processes of physical activity. Throughout the world, sport pedagogy has also been referred to as physical education pedagogy or pedagogy of physical activity. Regardless of the term used, each of these places an emphasis on curriculum and instruction (i.e., teaching) and

teacher education.[1,2] Furthermore, sport pedagogical work is primarily emphasized in K–12 physical education and sport coaching. For the purpose of this chapter, sport pedagogy will focus on physical education teaching in K–12 schools.

Physical education is the subject matter taught in schools that provide K–12 students with opportunities to learn and have meaningful content and appropriate instruction. Quality physical education programs focus on increasing physical competence, health-related fitness, self-responsibility, and enjoyment of physical activity for all students so that they can be physically active for a lifetime.[3] For this to occur, the National Association for Sport and Physical Education developed physical education content standards that provide outcomes for elementary, middle, and high school students to achieve by the end of their grade band.

Sport pedagogy has a rich tradition in physical education, exercise science, and sport. For many years, physical education was considered the overarching field of the 12 subdisciplines. Today, there is no consensus on the name of the field. Some argue that the field should be called kinesiology, while others refer to the field as

LIFESPAN AND CULTURAL PERSPECTIVES: Sport Pedagogy

- How can students with low skill ability come to value physical activity?
- How does a school community's socioeconomic status influence students' learning opportunities in physical education?
- What impact do K–12 physical education experiences have on adults and older adults' enjoyment and engagement in physical activity?
- How often and for how long should elementary, middle, and high school students receive physical education?
- How should students with disabilities be integrated into physical education classes?
- What role should parents and the community play in students' physical activity in and out of school?
- Do students' gender and race play a factor in the development of physical education programs?

physical education, exercise science, and sport. Many scholars and professionals believe that physical education has transitioned into a subdiscipline, sport pedagogy. Thus, the scope of sport pedagogy is broad in nature as it intersects with other subdisciplines due to the emphasis on teaching and learning in relation to human movement and physical activity.

Historical Development

Sport pedagogy emerged as a specialized area of study in the 1960s. Sport pedagogy traces its roots from ancient Greece and Rome and the early modern European gymnastics programs of Germany, Sweden, and Great Britain in the 1700s and 1800s. The original field of physical education continues to influence the subdiscipline of sport pedagogy today.

The 1970s were a significant time period in the growth and development of sport pedagogy. Prior to 1970, research on curriculum and instruction, and doctoral programs to train experts in pedagogical research, did not exist in higher education; however, that changed in the late 1970s as doctoral programs were established and began to produce teacher educators in physical education.[1,4] Classic scholarly works such as Dunkin and Biddle's *The Study of Teaching* (1974) and Lawrence Locke's "New Hope for a Dismal

Science" ignited a plethora of research on sport pedagogy. John Nixon was one of the leaders in founding sport pedagogy as a scholarly line of inquiry within education, as he, along with Locke, wrote a chapter on sport pedagogy in the *Second Handbook of Research on Teaching* (1973).

Scholars such as William Anderson, Daryl Siedentop, Ann Jewett, John Cheffers, and Locke conducted descriptive-analytic research that used systematic observation instruments to describe events and the interactions between teachers and students in physical education classes.[1,4] Furthermore, in 1975, the American Alliance for Health, Physical Education, Recreation, and Dance (AAHPERD) created the National Association for Sport and Physical Education (NASPE) and established the Curriculum and Instruction Academy.

Although research was being conducted in sport pedagogy, it wasn't until the 1980s that research articles were published in journals such as *Research Quarterly for Exercise and Sport, Quest,* and the newly developed *Journal of Teaching in Physical Education.* Throughout the 1980s, sport pedagogues' research focus was on measuring student learning; thus, many researchers conducted studies on academic learning time in physical education.

In 1982, the first sport pedagogy meeting—the CIC Big Ten Symposium on Research on

Teaching in Physical Education—was held at Purdue University, and in 1986, Lynn Housner formulated a special interest group within the already established American Education Research Association (AERA) for research on learning and instruction in physical education.[1,4] The involvement in AERA and dissemination of research in scholarly journals decreased sport pedagogy's marginality and provided it some legitimacy within the larger educational community. Quality research and professional development continues to be at the forefront of the sport pedagogy community today.

In sport pedagogy, teachers educate students on the critical elements of skills and movements, such as jumping rope. Here, students are jumping rope in their personal space and at their own pace.

Areas of Study

Research in sport pedagogy has covered many topics of interest over the past 40 years. Researchers have investigated teacher characteristics, different methods of instruction, teacher and student behaviors, the relationship between teacher behaviors and student achievement, the amount of time students are engaged in physical education content, and curricular development. Furthermore, some scholars have studied varying social issues (e.g., gender, race, (dis)ability, socioeconomic status, sexuality) within the context of physical education and how they influence student learning.

Sport pedagogy research is conducted in K–12 schools with physical education teachers and students. Researchers in sport pedagogy may address questions such as:

- How does appropriate practice develop motor skills, improve performance, and enhance student learning?
- How much time are students engaged in physical activity throughout a physical education class?
- How do different curriculum models enhance students' participation, enjoyment, and learning in physical education?
- How does personal and social responsibility influence students' comfort, sportspersonship, and engagement in physical education?
- To what extent does the social and public context of physical education impact students' experiences in physical education?
- How does motivation influence student engagement, performance, and level of participation?
- What strategies can teachers utilize to implement assessments within their instruction to determine if their students have learned?
- How do teachers and students navigate or address social issues (e.g., (dis)ability, gender, race, socioeconomic status, sexuality) in the physical education setting?

These are only a few of the questions that can be addressed in sport pedagogy research. In answering these questions, researchers and teachers can learn the best practices and classroom environments that will best meet the needs of students and enhance learning opportunities. These questions also reflect an alignment with the NASPE physical education content standards and the three learning domains (i.e., psychomotor, cognitive, and affective) as researchers and physical education teachers attempt to teach and learn about the whole student. The next sections in this chapter focus on the primary components needed to develop a quality physical education program.

STANDARDS-BASED EDUCATION

As a major institution of our society, education significantly influences the life of our nation. Today, at the beginning of the twenty-first century, we are entering an era in which technological advances, scientific progress, exponential knowledge growth, and greater diversity within our population will transform our society in many dramatic ways. It is within this context that America's educational institutions face the challenge of preparing today's students to live and work in tomorrow's world.

NO CHILD LEFT BEHIND 2002

Stronger Accountability for Results

- Annual testing in reading and mathematics; periodic testing in science
- Adequate Yearly Progress reports documenting students' learning
- Attainment of proficiency in core subjects
- Closing achievement gaps among population groups
- Educational services for students with limited English proficiency

More Freedom for States and Communities

- Streamlined educational programs
- Greater budgetary control at local levels
- Discretionary use of educational funds to enhance student learning, upgrade educational technology, and increase pay for teachers and staff
- Emphasis on teacher and staff development

Proven Education Methods

- Use of methods proven to be effective in promoting student learning
- Recruitment and retention of qualified teachers and paraprofessionals

More Choices For Parents

- Parental involvement in school decision
- Parental choice with option to transfer child from school in need of improvement to better-performing school within district
- Opportunity to transfer child from unsafe school environment
- No-cost supplemental educational services, including tutoring, after school academic programs, and summer programs

Source: US Department of Education. Overview—Four Pillars of NCLB, the No Child Left Behind Act. (http://www2.ed.gov/nclb/overview/intro/4pillars.html). Retrieved 27 June 2010.

To successfully tackle these challenges, American education over the past 20 years has undergone significant reform as it entered into a standards-based education era. Prior to this movement, education throughout the country greatly varied from state to state and community to community. The national standards movement was not a quest to develop a national curriculum; rather, the charge was to formulate educational goals for the nation on "what a students should know and be able to do."[3,5] Another purpose of the national standards movement was to decrease the achievement gap between the economically advantaged and disadvantaged, whites and minority students, immigrant and natural-born children, and students with or without disabilities.[3,6] In 2001, federal legislation proposed a new educational initiative, the No Child Left Behind Act (NCLB), to narrow the achievement gap.[7] NCLB mandates greater accountability for student learning. The goal of NCLB is to have every child attain proficiency in reading and mathematics. Four

principles are the driving force behind achieving this goal: stronger accountability for results, more freedom for states and communities, proven education methods, and more choices for parents.[8] (For more information on the four principles, see the No Child Left Behind 2002 box.)

NCLB did not identify physical education specifically as a subject in which children should become proficient; however, it does have implications for physical education. As physical educators, we too must be committed to closing the achievement gap between those students who are fit and unfit, those who are skilled and unskilled, and those who are active and those leading a sedentary lifestyle. No child should be left behind, whether in reading or physical education.

Standards and assessment of learning are important in physical education, too, not just in math or reading. NASPE answered the call of the national standards movement in 1995 when it published the first edition of *Moving into the Future: National Standards for Physical*

The standards-based movement has influenced physical education programs to focus on student learning within the psychomotor, cognitive, and affective domains. At the end of each class, it is important for physical education teachers to summarize the class or bring it to a close by asking students questions about the focus of the lesson content.

Education—A Guide to Content and Assessment.[9] In 2004, NASPE revised the content standards and published the second edition, entitled *Moving into the Future: National Standards for Physical Education.*[3] The NASPE standards provide a framework for student learning, specifically "what a student should know and be able to do as a result of a quality physical education program."[3] These standards have been adopted by most states as their physical education content standards and have been used by teachers, school districts, and teacher educators to guide the development of program curricula, unit and lesson plans (i.e., instruction), and assessments.

For standards to have meaning, assessment must be conducted to measure student learning in relation to the performance outcomes. A plethora of scholars and physical education teachers have developed assessment tools over the past 15 years, including the NASPE Assessment Series.[10] However, until the recent development of the PE Metrics texts, physical education did not have valid and reliable assessment instruments to measure student achievement of the national content standards.[11,12]

The standards-based assessment movement has advanced learning for many students throughout the country. Unfortunately, not all students are achieving, thus many are left behind. For all students to be successful, quality teachers need to be hired, quality programs developed, and both held accountable for student learning.

CURRICULUM DEVELOPMENT

The standards-based movement significantly changed physical education curricula (i.e., programs) throughout the nation. A physical education curriculum "includes all knowledge, skills, and learning experiences that are provided to students within the school program."[5] Prior to the development of the national standards, most physical education teachers based their programs on specific activities (e.g., basketball, volleyball, flag football) they selected to teach, which were usually determined by their area of expertise and the number of students that could partake in an activity at one time. With the development of the national standards, the activity became the medium through which instruction was delivered for students to achieve performance outcomes. That is, the standards became the focal point rather than the activity. Figure 10-1 demonstrates how each component of a physical education program works or aligns with the rest.

Before we continue to discuss the changes in curricular development over the years, it is important for you to get a sense of your own experiences in physical education. What were your physical education programs like at the elementary, middle, and high school levels? Did your programs focus more on sports, fitness, cooperation, dance, or recreational activities? How did your teachers deliver the instruction? Did they make all of the decisions or were you (i.e., the students) included in some of the decision making? Did you work on skill development and then play a game or was the game the primary focus of your classes? What did you learn in physical education, and how do you know if you learned?

For physical education teachers who have been teaching for many years, the standards-based movement significantly shifted their thinking in regard to program, unit, and lesson plan development. As physical education teachers, unit and lesson planning is the primary focus of what occurs before teaching lessons to students. Although some teachers think well on their feet and can create activities and tasks on the spot, in a standards-based curriculum it is very important that planning occur in advance to ensure that the content taught is based on standards and objectives and ultimately has a purpose. A *unit of instruction* (e.g., basketball, dance) incorporates all of the goals, objectives, content (i.e., tasks, activities, key terms, and concepts), instructional materials, and individual lessons. The *unit plan* allows teachers to make sure the content and tasks taught from lesson to lesson connect with one another and align with the standards and unit objectives. A *lesson plan* is a specific outline of all of the objectives, tasks, and assessments that

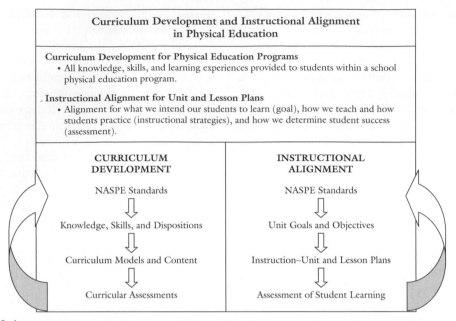

Figure 10-1   Curricular development and instructional alignment in physical education.

will be included for one particular lesson. Most often, physical education teachers first develop the unit plan and work off of that plan as they make changes to their instruction from lesson to lesson.

Over the past 15 years, many teachers have been challenged to reorganize a program they have delivered for an extended period of time. Professional development opportunities have been provided by college and university faculty in physical education teacher education programs, by each state's association, and at state, district, and national conferences. Even with the abundance of professional development opportunities and standards-based curricular texts, many physical education teachers have refused to restructure their program to be standards-based.

In addition to the education reform movement, other factors have contributed to the changes in physical education curriculum content. These factors include teachers' philosophies about physical education, geographic location, school and program context (e.g., facilities, equipment, class size), and time.[5,13]

Teachers' beliefs and philosophies about physical education provide the lens through which a program is developed. For example, do teachers emphasize teacher- or student-centered instruction? Will the content focus be on sport-related games or will other content, such as dance, gymnastics, self-defense, swimming, and outdoor pursuits be included in the curriculum? Should the focus be on competency and proficiency in motor skills or student engagement in physical activity regardless of performance? These questions need to be discussed with physical education faculty, especially at the secondary level, before a program can be developed.

Geographic location can also be a contributing factor when designing a physical education program. Do you live in the north, where you can include winter activities such as snowshoeing and cross-country skiing? Do you live around lakes or rivers, so you can teach units on canoeing, kayaking, or fishing? Are there hiking and biking trails in the vicinity to offer outdoor pursuits such as hiking or cycling? Most often, there are activities formulated that are specific to an area (e.g., cornhole is very popular in Ohio), which may pique students' interest if offered in physical education. Understandably, some of the activities are costly, which can prohibit programs from offering such units; however, physical education programs can connect with the physical education teacher education or recreation programs at state colleges and universities or apply for grants that are available to K–12 teachers. More than ever, it is important for physical educators to connect to physical activity options within the community as we encourage our students to be lifelong movers.

Physical educators are often challenged by the facilities in which physical education is taught, the equipment available for large or multiple classes, and large class sizes. Physical education classes are usually held in gymnasiums; however, elementary school teachers may have to teach in a gymnasium-cafeteria, may have a blacktop or outdoor grass space, and may at times have to teach in a hallway or classroom. Secondary school physical education teachers may have a gymnasium along with a wrestling room, auxiliary gym, weight room, fitness center, dance studio, or outdoor fields and tennis courts. The amount and type of equipment can vary from school to school and school district to school district. Funding is usually the primary factor in how much a physical education program will receive toward purchasing equipment. School systems with more funding, normally in higher socioeconomic communities, have more up-to-date equipment, compared to schools that receive less funding, which tend to be in lower socioeconomic communities. Lastly, class size significantly affects the curriculum, instruction, and form of assessment implemented in physical education. Physical education teachers need to know how many students are in each class and how many teachers are on each class period. School and program contexts such as facilities, equipment, and class size frequently influence one another.

Time is teachers' greatest challenge and barrier when developing a curriculum. Questions that need to be considered are, how long are the class periods, how often do the students have physical education, and how long should each unit last?

Geographic location, facilities, equipment, and time are some of the key factors that influence curricular development of physical education programs. Having access to facilities and equipment, such as tennis courts and racquets, creates valuable options to teach content that has potential to be a lifelong activity.

Since the educational reform movement and NCLB, the time students receive in physical education has significantly decreased, as pressure to spend more time on "academics" has increased. Currently, Illinois is the only state that has daily physical education.[14] Most elementary school students receive 30–60 minutes of physical education once or twice a week; middle school physical education programs vary from every other day for a full year to every day for a quarter or semester; and high school students receive as little as one quarter or semester of physical education throughout their 4 years in high school. Since 2008, there has been a 77% increase in the number of states that allow waivers and exemptions from high school physical education classes.[14]

CURRICULUM MODELS

As physical education teachers develop their curriculum, a teacher's philosophy, along with program goals and objectives, influences the focus of instruction. Teachers need to ask themselves if they are more focused on skill and motor competence, cooperation, and problem solving, or development of a personal fitness plan. Each of these foci aligns with the national standards; however, how instruction is delivered to students may differ. Thus, curriculum models have been developed by researchers, teacher educators, and physical education teachers over the past 20 years, as they believe these models are the "most effective way to deliver a meaningful and coherent physical education program. Curriculum models are focused, theme-based, and represent a particular philosophy."[5] (See the Curriculum Models in Physical Education box.)

Throughout this section, a brief introduction to the following curriculum models will be provided: skill themes, personal and social responsibility, teaching games for understanding and the tactical games model, sport education, fitness education, adventure education, outdoor education, and cultural studies. As you read about each of the models, it is important to remember that there is not a "one size fits all" model for all content taught in physical education. If teachers focus on sport-related games, the teaching games for understanding and the sport education models might be considered; whereas if the focus is on developing locomotor, nonlocomotor, and manipulative skills, the skill themes model should be the framework in which they base their planning.

Skill Themes

The skill themes approach, considered the "developmental model," is implemented in elementary school physical education. This approach has significantly evolved over the past 40–50 years. The skill themes approach originated in Great Britain and is based on Ralph Laban's movement analysis framework from the 1940s. This framework focuses on movement categories such as body awareness, space awareness, effort, and relationships. American teachers found the framework confusing and limited in regard to providing differentiated instruction for students of varying abilities. In 1980, Graham, Holt/Hale, McEwen, and Parker, in an effort to modify the framework with a movement education emphasis to address perceived shortcomings, developed the skill themes approach to games, sport, gymnastics, and dance.[5,15]

Movement skills and concepts are the basis of this model. Basic skills focus on performance and concepts describe how the skill is going to be performed. According to Holt/Hale, "teaching by skill themes is the teaching of skills, the combining of skills and concepts, to achieve the selected purpose or outcome."[16] There are four phases included in the skill themes approach:

1. Basic skill—mastery and achievement of the critical elements of the skill according to the age and developmental level of the students.
2. Combinations—addition of other skills and movement concepts once the basic skills and critical elements are mastered.
3. Skill in contexts—skills, movements, and combinations performed in a variety of contexts.
4. Culminating activity—application of the skill in different content areas within games, sport, gymnastics, and dance.[16]

The skill themes approach creates opportunities for all students to learn through developmentally appropriate skill theme progressions. Skill themes progress from simple to complex. All students may engage in the same skills and concepts; however, teachers will need to differentiate instruction according to students' skill development.

Personal and Social Responsibility

The personal and social responsibility model (PSRM) focuses on the development of the whole student, which includes how students think, feel,

CURRICULUM MODELS IN PHYSICAL EDUCATION

Models	Purpose/Goal	Grade Level
Skill Themes	Develops competence in fundamental movement skills and concepts; locomotor, nonlocomotor, and manipulative skills are taught within games and sports, gymnastics, and dance.	Elementary
Personal and Social Responsibility	Assigns students more responsibility for their personal and social development in physical activity settings both in and outside of school.	Elementary Middle High
Teaching Games for Understanding/ Tactical Games Model	Improves students' game performance by combining tactical awareness with skill execution to increase interest and excitement about games and sports.	Elementary—second and higher Middle High
Sport Education	Educates and develops students to be competent, literate, enthusiastic sportspersons through playing sports and undertaking various roles within the sport environment, such as coach, manager, official, and player.	Elementary—third and higher Middle High
Fitness Education	Uses many different approaches to incorporate fitness and wellness content into physical education programs by developing students' knowledge and skills to be physically active for a lifetime.	Elementary Middle High
Adventure Education	Involves activities that promote holistic student involvement (physical, cognitive, social, and emotional) in tasks that involve challenges and cooperation.	Elementary Middle High
Outdoor Education	Involves personal and group development, teamwork, trust, and taking on risks and challenges within a natural setting, typically in an outdoor environment.	Elementary Middle High
Cultural Studies	Develops knowledge to observe, analyze, and critique (i.e., question and challenge) physical activity and sport issues and topics in a variety of contexts.	Middle High

Elementary school physical education teachers have the opportunity to utilize the skill themes and personal and social responsibility models as the framework for their units of instruction. These students are working in pairs on the skill development of the forearm pass. Working in pairs allows students to have sufficient repetitions and provides teachers time to observe students' performance and give feedback based on the critical elements of the skill.

and interact with others. The model embraces students as individuals, provides them with a voice, allows them to make decisions on their own, and places less emphasis on skill development and academic achievement.[17] This model was initially developed for teachers to use in traditional classrooms in educational settings; however, in the 1970s, Don Hellison was the first physical educator to study and implement PSRM in physical education. The goal of PSRM is for students to take more responsibility for their personal and social development in physical activity settings both in and outside of school.

Hellison's model is widely used in elementary school physical education programs, as elementary school students learn how to have respectful behavior and take responsibility for their actions; however, many secondary school programs integrate PSRM into their curriculum. Teachers and students can assess their personal and social responsibility based on five different levels:

- Level I—respecting the rights and feelings of others
- Level II—participation and effort
- Level III—self-direction
- Level IV—helping others and leadership
- Level V—outside of the gym[18]

Level I is the lowest and most basic (i.e., students having self-control), whereas Level V is the highest and most challenging (i.e., being a role model). Teachers can create laminated posters of the levels and place them on bulletin boards and gym walls, making them visible for students to see. As teachers provide instructional strategies that center on personal and social responsibility, students can self-assess which level they are at within each lesson.

Four primary themes of this model are that these levels should be *integrated* across all physical education content, not taught separately; personal and social responsibility behaviors should be *transferred* outside of the physical education and school settings; students should be *empowered;* and teachers and students should develop a *relationship.*[18] The key to the success of this model is for teachers to find a balance between instructional tasks that focus on responsibility and on physical education content. It is believed that the more responsibility and ownership (i.e., voice, choice, empowerment) students have, the more open they will be to learning.

Teaching Games for Understanding/ Tactical Games Model

Teaching games for understanding (TGfU) is a problem-based approach to games teaching. When you played sports in physical education, did you ever ask your teacher, "When are we going to play a game?" Were you taught skill after skill long before you ever played a game? Thirty years ago, the answers to these questions were most notably yes. This led two teacher educators from England, David Bunker and Rod Thorpe, to develop a different approach to games teaching, which they named TGfU. The original TGfU model was based on modified game play that set up tactical problems for students to solve with different skills and movements. According to Mitchell and Oslin, *tactics* are "decisions about what to do in response to problems arising during a game."[19] In 1997, Griffin, Mitchell, and Oslin revised the TGfU model to be more user friendly for teachers, and they named it the tactical games model (TGM). The goal of the model is to improve students' game performance by combining tactical awareness with skill execution and increase students' interest in and excitement about games.[20]

Since the focus of both models is on solving tactical problems in sport-related games, a games classification system was designed to group similar games together based on the problems that need to be solved, which include: invasion (e.g., basketball, soccer), net/wall (e.g., volleyball, tennis), striking/ fielding (e.g., softball, kickball), and target (e.g., golf, bowling). Here is an example of how games are similar within each classification: In a game of basketball, Team A is trying to invade Team B's territory in order to score, while Team B is trying to prevent Team A from scoring. The same is true in games such as soccer, hockey, and football, which is why they are all classified as invasion games. Although different movements and skills are needed on the offensive and defensive sides of the ball (or puck) in each of these games, the tactics to score and prevent scoring are similar.

The tactical approach to games teaching includes a game-practice-game instructional format. This format begins with a modified game (i.e., Game 1) to set up the problem the teacher wants students to solve. Then, the teacher brings the students together to ask them thought-provoking questions to guide them to solve the tactical problem. Once students have solved the tactical problem, the teacher designs a gamelike practice task that emphasizes the solutions to the tactical problem. After students have had sufficient opportunities to practice the task, they play another modified game (i.e., Game 2) to see whether their skills or movements improve during game play. Improved game understanding and game performance is a primary focus of the TGfU/TGM models.

Sport Education

The sport education model (SEM), similar to TGfU, was first developed by Daryl Siedentop in 1984, to create an authentic sport experience for students in physical education that is developmentally appropriate and to provide opportunities for boys and girls to participate equally. SEM models genuine sport experiences enjoyed by athletes. The overall goal of the model is to educate and develop students to be competent, literate, enthusiastic sportspersons.[21] SEM can be implemented as early as the third grade, and at middle and high school levels.

The main features of the model include seasons, team affiliation, formal competition, record keeping, a culminating event, and festivity. *Seasons* include longer units, between 15 and 20 lessons, to provide students enough time for teams to practice together and compete against

In the teaching games for understanding, tactical games, and sport education models, students engage in sport-related games to improve their game performance and develop as competent, literate, enthusiastic sportspersons. Small-sided games, as shown with these boys, provide increased opportunities for students to get involved in game play and enjoy their sporting experiences.

shot attempts, batting averages, and points per game. These statistics can provide feedback for teams to help guide them in areas of the game in which they need to improve. Each season ends with a *culminating event* such as a championship in sport-related games or a final competition in gymnastics and dance. Normally, a winning team is declared in the culminating event. *Festivity* is included throughout the entire season as groups select their own team names and colors at the beginning of the season, take pictures or create posters that represent their teams, and perhaps even include an awards ceremony at the conclusion of the culminating event.

SEM is a student-centered, inclusive model that requires everyone to play and be involved with some aspect of the game in each lesson.

other teams in the class. *Team affiliation* can be developed since students are placed on the same team for the entire season (i.e., unit). This provides teams time to learn how to play and interact together as they work toward a common goal. *Formal competition* includes contests in formats such as preseason and regular-season play, tournaments, and leagues. All games are played according to a schedule designed by the physical education teacher. *Record keeping* primarily includes statistics taken by teachers or students during formal competitions. Records can include

In the fitness education model, it is important to apply the concepts discussed during classroom-based lessons in laboratory activities. These students may have learned about the muscular endurance component of health-related fitness, so are engaging in abdominal exercises with medicine balls to work on their abdominal endurance.

When engaging in fitness activities such as weight training, knowing how to spot is as important as understanding the training principles associated with quality form and performance of a particular exercise. These students are working together to ensure the safety of the student who is bench-pressing.

At the start of the season, each student signs a team contract where they select a role and responsibility to perform throughout the season. In addition to being team players, students also have the opportunity to participate in the following roles: head and assistant coach, captain, trainer, statistician, referee, judge, equipment manager, publicist, and scorekeeper. Not all of these roles need to be filled for each unit. For example, in a floor hockey unit, a judge will not be required, whereas that would be an important role in a gymnastics or dance unit. Furthermore, teams might comprise only three to five students, which would not

be enough to cover each role listed above. As in PSRM, the more responsibility and ownership students have in physical education, the more opportunities they will have to learn.

Fitness Education

Fitness education is a broad and general term that encompasses the various ways physical educators can incorporate fitness and wellness content into physical education programs. Fitness education can include units on the health-related components of fitness, walking or hiking, or weight training. Teachers may choose to include fitness during class warm-ups, as fitness Fridays, or integrated throughout other games and activities. In all of these units, the overall goal in fitness education is for students to develop knowledge and skills to be physically active for a lifetime.

The most formal approach to fitness education is the concepts-based fitness and wellness model, where students engage in classroom discussions, laboratory activities, and physical activity experiences.[22] The goal of this model is the development of an understanding of physical activity, that is, that students learn how to develop and execute their own physical activity programs that they can participate in in and out of school. The health-related components of fitness, goal setting, nutrition, stress management, program development, and self-assessment are concepts taught at the secondary school level in the concepts-based fitness and wellness model. In physical education programs where students have physical education every day of the week, teachers will need to decide how to divide the classroom-focused and activity-based lessons. Laboratory experiences should involve the students in active learning and self-evaluation, whereas the classroom lessons should focus on cognitive learning and application.[22] Collectively, the laboratory experiences should integrate and reinforce the concepts taught in the classroom lessons. Whether fitness education is integrated with other curricular approaches and content or stands as the defining curriculum, fitness education is important.

As obesity rates continue to rise and physical activity levels decrease across the lifespan, it is important more than ever for students to learn fitness, physical activity, and wellness concepts and how to apply these principles in the development of their own physical activity program. For students to be active outside of school, they need to be able to develop physical activity programs based on their own fitness levels and needs.

Adventure Education

Adventure education allows students to learn about themselves and their peers as they take on individual and group tasks and challenges. Dyson and Brown describe adventure education as

> activities that encounter holistic student involvement (physical, cognitive, social and emotional) in a task that involves challenges and uncertainty of the final outcome. Activities are carefully sequenced to ensure student safety while allowing them to take ownership of their learning.[23]

In adventure education, physical education teachers act as facilitators while students collaborate and problem-solve with one another to accomplish a task. Teachers support their students and ensure safety; however, students play a major role in their learning. A key component of adventure education is self and group reflection to discuss how tasks were accomplished and, most importantly, how they felt throughout the different activities.

The most widely known student-centered adventure education program integrated in physical education is Project Adventure.[23] Project Adventure is based on five philosophical concepts: challenge, cooperation, risk, trust, and problem solving. These concepts can guide students to develop personal goals in regard to achieving a particular task such as climbing a 25-foot climbing wall, walking across a high ropes course, or feeling safe during a trust fall.

Physical educators can base their instruction around the following three essential elements:

- Experiential learning cycle—The learning process begins with the learning experience,

then proceeds to observations and reflections (what happened?) followed by abstract concepts and generalizations (so what?), and concludes with application and transference of the lessons learned to other adventure-based activities (now what?).

- Full value contract—Group members design and agree to a contract in regard to the behaviors they feel should be demonstrated among all group members throughout the task, activity, or unit.
- Challenge by choice—Students, within a lesson or activity, choose which task they want to

The adventure education and outdoor education models provide students with opportunities to engage in activities in the natural environment, take risks, face challenges, and problem-solve. These students have taken safety precautions by wearing life preservers and helmets before they go kayaking, an activity that is conducted on lakes and rivers.

perform and the level of physical or emotional risk they would like to take.

Adventure education provides students with a variety of opportunities to take on challenges, gain support, build trust, problem-solve, cooperate, reflect upon their experiences, and most importantly, learn through the experiences they undertake within an adventure-based unit.

Outdoor Education

When you think about outdoor activities, such as backpacking, orienteering, snowshoeing, and kayaking, do you consider them activities that can be implemented in physical education programs? Hopefully, your answer to this question is yes! Although some of these activities can be costly (e.g., kayaking) and will need additional funding from the school or grants awarded, others have minimal to no cost (e.g., hiking). Comparable to other curriculum models, outdoor education can lead to increased physical activity for all students.

Outdoor education is similar to adventure education, as they both focus on personal and group development, teamwork, trust, and taking on risks and challenges. The key difference between the two models is that outdoor education occurs in the natural setting, where teachers and students have little to no control over the environment and potential hazards that may arise.[24] Dealing with hazards such as severe and unexpected weather, variable terrain, and wildlife must be discussed, researched, and assessed before students embark on an outdoor excursion. Outdoor education places more emphasis on skill development than adventure education does; however, the premise of both models is the student-centered, experiential learning process. Outdoor pursuits have considerable potential to provide students with enjoyment and appreciation of the great outdoors.

Cultural Studies

Over the past decade, Mary O'Sullivan and Gary Kinchin have developed and implemented a cultural studies curriculum model in physical education. This model significantly differs from the models discussed previously in this section, as this model emphasizes students' development as "literate and critical consumers of sport, physical activity, and the movement culture."[25,26] O'Sullivan and Kinchin define *movement culture* as the "infrastructure, norms, practices, policies, and values associated with sport, recreation, and physical activity at the local, national, and international levels."[26] In other words, the goal of this model is for students to be able to observe, analyze, and critique (i.e., question and challenge) physical activity and sport issues and topics in a variety of contexts.

The cultural studies model comprises two components, as learning experiences occur in both the classroom and the gymnasium. The first component is for teachers to select a specific content area (e.g., games, dance, track and field) as the physical activity instructional element of the unit. The second component of the model is for students to engage in group and class discussions, research projects, journal writing, and presentations. This classroom portion of the model is critical, because this is where students learn to "recognize the role and meaning of sport and physical activity in their lives and in the wider community in which they live."[26]

Although this model has tremendous potential in educating students to be lifelong movers, which has been demonstrated in other countries such as Ireland, England, Australia, and New Zealand, few American physical education programs integrate this model into their physical education curriculum. This could be due to physical educators who are unaware of this model, have limited knowledge of the content delivered in a cultural studies model, or do not believe that classroom discussions and activities should be a part of physical education. Given the growing emphasis on global awareness and diversity, this model offers physical educators the opportunity to promote these concepts within the physical education program.

The cultural studies model provides students with an in-depth understanding of the social issues integrated within our sport and physical activity culture. In today's society, where most of our knowledge and understanding of the world is influenced and constructed by our society, it is important for students to become critical consumers of the messages delivered from these societal influences.

ASSESSMENT AND ACCOUNTABILITY

The standards-based movement has had significant influence on educational programs across all content areas, including physical education. As discussed previously, physical education curricular had to change from a "busy, happy, good" philosophy to programs that emphasized student learning.[27] Although making changes to goals, objectives, and instructional processes was critical, standards and instruction meant very little without knowing what students know and are able to do. Assessment is the salient component needed to measure whether students have learned and are achieving the national

standards.[3] Furthermore, assessment holds physical education programs and teachers accountable for student achievement. Connecting the standards, instruction, and assessment components of physical education curricula and units of instruction is referred to as *instructional alignment*. With even just one of the components excluded in this alignment, physical education programs and lessons lack purpose and meaning.

Types of Assessment

Assessment can be implemented at the beginning of or during a unit of instruction (formative) or at the end of a unit (summative). Formative assessments are true to their name; they inform teachers whether students are learning and give them an indication of how to plan upcoming lessons for students to achieve the unit goals and objectives. Furthermore, teachers can notify students of their progress to give them a sense of where they are in

Assessment is the key to determining whether students have learned throughout the course of a lesson or unit of instruction. There are many types of assessments. This physical education teacher is observing his students' performance during an activity, which will inform him what feedback or changes he needs to make in upcoming activities or lessons.

TYPES OF ASSESSMENT

Formative Assessment

- Implemented at the beginning of or during a unit of instruction.
- Informs teachers and students whether students are learning.
- Suggests how to plan upcoming lessons for students to achieve the unit goals and objectives.

Summative Assessment

- Implemented at the end of a unit of instruction.
- Informs teachers and students about what students have learned over the course of the unit.
- Usually associated or equated with a grade.

Performance-based Assessment

- Measures higher levels of student learning, specifically students' understanding of concepts and ability to apply knowledge.

Examples of Assessments
- Observations
- Checklists
- Rubrics
- Journals
- Portfolios (print or electronic)
- Essays
- Role plays
- Projects
- Game performance

---

the learning process. Formative assessments tend to be ongoing throughout the instructional process within a unit.[5] Summative assessments inform teachers and students about what students learned over the course of the unit and are usually associated with a grade.

In the past, teachers conducted assessments such as skills tests, fitness tests, and written tests to measure students' knowledge and performance. Today, physical education teachers implement assessments that are performance-based, which are used to measure higher levels of student learning—specifically students' understanding of concepts and ability to apply knowledge while engaging in a meaningful or worthwhile task.[5] Teachers do not have to conduct all assessments, as they can educate students on how to conduct peer and self-assessments. Performance-based assessments include observations, checklists, rubrics, journals, portfolios (print or electronic), essays, role-playing exercises, projects, and game performance. (See the Types of Assessment box.)

Teachers continuously observe students' performance and behaviors during physical education

classes. Oftentimes, teachers provide students with feedback based on critical elements of skills or tactics and strategies that occur within game play. Teachers frequently make adjustments or think on their feet based on what they observe, deviating from the daily lesson plan. Without question, observation is important in physical education; however, it is even more critical that teachers document their observations in regard to student performance and learning. Checklists are an example of how teachers can document students' ability to perform the critical elements of specified skills. It allows teachers to assess performance systematically, which holds the teachers, along with the students, accountable for student learning. Students can also use checklists to conduct peer and self-assessments. Checklists can assess content taught within a variety of curriculum models.

Rubrics are frequently used by teachers as criteria to assess students' knowledge and performance.[11,12] Rubrics are based on descriptors of various levels, including "competent" (i.e., performing at the level teachers want all students to achieve), exceeding expectations (i.e., performing at a level higher than competency), and not meeting expectations or competency. Some teachers use "developing," "acceptable," and "target" as their different levels. Effective rubrics include detailed descriptors that make it clear how each level is differentiated from the next. For example, if a teacher is using a rubric to assess students' offensive skills in a game of basketball, and part of the criteria for competency is that students need to successfully complete two out of three passes, "exceeding" or "target" would be three out of three passes and "not meeting" or "developing" would be less than two out of three passes. If the criterion simply stated "successful passes," would one out of three be considered competent? The challenge for physical education teachers who develop their own rubrics is establishing the "competent" or "acceptable" level. This needs to be determined by the NASPE and state standards of performance outcomes for each grade band or level, as well as knowledge of their students' abilities. Rubrics can be used to assess student portfolios, projects, and role-playing exercises, along with other performance-based assessments not listed here. As with checklists, teachers can employ rubrics to assess content taught within a variety of curriculum models.

Journals are a great method of gathering information on students' thoughts, feelings, and cognitive knowledge about specific activities and experiences they have in physical education. Journals can be completed on a simple piece of paper, in a notebook or folder, on the computer, or by electronic recording. Journals are best used as a formative assessment, since it would be difficult to assign a grade to students' thoughts and feelings unless specific criteria were provided for the journal entries (e.g., number of entries, type of content, length). Journals are particularly used to assess NASPE standards 5 and 6, which focus on students' personal and social responsibility and valuing physical activity, especially in the PSRM, adventure education, outdoor education, and cultural studies curriculum models.

Assessing game performance is imperative when teaching sport and game units, particularly

Assessment can be conducted by teachers or students. This student is using a skills checklist to observe one of his classmates during physical education class.

at the middle and high school levels, because game play provides students the opportunity to apply the skills, knowledge, and tactics they have learned throughout the unit. Since game play is faster-paced than isolated skill practices, assessing students' offensive and defensive skills and movements or teamwork can be rather challenging. In units where teachers implement the sport education or TGfU/TGM curriculum models, the Game Performance Assessment Instrument can be used to assess students' base position, decision making, skill execution, support for teammates in possession of the ball, marking or guarding opponents, covering for teammates who are defending against opponents, and adjusting to the flow of the game.[19,20] Teachers can select several of the components out of the seven to assess students' game performance based on the unit of instruction. For example, skill execution and decision making can be assessed in all sports and games within the games classification system; however, support for teammates in possession of the ball is important in invasion games such as soccer or basketball, but not in golf or softball.

Over the years, teachers have struggled with implementing assessments within physical education lessons, because it takes up too much instructional time, it is too complicated to develop their own assessment tools, or it is difficult to assess hundreds of students alone. We will not deny that conducting quality and authentic (i.e., realistic, game-like) assessments is challenging; however, many resources have been developed (e.g., NASPE Assessment Series, PE Metrics) to provide teachers with examples of assessments they can implement in their classes.

For teachers to be successful at implementing assessment within instruction, they must first determine which standards and learning domains they want to assess, and they must take into consideration the number of students in each class, the frequency and duration of students' engagement in physical education, the aspects they want to assess within a single class period or unit, and whether the assessment will be formative or summative.[28] Then we suggest that teachers select one class or grade level to conduct the assessment, so they can determine management procedures, instructional processes, and potential changes they would like to make to the assessment tool before assessing a larger number of students.

Our hope is that teachers become aware of how important it is to conduct assessments that measure student learning. As the standards-based movement continues to steer education in the twenty-first century, administrators, teachers, and students are being held accountable for academic achievement in relation to content standards. Assessment is the key that provides purpose and meaning to instruction and informs teachers, students, parents, and administrators of students' achievement of the national and state standards.

CHARACTERISTICS OF EFFECTIVE TEACHING

Teaching can be defined as those interactions of the teacher and the learner that make learning more successful.[29] Although it is possible for learning to occur without a teacher's involvement, it is generally accepted that teachers facilitate the acquisition of knowledge, skills, and attitudes. Effective teachers use a variety of pedagogical skills and strategies to ensure that their students are appropriately engaged in relevant activities a high percentage of the time, hold positive expectations for their students, and create and maintain a classroom climate that is warm and nurturing.[30]

Salient teacher behaviors can be divided into several broad areas: organization, communication, instruction, motivation, and human relations. (See the Salient Teacher Behaviors box.) These characteristics are common to effective teachers, regardless of the skill to be learned, the age of the students, or the setting in which the teaching occurs.

Organizational skills are very important for establishing the learning environment and facilitating student involvement in activities. The manner in which the teacher structures instruction is of major importance. To be effective, a teacher must ensure that the lesson to be presented relates to the stated objectives, meets the needs of the individual learners, and is sequenced in a logical manner. Through efficient and thorough planning, effective teachers minimize transition time (i.e., the time to move students from place to place) and management time (i.e., time used for tasks such as taking attendance). Lessons are planned to ensure that students receive maximum opportunities to practice relevant skills and experience success. Actively supervising and monitoring student performance and providing students with appropriate feedback are characteristics of successful teachers. Skilled teachers bring each lesson to an end by summarizing what has been accomplished and by providing students with an assessment of their progress toward the stated objectives.

Communication skills needed by the teacher include verbal and nonverbal expressive skills,

SALIENT TEACHER BEHAVIORS

Organization

- Formulate plans with specific objectives and tasks that minimize transition and management time.
- Maximize opportunities for students to practice skills.
- Supervise and monitor student performance and provide feedback.
- Assess students' progress toward lesson plan objectives.

Communication

- Speak clearly and project your voice.
- Provide clear and precise directions, explanations, and instructions.
- Ask thought-provoking and critical-thinking questions to enhance students' involvement in the learning process.
- Use eye contact, smiles, and high fives.
- Articulate high expectations for all students.

Instruction

- Acquire expertise in instructional media, technology, and physical education content.
- Gather knowledge of students' needs and backgrounds.
- Sequence tasks progressively based on differing students' abilities and progress toward the lesson objectives.
- Modify lesson plans during instruction according to students' needs and abilities.

Motivation

- Learn students' interests and seek creative ways to involve students in the learning process.
- Use reinforcement techniques, such as checklists, contracts, and award systems.
- Give students a voice and provide them with choice and opportunities to be responsible.

Human Relations

- Listen to students and accept them for who they are.
- Provide students with opportunities to build their self-confidence and self-worth.
- Establish and maintain a rapport with all students.
- Have a sense of humor.

written competencies, and the ability to use various media. Effective verbal communication skills are essential in the teaching process. The ability to speak clearly and project one's voice in a pleasing manner is important. Other attributes of a successful teacher are the ability to give clear, precise directions and explanations and to use terminology and vocabulary that is appropriate to the activity and the level of the learners. The teacher's ability to use questions to elicit student input, to promote student involvement, and to clarify student understanding of the material being presented enhances the effectiveness of the learning process. Effective teachers are also aware of their nonverbal communication with students, such as use of eye contact, smiles, and high fives. Through their verbal and nonverbal behaviors, effective teachers model the kinds of behaviors they

Planning and organization are key characteristics of effective teacher behaviors. Teachers who plan in advance of a lesson and are organized, such as having the equipment set up before the students come into the gymnasium, usually have lessons that provide students with more opportunities to learn and engage in more activity time.

wish their students to exhibit, such as interest in and enjoyment of the activity and respect for other people's opinions and needs.

Written communication skills are also essential, especially in the planning and evaluation phases of teaching. Teachers who possess effective written communication skills are able to express themselves clearly. The ability to communicate with supervisors, participants, parents, and community members will help to establish a more successful program.

Expertise in the use of various instructional media and technology contributes to a teacher's

effectiveness. The use of computer programs, such as PowerPoint, to present information to students is an important skill. Increasingly, technology is being incorporated into teaching. The Internet, handheld devices, and fitness tools such as pedometers and heart rate monitors can enhance student learning. Computerized equipment, such as TriFit and Fitnessgram, can facilitate assessment of student fitness. Incorporation of media and technology into student learning activities can contribute to the accomplishment of instructional goals and objectives.

Competency in a variety of instructional skills is essential for effective teaching. When planning experiences for students, effective teachers use their knowledge of the content to be taught, in conjunction with instructional objectives and students' needs, to provide appropriate experiences leading to the attainment of stated goals. Effective teaching requires the ability to sequence movement tasks by increasing difficulty and complexity as students progress, and by providing opportunities for students to develop and apply skills. Good teachers not only must be able to implement planned experiences effectively, but also must be flexible so that they can appropriately modify planned experiences to suit the needs of the students and the situations that arise within the learning environment.

Effective teachers are able to maintain an orderly, productive learning environment, handling discipline problems appropriately while encouraging and providing opportunities for students to learn responsibility and to be accountable for their actions. A wide variety of teaching methods and instructional strategies are judiciously employed to maximize students' active and successful engagement in relevant tasks. The ability to present clear expectations and offer accurate demonstrations contributes to learning. Effective teachers actively monitor their students' performances and are concerned about the quality of their efforts. Teachers are aware of, and capably respond to, the myriad of events that occur within the instructional environment; this quality, called "with-it-ness," is often described as "having eyes in the

Teachers attempt to motivate their students by providing them with developmentally appropriate content and specific feedback based on their performance. This teacher is helping his student learn how to hold and shoot a basketball.

back of one's head." Evaluation skills are also important. Teachers must be able to observe and analyze student performance, focusing on the critical elements in relation to the goals, with feedback reinforcing or modifying responses as necessary.

The communication of high expectations for each student is also important. Teachers should hold high expectations for both student learning and behavior. Positive expectations, including the belief that all students are capable of learning, are important in establishing a warm, nurturing classroom climate and a productive learning environment.[30]

The ability to motivate students to perform to their potential is the goal of every teacher. Skillful teachers use a variety of teaching techniques to stimulate interest in participation and seek creative techniques to involve students in the learning process. They also use appropriate reinforcement techniques to maintain student involvement and promote a high level of student effort. These may include checklists, contracts, award systems,

and verbal and nonverbal feedback. Praise is used thoughtfully; it is contingent on the correct performance, specific in its nature and intent, and sincere. Successful teachers continually update their lessons in an effort to meet students' needs and to make the material relevant and challenging to the students.

Effective teachers possess superior human relations skills. They listen to students and accept and treat them as individuals. They strive to instill in each student a sense of self-worth. Effective teachers show concern for the well-being of each student in their classes and endeavor to provide students with opportunities that will enhance their self-confidence. The ability to establish and maintain rapport with students and staff and a readiness to acknowledge their own mistakes are also characteristics that many successful teachers possess. A sense of humor is a welcome attribute as well.

In summary, effective teachers are able to successfully utilize a variety of skills pertaining to organization, communication, instruction, motivation, and human relations. However, effective teaching requires more than these skills; it requires the ability to accurately assess the needs of the moment and tailor the skills to the specific context and situation. Although many of these skills appear to be innate in certain individuals, all of them can be developed or improved by individuals who desire to become effective teachers.

STUDENT PERSPECTIVES

In physical education, most often the teachers are the center of the instructional process and make all of the decisions about what occurs within the educational setting. If the teachers are the decision makers and are in charge of curricular decisions, what role do students have in the design and implementation of physical education programs? Should students be able to discuss and deliberate aspects of their learning in physical education with their teachers? Did you have an opportunity to voice your thoughts and feelings about which activities you would like to participate in or select a game you wanted to play that was recreational or more competitive?

Physical education research has made significant strides over the past 30 years; however, limited research has been conducted from the students' point of view. Research studies have included surveys that students completed to identify which activities they prefer, whether they like or dislike physical education, and if they would choose to take physical education if it were not mandated.[31,32] Other studies were based on interviews with students, to get a more in-depth understanding of how students think and feel in physical education. Although students liked the break from sitting at their desks and taking notes, the time to socialize and be with their friends, and the opportunity to play games, many disliked or resisted physical education because of concerns associated with their skill ability, body and gender issues, social dynamics with their peers, and dislike of activities offered.[33–38] It is important for physical education teachers to not overlook these issues that students encounter in physical education. Some of these concerns, such as gender and body issues, will specifically be addressed in the next section, on differences and diversity in physical education.

Whether students are highly skilled and excel in physical education, enjoy being physically active, or have negative feelings about physical education, most have more positive experiences in physical education when they have a sense of responsibility and ownership for their learning. Teachers can provide students with opportunities to be involved in the learning process by allowing them to have a voice, giving them a choice, and providing them with a sense of responsibility.[39]

Giving students a voice may involve letting them select the content for the period of time they have physical education (e.g., semester), decide the rules and behaviors they are expected to follow and perform in class, design their own activities, select the warm-up activity, or create their own practice task within teams. Providing students with a choice may include permitting them to select their own roles and responsibilities within a game, decide which classmates they would like on their team, elect whether they want to play in a recreational or competitive game, or choose the equipment they would like to use in a specified activity. In giving students a voice and providing them with a choice, teachers are inevitably giving students an opportunity to demonstrate personal and social responsibility.[39] For some teachers, it is not easy to let go of control by allowing students to take more ownership for their learning in physical education. These teachers may foresee management and behavioral issues if there is not a clear and specific order according to which the physical education program operates. Without question, chaos and disorganization may occur when students begin to take on more responsibilities, but similar to learning and developing new skills, it is up to the physical education teachers to provide these educational opportunities for students, with the hope that students will feel a sense of ownership and empowerment.

DIFFERENCES AND DIVERSITY IN PHYSICAL EDUCATION

As we begin this section on differences and diversity, we would first like you to think back to your own K–12 physical education experiences. At this point in the semester, you most likely have reflected upon your experiences, which might have included what you enjoyed and did not enjoy, what you liked and disliked, and what role your teachers played in these experiences. Once again, think back to those elementary, middle, and high school physical education classes and reflect upon the following questions: Were athletes and higher-skilled students given special privileges? Did students with disabilities participate with the rest of the class or were they off to the side, away from the action? Were girls and boys treated the same? Did teachers have high expectations for all students, regardless of race? It might take you some time to reflect upon these questions, and quite honestly, you might not remember the nuances that occurred in your physical education classes; however, the content of these questions are rarely discussed in physical education, which is concerning.

As demonstrated in previous sections on curriculum, there is an abundance of physical education content that can be taught by teachers and a variety of ways teachers can deliver instruction to their students. The goals and objectives of each unit and lesson are usually stated by the teacher so students are explicitly aware of what they are learning. However, there are times students learn additional lessons based on indirect messages teachers deliver. These messages are examples of what physical education teacher educators refer to as the *hidden curriculum,* which is based on unintended and implicit messages that are implied by teachers and learned by students.[1,40,41]

For years, social issues (e.g., gender, sexuality, (dis)ability, race) have been vastly ignored by physical education teachers.[40,42–45] Most often, the lessons learned by students from the hidden curriculum are more powerful than the content being taught in physical education classes. Few, if any, physical education teachers explicitly educate

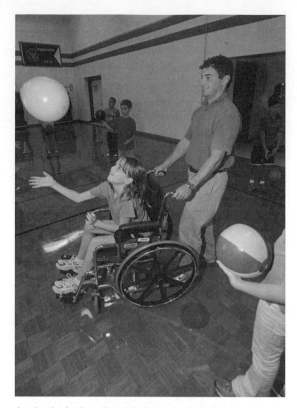

In physical education, it is important to include students with disabilities in the lesson. Here, students are using modified equipment to play volleyball with their classmate, who is in a wheelchair.

their students about gender, sexuality, race, or class issues. Instead, dominance by white, male, heterosexual, high-skilled, thin and athletic, able-bodied teachers and students in physical education and sport continues to be the center of physical education curricula, which leave many students and teachers feeling isolated, oppressed, and marginalized.[40,46,47] Physical educators have the potential to introduce students to and educate them about the ideas of privilege, oppression, and power relations. A positive first step to empowering all teachers and students would be to unveil the hidden curriculum—that is, to make the implicit messages explicit by including social issues (i.e., differences and diversity) in the physical education curriculum. In this section, the following social identities (i.e., how individuals associate or classify themselves relative to social categories) will be discussed in relation to differences and diversity within physical education: (dis)ability, gender, body issues, race, class, and sexuality.

(Dis)ability

On seeing the word *disability,* many may be quick to assume that it refers only to individuals with special needs, such as people who are in wheelchairs, are visually or hearing impaired, or have cerebral palsy. The reason "dis" is in parentheses is because students' ability, whether they are disabled or not, is observed, analyzed, and assessed by teachers and other students in the public arena of physical education.

We would be remiss to state that ability is not an important factor in physical education, since the psychomotor domain is the primary difference between physical education and other subject matter areas in schools. Students' experiences in physical education are often determined by their level of success in different sports and physical activities. Students who believe they are lower skilled tend to take positions where they are least likely to be involved in the game (e.g., right field in softball), pace back and forth during a game of basketball to look like they are participating, and avoid opportunities to be embarrassed in front of their peers.[48] Over the years, lower-skilled students have had negative experiences in physical education due to lack of success, being ousted first in elimination games, and dominance by highly skilled students, particularly boys.[1,34,38]

Students with disabilities are even more marginalized than students who are lower skilled, as they are often left on the sidelines, placed in a corner, or completely ignored by teachers and students, despite federal laws (i.e., the Education of All Handicapped Children Act, the Individuals with Disabilities Education Act, the Americans with Disabilities Act) that require the inclusion

Differences and diversity are present in physical education classes. Students will face and navigate different social issues, such as gender, (dis)ability, race, socioeconomic status, and body issues. It is important for the teacher to not only make students aware of these issues, but educate them about the issues.

of students with disabilities in physical education. By law, each identified student with a disability must have an individualized educational plan, which must include physical education. Students with disabilities include those with mental and emotional impairments, physical challenges such as cerebral palsy or amputation, vision and hearing problems, speech disorders, learning disabilities, and other health impairments such as asthma, heart problems, and cancer.

Physical education teachers often find it difficult to include students with disabilities and those that are lower skilled into daily instruction. It is much easier for teachers to focus on students who are able-bodied and higher skilled rather than students who are less skillful or have physical, mental, or emotional challenges. Unfortunately, physical educators are not completely at fault for their lack of knowledge on how to include these students. In many teacher preparation programs in higher education, students will take one or two courses in special education or adapted physical education to learn how to work with students with disabilities. In field experiences, including student teaching, few students actually formulate lesson plans and deliver instruction that integrate students with disabilities. Thus, physical education teachers are not prepared when they begin their teaching jobs in the K–12 schools. Physical educators, however, are prepared to individualize instruction for all students, including those who are lower and higher skilled. It is up to teachers to further educate themselves on how to teach students with disabilities and differentiate their instruction for students with varied abilities.

Gender

Gender had limited consideration in educational policies and school reform in the USA, until the enactment of Title IX in 1972. Title IX is the only federal policy that addresses gender in physical education.[49] Although physical education is not specifically mentioned within the law, requirements for physical education are provided in the Title IX regulations. Equal opportunities for boys and girls had to be established in activities, facilities, equipment, curriculum, testing and grading requirements, and behavior and dress codes.[50] These changes meant that a shift from same-sex to coeducational physical education classes was needed to ensure that males and females were provided comparable educational opportunities. For many teachers, this posed a challenge, as male teachers were used to teaching boys and female teachers were used to teaching girls.

Physical education teachers were not provided pedagogical strategies to teach students of both genders. They had limited knowledge of and experience with the other gender's physical abilities, attitudes, and behaviors—or, most importantly, with the skills, activities, and sports that were geared toward the other gender. Whether because they lacked knowledge, felt comfortable with the same-sex curriculum, or were challenged by change, some teachers bypassed the law and still conducted same-sex classes, which continued to perpetuate the male and female ideologies.[51] For example, teachers would offer football and dance, with male teachers teaching all of the boys football, while female teachers would teach the girls dance. On the other hand, some teachers attempted coeducational classes, but the emphasis was placed on traditional male-dominated activities and sports (e.g., team sports).

Pat Griffin was one of the first researchers to study students' participation patterns[43,44] and teachers' perceptions[45] in coeducational classes. Through extensive observations of the participants and interviews with their teachers, she found six "styles" of female participation in team sport activities: as athletes, JV players, cheerleaders, lost souls, femmes fatales, and system beaters.[43] The six styles were based on the researcher's and teachers' perceptions of the participants' skill ability and engagement in the sport. Collectively, students' behavior in the studies showed a clear difference in participation for the boys and the girls in the coeducational classes. The majority of the boys teased the girls, dominated team games, and exhibited overaggressive behavior toward others, while the girls shied away from game play and demonstrated a lack of skill in team games.[45] Despite these behaviors, Griffin found that coeducational classes were not positive for all boys or negative for all girls.

Griffin's studies were paramount to sex equity in the mid-1980s; unfortunately, little has changed over the past 25 years. Girls continue to feel that boys dominate game play, are excessively competitive, and tease, ridicule, and make fun of them, causing many girls to have negative experiences in physical education.[35,52,53] Girls' experiences are often made worse by teachers who make comments to boys such as "Don't throw like a girl" or rules such as "At least one girl must touch the ball before you shoot," along with boys' competitive and aggressive nature and dominating game play. The same is true for lower-skilled, noncompetitive, or non-sports-oriented boys who choose to not conform to the masculine stereotype. Oftentimes, these boys are bullied, teased, and laughed at by other boys. These problems tend to occur during the middle and high school years, but gender issues are becoming more and more prevalent in elementary school, even as early as first and second grade. There is significant concern with girls' and boys' negative experiences in physical education, since there is a likelihood that they will associate other physical activity with those negative experiences. From ages 9 to 15, when girls' physical activity significantly drops off, it is imperative that physical education teachers implement unit and lesson plans that are equitable and inclusive for all students.

Body Issues

In physical education, students' bodies are exposed and placed on display due to the public nature of the environment. Students, particularly girls, are concerned about other students observing their bodies in motion and feeling as if their bodies are objectified. During the adolescent years, when students' bodies are developing and changing, this public exposure creates a great challenge for students, which often supersedes their ability to focus on learning the physical education content.

Students are faced with many challenges in physical education, including the public nature of the environment. It is important for teachers to provide support to students of varying abilities.

Students should be treated fairly, regardless of race, gender, or ability. Teachers need to have the same expectations for all students, regardless of their social identity.

In today's society, when bodies are socially constructed (i.e., influences within our society tell us what, who, and how we should be) and gender roles and expectations are formulated, students tend to compare their own bodies with those of their classmates and the idealized male and female bodies they view in the media and consumer culture. The socially constructed, gendered ideal bodies are based on body size, shape, and appearance. Specifically, males are to be muscular and athletic and females slender, skill-less, and nonmuscular.[33,41] The physical education context (i.e., same-sex or coeducational) and the design of the physical education program influence students' feelings about their bodies, particularly in coeducational classes where the dominant male culture is promoted.

As our country's obesity rates continue to rise and physical activity levels decrease, it is imperative that physical educators teach students at all grade levels about body issues. In an educational institution, including physical education, that perpetuates the hidden curriculum, it is up to

physical education teachers to break the silence and bring these important, yet uncomfortable and vulnerable issues to the forefront of physical education curricula. The hope is for physical education teachers to give students a voice and create a physical education context that challenges dominant body ideals.

Race, Class, and Sexuality

Along with (dis)ability, gender, and body issues, race, class, and sexuality are also differences that teachers need to educate students about in physical education. As discussed in Chapter 8, students get assigned certain positions based on their race. For example, white students tend to play positions that are considered more intellectual, such as quarterback or pitcher, whereas black students play running back, wide receiver, or forward in basketball, because those are positions that are considered more athletic. Teachers are predominantly white, yet the racial diversity of our country continues to increase, causing a gap across racial groups.[41]

To navigate the superfluity of racial identities, teachers need to reflect upon their own identities and biases to have a better understanding of the students they teach.

Socioeconomic status or class also has an impact on physical education programs. In economically disadvantaged communities, particularly in urban settings, many physical education teachers are limited in regard to facilities, equipment, and space. Within these same communities, students may not have the appropriate attire to participate in physical education. This is considered a major problem for physical education teachers who continue to grade students on dress and participation. If students do not have the appropriate clothes, they usually sit in the bleachers, waiting out the time on the sidelines or talking to classmates. Since obesity is especially prevalent in individuals with lower socioeconomic status, and urban communities have less physical activity opportunities for youth, it is extremely important that students participate in physical education regardless of whether they have the appropriate clothes, unless it is a safety concern. To minimize the clothing issue, teachers can take clothing donations from others to provide to students when they do not have a change of clothes for physical education. Socioeconomic status also influences the out-of-school experiences that students have in sport and physical activity. Students who are from higher socioeconomic communities participate on traveling sport teams, attend specialized camps, and tend to have ample equipment at home to practice skills taught in physical education. On the contrary, students from lower socioeconomic communities cannot afford to play on traveling teams or go to camps and tend to live in neighborhoods that either are unsafe or do not have sidewalks and parks to engage in physical activity.

Sexuality closely intersects with gender. In the discussion on gender, we briefly mentioned gender stereotypes that are socially constructed. An example of a stereotype is that girls are associated with the color pink, whereas boys are aligned with the color blue. In your everyday conversations with friends and family, what is said if a boy wears pink? What if girls want to play football or wrestle, boys want to dance or be cheerleaders? Stereotypes are formulated, because our society influences our knowledge and understanding of what is, yet few individuals ever ask the question why. When answering these questions, many students most likely labeled these boys and girls as gay, because society says that boys are supposed to play football and wrestle, not girls, and girls are supposed to dance and cheerlead. If individuals break the dominant belief—that is, what is considered to be normal—then their sexuality is immediately questioned. According to society, girls can be skillful in "female" sports such as soccer and volleyball, as long as they look feminine. Boys' sexuality is also questioned if they are uninterested in sport or do not have large, ripped muscles, regardless of their actual sexual orientation. How do students, especially at the secondary school level, navigate these socially constructed gender and sexuality stereotypes in physical education? If teachers allow students to choose between football and fitness, who tends to select football, and who fitness? Do some boys who would prefer to participate in fitness and girls who would like to play football break those gender barriers and select the activity of their interest, or is the social pressure too much or too great of a risk to challenge those norms? Physical education teachers need to be aware of gender and sexuality stereotypes and expectations and be cognizant of the language they use and the implicit messages they send to students.

All of these social identities, along with ethnicity, religion, and language proficiency, are difficult to discuss in isolation; rather, identities tend to intersect with one another as demonstrated in the discussion of sexuality. It is imperative that physical education teachers, along with exercise scientists and sport leaders, have an awareness of the students, clients, and athletes. To gain this awareness, it is important for professionals to learn how their students, clients, and athletes identify, where they come from, and who they are. Before doing this, however, it is important for all professionals to reflect upon their own identities and assess their biases and stereotypes about individuals with differences from themselves. We must minimize the unintended, implicit messages we deliver to students and unveil the hidden curriculum by discussing and addressing differences and diversity in physical education. As Timken and Watson emphatically state, "As teachers, we need to be aware of and move beyond socially constructed and individual bias, beyond our preconceived expectations of students and their potential, in order to teach *all* kids."[41]

IMPLICATIONS FOR EXERCISE SCIENTISTS AND SPORT LEADERS

Although this chapter on sport pedagogy has focused on physical education teachers in K–12 schools, aspects of sport pedagogy have meaning and importance for other professionals in exercise science and sport.

As discussed in Chapter 2, all physical educators, exercise scientists, and sport leaders need to establish programs that are based on professional standards and have clear goals, objectives, and assessment outcomes. The concept of instructional alignment presented in this chapter should be taken into consideration by all professionals. For example, it is important for exercise scientists to assess their clients' performance before they design exercise and training programs, so that they can best meet the clients' needs.

Effective teaching behaviors and characteristics can also be valuable to coaches working with their players and physical therapists assisting their clients. All professionals who educate, teach, and convey information need to be organized (e.g., develop a lesson plan, playbook, or fitness program) and able to communicate (verbally and nonverbally), deliver instruction, motivate their students, clients, or players, and develop a rapport and build relationships with those whom they instruct (i.e., human relations). There clearly are differences between physical educators, exercise scientists, and sport leaders; however, most characteristics and behaviors are similar and necessary for all professionals to be effective and successful.

Lastly, let's remember that many of the adults you will work with have had their values regarding physical activity and their beliefs about their ability as physical movers influenced by their experiences in K–12 physical education classes. Whether they were selected last for a team, embarrassed by their poor skill performance, or favored and admired for their success as a skilled performer in physical education or athletics, these experiences may have influenced their beliefs and feelings about themselves and physical activity.

Collectively, all professionals have an appreciation for sport and physical activity. Thus, understanding curricular and program development, salient professional characteristics and behaviors, and students' (i.e., clients', players') needs is important to our unified shared mission of educating individuals across the lifespan about physical activity, human movement, and sport.

SUMMARY

Sport pedagogy is concerned with the study of teaching and learning processes of physical activity. The scope of sport pedagogy is broad in nature, as it intersects with other subdisciplines due to the emphasis of teaching and learning in relation to human movement and physical activity. Physical education is the subject matter taught in schools that provide K–12 students with opportunities to learn and have meaningful content and appropriate instruction. Quality physical education programs focus on increasing physical competence, health-related fitness, self-responsibility, and enjoyment of physical activity for all students so that they can be physically active for a lifetime.

Over the past 20 years, American education has undergone significant reform as it entered into a standards-based education era. In 1995 and again in 2004, the National Association for Sport and Physical Education answered the charge to formulate educational goals for the nation by developing standards to provide physical educators a framework for student learning, specifically, "what a student should know and be able to do" as a result of a quality physical education program. These standards have been adopted by most states as their physical education content standards and have been used by teachers, school districts, and teacher educators to guide the development of program curricula, unit and lesson plans (i.e., instruction), and assessments. The standards-based movement significantly changed physical education curricula throughout the nation. Although making changes to goals, objectives, and instructional processes was critical, standards and instruction meant very little without assessment. Assessment is the salient component needed to measure whether students have learned and are achieving the national standards. Furthermore, assessment holds physical education programs and teachers accountable for student achievement. Connecting the standards, instruction, and assessment components of physical education curricula and units of instruction is referred to as instructional alignment.

As physical education teachers develop their curricula, their philosophy, along with program goals and objectives, influences the focus of instruction. Curriculum models have been developed by researchers, teacher educators, and physical education teachers over the past 20 years to provide teachers with different approaches to delivering instruction to students. These curriculum models include skill themes, personal and social responsibility, teaching games for understanding and the tactical games model, sport education, fitness education, adventure education, outdoor education, and cultural studies. Although it is possible for learning to occur without a teacher's involvement, it is generally accepted that teachers facilitate the acquisition of knowledge, skills, and attitudes. Effective teachers use a variety of pedagogical skills and strategies to ensure that their students are appropriately engaged in relevant activities a high percentage of the time, hold positive expectations for their students, and create and maintain a classroom climate that is warm and nurturing. Salient teacher behaviors can be divided into several broad areas: organization, communication, instruction, motivation, and human relations.

In physical education, the goals and objectives of each unit and lesson are usually stated by the teacher so students are explicitly aware of what they are learning. However, there are times students learn additional lessons based on indirect messages teachers deliver (i.e., the hidden curriculum). For years, social issues (e.g., gender, sexuality, (dis)ability, race) have been vastly ignored by physical education teachers. Most often, the lessons learned by students from the hidden curriculum are more powerful than the content being taught in physical education classes. Physical educators have the potential to introduce students to and educate them about the ideas of privilege, oppression, and power relations. A positive first step to empowering all teachers and students would be to unveil the hidden curriculum—that is, to make the implicit messages explicit by including social issues (i.e., differences and diversity) in the physical education curriculum.

DISCUSSION QUESTIONS

1. What is your philosophy on physical education at the elementary, middle, and high school levels? How would your philosophy impact your selection of curriculum content?

2. Describe instructional alignment. What components should be aligned with each other? Why is it important for these components to be aligned with one another?

3. Discuss why it is important for teachers to know who their students are and where they come from. What are three ways teachers can engage students in the decision making process within physical education and provide opportunities for student empowerment?

4. How would you consider individual differences and diversity in planning units of instruction in physical education?

SELF-ASSESSMENT ACTIVITIES

These activities are designed to help you determine if you have mastered the materials and competencies presented in this chapter.

1. Due to No Child Left Behind and high-stakes testing, physical education programs are being reduced and eliminated throughout the country. What arguments will you present to the principal to advocate for physical education? Write a letter to your principal that includes specific arguments why physical education should be an important component of the school curriculum.

2. Select two curriculum models and describe the characteristics, components, and positive attributes of the model, and how you will assess student learning. Provide examples of how you will implement these models in your class.

3. Use the information provided in the Get Connected box to access the PE Central website. Review the information on assessment, particularly the assessment examples and ideas. What forms of assessment do they provide? How can these assessments be implemented into units of instruction? What steps would you take to construct your own assessment?

4. Refer to the 12 Steps to Understanding Research Reports box in Chapter 1. Complete Steps 10, 11, and 12 for the same article you selected in Chapter 1.

REFERENCES

1. Graber K and Templin T: Pedagogy of physical activity. In SJ Hoffman and JC Harris, editors, Introduction to kinesiology: studying physical activity, Champaign, Ill., 2000, Human Kinetics.

2. Tinning R: Pedagogy, sport pedagogy, and the field of kinesiology, Quest 60:405–424, 2008.

3. National Association for Sport and Physical Education: Moving into the future: national standards for physical education, ed 2, Reston, Va., 2004, AAHPERD.

4. Bain LL: Sport pedagogy. In JD Massengale and RA Swanson, editors, The history of exercise and sport science, Champaign, Ill., 1997, Human Kinetics.

5. Lund J and Tannehill D: Standards-based physical education curriculum development, ed 2, Sudbury, Mass., 2010, Jones and Bartlett.

6. US Department of Education: The condition of education 2000, Washington, D.C., 2001.

7. US Department of Education: No child left behind, Washington, D.C., 2001.

8. US Department of Education: No child left behind overview, 2004 (www2.ed.gov/nclb/overview/intro/4pillars.html). Retrieved 27 June 2010.

9. National Association for Sport and Physical Education: Moving into the future: national standards for physical education—a guide to content and assessment, Reston, Va., 1995, McGraw-Hill.

10. National Association for Sport and Physical Education: Assessment Series, 1995–2010 (www.aahperd.org/naspe/publications/products/asessment-series.cfm).

11. National Association for Sport and Physical Education: PE metrics: assessing the national standards, standard 1: elementary, Reston, Va., 2008, AAHPERD.

12. National Association for Sport and Physical Education: PE metrics: assessing national standards 1–6 in elementary school, ed 2, Reston, Va., 2010, AAHPERD.

13. Siedentop D: Introduction to physical education, fitness, and sport, ed 7, New York, 2009, McGraw-Hill.

14. National Association for Sport and Physical Education. 2010 shape of the nation report: status of physical education in the USA, Reston, Va., 2010, NASPE (www.aahperd.org/naspe/publications/Shapeofthenation.cfm).

15. Graham G, Holt/Hale S, and Parker M: Children moving: a reflective approach to teaching physical education, ed 8, New York, 2010, McGraw-Hill.

16. Holt/Hale S: The skill theme approach to physical education. In J Lund and D Tannehill, editors, Standards-based physical education curriculum development, ed 2, Sudbury, Mass., 2010, Jones and Bartlett.

17. Parker M and Stiehl J: Personal and social responsibility. In J Lund and D Tannehill, editors, Standards-based physical education curriculum development, ed 2, Sudbury, Mass., 2010, Jones and Bartlett.

18. Hellison D: Teaching responsibility through physical activity, ed 2, Champaign, Ill., 2003, Human Kinetics.

19. Mitchell S and Oslin J: Teaching games for understanding. In J Lund and D Tannehill, editors, Standards-based physical education curriculum development, ed 2, Sudbury, Mass., 2010, Jones and Bartlett.

20. Mitchell SA, Oslin JL, and Griffin LL: Teaching sport concepts and skills, ed 2, Champaign, Ill., 2006, Human Kinetics.

21. Siedentop D, Hastie P, and van der Mars H: Complete guide to sport education, Champaign, Ill., 2004, Human Kinetics.

22. McConnell, K: Fitness education. In J Lund and D Tannehill, editors, Standards-based physical education curriculum development, ed 2, Sudbury, Mass., 2010, Jones and Bartlett.

23. Dyson B and Brown M: Adventure education in your physical education program. In J Lund and D Tannehill, editors, Standards-based physical education curriculum development, ed 2, Sudbury, Mass., 2010, Jones and Bartlett.

24. Stiehl J and Parker M: Outdoor education. In J Lund and D Tannehill, editors, Standards-based physical education curriculum development, ed 2, Sudbury, Mass., 2010, Jones and Bartlett.

25. Kinchen GD and O'Sullivan M: Incidences of student support for and resistance to a curricular innovation in high school physical education, Journal of Teaching in Physical Education 22:245–260, 2003.

26. O'Sullivan M and Kinchen GD: Cultural studies curriculum in physical activity and sport. In J Lund and D Tannehill, editors, Standards-based physical education curriculum development, ed 2, Sudbury, Mass., 2010, Jones and Bartlett.

27. Placek JH: Concepts of success in teaching: busy, happy, and good? In T Templin and J Olsen, editors, Teaching in physical education, Champaign, Ill., 1983, Human Kinetics.

28. Fisette JL, Placek JH, Avery M, Dyson B, Fox C, Franck M, Graber K, Rink J, and Zhu W: Instructional considerations for implementing student assessments, Strategies 22(4):33–34, 2009.

29. Wuest DA and Lombardo BJ: Curriculum and instruction: The secondary school physical education experience, St. Louis, Mo., 1994, Mosby.

30. Siedentop D and Tannehill D: Developing teaching skills in physical education, ed 4, Mountain View, Calif., 2000, Mayfield.

31. Couturier LE, Chepko S, and Coughlin MA: Student voices—what middle and high school students have to say about physical education, The Physical Educator 62(4):170–177, 2005.

32. Hill G and Hannon JC: An analysis of middle school students' physical education physical activity preferences, Physical Educator 65(4):180–194, 2008.

33. Azzarito L and Solmon MA: A feminist poststructuralist view on student bodies in physical education: sites of compliance, resistance, and transformation, Journal of Teaching in Physical Education 25(2):200–225, 2008.

34. Carlson TB: We hate gym: student alienation from physical education, Journal of Teaching in Physical Education 14(4):467–477, 1995.

35. Fisette JL: Adolescent girls' embodied identities: exploring strategies and barriers to their success and survival in physical education, Saarbrücken, Ger., 2009, VDM Verlag Dr. Müller.

36. Hills L: Friendship, physicality, and physical education: an exploration of the social and embodied dynamics of girls' physical education experiences, Sport, Education and Society 12(3):335–354, 2007.

37. Oliver KL and Lalik R: Critical inquiry on the body in girls' physical education classes: a critical

poststructural perspective, Journal of Teaching in Physical Education 23(2):162–195, 2004.

38. Portman P: Who is having fun in physical education classes? Experiences of sixth-grade students in elementary and middle schools, Journal of Teaching in Physical Education 14(4):445–453, 1995.

39. Hastie P: Teaching for lifetime: physical activity through quality high school physical education, San Francisco, 2003, Benjamin Cummings.

40. Bain L: A critical analysis of the hidden curriculum in physical education. In D Kirk and R Tinning, Physical education, curriculum, and culture: critical issues in the contemporary crisis, London, 1990, Farmer Press.

41. Timken GL and Watson D: Teaching all kids: valuing students through culturally responsive and inclusive practice. In J Lund and D Tannehill, editors, Standards-based physical education curriculum development, ed 2, Sudbury, Mass., 2010, Jones and Bartlett.

42. Dodds P: Consciousness raising in curriculum: a teacher's model for analysis. In AE Jewitt, MM Carnes, and M Speakman, editors, Proceedings of the third conference on curriculum theory in physical education, Athens, Ga., 1983, University of Georgia.

43. Griffin PS: Girls' participation patterns in a middle school team sports unit, Journal of Teaching in Physical Education 4:30–38, 1984.

44. Griffin PS: Boys' participation styles in a middle school physical education sports unit, Journal of Teaching in Physical Education 4:100–110, 1985.

45. Griffin PS: Teachers' perceptions of and responses to sex equity problems in a middle school physical education program, Research Quarterly for Exercise and Sport 4(2):103–110, 1985.

46. McCaughty N: Learning to read gender relations in schooling: implications of personal history and teaching context on identifying disempowerment for girls, Research Quarterly for Exercise and Sport 75(4):400–412, 2004.

47. Penney D: Introduction. In J Penney, editor, Gender and physical education, London, 2002, Routledge.

48. Fisette JL: Getting to know your students: the importance of learning students' thoughts and feelings in physical education, Journal of Physical Education, Recreation, and Dance, 2010, 81(7):42–49.

49. O'Sullivan M, Bush K, and Gehring M: Gender equity and physical education: a USA perspective. In J Penney, editor, Gender and physical education, London, 2002, Routledge.

50. USA Department of Labor: Education act of 1972 (www.dol.gov/oasam/regs/statutes/titleix.htm).

51. Scranton S: Equality, coeducation, and physical education in secondary schooling. In J Evans, editor, Equality, education and physical education, London, 2003, Farmer Press.

52. Azzarito L, MA Solmon, and L Harrison Jr: ". . . If I had a choice, I would. . . ." A feminist poststructuralist perspective on girls in physical education, Research Quarterly for Exercise and Sport 77(2):222–239, 2006.

53. Derry J: Single-sex and coeducation physical education: perspectives of adolescent girls and female physical education teachers, Melpomene, Fall–Winter 2002, online version (findarticles.com/p/articles/mi_m0LJP/is_3_21/ai_94771954/?tag=content;col1).

PART

III

Careers and Professional Considerations

In Part II, the historical and scientific foundations of physical education, exercise science, and sport were described. In recent years, the expansion of the knowledge base has led to the development of subdisciplines in physical education, exercise science, and sport. This expansion, coupled with the tremendous growth of interest in sport and fitness in our society, has resulted in the development of many career opportunities for qualified physical education, exercise science, and sport professionals.

In Part III, diverse career opportunities within the field of physical education, exercise science, and sport are described. This section begins with a discussion of career preparation, professional responsibilities, and leadership development in Chapter 11. Chapter 12 discusses traditional career opportunities, such as teaching and coaching in the schools. The expansion of physical education, exercise science, and sport programs to nonschool settings and to people of all ages has resulted in teaching and coaching opportunities outside of the school setting. The tremendous interest in physical fitness and health has stimulated the growth of fitness-, health-, and therapy-related careers. These careers are examined in Chapter 13. Chapter 14 describes career opportunities in media, management, performance, and other related areas. The pervasiveness of sport in our society, combined with the growth of the communications media, has encouraged careers in sport communication, while the development of sport as big business has created a need for professionals trained in sport management. Opportunities for people interested in pursuing careers as performers have also increased during the last decade.

CHAPTER 11

CAREER AND
PROFESSIONAL
DEVELOPMENT

OBJECTIVES

After reading this chapter the student should be able to—

■ Identify career opportunities in physical education, exercise science, and sport.

■ Self-assess strengths, interests, goals, and career preferences.

■ Understand his or her professional preparation curriculum and how to maximize educational opportunities.

■ Discuss the role of practical experience in professional preparation.

■ Describe strategies to enhance his or her marketability.

■ Understand the importance of leadership and professionalism in one's career.

■ List several professional organizations in physical education, exercise science, and sport.

Career opportunities in physical education, exercise science, and sport have never been greater. Traditional careers of teaching and coaching have expanded from schools, colleges, and universities to nonschool settings such as community centers (e.g., YMCA) and commercial clubs (i.e., gymnastics or tennis). Many physical education, exercise science, and sport professionals are pursuing careers in the fitness field, working in health clubs or corporate fitness centers. Other professionals are employed in the areas of sport management, sports medicine, and sport media. The increased specialization within the fields of physical education, exercise science, and sport has created additional career opportunities. For example, biomechanists may work for sporting goods companies designing and testing sport equipment and apparel such as running shoes. Exercise physiologists may be employed in a corporate fitness center, a hospital cardiac rehabilitation program, or a sports medicine clinic. Career opportunities for a student who has studied physical education, exercise science, and sport have never been greater.

GET CONNECTED

Occupational Outlook Handbook—revised every two years, provides career information, including job responsibilities, working conditions, education needed, earnings, and future outlook in many occupations.
www.bls.gov/oco

Professional Organizations—these websites give information about the mission of the organization, services, membership, publications, limited access to resources, and educational opportunities. Some sites limit access to certain areas to members only.

AAHPERD	**www.aahperd.org**
AAASP	**www.appliedsportpsych.org**
ACSM	**www.acsm.org**
IAPS	**www.iaps.net**
NASSH	**www.nassh.org**
NASSM	**www.nassm.com**
NASPSPA	**www.naspspa.org**
NASSS	**www.nass.org**
NATA	**www.nata.org**

Gradschools.com—lists links to graduate programs, including programs in dance, exercise science, kinesiology, physical education, sport psychology, and sports management.
www.gradschools.com

Professional preparation for a career in physical education, exercise science, and sport will be discussed in this chapter.

CAREERS IN PHYSICAL EDUCATION, EXERCISE SCIENCE, AND SPORT

Career opportunities in physical education, exercise science, and sport have expanded tremendously during the past 30 years. The expanded career opportunities are a result of several factors. First, millions of Americans from all segments of society engage in fitness activities on a regular basis. They participate in a variety of activities, including working out at health and fitness clubs and engaging in community and commercial fitness programs. This has led to a need for competent physical education, exercise science, and sport professionals to design, lead, and evaluate physical activity programs. Additionally, people seeking to use their leisure time in an enjoyable manner have sought out physical activities and sports. Qualified individuals are needed to conduct recreational programs and to teach lifetime sport skills.

The increased interest in competitive sports by all segments of the population has served as the impetus for the growth of competitive sport programs, sport clubs, and leagues, and the associated career opportunities in coaching, sport management, officiating, and athletic training. Finally, the increase in the depth and breadth of knowledge in physical education, exercise science, and sport has led to the further development of subdisciplines and expanded career opportunities such as biomechanists, sport psychologists, exercise physiologists, and adapted physical activity specialists.

Career opportunities in physical education, exercise science, and sport are limited only by one's imagination. Lambert points out that one's definition of physical education can limit or expand one's horizons.[1] Defining physical education as only the teaching of sports, dance, and exercise in the public schools can limit job opportunities to the traditional teaching-coaching career. However, if you define physical education as the art and science of human movement, sport education, fitness education, or preventative and rehabilitative medicine, many career possibilities become evident. Similarly, defining physical education as the study of play, the study of human energy, perceptual-motor development, or an academic discipline that investigates the uses and meanings of physical activities to understand their effects and interrelationships with people and their culture opens up other avenues of employment.

Possible career opportunities are listed in the Physical Education, Exercise Science, and Sport Career Opportunities box. This list is by no means exhaustive but will help readers realize the number and diversity of career opportunities in physical education, exercise science, and sport. These career options will be discussed further in other chapters. Careers involving the teaching and coaching of physical activity skills in a variety of settings are discussed in Chapter 12. Health- and fitness-related careers are described in Chapter 13. Career opportunities in sport management, sport media, and other areas are addressed in Chapter 14.

You also can use your imagination to create new job opportunities suited specifically to your abilities and interests. The growth of the knowledge base, combined with the expansion of our services to diverse populations, has created many new and exciting career opportunities. By combining your abilities within a subdiscipline with your interest in working with a specific population and age group and within a particular setting, you can create a career opportunity uniquely suited to you. The Creating Career Opportunities in Physical Education, Exercise Science, and Sport box will assist you in exploring these various career options.

The broadening of career opportunities in physical education, exercise science, and sport is an exciting development. Selecting a career from the many available options requires careful consideration of a number of factors.

Choosing a Career

Have you already chosen a career in physical education, exercise science, and sport? Perhaps you decided years ago to pursue a career in teaching, athletic training, or sport broadcasting. On the other hand, you may be like many other students—undecided about a specific career. However, you do know that the field of physical education, exercise science, and sport is of interest, and you have decided to explore the many options in this area. Whether you are committed or undecided about a career, college offers a wonderful opportunity to broaden your base of knowledge about careers in these dynamic fields and to explore the growing number of opportunities that are available.

How do you choose a career from the many available? First, it is recommended that you select a career pathway, as opposed to a specific job. A career pathway allows you to pursue many different jobs within a specific area, such as sport management. Second, you can remove some of the stress and anxiety associated with choosing a career by realizing that a career decision is not irreversible. Many students change their minds about the career they desire several times during the course of their college education. Third, a career is not a lifelong commitment. Changing careers has become increasingly common. Some people deliberately plan to pursue one career for a while to provide a foundation for a second career. For example, a student may choose to pursue a career as a teacher and coach for several years before returning to school for training as a sport psychologist. The practical experience gained from coaching enhances the individual's new career as a practicing sport psychologist with a professional team. Additionally, you should periodically evaluate your satisfaction from your chosen career. If you feel little satisfaction from your career, you may want to pursue opportunities in other career fields.

Choosing a career is a decision making process. This involves gathering facts, evaluating information, and making a selection from the alternatives available to you. The most important factors influencing your choice of a career are your strengths, interests, goals, and preferences.

Having a realistic perception of your strengths and abilities is important in finding a satisfying and fulfilling career. In selecting a career, you should

PHYSICAL EDUCATION, EXERCISE SCIENCE, AND SPORT CAREER OPPORTUNITIES

Teaching Opportunities

School Setting		Nonschool Setting	
Elementary School	College	Community Recreation	Youth-Serving Agencies
Secondary School	Basic Instruction	Corporate Recreation	Preschools
Community College	Professional	Commercial Sport Clubs	Health Clubs
Adapted Physical	Preparation	Correctional Institutions	Military Programs
Education	Military Schools	Geriatric Programs	Resort Sport Programs
International Schools			

Coaching Opportunities

Interscholastic Programs	Commercial Sport Clubs
Intercollegiate Programs	Community Sport Programs
Commercial Sport Camps	Military Sport Programs

Fitness- and Health-Related Opportunities

Cardiac Rehabilitation	Worksite Programs	Corporate Fitness	Dance Therapy
Athletic Training	Personal Training	Programs	Physical Therapy
Health Clubs	Space Fitness Programs	Sport Nutrition	Kinesiotherapy
Community Fitness	Movement Therapy	Health Spas	Recreation Therapy
	Medical Fitness	Military Personnel Fitness	Chiropractic Care

Sport Management Opportunities

Athletic Administration	Sport Organization Administration
Facility Management	Health Club Management
Commercial Sport Club Management	Sports Retailing
Community Recreation/Sport Management	Worksite Recreation Management
Campus Recreation	Resort Sport Management

Sport Media Opportunities

Sport Journalism	Sport Broadcasting
Sport Photography	Sports Information
Sport Writing	Web Design
Sport Art	Social Media Direction

Sport-Related Opportunities

Sport Law	Sport Officiating
Professional Athletics	Dance
Entrepreneurship	Sport Statistics
Research	Equipment/Clothing Design
Sport Psychology	

Note: Some of these career opportunities require additional education beyond a bachelor's degree.

CREATING CAREER OPPORTUNITIES IN PHYSICAL EDUCATION, EXERCISE SCIENCE, AND SPORT

Explore career options by combining an area of study with a population group, an age group, and a setting or environment that matches your individual interests. Add additional items to each column as you think of them.

Area of Study	Population	Age	Setting
Adapted physical activity	Athletes	Adolescents	Athletic contests
Biomechanics	Cardiac risks	Adults	Clinic
Exercise physiology	Disabled	Children	College/university
Motor development	Inmates	Youth	Community
Motor learning	Military	Infants	Corporation
Sport history	Obese	Elderly	Correctional institution
Sport management	Patients		Geriatric center
Sports medicine	Students		Health/fitness club
Sport nutrition	Healthy fit		Health spa/resort
Sport pedagogy	Healthy unfit		Home
Sport philosophy	Chronically diseased		Hospital
Sport and exercise psychology			Media setting
Sport sociology			Park
Measurement and evaluation			Professional/sport organization
			Research laboratory
			Retail establishment
			School
			Space
			Sport facility

Create your own job title and define your responsibilities. In the first example below, exercise physiology is combined with an interest in working with adolescents with disabilities in the home setting to create a job as a personal fitness trainer to an adolescent with a disability, working in the youth's home.

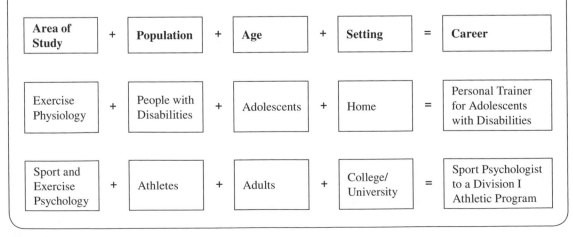

draw on your current strengths and abilities as well as the ones that you have the potential and desire to develop. Identifying your strengths and abilities involves the process of self-assessment. Self-assessment should be positive and ongoing.

Ask yourself the following questions about your strengths and abilities:

- What are my strengths?
- What are my best personal characteristics?
- What personal abilities are reflected in my accomplishments?
- What abilities would I like to improve?
- What do I like to do?

Reflect on the compliments you have received from your parents, teachers, and peers to gather additional information about your abilities. Have you received frequent compliments on your leadership? On your organizational ability? On your work with very young children?

You must also consider your academic abilities and interests.

- What are your academic strengths? Math? Science? Computers? History?
- What areas of study do you enjoy? Music? Language? Math? Psychology?
- What special talents or skills do you possess? Are you an accomplished photographer? Golfer? Painter? Basketball player? Web page designer?
- What talents and skills are you interested in developing?

Your decision to pursue a career in the area of physical education, exercise science, and sport reflects your interest in this area. Pursuit of a career in this area also reflects to a great extent an interest in working with people.

In weighing your career options, ask yourself what your personal and professional goals are.

- What are your goals?
- What are you striving to accomplish at this point in your life? What do you wish to accomplish in 5 years, in 10 years, or in 20 years?

Obviously your goals will have a great deal of impact on your selection of a career.

Finally, what are your preferences in terms of your lifestyle and your work?

- Do you want to work in an urban, suburban, or rural setting?
- What kind of environment do you want to live in?
- What ages of people do you prefer to work with?
- Do you prefer to work with people in groups or on an individual basis?
- What kind of facility do you want to work in? School or college gymnasium? Hospital? Health spa? Community center? Corporation?
- What are your salary expectations? Would you be comfortable with a salary based on commissions? Merit?
- Is salary the most important consideration in your selection of a career, or do you value other rewards associated with the job more? For example, is the personal satisfaction gained from helping a cardiac patient resume a normal activity level more important than your salary?
- What hours and days of the week do you prefer to work?
- How much vacation time would you like each year? Would you be satisfied having two or three weeks off a year, or does two months off appeal to you more?
- How important is job security? Career advancement? Fringe benefits?

As a result of this self-assessment process, you will become more cognizant of your strengths, interests, goals, and lifestyle and work preferences.

If you had difficulty in determining your personal characteristics, you may want to take advantage of services offered by the career planning office or the counseling center at your college or university. Trained personnel can help you recognize your assets and articulate your goals. You can take a variety of computerized inventories to help identify your abilities and preferences for different types of careers.

Talking and soliciting advice from others may also be helpful in the process. Discuss your self-assessment findings with your family, professors, and friends. Listen to the advice they have to offer, but remember that ultimately the career decision is yours alone to make. You are the one who has to find the career satisfying and rewarding.

Information about yourself—your abilities, interests, goals, and preferences—should be matched to the characteristics of your prospective career. For example, you can combine your organizational ability with your mathematical ability to pursue a career in sport management. However, before you can accurately match your own assets with a career, you need to obtain further information about your possible vocation.

Matching assets with careers requires an understanding of the nature of the career you are considering. This information is available from a variety of sources. Career planning or counseling center personnel are excellent resources. They can provide you with information about careers and job characteristics as well as prospects for employment in your selected career. College and university libraries are also good sources of information. Ask the reference librarian for assistance if necessary.

Two publications that might be helpful are the *Occupational Outlook Handbook*[2] and the *College Placement Annual*.[3] The *Occupational Outlook Handbook* is published annually and provides information about the job market in numerous areas. It is also available on the World Wide Web. The *College Placement Annual* provides information on potential employers in your specific interest area. Another source is the *Encyclopedia of Associations*; this reference lists professional organizations active in your career area.[4] For example, a search for fitness lists the American Council on Exercise and the American College of Sports Medicine, to name just a couple. If you want further information about wellness, you can write to the Wellness Council of America. Browsing through the athletic section of the encyclopedia, you will discover career opportunities that perhaps you never even realized existed. An expanded version, *Associations Unlimited,* can be accessed online.

Another excellent way to find out about potential careers is to talk to practitioners. Most people will be happy to talk with you about their career and share their perceptions. Ask practitioners the following questions:

- What is a typical workday like?
- What are the specific responsibilities of the job?
- What do you like and dislike about your work?
- What are the rewards associated with this career?
- What are the negative aspects of this line of work?
- What motivated you to seek employment in this area?
- How did you prepare yourself professionally for this position?
- What is the typical beginning salary associated with this position? What fringe benefits are available?
- What opportunities are there for advancement in this field? What are the qualifications for advancement?
- To what professional organizations do you belong? What conferences or workshops do you typically attend?
- What are the opportunities in your organization to further develop your skills? Does your organization pay for additional training? Attendance at conferences and workshops?
- What advice would you give someone seeking to enter this field?

Try to talk to several people in the same career area, because individuals' perceptions will vary, as will their experiences.

Still another way to find information about various careers is through your own practical experience. This will be discussed later in the chapter.

Your professional preparation courses will also provide you with information about various career opportunities and their requirements. It is hoped that reading this text and participating in this class will assist you in making a career choice or in solidifying one made previously.

After gathering information about yourself and the characteristics of the career you are choosing, try to make a match between your

Many teaching opportunities are available outside of the school setting.

assets and the requirements and characteristics of your potential career. Although you may already have a career in mind, as you embark on your professional preparation program, be open-minded, flexible, and ready to explore other career opportunities that interest you.

Maximizing Professional Preparation

The process of preparing for a career is referred to as **professional preparation.** Professional preparation is the attainment of knowledge necessary to be an educated person as well as knowledge essential to understanding the field of physical education, exercise science, and sport.

Professional preparation also includes maximizing strengths and developing abilities with reference to one's chosen career. In addition to providing the knowledge and skills necessary to be a successful practitioner, professional preparation may be thought of as the process of increasing personal competence and marketability. When viewed

from this perspective, professional preparation includes not only one's coursework and academics, but related career experiences as well.

Education

Typically, professional preparation curriculums have been oriented toward preparing individuals for careers in teaching and coaching. The growth of the subdisciplines and the changing job market have stimulated the development of curriculums to prepare individuals for these expanded opportunities in physical education, exercise science, and sport. Although professional preparation curriculums at different institutions vary, these curriculums do have some commonalities.

Liberal Arts   Professional preparation curriculums typically include liberal arts courses. Liberal arts courses provide the opportunity to obtain a broad base of knowledge. These courses are the sciences, math, languages, English, art, and music. All students must complete a certain number of liberal arts courses for their degree. Some courses are required, such as writing and speech. Other courses are elective, and students can select the courses they wish to take to fulfill their degree requirements. In some states, the state education department mandates that students take certain liberal arts courses, such as history and mathematics.

Professional Courses   Building on this liberal arts foundation are the professional physical education, exercise science, and sport courses. Professional theory courses focus on conveying knowledge within the discipline. Professional theory courses required for physical education, exercise science, and sport majors pursuing the same career paths may vary among institutions.

The professional theory courses provide students with knowledge relative to the discipline and are designed to prepare majors for their chosen career. Thus, students preparing for a career in teaching and coaching may take courses in physical education that include curriculum design, teaching methods, activity, performance analysis, and coaching; courses taken outside the area include education and psychology. Students preparing for a career in exercise science may take professional science courses and outside courses focusing on exercise science (e.g., chemistry and physiology), psychology, and nutrition. In addition to the required professional courses, students may take electives in this area.

Electives   Most curriculums have electives, although the number of electives varies from program to program and from institution to institution. Electives may be used to pursue a special interest, to broaden your liberal arts background, and/or to enhance your marketability by complementing and strengthening your career preparation.

Electives should be chosen carefully to help you achieve your goals. If you anticipate attending graduate school, check carefully to see if you have satisfied all the prerequisites for admission. Students who are planning on pursuing graduate study in another area to complement their degree may have to satisfy several requirements. For example, someone majoring in athletic training who wishes to obtain a master's degree in physical therapy may have to take additional courses in biology, chemistry, and physics. You can use your electives to take these courses.

Minors   An increasing number of students are taking advantage of their electives to pursue minors or concentrations or areas of specialization. By doing so, they broaden their career options and increase their marketability. Some physical education, exercise science, and sport major curriculums require a minor or a concentration. Sport management majors may be required to have a minor in business. Sport communication majors may have a minor in journalism, photography, or speech. Exercise science majors may choose a minor in science or perhaps nutrition and health.

In some states, if physical education teaching majors take enough credits in a second specific academic area, they can become certified to teach in that area as well. Often, the number of credits required for certification is only a few more than the number required to complete a minor at your institution. Thus, physical education teacher majors can

become certified to teach math, science, or health. Using credits judiciously can pay big dividends for all students, regardless of their course of study.

Practicums   Provision for practical experience is a common feature of many physical education, exercise science, and sport curriculums, regardless of the career being pursued. In teaching, this practical experience has long been a tradition and is referred to as student teaching. Student teaching typically takes place in the latter part of the student's junior year or during the senior year; this experience may last for a quarter or for a semester. In recent years, a concerted effort has been made by professionals to provide their prospective teachers with practical or field-based experiences prior to their student teaching. This allows students to practice the teaching skills learned in their courses and can help them solidify their career decision.

Practical experiences associated with nonteaching physical education, exercise science, and sport programs are commonly referred to as fieldwork or internships. Fieldwork is typically shorter in duration than an internship; an internship may be similar in length to the student teaching experience. These courses focus on placing students in a practical setting on or off campus. Exercise science majors enrolled in fieldwork may work with clients in a commercial fitness center or health club. As interns, exercise science majors may work in a hospital cardiac rehabilitation program or in a corporate fitness center. Sport management majors may intern with a professional athletic team, whereas sport media majors may gain practical experience with a radio or television station. Athletic trainers usually gain practical experience on campus, putting in hundreds of hours working in the training room and serving as the trainer for various athletic teams. Many professionals view the practical experience gained through fieldwork, internships, and student teaching as vital in career preparation.

Certifications

You can enhance your professional credentials by taking advantage of various certification programs offered through your school or reputable outside agencies. For example, many students take a first aid or CPR course offered by the American Red Cross as part of their school's curriculum. You can enhance your credentials by taking the next step and becoming certified as a first aid or CPR instructor. The instructor certification allows you to teach CPR or first aid to others and certify them as qualified. If you were working as a fitness instructor in a corporate wellness program, you would be able to certify employees in first aid or CPR. A variety of certifications in first aid and water safety are offered by the American Red Cross and may be a wonderful addition to your professional skills.

Many professional organizations offer certifications, and you may find that certification is a necessary requirement for a job. The National Athletic Trainers' Association (NATA) offers certification for athletic trainers. Fitness certifications are offered by the American College of Sports Medicine (ACSM) and the National Strength and Conditioning Association (NSCA). The ACSM offers two health-fitness certifications, two clinical exercise certifications, and three specialty certifications in physical activity leadership. The NSCA offers certification as a strength and conditioning specialist and as a personal trainer. More information about these certifications is found in Chapter 13.

Certifications also can be obtained in specific sport areas. For example, you can work toward becoming certified as a golf professional or a scuba instructor. Certification by the American Red Cross as a water safety instructor will enable you to teach all levels of swimming. Aerobic dance certification is becoming increasingly popular. Certification and training programs are offered by many professional organizations, such as the Aerobics and Fitness Association of America. Officiating ratings in various sport areas can also be obtained from the specific sport officiating governing body.

Some of these certifications may be available through your institution. If not, you can obtain them on your own through appropriate agencies and professional organizations. Be sure to check, however, to ensure that the certifying agency is reputable and the certification is highly regarded by professionals in the field. It may be helpful to

Practical experience and certifications, such as those offered by the American Red Cross in swimming, can be assets in preparing for a career.

Your academic performances influences your opportunities for employment and advanced study.

ask your instructors and practitioners in the field about the appropriate credentials and certifications.

Academic Performance

A major determinant of your career opportunities and professional success is your academic performance. Potential employers view academic performance as a strong reflection of a prospective employee's abilities and often as a reliable indicator of one's potential to succeed. You should make a commitment to your academic performance at the start of your college years. Additionally, your academic performance may affect your ability to enroll in graduate school.

Many students enter graduate school immediately after completing their undergraduate degree. The increased specialization within the field has made graduate school a necessity for some students and an attractive option for those seeking to increase their knowledge in their area of interest. Attending graduate school for further work in exercise physiology, biomechanics, sport management, sport psychology, sports medicine, adapted physical education, and pedagogy is the choice of many undergraduates. However, this option may not be open to someone who has a poor academic record.

Most graduate schools require a minimum grade point average (GPA) of 3.0 on a 4.0 scale. An even higher GPA may be required for you to get into the graduate school of your choice. Your undergraduate academic average may influence whether or not you are awarded a graduate assistantship to defray the expenses of graduate study. Graduate assistantships are also highly prized because of the practical experience they afford the recipient.

Personal Development

Development of personal skills and abilities is an important part of the educational process. As part of the self-assessment process, you were able to identify areas of strength and areas needing improvement. Additionally, you should carefully consider how you can develop transferable job skills, skills that can be used in many different positions. Communication, leadership, and human relations are applicable to working with people in many different settings. The Transferable Skills box identifies these highly marketable job skills.

Effective physical education, exercise science, and sport professionals can educate and motivate others to adopt a healthy, active lifestyle. Are you a role model for a healthy lifestyle? Do you incorporate physical activity into your life on a daily basis? Eat a low-fat diet? Deal with stress in a healthy manner?

Research conducted by Eastern Washington University showed that although an applicant's fitness level is not normally listed as an official job criterion or even discussed at a job interview, it is an important factor in hiring. The university initiated a Fit for Hire program designed to help majors achieve a healthy lifestyle and recognize those who exemplify active living.[5] Three basic components are included in the program: fitness testing, lifestyle or wellness assessment, and individual advising.[5] Students who satisfy program requirements are issued a Fit for Hire certificate. The certificate lets employers know that the students are fit and are role models.

As a student, it is important that you become familiar with your curriculum so you can plan your education and strengthen your qualifications

TRANSFERABLE SKILLS

Transferable skills are those skills that have application to many different careers. They can be developed through course work, related experiences, and personal activities. Examples of how these skills are important to professionals in different careers in physical education, exercise science, and sport are provided.

Speaking

Develop your skills as a public speaker through classwork and leadership experiences. Learn how to prepare remarks, effectively communicate ideas, and motivate people. (Applications: Appearing before the school board to justify your coaching budget; giving an update on the local television about your sports program.)

Writing

Write often and learn how to write for different audiences. Shape your skills by writing letters to the editors of the college newspaper and publications that you read routinely. Write a newsletter for a club or organization to which you belong. (Applications: Writing a brochure to promote your personal training business; publishing a newsletter for participants in a corporate fitness program.)

Teaching/Instructing

Refine your ability to explain things to people of different ages. Much of our work involves educating individuals with regard to skills, fitness, and healthy lifestyle. Develop your ability to share information and instruct. (Applications: Teaching students in the school setting; instructing an athlete how to rehabilitate an injured knee.)

Interviewing

Learn how to obtain information from people through direct questioning. Learn how to put a person at ease even when talking about difficult subjects. (Applications: Conducting intake interviews for fitness and rehabilitation programs; gathering information to resolve a problem under your athletic administration.)

Public Relations

Accept roles in which you must meet or relate to the public, such as greeting people, answering the phone and dealing with complaints, fund-raising, and making presentations to the public. (Applications: Engaging in athletic fund-raising at the professional organization where you are a staff administrator.)

Leadership

Assume responsibility for directing an event, supervising the work of others, initiating an activity, and directing it to completion. Learn how to advocate on behalf of yourself or others and promote change. (Applications: Advocating for additional community sports opportunities for people with disabilities; directing a corporate fitness program.)

Budget Management

Gain experience in working with a budget, even if it is small. Manage how the funds are dispersed, balance the books, and prepare reports. (Applications: Managing a facility; selling tickets.)

Negotiating

Learn how to bring opposing sides together, help people discuss their differences, and resolve difficult situations; learn how to negotiate with those in power. (Applications: Resolving conflicts among employees of a fitness club; negotiating with the publisher of the local paper for more coverage of your events.)

Organizing

Take charge of an event. Manage projects and learn how to delegate and follow through. (Applications: Organizing a community health awareness fair; hosting a conference for local teachers to share ideas and activities.)

Computer and Analytical Skills

Develop skills in word processing, spreadsheet, database, and presentation software; data analysis and presentation; and web page construction. (Applications: Constructing a database to monitor the progress of your personal training clients; developing a web page to promote your program.)

Source: Adapted from Career Planning and Placement presentation and handout, Career Planning, Ithaca College, October 14, 2005, Ithaca, N.Y.

Participation in athletics can later prove valuable in securing employment as a coach.

for your chosen career. Most institutions assign professors to serve as academic advisors. Work closely with your advisor in planning your program of study. Take advantage of all your education has to offer to become an educated individual and a professional. Create options along your chosen career pathway through judicious selection of courses and commitment to your academics. Your activities and related experiences also can contribute to your professional development.

Related Experiences

Your activities and related experiences can significantly enhance your career preparation. Your extracurricular activities can help you develop skills that are relevant to your chosen career. Perhaps it would help to view your extracurricular activities

as an unofficial fieldwork or internship of sorts. Certainly, participation on an intercollegiate athletic team as a player, manager, or statistician can enhance your expertise in that sport. Your experience as a sport photographer, sport writer, or editor of the campus newspaper provides you with excellent training for your career in sport media. Being active in the physical education or exercise science majors club contributes to your professional growth. Serving as a member of the student government may develop leadership, planning, and organizational skills applicable to a diversity of careers.

Your work experience can contribute to your professional development as well. Work experience gained through part-time and summer employment can give you valuable on-the-job experience. Although employment opportunities may be difficult to secure, try to find work that relates to your career goals. In the summer, gain experience teaching and organizing activities for people of all ages by working in a community recreational program. Or try to get a job working in a fitness or health club, teaching clients how to use the various pieces of exercise equipment, supervising their workouts, and teaching aerobic dance. To gain practical experience, you may want to consider forgoing a higher-paying job in favor of working the career-related job and getting a second job to make ends meet.

Another source of practical experience is on-campus jobs. If you have financial need, you may qualify for a work-study job. As a first-year student, you may not be able to get the job you want and have to settle for working in the cafeteria, but after your first year you will have a better chance to secure the job you desire. Work-study jobs may be available as an intramural assistant, researcher, tutor, lab assistant, or computer assistant. Of course, you must have the skills to perform the job or the willingness to learn if afforded the opportunity to do so. Another campus employment opportunity open to qualified students is being a resident assistant in the dormitories. As a resident assistant, you will learn how to work closely with people and develop counseling and programming skills.

Volunteering is another means to gain practical experience. Although volunteering does not pay you any money, try to view it as an investment in your future. Perhaps you would have liked to work for the summer at a corporate fitness center, but have found that the center is unable to hire you due to budgetary constraints. Ask if the center would be willing to accept your services as a volunteer. This means that if you need money for tuition and related costs, you may have to work nights and weekends to secure the necessary funds for school. However, volunteering may pay big dividends when it comes to your career. One word of advice: Even if you are a volunteer, devote as much time and energy to the job as if you were a paid employee. You are being viewed by the management as a potential employee. Perhaps if you do a good job this summer, you may be hired on a regular basis for the next summer.

Volunteering is a good way to gain entry into your career field. Considering a career in sport broadcasting? Volunteer to be a gofer at a local television station to gain exposure to life behind the scenes. Perhaps this will put you in the right place at the right time to take advantage of any opportunities that may come your way. Volunteering will also allow you to make professional contacts for the future.

As mentioned previously, fieldwork and internships are a good way to gain practical experience. If they are not mandated by your program, find out if you could do one for credit or on a volunteer basis. Many professional organizations are delighted to provide internship experiences for volunteers. The American Alliance for Health, Physical Education, Recreation, and Dance (AAHPERD), for example, offers internships to interested students. Contact professional organizations within your field of study to see if they would be willing to accept an intern.

Consider volunteering to work with one of your professors on a research project he or she is conducting in your area of interest. If you are attending an institution with a master's or doctorate program in physical education, exercise science, and sport, volunteer to help one of the graduate students collect data for a research project. This research experience will prove enlightening and can be helpful when you are involved in your own graduate education. Again, a reminder: Make a commitment to the

research project and let the researcher know you can be counted on to fulfill your responsibilities.

Extracurricular activities, work experiences, and volunteer activities can contribute to your professional development. These practical experiences provide you with the opportunity to work in your chosen career, learn necessary skills, and develop professional contacts. Even though you are just starting your professional for your career, it is not too early to start thinking about being a professional and planning for the future.

Professional Involvement

Start early to become a professional. Professional activities are a source of knowledge and growth. One way to start is by becoming active in the physical education, athletic training, sport management, or exercise science majors club at your institution. If there is not a professional club, try to start one with the help of fellow students and interested faculty.

Join the national association affiliated with your career choice (e.g., AAHPERD, ACSM, or NATA). Many professional organizations offer student memberships at reduced rates. Attend the national conventions, where you will have the opportunity to meet professionals, make personal contacts, and attend meetings and workshops on research findings and new techniques. In addition to national meetings, many organizations have state or regional associations that hold their own conventions. These may be more convenient to attend and allow you to meet professionals within the same geographical area. Association members, as part of their membership fee, receive professional periodicals. For example, AAHPERD members can select JOPERD, the *Journal of Physical Education, Recreation and Dance,* or *the Research Quarterly for Exercise and Sport* as one of their publications.

Start to build a professional library. In addition to the professional periodicals to which you subscribe, organize and retain your class notes, handouts, and texts. Many a student who threw out notes for a particular class or sold textbooks found it meant a lot of additional work and money

TABLE 11-1 4-Year Timeline for Professional Preparation

Focus	First Year	Second Year	Third Year	Fourth Year
Academic	Learn about requirements of your major, including liberal arts and professional courses; determine how many electives you have to explore areas of interest or to use for a minor.	Begin working on requirements for a minor; carefully monitor your academic performance; remember that many graduate schools require a minimum GPA of 3.0 for admission.	Determine prerequisites for graduate school and plan how to satisfy them; check to make sure that you are on track to graduate; take advantage of opportunities to join academic honor societies.	Review carefully your requirements for graduation to make sure you have completed them.
Career Goals	Identify short- and long-term career goals.	Identify a unique skill and formulate a plan for its development.	Work on strengthening your transferable skills; reevaluate your short- and long-term career goals.	Solidify career goals for the next 1 year and for the next 5 years.
Campus Activities	Become involved in some capacity in one sport or one fitness-related activity.	Continue involvement in sport and fitness activity; add involvement in another campus organization or other activities.	Undertake some leadership activity in a professional organization, such as chairing a committee or being an officer.	Advance in leadership responsibilities by taking on more challenging and responsible positions.
Professional Activities	Join your majors club; join a local affiliate of a professional organization (e.g., state athletic trainers organization).	Join a national professional organization; attend a professional conference and take advantage of special opportunities for students.	Attend a professional conference and become involved in the organization in a leadership capacity.	Attend a professional conference; take advantage of placement opportunities offered by professional organizations.
Volunteer Activities	Check out opportunities for volunteering in school and hometown communities.	Volunteer for a few hours a week in an organization of interest to you (e.g., Special Olympics, American Heart Association).	Increase volunteer hours or consider volunteering in a different area of interest.	Undertake some leadership responsibilities as a volunteer (e.g., volunteer recruitment).

Related Work	Seek out related work experiences during the school term or summer.	Work in related area during the summer or the school year (e.g., aerobics instructor on campus, fitness trainer in a health club).	Advance in responsibilities you undertake at work; consider a different job to broaden your expertise.	Continue to work and expand responsibilities undertaken; advance to a position of leadership or supervision.
Practicums	Explore practicum opportunities, including both short- and long-term opportunities.	Participate in a short-term practicum, such as fieldwork.	Investigate internship opportunities in your major; continue to participate in practicum experiences.	Complete full-time internship or student teaching experience lasting at least 10 weeks.
Career Planning	Visit your career planning office; take advantage of self-assessment and guidance programs to clarify your interests, strengths, and areas needing improvement.	Write a draft of your resume and have it reviewed by a professional or career planning counselor.	Take advantage of career planning seminars on interviewing, writing cover letters, and conducting effective job searches; update your resume.	Update your resume; attend on-campus job fairs; take advantage of alumni networks; use career planning, the Internet, and other resources to identify potential job openings.
Networking	Get to know faculty and students within your school; interview practitioners about their work.	Take advantage of local professional opportunities, such as conferences, to meet professionals in your field.	Widen your professional contacts and expand your network.	Network with faculty, professionals, friends, and family to identify employment opportunities.
Certifications	Identify certifications that will enhance your professional skills and contribute to your marketability.	Begin to acquire certifications such as CPR, first aid, or water safety.	Add additional certifications as appropriate; find out the requirements to take major certification exams in your career field—athletic training, fitness, and teaching.	Take certification exams for athletic training, fitness, and teaching.
Application for Employment after Graduation	Become familiar with employment opportunities in the field.	Practice job search skills in securing summer employment, fieldwork, and internship experiences.	Establish a credential file; secure letters of recommendation for your file.	Apply for jobs.
Application for Graduate School	Become familiar with areas of advanced study within the field.	Explore graduate school options and identify general program pre-requisites; develop a plan to satisfy prerequisites.	Write for graduate school applications and determine entrance requirements; take examinations for entry.	Apply for graduate school and assistantships.

later on when the materials were needed for a job. These materials serve as resources when you are starting out in your career. Undergraduate notes and materials may prove helpful in your course work in graduate school.

Attaining a Professional Position

Whether you are seeking full-time employment following graduation, part-time or summer employment, an internship, a graduate assistantship, or a position as a volunteer, obtaining the desired position requires a well-planned, concerted effort. Highly desirable positions attract numerous applicants, and competition is strong. Therefore, it is important to market yourself effectively and prepare thoroughly for this effort.

Preparing yourself to attain a professional position can be viewed as a 4-year ongoing effort. Each year can be viewed as a stepping stone toward achieving your long-term goal of employment as a professional or entry into graduate school. A 4-year timeline for achieving your goal is presented in Table 11-1. If you proceed in a systematic manner, you will maximize your professional preparation and enhance your marketability.

Resume Building

Early in your educational career you should begin the process of developing a resume. A resume is a summary of your qualifications and experiences. To facilitate the writing of your resume, keep a record of all your activities on an ongoing basis throughout your career. People who fail to do so often inadvertently exclude important activities or honors from their resume because they have been forgotten. Some examples of activities that are important to include are honors, internships, athletic participation, employment, professional memberships, and volunteer activities.

One way to keep track of your activities is to use an index card system. Label a file folder "Resume," and each time you participate in a professional activity, engage in an extracurricular activity, or receive an honor, make note of it on an index card and put it in the folder. Some students use a computer to effectively keep track of their accomplishments and activities.

Make sure the information you record, whether it is on an index card or a computer, is accurate and complete. For student teaching, internships, work, and related experiences, be sure that you have the correct title, the correct spelling of the organization, the address, and the name and the title of the person who supervised you. Carefully and accurately portray the responsibilities you performed and give the relevant dates. For example, if you just completed an internship at Xerox Corporation in its corporate fitness program, you would write in your resume file:

> Internship at Xerox Corporation. Industrial Drive, Rochester, NY, 14859. Supervisor: Dr. Richard Smith, Director of Corporate Fitness. Responsibilities: Assisted with the administration of stress tests; designed individual exercise prescriptions; supervised individual exercise programs; counseled participants in the areas of nutrition, smoking cessation, and stress management. Dates: January–May 2010.

Have you ever been awarded any honors, such as being named to the Dean's List? Make note of it: Dean's List, Fall 2010. Write down extracurricular activities on a yearly basis as well—intramurals, intercollegiate athletics, physical education majors club member, representative to student government, attendance at the state Association for Health, Physical Education, Recreation and Dance convention, volunteer for Special Olympics, and so on. Make note of the dates that you obtain certifications as well: For example, "2009: certified by the American Red Cross as a Community CPR Instructor." It is also helpful to make a note of your special skills, such as speaking a foreign language or having a high level of competency with computers.

There are many different formats for writing a resume, depending on the purpose for which it is being used. For example, resumes can be used to obtain an interview, as a follow-up to an interview, as a means of highlighting your qualifications for the position, and as a complement to a letter of application. Career planning and counseling centers offer students guidelines for constructing resumes. A sample resume is shown in Figure 11-1. There are also computer programs and websites available that can be used to write a resume.

Customize your resume for the particular position that you are pursuing. This may involve developing several different resumes, tailoring your background, strengths, and experience to fit the position being sought. Your index cards or computer records serve as a master list from which to select information and activities to present the best picture of you to the potential employer and enable you to include all relevant information on the resume. Preparing your resume on a computer will allow you to easily edit it and to create different versions. There are also several online sites that help you write a resume.

Resumes should be prepared meticulously and proofread several times to ensure that there are no errors. The resume serves as a writing sample and reflects how well you can communicate. It also reflects your neatness and attention to detail. Organize the resume so that the reader's attention is easily drawn to the most important information. Print your resume on high-quality, standard-size bond paper using a high-quality photocopier or laser printer.

Portfolios

Portfolios are used by some individuals to showcase their work and document their attainment of stated standards for the field. Although primarily used in teaching, other physical education, exercise science, and sport professionals, such as those entering the field of sport media, may find portfolios useful to highlight their qualifications for a job and document their professional competence and achievements.

To create a portfolio, samples of work—artifacts—are collected over the 4-year professional preparation program. Artifacts can include a wide variety of objects, such as essays (e.g., professional philosophy), samples of work (e.g., case study or unit plan), videos (e.g., instructional video of you leading an exercise class or teaching a class in a public school), photographs (e.g., programs in action or a bulletin board you designed), computer disks (e.g., web page of an instructional unit), and

published works (e.g., journal article or news article you authored). Additionally, your resume, a statement of professional philosophy, a transcript, copies of relevant certifications (e.g., teaching license or ACSM certification), and letters of recommendation are included. These artifacts should represent a sample of your abilities, strengths, quality of work, and attainment of specific competencies for the field.

Take care in how you organize your portfolio. Often, a three-ring binder with a clear cover insert on the front is used for the portfolio. Artifacts are typically placed in plastic sheets before being inserted into the binder. A table of contents and section dividers separate artifacts and organize them for easy review. A brief explanation of the artifacts included in the section and a reflective statement on their importance and significance helps the reader—the potential employer—to understand the material presented. The portfolio used for employment should be neat, free from grammatical and spelling errors, and easy for the employer to use. Not all artifacts are used in construction of a portfolio for employment, only those relevant to the specific situation. The portfolio can either be sent to the potential employer in advance of the job interview or presented during the job interview.

Electronic portfolios or e-portfolios are popular today. E-portfolios are displayed via the web. They are easy to update and modify according to the position being sought for employment. In setting up your e-portfolio, make sure that it is easy to navigate and that the menu reflects the organization of your portfolio. When possible, convert your documents to PDF files so that they can be easily read, even by those who do not have the software you used to create your work. Another advantage is the ability to upload and then view videos demonstrating specific skills or a presentation you made about your professional philosophy. Make sure that all links function. Students can include the web address in their cover letter, enabling a potential employer to easily review their portfolio. Some prospective employers now require all job credentials to be submitted via the Web, and ask students to provide samples of their work. Having

ROBYN LEE WEST

School Address   Permanent Address
  221 Eastview Road, Apt. 1   312 Cherry Lane
  Ithaca, NY 14856   Floral Estates, NY 11003
  Phone: 607-111-5555   Phone: 516-222-5555

CAREER OBJECTIVE   To teach physical education in an elementary school, work with children with disabilities
                          to improve their motor performance, and coach soccer and track

EDUCATION   Ithaca College, Ithaca, NY, May 2010
                             Bachelor of Science in Physical Education
                                 Provisional certification K–12
                                 Minor in Health
                                 Concentration in Adapted Physical Education

PROFESSIONAL   Student teacher, Pine Elementary School (1/3–3/7 2010)
EXPERIENCE   Student teacher, Cayuga High School (3/10–5/14 2010)
                          Fieldwork in adapted physical education, United Children's Center (1/4–5/2 2009)
                          Youth Bureau volunteer soccer coach (Fall 2008, 2009)
                          Counselor for children with special needs, Floral Estates Youth Summer Camp
                             (Summers 2007–2009)

HONORS AND AWARDS   Dean's List (Fall 2007, 2008; Spring 2008)
                          Who's Who in American Colleges and Universities
                          Ithaca College HPER Professional Achievement Award

COLLEGE   Physical Education Majors' Club (2007–2010; Vice-President 2008–2009)
ACTIVITIES   Intercollegiate Soccer Team (2007–2009; Captain 2009)
                          Intercollegiate Track and Field Team (2005–2006)
                          Intramural volleyball and basketball official (2007–2010)
                          Peer counselor, Health Center (2006–2008)
                          President's Host Committee for Admissions (2006–2009)

CERTIFICATIONS   American Red Cross Community First Aid Instructor
                          American Red Cross Water Safety Instructor
                          American Red Cross Adapted Aquatics Instructor
                          American College of Sports Medicine Health Fitness Instructor
                          Rated official in volleyball and basketball

PROFESSIONAL   American Alliance for Health, Physical Education, Recreation, and Dance
AFFILIATIONS   New York State Association for Health, Physical Education, Recreation, and Dance
                          American College of Sports Medicine
                          Finger Lakes Board of Officials

REFERENCES   Available from the Placement Office, School of Health Sciences and Human
                             Performance, Ithaca College

Figure 11-1   Sample resume

a well-designed e-portfolio that highlights your accomplishments and showcases your competencies is a valuable employment tool.

Placement File

As a senior, open up a placement file at your institution's placement office. Placement files generally contain demographic information, a resume, and letters of recommendation. Letters of recommendation should be solicited from people who are well acquainted with your abilities. Professors familiar with your work, student teaching or internship supervisors, and individuals for whom you worked or volunteered may be able to accurately assess your abilities and qualifications for employment or further study.

Searching for a Job

Many sources will assist you in locating job openings. College and university placement offices maintain job listings and update them on a continuing basis. Some professional organizations offer placement services to their members and periodically disseminate information about job openings. AAHPERD, NATA, and the ACSM offer placement services and job listings to their members. Newspapers, state employment offices, and some state education departments have lists of job openings. Job listings are also posted on the World Wide Web.

Networking is one of the most important job search strategies. Contact faculty members, friends, relatives, former employers, and practicum supervisors to see if they know of any job openings. It is through personal contacts that people learn about jobs before they are even advertised. Attending conferences or participating in professional organizations is a great way to build contacts and expand your network. Be sure to follow up on all leads in a timely manner.

Applying for a Job

Once you are aware of possible vacancies, send a copy of your resume along with a cover letter requesting an interview or application. The cover letter's purpose is to interest an employer in hiring you. When possible, address the letter to a specific person. It should set forth the purpose of the letter, refer the reader to the resume to note certain qualifications particularly relevant to the position, and relate why you are interested in the position, emphasizing your career goals and potential contributions to the organization. The letter should close with a request for action, either an interview or an application, and should thank the reader for his or her time.

Interviewing

If you are invited for an interview, prepare carefully—in other words, do your homework. Find out as much as possible about the organization, the job responsibilities, and other relevant information. Before the interview, take some time to formulate answers to commonly asked interview questions. The following list contains some common questions.

- What are your career plans and goals?
- When and why did you select your college major?
- How has your education prepared you for this job?
- Which of your experiences and skills are particularly relevant to this job?
- What are your greatest strengths? What are your major weaknesses?
- What is your professional philosophy? Can you give an example of how your philosophy has guided your actions?
- What jobs have you held? How did you obtain them, and why did you leave? What would your former supervisors tell us about your job performance?
- What can you tell me about yourself?
- What accomplishments have given you the greatest satisfaction?
- What have you done that shows leadership, initiative, and a willingness to work?
- What salary do you expect to receive? How many hours per week do you expect to work?
- Why should I select you above all other candidates for this position?
- What questions do you have about our organization?

As part of the preparation process, you also should prepare a list of questions to ask the interviewer. Some possible questions are:

- What are the opportunities for personal growth?
- What are the training programs or educational opportunities offered to employees?
- What are the challenging aspects of this position?
- What are the organization's plans for the future?
- What qualities are you looking for in new employees?
- What characteristics distinguish successful personnel in your company?
- How would you describe the organization's management style?
- How would you best use my skills within the organization?

Develop additional questions appropriate to the specific job for which you are interviewing.

First impressions are critical, so create a positive one by your professional appearance, attitude, and personality. Dress appropriately for the interview. To be sure to be on time, plan on arriving ahead of the scheduled appointment time. Greet the interviewer with a firm handshake and be courteous, poised, interested, responsive, and enthusiastic. Be prepared to discuss your accomplishments, skills, interests, personal qualities, and work values in an honest, self-confident manner. Be self-assured, not arrogant or aggressive. Listen to each question carefully and take some time to formulate a thoughtful, concise answer. Remember that you are being evaluated not only on your achievements, but on your ability to think and communicate. At the close of the interview, thank the interviewer for his or her time.

Follow-Up

Follow each interview with a thank-you letter. The letter should stress your interest in the position and highlight important topics that you believe went particularly well in the interview. Be sure to thank the interviewer for his or her time and consideration. If you decide after the interview that the position is not for you, thank the interviewer for his or her time and say politely that you are not interested in the position.

Accepting a Position

When offered a position, again carefully weigh the characteristics of the job with the results of your self-assessment pertaining to your skills, interests, personal and work values, and career goals. If you accept the position, your letter should confirm previously agreed-on terms of employment and reflect your excitement at meeting the challenges of the position. If you decide to decline the offer of employment, the letter of rejection should express your regrets as well as your appreciation to the employer for his or her time, effort, and consideration.

Attaining a desired position requires a commitment to marketing yourself effectively. Actively seeking information about position vacancies and diligently pursuing all leads are important for conducting a successful job search. Your resume should truthfully portray your abilities and accomplishments and be tailored to fit the position. Prepare thoroughly for each interview and present yourself as a professional. Make your final decision thoughtfully and communicate this decision to your potential employer in a professional, timely manner.

LEADERSHIP AND PROFESSIONALISM

Leadership and professionalism are critical to attaining our mission of promoting health and active lifestyles for all people. The advancement of knowledge, the growth of programs to reach people of all ages, and our ability to significantly contribute to the health of society depend on leadership. Professionals entering the field must commit themselves to assuming a leadership role.

Professionalism is also critical to attaining our mission of lifespan involvement in physical activity for all people. Professionalism encompasses competency, credibility, accountability, and cultural competency. Ethical behavior, commitment to being a role model, active involvement, and service are critical aspects of professionalism.

Leaders have a vision, a strong belief in the value of their endeavors, and a commitment to their profession. Head coach Mike Krzyzewski, of Duke University, exemplifies leadership. Photo courtesy Duke University Sports Information Office.

Leadership

Leadership is essential to the success of physical education, exercise science, and sport programs. Leaders have passion, vision, and commitment. They inspire and motivate others to achieve their potential. Leadership is the art of influencing individual people or a group to work to achieve established goals. According to Smith, "leaders have the ability to develop a vision, the skill to articulate that vision in practical terms, and the skill to direct and assist others in executing various aspects of that vision."[6] Leaders influence individuals' and group members' feelings, beliefs, and behaviors. Leaders are conscious of the need for self-realization by participants in our programs. Each individual needs to believe that he or she is valued and respected. Leaders need to recognize that each individual has different interests, needs, abilities, attitudes, and talents.

Many traits, characteristics, skills, responsibilities, and roles have been used to describe effective leaders. (See Leadership Qualities, Traits, and Skills box.) Early research on leadership focused on personality traits possessed by effective leaders. Personality characteristics such as confidence and empathy were identified as characteristics of effective leaders. Current research suggests that effective leadership is highly interactive and situational. Physical education, exercise science, or sport professionals possessing certain characteristics and traits may be effective as leaders in one situation but not in another. The characteristics of the group (e.g., class, team, exercise participants, clients) also influence the behaviors necessary for effective leadership. Among the important characteristics of the group to consider are gender, age, ability level, personality, ethnicity, and experience. Peterson and Bryant point out that there is no one single recipe for leadership: The traits and qualities needed to be an effective leader "vary from situation to situation and from individual to individual."[7] Leadership is like a mosaic composed of different traits.[7] As situations change, so does the mosaic of effective leadership.[7] The challenge to professionals is to determine which leadership behaviors will be most effective in a specific situation.

Effective leadership is essential to those who aspire to work in the health and fitness setting. Peterson and Bryant describe attributes for successful leadership by personal trainers; many of these attributes are relevant to professionals working in the realm of health, fitness, and wellness.[7] Successful leaders possess some, if not all, of these attributes.

- Values-oriented behavior and ethically guided principles (e.g., integrity, trustworthiness).
- Adequate preparation, including well-defined goals, ability to prioritize time and resources to achieve goals, and flexibility to adapt to changing circumstances.
- Self-discipline, including a strong work ethic and commitment to doing what is necessary to get the job done and a moral ethic to guide actions. Self-control is important, and influences one's response to situations, utilization of time and

LEADERSHIP QUALITIES, TRAITS, AND SKILLS

Weinberg and Gould[8] (Coaches)	Intelligence Assertion Empathy Intrinsic motivation	Flexibility Ambition Confidence Optimism
Anshel[9] (Coaches)	Genuine concern for people Respect for others Ability to teach Excellent communication skills	Knowledge (of sport) Strong relationship skills Fairness Positive reinforcement
Peterson and Bryant[7] (Personal Trainers)	Vision-oriented behavior Ethical principles Self-discipline Strong work ethic Knowledge Competency Credibility Performance-oriented attitude	Passion Dedication Effective communication Preparation Motivational abilities Problemsolving skills Opportunistic outlook Courage
McIntrye[10] (Administrators)	Peer skills (fostering group and individual relationships) Leadership skills (styles, planning skills, morale building) Conflict resolution skills (resolving conflict in a positive manner) Information processing skills (gathering, evaluating, planning, disseminating) Decision making skills (problemsolving) Introspective skills (sensitivity to own behavior and its impact)	
Mack[11] (Coaches)	Create an environment for self-motivation and commitment Maintain integrity Lead by example Give credit for success and accept responsibility for failure Praise the contributions of the group Communicate effectively Delegate Practice the Golden Rule—treat others as you wish to be treated	
Smith[6] (Executives)	Vision (creating and communicating vision, goal setting, motivating) Relationships(nurturing relationships, team building, networking) Control (prioritizing, allocating resources) Encouragement (recognizing contributions, supporting) Information (maintaining channels of communication)	
Armstrong[12] (Coaches)	Emphasize ethical behavior Develop leadership among team and group members Share vision and goals Lead by example—model appropriate values Use encouragement and praise effectively	

resources, acceptance of responsibility for time and resources, and ability to maintain focus.

- Knowledge, which serves as a source of competency and credibility. Competency engenders respect and enhances one's credibility as a leader.
- Performance-oriented attitude that leads to the creation and definition of a vision, development of a plan to attain that vision, and ongoing assessment of progress. Passion and dedication help ensure that plans are successful. Vision is the "touchstone that helps guide the behavior of the leader."
- Effective communication, encompassing several essential skills which have an impact on leadership. These include verbal communication, listening, written communication, feedback, electronic communication, and nonverbal communication.

A leader must understand the scientific foundations of his or her field.

- Motivational abilities that enable them to help clients achieve personal goals and help organizations attain their vision. Effective leaders understand and respond appropriately to the unique needs and other factors that affect the motivation of individuals within the health and fitness environment.
- Problem solving skills to solve problems in a timely, systematic manner while remaining focused on what's important in each situation.
- Opportunistic outlook that enables them to identify and take advantage of opportunities that will have a positive impact on their professional lives, the lives of their clients, and the organization.
- Courage, "the personal strength that enables a leader to handle fear, make difficult decisions, take risks, confront change, accept responsibility, and remain self-reliant. . . . It empowers individuals to be themselves, follow their conscience (instincts), and pursue their visions."[7]

Physical education, exercise science, and sport professionals must develop the qualities and attributes essential to the leadership mosaic. Leadership contributes to your effectiveness as a practitioner, and it is important to take steps to develop your leadership abilities.

Another perspective on leadership is offered by Mack, who describes leadership skills as a coach's greatest asset.[11] In a coaching situation, leadership may be the critical factor in determining success. Coaches need to utilize their leadership skills not only in competition but every day in practice. Mack's principles of effective leadership have great relevancy for professionals in physical education, exercise science, and sport. These principles include the following:

- *Create a vision and commitment.* Creating a vision is the most critical of all leadership skills. Effective leaders create a shared vision and foster a sense of commitment. They align and motivate the group toward the attainment of the vision.
- *Maintain integrity.* Effective leaders have a strong sense of ethics and moral values. They remain firmly committed to their beliefs and never compromise their values.

- *Lead by example.* Effective leaders model the behaviors they seek to develop in their group members. They "practice what they preach"; they "walk the talk." They understand the powerful effects of their actions. They serve as an energizing force.
- *Give credit for success and accept responsibility for failure.* Effective leaders recognize the contributions of others to their successes. They acknowledge their failures and learn from their mistakes.
- *Praise the contributions of the group.* Effective leaders try to catch group members doing something right. The use of positive reinforcement engenders enthusiasm, builds self-confidence, and fosters commitment.
- *Communicate effectively.* Effective leaders display skillful use of a wide array of communication techniques, including listening.
- *Delegate.* Effective leaders delegate wisely, giving group members tasks to complete and responsibilities to fulfill. They facilitate the completion of the tasks by giving members the necessary resources, encouraging their efforts, and supporting their actions.
- *Practice the Golden Rule.* Treat others as you wish to be treated. Be respectful, considerate, and kind. The age-old Golden Rule, "Do unto others as you would have them do unto you," offers leaders a good standard to follow in their endeavors.
- *Create an environment for self-motivation.* Although leaders are often given credit for motivating others, most motivation comes from within the individual. Effective leaders nurture the strengths of the group members, provide meaningful yet challenging opportunities to achieve success, and promote the development of self-confidence and independence.[11]

As you can see, there are many qualities, characteristics, traits, principles, and skills associated with effective leadership.

Many people believe that leaders are born, not made. Smith, in disputing the "born to lead" myth, states, "Leadership skills can be described and learned. The key to leadership lies not in having the right stuff from birth, but in getting it."[6] Physical education, exercise science, and sport professionals should carefully assess their leadership behaviors and develop a plan to strengthen them further as they continue their career. Mack writes, "Failure to hone leadership skills is an opportunity lost."[11] Future professionals should actively seek out experiences and opportunities that allow them to further develop as leaders.

Opportunities for leadership development are plentiful. Smith advises that individuals take the opportunity to practice leadership skills at all levels of responsibility, from working with one person to working at the highest level of an organization.[6] For example, an aspiring professional can learn leadership skills by helping a roommate begin and continue an exercise program, by assisting a friend in learning a new sport, by volunteering to serve as a coach of a youth sport team, or by officiating at intramurals. Taking on progressively more challenging leadership roles in various campus, community, and professional organizations allows a professional to further develop and refine his or her leadership abilities.

Professionalism

Professionalism is a deep commitment to all aspects of the field of physical education, exercise science, and sport. Professionalism means many different things to people and includes several dimensions. Professionalism means exhibiting high levels of professional competence and conduct, possessing required credentials, presenting accurate and truthful information about the programs and services provided, and exemplifying a commitment to a healthy, active lifestyle. Professionals demonstrate an enthusiasm for their work, an interest in new developments, leadership skills, and involvement in the further advancement of the field.

Accountability

Professionals exhibit accountability. They fulfill their many professional obligations in an exemplary fashion. Programs are planned, have established goals, are implemented according to current standards of professional practice, are conducted in the best interests of the participants, are monitored for quality on a continuous basis, and are evaluated periodically using accepted assessment techniques. Equally important, the public statements and claims that professionals make about their credentials, programs, and outcomes are accurate and truthful.

Cultural Competency

Cultural competency is important for all professionals. Our society is becoming increasingly diverse. In order to effectively provide services in this dynamic, multicultural environment, professionals need to develop skills relating to cultural competency. Tritschler describes cultural competency as an "ongoing engagement in a process of respectful interaction with clients and their communities."[13] Tervalon and Murray-Garcia describe this process as part of the self-reflection that professionals engage in as part of their commitment to lifelong learning.[14] This process requires that we critically examine our biases and develop an understanding of traditional power imbalances within our society.[14]

Professionals who strive to become culturally competent are more likely to be able to work effectively in our multicultural environment. Professionals need to become attuned to issues of language, culture, and ethnicity, and sensitive to cultural beliefs regarding the cause, prevention, and treatment of illness and the maintenance of good health. Culturally competent health care has been shown to have a positive impact on the health of minority populations. Sensitivity, respect for culture, and integration of cultural beliefs into preventative (e.g., worksite health promotion programs) and rehabilitative (e.g., cardiac rehabilitation) programs can increase the likelihood that participants will achieve their goals.

As Tritschler points out, we "cannot ignore the reality of physical activity disparities for minority groups."[13] The increasing diversity of the United States requires that professionals who work in physical activity settings take steps to increase their cultural competence. Tritschler writes, "Specifically, each and every one of us must learn to skillfully and respectfully negotiate

Conventions offer professionals opportunities for communication and fellowship.

the implications of this multicultural diversity in our physical activity programming. In order to be truly effective 21st-century physical activity leaders, we must develop our 'cultural competence.'"[13]

Ethics

Professionals adhere to ethical standards of conduct in their dealings with participants in their programs. These ethical standards serve as guidelines for actions and aid in decision making. Interactions with participants in programs should be appropriate. For example, many codes of conduct and common professional consensus prohibit inappropriate personal relationships between coaches and their athletes, disclosure of confidential information about an employee by a worksite health professional, or discrimination by athletic trainers in their treatment of starting and nonstarting athletes (see Table 11-2). Actions toward program participants and other professionals in the field reflect honesty, respect, and fairness.[15]

Role Modeling

Professionals remember that they are in a position of influence and serve as role models for participants in their programs. Initially, young professionals may want to discount the idea that appearance is important and believe that competence is what matters the most. Yet first impressions and appearances do influence people's perceptions and beliefs. What impression does a sloppily dressed, overweight, out-of-shape, smoking, inarticulate physical education, exercise science, and sport professional make on participants in their program? Compare that impression to the one made by a professional who is nicely groomed, well-spoken, fit, dynamic, and enthusiastic and possesses good health habits. Which professional has more credibility? Effective professionals are exemplary role models; they practice what they preach.

It is important for physical activity professionals to model an active lifestyle and physical fitness. NASPE, in a position paper entitled

Personal trainers and other physical activity professionals should engage in regular physical activity at a sufficient level to promote health fitness. Practicing what we preach enhances our credibility as professionals.

TABLE 11-2	Examples of Codes of Ethics and Conduct for Physical Education, Exercise Science, and Sport Professionals
National Association for Sport and Physical Education (NASPE) Code of Conduct for Sport and Physical Educators[16]	• "Sport and Physical Education practitioners . . . maintain their professional and personal standing through the highest standards of ethical behavior." • "Sport and Physical Education practitioners . . . seek out and implement appropriate instructional methods that reflect best practice in teaching physical education and coaching sport."
National Association for Sport and Physical Education (NASPE) Coaches Code of Conduct[17]	• "Coaches have the knowledge and preparation to lead their teams" as outlined in the National Standards for Athletic Coaches. • "Coaches are responsible to ensure that the health, well-being, and development of athletes take precedence over the win/loss record."
Association for Applied Sport Psychology (AASP) Code of Ethics[18]	• "AASP members recognize that differences of age, gender, race, ethnicity, national origin, religion, sexual orientation, disability, language, or socioeconomic status can significantly affect their work. AASP members working with specific populations have the responsibility to develop the necessary skills to be competent with these populations, or they make the appropriate referrals."
North American Society for Sport Management (NASSM) Canons or Principles[19]	• "That professionals shall (a) hold as primary their obligations and responsibilities to students/clients; be a faithful agent or trustee when acting in a professional matter; (b) make every effort to foster maximum self-determination on the part of students/clients; (c) respect the privacy of students/clients and hold in confidence all information obtained in the course of professional service; and, (d) ensure that private or commercial service fees are fair, reasonable, considerate, and commensurate with the service performed and with due respect to the students/clients to pay."
National Athletic Trainers' Association (NATA) Code of Ethics[20]	• "Members shall accept responsibility for the exercise of sound judgment. Members shall not misrepresent in any manner, either directly or indirectly, their skills, training, professional credentials, identity or services." • "Members shall maintain and promote high standards in the provision of services."
American College of Sports Medicine (ACSM) Code of Ethics[21]	• "Members should continuously strive to improve knowledge and skill and make available to their colleagues and the public the benefits of their professional attainment."
National Strength and Conditioning Association (NSCA) Code of Ethics[22]	• "Members shall respect the rights, welfare and dignity of all individuals. . . . Members shall maintain and promote high standards . . . [and] shall not misrepresent, either directly or indirectly, their skills, training, professional credentials, identity or services."

Quotations from references 15 through 21.

Physical Activity and Fitness Recommendations for Physical Activity Professionals, states:

> Participation in regular physical activity at a level sufficient to promote health-related physical fitness is an essential behavior for all professionals in all fields of physical activity at all levels (this includes coaches, K–12 teachers, physical education and kinesiology faculty in higher education, fitness professionals, athletes, all advocates of a physically active lifestyle).[23]

In support of this position, NASPE notes that modeling is an important factor in changing the behaviors and attitudes of others. Modeling influences health practice, motor skill acquisition, and adoption of a physically active lifestyle. Physical activity professionals are important models for the individuals with whom they work. They should model the most current recommendations for improving health and fitness. Besides modeling appropriate behavior and commitment to what they preach, professionals will realize the associated health benefits. Additionally, they will enjoy greater credibility and exemplify the value of a physically activity lifestyle.

Involvement

The field of physical education, exercise science, and sport is growing rapidly. Professionals are committed to staying up-to-date with new research findings and changing techniques. They are interested in learning and take advantage of continuing education courses, workshops, conferences, and professional journals to stay abreast of the latest changes. Professionals take an active role in advancing the field through conducting and sharing research, exploring new ideas, and undertaking leadership responsibilities at various levels (e.g., local to regional to national levels). Through networking, professionals exchange ideas and support each other's efforts.

Service

Professionalism includes service not only to the profession but to society. Professionals recognize their responsibility to be involved in community service, not only to offer leadership in their area of expertise, but to participate in activities that enrich the community as a whole. Professionals advocate for increased opportunities in physical activity and sport for those who have been denied or have limited access to services.

Noted adapted physical activity specialist Claudine Sherrill views service as the most critical aspect of professionalism. Sherrill states that professionalism "is manifested in SERVICE to one's place of employment, SERVICE to the community, SERVICE to one's professional organizations, and SERVICE to one's discipline or body of knowledge (generating, using, and disseminating research) justifying and strengthening the existence of the profession."[23] According to Sherrill, "SERVICE is the closest synonym to professionalism."[24]

Professionalism is a concept with many different meanings. It reflects commitment to the field and people whom we serve, respect and consideration for others, and responsibility to oneself, others, and society.

PROFESSIONAL ORGANIZATIONS IN PHYSICAL EDUCATION, EXERCISE SCIENCE, AND SPORT

Professional organizations play an important role in the growth and development of the fields of physical education, exercise science, and sport. Many of the greatest changes in the field have their beginnings in organizational meetings and conferences. Scholarly research, curricular development, certification requirements, and hundreds of other topics are discussed in detail at conferences and other activities associated with professional organizations. The physical education, exercise science, and sport field, both in the United States and in other countries of the world, has an imposing list of associations concerned with its every aspect.

All physical education, exercise science, and sport professionals should belong to the national and state associations in their areas of interest. If all professionals belonged to and worked for their professional organizations, the concerted effort of such large professional groups would result in greater benefits and more prestige for the field.

Besides the many national organizations, there are a myriad of international organizations for professionals in the field. Involvement in an international organization provides the opportunity for professionals to contribute to the building and shaping of the field worldwide.[25] Through their involvement in international organizations, professionals can work with people from other countries to promote physically active lifestyles for all people on a global scale.[24]

Why Belong to a Professional Association?

Belonging to a professional organization has many advantages:

1. *It provides an opportunity for service.* With the many offices, committee responsibilities, and program functions that professional associations provide, the individual has an opportunity to serve to better this field of work.
2. *It provides an opportunity to shape the future of the profession.* Members can work actively to influence the direction of the field in the future. This can be accomplished through involvement in committees, task forces, and governance. Members can also be active in influencing legislation that will benefit the profession. For example, NASPE, an association of AAHPERD, is actively crusading for daily physical education for all schoolchildren and is using its congressional lobby as one means to achieve this objective.
3. *It provides a way to gain new skills and knowledge.* As a professional, it is the individual's responsibility to stay abreast of the latest developments in the field. Through conferences, workshops, publications, and the Web, organizations help professionals learn the latest techniques, gain additional knowledge, and become aware of the many trends that emerge continually in a growing field. Continuing education offerings, online courses, and Webinars are just some of the ways organizations help professionals continue to learn and grow as members of the field.
4. *It provides a means for interpreting the field.* Physical education, exercise science, and sport must be interpreted to the public on national, state, and local levels. This interpretation is essential to achieve public support for the services rendered by the professional practitioner. The professional association provides an opportunity for the best thinking and ideas to be articulately interpreted far and wide. As a result of such endeavors, the profession can achieve recognition, respect, prestige, and cooperation with other areas of education, professions, and the public in general.
5. *It provides a source of help in solving professional problems.* Often, physical education, exercise science, and sport professionals encounter professional problems. Through their officers, members, conferences, and other activities, professional associations can play an important role in solving these problems. The associations can be of assistance, for example, in solving a professional problem involving the administration of an adapted physical activity program or even a personal problem with liability insurance.
6. *It provides an opportunity for fellowship.* Through association conferences and meetings, physical education, exercise science, and sport professionals get to know others doing similar work; this common denominator results in friendships and many enjoyable professional and social occasions. The opportunity to build and sustain networks is an important benefit of belonging to a professional organization.
7. *It provides a forum for research.* Professionals must continually conduct research to determine the effectiveness of their programs, the validity of their techniques, and the quality of their contributions to society. Professional associations aid in the dissemination of research findings through conferences, workshops, newsletters, and publications. They also support research efforts by promoting collaborative projects or by offering grants to help defray costs. Through research, associations also seek knowledge that will enable the profession to move ahead and expand its services.
8. *It provides a means for distributing costs.* The work undertaken by a professional association is intended to benefit the members. This work requires money. By joining a

professional association, professionals rightfully assume their responsibility to share in these costs. If one participates in the benefits, one should also share in the costs of achieving these benefits.

9. *It is valuable in gaining employment.* Through organizations, physical education, exercise science, and sport professionals can develop professional contacts that may prove useful in gaining employment. Through such contacts, professionals can learn of prospective employment opportunities or obtain a letter of recommendation for a desired position. Many professional organizations offer placement services for their members. They send their members updates of job openings, have job openings posted on their websites, and have placement services at their national conventions. These services help a person in gaining his or her first job, as well as in changing jobs.

Numerous professional organizations exist within the realm of physical education, exercise science, and sport to meet the diverse interests and needs of professionals in the field. From the many organizations available, you should select carefully those that best meet your needs and interests. Become involved. Be a committed, active professional willing to work hard to shape the direction and future of this dynamic field.

Professional Organizations

It would be difficult to discuss all the organizations that pertain to the physical education, exercise science, and sport field. The growth of the field has led to the formation of numerous organizations; it seems that for every specialized area of study, as well as for each sport, there are organizations for interested professionals.

You can find out about organizations in your areas of interest in several ways. First, talk to other professionals, such as faculty at your undergraduate institution, that may share the same interests. Talk to practitioners in your prospective field of employment and find out the organizations in which they hold membership. Second, you can search the World Wide Web for organizations in your area of interest. Third, a comprehensive listing of all organizations in the United States is given in the *Encyclopedia of Associations.* The listing for each organization includes the purpose of the organization; name, address, and phone number of the person to contact for further information; size of the membership and the association staff; and publications of the association. The *Encyclopedia* is probably available at the reference desk or in the reference section of most college and university libraries.

The American Alliance for Health, Physical Education, Recreation, and Dance (AAHPERD), the American College of Sports Medicine (ACSM), and the National Athletic Trainers' Association (NATA) will be described here. Examples of associations for individuals interested in sport and exercise psychology, sport sociology, sport philosophy, and sport history are mentioned. Finally, examples for professionals interested in specific sport areas are provided. Since many professional organizations now have websites, it is easy to obtain information about professional organizations and even to visit online.

American Alliance for Health, Physical Education, Recreation, and Dance (AAHPERD)

AAHPERD was established in 1885 as American Association for the Advancement of Physical Education. AAHPERD is committed to developing and maintaining healthy, active life-styles for all Americans and to enhancing skilled and aesthetic performance. AAHPERD's mission is to "promote and support creative and healthy life-styles through high-quality programs in health, physical education, recreation, dance, and sport and to provide members with professional development opportunities that increase knowledge, improve skills, and encourage sound professional practices."[26] AAHPERD has over 30,000 members representing many different areas of interest within health, physical education, recreation, and dance. These include administrators, teachers and coaches at all levels, sports medicine professionals, athletic trainers, dancers, fitness professionals, recreators, and physical activity specialists.

AAHPERD comprises five national associations. These associations and their purposes are presented in the American Alliance for Health, Physical Education, Recreation, and Dance Associations box.

The Research Consortium is also an important part of the alliance. The Research Consortium provides services and publications that assist professionals in becoming aware of new research in the fields. The consortium promotes the exchange of ideas and the dissemination of scientific knowledge.

Nationally, AAHPERD is divided into six district or regional organizations. The Eastern, Southern, Central, Midwestern, Southwestern, and Northwestern districts have a similar purpose to that of AAHPERD and elect officers and hold district conventions. These district organizations provide leadership opportunities for professionals and allow AAHPERD to present programs specific to regional needs.

State associations provide services to professionals in each state. Membership in the state organization requires a fee; membership in the national organization is optional. State associations provide wonderful opportunities for young practitioners to become involved in their profession.

The publications of the alliance serve to disseminate knowledge about the field to its many members. Among its many publications are JOPERD (the *Journal of Physical Education, Recreation, and Dance*), the *Research Quarterly for Exercise and Sport, Strategies, Update,* and *Health Education*. In addition, AAHPERD publishes many other materials pertinent to the work of the alliance, such as the *National Content Standards for Physical Education*.

AMERICAN ALLIANCE FOR HEALTH, PHYSICAL EDUCATION, RECREATION, AND DANCE ASSOCIATIONS

AAPAR	**American Association for Physical Activity and Recreation** serves professionals who strive to "promote meaningful physical activity and recreation across the lifespan," with a focus on "inclusive community-based programs." Fitness for older adults, adapted physical activity, outdoor adventure education, and aquatics are just a few of the many areas encompassed within this association.
AAHE	**American Association for Health Education** "encourages, supports and assists health professionals concerned with health promotion through education and other systematic strategies."
NAGWS	**National Association for Girls and Women in Sport** addresses equity issues in and "champions equal funding, quality, and respect for girls' and women's sports."
NASPE	**National Association for Sport and Physical Education** strives to "enhance knowledge and professional practice in sport and physical activity through scientific study and dissemination of research-based and experiential knowledge to members and the public."
NDA	**National Dance Association** promotes and supports "creative, artistic and healthy lifestyles through quality services and programs in dance and dance education."

Source: From American Alliance for Health, Physical Education, Recreation, and Dance. Statements of mission and purpose (www.aahperd.org).

The services performed by the Alliance include:

- Research on a variety of topics and the dissemination of research through conferences, workshops, and published materials.
- Professional development through numerous conferences, workshops, and training sessions.
- Advocacy at all levels of government and with other national agencies on behalf of members for such issues as gender equity, coaching certification, and maintenance of educational programs.
- Job placement services and professional development services offered to members.
- Recognition of excellence through presentation of numerous awards.

The AAHPERD Student Action Council (SAC) is an organization of students that works for the benefit of its members through student involvement. The group's objectives include greater student involvement in AAHPERD, promotion of professionalism among majors, and promotion of professional interest groups. The alliance, in cooperation with the SAC, has made available special membership plans for students.

For more information about AAHPERD, visit their website at www.aahperd.org.

American College of Sports Medicine (ACSM)

ACSM, founded in 1954, is the largest sports medicine and exercise science organization in the world. The purpose of ACSM is to promote and integrate "scientific research, education, and practical applications of sports medicine and exercise science to maintain and enhance physical performance, fitness, health, and quality of life."[27] From astronauts to athletes to those people chronically diseased or physically challenged, ACSM seeks to find methods that enable people to live longer, work more productively, and enjoy a better quality of life.

Nationally, ACSM is divided into several regional chapters, such as the Mid-Atlantic chapter. Many states have their own chapters as well. The 18,000 members of ACSM include physicians, fitness professionals, cardiac rehabilitation specialists, sports medicine practitioners and athletic trainers, physical education teachers, and coaches. ACSM is affiliated with the International Federation of Sports Medicine, an organization that has played an important role for many years in Europe and South America.

ACSM supports many different activities related to health, fitness, exercise, and sports medicine. These activities include:

- Promoting public awareness and education about the benefits of physical activity and exercise for people of all ages and abilities.
- Sponsoring certification programs for professionals interested in preventative and rehabilitative exercise.
- Holding conferences and workshops throughout the year for professionals in the field.
- Publishing journals, including *Medicine and Science in Sports and Exercise, Exercise and Sport Sciences Reviews,* and *Current Sports Medicine Reports.*
- Supporting scientific studies and encouraging research efforts to advance the field.
- Cooperating with other organizations concerning sports medicine and related areas.

Additional information about ACSM can be found at www.acsm.org.

National Athletic Trainers' Association (NATA)

The mission of NATA, founded in 1950, is to "enhance the quality of health care for athletes and those engaged in physical activity and to advance the profession of athletic training through education and research in the prevention, evaluation, management, and rehabilitation of injuries."[28] There are more than 28,000 members nationwide and 22,000 of the membership are certified by the NATA Board of Certification, earning the title certified athletic trainer (ATC).

NATA establishes the standards for athletic trainers through its education programs. Nationwide, over 100 colleges and universities offer NATA-approved curricula. Each year, 1,200

SELECTED INTERNATIONAL AND SUBDISCIPLINE PROFESSIONAL ORGANIZATIONS

NASPSPA	**North American Society for the Psychology of Sport and Physical Activity** (www.naspspa.org) focuses on the "scientific study of human behavior when individuals are engaged in sport and physical activity."[29] Members are interested in the areas of motor behavior, motor development, motor learning, motor control, and the psychology of sport and exercise. Journals include *Motor Control* and the *Journal of Sport and Exercise Psychology.*
IAPS	**International Association for the Philosophy of Sport** (www.iaps.net) strives to "foster philosophic interchange among scholars interested in better understanding sport."[30] IAPS publishes the *Journal of the Philosophy of Sport.*
NASSH	**North American Society for Sport History** (www.nassh.org) strives "to promote, stimulate, and encourage study and research and writing of the history of sport"[31] and physical activity across different time spans and within diverse historical contexts. NASSH publishes the *Journal of Sport History.*
NASSS	**North American Society for the Sociology of Sport** (www.nasss .org) seeks to "promote, stimulate, and encourage the sociological study of play, games, and sport . . . and shall recognize and represent all sociological paradigms for the study of play, games, and sport."[32] The *Sociology of Sport Journal* is a publication of NASSS.
NASSM	**North American Society for Sport Management** (www.nassm.org) endeavors to "promote, stimulate, and encourage study, research, scholarly writing, and professional development in the area of sport management (broadly interpreted)."[33] The society focuses on both the theoretical and applied aspects of sport management as related to sport, exercise, dance, and play as these activities are engaged in by diverse populations. Its official publication is the *Journal of Sport Management.*

to 1,500 athletic trainers earn certification through its program.

NATA provides a variety of services to its members, including:

- Establishment of professional standards and a code of ethics for athletic trainers.
- Administration of the certification program.
- Continuing education opportunities through conventions and workshops.
- Annual conventions for the benefit of its members.
- Advocacy efforts to influence legislation beneficial to the field.
- Promotion of athletic training through public relations efforts.

- Job placement services for its membership.
- Publication of journals and newsletters, including the *Journal of Athletic Training,* a quarterly scientific journal, and *NATA News,* a monthly membership magazine.

For furthter information, visit the NATA website at www.nata.org.

Organizations for the Subdisciplines of Physical Education, Exercise Science, and Sport

Many of the subdisciplines of physical education, exercise science, and sport also have professional organizations or associations. The number of these specialized organizations continues to grow each year as professionals with specific areas of interest start new organizations in their areas of expertise. Information about selected international and subdiscipline organizations is shown in the Selected International and Subdiscipline Professional Organizations box.

Sport Organizations for Coaches and Interested Professionals

Numerous organizations are affiliated with specific sport areas. Many of these organizations sponsor annual conferences and clinics for interested professionals, conduct certification programs, and publish newsletters and journals related to the sport. Professionals who are coaching or teaching in the specific sport are good sources of information about these sport associations.

Some professional organizations may have certain requirements for membership, whereas others may be open to any interested individuals. They provide a wonderful means to network with other professionals, learn new skills and techniques, and stay up to date with new advances in the sport.

SUMMARY

Many exciting career opportunities are available today for people interested in pursuing a career in physical education, exercise science, and sport. Teaching and coaching in schools at all levels remains a popular career choice. Teaching and coaching opportunities have also expanded to nonschool settings. With the growth of the field of physical education, exercise science, and sport, additional career opportunities are available for qualified individuals in fitness, health promotion, cardiac rehabilitation, athletic training, sport management, and sport media, to name a few of the many career choices available.

Selecting a career pathway from the many available options requires careful consideration of many factors. To make an informed decision, you must gather information from the appropriate sources and evaluate it. Your personal strengths, interests, goals, and preferences are the most important considerations in choosing a career. In selecting a career, you must also consider information about the career itself. This information may be gathered through research and by talking to practitioners in your prospective career.

Professional preparation for a career involves academic studies, related experiences, and professional activities. Planning for a career demands understanding the nature of the work to be performed and the requirements of the job. As you read about different career opportunities in physical education, exercise science, and sport, be flexible and open-minded and explore career opportunities that interest you.

Leadership and professionalism are needed to ensure the continued growth and vitality of the field of physical education, exercise science, and sport. Leadership is also critical in helping participants in our programs achieve desired goals. Leaders are not born, but made. Leadership qualities and skills can be developed and improved by professionals who desire to enhance their effectiveness. Professionalism embodies competence, credibility, accountability, and cultural competency. Critical aspects of professionalism are ethical behavior, role modeling, active involvement, and service.

There are many advantages to belonging to a professional organization. Professional organizations provide opportunities for service, facilitate communication, and provide a means to disseminate research findings and other information to professionals. Membership in a professional organization provides opportunities for networking and a resource for resolution of problems and may enhance one's employment opportunities.

Numerous professional organizations exist. To find out about a professional organization in your specific area of interest, you can consult a professional or practitioner in the field, or the World Wide Web.

DISCUSSION QUESTIONS

1. What were the most significant factors influencing your choice of a career in the area of physical education, exercise science, and sport?

2. As a professional, do you believe it is important to be a role model? Why or why not? Do you have a professional role model? What qualities does that individual exhibit?

3. Reflect on your cultural heritage. What are some beliefs within your culture about physical activity, body image, health, and illness? How do these beliefs influence your actions?

SELF-ASSESSMENT ACTIVITIES

These activities are designed to help you determine if you have mastered the materials and competencies presented in this chapter.

1. Identify five career opportunities in physical education, exercise science, and sport. Using the information provided in the Get Connected box, access the *Occupational Outlook Handbook* site and search for information about physical activity careers. Find out the skills required, potential employers, future outlook, and salary associated with each career.

2. Using the information provided in the chapter, access the website of one of the professional organizations in your area of interest. Find out the fees for membership, membership benefits, and publications.

3. Develop a multiyear plan to enhance your credentials. Specifically, in addition to the requirements of your professional preparation program, what other opportunities will you pursue (e.g., certifications, extracurricular activities, employment) to enhance your professional qualifications?

4. Through self-reflection, determine what leadership qualities and skills you possess. What qualities do you need to develop?

5. Carefully read the statements in Table 11-2 regarding codes of ethics and conduct for professionals. Working as a group, select one career area and develop a five-point code of conduct for that career.

6. Using the information provided in the Get Connected box, access the list of associations. Locate information about two associations in your areas of interest. Find out the fees for membership, membership benefits, and publications.

REFERENCES

1. Lambert CL: What is physical education?, JOPERD 51(5):26–27, 1980.

2. US Department of Labor: Occupational outlook handbook, current edition, Washington, D.C., Department of Labor.

3. College Placement Council: CPC annual, current edition, Bethlehem, Pa., College Placement Council, 2010

4. Akey DS, editor: Encyclopedia of associations, Detroit, Gale Research Co., current edition.

5. Krause JV and Melville DS: Fit for hire—a model for promoting the health and fitness of physical education students, JOPERD 64(4):61–65, 1993.

6. Smith DM: The practical executive and leadership, Lincolnwood, Ill., 1997, NTC Business Books.

7. Peterson JA and Bryant CX: A personal trainer's guide to effective leadership, Fitness Management, October 2001.

8. Weinberg RS and Gould D: Psychology of exercise and sport, Champaign, Ill., 1995, Human Kinetics.

9. Anshel MH: Sport psychology: from theory to practice, ed 3, Scottsdale, Ariz., 1997, Gorsuch Scarisbrick.

10. McIntrye M: Leadership development, Quest 33(1):33–41, 1981.

11. Mack R: Leadership skills: a coach's greatest asset, Coach 16(4):3–4, 1996.

12. Armstrong S: Are you a "transformational" coach?, JOPERD 72(3): 44–46, 2001.

13. Tritschler K: Cultural competence: a 21st-century leadership skill, JOPERD 79(1):7–9, 2008.

14. Tervalon M and Murray-Garcia J: Cultural humility versus cultural competence: a critical distinction in defining physician training outcomes in multicultural education, Journal of Health Care for the Poor and Underserved, 9(2):117–125, 1998.

15. Stoll SK and Beller JM: Professional responsibility—a lost art, Strategies 9(2):17–19, 1995.

16. American Alliance for Health, Physical Education, Recreation, and Dance, National Association for Sport and Physical Education: Code of conduct for sport and physical educators, Reston, Va., 1999, AAHPERD (www.aahperd.org).

17. American Alliance for Health, Physical Education, Recreation and Dance, National Association for Sport and Physical Education: The coaches code of conduct, Reston, Va., 2001, AAHPERD (www.aahperd.org).

18. Association for the Advancement of Applied Sport Psychology: Ethical principles and standards of the Association for the Advancement of Applied Sport Psychology (www.aaasponline.org).

19. North American Society for Sport Management: Position statement (www.nassm.com).

20. National Athletic Trainers' Association: Code of ethics (www.nata.org).

21. American College of Sports Medicine: Code of ethics. (www.acsm.org).

22. National Strength and Conditioning Association: Code of conduct (www.nsca-lift.org).

23. National Association for Sport and Physical Education: Physical activity and fitness recommendations for physical activity professionals, College and University Physical Education Council, NASPE, 2002.

24. Sherrill CL: Giants, role models, and self-identity: issues in professionalism, Palaestra 22(3):56–58, 2006.

25. Kluka DA: Finding our rightful place in the world, JOPERD 74(6):6, 2003.

26. American Alliance for Health, Physical Education, Recreation, and Dance (www.aahperd.org).

27. American College of Sports Medicine (www.acsm.org).

28. National Athletic Trainers' Association (www.nata.org).

29. North American Society for the Psychology of Sport and Physical Activity (www.naspspa.org).

30. International Association for the Philosophy of Sport (www.iaps.net).

31. North American Society for Sport History (www.nassh.org).

32. North American Society for the Sociology of Sport (www.nasss.org).

33. North American Society for Sport Management (www.nassm.com).

CHAPTER 12

TEACHING AND COACHING CAREERS

OBJECTIVES

After reading this chapter the student should be able to—

- Describe the advantages and disadvantages of pursuing a teaching career in a school or nonschool setting.
- Describe the similarities and differences between teaching and coaching.
- Discuss the problem of burnout and its effects on teachers and coaches.
- Identify strategies to maximize opportunities for employment in a teaching or coaching position.

Teaching and coaching opportunities for physical education, exercise science, and sport professionals have expanded from the school to the nonschool setting and from school-aged populations (i.e., ages 5–18) to people of all ages, ranging from preschoolers to senior citizens. Although traditional opportunities in the public schools are available, some professionals are seeking other avenues for teaching and coaching careers. The national interest in fitness and sport has contributed to the opening of these alternative areas of employment. Moreover, the continued emphasis on fitness, physical activities, and sport opportunities for all age groups presents an encouraging employment picture to potential physical education teachers and coaches.

The challenge to those who wish to enter the teaching or coaching professions is reflected in the words of Aristotle. He said that those who educate children well are to be honored more than those who produce them, for those who produce children give them only life, but those who educate them give them the art of living well.[1] A physical education teacher or coach has the responsibility to inspire students or athletes with the desire to learn, to have them recognize the need to develop physical skills and be physically active, and to see that each one develops to his or her capacity.

Cultural competency is important for both teachers and coaches (see Chapter 3). In our increasingly multicultural society, both teachers and

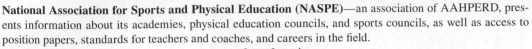

GET CONNECTED

National Association for Sports and Physical Education (NASPE)—an association of AAHPERD, presents information about its academies, physical education councils, and sports councils, as well as access to position papers, standards for teachers and coaches, and careers in the field.

www.aahperd.org/naspe

PE Central—serves as a major resource for physical educators of all levels, offering access to lesson plans for all levels of physical education and adapted physical education, information on assessment, positive learning environment, professional links, jobs, and resources.

www.pecentral.org

PE Links4U—offers information, lesson ideas, and tips for teachers and coaches of all levels as well as current news in the field of physical education and sport. Areas include technology, interdisciplinary learning, coaching, teaching, and current events.

www.pelinks4u.org

National Consortium for Physical Education and Recreation for Individuals with Disabilities—presents information about the Adapted Physical Education National Standards project, fact sheets, monographs, and links to resources.

www.ncperid.org

coaches must be committed to conducting culturally responsive programs that are sensitive to the needs of students and athletes from diverse cultural backgrounds. This includes being committed to the equitable treatment of all people, regardless of race, gender, socioeconomic background, abilities, sexual orientation, or religion.

THE TEACHING PROFESSION

Teaching has been the traditional focus of the field of physical education and sport. Even though many types of jobs are now available in the field, many young people still choose to teach and to coach. The school setting remains the most popular setting for teaching, and job opportunities look promising. It is estimated that during the next decade, 2 million new teachers (all subjects) will need to be hired to replace the generation of teachers about to retire and to respond to a growing need.

Teaching in school and nonschool settings has many benefits as well as some drawbacks.

Regardless of the setting, effective teachers hold high expectations for their students, keep them involved in relevant learning activities, and create an atmosphere that promotes learning. Beginning teachers possess competencies in many different areas that enable them to enhance student learning. The use of developmentally appropriate teaching practices helps teachers more effectively address the needs of their learners.

Choosing a Teaching Career

Teaching offers many rewards, regardless of whether it takes place in the traditional school or an alternative nonschool setting. Probably most important is that it offers an opportunity to help influence people's lives and promote a healthy lifestyle. Students select teaching as a career for many reasons.

Many physical educators want to teach because of their love of children and their desire to help others. The conviction that involvement in a sound physical education program can have a significant impact on the quality of life of its participants motivates some individuals to enter the teaching profession. Prospective teachers who have been fortunate to reap the benefits of participation in a quality physical education program often express the desire to share with others the same benefits that they themselves have realized. Other individuals, who had poor experiences while students in physical education, enter the teaching profession because they want to improve physical education programs so that the benefits of quality programs can be attained.

Certainly personal interests, likes, and dislikes influence the decision to enter the teaching profession. Many choose to teach physical education because of their love for sport and perhaps the desire to transmit this love to others. The opportunity to be outdoors, to work out and stay physically fit, and to have fun are often given as reasons for entering the teaching profession.

The nature of the job attracts many individuals. In the school setting, the long vacations, the informality of teaching in the gymnasium as compared with the classroom, and the security offered by tenure are some of the benefits that prompt some people to seek a teaching career. Others may enter teaching because they desire to coach, and in many schools teaching is a requirement for coaching. Teaching may also be used as a stepping stone to other careers, such as athletic administration.

Many of these reasons for entering the teaching profession are valid for those seeking to work in nonschool settings. The opportunity to capitalize on one's proficiency in a sport, the desire to share the benefits of participation with others, and the love of working with people may motivate physical educators to prepare for a teaching career in a nonschool setting.

The rewards that accrue from teaching depend to a large degree on the individual and what each person makes of his or her opportunities. The rewards can be great for people who commit themselves to teaching.

Benefits and Drawbacks Associated with Teaching

The teaching profession is considered a service-oriented profession. As with other service-oriented professions, those who enter teaching must often be satisfied with intrinsic rather than extrinsic rewards. Several benefits are associated with teaching physical education in the school setting.

Teaching salaries vary widely from state to state, district to district, and community to community. According to the latest American Federation of Teachers salary survey, average teacher salaries in 2006–2007 were highest in the states in the New England, Mid-Atlantic, and Far West regions, and lowest in the Plains region.[2] The national average teacher salary in 2006–2007 was $51,009, with teachers in California earning the highest average salary—$63,340 a year—and teachers in South Dakota earning the lowest—$35,378 a year.[2] Beginning teachers' national average salary was $35,284 a year.[2] For beginning teachers, average salary in New Jersey was the highest, at $44,523 a year, and South Dakota the lowest, at $26,988 a year.[2] In reviewing teacher salaries, as with any other job, you should keep in mind that the cost of living considerably varies from place to place.

At first glance, teachers' salaries appear to be low compared to those offered in other professional careers. However, remember that teachers typically work 9 months or about 180 days a year. Additionally, many teachers receive additional compensation for coaching or for directing or supervising extracurricular activities, such as intramurals and fitness clubs or even the student yearbook staff. The long vacation periods provide the opportunity to earn additional money, to travel, or to continue one's education. Although teaching is not a lucrative career, the financial picture in many cases is not bleak as is sometimes thought.

Second, teaching in an educational setting offers job tenure. The primary objective of tenure is to enhance the academic freedom of teachers. However, it can also be perceived as providing teachers with

Elementary schoolchildren practice their ball handling skills.

job security. Tenure is typically granted in the public schools after 3 years of satisfactory service to the school district. At the college and university level, tenure is typically granted after 6 years.

Many other benefits associated with teaching attract young people to the field. The intrinsic rewards are great. These include the opportunity to serve as a role model to young people. As many of you know from your own experiences, teachers can exert a great influence on the lives of young students, contributing greatly to their development. Others are attracted to the field because of the chance to teach a diversity of activities. For many young people, one great benefit to teaching physical education is that it offers them the opportunity to coach.

On the other hand, one should be aware that there are several disadvantages to pursuing a teaching career in a school setting. Although the public's confidence in teachers appears to be improving, the lack of wholehearted commitment has resulted in problems of morale, lack of financial support, and pressure to do more with less money and to get by with often inadequate facilities. The teacher is often beset with discipline problems, confronted with overpopulated

classes that contain unmotivated students, and required to absorb teaching loads that are too heavy. Teachers often do numerous tasks not related to teaching, such as lunchroom and study hall supervision, hall duty, and playground or bus patrol.

Several benefits are associated with teaching in the nonschool setting. Examples of teaching opportunities in the nonschool setting include working as a tennis or golf professional and teaching in a community recreation program, YMCA/YWCA, or commercial sport club, such as a gymnastics club, swim club, or racquetball club. First, since participation in these programs is voluntary, the teacher generally works with individuals and students who are highly motivated and eager to be involved in the activity. Second, many physical educators elect to teach in the nonschool setting because of the opportunity to specialize; many physical educators like the idea of teaching just one activity, such as golf, tennis, or swimming. However, many nonschool settings such as YMCA/YWCA and community recreation programs require the ability to teach a diversity of activities.

There are some drawbacks to teaching in the nonschool setting. Unlike teaching in the schools, there is a lack of job security. The number of participants enrolled in a program may determine whether it continues to be offered and may also determine the teacher's salary. Salaries vary widely as well. In contrast to school, where the working hours are confined to weekdays (unless one is coaching), working hours at a nonschool setting may be late afternoons and evenings and often weekends. Working hours need to be responsive to the hours the clients have available for leisure-time pursuits. Work may also be seasonal, but this depends on the nature of the activity and the location. For example, golf professionals in the Northeast may find work only from May to September, but those pursuing this profession in the South may be able to work year-round.

Prospective teachers should identify their reasons for entering the teaching profession as well as evaluate the benefits associated with this career in terms of their personal priorities and goals. Advantages and disadvantages are associated with teaching in both the school and nonschool settings. These must be considered in making a career choice.

Competencies for Beginning Teachers

What should beginning teachers know? What should they be able to do? How well should they be able to perform these tasks? What is competent beginning teaching? In an effort to address these questions, a committee of teachers, teacher educators, and state agency officials met to determine what constitutes competent beginning teaching. As a result of these shared efforts, in 1992, the Interstate New Teacher Assessment and Support Consortium (INTASC) identified the knowledge, dispositions, and performances that beginning teachers at all levels and across all subject areas should demonstrate.

In 1995, the National Association of Sport and Physical Education (NASPE) developed standards for beginning physical education teachers. Revised in 2003, these standards identify what

competencies should be possessed by beginning physical education teachers.

INTASC

INTASC's performance-based standards represent a common core of teacher knowledge that transcends different disciplines, grade levels, and states. Guiding the development of these standards was one key premise: "An effective teacher must be able to integrate content knowledge with the specific strengths and needs of students to assure that all students learn and perform at high levels."[3]

INTASC's standards provide information for beginning teachers about behaviors and expectations for performance. According to INTASC standards, beginning teachers should have an understanding of the content they are teaching, the ability to work with diverse learners, and competency in a variety of instructional strategies. Beginning teachers also need to be able to motivate students, actively engage students in learning, and create a positive learning environment. Beginning teachers use a multitude of communication strategies to foster inquiry, active engagement, and self-motivation.[3]

As beginning teachers plan for instruction, they take into account the subject matter, the needs of the students, the curriculum goals, and the community in which students live. Formal and informal assessment strategies are used to ensure the intellectual, social, and physical development of students.[3]

Beginning teachers strive to learn from their experiences, engaging in systematic reflection on their teaching and considering the effects of their choices and actions on their students, parents, and other professionals in the school. Beginning teachers seek opportunities to grow professionally, further developing their skills and acquiring new competencies. Recognizing that teachers are part of a learning community, beginning teachers foster relationships with school colleagues, parents, and agencies within the community, seeking to expand students' learning opportunities and support their well-being.[3]

These standards identify what beginning teachers should know, the skills they should possess, and expectations for performance. INTASC standards have helped shape teacher preparation programs as well as teacher licensing.

Competencies for Beginning Physical Education Teachers

What competencies should beginning physical education teachers possess? In response to this question, both the INTASC standards and the NASPE Content Standards that identify what students should know and be able to do as a result of participating in a quality physical education program were considered by professionals in developing a set of standards (see Chapter 2).[4] Ultimately, NASPE identified 10 standards that competent beginning physical education teachers should possess to facilitate student learning in physical education. (See the Beginning Physical Education Teachers National Standards [NASPE] box.)

Associated with each standard are dispositions, knowledge, and performance competencies. Dispositions are fundamental attitudes and beliefs about teaching that underlie the professional and ethical basis for practice. Knowledge is the subject matter that a beginning teacher needs to know and understand. Performance refers to the demonstrated outcomes or teaching skills that the teacher should exhibit or possess. An example of a standard and an associated sample disposition, knowledge, and performance competency is shown in the

Beginning Physical Education Teacher Standards: Example of Standard, Disposition, Knowledge, and Performance Competencies box.

QUALITY PHYSICAL EDUCATION

Conducting a quality physical education program requires dedicated and competent teachers. Beginning teachers should be aware of the characteristics of a high-quality program so that they can strive to focus their efforts on these desired outcomes. Additionally, beginning teachers should be cognizant of appropriate and inappropriate instructional practices in physical education.

Conducting Quality Programs

One challenge facing physical educators is providing a high-quality physical education program for all their students. According to NASPE, quality physical education programs help students develop health-related fitness, physical competence, and cognitive understanding of the many different facets of physical activity.[5] High-quality programs focus on meeting the developmental needs of students and developing the skills, knowledge, and attitudes essential to adopting a healthy and physically active lifestyle. The essential features of a high-quality program include the opportunity to learn, incorporation of meaningful content, and appropriate instruction.[5]

According to NASPE guidelines, opportunities to learn are enhanced when students receive instruction from a qualified physical education specialist who is skilled in providing a developmentally appropriate program.[5] Students need a sufficient amount of instruction time in order to learn, and NASPE recommends 150 minutes per week of instruction at the elementary school level and 225 minutes per week at the middle and secondary school levels.[5] Adequate facilities and equipment are also important to learning.

A quality program features meaningful content, sequenced and organized to provide instruction in a variety of motor skills. Fitness education helps students understand their current level of fitness,

---

BEGINNING PHYSICAL EDUCATION TEACHERS NATIONAL STANDARDS (NASPE)

Content Knowledge	Communication
Growth and Development	Planning and Instruction
	Student Assessment
Diverse Learners	Reflection
Management and Motivation	Technology
	Collaboration

Source: National Association for Sport and Physical Education. *National Standards for Beginning Physical Education Teachers* (2nd ed.). Reston, Va.: AAHPERD, 2003.

BEGINNING PHYSICAL EDUCATION TEACHER STANDARDS: EXAMPLE OF STANDARD, DISPOSITION, KNOWLEDGE, AND PERFORMANCE COMPETENCIES

Standard 1.	"Understand physical education content and disciplinary concepts related to the development of a physically educated person."
Disposition	"The teacher believes physical activity and fitness are important to the health and well being of individuals."
Knowledge	"The teacher has knowledge of critical elements and sequencing of basic motor skills."
Performance	"The teacher demonstrates basic motor skills and physical activities with competence."

Source: National Association for Sport and Physical Education. *National Standards for Beginning Physical Education Teachers* (2nd ed.). Reston, Va.: AAHPERD, 2003.

---

maintain it, or improve it. The program content is designed not only to promote the development of motor skills and fitness, but to teach related cognitive knowledge, promote social development, and help students acquire a multicultural perspective. The program focuses on helping students incorporate regular amounts of appropriate physical activity into their lives throughout their lives.

Provision of appropriate instruction is a key element of a high-quality physical education program. Appropriate instruction is designed to fully include all students in developmentally appropriate physical activity using lessons designed to facilitate learning. Physical activity is not used for punishment, but valued for its contribution to one's health and life. To monitor and reinforce physical activity, assessments of students' learning are conducted on a regular basis.[5]

High-quality physical education programs are important for all students. High quality programs feature adequate opportunities to learn, student engagement in meaningful content, and appropriate instruction provided for all students. The goal of high-quality physical education programs is to foster development in the motor, cognitive, and affective domains while fostering the adoption of healthy, physically active lifestyles.

Although these guidelines were designed for teaching physical education in grades K–12, they are appropriate for physical activity programs in higher education as well. Many of these guidelines may also be helpful to physical educators who offer physical activity programs in nonschool settings.

Prospective physical education teachers may find it helpful to read some of the position papers and guidelines developed by NASPE to help professionals conduct high-quality programs in their schools. Some of these relevant documents are shown in the NASPE Position Papers and Guidelines Relative to Teaching Physical Education and Physical Activity box and can be accessed online from the NASPE website.

Providing Appropriate Physical Activity Experiences

Traditionally, the teaching of motor and sport skills has taken place in physical education programs and in athletic programs associated with the schools. However, in the past decade there has been a proliferation of programs to teach movement and sport skills outside of the school setting. Some examples are preschool and day care motor development programs, community youth sport programs, exercise programs in senior citizen centers, recreational programs in community settings, private sport clubs, and corporate fitness programs. These programs encompass people of all ages and abilities.

Strong leadership and appropriate program design are important if these physical activity

NASPE POSITION PAPERS AND GUIDELINES RELATIVE TO TEACHING PHYSICAL EDUCATION AND PHYSICAL ACTIVITY

- *Moving into the Future: National Standards for Physical Education*
- *National Standards for Beginning Physical Education Teachers*
- *What Constitutes a Quality Physical Education Program? 2003*
- *Active Start: A Statement of Physical Activity Guidelines for Children Birth to Five Years*
- *Physical Activity for Children: A Statement of Guidelines for Children 5–12*
- *Appropriate Practices in Movement Programs for Young Children Ages 3–5*
- *Appropriate Practices for Elementary School Physical Education*
- *Appropriate Practices for Middle School Physical Education*
- *Appropriate Practices for High School Physical Education*
- *Guidelines for After School Physical Activity and Intramural Sport Programs, 2002*
- *Opposing Substitution and Waiver/Exemptions for Required Physical Education*
- *Recess for Elementary School Students, 2006*
- *Position on Dodgeball in Physical Education*
- *Co-Curricular Physical Activity and Sport Programs for Middle School Students, 2002*
- *Physical Education Is Critical to a Complete Education, 2001*
- *Code of Conduct for Sport & Physical Educators, 1999*

Note: These position papers and guidelines are available through NASPE. Some of these are free and can be downloaded at www.aahperd.org/naspe; click "Standards and Position Statements."

programs are to provide a positive experience for the participants and achieve desired outcomes. How then should these programs be structured to enable the maximum amount of learning to occur and to provide an enjoyable experience for the participants? Perhaps some guidance can be gained from a document entitled *Developmentally Appropriate Physical Education Practices for Children,* written by the Council on Physical Education for Children (COPEC), part of NASPE.[6] This document outlines appropriate and inappropriate practices in teaching physical education to young children. Although it was designed for school physical education, many of the guidelines presented are appropriate for physical education programs for all school levels and physical activity programs for people of all ages in community and commercial settings.

Selected guidelines, modified to include all people and settings, are presented in Table 12-1. As you read each guideline, first reflect on your own experiences in physical education classes and determine whether the practices you experienced were appropriate or inappropriate. Next, reread the guidelines and expand your thinking to conceptualize how these guidelines would apply to leaders (teachers) and participants in a variety of different physical activity programs. For example, what are the implications of these guidelines for the conduct of interscholastic sports, youth sport programs, programs for the elderly, corporate fitness programs, cardiac rehabilitation programs, and preschool motor development programs?

As professionals, we can play a significant role in the nation's health by conducting programs to help participants acquire the skills, knowledge, and attitudes to incorporate physical activity into their lives. For us to contribute in a meaningful way, however, we must make sure our programs are of high quality and appropriate to the needs of the participants.

Noted fitness leader and author Charles Corbin offers sage advice for teachers regarding the conduct of physical education programs.

TABLE 12-1 Developmentally Appropriate Physical Activity Program Practices

Program Component	Appropriate Practice	Inappropriate Practice
Curriculum	The physical activity curriculum has a scope and sequence that is based on goals and objectives that are appropriate for the participants. It includes a balance of activities designed to enhance the cognitive, motor, affective, and physical fitness development of each participant.	The physical activity curriculum lacks developed goals and objectives and is based primarily on the leader's interests, preferences, and background, rather than those of the participants.
Development of movement concepts and basic skills	Participants are provided with frequent and meaningful age-appropriate practice opportunities that enable individuals to develop a functional understanding of movement concepts (body awareness, space awareness, effort, and relationships) and build competence and confidence in their ability to perform a variety of motor skills (locomotor, nonlocomotor, and manipulative).	Individuals participate in a limited number of activities in which the opportunity for them to develop basic concepts and motor skills is restricted.
Cognitive development	Physical activities are designed with both the physical and the cognitive development of participants in mind; leaders provide experiences that encourage individuals to question, integrate, analyze, communicate, apply cognitive concepts, gain a multicultural view of the world, and integrate physical activity experiences with their other life experiences.	Leaders fail to recognize and explore the unique roles of physical activities that allow individuals to learn to move while also moving to learn. Individuals do not receive opportunities to integrate their physical activity experiences with other experiences.
Affective development	Leaders intentionally design and teach activities that allow participants the opportunity to work together to improve their social and cooperation skills. These activities also contribute to the development of a positive self-concept. Leaders help all individuals experience and feel the satisfaction and joy that results from regular participation in physical activity.	Leaders fail to intentionally enhance the affective development of individuals when activities are excluded that foster the development of cooperation and social skills. Leaders ignore opportunities to help individuals understand the emotions they feel as a result of participation in physical activity.
Concepts of fitness	Individuals participate in activities that are designed to help them understand and value the important concepts of physical fitness and the contribution they make to a healthy lifestyle.	Individuals are required to participate in physical fitness activities, but are not helped to understand the reasons why.

Source: Adapted from National Association for Sport and Physical Education Council on Physical Education for Children. *Developmentally Appropriate Physical Education Practices for Children.* Modified to reflect developmentally appropriate physical activity programs for people of all ages in a diversity of settings, AAHPERD, Reston, VA. 2008.

Continued

TABLE 12-1 —cont'd

Program Component	Appropriate Practice	Inappropriate Practice
Physical fitness tests	Ongoing fitness assessment is used as a part of the ongoing process of helping individuals understand, enjoy, improve, or maintain their physical health and well-being. Test results are shared privately with individuals as a tool for developing their physical fitness knowledge, understanding, and competence. Individuals are physically prepared for the fitness assessment tests.	Physical fitness tests are given infrequently, solely for the reason that they are required. Individuals are required to complete a physical fitness test battery without understanding why they are performing the tests or the implications of their individual results as they apply to their future health and well-being. Individuals are required to take physical fitness tests without adequate conditioning.
Calisthenics	Appropriate exercises are taught for the specific purpose of improving the skill, coordination, or fitness levels of individuals. Individuals are taught exercises that keep the body in proper alignment, thereby allowing the muscles to lengthen without placing stress and strain on the surrounding joints, ligaments, and tendons (e.g., sitting toe touch).	Individuals perform standardized calisthenics with no specific purpose in mind (e.g., jumping jacks, windmills). Exercises are taught that compromise body alignment and place unnecessary stress on the joints and muscles (e.g., deep knee bends, ballistic or bouncing stretches).
Fitness	Fitness activities are used to help individuals increase personal physical fitness levels in a supportive, motivating, and progressive manner, thereby promoting positive lifetime fitness attitudes.	Physical fitness activities are used by leaders as punishment for individuals' misbehavior (e.g., individuals running laps or doing push-ups because they are off-task or slow to respond to instruction, or the leader wants to teach them a lesson).
Assessment	Leaders' decisions are based primarily on ongoing individual assessments of people as they participate in physical activities (formative evaluation), and not on the basis of a single test score (summative evaluation). Assessment of individuals' physical progress and achievement is used to personalize instruction, plan the program, identify individuals with special needs, and evaluate program effectiveness.	Individuals are evaluated on the basis of fitness test scores or on a single physical skill test.
Regular involvement	Individuals participate on a regularly scheduled basis because they recognize that it is an important part of their life and essential to their health.	Individuals participate infrequently or fail to recognize the value and contribution of regular participation to their life and health.

Continued

TABLE 12-1 —cont'd

Program Component	Appropriate Practice	Inappropriate Practice
Active participation	All individuals are involved in activities that allow them to remain continuously active. Classes are designed to meet an individual's need for active participation in all learning experiences.	Activity time is decreased because of waiting for a turn, insufficient equipment, or organization into large groups. Individuals are eliminated from activities with no chance to reenter the activity.
Activities	Activities are selected, designed, sequenced, and modified by teachers or individuals to maximize learning and enjoyment.	Activities are taught with no obvious purpose or goals other than to keep individuals "busy, happy, and good."
Equity	All individuals have equal access to activities. All individuals are equally encouraged, supported, and socialized toward successful achievement in all realms of physical activities, regardless of race or sex. Statements by leaders support leadership opportunities and provide positive reinforcement in a variety of activities that may be considered equitable.	Individuals' opportunities are limited because of traditional roles (feminine or masculine) and stereotypes. Prejudice and discrimination reduce opportunities for equitable participation.
Success rate	Individuals are given the opportunity to practice their skills at high rates of success adjusted for their individual skill levels.	Individuals are asked to perform activities that are too easy or too hard, causing frustration, boredom, or misbehavior. All individuals are expected to perform to the same standard with no allowance for individual abilities and interests.
Time	Individuals are given the opportunity to participate daily at a scheduled time; the length of time is appropriate for the developmental level of the individual.	There is no provision for regular physical activity. Individuals' age and maturational levels are not taken into account when the physical activity program is developed.
Facilities	Individuals are provided an environment in which they have adequate space to move freely and safely.	Classes are held in spaces not free from obstructions, where opportunities to move are restricted.
Equipment	Enough equipment is available so that each individual benefits from maximum participation. Equipment is appropriate to each individual's size, skill, and confidence level so that they are motivated to participate.	An insufficient amount of equipment is available for the number of individuals present. Equipment used is inappropriate and may hamper skill development or injure or intimidate individuals.

The assumption that promoting lifelong physical activity is the primary goal of physical education programs is a premise that should underlie our programs at all levels. As Corbin notes, this primary goal is consistent with the NASPE guidelines.[7] The focus on promoting lifelong physical activity supports the public health role of physical education and is congruent with the emphasis on using physical activity to promote better health for youth as advocated by the Centers for Disease Control and

Prevention.[7] Quality programs should progressively build toward this goal, with physical education at each level of instruction helping students acquire the skills, knowledge, and attitudes to be physically active for a lifetime.

TEACHING RESPONSIBILITIES

Teachers in both school and nonschool settings perform a myriad of tasks every day. Prospective teachers need to be cognizant of their responsibilities. In addition to actually teaching, teachers perform many administrative and professionally related tasks. Gensemer groups the activities of teachers into three areas: instructional tasks, managerial tasks, and institutional tasks.[8]

Instructional tasks are responsibilities and activities that relate directly to teaching. These tasks include explaining and demonstrating how to perform a skill, describing how to execute a particular strategy in a game, evaluating students' performance, motivating students through the use of various techniques, and using questions to check

students' comprehension of the material being presented to determine the clarity of the presentation and to elicit student input.

Managerial tasks are activities related to the administration of the class. In the school setting, these activities may include taking attendance, dealing with discipline problems, and patrolling the locker room. In a nonschool setting such as a commercial health club or sports center, managerial responsibilities may include setting up and dismantling equipment, repairing equipment, handing out towels, distributing workout record sheets, and recording individuals' progress.

Institutional tasks are activities related to the institution in which teaching occurs, that is, the school or organization for which the teacher works. In the school setting, teachers may be expected to assume hall duty or lunchroom supervision, attend curriculum or departmental meetings, and conduct parent-teacher conferences. Many physical educators note that counseling students about matters that affect the development of their physical selves and advising students on personal problems occupy

Locker-room supervision is one of a teacher's managerial responsibilities.

a great amount of their time, but the opportunity to be of service to students in this manner is rewarding. In the nonschool setting, teachers may also perform institutional duties such as checking membership cards at the front desk, mailing promotional brochures to attract new members, and filling out a variety of reports. In some situations, managerial and institutional responsibilities occupy more of a teacher's time than actual instructional tasks.

Teachers have numerous professional responsibilities in addition to the responsibilities previously described. They may conduct research in an effort to push forward the frontiers of knowledge. Another professional responsibility is interpreting the worth of physical education and sport to the public. This requires that physical educators be well versed in the scientific foundations of the discipline so that they may accurately interpret the worth of physical education and sport to others. Physical educators need to be cognizant that the programs they conduct reflect the aims and the worth of the field. Physical educators symbolize their commitment to the profession by being role models for what they preach; they should exemplify a healthy, active lifestyle. Professionals need to take advantage of opportunities to speak to educators, the community, and civic and other groups about their field of endeavor.

Many physical educators may also have community responsibilities. These are usually engaged in voluntarily. However, the special qualifications and skills of physical educators make them a likely target for requests from community groups to assist with youth and other sport programs such as Little League or adult recreational programs. By assuming a leadership role, physical educators can help ensure that such programs are organized and administered in the best interests of youths and adults. By their participation, physical educators are afforded an opportunity to interpret physical education and sport to the public in general. In doing so, physical educators become respected and important leaders in the community and gain greater support for their program.

Teachers' responsibilities are not limited to teaching. They perform a wide variety of activities during the course of their workday. Managerial, administrative, institutional, and professional responsibilities are associated with teaching. The exact nature of these tasks may vary from setting to setting. Teaching opportunities in school and nonschool settings and with people of all ages will be discussed in the following section.

TEACHING CAREERS

If teaching is your career goal, there are many different opportunities for work. Traditionally, physical education teachers have worked in the school setting with children and youths. Today, however, there are teaching opportunities available in many settings outside of school, giving teachers the wonderful opportunity to work with people of all ages. (See the Lifespan and Cultural Perspectives box.)

Teaching in the School Setting

Teaching positions in the school setting are available in public and private school systems, higher education, and specialized schools. Public and private schools are organized according to various administrative patterns. Today the most typical pattern is the elementary school, middle school, and high school configuration.

The number of preschool programs in the United States is growing rapidly. The National Education Association recommends that a greater emphasis be placed on early childhood education for all children.[9] The growth of preschool programs has created additional opportunities for physical educators to work with young children to develop motor skills and promote the development of a healthy lifestyle.

In higher education, professional opportunities include teaching in 2-year junior colleges or community colleges and 4-year colleges or universities. There are also teaching positions for those professionals who want to work with people with disabilities and for those who aspire to instruct in a professional preparation program. Teaching opportunities also exist in specialized schools, such as vocational and technical schools, as well as in developmental centers.

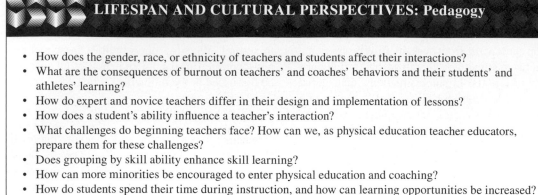

LIFESPAN AND CULTURAL PERSPECTIVES: Pedagogy

- How does the gender, race, or ethnicity of teachers and students affect their interactions?
- What are the consequences of burnout on teachers' and coaches' behaviors and their students' and athletes' learning?
- How do expert and novice teachers differ in their design and implementation of lessons?
- How does a student's ability influence a teacher's interaction?
- What challenges do beginning teachers face? How can we, as physical education teacher educators, prepare them for these challenges?
- Does grouping by skill ability enhance skill learning?
- How can more minorities be encouraged to enter physical education and coaching?
- How do students spend their time during instruction, and how can learning opportunities be increased?
- How does cultural competency influence adherence to physical activity programs for adults?
- How do teachers' personal preferences for sports affect their curriculum decisions?
- How can physical education be used to promote student responsibility?
- What is the most effective way to design instruction to meet the needs of students with specific disabilities?
- How can physical educators more effectively promote lifelong physical activity?

Teaching in an Elementary School

Providing a quality physical education program for young children is critical. Participation in a quality program during these formative years will likely instill in the child a love for physical activity that may last a lifetime, and a favorable attitude toward physical education. If the experience is negative, the youngster may come to hate physical education as well as physical activity, a feeling that could remain with him or her for life. Because of the close relationship between physical activity and health, this could have a significant impact on the quality of the child's life.

Movement experiences are recognized as educationally desirable in the early life of the child. This is the time when a solid movement foundation can be developed, providing children with a base for future physical development and achievement in various forms of physical activity. Furthermore, it is through movement that children express themselves, are creative, develop self-image, and gain a better understanding of their physical selves. It is through such movement experiences that young children explore, develop, and grow in a meaningful manner.

In the primary grades K through 3, great emphasis is placed on learning fundamental motor skills such as running, jumping, climbing, throwing, catching, kicking, and striking. Children participate in guided discovery and problem solving activities focused on movement concepts, including body awareness, spatial awareness, qualities of movement, and relationships. Conceptually based programs further enhance the child's understanding of movement. Perceptual-motor activities help children to develop such necessary skills as eye-hand and eye-foot coordination, laterality and directionality, and tracking of an object.

The primary-grade curriculum is concerned with developing within each child a positive self-image as a mover. Attention also should be given to developing desirable social skills, such as working with others. Individualized learning, in which students learn at their own pace, is compatible with problem solving and a creative approach to learning for primary school children.

In the upper elementary school grades, the physical education curriculum focuses on refining fundamental motor skills and applying these skills

Young children like to test their abilities, such as balance, in a variety of environments.

to the development of sport-related skills. During this time, all children should be given the opportunity to participate in a wide range of sport and physical activities rather than be encouraged to specialize in a few selected sports. In addition to being exposed to traditional team sports, students at this level should receive instruction in dance, gymnastics, and individual activities (e.g., track and, whenever possible, aquatics). Acquisition of knowledge relative to physical education and the development of qualities of good sportspersonship, leadership, and fellowship should be encouraged.

Elementary school physical educators may find the guidelines developed by COPEC, helpful in designing and implementing their programs. COPEC recommends that a quality instructional program provide opportunities for each child to develop motor skills and efficient movement patterns, attain a high level of fitness, learn to communicate through movement, acquire self-understanding, interact socially, and achieve desired psychomotor, cognitive, and affective outcomes.[10] COPEC guidelines also suggest that elementary school-children participate in a quality physical education program for a minimum of 150 minutes per week.[10]

Many reasons are given by physical educators for preferring teaching in the elementary schools. At this level, students typically are eager and enthusiastic about moving and take pride in their progress. Children at this age enjoy being active and have boundless energy. Many physical educators enjoy the challenge of working with children during their most impressionable and formative years. The rapid, visible skill improvement typical of elementary school students is rewarding and motivating to the teacher.

Teaching in a Middle School

Teaching students enrolled in a middle school presents a unique series of challenges to physical educators. Students are in a period of their development that is fraught with physical, social, and emotional changes. Because of the anatomical and physiological characteristics of this age group, activities must be selected with care. Students at this level are in a period of rapid growth that causes them difficulty in coordinating their actions and often results in awkwardness and excessive fatigue. Students are faced with the task of coping with the myriad changes associated with puberty, including the development of secondary sex characteristics. Social and emotional changes are also experienced. The desire to be independent and the influence of peers are particularly strong. Physical educators need to be aware of and sensitive to the many changes students are experiencing.

At this level, physical education programs should include a balance between individual and dual sport activities such as aquatics and tennis and team sport activities such as soccer and basketball. Dance, gymnastics, and fitness activities also should be an integral part of the curriculum. It is important to build on the skills and positive experiences of the elementary school level. Those students who have not progressed as rapidly as their peers in motor development should receive special attention to help them improve their skills. Students' knowledge of physical education should be further expanded and opportunities to apply this knowledge be provided. During these school years, students begin to specialize in certain physical activities and actively pursue those interests.

NASPE's Middle and Secondary School Physical Educaton Council recommends that middle school physical education programs provide opportunities for each student to engage in activities that promote motor skill and fitness development throughout life.[11] Programs at this level should advance knowledge of physical education while enhancing social and emotional development through increased self-responsibility and self-direction. Within the physical education program, students should be grouped by interest and ability, and careful attention should be given to avoiding sex-role discrimination and stereotyping. A minimum of 225 minutes of physical education per week, distributed over at least 3 days, is recommended. Additional opportunities for students to participate

in physical activity experiences should be provided through intramural programs, club activities, and, when appropriate, interscholastic sports.

Teaching in a High School

At the high school level, students exhibit increased physical, mental, social, and emotional maturity. This is the time of transition from adolescence to adulthood.

One of the primary goals for physical educators teaching at the secondary school level is to socialize students into the role of participants in physical activities suited to their needs and interests. Pangrazi and Darst state that "the most important goal of a secondary physical education program should be to help youngsters incorporate some form of physical activity into their lifestyle."[12] This means that teachers must design and implement physical education programs in such a manner that the students' attitudes, knowledge, and skills are developed with a view to realizing this objective. Pangrazi and Darst contend that the ultimate measure of a successful high school physical education program is the "number of students who incorporate physical activities such as exercise, sport, dance, and outdoor adventure activities into their lifestyles."[12]

The curriculum is generally oriented toward lifetime sports, although team sports also may be popular. It is critical that the physical educator take into consideration the interests and needs of the students in planning the curriculum. During this time, students should have the opportunity to develop sufficient skills so that when they leave school they will have the desire and the knowledge to participate in physical activities and sport successfully and enjoyably. Because many students do not continue on to college, it is essential that they acquire the competencies and interest before they leave high school.

NASPE's Middle and Secondary School Physical Education Council recommends that programs at the high school level focus on refining skills in a wide range of activities and on developing advanced skills in lifetime activities personally selected by the student.[13] Students should learn how to develop personal programs to gain and maintain optimal levels of fitness throughout their lifetime. Knowledge of the scientific principles related to physical education, self-direction in the conduct of individual physical activity programs, and an appreciation of the role of physical activity and sport in society are also outcomes of a quality secondary school physical education program. It is recommended that daily physical education be provided for all students, and instructional periods total at least 225 minutes per week. The length of the class period, the size of the class, and the quality standards used for credit should be comparable to those used for other subject areas within the curriculum.

Many high school physical education programs, while required of the students, offer students the opportunity to select units in which they want to participate. An increasing number of schools have expanded their course offerings by using off-campus community facilities such as a golf course, an ice rink, an aquatics center, or a ski slope. The trend is toward providing students with increased knowledge and understanding of physical education concepts. This is often accomplished by offering minicourses on topics of interest, such as fitness or weight management, or by the integration of concepts, such as those pertaining to force production, into regular activity classes. Intramurals, interscholastic sports, and sport clubs offer students additional opportunities to participate in sport, develop expertise, and realize other desirable outcomes.

Teaching Physical Education in Higher Education

Prospective physical education teachers may also take advantage of opportunities to teach in higher education. Opportunities may be found to teach at 2-year community colleges or at 4-year colleges or universities. Usually a master's degree in an area of physical education is a prerequisite to obtaining a job at this level. In some institutions, coaching responsibilities may be associated with teaching positions, whereas in other institutions, coaches carry no teaching responsibilities.

The status of general or basic-instruction physical education programs* in colleges and universities in the United States has changed in recent years. At one time, many colleges and universities required all students to take a physical education course each semester—for example, one course a semester for 2 years. Today, physical education at this level is usually voluntary, thus placing responsibility on the physical education department to offer courses that are appealing to students. Because of this need, curriculums at this level tend to be more flexible and to change more often in response to students' interests and needs.

Lifetime sports and recreational activities are emphasized at this level, including such activities as tennis, golf, self-defense, aerobic dance, and personal fitness; outdoor pursuits such as canoeing, camping, and rock climbing; and aquatic activities. Students may have the opportunity to enroll in theory courses. Class topics may include health concepts, cardiovascular fitness, principles of exercise, biomechanical principles, and development of personalized fitness programs. Some colleges offer courses called Wellness for Life or Fitness for Life. These courses combine theoretical information with laboratory experiences designed to help students acquire the knowledge and skills necessary to lead a healthy lifestyle.

Sport clubs provide interested participants an opportunity for social group experiences and enjoyment of a particular sport activity. Intramurals and intercollegiate sports play an important part in college and university physical education programs. They offer students additional opportunities for participation according to their abilities, needs, and interests.

Teaching Physical Education and Sport in Professional Preparation Programs

Professional preparation programs at colleges and universities educate students for careers in physical education, exercise science, and sport. About

---

*These programs are designed to serve all students on campus and are not to be confused with programs designed to educate prospective physical education and sport majors; those programs are referred to as professional preparation programs.

700 institutions offer professional preparation programs. Physical education, exercise science, and sport professionals who aspire to teach in these programs have the opportunity to train students to be leaders in the field and shape its direction.

Physical education, exercise science, and sport professionals who teach in these programs typically possess advanced degrees, a strong academic record, and, many times, previous experience in their area of interest. For example, a physical education, exercise science, and sport professional desiring to teach in a professional preparation program to prepare future teachers may find it advantageous to have at least 3 years of teaching experience in the public schools, at the elementary, middle, or secondary school level. Similarly, a professional desiring to teach in a professional preparation program focusing on exercise science may find it helpful to have several years of practical experience, such as working in a fitness center, corporate wellness program, or cardiac rehabilitation program.

A professor in a professional preparation program may teach theory courses in the subdisciplines and related areas such as history and philosophy of physical education, assessment, motor control, motor learning, motor development, biomechanics, exercise physiology, curriculum and methods, organization and administration, sociology of sport, sport psychology, and adapted physical education. These individuals typically possess doctorate degrees in their areas of expertise. Individuals who aspire to teach in professional preparation programs may also teach professional activity and skills courses, as well as courses in coaching methods. These individuals usually possess a high degree of skill in their areas of expertise. Professionals teaching activity and skills courses possess master's degrees, and some individuals may have earned doctorate degrees.

In addition to their teaching responsibilities, teachers are expected to conduct research, participate on department and college or university committees, and advise and counsel students. These teachers are expected to write for professional publications, perform community service, consult, and participate in the work of professional organizations.

Teaching in a professional preparation program is very rewarding. The joy and satisfaction derived from teaching students who are entering your own field are tremendous. Helping these future professionals acquire the knowledge, competencies, and dispositions essential to contribute to the growth of the field and to becoming an outstanding professional is very gratifying. As a professor, mentoring these young future professionals provides you with the opportunity to help shape the future of the field, and it is exciting to realize that your students will mature as individuals and professionals and become your future colleagues.

Teaching Adapted Physical Activity

Teaching physical education to students with disabilities is another career opportunity. About 13% of the school population, or more than 6.6 million students, have a disability.[14] These students include those with physical challenges such as cerebral palsy or amputations, mental or emotional impairments, hearing and visual impairments, learning disabilities, and other health impairments such as asthma or heart problems. Adapted physical activity focuses on adapting or modifying physical activity to meet the needs of students. Good physical education is adapted physical education, for the heart of quality physical education and adapted physical activity is education that is developmentally appropriate for the needs of the individual student. The Education of All Handicapped Children Act and other legislation gives students with disabilities the right to participate in physical education.

By law, each identified student with a disability must have an individualized education plan, or IEP. Physical education is mandated by law to be included in each student's educational program. Physical education teachers have the opportunity to participate in the design of the individual plan.

There are several approaches to the inclusion of children with disabilities into the educational setting, including physical education. The least restrictive environment approach places students with disabilities in an educational setting that matches the students' abilities and provides as much freedom as possible. For some students, this may be a placement, with or without an aide, in a "regular" physical education class with peers who are not disabled, or it may be placement into a special class or adapted physical education. These classes are generally smaller and contain only children with special needs. The placement of students with disabilities into the regular class is referred to as *mainstreaming.*

In the 1990s, some educators advocated that students with disabilities be placed in the regular class setting, including physical education. This inclusive approach insists that all students, regardless of their disability and its severity, be placed in the regular classroom in the neighborhood school. Supplemental aids and services are used to help students with disabilities achieve success in the regular class setting. There is considerable debate within many communities about the use of inclusion. Many regular teachers do not feel qualified to include children with special needs in their classes. They feel they lack the specialized training to provide them with a quality educational experience.

Physical education teachers provide many different services to individuals with disabilities. Some schools or school districts have an adapted physical education specialist who provides direct services to individuals with disabilities. In other settings, the adapted physical educator serves as a consultant to help other teachers provide needed services.

All physical education teachers should be prepared to work with students with disabilities. Physical educators will be involved in the writing of IEPs. These plans may focus on helping the student to correct physical conditions that can be improved with exercise, assisting each student in achieving the highest level of physical fitness within his or her capabilities, aiding the student in identifying physical activities and sports suited to his or her abilities and interests, and providing each student with positive experiences conducive to the development of a healthy self-concept.

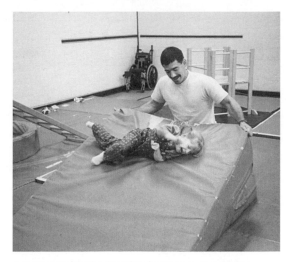

Adapted physical education focuses on modifying activities to meet students' needs.

Prospective physical education teachers interested in working with individuals with disabilities should prepare for this opportunity by taking additional course work in the area of adapted physical activity and special education. Try to obtain practical experience working with individuals with disabilities as part of your preparation for a physical education career.

Physical education teachers can also become certified as adapted physical educators. The Adapted Physical Education National Standards project was designed to ensure that physical education for students with disabilities is provided by qualified physical educators. As part of this project, national standards were developed and a certification examination was designed to measure knowledge of these standards.[15] (See Adapted Physical Education National Standards box.)

Physical educators interested in taking the certification examination must demonstrate that they have a bachelor's degree in physical education, 200 hours of documented practicum experience in teaching physical education to individuals with disabilities, and at least one 3-credit-hour course in adapted physical education. They should also study the Adapted Physical Education National Standards to make sure that they have

ADAPTED PHYSICAL EDUCATION NATIONAL STANDARDS

Human Development	Instructional Design and Planning
Motor Behavior	Teaching
Exercise Science	Consultation and Staff Development
Measurement and Evaluation	Student and Program Evaluation
History and Philosophy	Continuing Education
Unique Attributes of Learners	Ethics
Curriculum Theory and Development	Communication
Assessment	

Source: *Adapted Physical Education National Standards*, ed 2, National Consortium for Physical Education and Recreation for Individuals with Disabilities. Luke Kelly (ed.) Human Kinetics, Champaign, IL, 2008 (www.apens.org). For a complete description of each standard, visit the website.

the broad-based knowledge of physical education required of adapted physical education specialists. Teachers who pass the exam are certified for 7 years and can use the acronym CAPE (Certified Adapted Physical Educator) after their name. They are listed in the National Registry of Certified Adapted Physical Educators that is distributed to each state education department.

A diversity of opportunities exists for individuals interested in teaching in the school setting. Many opportunities also can be found for the physical educator who is interested in working overseas. Teacher exchange programs and the Peace Corps offer the opportunity to teach in elementary and secondary schools, as well as colleges and universities, in other countries. The United States armed forces also operate elementary and secondary schools on overseas bases for students of personnel; it is not necessary to be a member of the military to teach in these schools. Job possibilities are numerous for the prospective physical education teacher who actively seeks a position teaching in the schools.

Teaching in Nonschool Settings

Obtaining teacher certification in physical education opens up many doors for you. Opportunities to teach physical education outside of the school setting

continue to increase. The growth of interest in sport by people of all ages has stimulated the development of these additional teaching avenues. Teaching opportunities may be found today in commercial sport clubs, community recreational and sport programs, resorts, the armed forces, senior citizen and retirement centers, and correctional institutions.

The requirements for employment in these positions, working conditions, and salaries and other benefits vary widely. Some of these teaching positions require a high level of expertise in a particular sport, whereas others require individuals to teach a diversity of activities. Working hours vary a great deal as well. For some positions, hours are often dictated by the times clients or students are available. If one is working with youths, hours are likely to be after school and on the weekends. If one is working with adults, hours tend to be on the weekends and in the evenings. Daytime work is also available, however. These positions may pay on an hourly basis, have a set salary, or pay based on the number of students taught. Benefits may vary from none to complete medical, dental, and life insurance plans.

Some teaching positions in nonschool settings require that individuals assume other responsibilities as well. These may include public relations work, soliciting memberships, record keeping, and equipment and facility maintenance.

Some work may be seasonal in nature, depending on the climate or type of facility. For example, if you were a teacher or director of aquatics at an outdoor facility in the northeastern United States, your employment would probably last from June to September; working at an indoor facility in the Northeast would likely result in a year-round position. In the Southwest, the same job might be year-round regardless of the type of facility.

Because these jobs, in essence, require teaching skills, many physical educators who desire to teach in the nonschool setting also complete the requirements for teaching certification. By doing so, they increase their range of job opportunities. Other physical educators, having prepared for teaching in the schools, look to these other avenues of employment when they are unable to find a teaching position suited to their needs and interests, or as a means of part-time and summer employment. Many employers hiring physical educators to fill these positions also view favorably the credentials of those applicants able to list a teaching certificate on their resume. For some positions, special certificates may be required, such as certification by the PGA or LPGA as a golf professional.

The physical educator should also understand why adults and youths seek instruction. Adults seek instruction at these organizations for many reasons. First, they may not have had instruction in the activity or activities during their youth in their physical education classes. Second, they may seek instruction for their own personal growth and pleasure. Instruction may be sought for social reasons, such as the desire to be able to participate in specific activities with friends and family. For example, some adults may seek instruction in golf to be able to successfully participate with business associates in this accepted social activity. The desire to improve and refine one's performance by seeking instruction from a professional is often cited as the reason for enrolling in instructional classes.

Youths enroll in these organizational programs and classes for many of the same reasons as adults. Additionally, youths may enroll in certain activity classes because instruction or interscholastic

Physical educators may find teaching and coaching opportunities outside the school setting in sport clubs.

competition in that activity is not offered in their school. Youths desiring to develop more advanced skills, such as in gymnastics, or to compete in certain sport activities such as swimming may find that these organizations offer experiences that meet their needs. Youths and their parents may seek expert instruction because of aspirations to be a professional player, such as in tennis, or because of the desire to successfully compete for a college scholarship in certain sport areas; they may find nonschool instructional opportunities essential to the realization of these goals.

Teaching in Commercial Sport Clubs

In recent years the number of commercial sport clubs and facilities has grown tremendously. Tennis and racquetball clubs, gymnastics clubs, swimming clubs, country clubs offering golf and tennis, karate and judo schools, and bowling establishments are examples of commercial sport enterprises.

Since commercial sport clubs usually focus on a particular sport, physical educators who desire to teach in such an organization should possess a high level of expertise in that sport. In many instances, this expertise can be gained through participation in intercollegiate athletics. Many physical educators also have gained expertise by participating in private clubs such as gymnastics clubs during their youth and continuing their participation throughout their college years. Teaching responsibilities may include private lessons as well as group lessons. There may be the opportunity to coach high-level performers as well. Additional responsibilities may include setting up tournaments, such as in a tennis and racquetball club, selling sport equipment and apparel, such as in a golf pro shop at a country club, or transporting individuals to competitions, such as in a swimming club or a gymnastics club. Many commercial clubs also expect the teachers to assume managerial responsibilities at times.

Employers, in addition to requiring a high level of expertise as a condition of employment, may also require certification. In the aquatics area, certification as a water safety instructor and lifeguard instructor and in pool management may be required. Certification as a golf professional such as through the PGA or LPGA may be necessary. Where not required, certificates may enhance one's employment opportunities.

Teaching in Youth and Community Organizations

The Young Men's Hebrew Association (YMHA), the Young Women's Hebrew Association (YWHA), the YMCA, the YWCA, and similar organizations such as the Boys and Girls Clubs and 4-H serve both the youth and adult populations in the community. Religious training was originally the main purpose of many of these organizations. However, sport and fitness are now an important part of their programs. Included in the programs are classes in various physical activities; athletic

leagues for corporate employees, youth, and adults; and youth groups. The cost of financing such organizations is usually met through membership dues, community and business contributions, and private contributions.

These organizations are designed to improve participants socially, physically, morally, mentally, and spiritually through their programs of physical activity. Usually these organizations employ physical educators and recreation specialists to teach a wide diversity of activities. In many communities, events are scheduled from early morning to late at night—early-bird swim at 6 A.M. for business and professional people before work and late-hour racquetball games. Besides instructing clients in sport activities, the physical educator may have the opportunity to serve as a coach of a team. Many

Teaching opportunities outside of the school setting include working with adults providing specialized instruction in many different activities. This yoga instructor assists a student in attaining the correct posture.

youth clubs offer young people and adults the opportunity to compete on athletic teams at the local, state, regional, and national levels. Additional responsibilities include developing health and fitness programs, managing facility and budget, and supervising personnel. Many centers, in addition to physical activities, offer programs in exercise and fitness evaluation, cardiac rehabilitation, and health counseling. A background in these areas as well as in teaching would be helpful in seeking employment. Although salaries vary, they are comparable to public-school teaching positions.

Although the YMCA, YWCA, YMHA, and YWHA certainly constitute widespread organizations, they are not the only community organizations offering employment opportunities to the physical educator. Other opportunities include working for town and city recreation departments, community centers, youth centers similar in nature to the YMCA/YWCA, and playgrounds. Some of these opportunities may be seasonal, generally available in the summer, but the trend is for more and more programs to operate year-round. These programs provide instruction in physical activities for people of all ages, recreational sport leagues, and recreational activities. In addition to jobs teaching and coaching for these organizations, other job possibilities include the supervision of personnel and program development.

Teaching in Centers for the Elderly

In recent years, elderly people have received considerable attention from the US government and other agencies. The elderly comprise over 11% of the population, and this percentage is increasing yearly. There is also concern for the physical fitness of elderly people and their need to be physically active to maintain a state of optimum health. In recent years, programs for elderly people offered by recreational agencies, retirement centers, and health care facilities have expanded in the number and types of offerings.

Many of these programs offer instruction in physical activities suited to the abilities and interests of the participants. Exercise is frequently included in these programs. In addition to the physical benefits, physical education programs provide the opportunity for socialization. Physical educators interested in working in such programs may benefit from classes in adapted physical education, sociology, psychology, and gerontology.

Teaching in Resorts

The increase in leisure time has stimulated an increase in the travel and tourism industry. The number of resorts has grown, and many resorts offer instruction in various physical activities as part of their programs. Activities offered may include sailing, scuba, tennis, golf, swimming, waterskiing, and snow skiing. Expertise in specific sport areas is required for employment in these resorts. Instruction is usually done in small groups or in private lessons. Additionally, responsibilities may include managerial activities and directing social activities. Pay varies, and depending on the location of the resort, work may be seasonal, although many resorts operate year-round. Working in a resort offers many desirable side benefits, such as working in an attractive location and usually lush surroundings, and the opportunity to work with changing clientele.

Teaching in the Military

The army, navy, marines, air force, coast guard, and national guard have extensive physical activity programs that aid in keeping service personnel in good physical and mental condition. In addition to the personnel used to direct the fitness and physical training programs of these organizations, physical educators are needed to instruct service personnel in physical activities and sport for use in their leisure time. The military sponsors extensive recreational programs on its bases, and qualified personnel are needed to direct these programs. Coaches are also needed to assist military athletes in their training for competitions throughout the world. The military also sponsors schools for children of military personnel. Physical educators who desire to teach overseas may wish to consider employment in these schools. For many of these positions, physical educators do not have to belong to the military. Physical educators interested in further information about these opportunities should talk to their local military recruiter or contact the Department of Defense.

TEACHING CERTIFICATION

Each state has established minimum requirements that prospective teachers must meet before they become legally certified to teach. The certification of teachers protects schoolchildren by ensuring a high level of teaching competency and the employment of qualified personnel. Many states require that candidates for teaching positions take a standardized test, such as Praxis. These standardized tests usually consist of a core battery that tests general knowledge (e.g., knowledge pertaining to art, literature, history, science), communication skills, and professional knowledge. Some states require that students take an additional test in their specialty area, such as physical education. Different states have different passing score requirements for the standardized tests. Some states have their own certification examinations. For example, New York requires that teachers take the New York State Teacher Certification Examinations.

Because certification procedures and requirements vary from state to state, prospective teachers should obtain the specific requirements from their college or university or by directly contacting the state education department. Because of variations in state requirements, a certificate to teach in one state is not necessarily valid in another state. However, reciprocity among states in a region is increasingly common. Sometimes, where there is not reciprocity, prospective teachers can become certified in another state by merely taking a few additional required courses.

Teaching certificates are required to teach in the public schools. Some private schools may not require their teachers to possess a certificate. Teaching certificates are also an asset to individuals desiring to teach in nonschool settings. Prospective employers may be impressed by candidates who have fulfilled the necessary requirements for certification.

COACHING CAREERS

Many prospective physical educators aspire to a career as a coach. Because a teaching certificate is required by many states to coach, many aspiring coaches enroll in a program of study leading to a teaching certificate in physical education. Some of these prospective coaches seek a dual career as a teacher and a coach, whereas others desire solely to coach and view a teaching career as a means to attain their ultimate ambition.

Within the last four decades, coaching opportunities have increased tremendously. The passage of Title IX promoted the growth of interscholastic and intercollegiate competition for girls and women. The increased interest in sport by people of all ages has also served as a stimulus to increase opportunities in competitive athletics.

As with teaching, coaching opportunities today exist in both the school and nonschool setting. In the school setting at the interscholastic level, coaches work with middle school, junior high school, and high school athletes. Intercollegiate coaching opportunities are found in 2-year community colleges as well as 4-year colleges and universities.

More and more people with disabilities are participating in sports and taking an active role in coaching. Helping to lead the way is Brad Parks, founder of the National Foundation for Wheelchair Tennis.

Outside of the school settings are many different coaching opportunities. Some young people aspire to coach at the professional level. An increasing number of coaching opportunities are available in commercial or private clubs, such as coaching elite gymnasts or promising young tennis professionals. Community-based programs offer a multitude of coaching opportunities.

In the past two decades, participation in sport by older adults and people with disabilities has increased. For example, in 2009, more than 10,000 world-class senior athletes participated in the US Summer National Senior Games—the Senior Olympics.[16] This is one of the premier competitions for athletes age 50 and over. There were over 800 events in 18 sports.[16] The Special Olympics for individuals with mental retardation, the Paralympics, and the Games for the Deaf are attracting record numbers of participants. Coaching opportunities within these populations are increasing as these athletes strive to be their best.

Teaching responsibilities may be associated with coaching. At the interscholastic level, it is expected that coaches will teach classes in the school; often coaches teach physical education. At the collegiate level, some coaches are hired solely to coach and have no teaching responsibilities. At other higher education institutions, coaches may have teaching responsibilities in the general physical education program or in the professional preparation program. Administrative responsibilities also may be associated with coaching.

Choosing a Coaching Career

Individuals aspire to a coaching career for many reasons: their love for the sport, their own previous involvement on athletic teams, and the enjoyment they derived from participation. The desire to continue this involvement and association with athletics, perhaps to share some of what one has learned through athletics, is a strong motivating factor in selecting a coaching career. Individuals may choose to coach because of the profound influence one of their coaches had on their lives. Having a coach who was a positive role model and

a desire to emulate this individual can influence one's decision to pursue a coaching career.

Many choose to coach because of their love of children. The opportunity to work with highly skilled and motivated individuals is often cited as a reason for coaching. Many coaches enter the profession because of their belief that participation in athletics can be a positive experience; they are committed to providing opportunities by which young people can develop to their fullest potential, both as athletes and as individuals.

Coaching is a highly visible occupation. Coaches may have a great deal of influence and power within both the institution and the community. The excitement, attention, influence, and recognition associated with coaching make it an attractive career choice.

Benefits and Drawbacks of Coaching

Like teaching, a coaching career has both advantages and disadvantages. Many intrinsic rewards are associated with coaching. The opportunity to work with athletes and strive side by side with them to achieve their fullest potential, the excitement of winning and the satisfaction associated with giving the best of oneself, and the respect accorded to a coach are some of the intrinsic benefits of coaching.

Several drawbacks are associated with coaching. The hours are often long and arduous. The practice hours and the hours spent coaching during a competition are the most visible indications of the amount of time involved in coaching. Untold hours may be spent in preparing practices, reviewing the results of games and planning for the next encounter, counseling athletes, performing public relations work, and, at the collegiate level, recruiting.

Salaries vary greatly depending on the level coached, the sport coached, and the coach's position as head or assistant coach. Salaries at the high school level can range from a small stipend to several thousand dollars, whereas coaches at the collegiate and professional levels may have contracts worth hundreds of thousands of dollars.

Coaches fulfill many different responsibilities, including helping athletes put winning and losing in perspective.

A high turnover rate is associated with coaching. Unlike teachers, coaches are often placed under tremendous pressure to achieve—to have a winning season. Many coaches are fired because of a lackluster win-loss record or for having a poor working relationship with the administration or alumni. Other coaches choose to leave the profession voluntarily, overwhelmed by the pressures and exhausted by the demands, suffering from burnout, disenchanted with the profession, or desirous of a career change.

Role conflict is one problem some teachers and coaches struggle with in an effort to balance their jobs as teacher and coach. Individuals occupy many different roles in our society, both personally and professionally. Both positions or roles—teaching and coaching—carry with them responsibilities and associated expectations for performance. Both roles carry a multitude of responsibilities that often consume many hours—preparing lessons, formalizing practice plans, teaching classes, conducting practices, and a host of other demands. Additionally, personal and external expectations

relative to performance induce pressure. Teachers are expected to teach challenging lessons to all students, maintain discipline, participate on school committees, and fulfill many other functions. Coaches are expected to conduct practices in preparation for games, motivate athletes to achieve, interact with the public and press, and many times go on the road to scout the opponent. These and many more demands are coupled with the pressure to win.

Sometimes the pressure to do it all and do it well can be overwhelming. Role conflict occurs when teacher-coaches, in an effort to fulfill the demands associated with these two roles, have to make choices about how to apportion their time and effort in order to juggle those demands. The perceived value of each of the roles affects how teacher-coaches choose to balance their demands. Teachers hired to instruct physical education and committed to delivering a quality physical education try to maintain that goal in the face of pressures to produce a winning team as a coach. To resolve this conflict, some teachers choose to spend less time on their teaching, perhaps to the extent that they offer a "roll out the ball" physical education program. This compromise in use of time and values allows teachers to spend more time on their coaching, a role for which there is often more public recognition and reward. However, achieving success in coaching, one role, may be the result of reducing effort directed toward the other role, teaching. Trying to resolve this conflict between multiple roles can be stressful and can result in a decrease in the quality of performance. Yet many teachers and coaches successfully balance the demands and conduct high-quality physical education programs while helping students to achieve in the athletic arena.

Teaching and Coaching

Because coaching is in essence teaching, the qualities that exemplify good teachers—organizational, communication, human relations, instructional, and motivational skills—may also be characteristics of effective coaches. Coaches must be able to organize their practices to provide maximum opportunities for all players to learn the skills and strategies essential for play. They must be actively engaged in monitoring the efforts of their athletes. They must be able to communicate what is to be learned in a clear manner and provide athletes with appropriate feedback to improve their performances. Coaches must instill in each athlete a feeling of self-worth and self-confidence, and be able to motivate all players to put forth their utmost effort to achieve their goals.

Many qualities characterize the outstanding coach. First, the coach has the ability to teach the fundamentals and strategies of the sport: he or she must be a good teacher. Second, the coach understands the player: how a person functions at a particular level of development, with a full appreciation for skeletal growth, muscular development, and physical and emotional limitations. Third, he or she understands the game coached. Thorough knowledge of techniques, rules, and so on is basic. Fourth, the coach is a model for the players, a person of strong character. Patience, understanding,

kindness, honesty, sportspersonship, sense of right and wrong, courage, cheerfulness, affection, humor, energy, and enthusiasm are imperative.

Although coaching is similar in nature to teaching, there are some dissimilarities. Both teachers and coaches are engaged in instructional activities and both must provide opportunities for the learners—students and athletes—to attain the skills and knowledge presented. However, coaches must have the expertise to teach their athletes more advanced skills and are held much more accountable for their athletes' learning than teachers are for their students'. The caliber of a coach's instruction is scrutinized by both the administration and the public. If a coach has failed to prepare the athletes for competition or their learning appears inadequate (by the often-used standard of the win-loss record), the coach may be dismissed. Teachers, on the other hand, have less pressure and less accountability for their students' learning, and even if their success rate is not high, they will most likely be allowed to retain their position. The coach must work in a pressure-filled arena, whereas the teacher works in a less stressful environment.

Teachers must work with a diversity of skill levels and interests within their classes. Students may be mandated to take gym class and may be difficult to motivate. In contrast, coaches work with highly skilled athletes who often possess a high level of commitment to their sport. Their decision to participate is voluntary, and they may be united in their effort toward a common goal. Thus, although there are some similarities between teaching and coaching, there are some striking differences.

Coaching Responsibilities

Many responsibilities are associated with coaching. As in teaching, these responsibilities may be classified as instructional, managerial, and institutional in nature.

The coach's instructional responsibilities include conducting practice and coaching during the game. Although the coach is working with highly skilled athletes, the coach must be a good teacher to instruct the athletes in the more advanced skills and strategies necessary to perform at this level. During practices and games, the coach must motivate the athletes to put forth their best effort so that their optimal level of performance can be achieved. In many cases, these instructional responsibilities may be the least time consuming of all the coach's responsibilities.

Many coaches spend untold hours evaluating practices and the results of competitions and then using this information to plan for forthcoming practices and competitions. For those coaches fortunate enough to have assistant coaches, time must be spent with them reviewing this information and delegating responsibilities for future practices and games. Team managers may relieve the coach of many of the necessary but time-consuming managerial tasks such as dealing with equipment or recording statistics. Additionally, the coach must take care of the necessary public relations functions, such as calling in contest results, giving interviews, and speaking in front of groups. Where allowed, recruiting occupies a tremendous amount of time. Phoning prospective athletes, arranging for campus meetings, talking with parents, and scouting contests for potential athletes adds many hours to the day.

The institutional responsibilities are many as well. Interscholastic coaches are expected to take part in many school activities in addition to their teaching responsibilities. Intercollegiate coaches may be expected to attend athletic department meetings or represent the institution on a community committee.

Many other responsibilities and expectations are associated with coaching. Coaches occupy highly visible positions in their institution. In institutions of higher education, it is not uncommon for more students to recognize the face of the football or basketball coach than the face of the college president. The coach is expected to reflect a positive image and the values associated with sport. The actions of the coach as the team wins or loses will influence the public's opinion of the sport program. Establishing and maintaining positive relationships with the community,

alumni, and parents is often seen as vital to a coach's success in generating support for the athletic program. Because of their influence and visibility, coaches may be sought after to take an active part in community and civic affairs. They may be called on to train volunteer coaches for community recreational and sport programs or to spearhead a fund-raising drive for United Way.

Many other duties are incumbent on the coach by virtue of his or her position. The coach, because of the close relationship that develops from the many hours of working with his or her athletes toward a common goal, often undertakes the role of counselor for athletes or assumes the role of a surrogate parent. Athletes turn to their coach for advice about myriad problems. Athletes may have problems associated with their athletic performance or financial, academic, or personal concerns. Because of their positions as leaders, coaches are viewed as role models. They are expected to exemplify the highest standards of conduct and are under pressure to live up to these expectations.

Coaches must fulfill many professional responsibilities. They must attend sport and rules clinics so that they are aware of the current trends and latest rule changes in the sport. They are often active in professional organizations related to the sport they coach as well as professional organizations such as AAHPERD. They may be called on to serve as clinicians at some of these groups' meetings or asked to write an article for a professional journal.

The responsibilities and expectations associated with coaching are many. Instructional, managerial, institutional, community, and professional responsibilities compose the work of the coach.

Securing a Coaching Position

Depending on the level you wish to coach, you can take several steps to enhance your chances of securing the coaching position you desire. First, coaching requires a great deal of expertise. Playing experience in the sport you wish to coach may be helpful in this respect. Attending clinics

University of Tennessee head women's basketball coach Pat Head Summitt demonstrates leadership and commitment to her sport and her athletes.

and workshops on advanced techniques and rules may add to your knowledge. Consider becoming a rated official in your sport. Take advantage of coaching certification and licensing programs, such as the one offered for soccer by the United States Soccer Federation. Second, particularly for coaching at the interscholastic level, a teaching certificate may be required. However, this depends on the state in which you wish to coach. Coaching at the intercollegiate level often requires a master's degree.

Prospective coaches should consider developing expertise in a second sport, preferably one that is not in season at the same time as your major sport. For example, if you aspire to coach soccer, a fall sport, you should develop expertise in a spring sport such as lacrosse, baseball, or softball. In many institutions, at both the interscholastic and intercollegiate levels, coaches may be required to coach two sport activities or sometimes be the head coach in one sport and serve as an assistant coach in a second sport. At other institutions, a coach may be involved in one sport throughout the year because of the length of the season.

Practical experience is helpful as well. Volunteering to serve as an assistant coach or working with a youth sport program as a coach during your undergraduate preparation is a step in the right direction and is an invaluable experience. It is important that prospective coaches realize that oftentimes one must be willing to work in other positions in the coaching organization before achieving the head coaching position desired. Serving as a junior varsity coach, working as a graduate assistant coach, or accepting a position as an assistant coach can be helpful in attaining a head coaching position at the desired level.

Certification of Coaches

Criteria for certification of coaches at the interscholastic level vary from state to state. In 1987, only 21 states mandated that interscholastic coaches possess a teaching certificate, although not necessarily in physical education.[17] Furthermore, the increased need for coaches and the lack of teachers available to fulfill these needs has led to the hiring of many nonteacher coaches. By 1997, the number of states allowing nonteacher coaches was 49.[17] As a result, many individuals who hold coaching positions lack the professional preparation and competencies so necessary to conduct educationally sound and safe programs. To address the lack of preparation, 28 states require coach education.[17]

Additionally, concern has been expressed by professionals regarding the qualifications and preparation of youth sport coaches. Millions of children participate in youth sport; millions of adults serve as volunteer coaches. Some of these coaches have excellent credentials and do an outstanding job in keeping winning in perspective and enhancing the development of the young

---

**NASPE POSITION PAPERS AND GUIDELINES RELATIVE
TO COACHING***

- Rights and Responsibilities of Interscholastic Athletes 2003
- Coaching the Parents, 2003
- Estimated Probability of Competing in Athletics Beyond the High School Level
- Coaches Code of Conduct 2001
- Sexual Harassment in Athletic Settings
- Program Orientation for High School Sport Coaches, 2005
- Quality Coaches, Quality Sports: National Standards for Sport Coaches, 2006

*These position papers and guidelines are available through NASPE. Some of these are free and can be downloaded at www.aahperd. org/naspe, then browse Publications for Position Papers, Appropriate Practices, and National Standards and Activity Guidelines.

---

athletes entrusted to their care. Other coaches lack preparation in safety, skill development, organization, training and conditioning, and the needs of young athletes. To address these concerns, coaching standards and numerous coaching education programs have been established.

NASPE developed *National Standards for Athletic Coaches* to provide a national framework for organizations and agencies that provide coaching education and training. Knowledge, skills, and values associated with effective and appropriate coaching of athletes are organized into 40 standards, grouped into eight domains.

The eight domains of coaching competency are:

- Philosophy and Ethics
- Safety and Injury Prevention
- Physical Conditioning
- Growth and Development
- Teaching and Communication
- Sports Skills and Tactics
- Organization and Administration
- Evaluation[18]

For each domain, several standards are identified, and for each standard, specific benchmarks listed. For example, for the domain "Philosophy and Ethics." Standard 1 states:

- "A well-developed coaching philosophy provides expectations for behaviors that reflect the priorities and values of the coach.

An appropriate coaching perspective focuses on maximizing the positive benefits of sport participation for each athlete."
- Benchmarks:
  - "Identify and communicate reasons for entering the coaching profession.
  - Develop an athlete-centered coaching philosophy that aligns with the organizational mission and goals.
  - Communicate the athlete-centered coaching philosophy in verbal and written form to athletes, parents/guardians, and program staff.
  - Welcome all eligible athletes and implement strategies that encourage the participation of disadvantaged and disabled athletes.
  - Manage athlete behavior consistent with an athlete-centered coaching philosophy."[18]

These standards are not a coaching certification program but a framework for the education of coaches.[18]

In 2001, the Coaches Council of NASPE published the *Coaches Code of Conduct*, to which coaches at all levels should be held accountable.[19] The *Coaches Code of Conduct* is designed to maximize the mental, physical, and social development of athletes. In addition to possessing the competencies outlined in the *National Standards for Athletic Coaches*, coaches should adhere to the 18 standards of conduct. Examples of the standards are:

- "Coaches are responsible to ensure that the health, well-being and development of athletes take precedence over the win/loss record.
- Coaches accept that they do serve as role models and there must be congruency between their actions and their words.
- Coaches exemplify honesty, integrity, fair play, and sportsmanship regardless of the impact that might have on the outcome of the competition.
- Coaches maintain a professional demeanor in their relationships with their athletes, officials, colleagues, administrators and the public, and treat them with respect and dignity.
- Coaches are committed to the education of their athletes and should encourage academic achievement."[19]

The *Coaches Code of Conduct*, in conjunction with the *National Standards for Athletic Coaches*, provides coaches with guidelines for their behavior and for enhancing the experience of athletes in their programs. Additionally prospective coaches may find it helpful to read other coaching-related documents offered by NASPE; these are shown in the NASPE Position Papers and Guidelines Relative to Coaching box.

There are several coaching certification programs sponsored by private and professional organizations. The American Sport Education Program (ASEP) is the most widely used coaching education program in the United States. Rainer Martens, founder of ASEP, states, "ASEP is committed to improving amateur sport by encouraging coaches, officials, administrators, parents, and athletes to embrace the 'athletes first, winning second' philosophy, and by providing the education to put the philosophy to work."[20] ASEP provides education at three levels: volunteer level primarily for youth sport coaches, leader level for leaders of scholastic and club sports, and master level for those who aspire to higher levels of competency. Educational programs are designed for sport parents, sport coaches, and sport directors. ASEP provides training in coaching the young athlete,

coaching principles, sports first aid, drugs and sport, teaching sports skills, and a variety of sport sciences. Some ASEP courses can be completed online. ASEP has been selected by the National Federation of State High School Associations, the YMCA, and thousands of high schools for their coaching education programs.

The National Youth Sports Coaches Association (NYSCA) has been active in the training, support, and continuing education of coaches of youth sports teams. NYSCA reports that 2.5 million individuals have become NYSCA-certified coaches since the inception of the program in 1981.[21] Volunteer coaches attend training clinics, pass an exam, and sign a pledge committing themselves to upholding the standards set forth in the NYSCA Code of Ethics. As a continuing member, a coach receives the quarterly *Youth Sports Journal,* excess liability insurance, and accident and medical insurance.

Other coaching certification programs are available, such as PACE (Program for Athletic Coaches' Education), a branch of the Institute for the Study of Youth Sports. PACE seeks to provide interscholastic coaches with the latest information pertaining to their day-to-day responsibilities.[22] Specific sports also may have certification programs for their coaches. Coaching certification programs may also be offered at the local level—for example, by the recreation department in charge of youth sport in a community.

Young professionals aspiring to coach should prepare carefully for assumption of this important responsibility. They may accomplish this through an undergraduate professional preparation program or by enrolling in a coaching certification program. Athletic participation and the practical experience of working as an assistant coach or a volunteer youth sport coach in a community program can enhance the professional qualifications of prospective coaches.

BURNOUT

Burnout is a problem among teachers and coaches. Noted researcher Christina Maslach defines job *burnout* as "a psychological syndrome

Excessive demands can lead to burnout among teacher-coaches.

in response to chronic interpersonal stressors on the job. The three key dimensions of this response are an overwhelming exhaustion, feelings of cynicism and detachment from the job, and a sense of ineffectiveness and lack of accomplishment."[23] *Exhaustion* refers to "feelings of being overextended and depleted of one's emotional and physical resources."[23] *Cynicism* is reflected in "a negative, callous, or excessively detached response to various aspects of the job."[23] *Reduced efficacy or accomplishment* refers to "feelings of incompetence and lack of achievement and productivity at work."[23] Because burnout can have a devastating effect on dedicated individuals, young professionals need to be aware of the causes and consequences of burnout and strategies they can use to prevent its occurrence.

There are many causes of teacher burnout: lack of administrative support, lack of input into the curriculum process, and public criticism and the accompanying lack of community support. Inadequate salaries, discipline problems, too little time to do the ever-growing amount of work, large classes, and heavier teaching loads may also contribute to this problem. The lack of challenge, inadequate supervisory feedback, and the absence of opportunities for personal and professional growth also may lead to burnout.

In the coaching realm, burnout may be caused by seasons that seem to go on without end, administrative and community pressures, and time pressures. Teacher-coach role conflict may also lead to burnout. This role conflict occurs when a disparity exists between the expectations associated with being a teacher and a coach; this results in a multitude of simultaneous, somewhat diverse demands. The teacher-coach, unable to satisfy these demands, experiences role conflict.

In both the teaching and coaching realms, personal problems may interact with professional problems to exacerbate burnout. Personal problems such as family conflicts, money difficulties, or perhaps even divorce or problems with relationships may cause additional stress for the individual. These stresses coupled with professional problems may hasten the onset of burnout.

The consequences of burnout are many and are often quite severe, affecting teachers as well as their students. Burnout is associated with absenteeism, intent to leave the job, and actual job turnover.[23] For people who continue to work, burnout leads to lower productivity and effectiveness.[23] Burnout can adversely affect instruction. Burned-out teachers may cope with the demands of teaching by sitting on the sidelines, going through the motions of teaching by "throwing out the ball." Infrequent and careless planning of classes, complacency, and behavioral inflexibility may occur as well. Teachers' interactions with their students may also suffer. Burned-out teachers may treat their students in a depersonalized manner, providing them with little encouragement, feedback, and reinforcement of their efforts, and many have lower expectations for student performance. Teachers who are burned out may feel dissatisfied with their accomplishments and believe they are wasting the best years of their lives. Burnout can result in deterioration of health. Insomnia, hypertension, ulcers, and other stress-related symptoms may manifest themselves in burned-out teachers.

What can be done to cope with burnout? The varied causes and consequences of burnout require a diversity of solutions. Supervisors such as principals and athletic directors can play a crucial role in the prevention and remediation of burnout. Supervisors can provide teachers and coaches with meaningful in-service programs, focusing on developing a variety of teaching and coaching techniques, learning efficient time management, and acquiring effective communication skills. They can also provide teachers and coaches with more feedback about their performance, which can serve as a stimulus for growth. Teachers and coaches can seek out new ideas, professional contacts, and opportunities through participation in professional organizations and conferences. Taking some time off to revitalize oneself during the summer is also a successful strategy. Developing and participating in hobbies

or nonwork-related activities are helpful ways to deal with burnout. Establishing and maintaining an appropriate level of fitness, practicing proper nutrition, and getting enough sleep are also positive approaches to dealing with burnout.

Some teachers and coaches seek to cope with the consequences of burnout by adopting inappropriate solutions such as alcohol or drugs. The pervasiveness of burnout and the serious consequences for teachers, coaches, students, and athletes should make dealing with burnout an important professional priority.

INCREASING YOUR PROFESSIONAL MARKETABILITY

If you are interested in a teaching career in the public schools or in nonschool settings, you can often enhance both your marketability and your ability to teach by building on your assets and interests. Through careful planning of your study program and wise use of your electives and practicum experiences, you can improve your chances of gaining the professional position you desire. Many of the same strategies are applicable to coaching as well.

You can enhance your opportunities to teach in the public schools in several ways. One way is to build on talents or skills you already possess. For example, the need is great for bilingual educators. Perhaps you have gained proficiency in a second language because of your family background, the location in which you grew up, or the foreign language you studied in secondary school. These language skills can be built on with further course work at the college or university level.

Second, additional course work can be beneficial in broadening the abilities of the prospective teacher. Courses in the area of adapted physical education are an asset whether or not one is interested in specializing in adapted physical education. Since adapted physical education emphasizes individualized instruction, the knowledge gained from its study can be applied to all children, including those with special needs mainstreamed into or included in regular physical

---

FOCUS ON CAREER: Teaching and Coaching

PROFESSIONAL ORGANIZATIONS	• American Alliance for Health, Physical Education, Recreation and Dance (www.aahperd.org) • American Association for Physical Activity and Recreation (www.aahperd.org/aapar) • American Federation of Teachers (www.aft.org) • National Association for Sport and Physical Education (www.aahperd.org/naspe) • National Education Association (www.nea.org)
PROFESSIONAL JOURNALS	• *Adapted Physical Activity Quarterly* • *JOPERD* • *Journal of Teaching in Physical Education* • *Palestra* • *Research Quarterly for Exercise and Sport* • *Sports and Spokes* • *Strategies*

---

education classes. Additional courses in health may be helpful because physical educators often find themselves teaching one or two health classes in addition to their physical education courses. The close relationship between wellness and fitness makes knowledge of health important to the practitioner.

Another possibility, depending on the state in which you plan to teach, is to gain certification to teach in a second academic area. If you enjoy other areas such as math, science, or health, dual certification would enable you to qualify for additional jobs such as a teaching position that has a teaching load of one-third math and two-thirds physical education or one-third health and two-thirds physical education. Certification in driver education is also a popular choice that enhances one's credentials. To gain dual certification, you are required to take several courses in your alternate area of study. Often the number of courses required for certification may not be many more

than are required by your college or university for a minor. The education department in the state in which you plan to teach can provide you with additional information about the requirements for certification.

Individuals interested in teaching in a non-school setting can enhance their marketability in a similar way as individuals preparing for a teaching position in the public schools. Depending on where one seeks employment, having a bilingual background might be an asset. Experience in adapted physical education will be useful in working with individuals of different abilities and ages. Courses in math and business may be helpful if one is employed by a commercial sport club or fitness center or community sport program, where the position often involves managerial duties. Because many of these organizations offer some type of health counseling and because of the interest of many of the clientele in health, courses in health will be an asset as well. Many employers may view possession of a teaching certificate by someone seeking to teach in these nonschool settings as an asset. Expertise in one or several sport areas may also be a plus, as is possession of specialized certifications.

In the coaching realm, one's previous experience as an athlete in the sport is an asset. Many former athletes have capitalized on their experience to secure coaching positions. Previous work as an assistant or head coach certainly is a positive asset. Professional contacts, official ratings in a sport, and membership in a professional organization are helpful in getting hired or advancing. Many states require that coaches hold teaching certification; holding such certification gives one more flexibility in selecting from job opportunities.

Finally, you can enhance your credentials by gaining as much practical experience as possible, working with people of all ages and abilities. This holds true whether you are seeking work in a school or nonschool setting or in coaching. This experience can be gained through volunteer work, part-time employment, summer employment, or supervised field experiences sponsored by your college or university. Being able to cite such practical experiences on your resume may prove invaluable when you are seeking to gain employment. Membership in professional organizations and professional contacts may also be helpful in securing employment.

Teachers and coaches can improve their marketability by acquiring skills in the use of technology. Technology can help teachers and coaches enhance their instructional effectiveness and manage their time more efficiently. Many teachers are now using heart rate monitors in their classes. These monitors, which attach to the student's wrist, provide immediate and ongoing feedback to students about their heart rate. Some heart rate monitors store the information so that it can be downloaded to a computer and later analyzed by the teacher. Some teachers use hand held computers to gather information about a student's

performance of different skills during class. Other teachers use computers for a myriad of tasks, such as record keeping, grading, and creating newsletters to promote their programs.

Coaches can use laptop computers and video editing technology to prepare scouting reports on their opponents. Spreadsheets help coaches quickly calculate statistics and keep track of their budgets. College coaches especially benefit from the use of databases to manage their recruiting activities.

The use of the World Wide Web as a resource for teachers and coaches is growing. There are many websites for physical education teachers to use as resources and a means to communicate with other teachers throughout the country. PE Central (Figure 12-1), established by Dr. George Graham and the doctoral students in the health and physical education program at Virginia Tech, is one of the premier websites for physical educators. It offers teachers access to lesson plans, instructional resources, assessment ideas, professional information on conferences and workshops, job openings, equipment purchasing, and related websites. Through its e-mailing list, physical education teachers can share information and engage in problem solving with other teachers throughout the nation.

Coaches find that the web offers them the opportunity to share information with coaches throughout the world. A coach may find posted on the web information about drills, training techniques, and upcoming conferences and clinics. Through several different sites on the web, college coaches can contact and recruit prospective athletes. Through various sport-specific e-mailing lists, coaches can communicate with colleagues worldwide.

Prospective teachers and coaches can enhance their marketability. Building on your skills, taking additional courses, and gaining as much practical experience as possible will increase your options and enhance your opportunities for employment.

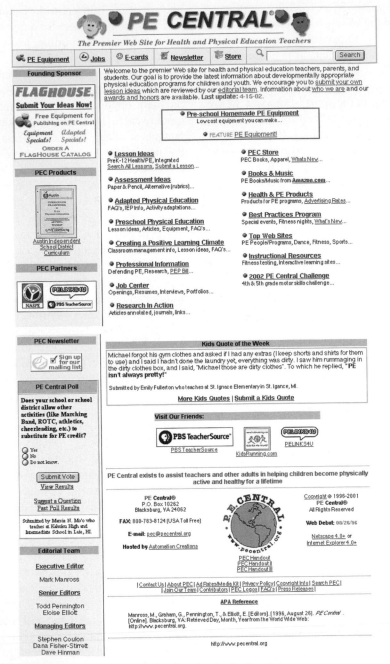

Figure 12-1   PE Central is a popular website for physical educators.
Source: Used by permission of PE Central (www.pecentral.org), the premier website for health and physical education teachers.

SUMMARY

Teaching and coaching opportunities have broadened from the traditional school setting to the nonschool setting and from school-aged populations to people of all ages, ranging from preschoolers to senior citizens. Teaching opportunities in the school setting are available at the elementary level, secondary level, and in higher education. Prospective teachers may also teach physical education in adapted physical education programs and in professional preparation programs. In the nonschool setting, opportunities exist in commercial sport clubs, community and youth agencies, resorts, corporate fitness programs, the armed forces, and preschool and day-care motor development programs. Many individuals choose a teaching career because of their strong desire to work with people, because of personal interests, and because of the nature of the job. Individuals desiring to pursue a teaching career, regardless of setting, should be cognizant of the numerous advantages and disadvantages of such a career.

Many prospective physical educators aspire to a career as a coach. Some seek a dual career as a teacher and a coach, whereas others desire solely to coach and view a teaching career as a means to attain their ultimate ambition. The prospective coach should be knowledgeable of the benefits and drawbacks of the career.

In an effort to improve teaching, researchers have sought to identify characteristics of effective teachers. They have determined that effective teachers possess organizational, communication, human relations, instructional, and motivational skills. Teachers have a myriad of responsibilities; those responsibilities may be classified as instructional, managerial, and institutional in nature. Coaching is similar in many respects to teaching. Effective coaches possess many of the characteristics of effective teachers and must assume many of the same responsibilities as well.

One problem that has become increasingly prevalent among teachers and coaches is burnout. Burnout is physical, mental, and attitudinal exhaustion. The causes of burnout are many, and personal problems may interact with professional problems to exacerbate burnout. There are a variety of solutions to this problem.

Many strategies can be used by prospective teachers and coaches to enhance their marketability. They can build on their talents and interests, take additional course work in a supporting area, and gain as much practical experience as possible.

DISCUSSION QUESTIONS

1. Review your educational experiences. Regardless of the subject, describe the characteristics of the most outstanding teacher you ever had. How do these characteristics align with the INTASC standards?

2. NASPE has published a position paper on the playing of dodgeball in physical education classes. Carefully read the position paper. Should dodgeball be banned in physical education? What is your point of view?

3. How are teaching and coaching different? How are they similar? Within the public school setting, should all coaches be required to be certified teachers? Certified physical education teachers?

SELF-ASSESSMENT ACTIVITIES

These activities are designed to help you determine if you have mastered the materials and the competencies presented in this chapter.

1. In light of the qualities of effective teachers and their responsibilities, assess your own qualifications for this field of endeavor.

2. Discuss the advantages and disadvantages of pursuing a teaching or coaching career in a school and a nonschool setting. If possible, try to interview a physical educator or coach presently working in each setting.

3. Using the information provided in the Get Connected box, access PE Central or PE Links 4U site on the World Wide Web. Explore the information contained within each site. Write a 1- to 2-page paper on the usefulness of the World Wide Web to teachers and coaches.

4. Using the information provided in the Get Connected box, access the AAHPERD website and read the National Standards for Athletic Coaches and the Coaches Code of Conduct. Carefully review your own athletic experiences and compare the actions and behaviors of your coaches to the standards. Did your coaches meet these standards?

Where did they fall short? Discuss the importance of standards for coaches, especially at the youth sport level.

5. Access the NASPE website and browse through the publications listings. Select one publication that is available online. Carefully read this document and then reflect on your experiences relative to this topic (elementary physical education, recess, etc.). How did your experiences compare to the recommended guidelines? Be specific in providing examples to support your answers. What are five things that you learned from this publication that you could use as a professional?

REFERENCES

1. Bucher CA and Koenig CR: Methods and materials for secondary physical education, St. Louis, Mo., 1983, Mosby.

2. Di Carlo M, Johnson N, and Cochran P: Survey and analysis of teacher salary trends, 2007, Washington, D.C., 2008, American Federation of Teachers (www.aft.org/pdfs/teachers/salarysurvey07.pdf).

3. Interstate New Teacher Assessment and Support Consortium Standards (www.ccsso.org/content/pdfs/corestrd.pdf).

4. National Association for Sport and Physical Education: National teachers, ed 2, standards for beginning physical education Reston, Va., 2003, NASPE, AAHPERD Publications.

5. National Association for Sport and Physical Education: What constitutes a quality physical education program? 2003 (www.aahperd.org/naspe).

6. American Alliance for Health, Physical Education, Recreation, and Dance: Developmentally appropriate physical education practices for children, Reston, Va., 1992, AAHPERD.

7. Corbin CB: Physical activity for everyone: what every physical educator should know about promoting lifelong physical activity, Journal of Teaching in Physical Education 21:128–144, 2002.

8. Gensemer RE: Physical education: perspectives, inquiry, and applications, Philadelphia, 1985, W. B. Saunders.

9. National Education Association: Building blocks for success, 2002 (www.nea.org).

10. Council on Physical Education for Children of the National Association for Sport and Physical Education: Opportunities to learn standards for quality elementary physical education, Reston, Va., 2000, AAHPERD Publications.

11. Middle and Secondary School Physical Education Council of the National Association for Sport and Physical Education: Appropriate practices for middle school physical education, Reston, Va., 2001, AAHPERD Publications.

12. Pangrazi RP and Darst PW: Dynamic physical education curriculum and instruction for secondary school students, Minneapolis, 1985, Burgess.

13. Middle and Secondary School Physical Education Council of the National Association for Sport and Physical Education: Appropriate practices for high school physical education, Reston, Va., 2004, AAHPERD Publications.

14. National Center for Educational Statistics: Children 3 to 21 years of age served under the Individuals with Disabilities Education Act, 2008 (http://nces.ed.gov/).

15. National Consortium for Physical Education and Recreation for Individuals with Disabilities: Adapted physical education national standards, ed 2, Luke Kelly (ed.) Human Kinetics, Champaign, IL, 2008 (www.apens.org).

16. National Senior Games Association: History of the National Senior Games (www.nsga.com/history.html).

17. American Sport Education Program: 1997 national interscholastic coaching requirements report: a shared mission, Champaign, Ill., 1997, Human Kinetics (www.asep.com).

18. National Association for Sport and Physical Education: Quality coaches, quality sports: national standards for sport coaches, Reston, Va., 2006, AAHPERD Publications.

19. National Association for Sport and Physical Education, Coaches Council: The coaches code of conduct, 2001, Reston, Va, AAHPERD Publications, American Alliance for Health, Physical Education, Recreation, and Dance (www.aahperd.org).

20. American Sport Education Program: About ASEP and human kinetics, 2001, Human Kinetics (www.asep.com).

21. National Youth Sport Coaches Association (www.nays.org/coaches).

22. Institute for the Study of Youth Sport: PACE (www.educ.msu.edu/ysi).

23. Maslach, C, Schaufeli, WB, and Leiter, MP: Job Burnout, Annual Review of Psychology, Annual 2001, 52:397–422.

C H A P T E R 13

Fitness- and Health-Related Careers

OBJECTIVES

After reading this chapter the student should be able to—

■ Discuss the responsibilities and opportunities of a physical education, exercise science, and sport professional working in a fitness-related career.

■ Discuss the responsibilities of a physical education, exercise science, and sport professional working in a health-related career.

■ Describe the opportunities available to an individual desiring to pursue a therapy-related career.

■ Discuss the various strategies that can be used to enhance one's professional marketability in fitness-, health-, and therapy-related careers.

Today there is great interest in preventative medicine and a wider public awareness of the values of physical activity. Research has substantiated the benefits of exercise and appropriate physical activity in reducing the incidence of cardiovascular disease and in enhancing the rehabilitation of those experiencing this common malady. The increased public awareness of the role of physical activity in health promotion and disease prevention, coupled with the interest in fitness by many segments of society, has stimulated the growth of community, commercial, and worksite wellness and fitness programs. As a result, employment opportunities for professionals with preparation as exercise and fitness specialists have grown tremendously. The number of physical education, exercise science, and sport professionals who have found employment opportunities working in preventative and rehabilitative physical activity programs has risen sharply, and it appears that this trend will continue in the years ahead.

Another field that has experienced growth is athletic training. Although athletic trainers have typically been employed by professional and college athletic teams, their employment at the secondary school level is rising. Furthermore, the public's increased participation in a variety of sport activities and the medical profession's interest in sport have led to increased employment opportunities for qualified athletic trainers in commercial

GET CONNECTED

American College of Sports Medicine—gives information about the organization, membership, certification, research reports, publication, and official position papers on a variety of topics.

www.acsm.org

American Council on Exercise—contains information on certification, fitness news and facts, and trends. Access the press releases to read information about research projects, such as the most effective exercises or tests of claims made for different fitness products.

www.acefitness.org

National Athletic Trainers' Association—provides information on NATA, membership, certification, position papers, and listing of undergraduate and graduate schools offering an approved NATA curriculum.

www.nata.org

National Strength and Conditioning Association—presents information on membership, certification, and research abstracts.

www.nsca-lift.org

Wellness Councils of American—offers an array of resources, many of them free, for professionals employed in corporate wellness programs. Free presentations, publications, and a newsletter help professionals stay abreast of developments in the field.

www.welcoa.org

sports medicine clinics, physical therapy clinics, hospitals, and even corporate worksite wellness programs.

Many employment opportunities are available for qualified individuals in weight management and health spas, resorts, and health clubs. Qualified individuals may be employed as dance exercise specialists, exercise leaders, exercise test technologists, and weight management counselors.

An increasing number of medical and health care professionals, as well as members of the general public, realize the significant physical and psychological benefits gained by individuals who participate in regular, appropriate physical activity. There is greater recognition of the therapeutic values of movement in helping individuals attain an optimal state of well-being, as well as recover from illness. Careers in therapeutic recreation and dance therapy are available to physical education, exercise science, and sport professionals who desire to work in a therapeutic setting. Some students build on their undergraduate degree

in physical education, exercise science, or sport and pursue advanced study in health-related fields. These students enroll in programs leading to careers as kinesiotherapists, physical therapists, and chiropractors.

FITNESS- AND EXERCISE-RELATED CAREERS

The awareness of the benefits of physical activity by the public, corporate sector, and medical profession has stimulated the growth of preventative and rehabilitative physical activity programs. Students aspiring to pursue careers in this growing area should familiarize themselves with the types of programs typically offered and the nature of responsibilities associated with them, the many career opportunities available, and strategies to prepare themselves for a fitness- and exercise-related career.

Preventative and rehabilitative exercise programs differ in their focus and in the nature of their participants; the setting in which these

Members work out at the state-of-the-art Taking Care Center in Hartford, Conn. In addition to the exercise equipment and indoor track, it has a pool and an aerobics studio.

programs are conducted often is different as well. Preventative exercise program specialists work with healthy adults to increase their level of fitness and realize concomitant gains in health. Rehabilitative exercise program specialists work primarily with individuals who exhibit the effects of coronary heart disease; they focus on helping these individuals attain a functional state of living and an enhanced quality of life. Preventative exercise programs are commonly found in corporate fitness centers, commercial fitness centers, and community agencies such as the YMCA/YWCA. An increasing number of hospitals are now offering wellness programs. Rehabilitative exercise programs are most often found in hospitals, although some may be found in medical clinics or community agencies or be affiliated with corporate fitness centers.

Preventative and rehabilitative programs often vary in their scope and comprehensiveness. However, some commonalities may be discerned. Although these programs typically focus on improvement of fitness, they may include other components such as educational programs, health promotion programs, and lifestyle modification.

Comprehensive wellness programs are growing in popularity. The fitness component of these programs typically includes some assessment of the individual's current level of fitness, prescription of a program of exercise and activity, opportunities to engage in exercise and activities, and periodic reevaluation of the individual's level of fitness. Educational efforts often focus on instructing individuals on the principles underlying the performance of exercises and physical activity so that individuals can learn to properly plan their own exercise and activity programs. Health promotion efforts may include health education, such as providing participants with nutritional information, as well as measures focusing on the early detection of disease, such as hypertension screening and cancer detection. Lifestyle modification may include counseling individuals regarding stress management, weight control, smoking cessation, and alcohol and drug abuse. In addition to these program components, recreational sport opportunities may be offered.

Cooper and Collingwood note that fitness and wellness programs vary in their structure and offerings.[1] In an effort to maximize the benefits

The trained exercise professional must be able to evaluate each participant's fitness level. This PepsiCo staff member is administering the sit-and-reach test to a program participant.

to be realized from participation and to promote adherence to these programs, the Institute for Aerobics Research identified several elements as "generic" services for such programs. Programs should make provisions for medical screening of their participants to ensure that they are safe exercise risks. Program personnel should also evaluate participants' levels of fitness and their lifestyles. Exercise programs should focus on individual goal setting; thus, exercise and nutritional prescriptions should be developed for each individual. To motivate participants to get started on their programs, supervised group exercise and activity programs should be offered. To sustain changes in fitness and lifestyle, educational classes should be held and provisions should be made for motivation and reinforcement of participants' efforts. Feedback should be ongoing in nature. These generic elements are critical to the success of preventative

exercise programs and seem appropriate for rehabilitative programs as well.[1]

The trained fitness professional working in preventative and rehabilitative exercise programs must be able to perform a wide variety of tasks and be capable of assuming responsibility for numerous aspects of the exercise program. Sol identifies the responsibilities of an exercise program specialist as:

- Directing the exercise program, which may be oriented to prevention or rehabilitation.
- Training and supervising staff.
- Developing and managing the program budget.
- Designing and managing the exercise facility and laboratories.
- Marketing the exercise program.
- Evaluating—in conjunction with a physician— each participant's medical and activity history,

administering a graded exercise test, pulmonary function tests, and assorted fitness tests.

- Developing individual exercise prescriptions for participants.
- Evaluating or counseling participants, on request, about nutrition, smoking, weight control, and stress.
- Accumulating program data for statistical analysis and research.
- Maintaining professional affiliations.
- Performing other program-specific duties.[2]

The responsibilities that each professional in the program will be asked to assume depend on several factors, including the scope and comprehensiveness of the program, the number of participants, the size of the staff, and qualifications of other staff members. In programs that have a broad range of services, a large number of participants, and several staff members, responsibilities tend to be more specialized. One staff member may direct the program, administer the budget, market the program, and conduct in-service training for other program staff. Some staff members may have as their sole responsibility the conducting of graded exercise tests and the writing of exercise prescriptions. Still other staff members may lead the fitness classes and provide instruction in activities. Providing participants with counseling for lifestyle modification or educating participants about exercise may be the responsibility of other staff members. Finally, another professional may be assigned to accumulate data and conduct statistical analyses. In programs that are narrower in scope or are conducted for fewer participants, the staff tends to be smaller and one professional will perform many more functions.

Opportunities for qualified individuals may be found in a diversity of preventative and rehabilitative exercise programs offered in a variety of settings. These include worksite health promotion and fitness programs, commercial and community programs, and rehabilitation programs. Some individuals are finding employment as personal fitness trainers. Salaries range from $20,000 to over $50,000 a year, depending on the qualifications of the individual, responsibilities assigned, and nature of the job.

Worksite Wellness Programs

Worksite wellness promotion programs have grown dramatically over the past decade. Physical activity and fitness programs are often an integral part of health promotion efforts at the worksite. Worksite wellness programs vary greatly in their scope and type of health promotion activities offered.

The proportion of worksites offering physical activity and fitness programs continues to grow. The larger the employer's workforce, the more likely it is the employer has a physical activity and fitness program. Thirty-eight percent of small corporations (50–99 employees) have worksite programs, compared with 68% of large corporations (more than 750 employees).[3]

Worksite physical activity programs are a critical component of the national health promotion and disease prevention effort because they have the potential to reach a large percentage of the population. Today's workforce spends most of the day at the worksite. The worksite offers an effective way to reach these adults and to provide them with education and access to the means to adopt and maintain a healthy lifestyle. Onsite programs are convenient for employees and offer the peer social support so important for continued participation.

Corporations invest in worksite wellness programs because it makes economic sense. Quality worksite wellness programs contribute to high productivity and help contain costs. Improvements in job performance, increases in productivity, and reduced absenteeism are some of the benefits for companies that choose to invest in health promotion programs.[4,5] Corporations also sponsor wellness programs as a cost containment measure. Health care costs are spiraling, and health insurance premiums continue to rise astronomically. Workplace programs have been associated with reduced injury rates, lower worker's compensation costs, and reduced health care costs.[4–6]

Aerobics are a popular offering in wellness programs and fitness clubs.

Reports show that the benefits realized from worksite programs vary widely. Benefit/cost ratios are most widely used to determine the economic benefits. A benefit/cost ratio divides the money saved by the money spent; a ratio of 3.43 means that for every $1 spent, $3.43 was saved. Benefit/cost ratios for physical activity programs range from 0.76 to 3.43.[7] When physical activity programs are included as part of a comprehensive health promotion program, benefit/cost ratios range from 1.15 to 5.52.[8] Recent studies have reported benefit/cost ratios averaging $3.93 to $5.07 in savings for every dollar invested in health promotion.[9] Shepard reports that the "cumulative benefit was estimated to be $500 to $700 per worker per year, enough to cover the cost of a modest wellness program."[5] However, researchers suggest that increasing productivity by as

little as one-third of 1% could pay for the wellness program.[10] Furthermore, the benefits that can be achieved from increasing productivity are 10 times greater than the savings realized by reducing medical costs.[11]

Corporations may also invest in worksite wellness programs because of the benefits in terms of human relations and enhancement of morale. Worksite wellness programs are also important in recruiting and retaining employees. Wellness and health promotion rank high among the top employee benefit health priorities.[12]

Worksite wellness programs vary widely in comprehensiveness—that is, the number and nature of activities offered. According to health promotion expert Larry Chapman, virtually all worksite wellness programs should address 12 "core" topics.[13] (See the 12 Core Components of Worksite Fitness Programs box.) These topics address a myriad of wellness concerns and health risk factors. Chapman points out that these topics have a "great deal of inherent synergy."[13] He explains, "For example physical activity programming has been shown to have collateral benefits effects on weight management, tobacco use, nutritional practices, back pain, stress management and blood pressure. Any program that offers a mix of interventions in these areas will naturally benefit from their natural synergy."[13]

Physical education, exercise science, and sport professionals aspiring to work in worksite wellness programs may find themselves working as part of a comprehensive health promotion team. As members of a health promotion team, professionals may benefit from additional training in wellness areas such as health, nutrition, and stress management.

The Wellness Council of America offers several suggestions to enhance the success of wellness and health promotion programs. These include the following:

- Make the program voluntary.
- Continually market the program.
- Be sensitive to individual differences with respect to age, culture, and health status.

12 CORE COMPONENTS OF WORKSITE WELLNESS PROGRAMS

Back Care and Injury Prevention
Exercise/Physical Fitness
Stress Management
Smoking Control
Substance Abuse
Weight Management

Medical Self-Care
Consumer Health Education
Cholesterol Reduction
Nutritional Intervention
Select Biometrics Screenings
Hypertension Management

Source: Chapman LS. "Fundamentals of Wellness" *Absolute Advantage*, Winter 2006 (www.welcoa.org).

- Evaluate the program often.
- Make sure that the program staff model healthy behavior.
- Recognize and reward people who develop the programs.
- Maintain good records in order to properly evaluate the program.
- Offer a balance between programs that are fun and those that are clinically significant.
- Personalize the programs to the employees' needs.[14]

Worksite wellness programs offer a great opportunity to improve the health of the nation. However, the effectiveness of this effort must be measured in not only the number of worksite programs but the degree of involvement of employees.

Worksite wellness programs, especially for physical fitness and activity, are most effective when they can attract at-risk employees, that is, those employees who will benefit the most from the program.[5] At-risk employees are those members of the workforce who are sedentary or obese, possess high cholesterol levels, are hypertensive, experience high levels of stress, and smoke.[15] It has been found, however, that participants in the fitness program tend to already be healthier than nonparticipants.[5,15] Efforts should be directed at attracting at-risk individuals into the fitness program.

Physical education, exercise science, and sport professionals must realize that part of their job responsibilities will be the active and ongoing recruitment of employees to participate in the program. Employee recruitment is one of the key factors in program success. Once employees have begun a program, efforts need to be directed at maintaining involvement so that desirable health benefits can be achieved.

Worksite facilities vary greatly. Some corporations have invested in multimillion-dollar facilities—gymnasium, pool, indoor track, aerobics studio, racquetball courts, weight rooms, and playing fields—for sport activities. Facilities at other corporations are more modest, perhaps only a weight room and a multipurpose gymnasium.

Within the last decade, there has been an increase in worksite health promotion and fitness programs for school faculty and staff. These programs vary in nature and scope. Like those found in corporate settings, school programs focus on protecting and improving employees' health status. These worksite programs are seen by professionals in the health field as an integral part of a comprehensive school health program.[16]

Colleges and universities also are offering programs for their employees. These programs typically emphasize prevention and improvement of health through appropriate lifestyle management. Some institutions offer wellness and fitness programs to their students, on either a credit or noncredit basis. The emphasis is on learning skills and acquiring knowledge to lead a healthy, active life.

Many worksites offer recreational sport programs as well. These recreational programs may include softball and bowling leagues as well as competitive teams. Instruction in physical activities may be offered to employees.

Opportunities for employment in worksite programs are increasing for qualified professionals. A physical education, exercise science, and sport professional may work as a group aerobics or group exercise instructor. As a professional, you may work with people of all fitness levels and all ages, or you may offer specialized classes for women who are pregnant or for people with lower back pain. Class offerings vary widely, ranging from low-impact aerobics to high-intensity cardiovascular workouts and from water-based resistance programs to cycling.

Another opportunity is working as the director of the employee fitness or wellness program. In this capacity, you may lead a variety of wellness and fitness classes, train and supervise other instructors in the program, and educate employees

WORKSITE HEALTH PROMOTION BEST PRACTICES

Building top management support
Integrating program with organization or
    business goals
Communicating soundly
Using the stages of change concept to design
    programs
Creating supportive cultures
Offering recruitment incentives
Operating by personal contact or word of mouth
Targeting personal invitations
Targeting personal communication
Making announcements during meetings
Instilling a sense of program ownership
Using the self-efficacy concept
Using health website, Internet, and intranet
    strategies
Using a program database of informational
    structure

Source: Adapted from Chapman LS. "Expert Opinions on 'Best Practices' in Worksite Health Promotion (WHP)." *The Art of Health Promotion,* July-August 2004, 1–6.

on a variety of topics, such as worker safety or stress management.

Worksite health promotion programs also employ exercise physiologists. Exercise physiologists administer and evaluate exercise tests and supervise exercise sessions. Exercise physiologists work with both healthy individuals and those with special medical concerns. Depending on the scope of the worksite health promotion program, exercise physiologists may direct a cardiac rehabilitation program.

Commercial and Community Fitness Programs

The number of health clubs has grown dramatically within the past decade. Both commercial and community programs have increased, involving people of all ages. (See the US Health Club Industry Facts and Figures box.) The International Health, Racquet, and Sportsclub Association (IHRSA) reports that there are more than 30,000 US health and fitness clubs, including nonprofits such as YMCAs and community centers. These clubs generate more than $19.1 billion dollars in revenue. More than 45 million people are members, with people aged 35 to 54 accounting for 34% of the membership. This segment is rapidly growing and has increased by 122% since 1990. Women account for more than half of club memberships.[17]

Income is one factor that influences health club membership. According to IHRSA, 51% of health club members have an income of greater than $75,000. The average health club member's household income is $82,000. Over 33% of health club members have an income in excess of $100,000. The average attendance per member has climbed to 90 days per year. The average retention rate of the members is above 70%.[17]

The types of programs offered at clubs and fitness centers are extremely diverse. Graded exercise tests, individualized fitness evaluation and prescription, educational programs, and lifestyle modification are some services offered by more comprehensive programs. Group exercise programs of all sorts, ranging from aerobic dance

US HEALTH CLUB INDUSTRY FACTS AND FIGURES

Industry Status	Number of US health clubs	30,022
	Membership	45.5 million
	Industry revenues	$19.1 billion
Most Prevalent Type of Club	Commercial—multipurpose	25%
	Commercial—fitness-only	21%
	Nonprofit—YMCAs, etc.	17%
	University-based	8%
	Hospital-based	5%
	Municipal/town recreation facility	4%
	Corporate	3%
Attendance	Average member attendance	90 days per year
Membership by Age	6–11 years	3%
	12–17 years	6%
	18–34 years	33%
	35–54 years	34%
	>55 years	24%
Membership by	Female	57%
Gender	Male	43%
Membership by Income	<$25,000	9%
	$25,000–$49,999	22%
	$50,000–$75,000	18%
	>$75,000	51%

Source: International Health, Racquet, and Sportsclub Association (www.ihrsa.org) Retrieved July 15 2010.

class to yoga instruction to cardiac rehabilitation to sport specific training, are offered to members. Resistance training has increased in popularity. Programs that are less comprehensive may offer fewer choices for their members. As with the employee fitness programs, there is a trend toward offering wellness programming. More clubs are offering personal training services and 50% of the clubs surveyed reported that personal training is one of their most profitable services.[17] (See the Popular Fitness Programs Offered at Clubs box.)

Fitness programs tailored to meet the needs of different groups are becoming more common. Toddler and preschool programs, as well as programs for the aged, are being offered by both community and commercial agencies, and increasingly by schools. There is also a growth of single-sex health clubs, women- or men-only clubs. Professionals

POPULAR FITNESS PROGRAMS OFFERED AT CLUBS

Program	Percentage
Personal Training	91
Fitness Evaluation	76
Step/Aerobics	74
Strength Training	74
Yoga	67
Group Cycling Class	56
Nutrition Counseling/ Classes	53
Weight Management	52
Cardio Kickboxing or Similar Activities	51

Note: This box reflects the percentage of clubs that listed these programs among their top programs in the 2008 survey by the International Health, Racquet, and Sportsclub Association.

Source: www.ihrsa.org

working within these programs must be particularly attuned to the developmental characteristics of the group and adapt programs accordingly.

An increased number of fitness programs are available to address the fitness needs of individuals with disabilities. For example, the Fitness Clinic for Physically Disabled at San Diego State University provides fitness programming to individuals with a wide range of physical disabilities.[18] Fitness programming at the clinic focuses on both improvement of fitness and functional independence. Improvement of functional independence allows participants in the program to assume a greater responsibility for their personal care and other activities of daily living. For individuals with severe limiting conditions, such as quadriplegia or multiple sclerosis, increasing their basic muscular strength, endurance, and balance allows them more independence and greatly enhances the overall quality of their lives.

A growing site for community fitness and wellness programming is medical fitness centers. These centers focus on providing services to individuals with chronic diseases and multiple risk factors. They are also open to healthy individuals, and focus on disease prevention and health promotion. These medical fitness centers strive to offer a continuum of care for people within their community, ranging from rehabilitation to prevention, with the goal of improving the health status of the entire community.[19] Medical fitness centers may be incorporated within a hospital or, most commonly, as a stand-alone center, often in partnership with a local community fitness or wellness center. The Medical Fitness Association reports that public demand for medically integrated programs and facilities has reached record numbers. Medical fitness facilities serve more than 4 million people.[19] The majority of their members are adults in their 40s and 50s, but membership is open to people of all ages.[19]

These medical fitness centers offer an array of clinical services. These services focus on meeting the needs of special populations such as cardiac patients, arthritics, diabetics, and cancer patients. Services range from cardiac and pulmonary rehabilitation, weight management, and physical therapy to sports and occupational medicine. Like many health clubs, these fitness centers make available cardiovascular and weight training equipment, group exercise programs, and personal training. Some have swimming pools and indoor running tracks.[19] Medical fitness centers also focus on meeting the needs of healthy community members, and offer an array of services such as health screenings for cholesterol and health education seminars on nutrition, smoking cessation, and stress management.

Medical fitness centers involve physicians as directors or part of a medical advisory board.[19] The staff typically have degrees in exercise physiology and certifications that reflect their ability to meet the needs of individuals with specific medical conditions. Medical fitness centers are a growing trend, and provide opportunities for physical education, exercise science, and sport professionals who have the proper credentials and an interest in being part of the continuum of care within a community.

Professional responsibilities within commercial enterprises and community programs are similar to those associated with worksite programs. Employment opportunities within these areas have grown dramatically within the past few years.

Many people prefer to exercise at home. Sales of home exercise equipment have reached an all-time high.

One factor that may counter the growth of employment opportunities is the tremendous increase in the sales of home exercise equipment. Many adults who in the past would have paid a membership fee to participate in these programs have chosen to invest the money in home exercise equipment, such as home gyms, bicycle ergometers, treadmills, and rowing machines. These individuals prefer the convenience of being able to exercise at home. Some professionals have capitalized on this trend by working as personal trainers, offering one-on-one fitness instruction in the home.

Personal Trainers

A number of physical education, exercise science, and sport professionals have pursued careers as personal fitness trainers. They meet with clients individually in their homes on a regular basis, sometimes as often as 5 or 6 days per week. For each client, the personal trainer conducts a fitness assessment, develops specific goals and designs a program leading to their attainment, coaches the individual through the workout, and monitors progress. Additional services often include nutritional counseling. Personal trainers can earn from $30 to over $100 an hour; rates vary by location and clientele.[20]

Some fitness programs and health clubs also offer members the services of a personal trainer at an additional cost. Members like the one-on-one attention offered by a personal trainer, believing it enhances their motivation and their effort in performing their program.

Some personal trainers work for a health club or fitness center. Members have the option of paying an additional fee to utilize the services of the personal trainer. In these circumstances, trainers may be required to give the club a percentage of their earnings. Other professionals run their own personal training business; they may be the sole provider of care or have other professionals who work for them.

One new trend is the use of the web for personal training. Clients who live too far away from a club, prefer to work out at home, or are too busy to visit a fitness center sign up with a personal trainer online. Via e-mail or phone, the personal trainer and the client establish fitness goals, and then the trainer prescribes a fitness regimen tailored for the needs of the client. Clients typically e-mail their personal trainer the results of each workout, and the personal trainer monitors the clients' progress, e-mailing workout modifications and encouragement. Hiring a virtual personal trainer saves money—the cost is about $30 to $40 a month, compared to $30 or more per hour at the club or home.

Strength and Conditioning Professionals

According to the National Strength and Conditioning Association, strength and conditioning professionals "assess, motivate, educate, and train

Personal trainers work with individuals typically in the home or club setting. Personal trainers tailor the fitness program to meet the client's needs.

They work closely with coaches, athletic trainers, medical staff, and nutrition specialists to ensure the health and well-being of athletes. Record keeping, management of the fitness facility, and administration of the program often are part of the strength and conditioning professionals' responsibilities.

Many strength and conditioning professionals work with collegiate athletes, although an increasing number of professionals work in scholastic settings. Recognizing the critical role that fitness and sport-specific conditioning can play in enhancing performance and helping athletes remain healthy and injury-free, many colleges and university athletic departments hire strength and conditioning specialists.

The National Strength and Conditioning Association identifies several competencies needed by strength and conditioning coaches. Strength and conditioning professionals need competency in the scientific foundations of sport and exercise science and nutrition. Competency is also needed in the practical and applied areas of the field, such as exercise leadership and program design. Sport and exercise science competencies include an understanding of human physiology, exercise physiology, motor learning, sport pedagogy, and biomechanics, and the ability to utilize these understandings in the design and implementation of muscular strength and endurance training programs, as well as aerobic and anaerobic fitness programs. Sport and conditioning professionals must be able to utilize techniques from sport psychology to maximize the training and performance of athletes. Professionals must also be cognizant of risks and the effects of performance-enhancing substances. In terms of nutrition, strength and conditioning professionals should be knowledgeable of how nutrition affects health and performance.[21]

Within the applied realm, strength and conditioning coaches need to be able to design training programs that take into account an athlete's health status, current fitness level, and training and performance goals. They need to be knowledgeable about many different forms of exercise, including flexibility, plyometrics, strength training,

athletes for the primary goal of improving sport performance."[21] Strength and conditioning professionals work with interscholastic, intercollegiate, amateur, and professional athletes. They are employed in colleges and universities, high schools, sports medicine and physical therapy clinics, and health and fitness clubs.

Strength and conditioning professionals have a rather varied job description. They assess athletes' health status and fitness levels by conducting a multitude of tests, including evaluation of sport-specific abilities. Based on the results of the assessment, they design and implement safe and effective training programs to maximize performance and help athletes achieve their goals. Additionally, they provide guidance to athletes, as well as their coaches, in areas such as injury prevention and nutrition.[21]

and conditioning, and be able to instruct athletes in these exercise techniques, including spotting when appropriate.[21] Competencies also include assessment and evaluation, as well as administration and record keeping.[21]

Physical education teachers, coaches, exercise and fitness specialists, physical therapists, and athletic trainers pursue opportunities as strength and conditioning professionals. Certification as a strength and conditioning specialist is often required for many of these job opportunities.

Rehabilitation Programs

As the role of exercise in the rehabilitation of individuals with illness, particularly cardiovascular diseases, has become increasingly well documented, the number of rehabilitation programs has grown. Typically, rehabilitation programs are offered at hospitals and clinics, although some programs may be offered through community agencies such as the YMCA/YWCA. Besides the development of fitness, health promotion and lifestyle modification are integral parts of these programs.

Clinical exercise physiologists work in rehabilitation settings.

The scope and responsibilities of clinical exercise physiologists are quite broad. They work with clients with a host of conditions, such as cardiovascular and pulmonary disease, as well as those who may have orthopedic or musculoskeletal problems; these clients are referred by a physician. Their responsibilities include exercise evaluation, exercise prescription, exercise supervision, exercise education, and assessment of exercise outcomes.[22] Clinical exercise physiologists work closely with physicians and medical personnel to meet the needs of their diverse clientele. To plan rehabilitation programs, clinical exercise physiologists must be familiar with the medical aspects of their clients' diseases or conditions, cognizant of the limitations faced by clients, and aware of drugs commonly used to treat the diseases or conditions and their effects. Clinical exercise physiologists must be prepared to help their clients deal with some of the psychological aspects associated with participation in an exercise program, such as the often-expressed fear that exercise will lead to another heart attack.

Career Preparation

Preparation for a career in this area requires a strong background in the exercise sciences and fitness and practical experience. Students will also benefit from obtaining certification from a recognized organization and becoming involved in professional organizations.

Preparation

Today, many colleges and universities offer undergraduate and graduate degrees in areas related to health promotion, fitness, or exercise. Undergraduate degree programs are available in exercise science, fitness and cardiac rehabilitation, clinical exercise science, adult fitness, corporate fitness, and fitness programming. Although the requirements for the degree vary by institution, in the typical program, the student takes core courses such as foundations of exercise science, anatomy and physiology, kinesiology, biomechanics, exercise physiology, injury prevention and care, sport and exercise psychology, sport sociology, and assessment.

In addition to these core courses, more in-depth instruction is provided in exercise science, focusing on assessment of cardiopulmonary function and health status, exercise prescription, exercise leadership, and fitness programming. Certification in cardiopulmonary resuscitation (CPR) is commonly required. Because of the strong relationship of this field to health promotion, students may take courses in nutrition, drug education, pharmacology, and stress management. In completing their preparation, students may find it helpful to take several psychology courses, such as motivation, behavior modification, and individual and group counseling. Computer science courses, statistics, and research methodology are helpful to students in preparing for the administrative and evaluative

Weight training for children is becoming popular. Professionals working with young children and adolescents must be aware of their special needs.

responsibilities associated with a position in this field. Finally, business courses assist students in dealing with the myriad responsibilities associated with exercise programs, such as budgeting, marketing, and personnel supervision.

To provide students a supervised practical experience in which they have the opportunity to apply and further develop their competencies, most programs require an internship. This internship can take place in a diversity of settings, such as a hospital, corporate fitness center, campus fitness program, or commercial enterprise. The internship typically occurs near the end of the program and serves as a capstone experience.

Also, many programs across the country offer a graduate degree in this area. These programs provide advanced training and an opportunity to specialize. Programs are offered in exercise physiology, fitness programming, cardiac rehabilitation, strength development and conditioning, fitness management, corporate fitness, health fitness, and health promotion. These programs may require that students complete an internship, research project, or thesis to graduate.

Certification

Certification programs offered by professional organizations have grown within the last 10 years. These programs try to ensure that individuals who receive certification have the necessary skills and knowledge to competently plan and administer programs.

Certifications reflect attainment of a prescribed level of competence, knowledge, skills, and abilities. There are more than 400 certifications, offered by more than 50 organizations, in the area of fitness.[23] Certifications vary by prerequisites, requirements, and price. Some certifications require at least an associate degree in a health-related or exercise science–related field; others require a bachelor's degree before taking the certification exam. Certification exams vary as well. Some certification programs require a written and a practical exam; others only a written one. For some certification programs, candidates must accumulate a certain number of hours of experience prior to sitting for the exam. Continuing education requirements vary by program. Given so many certifications available, it is important that physical education,

TABLE 13–1	**Fitness Certifications**
Organization	**Certifications**
American College of Sports Medicine (ACSM) www.acsm.org	• ACSM Certified Personal Trainer • ACSM Certified Health Fitness Instructor • ACSM Certified Clinical Exercise Specialist • ACSM Registered Clinical Exercise Physiologist
American Council on Exercise (ACE) www.acefitness.org	• Personal Trainer • Group Fitness Instructor • Lifestyle and Weight Management Consultant • Advanced Health and Fitness Certification
Aerobics and Fitness Association of American (AFAA) www.afaa.com	• Personal Trainer • Primary Group Exercise Leader
National Strength and Conditioning Association (NSCA) www.nsca-lift.org	• Certified Strength and Conditioning Specialist (CSCS) • Certified Personal Trainer (NSCA-CPT)

exercise science, and sport professionals check with their professors and respected professionals in the field to make sure that the certification is rigorous and well respected within the field. Selected certification programs generally recognized within the field are shown in Table 13.1.

The American College of Sports Medicine (ACSM) offers one of the most widely recognized certification programs. The ACSM certification program offers certifications in the area of preventative and rehabilitative fitness programs. There are two tracks: health fitness and clinical.

The health fitness track is designed for professionals working in fitness programs in which the participants are apparently healthy, have a controlled medical condition for which exercise is not prohibited, and engage in exercise for the maintenance of health.[24] The two certifications included within this track are ACSM Certified Personal Trainer and ACSM Health Fitness Certified Specialist.[24]

The clinical track certifications are for appropriate for "individuals who work in clinical settings to provide cardiac or pulmonary rehabilitation or exercise programs for persons who have a chronic disease, such as diabetes."[24] There are two certifications associated with this track: ACSM Certified Clinical Exercise Specialist and ACSM Registered Clinical Exercise Physiologist.[24]

Certifications within both program tracks reflect a progressive level of skills, competency, knowledge, and experience. Additionally, the ACSM offers a Registry for Clinical Exercise Physiologists that promotes ethical standards and competent health and medical services and requires that professionals provide services to patients in a compassionate and respectful manner.[24]

ACSM certification requires satisfactory performance on both a written and a practical examination. Prior to the examination, optional workshops and seminars are usually offered that cover the competencies for each level of certification. Information about certification can be obtained from ACSM's website (www.acsm.org).

Other organizations have also developed certification programs, including the American Council on Exercise (ACE), the Aerobics and Fitness Association of America (AFAA), and the National Strength and Conditioning Association (NSCA).

ACE offers four types of certifications for fitness professionals. The Personal Trainer certification is for individuals who provide one-on-one fitness training. The Group Fitness Instructor certification is for fitness instructors who lead group exercise programs. The Lifestyle and Weight Management Consultant certification is for those individuals who want to offer comprehensive weight management consulting that addresses nutrition, behavior modification, and fitness. The Advanced Health and Fitness certification is designed for personal trainers who have the experience, skills, and knowledge to work with special populations, including individuals who suffer from chronic disease or who have an injury. It is an advanced personal trainer certification that reflects the individual's ability to screen, assess, design, implement, and evaluate exercise programs to meet the needs and match the abilities of special population groups.[25] ACE offers a variety of training workshops and opportunities to gain expertise in specialty fitness areas. ACE can be found on the web at www.acefitness.org.

AFAA conducts a certification program, training workshops, and continuing education workshops for fitness professionals. Certification programs include Personal Trainer and Primary Group Exercise Leader.[26] Specialty workshops in prenatal fitness, aqua fitness, senior fitness, mat science, and resistance training are offered. Certification requires a written and a practical exam. AFAA workshops and home study programs may also be applied toward ACSM continuing certification. AFAA also offers continuing education via the web at www.afaa.com.

NSCA's focus is on strength development to improve athletic performance and physical fitness. Membership in NSCA brings together professionals in the areas of sport science, athletic training, and fitness industries. Two certifications are offered: Certified Strength and Conditioning Specialist (CSCS) and Certified Personal Trainer (NSCA-CPT). Candidates for CSCS certification must hold

a bachelor of arts or science degree or be enrolled as a senior at an accredited college or university, be CPR-certified, and pass the exam.[27] The NSCA-CPT is designed for professionals who train clients in a one-on-one situation, such as in a client's home, in a fitness or health club, or in organizations such as the YMCA.[27] These professionals often have areas of expertise to accommodate the diverse needs of their clients. They may work with clients who have orthopedic, cardiovascular, and weight problems or who are elderly or have physical disabilities. Both certification programs require practical and written exams. NSCA also sponsors conferences and offers continuing education. NSCA can be contacted via the web at www.nsca-lift.org.

As the number of certification programs continues to grow, students are cautioned to check the quality of the program with professors and professionals in the field before pursuing certification. And, as Siedentop points out, "remember that a 1-week 'intensive' workshop does not provide the level of preparation that a physical education major receives during a 4-year college program."[28]

Professional Organizations

Membership in organizations and establishment of affiliations are important for young professionals. Membership will facilitate the development of professional contacts. It provides the opportunity to update one's skills and knowledge through continuing education programs, workshops, and conventions. Students preparing for a career in this area may find membership in the American Alliance for Health, Physical Education, Recreation, and Dance (AAHPERD), ACSM, and NSCA to be a valuable professional experience.

HEALTH-RELATED CAREERS

Health-related career opportunities in the realm of physical education, exercise science, and sport have expanded. Careers in athletic training have become increasingly available. Career opportunities also exist for physical educators, exercise scientists, and sport leaders in health and weight control clubs and spas.

Athletic Training

In recent years, employment opportunities have increased for professionals with expertise in athletic training. Traditional employment opportunities can be found at the college and professional levels. Employment opportunities at the secondary school level also exist and are growing, although there are still many high schools that do not employ athletic trainers. It is likely that employment opportunities at this level will increase in the near future as states and school systems, concerned about the safety of their athletes and their legal liability, mandate the hiring of certified athletic trainers for interscholastic sports.

Another avenue of employment that is available to athletic trainers is in sports medicine clinics. These clinics can be commercial enterprises, affiliated with hospitals, or associated with physical therapy practices. The increase in sport participation by all segments of society has resulted in the need for qualified individuals to evaluate, treat, and rehabilitate injuries.

An increasing number of athletic trainers are employed in the industrial and corporate settings.

Many employment opportunities are available to men and women at the college and university level.

As part of the wellness programs, athletic trainers can use their knowledge as allied health professionals to provide health education on a diversity of topics and educate employees about the prevention of injury.[29] They may also work in onsite rehabilitation programs. The opportunities in this setting are likely to increase as employers seek to provide their employees with more comprehensive health care at the worksite.

An athletic trainer's responsibilities are numerous and varied in nature, focusing primarily on the prevention of injury and the rehabilitation of injured athletes. In terms of injury prevention and safety, the athletic trainer performs such preventative measures as taping the ankles and knees of athletes prior to practices and competitions. The athletic trainer works closely with coaches in designing and supervising conditioning programs. Advising coaches and athletes regarding the prevention of injuries is an important responsibility of the athletic trainer. Athletic trainers may also assist in preseason physicals. Checking equipment and checking facilities for safety are tasks often performed by the athletic trainer.

The athletic trainer is often the first person to reach an injured athlete. Thus, the athletic trainer must be prepared to deal with a variety of emergencies. The athletic trainer diagnoses injuries and refers athletes to the appropriate medical personnel for treatment. Working closely with the physician, the athletic trainer implements the prescribed rehabilitation program and administers the appropriate therapeutic treatments. The athletic trainer closely monitors the athlete's efforts and progress during the rehabilitation program. Rehabilitation may be a long and arduous process, and the athletic trainer may need to motivate and encourage the athlete during this trying period to put forth the necessary effort to attain complete recovery. Keeping accurate records of athletes' injuries, the treatment program prescribed, and each athlete's progress during the rehabilitation program is part of the athletic trainer's job.

In addition to competencies pertaining to training, an athletic trainer must possess excellent interpersonal skills. The athletic trainer must work closely with the coaches and the team physician. Establishing and maintaining good rapport with these individuals contributes to a harmonious working relationship. Often, the athletic trainer is placed in a position of telling a coach that an athlete cannot practice, play in an upcoming game, or return to the competition after an injury. Professional competency and a good rapport help make these difficult tasks a bit easier. The athletic trainer often finds himself or herself serving as a counselor to the athletes. Athletes may talk to the athletic trainer about problems relating to their own performance or that of their teammates or about problems on the team. The athletic trainer must be able to deal with the concerns of injured athletes; injured athletes may be fearful that they may not be able to return to 100% of their ability, that the injury will limit their performance in some way. The athletic trainer may also be sought out by athletes for advice about their personal and academic problems. The athletic trainer must be able to deal with these numerous problems and concerns in an appropriate and professional manner.

The hours worked by trainers are long. In addition to being in the training room before practice and on the sidelines during practice and competition, the trainer must often spend several hours in the training room at the conclusion of practices and competitions, dealing with any injuries that may have occurred and giving treatments. Trainers may have to come in on weekends for practice or contests and to give athletes treatments.

> ## ATHLETIC TRAINING PRACTICE DOMAINS
>
> Prevention
> Clinical Evaluation and Diagnosis
> Immediate Care
> Treatment, Rehabilitation, and Reconditioning
> Organization and Administration
> Professional Responsibility
>
> Source: Board of Certification for Athletic Training. Defining Athletic Training, 2006 (www.bocatc.org).

During the season, the athletic trainer travels with the team, and this travel can be quite extensive. Because athletic trainers frequently work several sport activities during the year, the season can go on without end. Less visible responsibilities also consume quite a bit of the athletic trainer's time. Cleaning up the training room, rerolling bandages, sterilizing the whirlpool, and ordering supplies are some of the other responsibilities of the athletic trainer. The long and demanding hours and lack of days off have resulted in some athletic trainers experiencing burnout, just as teachers and coaches do. (See Chapter 12 for a further discussion of burnout and its solutions.)

Despite the long hours and other demands, many individuals pursue careers in athletic training because of the opportunity to help athletes

ATHLETIC TRAINING CURRICULUMS

- Assessment and Evaluation
- Acute Care
- General Medical Conditions and Disabilities
- Pathology of Injury and Illness
- Pharmacological Aspects of Injury and Illness
- Nutritional Aspects of Injury and Illness

- Therapeutic Exercise
- Therapeutic Modalities
- Risk Management and Injury Prevention
- Health Care Administration
- Professional Development and Responsibilities
- Psychological Intervention and Referral

Source: Board of Certification for Athletic Training. Defining Athletic Training, 2009 (www.bocatc.org).

attain their fullest potential and the desire to be closely associated with athletics. The intrinsic rewards, such as the satisfaction in helping an injured athlete return to competition quickly and at full potential, are many.

At the professional level, the athletic trainer's responsibilities include injury prevention and the care and rehabilitation of injured athletes. (See the Athletic Training Practice Domains box.) At the collegiate level, the athletic trainer's responsibilities may be expanded to include teaching courses in the physical education or health program. In an institution that offers an approved athletic training curriculum, athletic trainers can teach courses within the curriculum as well as supervise student athletic trainers.

At the secondary level, an athletic trainer may be employed in several different capacities. A school may employ a full-time athletic trainer, or the district may employ a full-time athletic trainer to serve all of the schools within the district. An individual may also be hired as a teacher and athletic trainer. Therefore, athletic trainers may find it advantageous to possess a teaching certificate in physical education or another academic area. Some schools may contract with a sports medicine center for an athletic trainer and for related services.

Athletic trainers affiliated with clinics generally work fewer hours than individuals in a school or professional setting, and their work schedule is often more regular. Trainers who work in these settings typically work on a one-on-one basis with the athlete. However, an increasing number of schools and community sport programs are contracting with these clinics for services. Therefore, hours worked and working schedules may be similar to those of trainers employed in a school setting.

Salaries for athletic trainers vary widely. The work setting, responsibilities, and amount of experience possessed by the individual influence the salary. The *National Athletic Trainers' Association 2000 Salary Survey* revealed that athletic trainers with 5 or fewer years of experience averaged $27,623 a year. Athletic trainers with 20 or more

years of experience averaged $62,975 (these figures include salary and benefits).[30]

The National Athletic Trainers' Association (NATA) offers a certification program in athletic training; increasingly, this certification is becoming required to obtain a position. Effective in 2004, in order to obtain certification, an individual must be a graduate of an approved athletic training curriculum. An approved athletic training curriculum includes courses in biological and physical sciences, psychology, first aid, and specific courses relative to training. (See the Athletic Training Curriculums box.) Certification requires membership in NATA and passing a written and a practical exam. Information regarding certification procedures can be obtained from NATA's website (www.nata.org).

Some athletic trainers choose to continue their education and obtain a master's degree in physical therapy to add to their skills. Prospective athletic trainers interested in pursuing work in physical therapy should check early in their undergraduate career with institutions offering master's degrees in physical therapy as to requirements for admission, including course prerequisites. Often, courses in physics, chemistry, and math are required for admission to these schools. By knowing the prerequisites early, students may be able to use these courses as electives in their undergraduate professional preparation program. Other athletic trainers choose to continue their education by enrolling in a program leading to a master's degree in athletic training. Being active in professional organizations provides the opportunity to continue one's education through attendance at professional meetings and workshops.

Health and Weight Management Clubs and Spas

The number of health and weight control clubs and spas has increased greatly during the last decade. Many commercial enterprises have been established to capitalize on people's desire to be physically fit and healthy, and to look their best. Spas can be found at resorts, hotels, and mineral springs, and aboard cruise ships. Some spas are residential and others are club and day spas. Some of these businesses are independently owned, whereas others are franchises. It is a multibillion-dollar industry. As a result, some health and weight control clubs and spas are only seeking the public's dollar rather than trying to be of service. However, many spas are reputable, are hiring trained personnel, and have excellent programs. Physical education, exercise science, and sport professionals not only will find an opportunity for employment in health and weight management clubs and spas, but they also can contribute by upgrading the standards of these businesses.

The activities and services offered by health clubs and spas vary widely. Fitness activities are an integral part of many spas. Some spas may even offer graded exercise tests as part of their program. Many spas provide their clients with instruction and opportunities to practice a variety of sport activities such as tennis, racquetball, volleyball, and swimming. Aerobic dance, swimnastics, weight training, and a diversity of exercise classes are common. Facilities may include pools; racquetball, handball, squash, and tennis courts; and such amenities as whirlpools, saunas, steam rooms, tanning booths, and massage rooms. Health promotion activities such as diet and nutritional counseling, stress management, and massage are often offered to the clients.

In recent years, the number of resort-type spas has grown; individuals desiring to shape up and lose weight check into the spa and stay from one to several weeks. Another pronounced trend is the growth of commercial diet centers and weight management spas and clubs. Like health clubs and spas, these may be independently owned or franchises. The focus of these businesses generally is on weight reduction. Exercise classes and fitness activities, similar to those offered in health clubs and spas, may be part of the weight reduction programs at these commercial enterprises.

The growth of these health and weight control clubs and spas has led to a diversity of employment opportunities for physical education, exercise science, and sport professionals interested in working in these health-related careers. Responsibilities associated with these positions vary widely. Professionals may gain employment in these commercial enterprises as activity instructors or as exercise leaders. They may be responsible for leading an aerobic dance class or for setting up a weight training program for clients and monitoring their performance. In large clubs, professionals may be responsible for training the club's instructors in various exercise techniques and supervising their work with the club's clients. Where weight control and nutritional counseling are primary concerns, professionals may evaluate the clients' dietary habits, design a diet to help them reach their goal, plan individual exercise programs to be followed in conjunction with the diet, and offer nutritional counseling. In many cases, the professional will be required to attend in-service workshops on the

LIFESPAN AND CULTURAL PERSPECTIVES: Fitness, Exercise, and Health

- How can access to health and fitness facilities be improved for underserved populations?
- What modifications to adult exercise tests (e.g., treadmill tests) need to be made to safely and accurately assess fitness in children and adolescents?
- What factors influence employees' use of corporate wellness programs?
- How does one's body image influence enrollment and continued participation in a health club?
- What are the effects of long-term resistance training on fitness levels, body image, and self-concepts of adolescents? On adults over 55?

Yoga and meditation are popular offerings at health clubs and spas.

specific diet approach espoused by the business and will also receive training in nutritional counseling and psychological techniques such as behavior modification.

Physical education, exercise science, and sport professionals may also be employed to manage these facilities. Even if professionals are employed as fitness instructors, they have many other responsibilities that are managerial in nature. These responsibilities may include record keeping, training and supervising employees, developing and implementing social programs, and soliciting memberships. The varied responsibilities associated with these jobs suggest that in addition to courses in fitness, students should take courses in health, business, psychology, and recreation. Salaries can range from $25,000 to $45,000. Hours and days worked vary. As the interest in being fit and healthy in our society grows, opportunities for employment in these settings appear to be excellent.

THERAPY-RELATED CAREERS

There are several therapy- and health-related careers where physical activity plays an important role in working with clients. Dance therapy and therapeutic recreation are two careers in which professionals use physical activity to help their clients improve their well-being. Kinesiotherapists, physical therapists,

and chiropractors also use physical activity in working to help their clients achieve their goals.

Dance Therapy

The use of dance has proved very helpful in alleviating physical, emotional, and social problems. It has received wide acceptance as a psychotherapeutic means of physical and emotional expression. Through dance, the patient or client has freedom of movement and gains a sense of identity. Dance encourages individuals to recognize their emotions and express them. Through dance, by varying movement qualities, individuals can convey their feelings and ideas to others and perhaps portray emotions that they cannot verbally express. Dance provides a means not only to express one's feelings and emotions to others but also to gain insight into oneself. Dance, by its very nature, can promote sensitivity and awareness.

Dance therapy is one of the fastest-growing professions. It is used in rehabilitation centers, psychiatric centers, geriatric programs, hospitals, and programs for people with disabilities. Dance therapy is used with all segments of the population, from very young to very old people. Certification standards for dance therapists have been established by the American Dance Therapy Association (ADTA) (www.adta.org).

Therapeutic Recreation

Therapeutic recreation is concerned with problems of individuals with physical, mental, and social disabilities and with elderly people. Recreation therapists work in community and institutional settings where these individuals are located. Therapists use techniques of play and other recreational activities to help individuals achieve appropriate goals in physical, emotional, mental, and social development. Games, sports, arts and crafts, and social activities are modified to meet the needs of the patients or clients so that the goals of the program can be realized. Job opportunities for recreation therapists exist in nursing homes, senior citizen centers, child- and day-care centers, recreational programs, YMCAs/YWCAs, hospitals, clinics, and private agencies.

Indoor rowing machines are popular among fitness enthusiasts. Competitions allow participants to test their ability.

Degree programs in therapeutic recreation are available. However, there are employment opportunities for physical education, exercise science, and sport professionals who have the background and desire to work in this area. Physical educators and sport leaders working in a community recreation agency may direct therapeutic recreation programs in addition to teaching physical skills and leading activities. More information about therapeutic recreation is available from the American Therapeutic Recreation Association (www.atra-online.com) and the National Therapeutic Recreation Society (www.nrpa.org/ntrs).

Kinesiotherapy

According to the American Kinesiotherapy Association, a kinesiotherapist is a "health care professional who, under the direction of a physician, treats the effects of disease, injury, and congenital disorders, through the use of therapeutic exercise and education."[31] According to the Commission on Accreditation of Allied Health Education Programs, kinesiotherapists "emphasize (a) prevention of deconditioning and debilitation and (b) development and maintenance of functional fitness in persons with chronic disease or disability."[32] The American Medical Association reports that the types of treatments used by kinesiotherapists focus on "therapeutic exercise, ambulation training, geriatric rehabilitation, aquatic therapy, prosthetic/orthotic rehabilitation, psychiatric rehabilitation, and driver training."[33]

Kinesiotherapists are employed in many different settings, including medical centers, hospitals, sports medicine facilities, rehabilitation facilities, schools, private practice, and exercise consultancies.[32] The average starting salary for kinesiologists is about $28,000 a year, but varies according to the job setting and associated responsibilities.[33]

The American Kinesiotherapy Association offers certification for qualified individuals. Kinesiotherapists may have a degree in physical education or exercise science and must meet specific coursework requirements. Additionally, to qualify for certification, an individual must successfully

Exercise is important for people of all ages. Flexibility exercises help the elderly retain their range of motion, allowing them to be more independent.

complete a 1,000-hour clinical internship at an approved site and pass a national certification exam. To maintain their certification, kinesiotherapists must participate in continuing education every year. For more information, contact the American Kinesiotherapy Association (www.akta.org).

Physical Therapy

Physical therapists provide services directed at the restoration, maintenance, and promotion of overall health. Physical therapists work with individuals of all ages to prevent or limit physical disabilities of patients who are injured or who are suffering from disease.[34] Physical therapists work with their patients to restore function, improve mobility, and limit pain.[34]

After reviewing patients' medical histories, physical therapists assess the patients' abilities, including strength, range of motion, balance, coordination, posture, and motor function. A treatment plan is developed and implemented. Treatments might include exercises to help patients who have been immobilized regain their strength, flexibility,

and endurance. To help patients improve their ability to function, physical therapists use many techniques, such as electrical stimulation, hot packs, cold compresses, ultrasound, traction, and massage.[34] Physical therapists teach patients how to effectively and efficiently use adaptive and assistive devices, such as crutches and prostheses.[34] Physical therapists also teach patients exercises to do at home.

Physical therapists often practice as part of a health care team that includes physicians, therapists, educators, occupational therapists, and speech-language pathologists. Some physical therapists are generalists who treat a wide range of patients and needs. Others are specialists, focusing on pediatrics, geriatrics, orthopedics, sports medicine, and cardiopulmonary physical therapy. Physical therapists are employed in many different settings, most often in hospitals, clinics, and private offices. Some physical therapists work in homes. Median salary for physical therapists is about 72,000, although some earn more than 100,000 a year.[34]

Some physical education, exercise science, and sport professionals decide to build upon their education and obtain a master's degree in physical therapy. For those who aspire to continue their education in this area, it is important to note that physical therapy programs have strict admission requirements. Biology, chemistry, and physics are just some of the many requirements that must be satisfied. Additionally, most programs require prospective students to work as volunteers in a physical therapy setting for a specified number of hours. For more information about physical therapy, contact the American Physical Therapy Association (www.apta.org).

Chiropractic Care

Chiropractors, also known as doctors of chiropractic, work with individuals to help them regain their health and improve the function of their body. Chiropractors believe that interference with the muscular, nervous, and skeletal systems of the body, particularly the spine, leads to health problems.[35] Spinal or vertebral dysfunction affects the

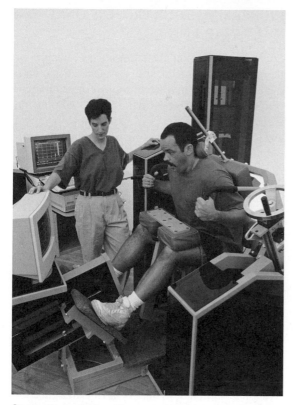

Some physical education, exercise science, and sport professionals build on their undergraduate preparation and obtain a degree in physical therapy.

nervous system, interfering with regulation of many important body functions.[35]

Chiropractors emphasize a holistic approach to health care. They recognize that many factors affect patients' health, including diet, physical activity, environment, and heredity. Their treatment approaches emphasize reliance on the body's inherent recuperative abilities, and they use nonsurgical interventions. Chiropractors also assist their patients in recognizing aspects of their lifestyle that could be changed—such as diet, exercise, and sleeping habits—that would improve their health. Chiropractors also consult with and refer patients to other health practitioners, when necessary.

In working with a patient, the chiropractor takes the patient's medical history and then uses a variety of techniques to diagnose the patient's condition. These include physical, neurological, and orthopedic examinations as well as X-rays and other diagnostic imaging techniques. A postural and spinal analysis is an important part of the diagnostic procedure.

A wide variety of treatment approaches are used by chiropractors. Typically, when the patient's problem involves the musculoskeletal system, the chiropractor manually adjusts the spinal column using a variety of techniques.[35] Other treatment approaches involve massage, ultrasound, acupuncture, electrical stimulation, and heat therapy. Supports such as braces may also be used to help the patient regain function.[35] As part of their holistic approach, chiropractors counsel patients about many different facets of wellness, including nutrition, physical activity, stress management, and lifestyle changes. Chiropractors do not prescribe drugs or perform surgery.

As more Americans embrace a holistic approach to health and health care, chiropractic treatment has become more popular. The tenets of chiropractic care are compatible with this holistic approach. The emphasis on lifestyle management and nonsurgical, noninvasive interventions has led more people to seek chiropractic care for problems related to their back, neck, extremities, and joints. The willingness of more health insurance companies to pay for such care has also contributed to its growth in popularity.

Most chiropractors are self-employed or work as part of a group practice. There are few chiropractors employed by major health care organizations. As in many professions, chiropractors' earnings are relatively low when starting out and increase as their practice grows. In 2009, the average salary was $94,454.[35]

Some physical education, exercise science, and sport professionals decide to pursue their education further and study to be chiropractors. Their preparation in the areas of anatomy and physiology, natural sciences, physical activity, and health provides a strong background for study in this area. Additionally, since chiropractors often discuss physical activity, health, and nutrition with their patients, physical education, exercise science, and sport professionals are well qualified to address these areas of health promotion.

To become a chiropractor, an individual must have at least 2 years of undergraduate education, although more schools are requiring a 4-year bachelor's degree. The individual must then complete a 4-year program at an accredited chiropractic college, which culminates in a doctor of chiropractic degree. Chiropractors must take a state licensing exam and pass the National Board of Chiropractor Examiners test. Chiropractors can specialize in sport injuries, orthopedics, pediatrics, radiology, nutrition, physiotherapy, and geriatrics.[35] Physical education, exercise science, and sport professionals who wish to become chiropractors should familiarize themselves with the admission requirements for advanced study in this area. For more information about becoming a chiropractor, students should contact various chiropractic colleges, as specific admission requirements vary.

• • •

Individuals interested in pursuing careers in dance therapy, therapeutic recreation, and kinesiotherapy may benefit from courses in adapted physical education, psychology, health, recreation, and counseling. Some physical education, exercise science, and sport professionals build on their background in physical education, athletic training, or exercise science at the undergraduate level to pursue master's degrees in physical therapy or become a doctor of chiropractic. Physical education, exercise science, and sport professionals aspiring to continue their studies and pursue careers in these areas should, early in their professional preparation, identify courses that are needed as prerequisites for entry into master's and doctoral programs in these areas. Students may then use these prerequisite courses as electives in their undergraduate curriculum.

As recognition of the therapeutic, recreational, and social benefits of movement increases, employment opportunities for physical education, exercise science, and sport professionals in these areas will expand.

INCREASING YOUR PROFESSIONAL MARKETABILITY

Students who are interested in fitness-, health-, or therapy-related careers can do much to increase their professional marketability. Taking additional course work, pursuing certification, building on their talents and interests, and gaining practical experience will enhance the credentials of individuals seeking a position in these areas.

Additional courses in health will increase one's marketability. Conducting health promotion programs—nutritional counseling, weight management, substance abuse, smoking cessation, and stress management—is often a responsibility associated with positions in this career area. Thus, courses in nutrition, stress management, pharmacology, and drug education are helpful to students preparing for careers in these areas. Courses in counseling, psychology, and sociology will be helpful as well. Prospective professionals need to develop the skills necessary to help individuals change their fitness and health habits. By understanding various decision making approaches, motivational techniques, and behavior modification strategies, physical education, exercise science, and sport professionals can help their clients achieve their goals, whether those goals are increased fitness, weight loss, or learning to manage stress. Because many fitness- and health-related careers include responsibilities such as budgeting, program promotion, membership solicitation, and bookkeeping, courses in business and computer science help professionals perform these aspects of the job.

Obtaining certification may also increase one's marketability. In many exercise specialist and fitness-related jobs, ACSM certification is becoming an increasingly common requirement. Even if such certification is not required for employment, certification as a Health Fitness Instructor, for example, may be viewed positively by a prospective employer. Although certification in CPR and first aid may be required, it may be helpful to pursue additional certification as a CPR or first aid instructor. These certifications enable one to teach CPR or first aid in a corporate fitness center. Professionals interested in working as exercise specialists or athletic trainers may wish to become certified as Emergency Medical Technicians (EMTs). This will provide additional expertise in the area of emergency care. Belonging to professional organizations such as AAHPERD, ACSM, NSCA, or NATA will also allow one to take advantage of workshops and clinics in one's area of interest.

Building on one's interests and strengths through extracurricular and outside experiences can contribute to one's professional expertise. If you are interested in weight training, for example, and work out frequently, take the time to learn about the different approaches to weight training. Expertise in dance is necessary for those seeking a career in dance therapy and can also enhance the skills of individuals seeking to work in corporate and community fitness centers and preschool programs. Aerobic dance has become a very popular approach to fitness and is often used in fitness centers.

Gaining practical experience through internships, fieldwork, volunteering, or part-time or summer employment can enhance one's marketability. There is no substitute for experience. Take advantage of the opportunities to work in potential places of employment to gain insight into the day-to-day work. Working as an assistant to a recreational therapist or physical therapist in a hospital, assisting in a sports medicine clinic, supervising clients working out in a health spa, and interning in a corporate fitness center provide practical experience and the opportunity to put theoretical knowledge gained in your undergraduate preparation into practice, as well as teach you the skills necessary for employment in these positions. Through various practical experiences, professional contacts can be developed as well.

Physical education, exercise science, and sport professionals can increase their opportunities for employment in fitness-, health-, and therapy, related careers by several means. Taking additional course work, building on one's interests and strengths, obtaining relevant certifications, and gaining practical experience are strategies that will enhance your marketability.

FOCUS ON CAREER: Health, Fitness, and Sports Medicine

PROFESSIONAL ORGANIZATIONS	• American Association for Physical Activity and Recreation www.aahperd.org → AAPAR • American College of Sports Medicine www.acsm.org • National Athletic Trainers' Association www.nata.org • National Strength and Conditioning Association www.nsca-lift.org
PROFESSIONAL JOURNALS	• *Clinical Exercise Physiology* • *Journal of Athletic Training* • *Journal of Sport Rehabilitation* • *Journal of Strength and Conditioning Research* • *Medicine and Science in Sports and Exercise* • *The Physician and Sportsmedicine* • *Strength and Conditioning Journal*

SUMMARY

Within the past decade, opportunities for physical education, exercise scientists, and sport professionals desiring to pursue a career as a fitness or exercise specialist have increased tremendously. Career opportunities exist in preventative and rehabilitative exercise programs. Preventative exercise programs are conducted by corporations, community agencies, and commercial fitness clubs. Rehabilitative exercise programs are typically conducted in a hospital setting, but may be affiliated with corporate fitness programs or community agency programs.

Opportunities for physical education, exercise science, and sport professionals to pursue health-related careers have also grown rapidly. Professionals possessing qualifications in athletic training may find employment working with athletic programs at the professional, collegiate, and, increasingly, secondary level. Employment opportunities also are available in sports medicine clinics, physical therapy clinics, and hospitals. Physical educators, exercise science, and sport leaders have also been successful in securing employment in health and weight control spas and clubs.

The recognition that participation in movement and physical activities has therapeutic and psychological benefits as well as physical benefits has stimulated the growth of therapy-related careers. These include careers as dance therapists, recreational therapists, and physical therapists. Kinesiotherapy and chiropractic are also potential careers for physical education, exercise science, and sport professionals willing to continue their studies.

If you are seeking employment in fitness- and health-related careers, you can increase your marketability by taking additional course work in health, business, and psychology. Gaining as much practical experience as possible will also be an asset in securing employment.

It appears that opportunities for qualified individuals in fitness- and health-related careers will continue to increase in the future.

DISCUSSION QUESTIONS

1. Fitness and health clubs have gained in popularity. However, more than one-third of health club members have a household income of more than $100,000 a year and the average income is over $80,000 a year. What can professionals do to reach more individuals whose income is less than the average and provide opportunities for them to be physically active?

2. Should health clubs be mandated to hire only certified fitness professionals? Explain your reasoning. If you believe that health clubs should hire only certified fitness professionals, from what organizations would you accept certifications and why?

3. What is burnout? Why may athletic trainers be susceptible to burnout? What can be done to prevent burnout?

SELF-ASSESSMENT ACTIVITIES

These activities are designed to help you determine if you have mastered materials and competencies presented in this chapter.

1. Describe the responsibilities of a fitness or exercise specialist. If possible, interview a professional in this career regarding his or her responsibilities and qualifications.

2. Describe the various employment opportunities for a fitness or exercise professional. Review the want ads in several large city papers for 2 weeks for employment opportunities in this area or search for jobs online; describe the positions that you found available and qualifications required for employment.

3. Using the information provided in the Get Connected box, read about one of the certification programs available through the American College of Sports Medicine, American Council on Exercise, National Athletic Trainers' Association, or the National Strength and Conditioning Association. For the association you selected, investigate the certification programs, benefits offered to members, costs for certification and membership, and opportunities for continuing education. How could this certification be beneficial to you in your chosen career?

4. Using the information provided in the Get Connected box, locate new research, industry news, and position papers pertaining to health and fitness. Summarize your findings in a brief report.

REFERENCES

1. Cooper KH and Collingwood TR: Physical fitness: programming issues for total well-being, JOPERD 55(3):35–36, 44, 1984.

2. Sol N: Graduation preparation for exercise program professionals, JOPERD 52(7):76–77, 1981.

3. US Department of Health and Human Services: Healthy people 2010, ed 2, Washington D.C., 2000, US Government Printing Office.

4. DiNubile NA and Sherman C: Exercise and the bottom line: promoting physical and fiscal fitness in the workplace: a commentary, The Physician and Sportsmedicine 27(2), 1999.

5. Shepard RJ: Do work-site exercise and health programs work?, The Physician and Sportsmedicine 27(2), 1999.

6. Riedel JE, Lynch W, Baase C, Hymel P, and Peterson KW: The effect of disease prevention and health promotion on workplace productivity: a literature review, American Journal of Health Promotion 15(3):167–191, 2001.

7. President's Council on Physical Fitness and Sports: Economic benefits of physical activity, Washington, D.C., 1996, The President's Council on Physical Fitness and Sports Physical Activity Research Digest.

8. US Department of Health and Human Services: Physical activity and health: a report of the surgeon general, Atlanta, Ga., 1999, US Department of Health and Human Services, Centers for Disease Control and Prevention, National Center for Chronic Disease Prevention and Health Promotion.

9. Aldana SG: Financial impact of health promotion programs: a comprehensive review of the literature, American Journal of Health Promotion 15(5):296–320.

10. Learning about health and productivity: The Health Enhancement Research Advocate 3(1), 2000.

11. Chapman L: American Journal of Health Promotion, January–February 2001, 117.

12. US Department of Labor Bureau of Labor Statistics: National compensation survey: employee benefits in private industry in the United States, 2006.

13. Chapman LS: Planning wellness: getting off to a good start, Part 1, Absolute Advantage 5(4), 2006 (www.welcoa.org).

14. Wellness Councils of America: Health, wealthy and wise—fundamentals of workplace health promotion, Omaha, Neb., 1993, Wellness Councils of America.

15. Lewis RJ, Huebner WW, and Yarborough CM, III: Characteristics of participants and nonparticipants in worksite health promotion, American Journal of Health Promotion 11(2):99–106, 1996.

16. Drolet JC and Fetro JV: State conferences for school worksite wellness: personal health practices of conference participants, Journal of Health Promotion 24(3):174–178, 1993.

17. International Health, Racquet, and Sport Club Association: Industry statistics, 2009. (www.ihrsa.org).

18. Aufsesser PM and Burke JP: The fitness clinic for physically disabled, Palaestra 13(1):18–20, 1997.

19. Popke M: Healthy prognosis, Athletic Business, updated October 1, 2005 (athleticbusiness.com/articles/article.aspx?articleid=1090&zoneid=22).

20. American Council on Exercise, 2005 salary survey results, 2006 (www.acefitness.org).

21. National Strength and Conditioning Association (www.nsca-lift.org).

22. American College of Sports Medicine endorses clinical exercise physiologist profession (www.acsm.org).

23. McDermott B: Certification: a connection to competence, 2006 (www.athleticbusiness.com).

24. ACSM Certifications (www.acsm.org).

25. American Council on Exercise: Certifications (www.acefitness.org).

26. Aerobics and Fitness Association of America: Certifications (www.afaa.com).

27. National Strength and Conditioning Association Certification Commission: Certifications (www.nsca-cc.org).

28. Siedentop D: Introduction of physical education, fitness, and sport, Mountain View, Calif, 1990, Mayfield.

29. Kaiser DA: Location, location: where are athletic trainers employed?, Athletic Therapy Today 11(6):6–11, 2006.

30. NATA 2000 Salary Data Survey Results: National Athletic Trainers' Association (www.nata.org).

31. American Kinesiotherapy Association (www .akta.org).

32. Commission on Accreditation of Allied Health Education Programs: Kinesiotherapist, 2002 (www.caahep.org).

33. American Medical Association: Kinesiotherapist. (www.ama-assn.org).

34. US Department of Labor Bureau of Labor Statistics. Occupational Outlook Handbook, 2010–2011 ed, Physical Therapists (www.bls .gov/oco/ocos080.htm) Retrieved July 10, 2010.

35. US Department of Labor Bureau of Labor Statistics. Occupational Outlook Handbook, 2010–2011 ed, Chiropractors (www.bls.gov/oco /ocos071.htm) Retrieved July 10, 2010.

C H A P T E R 14

SPORT CAREERS

OBJECTIVES

After reading this chapter the student should be able to—

■ Identify opportunities for professionals in sport management and entry-level positions in these careers.

■ Describe career opportunities in sport media and explain how preparation in physical education, exercise science, and sport can assist individuals in these careers.

■ Describe career opportunities in performance and other sport-related careers.

■ Discuss how professionals can increase their professional marketability.

Participation in fitness activities and sport at all levels is at an all-time high, and it appears that participation will continue to increase in the future. One indication of this growth is the sale of fitness and sports products. According to the Sporting Goods Manufacturers Association (SGMA), the sporting goods industry enjoyed $71.8 billion in wholesale business in 2009.[1] This includes the sales of sporting goods equipment, fitness equipment, sport apparel, athletic footwear, and licensed merchandise in the United States. Sales are projected to increase in future years, with athletic footwear and consumer fitness equipment driving the growth.[1]

Some highlights that reflect the state of the industry include the following:

• Sporting goods equipment registered sales of $20.2 billion. Golf equipment accounted for $2.48 billion in sales.

• Exercise equipment reached $4.2 billion in sales. Treadmill sales accounted for nearly 25% of those sales. The next two largest sales categories were elliptical machines, accounting for $913 million in sales, and exercise cycles, reaching $442 million in sales. Nearly 80% of the sales of exercise equipment is accounted for by consumer and retail expenditures.

• Wholesale sales of sport apparel, which includes branded athletic apparel, performance apparel, fitness apparel, and branded active wear, were $28.17 billion.

• Team uniform spending was $1.131 billion, with football, baseball, basketball, soccer and volleyball leading sales.

• Athletic footwear reached $12.3 billion in sales. Running shoe sales accounted for more than $3.35 billion in revenue.

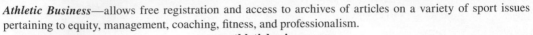

GET CONNECTED

Athletic Business—allows free registration and access to archives of articles on a variety of sport issues pertaining to equity, management, coaching, fitness, and professionalism.
www.athleticbusiness.com

North American Society for Sport Management—contains information about the organization, membership, publications, and conferences.
www.nassm.com

ESPN and *Sports Illustrated*—provide up-to-date information about sports and sport issues.
http://espn.go.com

http://sportsillustrated.cnn.com

Women's Sports Foundation—gives access to research, information about career opportunities in sport, articles on a variety of topics, and internships.
www.womenssportsfoundation.org

• Retail sales of licensed sport products in the United States were $8.02 billion. Products with team logos or stars' names on them from the National Basketball Association (NBA), National Football League (NFL), NASCAR, and college and universities were popular, and sales continue to rise.[1]

As can be seen from these figures, interest in sports and fitness is tremendous, and the industry has become a big business. As participation and the sporting industry continue to grow, career opportunities in the various areas of sport management will expand.

Spectator interest in all sports at all levels is rising. Within the last decade, many sports recorded record high attendance at contests. The National Collegiate Athletic Association's (NCAA) women's basketball Final Four championships continue to sell out, as do the men's. The Women's National Basketball Association (WNBA) draws almost 1.7 million million fans a season. Over 22 million fans attended regular-season NBA games. In 2009, nearly 73 million people attended Major League Baseball (MLB) games. The growth of spectator interest in sport at all levels widens the career opportunities for physical education, exercise science, and sport professionals.

The coverage of sport by the media continues to grow. Newspapers, magazines, radio, and television are traditional channels to deliver sport news and game coverage to the fans. Two of the greatest areas of growth are cable television and the Internet. Monies paid for broadcasting rights to sport events indicate the extent of the public's interest in—and the profit associated with—the coverage of sports. For example, the NFL earns more than $3.1 billion a year from fees paid by CBS, ESPN, Fox, NBC, and DirecTV to broadcast its games. CBS paid $6 billion to telecast the NCAA men's basketball tournament for 11 years. In 2010, ABC/ESPN signed a $1.86 billion 12-year deal with the Atlantic Coast Conference for the right to broadcast football and basketball games.[2] This is about $155 million a year. Other conferences, such as the Southeastern Conference (SEC), have signed more lucrative deals. The SEC secured a 14-year deal with CBS and ESPN for $205 million a year. Most of these deals are wide-ranging, encompassing not only television but digital rights associated with online and broadband delivery of programming. Longtime Olympics broadcaster NBC purchased the broadcast, cable, and digital rights for the 2010 Winter Games and the 2012 Summer Games for $2.201 billion.

Premier sport events such as the Olympics, the Super Bowl, the NCAA basketball Final Four, the NBA championships, and MLB's World Series are watched by millions of people worldwide. Soccer's quadrennial World Cup attracts the largest television audience. It was estimated that during the last World Cup in 2006, more than 30 billion viewers watched the matches during the course of the tournament. For the 2010 World Cup, new online and mobile broadband technologies in conjunction with television attracted record audiences. Given the growth of the popularity of sport and the emergence of new technologies that transform viewing, opportunities for qualified professionals seeking a career in these areas will increase.

Sport at many levels is big business. It is estimated that in the United States, sport is a $410 billion industry, with billion-dollar franchises and multimillion-dollar contributing to this business.[3] In the United States, the NFL, the NBA, MLB, and the National Hockey League (NHL) are the top professional leagues. Of these, MLB and the NFL are the most profitable, with revenues estimated at $6 billion a year.[3] Players' salaries in professional sports are at levels unheard of 10 years ago. For example, Los Angeles Lakers star Kobe Bryant has a 7-year contract worth an estimated $136 million. For top players, their earnings are supplemented with millions of dollars in lucrative endorsement deals with such sport giants as Nike and Adidas.

As you can see sport is a megabusiness, one that is constantly expanding. The magnitude of the industry as well as its diverse nature offers students with an interest in sport a multitude of career opportunities. Before describing some of the many opportunities available, a short overview of sport management, an ever-expanding area of study, is presented. Examples of careers associated with sport management, including sport media, are next highlighted. In addition to careers in these areas, some individuals aspire to careers as performers. Others pursue careers in officiating and sport law. Entrepreneurship captures the interest of other individuals, who develop their own business or services.

SPORT MANAGEMENT

Sport management is a rapidly growing area of knowledge. Professional opportunities for individuals trained in this area are diverse and challenging. Sport management can be defined in many different ways. According to DeSensi, Kelley, Blanton, and Beitel, sport management is "any combination of skills related to planning, organizing, directing, controlling, budgeting, leading and evaluating within the context of an organization or department whose primary product or service is related to sport."[4] Opportunities within this broad field include, but are not limited to, the management of facilities, hotels, resorts, fitness clubs, merchandising, and sports at all levels, within the public and private sectors.

The growth of the sport business industry, a multibillion-dollar-a-year industry, has created additional opportunities within the field. Given the expanding dimensions of sport, Parkhouse and Pitts suggest that a more contemporary definition of sport management may be needed. They define sport management as:

> the study and practice involved in relation to all people, activities, organizations, and businesses involved in producing, facilitating, promoting, or organizing any product that is sport-, fitness-, and recreation-related; and, sport products can be goods, services, people, places, or ideas.[5]

Sport can include a wide range of activities, ranging from the spectator sport industry and its focus on consumer entertainment to the fitness and sport industry and its focus on consumer participation.

A conceptual analysis of the dimensions of sport management developed by Blann is shown in Figure 14-1.[6] Sport management is conceptualized as encompassing the sport world, organized sport, management of sport experiences, and the sport enterprise.

During the past five decades, the academic study of sport management has grown tremendously. Historically, the study of sport management, like that of the other subdisciplines, was based in physical education. Today, sport management

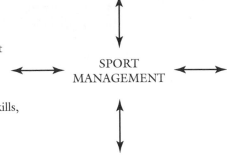

The Sport World

Analysis of the sport environment. Consideration of sport experiences, types of clients, types of activities.

Managing Sport Experiences

Analysis of management principles in sport. Consideration of management functions, processes; managerial skills, roles, responsibilities.

SPORT MANAGEMENT

Organized Sport

Analysis of cultural-philosophical, institutional-organizational aspects of sport. Consideration of sport roles, functions, expectations.

The Sport Enterprise

Analysis of the sport domains. Consideration of purposes, objective, goals, clients of sport organizations, broad career paths, specific career opportunities.

Figure 14-1   Four-factor analysis of sport management

continues to grow and develop its own specialized programs of study.

There are several major professional organizations for sport management professionals. The North American Society for Sport Management (NASSM) was established in 1985 to promote sport management and to encourage the growth of research, scholarly writing, and professional development in the field. NASSM sponsors an annual conference and publishes the *Journal of Sport Management*. The National Association for Sport and Physical Education (NASPE), one of the associations of the American Alliance for Health, Physical Education, Recreation, and Dance, established a Sport Management Council (SMC). The SMC strives to provide the development of quality programs in sport management, to work to develop research and projects of benefit to professionals, and to establish mutually beneficial relationships with professionals in sport industry. Two other associations deal with specific

aspects of the sport management field. The Sport and Recreation Law Association (SRLA) focuses on the legal aspects of sport. In addition to its annual conference, SRLA publishes the *Journal of Legal Aspects of Sport*. The Sport Marketing Association provides professionals an opportunity to interact with others who share a similar interest in sport marketing.

As the area of sport management evolved from physical education, new programs were developed to prepare professionals in this specialized area. Today there are over 200 programs offering degrees in sport management at the undergraduate and graduate levels. In an effort to ensure that students entering the field were prepared with the appropriate knowledge and skills, a joint task force was established by NASPE and NASSM to develop standards for sport management professional preparation programs.

NASPE-NASSM defines sport management as "the field of study offering specialized training and education necessary for individuals seeking careers in any of the many segments of the industry."[7] The NASPE-NASSM Task Force developed a comprehensive set of competencies to be included in a sport management professional preparation curriculum. The undergraduate content areas include:

- Sociocultural dimensions.
- Management and leadership in sport.
- Ethics in sport management.
- Marketing in sport.
- Communication in sport.
- Budget and finance in sport.
- Legal aspects of sport.
- Economics in sport.
- Governance in sport.
- Field experience in sport management.[7]

The field experience is considered a critical aspect of preparation for a career in sport management. An internship is commonly required. Students usually work in a sport management setting for a semester or summer, working at least 40 hours a week and accumulating at least 400 hours. This experience is supervised by a faculty member from the undergraduate institution, as well as by a professional at the internship site. Additional practical experiences can be gained by students through fieldwork (short periods of supervised work in a professional setting), volunteering, or working in a sport management position during the summer or on a part-time basis during the school year. Practical experiences are also a good way to investigate the growing number of career opportunities in this rapidly expanding field.

Just recently, in 2008, the Commission on Sport Management Accreditation (COSMA) was established by NASPE and NASSM.[8] This accrediting body strives to promote and recognize excellence in sport management education, at both the undergraduate and graduate levels. Programs that meet the standards are accredited for a period of 7 years.

The increased growth of athletics, sport participation by all segments of our society, and sport-related businesses has created a need for individuals trained in sport management. There are many different career paths that students with an interest in sport management can pursue. The dynamic nature and growth of the field lead to new and plentiful career opportunities for students well prepared in this area. Figure 14-2, developed by Blann, shows some of the sport management career paths.[9] Employment opportunities include sport administration, management of sport clubs and facilities, sport and leisure social services, sport marketing, and sport communication.

Individuals interested in pursuing a career in sport management need to realize that they will likely begin their career working in an entry-level position, often with limited responsibilities. From this position, competent individuals can work their way up the career ladder to middle and top management positions. Each step up the ladder typically requires assuming increased and broader responsibilities. Salaries in this field vary widely, ranging from $30,000 to $50,000 per year, although some salaries may be greater than $100,000 a year.

CAREERS IN SPORT MANAGEMENT

Athletic administration, campus and corporate recreation management, sport facilities management, sport retailing, and sport tourism opportunities are described in the next section. Additionally, a myriad of opportunities exist for qualified individuals in professional organizations, conferences, and leagues.

Athletic Administration

There are many job opportunities in the field of athletic administration. At the high school level, administrative positions are available as an athletic director and, depending on the size of the school, as an assistant athletic director. At the collegiate level, many administrative opportunities exist, with the number of administrative positions and associated responsibilities depending on the nature and size of the athletic program. Among the administrative positions are athletic director, associate athletic director, and assistant

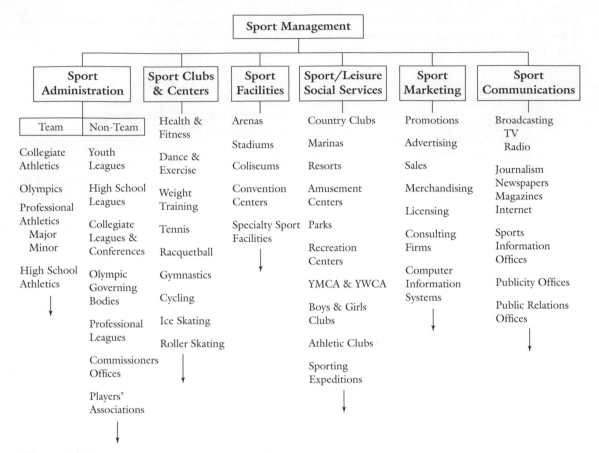

Figure 14-2 Sport management career paths

athletic director. Other administrative positions that might be found in collegiate athletic programs include program fund-raising director, marketing director, recruiting coordinator, compliance coordinator, and academic counseling coordinator. Not all colleges and universities have these positions; oftentimes, the athletic director and his or her associate or assistant director may fulfill the responsibilities of with these positions.

The director of athletics is responsible for the administration of the athletic programs. This position may be found at high schools as well as at colleges and universities. Typically, at the high school level, the athletic director may be employed as a teacher and, in smaller schools, also

as a coach. At the collegiate level as well, athletic directors also may have teaching and coaching responsibilities. In many schools, however, particularly those with large competitive programs, the athletic director may have as his or her sole responsibility the conduct of the competitive program. In many instances, athletic directors have associate and assistant athletic directors to help them in the performance of their work.

The athletic director is responsible for performing a variety of tasks. The athletic director may delegate these tasks to assistants or perform them himself or herself. The athletic director is responsible for the administration of men's and women's athletics. This includes both the hiring and ongoing supervision of coaches and assistant coaches. The athletic director must be knowledgeable regarding the rules and regulations governing athletic competition, including rules pertaining to the recruitment and eligibility of athletes. Other tasks are scheduling athletic contests; arranging for officials; and, for competitions involving travel, planning for transportation, lodging, and meals.

The athletic director is also responsible for the safety of the coaches, athletes, and spectators at home contests. This involves working closely with security personnel and making careful provisions for crowd control. At home contests, the athletic director supervises the ticket office and concessions. The athletic director must work closely with other personnel involved in athletics such as the athletic trainers and sport information directors. Establishing a good working relationship with the facilities manager and maintenance staff is important as well.

Development and management of the athletic budget is an important function of the athletic director, who is often expected to work as a fund-raiser. Establishing and maintaining good relationships with the community, local support groups such as booster clubs, and alumni is seen as vital to the success of the athletic program. The athletic director must also attend professional meetings to keep abreast of changes in rules and governance.

In large athletic programs, such as those at major colleges and universities, there may be a fairly large administrative staff with specific job responsibilities assigned to each person. Many large institutions employ associate or assistant athletic directors. A few institutions employ directors of fund-raising who are charged with obtaining money to supplement the athletic budget. Some institutions have employees who monitor the institution's compliance with the growing number of rules and regulations of the athletic governing bodies, most notably the NCAA.

More and more institutions have academic support programs for their student-athletes. Through these programs, student-athletes have access to tutoring, supervised study tables, and courses in life skills. The academic coordinator also works with faculty and other academic resources across campus to help student-athletes fulfill their academic obligations. Some tutors travel with the team, providing student-athletes with academic support when they are on the road for an extended period of time. Some institutions have an administrator who coordinates the academic support program; in other institutions, this responsibility is undertaken by the athletic director or one of his or her assistants. Opportunities exist within these programs for program coordinators, tutors, and instructors of life skills courses.

Salaries associated with the various jobs in athletic administration vary widely, depending on the extent of the responsibilities and the size of the program. Salaries can range from $25,000 to over $100,000. For individuals who enjoy working with athletes, jobs in athletic administration can be very rewarding.

Students interested in pursuing a career in athletic administration may find it helpful to know that at the high school level, directors of athletics typically have a degree in physical education and coaching experience. At the collegiate level, athletic directors may have a physical education degree, a sport management degree, or a business degree. Additionally, oftentimes an advanced degree, either a master's or doctoral degree, is required. Students aspiring to a career in athletic administration may want to take advantage of opportunities to intern or volunteer at their college or a high school athletic department. Additionally, the NCAA offers scholarships for postgraduate internships in athletic administration.

Campus Recreation

In the past two decades, college and university campus recreation programs have grown tremendously. The intramural programs of the 1990s have expanded to include a wide array of recreational pursuits for students, faculty, and staff.[10] These opportunities include both formal and informal recreational activities, encompassing intramural sport, fitness and wellness programs, sport clubs, outdoor recreation, and aquatic programs.[10] The National Intramural-Recreational Sports Association estimates that 75% of the 16 million college students participate in campus recreation activities.[11] The development of multimillion-dollar facilities, the increasing comprehensiveness of campus recreational programs, and the growing interest in fitness and wellness have created an array of job opportunities for competent professionals.

Many titles have been used to describe the individual charged with the administration of these programs. These titles include director of campus recreation, director of recreational sports, and director of intramurals. Depending on the institution, the intramural and campus recreation programs may be administered through student services, the physical education department, or the athletic department. In schools with large programs, the director may have an assistant or several staff members to help conduct the program.

Responsibilities associated with this position are wide-ranging. One of the primary responsibilities is promoting participation. This requires scheduling activities and tournaments that are of interest to students, publicizing programs, and working closely with campus groups such as residential life and student government to promote these programs. Training and supervision of officials are essential if programs are to run smoothly and safely. The director may also be responsible for instructional programs and the supervision of sport and recreation clubs. Often, the director is assigned to supervise physical education and athletic facilities and open recreation programs such as recreational swimming. This may entail the training and supervision of numerous students to serve as lifeguards, gymnasium supervisors, or building security guards.

The intramural director may or may not have teaching responsibilities, depending on the size of the program. Programs are usually offered from late afternoon to late at night; frequently in schools with limited facilities, intramurals cannot start until the athletic teams have finished their practices. Programs also may be offered on weekends. Professionals who are interested in promoting educational values through activities and in providing opportunities for others to experience the satisfaction derived from participation will find working in intramural and campus recreation programs an enjoyable career. The National Intramural-Recreational Sports Association provides additional information on career opportunities and programming (www.nirsa.org).

Corporate Recreation

More and more companies are providing recreational and sport opportunities for their employees. As the number of programs has increased, so has the need for qualified professionals to direct these activities. The responsibilities associated with this position are similar to those associated with the director of intramurals or campus recreation. These responsibilities include establishing a program of activities, setting up athletic teams, scheduling contests, providing for instruction, and supervising personnel. Professionals may also direct team-building activities and ropes courses. As corporate recreation programs continue to grow, so will opportunities for qualified professionals.

Sport Facilities Management

Facilities manager positions can be found in a diversity of settings. Facilities managers are traditionally employed by colleges and universities, and are also are needed to direct community, municipal, and commercial facilities such as aquatic centers, ice arenas, domed stadiums, sport complexes, and golf courses. The growing number of fitness centers and health clubs has also increased opportunities for individuals interested in facilities management.

Depending on the size of the sport facility, nature of programs, and number of individuals using the facility, the sport facilities manager may perform all the responsibilities by himself or herself or may have an assistant or several staff

Job opportunities in collegiate and professional athletics have increased during the last decade.

members under his or her direction. In some situations, the facilities manager may have additional responsibilities; for instance, in a fitness club, the facilities manager may also teach exercise classes or monitor individuals' workouts.

One of the primary concerns of the sport facilities manager is the safety of individuals using the facility. This involves making sure that the facility and equipment are maintained according to accepted standards. Knowledge of building codes, health and sanitation requirements, and certain laws is necessary in this position. In facilities that are used for competitions, such as stadiums, the facilities manager must make provisions to ensure the safety and well-being of spectators as well as participants. The manager must be concerned with crowd control and is responsible for security personnel. The facilities manager also is concerned about the business aspects of managing the facility, and he or she can have an impact on the financial success of the facility. The facility must be scheduled for maximum use to ensure a profitable financial status. The manager may also supervise other financial aspects of the facility, such as ticket sales, concessions, and parking. As the number of facilities continues to grow, opportunities in this area for qualified personnel will expand.

Sport Retailing

Sales of sporting goods—equipment, apparel, and shoes—are at an all-time high. Exercise equipment and golf equipment top sporting goods sales. Sales of sport apparel, sport activewear, athletic footwear, and licensed sports products are in the billions of dollars. Sport retailing is a booming business. Additionally, the enormous growth of women's sports since the enactment of Title IX has created new markets for sporting goods.

Manufacturers are now designing equipment and apparel specifically for girls and women, rather than downsizing boys' and men's products. The public's growing interest in sport, fitness, and physical activity has stimulated sales, and the traditional markets such as schools, colleges, universities, and professional teams have remained strong. Consequently, job opportunities in sport retailing, in both management and sales, have increased and will continue to grow.

The area of sport retailing has several opportunities. Jobs are available as salespeople selling directly to the consumer in sporting goods stores. Job opportunities also are available as manufacturers' representatives. An individual employed in this capacity, perhaps as a representative for Nike, may sell to buyers for sporting goods stores and to athletic teams in a certain region. Manufacturers' representatives are committed to increasing their company's share of the market. This position entails a great deal of travel. Hours may be spent on the phone setting up appointments with potential buyers and following up on sales calls. Whether a manufacturer's representative is successful depends to a great extent on the quality and reputation of the product he or she is selling and the establishment of personal contacts with buyers for these stores and institutions. Manufacturers' representatives may often submit bids for equipment and goods wanted by stores and institutions. Successful bidding requires that the representative be able to meet the buyer's specifications for the equipment and goods at the lowest cost. Manufacturers' representatives may also set up sales booths for their companies at conventions such as the AAHPERD National Convention. Other opportunities in sport retailing include positions as a manager or owner of a company.

Salaries for sales positions vary widely. Salespeople may receive a set salary. More often, however, their income is based on commissions and bonuses for the sales they have completed; thus, their income may vary widely from month to month. Salespeople who travel may receive a company car or an allowance for the use of their personal car, as well as an expense account.

Job opportunities in sport retailing may involve direct sales, retail management, or serving as a manufacturer's representative.

Salespeople may receive free equipment and goods or be able to purchase them at substantial discounts.

Being a salesperson requires that an individual be extremely knowledgeable about the products that he or she is selling. The consumer in a sporting goods store often expects the salesperson to be an expert on all types of equipment. Buyers for institutions and stores expect manufacturers' representatives to know all the specifications for the equipment and goods they are selling.

A background in physical education and sport is helpful in understanding the demands and nature of various sport areas and the requirements for equipment and goods for these kinds of sports. Courses in business management and accounting are helpful for salespeople. Being a salesperson requires strong interpersonal skills and the ability to identify individuals' needs and to sell them a product that meets those needs. As interest in sport, physical activities, and fitness continues to grow, opportunities for salespeople will expand as well. For more information about the state of the sporting goods industry, contact the Sporting Goods Manufacturers Association (www.sgma.com).

Career Opportunities in Professional Organizations

Qualified physical education, exercise science, and sport professionals may find employment in one of the many professional or specific sport organizations such as AAHPERD, NCAA, NFHS, Ladies Professional Golf Association, (LPGA), the NHL, or the United States Tennis Association (USTA). Other jobs are available in athletic conferences, such as in the offices of the Big Ten or the Big East. Foundations, such as the Women's Sports Foundation, are yet another place for employment.

The jobs available in professional organizations vary, depending on the nature of the organization and its size. Entry-level managerial positions may be available dealing with the day-to-day operations of the organization. Other positions may entail fund-raising, handling public relations, conducting membership drives, and directing special projects. If the organization sponsors a national convention, professionals are needed to assist in this endeavor; providing support and guidance to members preparing for local and regional conventions and coordinating meetings of the organization may also be part of one's responsibilities. Writing for the organization's newsletter and editing its periodicals are also jobs performed by individuals working for professional organizations. Professionals are also needed to serve as liaisons with the various committees of the organization. Still other positions in the organization may involve conducting special research projects, gathering data, and performing statistical analyses.

Individuals interested in this kind of career can obtain further information by contacting professional organizations in their area of interest or speaking to knowledgeable faculty. Some organizations, such as AAHPERD, the NCAA, the Women's Sports Foundation, and the United States Olympic Committee, may offer internships to students. Students interested in internships should write to the organization requesting information on these opportunities.

Sport Tourism

A growing area of specialization is sport tourism. Gibson defines sport tourism as "leisure-based travel that takes individuals temporarily outside of their home communities to participate in physical activities, to watch physical activities, or to venerate attractions associated with physical activities."[12]

 LIFESPAN AND CULTURAL PERSPECTIVES: Sport Management, Media, and Performance

- What are the societal, personal, and situational factors that lead individuals to pursue a career as a professional athlete?
- How do the media influence gender, racial, and cultural stereotypes of participants in sport?
- What are societal factors that contribute to the low numbers of women and people of color in athletic administration?
- Does the media's coverage of disabled sports reinforce or change society's perceptions of individuals with disabilities?

Gibson identifies three types of sport tourism—active sport tourism, such as when participants travel to take part in a sport event (e.g., Boston Marathon); event sport tourism, such as participants' traveling to watch an event (e.g., NCAA Final Four basketball tournament); and nostalgia sport tourism, such as participants' traveling to visit sport attractions (e.g., Baseball Hall of Fame).[12]

Globally, sport tourism is a multibillion-dollar business. Sport tourism is one of the most rapidly growing segments of the $5.9 trillion global travel and tourism industry.[13] Sport tourism is estimated to account for $600 billion, or 10% of the global tourism industry.[13] Mega-events, such as the Olympic Games and the FIFA World Cup, have a significant impact on the economy of the host county. The 2010 World Cup is estimated to attract more than 3.5 million fans to the tournament. The benefit to the South African economy is estimated to be at least 2 billion dollars. The 2014 FIFA World Cup and the 2016 Olympics will draw millions to the host country of Brazil, while benefiting the local economy in many different ways. As you can see, sport tourism is a big business, generating significant revenues for cities, regions, and countries that host sport events.

The growth of sport tourism has created a multitude of job opportunities for qualified individuals. Event and travel coordination, marketing, and promotion are just a few of the many aspects of the sport tourism industry that provide exciting and challenging careers. Salaries and hours worked vary widely, based on the magnitude of the event, its popularity, and its location.

CAREERS IN SPORT MEDIA

The pervasiveness of interest in sport in our society, coupled with the growth of the communication media—television, radio, newspapers, and magazines—has contributed to the growth of career opportunities in sport communication. The last decade has also seen an increase in sport coverage by the media. The growth of media specifically dealing with sport has been phenomenal. For example, the number of sport periodicals has grown, including the number of periodicals dealing with specific sport areas such as running, body building, skiing, swimming, and bowling. Cable television channels such as ESPN provide round-the-clock coverage of sport. The growth of the Internet and the increasing sophistication of the World Wide Web have created a whole new host of media opportunities and related occupations. The ability of the World Wide Web to serve as a site for information containing text, graphics, sound, and streaming video makes it an exciting medium for sport. This growth has led to a number of career opportunities in sport media.

An individual interested in sport media can pursue many careers. These careers include sport broadcasting, sportswriting, sport journalism, sport photography, and sports information.[14] A job in web development or social media is another career option.

Sport Broadcasting

Sport broadcasting is one career that has become increasingly popular. Sport broadcasting opportunities may be found with radio and television stations, including cable television, at local, regional, and national levels. Sport broadcasting requires not only knowledge of the game but also the ability to communicate in a clear, articulate fashion.

Preparation in physical education, exercise science, and sport will be helpful to the sportscaster. Sportscasters need to be knowledgeable about the skills, strategies, tactics, and rules used in sport, including the techniques of officiating. A background in physical education, exercise science, and sport enables the sportscaster to be cognizant of the sport skills used in the competition and be readily able to detect errors in the athletes' performances. Studying physical education, exercise science, and sport provides the sportscaster with an understanding of the manner in which athletes train for competition and of the physiological effects of performance, as well as psychological insight into the athletes' actions. Sportscasters must be able to relate this information to the public in easily understood terms, providing the public with insight into the nature of the competition and the essence of the athletes' efforts. Familiarity with the sport enables the sportscaster to fluidly and accurately describe the play-by-play or moment-to-moment action and to present to the listening and watching public a vibrant portrayal of the athletes' actions.

Sportscasters need to have an in-depth knowledge of sport; in the eyes of the public, the sportscaster is regarded as an expert on the sport he or she is covering. Therefore, it is important that the sportscaster have an extensive preparation in sport. In a physical education, exercise science, and sport professional preparation program, the potential broadcaster may be exposed to the more common sport areas such as football, basketball, baseball and softball, aquatics, golf, track and field, tennis, and gymnastics. The sportscaster also needs to be familiar with other sports, such as auto racing, horse racing, skiing, surfing, boxing, ice hockey, and figure skating.[14] Because instruction in many of these sport areas is typically not provided in professional preparation programs, the sportscaster must seek out experts in these sport areas for instruction, learn through on-the-job experience, or acquire knowledge by research.

Sportscasters' days are often long. Hours spent in front of the camera or the microphone are most visible, but in preparing for a broadcast, the sportscaster may put in numerous hours researching the upcoming competition, compiling statistics on athletes' performances, writing scripts, rehearsing certain aspects of his or her performance, arranging and preparing for on-air interviews, gathering background information on the athletes, and preparing in numerous other ways. Although many top sportscasters have help with these aspects of the job, individuals just starting their career may have to do all this preparation on their own. In fact, many individuals begin their broadcasting careers by performing just such tasks for established sportscasters.

Individuals desiring to pursue a career in sport broadcasting must be able to speak well and not be inhibited by speaking into the microphone or in front of the camera. The ability to think on one's feet is important because the

Sportscasters must give the audience play-by-play information, as well as insight into the game and the athletes' efforts.

action must be described as it unfolds. Course work or a minor in communication, particularly courses in speaking and interviewing, is critical. Course work or a minor in radio and television is valuable as well.

Practical experience can greatly contribute to one's success in attaining an entry-level position in this career field. If your college or university has its own television or radio station, become involved in some aspect of its work. Understand that in many situations, to gain a foothold, you may find it necessary to work on behind-the-scenes chores, such as researching material for the upcoming competition, before being afforded the opportunity to work in front of the microphone. If your college or university does not have a station or you are unable to attain a position at the station, perhaps you can gain experience by volunteering to announce and provide live commentary at college or university sporting events or events at the local high school. Try to gain employment or even serve as a volunteer at a local television or radio station for the summer or on a part-time basis throughout the year. Take advantage of opportunities provided by your college or university for fieldwork or internship at radio and television stations. The prospective sportscaster should also collect samples of his or her work to share with future employers. Audio and video recordings of one's performance as a broadcaster and copies of any reviews received can be an asset in gaining employment in this field.

The hours worked by a sport sportscaster may be varied; they are usually at night and on the weekends. Depending on the position, a lot of travel may be associated with the job. Rewards are great; there are opportunities to meet athletes, watch numerous contests, share one's love of sport with the listening or viewing public, and become intimately involved with the sport. Salaries vary according to one's location (i.e., working for a local station as compared to a national network); one's reputation as a broadcaster (well known or just beginning and without a reputation); and the sport covered.

Sportswriting and Journalism

Individuals with a talent for writing may decide to pursue a career as a sport journalist or a sportswriter. Writing for online sports sites is another growing career. The sport journalist may find opportunities for work with newspapers and in sport magazines, the number of which is increasing all the time. Sport magazines, such as *Sports Illustrated,* may provide coverage of several areas or, like *Runner's World,* provide coverage of one specific sport.

Sportswriters and journalists may cover events live or write in-depth or feature articles about athletes or various topics in the sport world. As in sport broadcasting, covering the athletic event and reporting it is the most visible part of this occupation. Researching stories, compiling statistics, and interviewing athletes and coaches are all functions of the sportswriter and journalist. The ability to meet deadlines and to write stories under time pressures is required. The work hours, opportunities to travel, and the rewards associated with this profession are similar to those associated with sport broadcasting.

A background in physical education, exercise science, and sport is helpful to the sportswriter and journalist. It provides the writer and

Media coverage of girls' and women's sports is increasing.

journalist with a broader understanding of the demands and nature of sport. For example, a sport journalist with course work in sport psychology may be better able to explain to the public why some athletes fail to perform under pressure, or "choke," whereas other athletes appear to rise to the occasion. A sportswriter with an understanding of exercise physiology may be better able to explain what happens physiologically to athletes as they endeavor to complete the rigorous marathon. Sportswriters can call on their background in sport philosophy to describe the transcendental experience of an athlete winning an Olympic gold medal.

Prospective sportswriters and journalists can benefit from course work or a minor in writing and journalism. Practical experience, as in all careers, is an asset in gaining employment. Many sportswriters and journalists have gotten their start covering sports for their high school papers and have continued this work for their collegiate newspaper. Experience working as an editor of the high school or college paper is an asset as well. These experiences can help prospective sportswriters and journalists gain internships or employment with local newspapers and sport publications. To assist in gaining employment in this field, individuals should keep a well-organized scrapbook of their work.

Some physical education, exercise science, and sport professionals engage in sportswriting as a full- or a part-time career. For example, professionals may use their expertise to write textbooks and sport skills books. Another career opportunity in this area is working for a publishing company, editing physical education, exercise science, and sport texts.

Sport Photography

A career as a sport photographer may be attractive to physical education, exercise science, and sport professionals who have a strong interest in photography and the desire to communicate to others the essence and meaning of sport through photographs. Talent as a photographer is a prerequisite to such a career. Opportunities for sport photographers exist with newspapers and sport publications; many sport photographers pursue their careers independently as freelance photographers.

One's background and preparation in physical education, exercise science, and sport can enhance one's career as a sport photographer.[14] Knowing the essentials of sport skills from work completed in biomechanics can help the photographer understand the critical aspects of the skill performance and where to position himself or herself to get the best angle for the photograph. Knowledge gained from exercise physiology of the stress endured by athletes working at their utmost level of effort, understanding gained from the sociology of sport of the significance of sport in our society, and appreciation gained from sport philosophy of the personal meaning that sport holds for its participants can help the sport photographer better capture the true nature and meaning of sport in pictures.

Courses in photography, graphics, and art will be of assistance to the potential sport photographer. Take advantage of opportunities to gain practical experience. Covering sporting events for the campus or local newspapers, taking sport photographs for the yearbook, and contributing photographs to the sports information office to be used in promotional brochures are several ways to gain practical experience and exposure. Sport photographers should maintain a portfolio of their work so that potential employers may readily discern their talent.

Sports Information

The sports information director's primary function is to promote athletic events through the various media. Opportunities for employment as a sports information director are found mainly at colleges and universities. At the professional level, many of the same responsibilities performed by the sports information director are handled by the director of public relations.

Among many responsibilities, the sports information director must maintain records and compile statistical information on all teams. He or she must design and prepare promotional brochures; this involves writing the copy for the text, obtaining photographs of the athletes, preparing the layout, and making arrangements for printing. Preparation of programs for various contests, including obtaining advertisements for the programs, is another responsibility of the sports information director. Another responsibility is to prepare material for and even design the institution's web pages for athletics. The sports information director provides assistance to the media covering home contests, phones in contest results to various media, writes press and television releases, writes commercials, and arranges press conferences and interviews for the media with coaches and athletes. Organization of special promotional events is also the responsibility of the sports information director. In a small school, the sports information director may handle all these responsibilities personally, whereas in a larger school, the sports information director may have several assistants. The hours are long, because the sports information director may be expected to personally cover many of the athletic events, and quite a bit of travel may be required.

Being a sports information director requires the ability to work closely with the members of the college and university administration, as well as the athletic administration, coaches and athletes, and members of the various media. Excellent communication skills—writing, speaking, and interpersonal skills—are essential to this profession. In addition to a background in sport, courses in public relations, advertising, writing, speech, and web development are helpful. Experience gained in covering high school or college sport as a sportswriter or journalist or as a sport broadcaster is valuable. Faced with numerous responsibilities and demands, many college sports information directors would welcome volunteers interested in working in this career field. Volunteers may be assigned to work on promotional brochures, travel with teams to cover the competition, or work with the media covering home events. Volunteers should keep a file of their work. Prospective sports information directors may

wish to obtain additional information from the College Sports Information Directors of America (COSIDA) (http://cosida.fansonly.com).

Web Development/Social Media

The growth of the Internet and World Wide Web has created new opportunities for individuals interested in sport communication. The online sport industry is rapidly expanding, and there is a need for individuals who have the technological qualifications and sport expertise to work in this area. Web developers design, create, and update sports sites for college athletic departments, professional teams, sport organizations, newspapers, and television networks. The web developer

Marketing of events, such as basketball games, is one career option in sport management.

writes the material, creates the layout, attractively incorporates graphics and other electronic media into the site, and uploads the site to the organization's server. The web developer updates the site and constantly seeks to improve the site's presence on the web.

The social-media marketing director assumes responsibility for promoting the sports program through the use of social media such as Facebook, MySpace, and Twitter as well as through blogging. The use of social media is typically part of an integrated marketing program that allows organizations to communicate, share information, and connect with their target audiences. Organizations can use social media to readily implement marketing campaigns, not only focusing on reaching their target audiences but receiving communication from them as well. Opportunities for individuals skilled in the use of social media continue to increase as many elements of their sport industry see this as a valuable addition to their organizations.

PERFORMANCE AND OTHER SPORT CAREERS

Dance

Individuals talented in the various forms of dance may aspire to careers as professional dancers. Although college and university programs offer a major or a minor in dance performance, most college-age dancers have developed their talents through many years of private lessons, often commencing at an early age. Opportunities for professional dancers may be found with dance companies, theater companies, and television shows. Resorts and clubs where nightly entertainment is offered to guests are other settings for employment.

Individuals who enjoy dance but do not aspire to careers as professional dancers may decide to transmit their love for dance to others through teaching. Opportunities for dance teachers may be found at schools, colleges, and universities. Many individuals choose to teach dance at private studios; some start their own studios as well.

Professional dance requires a great deal of preparation and a high level of skill.

A career as a dance therapist (Chapter 13) is also a viable career choice.

Expanding opportunities for individuals interested in a dance-related career can be found in dance administration. Dance administration may be an attractive choice for young dancers as well as dancers who are ready to retire from their performing careers. Lee states that "dancers should capitalize on their professional strengths of fund raising, promotion, management, and administrative skills while integrating their knowledge of dance in such careers in dance company management as artistic director, managing director, development officer, public relations officer, and booking agent." [15] Further information on dance careers may be obtained from the National Dance Association (NDA) (www.aahperd.org/nda).

Professional Athletics

Highly skilled athletes may desire to pursue a career in professional athletics. Although many aspire to a career as a professional athlete, few individuals actually attain this goal. The expansion of men's teams and greater opportunities for women desiring to compete at this level have contributed to increased opportunities for skilled athletes of both sexes to pursue a professional career. Even though the opportunities are greater than in the past, the number of positions for individuals in professional sports is very limited. The NCAA estimates that only 1.3% of NCAA men's basketball players enter the professional ranks, compared to 1% of women basketball players. [16] The NCAA estimates that the percent of NCAA football players that enter the professional ranks is 2%; baseball players have the greatest percentage entering the professional league—10.5%. [16]

The salaries paid to top professional athletes are astronomical and range from hundreds of thousands to millions of dollars. Well-known athletes earn even millions of dollars more in commercial endorsements. Other professionals may not fare as well. Baseball players may spend years in the minor leagues before being sent to the majors, and golfers may spend years on the

Opportunities to participate in sports after high school and college are limited. However, sport participation is an asset to physical educators who aspire to teach and coach.

professional tour, struggling to make ends meet, before attracting a sponsor or winning enough money to break even. [12]

Because of the limited opportunities in professional sports, and because many professional careers can be short-lived, individuals who desire to pursue this career should make every effort to complete their college degree. All aspiring professional athletes should take it upon themselves to ensure that they have the skills to earn a living should they fail to attain the professional ranks, or have to leave the professional arena after a few years. One effort to help former professional and collegiate athletes complete their college degree is the National Consortium for Academics and Sports (NCAS) program, which was founded by

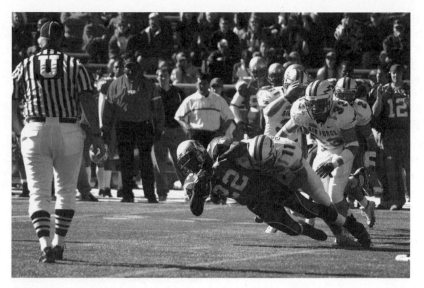

Officiating is a challenging career option that can be pursued on a full- or part-time basis.

the Northeastern University Center for the Study of Sport in Society. NCAS colleges and universities bring back, tuition-free, their former athletes, and help them to continue their pursuit of a college degree while working in the community addressing social issues.

Officiating

Sport officiating usually starts out as a part-time job, but some individuals elect to pursue it on a full-time basis. The growth of competitive athletics at the high school and collegiate levels has created a need for qualified officials for all sports. Opportunities are also available at the professional level.

Part-time officials can increase their chances for year-round work by becoming certified or rated in two or more sports, each with a different season. Attaining a rating typically requires passing a written exam as well as a practical exam. In some sports, beginning officials must spend a certain period of time working with experienced officials before being able to officiate alone. Individuals interested in information about becoming a rated official should ask an official in

the sport, coach, faculty member, or director of recreational sports. You can also contact the local officials association or board of officials.

Individuals interested in officiating should take advantage of opportunities to practice. Officials are needed for high school and college intramurals, summer adult recreational leagues, and youth sport leagues. Volunteering to work at home contests at your college or university as a scorekeeper or in some other capacity is another way to gain experience in this area. In officiating, one must not only know the rules but possess good officiating mechanics. For example, being able to place oneself in the right position at the right time requires an understanding of the flow of the game. Practice will enhance one's officiating skills.

In addition to being knowledgeable about the rules of the sport and skilled at the mechanics of officiating, officials must be able to work under pressure. Officiating also requires good interpersonal skills and communication skills to work with coaches and athletes in highly competitive and stressful situations.

Officials usually work on afternoons, nights, and weekends because this is when most athletic contests are conducted. Some travel is involved. Salaries have improved considerably during the last few years, and officials are often reimbursed for their travel costs. Officiating can be a challenging career on a part-time or full-time basis.

Sport Law and Agency

One career that has attracted the interest of some physical education and sport professionals is sport law. In litigation involving sport, a physical educator's background and practical experience as a teacher and a coach can be an asset.

A career in sport law is not a career that can be prepared for directly through one's undergraduate academic experiences. The practice of sport law requires the completion of law school, which typically involves a 3-year program of study. Admission to law school is very competitive. It requires an excellent GPA, and many law schools also have prerequisites or prefer the candidate to have certain areas of undergraduate study. For practitioners with experience seeking to change their career focus, however, sport law may be an attractive area of study. The growth of sport management curriculums has also created a need for individuals with preparation in sport law to teach courses in sport law and liability.

Another career opportunity for individuals with expertise in sport law is working with professional athletes, serving as their agents in contract negotiations.

Contract negotiation is only one of the services performed by sport agents. Sport agents may also serve as financial consultants—managing athletes' finances, investing their income, and structuring their financial portfolio for retirement. Some sport agents manage athletes' endorsements; they negotiate the endorsement contract and arrange promotional opportunities. Some sport agents perform a myriad of services, while others prefer to specialize in one area, such as contract negotiations. While you do not have to have a law degree to be a sport agent, knowledge of the law, as well as a background in business, is helpful.

A career in sport law presents an array of options for qualified individuals. Some opportunities include working as an agent, involvement in contract negotiations, litigation, and teaching.

Entrepreneurship

An increasing number of professionals are using their skills and competencies to become entrepreneurs. These individuals develop services and products to meet the public's needs and interests. The broad area of physical education, exercise science, and sport offers many entrepreneurial opportunities to motivated professionals. You may choose to pursue these opportunities on a full- or part-time basis.

Perhaps the most visible of all entrepreneurs in the profession are personal trainers. As discussed in Chapter 13, these professionals work one-on-one with the client, designing and implementing fitness programs tailored specifically to the client's needs. Personal trainers typically visit the client's home to monitor the workout.

Programming in the area of fitness and health promotion offers many entrepreneurial opportunities.[17] Many individuals who are interested in improving their fitness and health are willing to pay professionals for the opportunity to learn the skills necessary to achieve a high level of wellness. Entrepreneurs can design and offer health enhancement programs to meet these needs. Programs can focus on fitness assessment and improvement, nutrition, stress management, or weight reduction. These programs can be presented to interested individuals during the afternoon or evening. These programs also can be marketed to corporations that wish to offer these services to their employees but do not have the expertise to conduct such programs. Creative individuals also can produce and market instructional books, videos, and websites focusing on fitness and health.

Some professionals with a strong background in exercise science and administration use their skills to serve as consultants. They visit various fitness sites, such as a health club, assess the current program, make recommendations for improvement, train employees, and organize a system for ongoing program and employee evaluation.

Another opportunity for enterprising individuals with competency in exercise science is the establishment of a mobile fitness and health appraisal business.[18] Using a van filled with appropriate equipment, the professional can travel to different worksites to offer fitness appraisal and health enhancement programs to employees.

Personal coaching is a viable opportunity for individuals with expertise in a specific sport and the ability to coach individuals to achieve a high level of performance.[18] Parents may be interested in obtaining private coaching to help their children further develop sport skills. Many amateur and professional athletes use the services of a personal coach on a regular basis. Opportunities for personal coaching are most commonly found in individual sports such as swimming, diving, golf, tennis, track and field, and ice skating, although participants in team sports (e.g., basketball) may use a personal coach on an intermittent basis to refine selected aspects of their performance.

Professionals with expertise in biomechanics can offer computerized skill analysis services to athletes, as well as to coaches interested in

Summer sport camps give children and young adults an opportunity to learn new skills and develop their athleticism. University of Tennessee coach Pat Head Summitt lectures at a basketball camp with the assistance of her staff and players.

furthering their team's performance.[23] The athlete is recorded on video and the performance is computer-analyzed. The analysis is reviewed with the athlete and suggestions for improvement are given. Instructional videos can be offered to complement this service. Sites for this service typically include golf courses, tennis clubs, sporting goods stores, and various other sport facilities. The professional can also contract for this service with interested individuals, such as a coach desiring an analysis of individual team members' skills or a parent wishing a more detailed assessment of his or her child's skill performance.

Throughout the United States, sport and fitness camps for individuals of all ages are proliferating. Instructional camps are available for virtually every sport, although the most popular sports tend to be soccer, baseball, softball, tennis, golf, and volleyball. The number of instructional sport camps for youths with disabilities also is

growing. There are also camp programs that focus on increasing fitness and reducing weight. Although camp programs traditionally have focused on children and youth, a growing number of programs target the adult population in the areas of both sport and fitness. Directing sport and fitness camps offers many fine entrepreneurial opportunities. Because many of these programs are offered during the summer months or school vacations, teaching and coaching professionals often find employment in such programs and welcome the opportunity to supplement their salary.

There are numerous entrepreneurial opportunities for motivated physical education, exercise science, and sport professionals. Individuals aspiring to such a career must ask themselves two critical questions: (1) Do I have a viable, marketable service or product? and (2) Is there a consumer desire for the service or product? Furthermore, professionals must make sure they have the dedication,

---

FOCUS ON CAREER: Sport Management, Media, and Performance

PROFESSIONAL ORGANIZATIONS	• College Sports Information Directors of America www.cosida.com
	• National Association of Collegiate Directors of Athletics www.nacda.com
	• National Association of Collegiate Women Athletic Administrators www.nacwaa.org/
	• North American Society for Sport Management www.nassm.org
	• National Intramural-Recreational Sports Association www.nirsa.org
	• National Interscholastic Athletic Administrators Association www.niaaa.org
	• Society for the Study of Legal Aspects of Sport and Physical Activity www.ithaca.edu/sslaspa/
PROFESSIONAL JOURNALS	• *Journal of Sport Management*
	• *Journal of Legal Aspects of Sport*
	• *Recreational Sports Journal*

enthusiasm, initiative, and self-confidence to pursue this career successfully. The amount of financial resources necessary varies; some services, such as personal fitness instruction, require very little financial investment, whereas other services, such as a mobilized health and fitness business, require considerable capital to purchase the necessary equipment. Young professionals who are innovative and aspire to be their own bosses will find a host of entrepreneurial opportunities available to them in the twenty-first century.

INCREASING YOUR PROFESSIONAL MARKETABILITY

Individuals interested in pursuing sport communication and sport management careers can increase their professional marketability in several ways. Taking course work and minors in appropriate areas can enhance one's marketability. For individuals interested in sport media careers, courses or a minor in speech, photography, journalism, and broadcasting is an asset. Those who are interested in sport management careers can benefit from courses in business, management, law, and communication. Students also need to take courses specifically applying knowledge from other disciplines to sport communication and sport management—for example, courses in sport journalism or sport law.

Individuals interested in pursuing sport media, sport management, performance, and other sport-related careers need to be cognizant that the positions described in this section are often top-level positions. Attaining them requires a willingness to work one's way up the ladder. Professionals typically gain access to these positions through entry-level positions. For example, if you aspire to a career as an athletic director, you may first have to work as an assistant athletic director to gain the necessary experience and skills.

Practical experience is necessary to move up the career ladder. It can be gained from volunteering one's services, summer employment, and collegiate fieldwork and internship opportunities. Practical experience not only allows one to gain and refine the necessary skills but also allows one to develop professional contacts and exposure. These skills and professional contacts contribute to one's gaining employment and advancing up the career ladder.

SUMMARY

Sport has developed into a big business. Consequently, individuals trained in sport management are needed. Qualified professionals interested in sport management may pursue careers as athletic directors, directors of intramurals and campus recreation, directors of corporate recreation, and sport facilities managers. Individuals interested in retail may choose a career in sport business management and sport sales. Managerial opportunities are also available in professional organizations or working in sport tourism.

The intensity of interest in sport in our society, coupled with the growth of the communication media, has resulted in the expansion of career opportunities in the field of sport media. Individuals interested in this area can pursue careers in sport broadcasting, sportswriting, sport journalism, sport photography, sports information, and web development.

Talented individuals may elect to pursue careers as performers. Other sport-related careers that may be attractive to qualified individuals are sport officiating and sport law.

Physical education, exercise science, and sport professionals can use many strategies to enhance their professional marketability. Taking course work in supporting areas and gaining practical experience help individuals attain the position that they desire after graduation.

DISCUSSION QUESTIONS

1. How have new technologies contributed to the development of sport and opportunities for viewing sport events?

2. Many entrepreneurs have been successful in establishing viable sport-related businesses.

3. Sport tourism is big business. How does a sport event, large or small, impact the economy—either directly or indirectly—of a community, state, or country?

4. Discuss the administration of athletic programs and campus recreation programs on your campus. What titles do the directors of these programs hold? How many participants are involved in these programs and what activities are offered? Do you have any suggestions for additional activities?

SELF-ASSESSMENT ACTITVITIES

These activities are designed to help you determine if you have mastered the materials and competencies presented in this chapter.

1. Discuss how a background in physical education, exercise science, and sport can be an asset to individuals pursuing a diversity of sport media careers.

2. If possible, interview individuals working in sport management positions. Ask each person to define his or her responsibilities and the skills that are the most helpful in the performance of the job. Determine the entry-level positions in this area. Ask each individual for suggestions about advancing to top-level managerial positions in the field.

3. Discuss the positive and negative aspects of pursuing a performance career. Since performance careers may be of short duration, how can individuals prepare for another career after the culmination of their performance career? Access Northeastern University's Center for the Study of Sport in Society at www.ncasports.org and read about the

National Consortium for Academics and Sports program to help athletes continue their higher education and complete their degree. What are some strategies that can be used to help current and former student-athletes attain their educational goals? You may find it interesting to read about the highlights from the Racial and Gender Report Card and the work of The Institute for Diversity and Ethics in Sport (www.tidesport.org).

4. Using the information provided in the Get Connected box, locate an article on a topic of interest related to sport management, sport media, dance, officiating, or athletics. Write a brief summary of the article, identifying five key points and what you have learned.

5. Search the World Wide Web to identify different job opportunities in sports. Note the requirements for each position, as well as responsibilities associated with each job. Share your information with the class.

REFERENCES

1. Sporting Goods Manufacturers Association, 2010. (www.sgma.com).

2. Ourand J and Smith M: ESPN fends off Fox for ACC rights, Street and Smith's Sports Business Journal, May 17, 2010.

3. Plunkett Research. Sport Industry (www .plunkettresearch.com/Industries/Sports/ tabid/209/Default.aspx).

4. DeSensi J, Kelley D, Blanton M, and Beitel P: Sport management curricular evaluation and

needs assessment: a multifaceted approach, Journal of Sport Management 4(1):31–58, 1990.

5. Parkhouse BL and Pitts BG: History of sport management. In BL Parkhouse, The Management of sport: its foundation and application, ed 4, New York, 2005, McGraw-Hill.

6. Blann W: Four-Factor analysis of sport management, Personal communication, December 20, 2004.

7. NASPE-NASSM: NASPE-NASSM Sport management curriculum standards and program review, Reston, Va., 2000, AAHPERD.

8. North American Society for Sport Management: Program Accreditation (www.nassm.com/InfoAbout/NASSM/ProgramAccreditation).

9. Blann W: Sport management career paths, Personal communication, December 20, 2004.

10. Zhang JJ, DeMichele DJ, and Connaughton DP: Job satisfaction among mid-level collegiate campus recreation program administrators, Journal of Sport Behavior 27:184–212, 2004.

11. NIRSA Membership (www.nirsa.org).

12. Gibson HJ: Sport tourism: an introduction to the special issue, Journal of Sport Management 17:205–213, 2003.

13. Sport Tourism (www.worldsportdestinationexpo.com/sport-tourism).

14. Lambert C: Sports communications. In WJ Considine, editor, Alternative professional preparation in physical education, Washington, D.C., 1979, National Association of Sport and Physical Education.

15. Lee S: Dance administrative opportunities, JOPERD 55(5):74–75, 81, 1984.

16. Estimated probability of competing in athletics beyond high school interscholastic level, NCAA (www.ncaa.org).

17. Westerfield RC: Entrepreneurial opportunities in health education, JOPERD 58(2):67–70, 1987.

18. Pestolesi RA: Opportunities in physical education: what the entrepreneur can do, JOPERD 58(2):68–70, 1987.

PART

IV

Issues, Challenges, and the Future

Physical educators, exercise scientists, and sport leaders need to be aware of the issues and challenges facing the field today. If professionals hope to influence the future direction of physical education, exercise science, and sport in our society, they must lead the way.

Chapter 15 examines four of the issues and four of the challenges confronting professionals today. Addressing these require that professionals advocate on behalf of their programs and the value of physical activity.

ISSUES, CHALLENGES, AND FUTURE TRENDS

OBJECTIVES

After reading this chapter the student should be able to—

- Discuss the importance of leadership relative to lifespan participation in physical activity and fitness.
- Discuss how professionals can promote the development of values in physical education, exercise science, and sport.
- Interpret the role and contribution of physical education, exercise science, and sport professionals in the conduct of youth sport programs.
- Identify suggested names for the field currently entitled physical education, exercise science, and sport and discuss the implications of the growth of the field.
- Discuss the gap that exists between research and practice, and describe how this gap can be reduced.
- Identify and describe strategies that professionals could use to promote quality daily physical education.
- Explain the importance of advocacy in a variety of physical activity settings.
- Define the role of physical education, exercise science, and sport professionals in attaining national health goals.
- Describe specific strategies that could be used to help promote lifespan involvement in physical activity and sport.
- Indicate how physical education, exercise science, and sport professionals can capitalize on the increased public interest in health and physical activity.
- Discuss how the changing nature of education and technological advances will influence physical education, exercise science, and sport in the future.
- Show how physical education, exercise science, and sport professionals can establish jurisdiction over their own domain.
- Describe how physical education, exercise science, and sport can improve its delivery system.

GET CONNECTED

American Heart Association—site highlights information about many different aspects of coronary heart disease, including statistics, diseases, advocacy, publications, and resources.

www.heart.org/HEARTORG/

National Academies Press—provides free online access to a wide range of health publications, including health promotion.

www.nap.edu

World Health Organization (WHO)—gives access to reports on the health of the world, including health disparities, current issues, and health initiatives. WHO offers a global perspective on health issues such as aging and poverty.

www.who.org

Many issues and challenges confront physical education, exercise science, and sport today. As professionals, we need to be cognizant of the issues concerning the profession at all levels. As a professional, you will likely be perceived by the public as an expert in matters involving physical education, fitness, and sport. As such, you need up-to-date information on current issues so that you may give accurate, knowledgeable, and easily understood answers to the public's queries. This requires that you keep abreast of events and developments through newspapers, television, the World Wide Web, professional journals, and professional meetings and conferences.

Professionals are also facing a great number of challenges. As professionals, we must take an active role in meeting these challenges. This requires commitment and professional leadership at all levels. The continued growth of the field, its vitality and its future, depends on professionals' commitment and leadership.

This chapter focuses on some issues and challenges confronting physical education, exercise science, and sport. To address all of these issues and challenges would require a separate text. The purpose of this chapter is to introduce issues and challenges facing the field today. The chapter concludes with a discussion of selected trends and developments that could potentially have an impact on physical education, exercise science, and sport in the future.

ISSUES IN PHYSICAL EDUCATION, EXERCISE SCIENCE, AND SPORT TODAY

Numerous issues and problems confront professionals today. Resolution of these issues and problems requires thoughtful, visionary, and committed leadership. Four of these issues are addressed within this chapter: leadership in physical activity, leadership in youth sport, the growing field and our and identity, and the gap between research and practice.

Leadership in Physical Activity

Physical education, exercise science, and sport professionals must step forward and assume a greater leadership role in the promotion of physical activity. Substantial evidence supports the positive contribution of physical activity to health and quality of life. Physical inactivity has been related to premature mortality and morbidity, which exert a tremendous toll on society, both in human terms and monetary costs. Individuals who engage in physical activity on a regular basis reduce their risk for many chronic diseases and increase their chances for living a long, healthy life.

As professionals, we are in a unique position to take a more central, active role in responding to society's needs and engaging its members in physical activity so that they can realize the powerful concomitant health benefits. We have a responsibility to educate the public about the benefits of physical activity and fitness, and we must make a greater effort to disseminate a national message about the relationship between physical activity and health. One way we can do this is to collaborate with other professionals concerned with physical activity and take part in the activities of the National Coalition for Promoting Physical Activity.

During the past four decades, we have witnessed dramatic increases in participation in fitness and physical activities by people of all ages. An unprecedented proliferation of programs and products designed to capitalize on these interests has occurred. Although many programs are sound in nature and products are safe and live up to their claims, there are some programs that are not reputable and the validity of claims for some products is highly questionable.

Commercial sports clubs, community fitness centers, health and fitness clubs, and health spas all offer opportunities for people to engage in physical activities. Some of the programs offered are highly reputable, meet the health and fitness industry standards, and are staffed by qualified personnel. On the other hand, there are programs that advertise their services as leading to quick and dramatic results, fail to meet industry standards, and are staffed by personnel hired more for their appearance than their credentials.

Although some organizations, such as the International Health, Racquet, and Sportsclub Association (IHRSA), establish standards for clubs and others offer guidelines for exercise leaders and participants' safety, such as the American College of Sports Medicine (ACSM), there is no way to determine the number of programs that comply with accepted standards. For people who want to begin a physical activity program, where can they turn to find out whether the program meets industry standards or the staff is certified? What type of certification should the staff have? Is the program safe? Will it enable them to accomplish their goals?

Along with the proliferation of physical activity programs came the growth of fitness and health products, now a multibillion-dollar-a-year industry. The marketplace offers the consumer a wide choice of exercise equipment, websites sell diet products and fitness services, infomercials extol the merits of various types of ab machines, and magazine ads exhort readers to try products that guarantee weight loss. Books, magazines, and periodicals concerned with health, fitness, self-improvement, and sport are best-sellers. DVDs of celebrity experts leading specially designed workout programs are popular purchases for those people who like to work out at home. How are consumers to know what works and what doesn't?

Given the wide range of programs and products relating to physical activities and fitness, it is important that the members of the public make an educated choice from among the services and goods available; participation in programs that fail to meet recognized standards of care or the use of products that are of questionable value can have harmful results. Professionals can play a critical role in educating consumers about physical activities and fitness.

Professionals must be more active in making the public aware of their expertise in physical activity. Now is the time for us to step to the forefront and take a more significant role in promoting physical activity, leading the fitness movement, and exerting a significant influence on its direction.

Corbin, in a *Journal of Physical Education, Recreation, and Dance* editorial, asks, "Is the fitness bandwagon passing us by?"[1] He points out that physicians, self-appointed experts, and movie stars are at the vanguard of the fitness movement. Many of these people lack the qualifications, training, and expertise to be directing this movement. Corbin asks, "What is the problem?" He states:

> While many physical educators are experts, many are not. Some have no desire to be! I *am not* arguing that we should devote all our

efforts to physical fitness or exclude other important educational objectives. I *am* arguing that one of the most important social services we can provide is to teach about fitness and exercise. Like no other profession, we should be knowledgeable in this area.[1]

Corbin suggests that professionals can do several things to "lead the parade," and should actively seek leadership roles in the fitness movement. First, as experts, professionals should be cognizant of current findings in the field. Second, the public needs to be made aware that physical education, exercise science, and sport professionals are experts in this field and are a resource for answers as well as advice. Professionals should educate their students and the public to be wise consumers of exercise programs and products. Additionally, professionals should provide their clientele with the knowledge and the skills to solve their own exercise and physical activity problems and to evaluate their own fitness needs.

Ewers echoes Corbin's call for professionals to lead the "exercise parade."[2] He encourages professionals to be "pace setters" by "practicing what you know and believe about the benefits of movement."[2]

Overdorf sees leadership as essential if we, as a profession, want to make a difference in the lives of tomorrow's citizens and effectively deal with the problem of physical inactivity.[3] More of us need to assume positions of leadership and become agents of change. Furthermore, Overdorf stresses that collaboration among the subdisciplinary areas is essential in addressing the rampant physical inactivity among all segments of society and achieving the vision of lifespan participation in physical activity.[3] Like Ewers, Overdorf emphasizes the critical importance of each professional within our field being a role model and practicing what we preach. She writes, "If we want to influence others to embrace healthy lifestyles that include physical activity, we have to be healthy and fit ourselves. . . . Who will heed my message if I am not active? To have influence in producing behavioral change, we must, in the vernacular, walk our talk."[3]

As professionals, we must step forward and provide leadership for the physical activity movement because it falls within our domain. Collaborative, committed leadership is essential in reducing physical inactivity and promoting a physically active lifestyle.

Leadership in Youth Sport

Participation in youth sport programs has grown dramatically in the past decade. Most communities now offer youth sport programs, often in several sports and with varying levels of competition. It is estimated that close to 25 million boys and girls participate in these programs. Adult volunteers, without which these programs could not function, number approximately 3 million.

The generally stated purpose of youth sport programs is to promote the healthy physical, psychological, and social development of participants. Additionally, a positive experience in youth sport can lay the foundation for a lifetime of participation in physical activity. Although this goal is worthy, youth sport programs have been severely criticized by educators, physical educators, physicians, parents, and the media for the manner in which this goal has been pursued and for the failure in many cases to achieve it.

The criticism has been directed at the overemphasis on winning and competition, which makes it difficult to attain many of the stated developmental objectives. "Untrained adult volunteers are often the focus of this criticism. The lack of volunteers' knowledge about growth and development factors, psychological processes, training principles, nutrition, equipment use, safety, and injury prevention and treatment has precipitated the criticism."[4]

Because of the controversy surrounding youth sport programs and criticism directed at their endeavors, the American Academy of Kinesiology and Physical Education recommended that professional preparation programs provide prospective teachers and coaches with more information about teaching the young child. The developmental approach to skill acquisition, practical opportunities for students to work with young learners of all skill levels, and remediation techniques for gross motor skills should receive more emphasis in undergraduate professional preparation. The academy also urged that professionals assume a greater role in the conduct of these programs.[5]

There are several ways that professionals can help make the sport experience a more positive one for children and youths. Professionals can work collaboratively with youth sport program administrators and volunteers to develop sound program guidelines. The Bill of Rights for Young Athletes, developed by AAHPERD, offers coaches and parents guidance in structuring the sport experience to achieve more positive outcomes (see the Young Athletes' Bill of Rights box).

Professionals can serve as a resource for program personnel. Through leading in-service workshops, professionals can share with the adult volunteers information about skill development, psychological development, officiating, and safety and first aid that is essential to the conduct of sound programs. Professionals can also assist in developing minimal competencies in skill and knowledge and possibly establishing certification programs for volunteers. Training volunteers to attain these standards is another way that professionals can contribute to the development of sound programs. The American Sport Education Program,[6] one of the most widely used programs, can assist professionals in this endeavor.[6] This program provides a comprehensive, progressive sequence of objectives and knowledge to be used by program directors and professionals in the training of youth sport volunteers.

Vern Seefeldt, a former director of the Institute for the Study of Youth Sports, encourages program volunteers to focus on promoting the continued sport involvement of children rather than emphasizing winning.[4] Coaches must be aware of the reasons children participate in these activities. "Children become involved in sports to have fun, learn specific motor skills, socialize with their friends, and experience the excitement of competition on their own terms. These objectives are so wholesome and compelling that

coaches should strive to incorporate them into every practice and contest."[4]

If youth sport is to achieve the desired outcomes, three interdependent changes are necessary, according to Seefeldt. First, youth sport program directors must "resist the temptation to maintain the status quo."[4] Changes must be made in youth sport programs to accommodate children of all abilities and interests, not just those children who are highly skilled and competitive. Second, more research must be undertaken. Research is essential if programs are to be based on sound principles. Numerous questions require answers. Areas that need to be addressed include the nature and extent of injuries, optimal ages for learning specific skills, length of practices and duration of playing season, influence of different coaching methods on children's behavior and psychological development, and team selection for greatest equality. Third, sound training programs for youth sport coaches and personnel need to be

---

YOUNG ATHLETES' BILL OF RIGHTS

1. Right to the opportunity to participate in sports regardless of ability level.
2. Right to participate at a level that is commensurate with each child's developmental level.
3. Right to have qualified adult leadership.
4. Right to participate in safe and healthy environments.
5. Right of each child to share in the leadership and decision making of their sport participation.
6. Right to play as a child and not as an adult.
7. Right to proper preparation.
8. Right to an equal opportunity to strive for success.
9. Right to be treated with dignity by all involved.
10. Right to have fun through sport.

Source: *Guidelines for Children's Sports,* Martens, R. and Seefeldt, V. (eds.), Washington, D.C. American Alliance for Health, Physical Education, Recreation and Dance, 1979.

developed and implemented. These programs should focus on the acquisition of basic competencies in skills, teaching, knowledge, first aid, and psychology that are prerequisites for coaching. In-service workshops are needed to help the millions of adult volunteers acquire these competencies.

Rainer Martens, founder of the American Sport Education Program, also stresses the importance of providing physical activity experiences for children and youth that will "turn kids on to physical activity for a lifetime."[7] According to Martens, to accomplish this objective, physical education and sport professionals must take into account several behavioral principles: (1) the Modeling Principle, which states that children model the behavior of significant others in their lives, (2) the Reinforcement Principle, which emphasizes that children are more likely to repeat behaviors for which they are positively rewarded and to avoid behaviors for which they are punished, and (3) the Self-Determination Principle, which recognizes that children typically prefer activities that they select themselves rather than those activities imposed upon them.[7] However, Martens states that the two most fundamental principles influencing participation in physical activity are the Self-Worth Principle and the Fun Principle.

The Self-Worth Principle recognizes that we all need to feel we are competent, have the opportunity to experience success, and believe that we are worthy individuals. Martens explains, "If children initially have positive experiences when being physically active, whether it be in sports or other forms of physical activity, the internal feedback of accomplishment and the external recognition of success deliver a powerful message of achievement and thus greater worthiness."[7] This promotes future participation in physical activity. On the other hand, when children's experiences in physical activity are negative, their feelings of competency are diminished and they become less likely to seek out physical activities. They turn to other activities to engender their feelings of self-worth.

The Fun Principle is integral to promoting involvement in physical activity. Though we know this, we often fail to apply this principle in designing and conducting physical activities for children. Martens asserts, "As we take the fun out of physical activities, we take the kids out of them. They turn their interests elsewhere."[7] How do we take the fun out of physical activity? Martens believes that professionals and adults take the fun out of physical activities and sports by overorganizing the activities, by constantly instructing and evaluating rather than allowing children to play and to apply what they have learned without fearing the consequences of failing or performing poorly. Often there is a discrepancy between the goals of the adults involved in running the activity and the children participating; adults focus on performance while the children focus primarily on having fun. Teaching skills by using boring drills, developing fitness by using calisthenics, using physical activity as a punishment, and placing children in a position of being publicly embarrassed by their performance are some ways in which fun is taken out of physical activity.[7]

As professionals, we can take an active role in promoting physical activity programs for children that incorporate these principles and have the vision of lifetime physical activity as the primary objective. This active role extends to making a commitment to provide training for adult volunteers in youth sports so that they understand the importance of these principles and how to apply them to their situation. Furthermore, it is important as professionals to allow children to have some say about the activities in which they participate and to give children the opportunity to experience a wide range of activities so that they can find activities that are enjoyable and satisfying to them.

It is important as professionals in the field to understand how children perceive the actions of adults involved in youth sports. To find out what problems children perceive in youth sports, Stuart interviewed 15 children, aged 10 to 12, who had youth sport experience.[8] The children were asked to describe things in their team sport experiences that they perceived to be a problem. The issues identified by the children revolved around three primary themes: fairness of adult actions, negative game behaviors, and negative team behaviors.

It is important that professionals understand how children perceive their youth sport experiences if we are to address issues within this arena. Children's perceptions offer us valuable insight about how the nature of the youth sport experience can be changed to create more positive experiences for all those involved.

Youth sport programs have grown dramatically, and this growth will likely continue. If children are to benefit from participation in these programs, professionals need to take a more active role in their direction. Sound training programs for the millions of volunteers need to be developed and implemented so that the sought-after physical, psychological, and social benefits are realized, and, most importantly, so that millions of children become lifetime participants in physical activity and sports.

The Growing Field and Our Identity

Since the early 1960s, the body of knowledge about physical education, exercise science, and sport has expanded tremendously. Because of the proliferation of research and scholarship, the theoretical base of physical education, exercise science, and sport is becoming increasingly sophisticated and complex.

The expansion of the depth and breadth of knowledge has led to the development of subdisciplines within the field of physical education, exercise science, and sport that have emerged as areas of study in their own right. These distinct subdisciplines, which once were joined under the umbrella of physical education, have become separate, specialized areas with their own research traditions, professional organizations and publications, and specialized occupations. This specialization is currently increasing. Specialized areas of study are now emerging within the subdisciplines; for example, cardiac rehabilitation is becoming a specialized area within the subdiscipline of exercise physiology.

Many professionals have voiced concern about the increasing fragmentation and specialization of the discipline.[9,10] Lack of communication and cooperation among the increasingly specialized areas is a major concern. Moreover, the increased splintering of physical education, exercise science, and sport into narrow specialties may be harmful to our central mission of helping individuals learn the skills, knowledge, and understandings necessary to move effectively, to enhance health and well-being, and to be physically active throughout their lifespan.

It must be remembered that we as professionals are concerned with the development of the whole person through the medium of human movement, not just with the development of children's motor skills, physical fitness in adults, or psychological skills enabling elite athletes to perform at an optimum level. It is important not to forget that these specialized areas are actually parts of the greater whole. It is equally important that we not lose sight of our purpose.

Despite the calls for integration by many professionals, it is likely that the specialized areas of study will continue to further develop and become increasingly separate. However, there is a positive trend toward inter- and cross-disciplinary research. There is a growing realization of the need to help professionals integrate the growing knowledge base to respond better to the needs of the individuals with whom they work.[10] This integration of knowledge would take into account the population being served, the population's needs, and the setting in which the services are provided. Calls also abound for closing the gap between research and practice, with a greater effort being made to link theory and practice.

Many professionals are becoming dissatisfied with the traditional term used to represent the field: *physical education*. Within the past 30 years, our professional emphasis on teacher preparation has changed. Whereas teacher preparation was once the primary focus, it is now only one of many professional programs. The emergence of the exercise and sport sciences has led to many new professional programs, such as cardiac rehabilitation, adult fitness, sport management, sports medicine, and sport communication. Many professionals feel that the term *physical education* does

Professionals have adopted titles that more accurately reflect what they do. Athletic trainers, for example, help athletes prevent and manage injuries.

not accurately describe the current nature of the field. They believe a new term is needed to represent this field more accurately and to describe what professionals in the field do.

Today, practitioners in the schools continue to refer to themselves as physical educators. However, professionals working with other populations and in other settings have adopted different terms to represent the specialized nature of their work. These professionals may refer to themselves as athletic trainers, sports medicine specialists, adapted physical educators, exercise physiologists, sport psychologists, sport sociologists, fitness instructors, sport specialists, recreation leaders, and so on.

Many terms have been suggested to describe the academic discipline of what has been traditionally called physical education. In 1989, the American Academy of Kinesiology and Physical Education endorsed *kinesiology* as the new umbrella term for the field. *Kinesiology,* defined as the art and science of human movement, was believed to reflect the true focus of our efforts. Other terms frequently used are *physical education and sport, sport sciences, exercise science, human movement sciences,* and *exercise and sports sciences.*

Massengale points out that the "lack of a common conceptual label to represent the evolving discipline" has allowed literally hundreds of descriptors to be used, much to our disadvantage.[11] This situation has led to "a confused identity that lacks an accurate concept of who we are, what we do, and where we are going."[11] It is important that we agree on a common conceptual label that reflects our mission and our identity. Corbin suggests that the term *physical activity* be used as a conceptual focus for our endeavors.[12] As a conceptual label, *physical activity* could provide a means to draw together all of our subdisciplines, allowing us to deliver specialized services to different populations through the medium of physical activity.[11]

The Gap between Research and Practice

One of the major problems facing the profession is the need to close the gap between research and practice.[13] A significant time lag is often seen between the publication and presentation of research and the utilization of relevant findings. If our programs, regardless of their setting, are to be based on sound principles, then this gap must be narrowed.

Factors responsible for the gap between research and practice are many. Some of these factors may be attributed to the practitioner, while others are associated with the researcher. For example, one factor contributing to this gap is inadequate knowledge of research by the practitioner.[14] Practitioners, in both their undergraduate and graduate preparation, may not have been adequately instructed in research methods and the technical and conceptual skills necessary to conduct and interpret research. Locke writes, "The ordinary teacher, unfamiliar with basic terms and subtle distinctions in the vocabulary of research, is likely to find the usual research report nearly incomprehensible."[15] The lack of preparation hinders communication between researchers and practitioners and the consumption of research reports by practitioners. Practitioners who receive a sound background in research and statistics will be better equipped to communicate with the researcher who conducted the study and to interpret the findings.

Another factor that contributes to the gap is a negative attitude toward research held by practitioners. This attitude may deter them from using information revealed through research. Several reasons have been suggested to account for this negative attitude, including the view that research is irrelevant and impractical to the concerns of practitioners,[14,16] an inadequate understanding of research,[15] and failure to answer specific questions practitioners want answered[17] such as those about the teaching-learning process. Whatever the reason for this negative attitude, it militates against the effective use of research findings that may optimize learning.

The lack of time and resources to apply research findings to practical situations also contributes to the gap between research and practice.[18] For example, it is often heard that teachers are too busy to deal with theoretical matters; they must concentrate on daily tasks. In addition to teaching, teachers often are assigned homeroom duty, bus duty, locker room duty, hall duty, or study hall supervision, and may have coaching responsibilities as well. These extra, but required, responsibilities fill up the teacher's day and inhibit the implementation and utilization of research by the teacher. The lack of facilities and equipment with which to implement many of the research findings exacerbates the problem. Other professionals face similar constraints.

Application of research findings to practical settings is also hindered by the limited availability of the research findings. Many researchers publish their results in prestigious professional journals, many of which are not readily available to practitioners. Another source of research is theses and dissertations. Although theses and dissertations are available at college and university libraries, these unpublished sources of research are not readily available to practitioners at a distance from these sites. The growth of the Internet as a medium for the dissemination of research findings makes access to research and current developments easier. Online access to research and significant documents, such as *Physical Activity and Health: The Surgeon General's Report,* will make it easier for practitioners to keep abreast of current developments.

The relatively poor quality of some research and few conclusive research findings contribute to the gap between research and practice. Many research studies suffer from inadequacies, especially with regard to methodological concerns. Locke notes: "Research that is poorly designed, inadequately reported, and seriously misleading constitutes a major impediment to the intelligent guidance of physical education."[15] The fact that different researchers reach disparate conclusions regarding the same research topic makes it difficult for practitioners to apply these findings in a practical setting. The conflicting results of studies present problems for practitioners who wish to use the findings to guide and support their endeavors.

Finally, the unwillingness of researchers to be concerned with the application of their findings contributes to the gap between research and practice. The failure of investigators engaged in basic research to be concerned with the application of their findings might be a cause of lag in some cases. Complicated theoretical propositions that are sometimes advanced by researchers engaged in pure or basic research without some explanation of their practical uses are of little value to practitioners. If significant information provided by basic researchers is to be useful, investigators engaged in basic research should devote a portion of their time to development and dissemination.

How can we close the gap between research and practice? We have taken the initial step by recognizing that the gap does exist. There are several means by which this gap can be reduced. Professional preparation programs can do a better job of preparing professionals to read and interpret research. A thorough background in research and statistics will enable physical education, exercise science, and sport professionals to develop a knowledge of research theory and statistics, locate research reports, and evaluate research studies and interpret their findings. Another approach is for practitioners and researchers to work cooperatively on joint research projects. Researchers also must make a concerted effort to bridge this gap. They can do this by addressing the practical implications of their work when reporting their investigations in journals.

Although it is difficult to delineate the size of the chasm between research and practice, it is important that both researchers and practitioners work to bridge it. Over the last 20 years, we have experienced a tremendous growth in knowledge. If this knowledge is to influence the manner in which professionals conduct their programs, a concerted effort must be undertaken to narrow the gap between research and practice.

Finally, individuals are needed to serve as translators of research findings. These translators consolidate research findings, identify practical applications, and disseminate this information to practitioners in an easy-to-understand format. This job needs to be done on a large scale if research findings are to be put to use without the normal research lag.

CHALLENGES

The challenges facing physical education, exercise science, and sport professionals will increase as we move into the future. Only four of the many challenges will be discussed in this section: providing high-quality, daily physical education; advocating for our programs; working to achieve the nation's health goals; and encouraging lifespan involvement for all people.

High-Quality, Daily Physical Education

The provision of high-quality, daily physical education programs in the nation's schools is a challenge to all physical educators. There is evidence that many of the nation's children and youth are inactive and unfit.[19] Inactive lifestyles, sedentary leisure pursuits, and the lack of quality and regular physical education programs in the schools contribute to the poor fitness level of American children and youth.

Increasingly strong support for the idea that regular and appropriate physical activity can contribute to good health and enhance the quality of life for individuals of all ages.[18] There is also increased recognition that to achieve the maximum benefits of physical activity, an individual must begin to be physically active early in life and continue to be active throughout the lifespan. Daily physical education in school is one of the best means to help individuals learn the skills, knowledge, and values necessary to incorporate physical activity into their lifestyle. There is a concern that too many students lack the opportunity to participate in daily physical education.

There is also concern about the quality of the programs offered in schools. Although there are many exemplary programs throughout the United States, many programs are of low quality. The adverse effects of low-quality programs are not limited just to the children and youth in these programs. Poor-quality programs contribute to the administrators', teachers', and parents' perceptions that physical education programs have little to offer students in our schools. Children and youth who have low-quality physical education experiences may get "turned off" to physical activity for a lifetime. As adults, they may see little need to support physical education programs in the schools, even though the programs may have changed since they were students.

The National Association for Sport and Physical Education (NASPE) established content standards for physical education programs that clearly identified "what students should know and be able to do" as a result of participation in a high-quality physical education program.[20] These standards identified what students should learn with adequate support and sustained effort.

A variety of activities should be included within the physical education curriculum, carefully selected for their contribution to the attainment of the NASPE standards and to learning in the cognitive, affective, and psychomotor domains. Periodic assessment of achievement allows teachers to monitor students' progress toward attainment of the standards.

NASPE has also identified aspects of a quality physical education program. (See the What Constitutes a Quality Physical Education Program? box.) The incorporation of all these activities and program components and the realization of the maximum benefits from participation in a high-quality physical education program depend on the program being offered on a daily basis for a sufficient amount of time throughout all the school years. Equally important, physical education should be taught by certified physical education instructors. Just as noncertified and unqualified teachers are not tolerated in other academic areas, they should not be tolerated in physical education. Qualified and dedicated leadership is needed if the benefits associated with daily high-quality physical education programs are to be achieved.

Each physical education teacher must be willing to take part in the crusade for daily high-quality physical education. Evidence supporting the value of regular and appropriate physical activity continues to mount. Furthermore, there is recognition that health behaviors are formed at an early age and that it is easier to shape positive health behaviors in children than to change unhealthy ones in adults. Moreover, while the current societal interest in wellness and fitness remains strong, now is the time to engender support for daily high-quality physical education programs. Improving the status of physical education in the schools and helping make the dream of daily, high-quality physical education a reality for all children and youth are important priorities for all physical education, exercise science, and sport professionals.

Advocacy

Advocacy is an important responsibility of physical education, exercise science, and sport professionals. The decline of physical education programs in the schools, the increased privatization of sports resulting in decreasing opportunities for individuals with limited economic resources, and the growing need for health promotion and physical activity programs in the worksite, community, and medical settings make it important that each professional take a role in promoting the value of our programs. Advocates need a strong voice to clearly articulate the benefits of participation in quality physical education, exercise science, and sport programs. Additionally, addressing the health disparities among population groups and inequities of opportunities for women, minorities, and people with disabilities in sport requires that we be willing to work as agents for social change and for social justice. We must assume more social responsibility and take a more active

WHAT CONSTITUTES A QUALITY PHYSICAL EDUCATION PROGRAM?

According to NASPE guidelines, a high-quality physical education program includes the following components:

OPPORTUNITY TO LEARN:
- Instructional periods totaling 150 minutes per week (elementary) and 225 minutes per week (middle and secondary school).
- Qualified physical education specialist providing a developmentally appropriate program.
- Adequate equipment and facilities.

MEANINGFUL CONTENT:
- Instruction in a variety of motor skills that are designed to enhance the physical, mental, and social and emotional development of every child.
- Fitness education and assessment to help children understand, improve, or maintain their physical well-being.
- Development of cognitive concepts about motor skill and fitness.
- Opportunities to improve their emerging social and cooperative skills and gain a multicultural perspective.
- Promotion of regular amounts of appropriate physical activity now and throughout life.

APPROPRIATE INSTRUCTION:
- Full inclusion of all children.
- Maximum practice opportunities for class activities.
- Well-designed lessons that facilitate student learning.
- Out-of-school assignments that support learning and practice.
- No physical activity for punishment.
- Use of regular assessment to monitor and reinforce student learning.

Source: National Association for Sport and Physical Education. *What Constitutes a Quality Physical Education Program?* Position statement. Reston, VA: National Association for Sport and Physical Education, 2003.

leadership role if we are to accomplish our mission of lifespan physical activity for all people.

The Advocacy Institute defines advocacy as the "pursuit of influencing outcomes—including public policy and resource allocation decisions within political, economic, and social systems and institutions—that directly affect people's lives."[20] Advocacy consists of organized efforts to change what is—to "highlight critical issues that have been ignored and submerged, to influence public attitudes, and to enact and implement law and public policies so that the vision of 'what

should be' in a just, decent society becomes a reality."[21] The overarching framework for advocacy is human rights. Advocates seek to influence and play a role in the decision making of relevant institutions; they challenge the dominance of those with political, economic, or cultural power and through their efforts bring an improvement in people's lives.[20,22]

Advocacy is the use of communication to influence others and "to make your views or the views of those you represent count in the decision-making process."[23] The National Dance Association believes there is a role for everyone in advocacy. Activities can include researching an issue, writing press releases, presenting your case to a group, talking to a legislator, planning special events, securing a grant, maintaining a website, networking with individuals, forging new partnerships with organizations, or working to stay abreast of current issues.[23] It is important that we communicate our message effectively via various formats and media to the public and decision makers if we are to bring about change.

Professionals must undertake a greater role as advocates for social justice. As Dr. Martin Luther King Jr. said, "Injustice anywhere is a threat to justice everywhere."[24] Inequities persist despite our professed societal value of equality and the passage of legislation such as the Civil Rights Act, Title IX, and the Americans with Disabilities Act. Much more needs to be done. We promote lifespan involvement in physical activity for all people as important to their health and well-being, yet there are tremendous disparities in physical activity and disease conditions according to race, ethnicity, gender, age, education, sexual orientation, ability/disability, and income. Sport participation for males and females of all ages has increased dramatically, yet opportunities at all levels of sport and within sport administration and the sport industry remain inequitable.

We view school physical education as the means to provide all children with the skills, knowledge, and attitudes to participate in lifelong physical activity. As Larry Locke points out, the public schools provide us with a means to reach across barriers of race, ethnicity, gender, social class, and economic conditions to reach millions of children and youth.[25] In theory, the schools afford us the opportunity to ensure that all children learn what they need to know to be physically active for a lifetime. Yet in reality, the physical education experience of children and youth in inner-city schools in Los Angeles is likely to be quite different from that of students in an upper-class suburb of Chicago or those of students in a rural area of Maine.

As professionals, it is our responsibility to address these inequities. Are you ready to make a commitment to social justice and diversity? Are you ready to work in some way to close the gap between the haves and the have-nots? What will you do to promote daily, high-quality physical education K–12 for all children and youth? What will you do to ensure greater opportunities in sport for girls and women, for people with disabilities, and for minorities? What steps will you take to ensure that all high schools have certified athletic trainers on their staff? Are you ready to take an active role in working to ensure that medical insurance will cover preventative physical activity programs or that worksite health promotion programs will be open to all employees, not just the upper management?

As professionals, we must be ready and willing to work as agents of social change—as advocates to change public policies, to increase access for underserved populations, to provide services to those in need, and to empower people to make a difference in their own lives. We must be concerned not only with strengthening our programs, but with increasing access to our services for all segments of our population.

Public relations is an important component of program promotion and advocacy efforts. Now is the time to capitalize on the widespread public interest in sport, physical fitness, and health. Professionals teaching in the school setting; instructing in community and recreational sport programs; working in commercial sport clubs, fitness centers, and health spas; and directing corporate and community fitness programs must use public relations techniques to market their programs. Professionals must inform the public and prospective clientele of the values that accrue from participation in a sound physical activity and exercise program.

In the school setting, where physical education is often regarded as an extra or is cut to make more time for academic subjects, where budgetary cutbacks are becoming increasingly common, and where class sizes are expanding, teachers must be willing to advocate on behalf of their programs to gain the personal and budgetary support of school administrators, politicians, and parents. Dunn states that "the school board is recognized as one of the most influential organizations for developing and shaping policy at the local level. Without the support and advocacy of the local board, efforts to promote physical education and healthful activity will not be achieved."[26] Other legislative bodies and state education commissions must also be addressed because of the power they wield as decision making bodies.[26]

Advocacy can result in the passage of federal and state legislation that has a favorable impact on physical education programs. One example of this effort is the passage by the US Congress of the Physical Education for Progress Act, now known as the Carol M. White Physical Education Program. This bill provides millions of dollars a year in grants (PEP grants) for schools to revitalize their physical education programs. This act underscores the importance of physical education and its contribution to our nation's well-being.

Advocacy is just as important in physical activity programs that are conducted outside of the school setting. Advocacy in these settings can take many different forms. Professionals may work to initiate programs, to expand services offered within programs, and to increase access to programs by underserved populations. Additionally, professionals must work to promote and market their programs.

Prospective clientele for community and commercial programs must be aware of the nature of the programs offered and the benefits to be derived from participation in such programs. In the corporate fitness setting, professionals must promote the values and benefits to be derived from participation to management as well as to employees. Corporate management personnel will be reluctant to invest corporate resources, particularly money, to support these programs if they are not aware of their value or if the stated benefits are not achieved.

Professionals must become more powerful advocates on behalf of their programs and take a greater role in promoting the incorporation of physical activity as part of daily living.[27] Booth and Chakravarthy urge professionals to take a greater part in the war against "Sedentary Death Syndrome" (SeDS), a phrase they coined to describe "sedentary lifestyle-mediated disorders that ultimately result in increased mortality."[27] SeDS disorders include cardiovascular disease, certain types of cancer, type 2 diabetes, and lower quality of life. Advocates for health promotion should use strategies that emphasize the cost savings of moderate physical activity—the substantial benefits that will accrue from reduction in health care costs and indirect costs associated with poor health as well as gains in quality of life. Activism and advocacy efforts should be directed at incorporation of physical activity into one's lifestyle.

Professionals should utilize specific strategies for different age groups in advocating physical activity for health. For example, Booth and

As you look at this father and his daughter finishing a "fun" mile, remember that it is important to encourage parents to be active role models for their children. Children whose parents are active are more likely to be active than are children of sedentary parents.

Chakravarthy suggest that for children and adolescents, we should promote lifetime physical activity in physical education classes; for older adults, they recommend free access to strength training equipment and recreational facilities.[27] Additionally, professionals must make efforts to lobby decision makers—legislators, corporate heads, and community leaders—to support a physically active America.[27] Professionals should not overlook the use of the various media to educate the public about the large body of scientific evidence supporting the significant contribution of a physically active lifestyle to good health.[26]

Active involvement by physical education, exercise science, and sport professionals is critical to attaining our goal of lifespan involvement in physical activity for all people. Every professional is urged to be an active member in his or her own community, "advocating for the inclusion of appropriate physical activity for health."[26] Contact organizations that promote physical activity and health and "advocate that these organizations become more proactive in presenting the facts . . . to those decision makers who in turn can make policies to facilitate a more physically active lifestyle, and thereby play a direct part in facilitating a healthier and more prosperous America."[27] Active professional involvement will help us reduce the morbidity and mortality associated with chronic disease and help people of all ages live healthier lives.

Achievement of National Health Goals

Another challenge facing physical education, exercise science, and sport professionals is working collaboratively with other health professionals toward the achievement of the national health goals set forth in the surgeon general's reports *Healthy People 2010*[28] and *The Surgeon General's Vision for a Healthy and Fit Nation.*[29] The reports reflect a commitment to improving the nation's health through a comprehensive health promotion and disease prevention effort and to ultimately helping Americans lead healthier lives through better nutrition, regular physical activity, and improved communities to support healthy choices. Americans showed limited progress in achieving previous goals, objectives, and recommendations suggested by *Healthy People* and "Calls to Action" from the nation's administration; thus *The Surgeon General's Vision for a Healthy and Fit Nation* and the upcoming *Healthy People 2020* have been developed in an attempt to combat the obesity epidemic and low physical activity levels of the American population.

The current fitness status of the American people, the trends set forth by these reports, and the specific objectives are described in Chapter 3. The objectives for the year 2010 were based on the assumption that increases in appropriate physical activity by people of all ages would result in concomitant health gains. The reports also assumed that the primary motive for participation in physical activity would be a personal commitment to improving one's health and enhancing the quality of one's life. The objectives for the year 2010 focused on improvement of the health status of all Americans, regardless of age; reduction of risk factors through increased participation in appropriate physical activity; increased knowledge by the public and professionals about the role of physical activity in the promotion of health; and improvement of access and expansion of services.

The *Healthy People 2010* specific objectives for physical activity are briefly described below. In terms of risk reduction, the objectives called for:

- Reducing the proportion of adults who engage in no leisure-time physical activity and increasing the proportion of adults who engage in moderate physical activity for at least 30 minutes a day and vigorous physical activity on a regular basis.
- Increasing the proportion of adolescents who engage in 30 or more minutes of moderate physical activity at least 5 days per week and encouraging more adolescents to engage in vigorous physical activity to promote cardiorespiratory fitness.

Increasing the amount of time physical educators spend teaching lifetime sports is important to lifespan involvement.

The growth of community and commercial sport programs has enabled more children to receive instruction and develop a lifelong interest in sport and fitness activities.

- Increasing the number of K–12 schools that require daily physical education and increasing the amount of time during physical education class when students are active.
- Improving the public's access to school facilities outside of the regular school day—before and after school, on weekends, during vacations, and throughout the summer.
- Increasing the number of worksites that offer comprehensive health promotion, physical activity, and fitness programs.
- Increasing the number of community health promotion and disease prevention programs.

As you can see, physical education, exercise science, and sport can make important contributions to the improvement of the health status of the American public. Professionals should take an active role in working with other health professionals to attain these objectives. Moreover, our involvement in attaining these objectives will contribute to increased public recognition of the worth and value of our field. Additionally, one benefit that will accrue from our participation in this endeavor is increased employment opportunities.

Employment opportunities for qualified professionals will increase, and new career opportunities will develop. The objective of promoting daily physical education will result in a demand for more teachers. Instructors also will be needed to teach physical activities to adults and the elderly and educate them about the benefits of such activities. The growth of corporate health promotion and fitness programs will create a need for more professionals qualified in this area. More hospitals are adding health promotion and fitness programs for their employees, patients, and community members.

Although Americans did not meet the objectives the objectives for 2010, some progress was made. For example, deaths from coronary heart disease have declined, worksite health promotion programs have increased, and some progress has been made in promoting involvement in moderate and vigorous physical activity. However, the

David Fischer—author of *The 50 Coolest Jobs in Sports, Do Curve Balls Really Curve?*, and *365 Amazing Days in Sports*—combined his undergraduate degree in physical education with his strong interest in journalism to pursue a writing career. Many exciting careers await qualified professionals.

decline in daily physical education is disturbing. Obesity has increased for both children and adults, and much more improvement needs to be made in the physical activity patterns of children and adults. Inequities in health and physical activity still persist. There is much more to be done to achieve our health goals. Professional organizations such as AAHPERD and ACSM provide us with strong leadership. However, whether or not we can achieve the stated objectives for physical activity depends on each professional's commitment to attaining these objectives and to advocating for increased programs and opportunities for all people.

Physical education, exercise science, and sport professionals must make a commitment to serve as role models for healthy, active lifestyles. In a position statement on physical activity and fitness recommendations for physical activity professionals, NASPE states:

Participation in regular physical activity at least at a level sufficient to promote health-related physical fitness is an essential behavior

for professionals in all fields of physical activity at all levels (this includes coaches, K–12 teachers, physical education and kinesiology faculty in higher education, fitness professionals, athletes, all advocates of physically active lifestyles).[30]

As professionals, we must take the mantle of leadership and undertake the responsibility of being role models. Research shows that role modeling is an important factor in changing human behaviors. Role models can influence attitudes and behaviors related to health practices, acquisition of motor skills, and adoption of physical activity patterns.[30] Physical education, exercise science, and sport professionals should teach and model currently recommended physical activity behaviors for improving health and fitness (e.g., participation in moderate physical activities for at least 30 minutes a day on all or most days of the week).[30] This will have a "positive influence on those who expect fitness and exercise leaders to be leaders in their profession and to set a positive example for young people and the community."[30] When we, as professionals, lead active lifestyles, it enhances our credibility among the public and vividly demonstrates the value of being physically active.

Being a role model requires that we make a commitment. Wilmore[31] states:

> Each of us in the profession must make a personal commitment to achieve or maintain a good level of physical fitness. How can we be effective in promoting health and fitness if our bodies are not living testimonies of our commitment? What we are communicates so much more than what we say![31]

As professionals, we must practice what we preach. Actions speak louder than words. What is your commitment to serving as a model of a healthy, physically active lifestyle?

Lifespan Involvement for All People

One of the most heartening changes in our field within the past 30 years has been the expansion of physical education, exercise science, and sport programs to people of all ages and to a diversity of settings. Traditionally, our programs have focused on children and youth and have been conducted in the school and community recreation settings. However, within the last three decades, the scope of our programs has expanded tremendously.

There is an increased recognition that regular and appropriate physical activity can make a vital contribution to the health and lives of all people. It can enhance the quality of one's life as well as its longevity. Additionally, it has become increasingly apparent that our efforts should focus on early childhood education and intervention. Individuals gain the maximum benefits from exercise and physical activity when they begin at an early age and continue their participation throughout the lifespan.

During childhood, fitness and leisure habits are developed; once developed, they become difficult to change. Moreover, it has been shown that such insidious diseases as obesity and coronary heart disease can begin in childhood. Therefore, it is important that efforts be made to assist children in acquiring the skills, knowledge, and positive attitudes conducive to good health. Children must be educated to form good health and physical activity habits early in life. Physical educators, parents, and other health professionals should focus their efforts on helping children adopt an active rather than a sedentary lifestyle and on providing them with the skills and knowledge to effectively manage their lifestyles as adults.

It is important to note that the number of programs being provided for preschoolers is growing; it is likely that the number of these programs will increase in the next decade. Motor development programs are being offered to infants and toddlers in hospital and clinical settings. Preschools and day-care centers are incorporating physical education programs into their curriculums.

In the past decade, the wellness movement and the fitness and physical activity movement have encouraged an increasing number of adults to incorporate regular physical activity into their lifestyles. Many adults are now engaging in physical activities and exercise of sufficient intensity, duration, and frequency to realize health benefits. Unfortunately, many more adults are not. The majority of adults lead sedentary lives or exercise only moderately. The incidence of physical inactivity increases with age and is influenced by such factors as gender, race, ethnicity, socioeconomic status, educational level, occupation, and geographic location. Currently, underserved populations such as minorities, Native Americans, and individuals with disabilities have less access to health promotion and physical activity programs.[32–35] (See Chapter 3 for further information.) As professionals, we need to help these people change their physical activity and health habits and adopt health-enhancing lifestyles. Creative education and individualized physical activity and health promotion programs are needed to accomplish this objective.

As we head further into the twenty-first century, the proportion of elderly in the population continues to increase. By the year 2025, it is

Winners belong to every age group.

Participation in sport, an important institution of our society, enables individuals with disabilities to become more involved in family and community activities. For example, children who have a visual impairment can use their proficiency in swimming to both compete and take part in water activities enjoyed by their families. For some individuals with disabilities, participation in sport contributes to self-actualization and feelings of empowerment.

Sport involvement among people of all ages continues to increase. Millions of children throughout the country participate in youth and interscholastic sport. Intercollegiate athletic participation continues to rise. Communities are developing more sport opportunities for adults of all ages. Competitive and recreational leagues offer adults the opportunity to continue their participation in organized sport at a desirable level of intensity. Master's competitions and competitions for seniors in a variety of sports and at a number of levels—local, state, national, and international—allow many adults and senior citizens across the country to continue their sport involvement. Sport organizations for individuals with disabilities also provide opportunities for competition in a wide range of individual and team sports.

As we continue to expand our focus to meet the needs of new populations, we must also continue to broaden our programs. Because the populations that are served are increasingly heterogeneous, a greater diversity of programs is needed to meet their needs. The minority population is increasing and their needs must not be overlooked. Changes in program content and the manner in which programs are conducted will be necessary to meet a wide range of individual differences. Culturally competent physical education, exercise science, and sport professionals are critical to promoting the involvement of minorities and underserved populations in our programs. This is essential if we are to eliminate health disparities and increase involvement in physical activity. Additionally, we must increase our efforts to recruit minorities into careers in our field; they are presently underrepresented.

Ensuring access to our programs is critical as they continue to expand from the school

estimated the elderly will compose 18.5% of the population. Furthermore, the elderly will be increasingly healthy and vigorous. Professionals must be prepared to meet the physical activity and leisure needs of this population group. Research shows that people with healthy habits live longer, are functionally independent for a greater period of time, and experience a higher quality of life. Never has our potential to improve the health and well-being of this population group been greater. We must reach out and involve members of this age group in our programs.

The last decade has also seen an increase in physical education, exercise, and sport opportunities available to individuals with disabilities. Participation in physical activity and sport makes a significant contribution to the health and fitness of individuals with disabilities. However, the benefits extend further. Dunn and Sherrill[36] state that, for some individuals with disabilities, engaging in physical activities contributes to their ability to perform the tasks of daily living, such as dressing, bathing, and preparing for work.[36] Fun, enjoyment, and satisfaction from meeting challenges are other meaningful outcomes of participation.

setting to the community, from the public sector to the private sector. The school setting will be used increasingly as a site for community programs for individuals of all ages. Programs in day-care centers, preschools, hospitals, developmental centers, senior centers, nursing homes, community settings, and corporations will continue to expand. Commercial programs in the private sector will continue to increase. Health clubs, fitness centers, private clubs offering sport instruction, and private sport leagues will develop more programs to meet the needs of paying clients. As programs expand to meet the needs of various populations, it is important to ensure that all individuals have access to these programs. Fitness and health opportunities should also be available to those who do not have the means to pay. Fitness and health opportunities should be available to all individuals regardless of socioeconomic background.

As the scope of physical education, exercise science, and sport increases and the focus of the programs offered expands, it is important that professional preparation programs ready students to capably assume responsibilities within these growing areas. Professional preparation programs have traditionally focused on preparing students to work with children and youth within the school setting. Today, professional preparation programs must provide students with the skills and knowledge necessary to conduct effective programs with different population groups and across the lifespan.

Promoting lifespan involvement in physical activity is a challenge to all professionals. Lifespan involvement can enrich the life and enhance the health of every person—regardless of age, gender, race or ethnicity, income, education, sexual orientation, religion, geographic location, or disability. As *Healthy People 2010* states, the diversity of our nation's population is one of its greatest assets, but it also represents one of the biggest challenges we must face in improving the nation's health.[28] Every person in every community in the United States deserves the right to equal access to comprehensive, culturally competent, community-based health care.[28]

Physical activity programs are an important part of health promotion and disease prevention efforts. Making lifespan involvement a reality for all people requires qualified and dedicated professionals willing to work toward attaining this goal.

What will our world be like in the future? What will physical education, exercise science, and sport be like in the future? More importantly, what is our vision for physical education, exercise science, and sport in the future? To make the most of the future requires a plan for predicting what the future may be like by generating some scenarios, selecting a preferred future, and then prescribing a course of action that will lead to its attainment. Achieving the future of our choice requires strong leadership, a charted course, marshaled efforts and resources to achieve our goals, and the active involvement of professionals at all levels in pursuit of this vision.

Today our world is experiencing greater cultural diversity, tremendous demographic shifts, growing political unrest and turmoil, increasing global interdependence, dramatic advances in science and medicine with tremendous implications for health and longevity, rapid growth of technology and information science, paradigm shifts in health and health care, alterations in the nature of education at all levels reflecting new ways to access knowledge and different roles for teachers, and widening gaps between the haves and the have-nots in our society. It is hard to say what tomorrow's world will be—yet we must be courageous and imaginative in directing and shaping that future to meet the needs of humanity. Futurists Marvin Cetron and Owen Davies state, "Our future will be constrained by demographic, economic, and political forces that should be under our control yet seldom are—but it will be driven by our expanding knowledge of science and mastery of technology."[37]

Preparing for the future means preparing to live and work in an increasingly complex, dynamic society. Today, we must prepare for the challenges of tomorrow—although we are not quite sure what tomorrow will bring. As physical education, exercise science, and sport professionals, meeting the challenges of the future requires that we be prepared to effectively deal with change—and that we are able to successfully direct this change to accomplish our mission and achieve our goals. We must be aware of new opportunities, evaluate them, and pursue them if they would help us meet the physical activity needs of society and people of all ages.

Planning for the future recognizes that rapid change is a characteristic of our way of life. With each day that passes, we live in a different world. Human beings who are age 70 or older have witnessed in their lifetime the start of the atomic age, the space age, and the computer age. They have seen more than 80 new nations appear, the world population double, and the gross world product double and then redouble. As C. P. Snow, the noted British scientist, said, "The rate of change has increased so much that our imagination can't keep up."

Recognizing that change is ever present, certain societal trends and developments can be identified that lend themselves to a better understanding of our future and that of physical education, exercise science, and sport. Examination of trends is one of the simplest forms of studying the future. It is based on the assumption that factors that have shaped the past will continue and be instrumental in forming the future. This approach has serious limitations, such as mistaking fads for real trends and allowing personal biases to cloud professional judgment.[38] However, careful examination of trends can provide us with a starting point for thinking about the future. Some selected trends and developments that are likely to have an impact on physical education, exercise science, and sport in the future include the health promotion and disease prevention movement, the educational reform movement and the changing nature of education, the growth of technology, and the changing demographics.

SOCIETAL TRENDS AND CURRENT DEVELOPMENTS

As you read about trends and developments and explore the potential implications for the future of physical education, exercise science, and sport,

you may find it helpful to contemplate the following questions suggested by Massengale:

- If the direction of the trend continues, what will be some positive and negative consequences?
- If the rate or speed of the trend continues, what will be some positive and negative results?
- What will occur if the trend levels off or reverses itself?
- Which forces are acting to perpetuate this trend? Will these forces continue into the future?
- How much is this trend shapable by human action?
- What type of action would it take to modify the trend?[38]

As you read about each trend and consider each question, try to carefully imagine the implications for professional practice and the influence it may exert on your day-to-day responsibilities as a professional within physical education, exercise science, and sport.

Health Promotion and Disease Prevention Movement

The emphasis on the enhancement of health and the prevention of disease is a significant trend in our society. Three related factors in this movement will be discussed: the wellness movement, the fitness and physical activity movement, and the health care reform movement.

Wellness Movement

The wellness movement represents one of the most opportune moments in our history. The wellness movement stresses self-help and emphasizes that one's lifestyle—the way in which one lives—influences greatly the attainment and maintenance of personal health. This movement supports efforts directed toward health promotion and disease prevention rather than focusing on the treatment of illness. The wellness doctrine is based on the premise that it is the responsibility of the individual to work toward achieving a healthy lifestyle and an optimal sense of well-being. A healthy lifestyle should reflect the integration of several components, including proper nutrition, regular and appropriate physical activity and exercise, stress management, and the elimination of controllable risk factors (e.g., smoking, excessive alcohol consumption).

Strong support for health promotion and disease prevention efforts has been given over the past 30 years with the following health reports: *Healthy People,*[39] *Promoting Health/Preventing Disease,*[40] *Healthy People 2000,*[41] *Healthy People 2010,*[28] *Physical Activity and Health,*[19] and *The Surgeon General's Vision for a Healthy and Fit Nation.*[29]

The corporate sector has become interested in the wellness movement. This has led to the development of comprehensive worksite health promotion and programs for employees. Corporations are willing to invest in these programs because they have found that they result in increased employee productivity, decreased absenteeism, better employee health, and lower insurance costs.

As more corporations institute worksite health promotion programs, professionals need to become more cognizant of the issues associated with their conduct. Roy Shepard raises some important ethical and professional issues about the "attempts to change the personal behavior of employees in the interests of a 'healthy' workplace. . . . Needs for successful wellness programs must be balanced against individual rights to remain unhealthy."[42] One concern is the tendency to attribute the development of a preventable disease to the individuals, assuming they have failed to take adequate care of their health and the illness is their own fault. But Shepard cautions that, before adopting a "judgmental attitude," it is necessary to consider the impact of other factors on individuals' health, including their genetic profile, overall socioeconomic conditions, and adverse environmental conditions encountered in the workplace and the home.[42] Other issues raised include bias in assessment of the effectiveness of the program, directing wellness resources to those employees with the highest salaries, initial medical clearance of participants, prescribing exercise at a lower level than would yield health benefits, advocacy of the purchase of special clothing prior to the start

of the program, and failure to develop an overall plan for active living.[42]

One trend is the growth of hospital fitness centers. Hospitals and managed care practices are establishing health promotion programs, including fitness. These medical fitness programs vary, but offer a vast array of services, sometimes in partnership with fitness clubs or organizations such as the YMCA. Typically, these programs take place onsite. Facilities vary but may include an indoor track, 25-meter swimming pool, cardiovascular area, aerobic dance studio, and weight training complex. Some of the programs offer exercise stress testing, cardiac rehabilitation, sports medicine, and aquatic therapy. Exercise programs range from aerobics to one-on-one personal training. Health promotion classes such as nutrition, diabetes management, and smoking cessation may also be conducted. These programs may be open to patients, community members, or hospital staff. They are predicted to expand as hospitals increase their emphasis on health promotion and disease prevention; this will create additional employment opportunities for physical education, exercise science, and sport professionals.

Fitness and Physical Activity Movement

Enthusiasm for physical activity and fitness is at an all-time high in the United States today and likely will continue to increase in the future. Sales of sport equipment, apparel, and home exercise equipment have reached astronomical levels. The number of individuals participating in exercise and sport activities continues to rise, and it appears that physical activity and fitness have become an ingrained way of American life. In 1996, the landmark report *Physical Activity and Health:* convincingly set forth the contribution of physical activity to health.[19] The positive effects of remaining physically active throughout one's life have motivated many adults to embark on a fitness program and millions of others to continue their participation past the typical stopping point, the end of the school years.

However, adult participation in physical activity is not as widespread as it seems. Less than

30% of adults engage in regular physical activity during leisure time. A decrease in physical activity and poor nutrition has led to over 67% of adults who are overweight or obese. In addition to adults, there is concern among professionals that the fitness movement is not reaching many of the children and youth of our country. Given that over 18% of the child and youth population are overweight and obese and that many chronic diseases have their beginnings in childhood, it is important for children to learn that good lifestyle habits, including being physically active on a daily basis, should begin early in life and continue throughout their lifetime.

Professionals must direct more of their efforts at preventing the decrease in physical activity as children age. Teaching students physical skills, promoting physical fitness, and helping them acquire knowledge about sports and physical activity is not enough. More attention must be directed to the affective domain—for example, enhancing students' self-efficacy, promoting self-esteem, and engendering feelings of competence. We need to restructure our traditional physical education programs to make them more responsive to the needs of children and adolescents—new activities, new approaches, greater sensitivity to individual differences, and increased emphasis on encouraging physical activity outside of the school setting. Additionally, we must make a greater effort to help adolescents make a transition from school-based physical education programs to involvement in community-based physical activity programs that would meet their needs as adults.

To promote lifespan physical activity and physical fitness, we need to take a more active leadership role in this effort. We need to more closely identify personal and societal barriers to participation in physical activity and seek to alleviate them. As advocates for lifespan activity, we need to work more closely with health-promoting organizations within the community to develop programs to address the physical activity and fitness needs of persons from infancy to old age. Additionally, we need to collaborate with community organizers and designers to help build communities that are friendly to physical activity—with safe places to walk, accessible bicycle paths, and fitness trails. More of our efforts also need to be directed toward increasing the use of the school as a site for community-based physical activity programs and developing and sustaining community recreation programs that are available to people at low or no cost.

Finally, more physical education, exercise science, and sport programs must be established to meet the needs of the elderly, the very young, and individuals who have disabilities. These populations will continue to grow in the future; thus, we must do more than we are currently doing. Also, programs need to be developed to reach individuals who are economically disadvantaged; they lack the financial resources to join health clubs or pay for private sport instruction. Equity in physical activity and fitness is an important professional concern.

Health Care Reform Movement

The 1990s was marked by calls for health care reform. Rising health care costs and the growing number of uninsured people were two of the primary factors underlying this reform movement. In 2008, health care costs were over $2.3 trillion.[43] Health care costs accounted for over 16% of the gross domestic product (GDP), up from 7% in 1970. Costs continue to escalate at an astronomical rate. It is projected that health care expenditures will reach $4.5 trillion, or 19.3% of GDP, by 2019.[43] Despite the fact that the United States spends over a trillion dollars a year on health care, over 45 million Americans are uninsured.

During the last few years, numerous health care reform bills have been introduced by Congress. The proposals have varied greatly, ranging from coverage for only catastrophic illnesses to comprehensive coverage for nearly all medical services. Other differences include the degree of emphasis placed on health promotion and disease prevention services and activities.

National public health reports such as *Healthy People 2010* have emphasized efforts to reduce disease, disability, and death through early intervention and prevention programs. These efforts can lead to improved health status for people of all ages and reduction in health care costs.

Health promotion and disease prevention are less costly than treatment of disease. Chronic and preventable diseases and injuries account for nearly half of all causes of mortality in the United States and almost 70% of all medical care expenditures.[44] Lifestyle behaviors (e.g., smoking, diet, inactivity) and social conditions (e.g., poverty) play a significant role in these disease and health disparities. Yet only about 5% of the massive expenditure on health care is devoted to reducing the risks associated with these conditions.[44]

As we move toward the future, more attention, research, and resources must be directed toward understanding behavioral and social influences on health and identifying broader public health interventions that will lead to greater improvements in health for all population groups. After an extensive review of the research, an Institute of Medicine committee charged with the identification of effective social and behavioral health interventions put forth 21 recommendations relative to the application of behavioral and social science research to improving health. According to the committee, interventions need to:

1. "focus on generic social and behavioral determinants of disease, injury, and disability;
2. use multiple approaches (e.g., education, social support, laws, incentives, behavior change programs) and address multiple levels of influence simultaneously (i.e., individuals, families, communities, nations);
3. take account of the special needs of target groups (i.e., based on age, gender, race, ethnicity, social class);
4. take the 'long view' of health outcomes, as changes often take many years to become established; and
5. involve a variety of sectors in our society that have not traditionally been associated with health promotion efforts, including law, business, education, social services, and the media."[44]

The committee notes that capitalizing on the promise of social and behavioral research to improve the public's health requires innovative, collaborative approaches. Such approaches will not only improve the nation's health but lead to reductions in our spiraling health care costs.[44]

Implementation of the Institute of Medicine committee's social and behavioral intervention recommendations requires that physical education, exercise science, and sport professionals work collaboratively with community groups and health agencies to deliver services—to incorporate their physical activity programs within a comprehensive community health promotion program. These professionals will also need to design and implement physical activity programs targeted to meet the needs of specific populations. To be able to do this effectively, we as professionals must become more emphatic and understanding of the impact of societal forces on the lives and health of people.

Education

The last four decades in the United States have been marked by calls for reform of the educational establishment. Advocates for educational reform proclaimed a need to place a greater emphasis on the basic subjects such as English, mathematics, science, social studies, and computer science. Criticism was also directed at teacher competency, school leadership, and professional preparation institutions.

In the 1990s and early 2000s, national school reform programs such as *Year 2000 Goals* and *No Child Left* Behind[45] focused on providing students with the skills and knowledge to be productive members of the workforce in our growing global economy. All children, regardless of race, ethnicity, gender, or socioeconomic background, are entitled to a quality education. To ensure that children were making educational progress, standards were established and periodic assessments were incorporated into educational curriculums. Schools were required to demonstrate student learning, and greater accountability measures were

Physical education programs should help students learn the benefits of physical activity and develop skills and habits for lifelong participation in physical activity.

instituted. Emphasis was on teacher development and school-parent-community partnerships to improve learning.

Futurist Marvin Cetron (president of Forecasting International, Inc.) and educator Kimberly Cetron cite four societal and economic trends that will have an enormous impact on our nation's schools. First, it is anticipated that funding for schools will become more limited.[46] Schools will be challenged to accomplish more with less. Schools can respond to this challenge by making more creative use of financial resources and maximizing the use of new technologies.[46] Schools can use the Internet to tap into information any place in the world and shift some instruction online. Teachers will increasingly serve as catalysts and mentors to help students learn how to "collect, evaluate, analyze, and synthesize information."[46]

The second trend is that the student population will be significantly larger than anticipated during the next two decades. Furthermore, the diversity of the population will increase, and minority groups will comprise a larger percentage of the population. The greatest change will be in the number of Hispanic schoolchildren. It is anticipated that the percentage of non-Hispanic white schoolchildren will decrease from about 65% today to 56% by 2020 and to less than 50% by 2040.[46] Schools will be challenged to work with a more diverse student body and meet the learning needs of all their students.

A third trend is the impact of technology on the workplace, as computer competency will be mandatory for most fields.[46] This necessitates the growth of computer and technology training at the middle and high school levels. Teachers will need to have the necessary skills to provide this training. For the majority of high school students who do not go on to attend college, establishment of high-tech vocational training will be important.[46]

Last, engagement in lifelong learning will become increasingly necessary.[45] Unlike generations of the past, when people remained in one career for their working lives, today's and tomorrow's generation of workers will pursue an average of five different occupations.[46] Workers will require continual retraining. This learning will take place in the schools after the normal school day as well as through industry and community partnership.[46]

School structure is changing as we move forward in the twenty-first century. More and more states are adding public-school prekindergarten programs for children aged 3 to 5. Calls for a longer school day and school year to provide increased opportunities for learning are occurring with more frequency. Marvin Cetron predicts that students may spend only 3 days a week in school. They will spend the rest of the time at home, learning through the use of computer-facilitated instruction and distance-learning approaches[47]. Textbooks will be supplanted by computers and multimedia learning packages. Distance learning will allow students at several schools within the district or even throughout the nation to receive instruction from a central source. This will help equalize the quality of education provided to all students. Adults will regularly return to school to keep abreast of rapidly growing advances in technology and knowledge in their field. Today, several colleges and universities offer online degrees at the bachelor's, master's, and doctoral levels.

The school's use as a community learning center and a service provider will continue to grow. The 21st Century Community Learning Centers program of the Department of Education will lead to the establishment and expansion of the school as a site for community learning. There will be an expansion of before- and after-school, weekend, and summer programs for children and youths. These programs include academic enrichment and recreational programs. Greater ties and increased collaboration among public and private agencies, business, institutions of higher education, and cultural and scientific organizations will expand the learning opportunities and services provided not only to children and youth but to adults.

What are the implications of these trends and the changing structure of the school for physical education? First, to solidify the place of physical education in the educational curriculum in the next decade, physical educators must educate the public and decision makers about the values to be derived from participation in physical education, both in terms of the education and the health of the individual.

Second, as more adults return to school to update their skills, physical educators need to be ready to conduct instructional programs to meet adult needs. Third, just as education must teach students to be lifelong learners, so must physical education. Students in physical education class need to have knowledge as well as skills so that they may be self-educative.

Fourth, as more and more education takes place outside of the school setting in the home, professionals need to develop new programs to meet the needs of these learners. Finally, as the school continues to grow as a community center for learning for people of all ages, professionals must be prepared to conduct physical activity programs in these settings and to work collaboratively

Video game play contributes to sedentary behavior. However, new video and computer games, such as Nintendo Wii, allow children and adults to perform fitness activities and exercise in their own home.

with other professionals in the community to develop comprehensive programs to meet a multitude of needs.

Technology

Technological advances will transform our lives in the twenty-first century. Cetron and Davies state, "Technology is not the only power that will shape our future for good or ill. Yet it is the critical force that more than any other single factor, although not uninfluenced by the rest, will determine what is possible for us."[37] Technology is the "one discipline whose entire purpose is to make the future different from the present."[37] The past decade has been one of rapid technological advances, many of which have had implications for the future of physical education, exercise science, and sport. Developments in computer technology combined with increasingly sophisticated research techniques have enabled us to widen our knowledge base and will contribute to further growth in the future. The Internet has begun and will continue to revolutionize education, communication, and many other areas of our professional endeavors in the twenty-first century.

Technology has enabled researchers and practitioners to more clearly understand the impact of physical activity on the body as well as more clearly delineate the relationship among physical activity, exercise, fitness, and health. According to Powers, Ward, and Shanely, the development of more powerful microcomputers has had an "unprecedented effect on research in the field."[48] Other technological advances in the past 30 years that have had a significant impact on the field include the "development of electronic gas analyzers and metabolic measurement carts, blood gas analyzers, computerized muscle ergometers, and the commercially available instruments of molecular biology."[48] These advances have enabled us to explore questions not previously possible, obtain more sophisticated data and perform more complex analyses, and reduce the amount of time needed to complete the research process.

Advances in technology enable physical education, exercise science, and sport professionals to electronically monitor physical activity in real-time situations in new, easier ways. According to Healey,

Wearable computers and tiny programmable microprocessors are allowing mobile monitoring and real-time in situation processing of digital signals from physiological sensors and cameras. These tiny sensor-oriented computers can be sewn into clothing and embedded into accessories such as shoes or jewelry. Mobile signal processing offers an unprecedented opportunity to collect a vast amount of digital data about a person's physical activity.[49]

As individuals engage in various tasks, a record of their physical activity, including heart rate, muscle activity, and respiration, is easily and noninvasively made. This information is "correlated with a digital photo diary composed of images from a computer controlled camera." Integrating the visual information with the physiological information, we can see how engaging in certain activities affects individuals' physiological parameters.

Computer technology has facilitated improvements in performance. In biomechanics,

computer-generated graphical representations of an athlete's performance are compared with a prototypical sport performance, facilitating skill analysis and enhancing corrections. Skiers practice in wind tunnels while coaches and sport scientists study their body position and technique to find ways to reduce resistance from drag and increase speed. Equipment has been designed or reengineered using computer-assisted programs, which has led to improvements in performance. For example, redesigned handlebars for cyclists create a more aerodynamically shaped body position for the racers and lead to decreased time to complete the course. Sport participants at all levels can benefit from many of these improvements.

Developments in biotechnology hold implications for the future of physical education and sport. Experts in tissue engineering estimate that within the next 5 to 10 years, people will routinely have tendons, cartilage, and bones grown, a breakthrough that will benefit injured athletes as well as other individuals whose injuries limit their opportunity to lead a physically active lifestyle. Today, muscle fiber typing allows researchers to identify whether an individual has a greater potential to succeed in athletic events requiring strength or endurance. Perhaps in the near future, genetic engineering will be used to program an individual's genes for success in certain sport activities. The first mammal cloned from an adult cell, Dolly the sheep, was heralded as the greatest scientific breakthrough of 1997. Ethicists and scientists are now engaged in sweeping debates about cloning humans. Genetic engineering can lead to the development of humans with specific traits. Hoberman states that "it is likely that this technology will be used to develop athletes before it is applied to the creation of other kinds of human performers."[50] How will we deal with these complex issues?

Developments in the field of telecommunication have and will continue to improve our ability to communicate and our delivery systems. The Internet, a web of thousands of computer networks, has dramatically changed how we interact and manage information. E-mail allows rapid, inexpensive communication with colleagues throughout the world. E-mailing lists allow individuals with common interests, such as fitness, to engage in discussions, pose questions, and share ideas.

The World Wide Web, the multimedia channel of the Internet, is used for many different purposes. Electronic professional journals and documents are posted on the web, enhancing the dissemination of information. Personalized information services seek out specific information, update it automatically, and send it to the subscriber's computer.[51] For example, personal trainers can receive daily updates on training techniques, nutrition, and cardiovascular research. Professionals have easier access to current research and are able to retrieve needed information from virtually anywhere in the world where they have computer access. Research data can be easily shared via the web or through file transfers.

Internet telephones and videoconferencing enhance communications with professionals throughout the world. The web and desktop videoconferencing are increasingly being used for distance learning. Courses and even entire degree programs can be completed via the Internet. Continuing education programs offered through distance learning will increase in popularity. For example, a professional in Alaska can "attend" a workshop on fitness hosted by an organization in New York.

Multimedia instruction and interactive tutorials using CD-ROMs or the web will allow physical education, exercise science, and sport professionals to tailor learning to the needs of each program participant. Participants in a fitness program or schoolchildren accessing various sites on the web or using a CD-ROM can see a heart pulsating as it beats, follow the course of circulation, and become familiar with the short- and long-term effects of exercise on this vital organ. Multimedia presentations let content be experienced in new ways.

Virtual reality is the use of computers and sensory mechanisms to create simulated, interactive three-dimensional environments and experiences. Head-mounted displays and sensor gloves may be a part of virtual reality. Virtual reality can also be a game or a simulation. It places the body of the user directly inside the three-dimensional environment. Virtual reality offers some of the most exciting possibilities for our field and is expected to grow tremendously.

Through virtual reality, real-life situations can be re-created, altered, or simulated, allowing the user to react and to rehearse constant or changing scenarios. It provides invaluable training to users and allows them to gain a vast amount of knowledge through their experiences. Haggerty suggests that virtual reality can be used to provide athletes in many sports (e.g., batters, goalies, football players) with a variety of simulated situations to improve their performance.[51] Virtual golf simulators give golfers the opportunity to play many of the great courses while receiving feedback on their shot, distance, and errors. Simulators are being developed for other sports such as baseball and snowboarding.

Technology offers exciting new possibilities for the field of physical education, exercise science, and sport. Computers help professionals complete their responsibilities more efficiently. Application of technology has led to improvements in sport equipment and performance, benefiting sport participants of all abilities. Biotechnology offers exciting possibilities, as well as confronting us with a host of ethical issues that must be addressed. Multimedia technology enhances learning, and distance learning increases access to learning. Telecommunication facilitates interactions with colleagues throughout the world. And virtual reality offers tremendous possibilities for training, education, and sport participation in the twenty-first century.

Changing Demographics

Demographic trends exert a tremendous influence on the structure of societal institutions and the services they provide to different populations. The age distribution of the population is shifting quite markedly. Longer life expectancies and a declining birthrate have increased the average age of the population.

American society is aging. The change is quite dramatic when viewed over the course of the century. In 1900, approximately 4% of the population was aged 65 or older.[49] This is estimated to increase to 18.5% of the population in 2025.[52] Furthermore, there will be an increasing number of very old people, many of whom will be healthy. The number of people aged 85 years and older is expected to increase from 3.8 million in 1996 to more than 7 million in 2025.[53] Minorities are projected to comprise 25% of the population aged 65 and older in 2030.[52]

America's population is also becoming more culturally diverse as the number of Asians, Hispanics, African Americans, and Native Americans increases. Minorities are estimated to comprise more than 40% of the US population by 2035.[53] We must not continue to overlook the needs of minorities if the health of our nation is to improve and if we are, indeed, to achieve our goal of lifespan involvement in physical activity for all people. Significant racial and ethnic disparities exist in health and health care. Many minorities, especially those with limited English proficiency, face a multitude of barriers to accessing health care and receiving appropriate treatment; consequently, they generally suffer worse health.[53] Addressing the needs of increasingly diverse and underserved populations is one of our greatest challenges as we move forward in the twenty-first century.

These forthcoming years will see continued changes in the structure of the family and growing societal problems that must be addressed. The number of single-parent families is rising, including the number of teenage mothers. Single-parent and dual-career families have led to an increase in latchkey children—children who come home at the end of the school day to an empty house. Preschool and day-care programs are increasing dramatically. Amidst the changing nature of the family is the problem of a growing array of threats to the health and well-being of our children and youth. Drug and alcohol abuse, violence, child abuse, suicide, and risky sexual behaviors adversely impact the lives of many young people. People and families living in poverty face many hardships and are at increased risk for poor health.

What are the implications of these changes for the conduct of physical education, exercise science, and sport programs? We must be prepared to effectively work with the changing population groups. Quality physical activity programs are needed for the growing elderly population to enhance their health and their quality of life and to provide enjoyable recreational pursuits. Professionals in both school and nonschool settings must be prepared to conduct programs that are sensitive to the needs of an increasingly culturally diverse population. Culturally competent techniques have the potential to improve access to health care and the delivery of services to minority populations, thus contributing to the reduction of racial and ethnic disparities

Recreational activities, such as skateboarding, frequently capture youths' interest and keep them active for hours.

in health. It is important that we, as professionals, work toward attainment of cultural competency if we are committed to promoting lifespan involvement for all people.

As physical education, exercise science, and sport shifts to an industry in which people pay for desired sport services (e.g., commercial fitness clubs), we must not lose sight of the needs of the economically disadvantaged who cannot afford to pay. Providing access to physical activity programs for children and youth through school physical education programs is only one part of the answer. Professionally, we must explore innovative approaches that will help make physical activity programs available to underserved populations. We must do more to overcome community, organizational, and personal barriers to physical activity.

PREPARING FOR THE FUTURE

It is tempting to look back on these past four decades, which have been a time of tremendous growth for physical education, exercise science, and sport, and bask in the glow of such accomplishments as the celebration of the one hundredth anniversary of AAHPERD, the growth in professional stature achieved by the various subdisciplines, the tremendous expansion of our knowledge base in both depth and breadth, our efforts to develop programs to meet the needs of people of all ages in a diversity of settings, and the increase in job opportunities within the field. However, if physical education, exercise science, and sport professionals are interested in being involved in the future of their profession, they must also look ahead to the future.

If the potential of our field to enhance the lives of people of all ages is to be realized, we must take a more active role in creating our future and shaping our destiny. We must take a proactive, rather than reactive, stance in dealing with the issues and challenges that confront us. Furthermore, both individually and collectively, we must reflect more critically upon social issues related to physical education, exercise science, and sport and question long-held assumptions,

sacrosanct beliefs, and traditional practices.[54] We must be introspective, engaging in a thoughtful examination of our actions and values. We also must look outward, beyond ourselves, and examine the broader societal issues and their impact on our lives, institutions, programs, and the people with whom we work. But we must move beyond reflection to consider alternatives to the problems that confront us. Personally and professionally, both individually and collectively, we must move toward solutions if the potential of our field is to be fulfilled.

Oberle,[56] in a discussion about the future directions for health, physical education, recreation and leisure, and dance, stressed the importance of exerting quality control within the profession.[55] He suggested that each of the disciplines consider the following actions to enhance their effectiveness:

- Establish minimum standards of competency.
- Develop programs and services that are flexible to meet changing needs while accomplishing avowed disciplinary objectives.
- Provide meaningful programs that will meet needs today as well as tomorrow.
- Reduce ineffective programs.
- Establish minimum standards for entry into professional preparation programs.
- Provide high-quality experiences for professionals within the discipline, such as in-service education and graduate education.
- Develop a system for relicensure for all professionals, not just public school personnel.
- Establish professional accrediting agencies, as the American Medical Association has done, to ensure quality control.
- Develop high-quality model programs and build facilities that can serve as the standard for the profession.[55]

As we move into the future, we must be willing to confront change, capitalize on opportunities, and meet many challenges.

Many challenges and opportunities await us in 2020. Charles reminds us that "health promotion and disease prevention, athletic performance in sport and recreation, and physical education teaching and learning in the schools and the community have been defining elements of our field in the past and promise to continue to be staples of our profession in the future."[56] The delivery of these services should reflect two trends: globalization and the lifespan involvement, from neonatal to geriatric.[56] The increased diversity of our population and a greater understanding of how race, ethnicity, gender, socioeconomic background, and a host of other factors influence access and opportunities relative to physical activity and health must be considered as we move toward the future. The growing recognition from the general public and health professionals that physical activity is an essential ingredient of living at all ages provides us with the opportunity to contribute to the well-being of individuals throughout their lifespan.

ESTABLISHMENT OF JURISDICTION OVER OUR DOMAIN

As we move toward the future, collaboration and focus are critical if we are to play a significant role in the lives of people throughout their lifespan. The growth of the subdisicplines, while increasing our depth and breadth of knowledge, contributed to the fragmentation of the field. Overdorf points out that if our profession is to take a lead in using physical activity to address societal problems such as premature death and chronic disease, interdisciplinary endeavors and collaborative leadership are needed.[3] Collaborative leadership should not be limited to our domain. We should work collaboratively with other professionals, such as medical professionals or sociologists, in addressing the health problems confronting society.

Physical education, exercise science, and sport professionals must become publicly recognized leaders in the field of physical activity. Many of the services with which physical education, exercise science, and sport professionals are presently associated lie within the public domain. Unfortunately, we are not directing many of these services. Entrepreneurs, muscle builders, and movie stars are associated with health spas promising "overnight" rejuvenation,

specialized exercise equipment guaranteeing "six-pack abs," and weight reduction programs highlighting dramatic weight losses in a matter of weeks.[1] Often, the people involved in these and other ventures do not have the proper credentials.[1] Additionally, the public is not often aware of the nature of physical education, exercise, and sport and the tremendous worth and substance of our field of endeavor. We must work to solidify our place as prominent leaders in physical activity. Rikli states that "the field is best served by having visionary leaders who can look into the future and make adjustments needed to best serve an ever changing society."[57]

As professionals, we must assume the challenge of leadership for the promotion of physical activity. We must work to strengthen physical education in the schools while developing a wide array of options to promote skilled physical activity among people of all ages and abilities in a wide range of settings. We need to highlight the contributions of physical activity to health. We need to provide sport opportunities that appeal to a wide range of interests and abilities. High-quality programs are essential. We must promote our programs and take steps to ensure that the people who participate in them accrue the stated and personally desired benefits.

ENHANCING OUR DELIVERY SYSTEM

In the future, our delivery system—the manner in which we provide services and the population we serve—needs to change. New developments in the field of technology and communication, as well as the changing nature of education, need to be reflected in our services. Our delivery system needs to be more responsive to individuals' needs. Use of technology, more personalized instructional approaches, and innovative programming will enable us to meet the diverse needs of our increasingly heterogeneous population. No longer can we rely on one program to meet all needs or, as Lawson[61] states, the "one size fits all" approach.[58] An improved delivery system will enable us to better meet the needs of various population groups, including the elderly, the very young, the growing number of racial and ethnic minorities, and the economically disadvantaged.

In improving our delivery system we need to provide closer articulation between school physical education and sport programs and programs within the community. We also need to take advantage of the growing trend of the school as a community learning center, offering instructional and sport programs in this setting to meet the needs of the community. A systematic, progressive curriculum of skills will allow participants to progress and to build on previous learning.

In planning for the future, we need to expand our use of distance learning and cable television programs. More than 12 states allow high school students to satisfy their physical education requirements through online courses; this trend is likely to continue in the future. Online coaching education programs are growing in number. Cable television brings a multitude of exercise and sport programs to the public 24 hours a day, with programs available on demand. Segments about exercise are incorporated into health shows on a regular basis.

Computers will play an even greater role in our delivery system. Electronic databases now facilitate the worldwide dissemination of research findings, allowing professionals to more easily keep abreast of current developments. Collaborative research with professionals at other institutions, both in the United States and throughout the world, is possible with computer networking. Computerized record keeping in physical education programs and at health clubs allows professionals to more easily identify individuals' needs and monitor progress toward attainment of their goals.

As we move forward in the twenty-first century, we must change our delivery systems to take advantage of new technologies in order to more effectively provide services. Our delivery systems should offer innovative programming offered in a culturally competent manner to reach all segments of our population.

THE FUTURE

As we prepare for the future, physical education, exercise science, and sport professionals must:

1. Provide ourselves with the proper credentials to establish jurisdiction over their domain.
2. Utilize technological advances to improve the delivery system.
3. Prepare for space and underwater living and for changes in our society.
4. Become a positive role model for a fit and healthy lifestyle so that others will be favorably influenced to emulate this lifestyle.
5. Help people to become increasingly responsible for their own health and fitness.
6. Recognize that individuals will live longer and become more fit and active in the years to come.
7. Provide for all persons, regardless of age, skill, disabling condition, and socioeconomic background, throughout their lifespan.
8. Remember that we are involved with the development of the whole person as a thinking, feeling, moving human being.
9. Make a commitment to conduct high-quality programs that are sensitive to individual needs so that physical education and sport's potential to enhance the health and quality of life for all people can be achieved.

Whether or not professionals meet these challenges will affect the future of our field.

Scenario planning is one approach that would allow us to see some alternative futures for physical education, exercise science, and sport. Anticipating and planning for the future requires foresight, self-awareness, imagination, strategy, and fitness. According to Charles, scenario planning is based on the "Foresight to consider the options that lie ahead, the Self-awareness of understanding personal capabilities and situational capacities, the Imagination needed to conceive of creative alternatives, the Strategy of figuring out how to implement a chosen solution, and the Fitness to vigorously pursue a course of action."[57] These skills provide structure to the scenario planning process. However, uncertainties always play a role in defining future scenarios.

Scenario planning invites stakeholders to envision different futures based on assumptions and driving forces, such as public policy or funding. Neiner, Howze, and Greaney[62] use scenario planning to identify ways in which a public health department could address chronic disease prevention and management with unhealthy diet and physical inactivity used as key risk factors.[59] They describe what it would look like if there was support and what it would look like if support was lacking. See Table 15-1 for some of the outcomes Neiner, Howze, and Greaney associate with strong public support and funding for nutrition and physical activity, and with a lack of that support and funding.

TABLE 15-1   Scenario Planning for Physical Activity in the Future

Potential Supportive Outcomes	Potential Negative Outcomes
• Increase in number of health promotion programs to promote good nutrition and physical activity. • Increase in number of adults who exercise and eat healthily as a means to prevent and control chronic disease. • Increased support from the medical community as well as Medicare and Medicaid coverage of gym membership costs, nutrition classes, and weight loss programs. • Decrease in health disparities among racial and ethnic, socioeconomic, and age groups. • Passage of a junk-food tax, the revenues from which are used to support physical activity and good nutrition initiatives. • Offering of healthy food alternatives at all fast-food restaurants, with supersizing and the use of cartoon characters to entice children a thing of the past. • Partnerships involving schools, workplaces, and community agencies that lead to comprehensive approaches to addressing inactivity and poor nutrition risk factors. • Media campaigns that use a variety of vehicles to expose the public to consistent messages reinforcing the value of an active lifestyle and good nutrition. • Tax breaks given to owners of fitness centers and builders of recreational structures who are willing to build them in poor communities. • Fitness staff and nutrition counselors certified in areas of expertise. • Primary care physicians trained to counsel patients on physical activity and nutrition. • Insurance companies required to cover the cost of physicians' referrals to registered dieticians and certified physical activity providers.	• Decreased funding for health promotion programs to promote good nutrition and physical activity, with the available limited funds directed toward care of those with chronic diseases. • Growing health disparities among population groups, with the poor most affected. • Increase in the prevalence of chronic disease factors, including sedentary behavior and poor diet. • Lack of partnerships to promote physical activity and nutrition, as agencies compete with each other for limited funding. • Competing priorities, such as poverty, reducing political support for health programs, including those related to health promotion. • Media campaigns to promote the value of healthy eating and physical activity not being funded. • Consumption of fast food continuing to rise because of convenience and affordability. • Access to physical activity venues becoming more expensive, with fewer options available for those in low-income communities. Physical activity professionals not certified. • Access to health care decreasing as the number of uninsured or underinsured individuals increases. Primary care physicians provide little counsel on physical activity and nutrition. Referrals to professionals to help patients manage their weight are not covered by insurance.

Source: Neiner JA, Howze EH, and Greaney ML. "Using Scenario Planning in Public Health: Anticipating Alternative Futures." *Health Promotion Practice*, 5(1):69–79, 2004.

The supportive scenario recognizes that disease prevention and health promotion make economic sense and that such efforts will lead to positive gains in the health of the entire population. This approach offers a very promising future for physical education, exercise science, and sport professionals.

On the other hand, a bleaker future emerges when there is a lack of public support and funding. This scenario reflects an orientation that will lead to higher levels of chronic diseases and increases in health disparities. This alternative future does not bode well for physical education, exercise science, and sport professionals.

Think carefully about some of the outcomes associated with each of these alternative futures. To create the future that is most beneficial to the people we seek to serve as well as to the field of physical education, exercise science, and sport, we must take an active role in its creation. We must take charge of our professional destiny and create a future that allows the full potential of physical education, exercise science, and sport to be fulfilled.

It is likely that all of us, at some time in our lives, will have a significant experience that, as years pass, will come to embody the personal meaning of physical education and sport. Charles Bucher, a noted physical education leader and author of previous editions of this text, relates an experience that helped him personally and perhaps will help you to realize anew the tremendous potential of physical education, exercise science, and sport in our society. Bucher wrote the following passage about the New York City Marathon, one of the largest marathons in the world:

> I was particularly enthralled as I watched the runners, some of whom took as many as five, six, and seven hours to cross the finish lines. Most runners gritted their teeth, gasped for breath, and put on an extra burst of speed as they pounded across. Some runners had given so much of themselves that they were helped onto a stretcher or were carried across.
>
> A runner from Italy, in fourth place, whipped off his sweatband and waved it to the crowd. A runner from California, in second place among the women, clenched her teeth and went the last few strides on sheer will before collapsing across the line. When a long-haired Polish woman, sweat streaming down her face, stumbled slowly toward the line, the crowd cheered and chanted, "Finish it! Finish it!" And *she did*.
>
> A few runners completed the race hand-in-hand. Some went barefoot and some carried their shoes. Each person got a tremendous cheer, but perhaps the loudest cheers of all were for two men who crossed the finish line in wheelchairs.
>
> The runners had done their best—not for acclaim, for a loving cup symbolic of supremacy, or to be a champion—but to prove to themselves that they could do it.
>
> No one could watch the sight without realizing that he or she was witnessing a great moment in America and the world.

Let's remember to promote fun when we promote lifespan involvement in physical activity.

No one in physical education and sport could be a part of that experience without feeling the power and potential for our field of endeavor—the power and potential for improving the quality of life for all our citizens.[13]

The marathon perhaps in many ways is symbolic of our society, of America, and of the qualities that we in our field try to develop. It recognizes that the training of the physical is important; but perhaps more important, it shows how the physical *can* and *should* be used as a vehicle that brings into play such desirable qualities as courage, a belief in oneself, a feeling of accomplishment, and, most important, a blending of the mind, body, and spirit in the accomplishment of worthy goals.

The vision of lifespan involvement in physical activity for all people is a powerful one, but its achievement requires dedicated and committed professionals. Excellence must be present in all our professional endeavors. After you have read this text, we hope that you have an appreciation for the tremendous substance and worth of the field that you have chosen to study. Physical education, exercise science, and sport has a tremendous potential to enrich and enhance the health and quality of life of all people. Whether this potential is realized depends on each professional's willingness to make a personal commitment to achieving this goal.

SUMMARY

Four important issues in physical education, exercise science, and sport today were examined. First, professionals must assume a greater leadership role in the physical activity movement. Second, we need to assume a greater role in the conduct of youth sports programs. Third, as our field continues to grow in scope and expand its focus, we need to more clearly define who we are, what it is that we do, and how we can work together

better. Last, as research continues at an unprecedented rate, we must take additional steps to close the gap between research and practice.

Four particularly important challenges that face physical education, exercise science, and sport professionals were discussed. First, professionals are faced with the challenge of promoting daily, high-quality physical education in the schools. The second challenge is to become more actively involved as advocates for our programs. Professionals in all settings must actively promote their programs. The third challenge is to attain the goals set forth in *Healthy People 2010* and the upcoming *Healthy People 2020*. These specific physical activity objectives focus on improving the health status of all Americans by increasing the span of healthy life. If these objectives are to be achieved, each professional must make a personal commitment to work with professional organizations to accomplish this task and to be a role model exemplifying a healthy, active lifestyle. Last, promoting lifespan involvement in physical activity requires professionals to provide a diversity of services to individuals of all ages. Physical education, exercise science, and sport has the potential to enhance the health and quality of life of people of all ages. Helping individuals to realize this potential is one of our biggest challenges.

Professionals must start planning for the future now. Such planning requires that professionals recognize that rapid change is characteristic of our way of life.

Several societal trends will influence the future of physical education, exercise science, and sport. The wellness movement and fitness and physical activity movement present excellent opportunities for professionals to involve individuals of all ages in appropriate physical activity. The educational reform movement and the changing nature of education indicate that, more than ever before, we need to inform the public and decision makers about the contribution of physical education to the educational process. Developments in communication and other technological developments will influence the future of physical education, exercise science, and sport as well.

Professionals can prepare for the future in several ways. First, we need to establish jurisdiction over our domain by obtaining the proper credentials and actively seeking leadership positions. Second, professionals need to improve the delivery systems. We must provide for people of all ages and utilize technological advances to facilitate learning. We must take an active role in helping individuals be active participants throughout their lifespan. The future of physical education, exercise science, and sport is promising, but we must take an active leadership role in shaping its direction.

DISCUSSION QUESTIONS

1. How can professionals promote the development of values in their programs, regardless of the setting?

2. How can physical educators, exercise scientists, and sport leaders, through various programming efforts, help individuals attain the fitness and physical goals set forth in *The Surgeon General's Vision for a Healthy and Fit Nation, Healthy People 2010*, and the upcoming *Healthy People 2020*? What strategies could be used to promote greater access to these programs for underserved populations?

3. What various strategies can be utilized to promote lifespan involvement of people of all ages, abilities, races and ethnicities, genders, and socioeconomic backgrounds?

4. What are the implications of the changing nature of education and the impact of technological developments on physical education and interscholastic sports in the future?

SELF-ASSESSMENT ACTIVITIES

These activities are designed to help you determine if you have mastered the materials and competencies presented in this chapter.

1. Discuss the role of the physical educator, exercise scientist, and sport leader in the physical activity movement. Formulate a list of strategies and next steps on what we can do to "lead the parade."

2. Research current state legislation and policies that focus on physical education. What are the policies and requirements? Discuss specific strategies that

could be employed to encourage the state legislature and local school boards to mandate physical education. Create a plan of action you would use to implement those strategies.

3. Discuss the importance of advocacy programs in the physical education, exercise science, and sport setting of your choice. What local organizations exist in your current community that offer health promotion programs? How would you work to organize these groups into a coalition to promote physical activity?

4. Develop a plan for the early 2000s that provides specific suggestions for improving physical education, exercise science, and sport's delivery system.

REFERENCES

1. Corbin CB: Is the fitness bandwagon passing us by?, JOPERD 55(9):17, 1984.

2. Ewers JR: You must be present to win, Quest 49:238–250, 1997.

3. Overdorf V: Images and influences in the promotion of physical activity, Quest 57:243–254, 2005.

4. Seefeldt V: Why are children's sports programs controversial?, JOPERD 56(3):16, 1985.

5. American Academy of Physical Education: The Academy papers: reunification, no. 15, Reston, Va., 1981, AAHPERD.

6. American Sport Education Program, Champaign, Ill., Human Kinetics (www.asep.com).

7. Martens R: Turning kids on to physical activity for a lifetime, Quest 46:303–310, 1996.

8. Stuart ME: Moral issues in sport: the child's perspective, Research Quarterly for Exercise and Sport 74:445–455, 2003.

9. Sage GH: The future and the profession. In JD Massengale, editor, Trends toward the future in physical education, Champaign, Ill., 1987, Human Kinetics.

10. Siedentop D: Introduction to physical education, fitness, and sport, Mountain View, Calif., 1990, Mayfield.

11. Massengale JD: Doing PE at the new university, Quest 52:102–109, 2002.

12. Corbin CB: Promoting lifelong physical activity: education's challenge for the new millennium, Paper presented at the National Conference for Promoting Lifelong Physical Activity, Salt Lake City, Utah, October, 1998. (Cited in Massengale JD: Doing PE at the new university, Quest 52:102–109, 2002.)

13. Bucher CA and Thaxton NA: Physical education and sport: change and challenge, St. Louis, Mo., 1981, Mosby.

14. Rothstein AL: Practitioners and the scholarly enterprise, Quest 20:59–60, 1973.

15. Locke LF: Research in physical education, New York, 1969, Teachers College Press.

16. Stadulis RE: Bridging the gap: a lifetime of waiting and doing, Quest 20:48–52, 1973.

17. Barnes FP: Research for the practitioner in education, Washington, D.C., 1963, Department of Elementary School Principals, National Education Association.

18. Broderick FP: Research as viewed by the teacher, Paper presented at the AAHPER National Convention, Detroit, 1971.

19. US Department of Health and Human Services: Physical activity and health: a report of the surgeon general, Atlanta, Ga., 1996, US Department of Health and Human Services, Centers for Disease Control and Prevention, National Center for Chronic Disease Prevention and Health Promotion.

20. National Association for Sport and Physical Education: Moving into the future: national standards for physical education, ed 2, Reston, Va., 2004, AAHPERD.

21. Advocacy Institute: What is advocacy? In Cohen D: Part I: reflections on advocacy, West Hartford, Ct, Bloomfield Conn., 2001, Kumarin Press (www.advocacy.org).

22. DePauw KP: Futuristic perspectives for kinesiology and physical education, Quest 50:1–8, 1998.

23. National Dance Association: Advocacy kit: you can make a difference, National Dance Association (*www.aahperd.org/nda/issues/advocacy*).

24. Advocacy Institute: Become a leader for social justice: fight for what you believe in, Washington, D.C., 2001, Advocacy Institute.

25. Locke LF: Advice, stories, and myths: the reactions of a cliff jumper, Quest 50:238–248, 1998.

26. Dunn JM: Communicating with school boards: position, power, perseverance, Quest 51:157–163, 1999.

27. Booth FW and Chakravarthy MV: Cost and consequences of sedentary living: new battleground for an old enemy, President's Council on Physical Fitness and Sport Research Digest 3(16), 2002.

28. US Department of Health and Human Services: Healthy People 2010: With understanding and improving health and objectives for improving health, ed 2, Washington, D.C., 2000, US Government Printing Office (www.healthypeople.gov/healthypeople).

29. U.S. Department of Health and Human Services. *The Surgeon General's Vision for a Healthy and Fit Nation*. Rockville, MD: U.S. Department of Health and Human Services, Office of the Surgeon General, January 2010.

30. National Association for Sport and Physical Education: A philosophical position on physical activity & fitness for physical activity professionals, NASPE, 2010, Physical activity and fitness recommendations for physical activity professionals, NASPE, 2002 (www.aahperd.org/naspe/standards/upload/Physical-Activity-for-PA-Professionals-final-10-16.pdf).

31. Wilmore JH: Objectives for the nation: physical fitness and exercise, JOPERD 53(3):41–43.

32. Kumanyilca SK and Yancey AK: Physical activity and health equity: evolving the science, *American Journal of Health Promotion* 23(6): S4–S7, 2009.

33. Redwood D, Schumacher MC, Lanier AP, Eerucci ED, Asay E, Heizer EJ, Tom-Orme L, Edwards SL, Murtaugh MA, and Slattery ML: Physical activity patterns of American Indian and Alaskan Native people living in Alaska and the southwestern United States, American Journal of Health Promotion, 23(6):388–395, 2009.

34. Kumanyilca SK and Whitt-Glover MC: Systematic review of interventions to increase physical activity and physical Fitness in African-Americans, American Journal of Health Promotion, 23(6):S33–S56, 2009.

35. Drum CE, Peterson JJ, Culley C, Krahn G, Heller T, Kimpton T, McCubbin J, Rimmer J, Seekins T, Suzuki R, and White GW: Guidelines and criteria for the implementation of community-based health promotion programs for individuals with disabilities, American Journal of Health Promotion, 24(2):93–101, 2009.

36. Dunn JM and Sherrill C: Movement and its implication for individuals with disabilities, Quest 48:378–391, 1996.

37. Cetron M and Davies O: Probable tomorrows: how science and technology will transform our lives in the next twenty years, New York, 1997, St. Martin's Press.

38. Massengale JD: The unprepared discipline: selection of alternative futures, Quest 40:107–114, 1988.

39. US Department of Health, Education, and Welfare: Healthy people: the surgeon general's report on health promotion and disease prevention, Washington, D.C., 1979, US Government Printing Office.

40. US Department of Health and Human Services: Promoting health/preventing disease: objectives for the nation, Washington, D.C., 1980, US Government Printing Office.

41. US Department of Health and Human Services: Healthy people 2000: national health promotion and disease prevention objectives, Washington, D.C., 1991, US Government Printing Office.

42. Shepard RJ: Issues in worksite health promotion: a personal viewpoint, Quest 54:67–82, 2002.

43. Centers for Medicare and Medicaid Services: Highlights—National Health Expenditure, Projections 2009–2019 (www.cms.gov).

44. Smedley BD and Syme SL: Promoting health: intervention strategies from social and behavioral research, American Journal of Health Promotion 15:149–166.

45. United States Department of Education, No Child Left Behind (www.ed.gov), Retrieved July 2010.

46. Cetron M and Cetron K: A forecast for schools, Educational Leadership 61(4):22–30, 2003.

47. Cetron M: Schools of the future. Presentation at the Convention of the American Association of School Administrators, Dallas, August 1985.

48. Powers S, Ward K, and Shanely RA: Contemporary exercise physiology research in The United States: Influence of technology, Quest 49:296–299, 1997.

49. Healey J: Future possibilities in electronic monitoring of physical activity, Research Quarterly for Exercise and Sport 71:137–145, 2000.

50. Hoberman J: Mortal engines: the science of performance and the dehumanization of sport, New York, 1992, Free Press.

51. Haggerty TR: Influence of information technologies on kinesiology and physical education, Quest 49:254–269, 1997.

52. US Administration on Aging and American Association of Retired Persons: A profile of older Americans, 1997, Washington D.C., 1997, US Government Printing Office.

53. Agency for Healthcare Research and Quality: Minority health: cultural competency for health care providers could reduce disparities in care related to race and ethnicity, November 2000 (www2.ed.gov/nclb/overview/intro/edpicks. jhtml?src=ln).

54. Bain LL: Beginning the journey: agenda for 2001, Quest 40:96–106, 1988.

55. Oberle GH: A future direction plan for our profession, JOPERD 59(1):76–77, 1988.

56. Charles JM: Changes and challenges: a 20/20 vision of 2020, Quest 57: 267–286, 2005.

57. Rikli RE: Kinesiology—A "homeless" field: addressing organization and leadership needs, Quest 56:288–309, 2006.

58. Lawson HA: School reform, families, and health in the emergent national agenda for economic and social improvement: implications, Quest 45:289–307, 1993.

59. Neiner JA, Howze EH, and Greaney ML: Using scenario planning in public health: anticipating alternative futures, Health Promotion Practice 5:69–79, 2004.

PHOTO CREDITS

C-1

INDEX

Note: Page numbers followed by *f* or *t* indicate figures or tables, respectively.

A

Academic discipline, 13
Academic progress rate (APR), 279
Academic support programs, 489–490
Acceleration, 192, 193, 197
Accountability, 346
    educational, 57
    professional, 402–403
Accuracy, *versus* speed, 163–164
Achievement, motivation and, 315
Acosta, R. V., 286
Action/reaction, 198
Activitygram, 60, 62*f*
Adams, Jack, 151
Adapted physical activity
    origins of, 131
    overview, 16–17
    teaching, 432–434
Adapted Physical Education National
    Standards, 433
Adenosine triphosphate (ATP), 226
Administrators, female, 286
Adolescents, 92; *see also* Youth sports
    health habits for, 79
    overweight trends for, 80, 91, 532
    participation of, 8
    physical activity/fitness of, 6–7, 88–93,
        136, 526, 531–532
Adrian, M. J., 208, 211
Adults
    overweight/obesity trends for, 80, 81*f*, 94,
        531–532
    physical activity/fitness of, 6–7, 93–96,
        531–532
Adventure education, 351, 356–357
Advocacy, 520–524
Aerobics, 219
Aerobics, 218

Aerobics and Fitness Association of America
    (AFAA), 134, 387, 468*t*
Aerobic system, 227–228, 232
Aesthetics, 30–31
Affective domain, 48–52
African Americans, 538; *see also* Black athletes
Agassiz Middle School (Fargo, N.D.), 47, 48
Aging, and physical activity, 99–100
Air displacement plethysmography, 240
Allied fields
    dance, 21–22
    health, 19–22
    recreation, 20–21
Amateur Athletic Foundation of
    Los Angeles, 107
Amateurism, 113
Amateur Sports Act (1978), 142
American Academy of Kinesiology and
    Physical Education, 133, 513, 517
American Academy of Pediatrics, 275
American Academy of Physical Education, 133
American Alliance for Health, Physical
    Education, Recreation and Dance
    (AAHPERD), 43, 108, 120, 129, 132,
    134–136, 149–150, 186, 219, 343, 397,
    408–410, 514, 526, 539, 544
American Association for Health, Physical
    Education, and Recreation, 127
American Association for Health Education
    (AAHE), 409
American Association for Physical Activity
    and Recreation (AAPAR), 409
American Association for the Advancement
    of Physical Education (AAAPE), 120
American Athletic Union (AAU), 120, 121
American Basketball League, 285
American Bowling Congress, 120
American College Athletics (Carnegie
    Foundation), 127
American College of Sports Medicine
    (ACSM), 3, 87, 129, 133, 136, 217, 219,
    223, 233, 234, 259, 384, 387, 397, 410,
    455, 468, 468*t*, 512, 526
American Council on Exercise (ACE), 384,
    455, 468*t*

American Dance Therapy Association
    (ADTA), 474
American Education Research Association
    (AERA), 344
American Heart Association, 511
American Journal of Physiology, 219
American Journal of Sports Medicine, 219
American Kinesiotherapy Association,
    475–476
American Medical Association, 475
American Physical Education Association
    (APEA), 127
American Physical Therapy Association, 476
American Psychological Association, 310
American Psychological Association Division
    of Exercise and Sports Psychology, 307
American Red Cross, 387
American Society of Biomechanics, 186
American Sport Education Program (ASEP),
    445, 514
Americans with Disabilities Act (ADA,
    1990), 142, 367–368, 522
American Therapeutic Recreation
    Association, 475
Anabolic-androgenic steroids, 260–261, 275
Anaerobic system, 227–228
Analysis, described, 46
Anderson, William, 120, 122, 131, 343
Angular acceleration, 192
Angular velocity, 192–193
Anorexia nervosa, 239
Anshel, M. H., 322, 323, 400
Anthropometry, 204
Anxiety
    nature of, 323–324
    performance and, 324–325
Application, described, 46
Aristotle, 185, 415
Armed forces, physical fitness in, 125,
    128–129
Arousal
    nature of, 323–324
    performance and, 324–325
Artest, Ron, 299
Articulation, 54